NEGOTIATED EMPIRES

Negotiated Empires

Centers and Peripheries in the Americas, 1500–1820

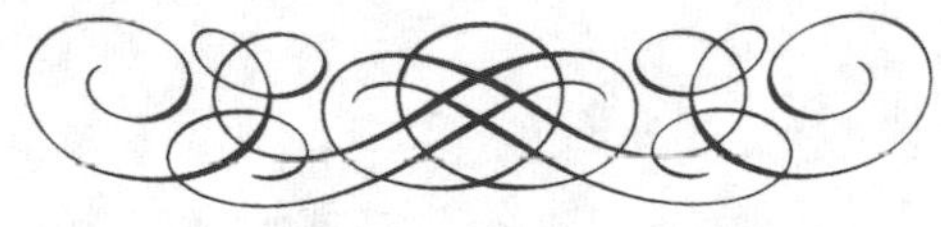

Edited by
Christine Daniels and Michael V. Kennedy

with an Introduction by Jack P. Greene & Amy Turner Bushnell

ROUTLEDGE
New York & London

Published in 2002 by
Routledge
29 West 35th Street
New York, NY 10001

Published in Great Britain by
Routledge
11 New Fetter Lane
London EC4P 4EE

Routledge is an imprint of the Taylor & Francis Group.

Printed on acid-free, 250-year-life paper.
Manufactured in the United States of America.
Design and typography: Jack Donner
10 9 8 7 6 5 4 3 2 1

Library of Congress Cataloging-in-Publication Data

Negotiated empires : centers and peripheries in the Americas, 1500–1820 /
edited by Christine Daniels and Michael V. Kennedy.
p. cm.
Includes bibliographical references and index.
ISBN 0-415-92538-X — ISBN 0-415-92539-8 (pbk.)
1. America—History—To 1810. 2. America—Colonization. 3. Europe—Colonies—America. 4. Indians of North America—First contact with Europeans. 5. Frontier and pioneer life—America. 6. Imperialism—History. 7. Central–local government relations—History. 8. Political geography—History. I. Daniels, Christine, 1953– II. Kennedy, Michael V., 1954–

E18.82. N44 2002
970—dc21

2001034982

Contents

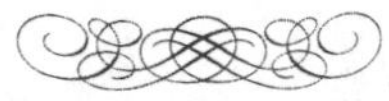

PREFACE

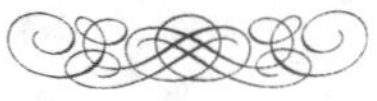

This volume grew out of a conference held at Michigan State University in the fall of 1997. That conference was made possible by an endowment provided by Jack and Margaret Sweet who have had a longstanding commitment to American history and the promotion of undergraduate education. Organized by the two inaugural Sweet Professors, Professors Amy Turner Bushnell of the College of Charleston and Jack P. Greene of the Johns Hopkins University, and their departmental sponsor, Professor Christine Daniels, this conference was attended by over 150 professors, graduate students, and undergraduates from Michigan State and other academic institutions throughout the Midwest. Nine of the fourteen substantive chapters in the volume originated as papers presented at this conference. Professors Bushnell, Daniels, and Greene subsequently recruited the remaining five chapters to cover areas not considered at the original conference. Professors Bushnell and Greene wrote the introduction, Professor Daniels and I edited the various chapters, I presided over the production of the volume, and Professor Daniels did the index.

As the volume editors, Professor Daniels and I wish to thank Jack and Margaret Sweet, the Michigan State University History Department, including particularly Dr. Leslie Page Moch who chaired the original committee on the Sweet Professorship, Amy Turner Bushnell, Jack P. Greene, the original conference participants, and most of all, the authors of the essays included here for their help in creating this volume. We also wish especially to thank Brendan O'Malley, formerly of Routledge Press, whose enthusiasm and early, sustained, and patient interest in this volume helped bring it to fruition.

Michael V. Kennedy
Flint, Michigan
January 2002

Peripheries, Centers, and the Construction of Early Modern American Empires

An Introduction

Amy Turner Bushnell and Jack P. Greene

The European encounter with the Americas inaugurated by the Columbian voyages provided the first step in the reconstruction of the Atlantic—and, more particularly, the American—world. Over the next 350 years, Europeans, operating under the aegis or with the blessing of the national polities taking shape on the northeastern fringe of the Atlantic Ocean, engaged in a plethora of efforts to bring the vast spaces and numerous peoples of the Americas under their hegemony. Sponsored by wealthy or well-connected individuals or by chartered trading companies, hundreds of thousands of European settlers flooded into the Americas. The pathogens they brought with them took millions of American Indian lives and, coupled with tactics of divide and conquer, made it possible for Europeans to overcome native resistance, expropriating lands and labor. As beachheads grew into settlements and settlements into colonies, settlers effectively presided over a wholesale reorganization of large regions of the Americas, transforming them, with the help of millions of enslaved Africans, into new political, social, economic, and cultural spaces. The product of the often unplanned and uncoordinated efforts of countless individuals, this reorganization represents one of the most profound transformations in human history.

Although Sweden participated in the early-seventeenth-century phase of this process, by the middle decades of the eighteenth century the seven states whose empires included significant spheres of jurisdiction in the Americas were Spain, Portugal, Great Britain, France, the Dutch Republic, Russia, and Denmark. Contemporary cartographers represented these spheres in the increasingly detailed and sophisticated maps they drew to depict the changes taking place in the Americas. In 1750, Spain, which had been engaged in the acquisition of American territory since the last decade of the fifteenth century, claimed to preside over a vast area organized into two great viceroyalties—the Viceroyalty of Peru covering half of South America, and the Viceroyalty of New Spain, stretching from Panama to New Mexico—plus significant portions of the Greater Antilles and the mainlands surrounding the Gulf of Mexico. Active in America since the mid-sixteenth century,

Portugal claimed jurisdiction over the loosely knit governor generalship of Brazil and Amazonian state of Maranhãoe Grão Pará, which together stretched from the Atlantic seaboard west to the Andes Mountains and south to the estuary of the Río de la Plata. Great Britain and France, neither of which managed to establish an effective settlement in America before the first decade of the seventeenth century, had by the mid-eighteenth attained vast cartographic empires. That of Britain stretched over much of the eastern coast of North America from Georgia north to Newfoundland and included several colonies in the West Indies, while that of France spread more thinly along the waterways of the Great Lakes and St. Lawrence and Mississippi Rivers, and included important settlements in both the Greater and Lesser Antilles. The Dutch Republic, Russia, and Denmark all had smaller spaces under their jurisdiction. The Dutch, having in the mid-seventeenth century lost their principal holdings in the Americas to the English and the Portuguese, presided over Surinam in the northeast corner of South America and several small Caribbean islands; Russia's series of trading posts and small settlements reached down the Pacific coast of North America from Alaska almost to San Francisco Bay; and Denmark held a few minor islands in the Caribbean.

Military and political events during the next three-quarters of a century significantly altered these arrangements. Defeat in the Seven Years' War deprived the French of their settlements in North America. In the American Revolution, inaugurating an era of settler and slave revolts, thirteen British colonies on the Atlantic seaboard joined to declare their independence. Bourbon Spain aggressively countered France in the Gulf, Russia in California, and Portugal in the Río de la Plata, only to lose the demographic contest for the North American borderlands to an expansionist United States in the early decades of the nineteenth century. These developments were only the latest of the profound changes wrought by Europeans and their African auxiliaries between 1492 and the Age of Revolution.

Cartographic representations of the Americas as spaces under European jurisdiction masked the unevenness of actual hegemony. In terms of control emanating from a colonial center, the *ecumene* was the immediate area over which settlers of European origin successfully asserted mastery, with or without numerical superiority.[1] Beyond the ecumene was the *sphere of influence*, an intermediate area in which European or Eurocreole traders, hunters, and other boundary crossers interacted with native peoples, serving as advance agents of settlement and contesting the presence of rival Europeans. Anything further was merely a European *claim* to exclusive development, a title other Europeans might or might not choose to respect. If in the late eighteenth century one-half of the vast expanse of the Americas was under the control of independent nations of Indians, as David J. Weber reports of Spanish America, the continental claims of European princes and colonists were moot.[2]

In its fullest sense, the Europeanizing of America was thus confined to ecumenes and core regions, implanted as separate political units and combining or dividing over time. Modern historians broadly refer to these units as colonies; contemporaries knew them by various national appellations: captaincies-general, presidencies, and *audiencias* in Spanish America; captaincies and governorships in Portuguese America; and plantations or colonies in British, French, and Dutch America. Whatever they were called, these units were defined in some major part by their constitutional, political, legal, economic, and cultural attachment to a particular European state culture.

In the mid-eighteenth century, remnants of Indian society could still be found in every colony; in areas of formerly dense indigenous population, such as Mexico and Peru, Indians and *mestizos* were the substantial majority. In areas where there had been massive importations of Africans to work in mines or on plantations, Africans and their creole descendants were similarly numerically predominant. The British colonies contained many people from other areas of Europe, especially the German. By virtue of their control over the machinery of politics, however, settler populations of Europeans from the sponsoring states and their creole offspring everywhere dominated the cores, transforming the cultural spaces they occupied by introducing and molding to local circumstances European systems of law, patterns of land occupation, and social, economic, political, and cultural institutions, practices, and forms.

Such core regions formed the foundations for the elaboration and development of creole cultures that earnestly sought to mirror the metropolitan European cultures to which they were attached, even as they departed from those cultures in their efforts to render the American "wilderness" tractable. These *charter* or *hearth* cultures proved to be eminently transportable to areas that were similarly environed; thus by a process of *secondary colonization* the original ecumenes served as staging areas for the expansion of creole cultures into the intermediate zone. Sometimes this hiving process enlarged the core region about a colonial center; sometimes it merely stranded a frontier community in a region where its values were contested and cultural influence flowed both ways. Over time, however, the heavily Europeanized centers and their lightly Europeanized peripheries formed increasingly complex political and economic systems. The nature and organization of these systems is the subject of this volume.

The volume's premise is that the concepts of *center* and *periphery* may be usefully applied to the historical understanding of colonial centers and their peripheries in the early modern Americas. As explicit scholarly explanatory devices, these concepts have a relatively short history. The sociologist Edward Shils first gave them currency in a seminal essay published in 1961 and simply titled "Centre and Periphery." Shils used these concepts less as a way of analyzing the organization than the workings of societies. For him, centers of societies were less a physical place than a sociointellectual construct. *Centrality* involved the "order of symbols, of values and beliefs, which govern the society" as well as the "structure of activities, of roles and persons, within the network of institutions" which, "through the radiation of their authority, give some form to the life of a considerable section of the population of the society." The authoritative elites who presided over those institutions possessed a particularly "vital relationship to the centre, the locus of the sacred, the order which confers legitimacy." Invariably, however, the central value system that legitimated the "central institutional system" was widely shared, albeit "with different degrees of intensity, wholeheartedness and devotion."[3]

In Shils's formulation, the periphery existed in a symbiotic but often uneasy association with the center. "As we move from the centre of society . . . in which authority is exercised . . . to the hinterland or the periphery, over which authority is exercised," Shils wrote, "attachment to the central value system becomes attenuated. . . . The lower one goes in the [social] hierarchy, or the further one moves territorially from the locus of authority, the less likely is the authority to be appreciated." In Shils's view, *peripherality* thus had both vertical (sociostructural) and horizontal (geographical) dimensions. In premodern societies, he observed, the mass of the population, existing on the peripheries of society, has mostly "been far removed from the immediate impact of the central value system." "As long as societies were loosely co-ordinated, as long as authority lacked the means of intensive control, and as long as much of the economic life of the society was carried on outside any market or almost exclusively in local markets," he noted, "the central value system invariably became attenuated in the outlying reaches." Indeed, often existing in what Shils referred to as "pockets of approximate independence," peripheries have usually "possessed their own value systems" that exhibited only an occasional and fragmentary articulation with the central value system and at best offered little more than "an intermittent, partial and attenuated affirmation" of that system.[4]

Their peripherality, Shils suggested, has meant that the "mass of the population in most pre-modern and non-Western societies have in a sense lived *outside* society," have been "far from full-fledged members of their societies," and "have very seldom been citizens." Moreover, their "low position in the hierarchy of authority has been injurious to them." Because "their convivial, spiritual and moral centre of gravity has lain closer to their own round of life," however, Shils denied that they have in general "felt their remoteness from the centre to be a perpetual injury to themselves." Only among the "most intensely sensitive or the more alertly intelligent," he contended, has this "distance from the centre" led "to an acute sense of being on 'the outside,' to a painful feeling of being excluded from the vital zone which surrounds 'the centre' of society."[5]

More familiar than Shils's formulation and more explicitly utilized by scholars of early modern colonizing ventures is the formulation that historical sociologist Immanuel Wallerstein employed in his ambitious three-volume study, *The Modern World-System*, published between 1974 and 1989.[6] For Wallerstein, the concepts of *core* and *periphery* represented a device to reconceptualize the nature and workings of the colonialist and mercantilist world system that came into being during the early modern era. In his analysis, a European core composed of "core-states" with "strong state machinery," integrated national cultures, and complex economies using a system of free labor presided over an emerging world economy in which it increasingly came to dominate peripheral areas with weak or nonexistent states, simple economies based principally on mining, agriculture, and various kinds of resource exploitation, and systems of forced labor. To these two categories, Wallerstein added a "third structural zone, the semiperiphery," which "represents a midway point on a continuum running from the core to the periphery" in terms of "the complexity of the economy, the strength of the state, and the degree of national integration." In this schema, the core always "dominated the periphery," albeit the core was never stable, structural shifts in the world economy pushing some core states into semiperipheral or even peripheral status.[7]

Although Wallerstein developed these categories to facilitate understanding of developments that had their origins in the early modern era, and although historians of Latin America and the Caribbean used his and other world-system perspectives in combination with the dependency theory that had emerged during the 1960s to explain modern underdevelopment, his specific conceptualization of core-periphery relationships has rather informed than been central to developing structures of explanation among colonial historians. Wallerstein's conceptual scheme, they have found, grants too much power to European cores, is too exclusively focused on the creation of international trading systems and other broad economic developments, is much too innocent of what one scholar has called a "peripheral vision," and is far too general to be widely applicable to the analysis of the rich histories of the complex imperial structures that emerged out of Europe's expansion into the Americas and elsewhere during the early modern era.[8]

That despite these problems, historians of the Spanish American peripheries, north and south, nonetheless attempted to fit their findings into Wallerstein's overarching system was indicative of the insufficiency of modes of explanation for the Spanish American frontier.[9] Frontier historian David Weber, for example, who in 1982 made explicit use of the Wallerstein schema, had by 1986 turned from world-systems theory to explanations taken from geography, anthropology, and ethnohistory, and in 1992, having examined the available explanatory models, resigned himself to eclecticism on the grounds that no single theory was satisfactory.[10] This shortfall of theory for the Spanish frontiers is due to a combination of factors, among them the dethroning of Frederick Jackson Turner's Eurocentric frontier hypothesis, the antitheoretical bias of Herbert Eugene Bolton and his Spanish Borderlands "school," the relative lack of enthusiasm among Latin American scholars for frontier studies, and a general "crisis of theory," attributed in Latin America to the growing disillusion of intellectuals with Marxism and anything else broadly explanatory.

In *Peripheries and Center: Constitutional Development in the Extended Polities of the British Empire and the United States, 1607–1788*, Jack P. Greene used center-periphery theory as a vehicle for the analysis of the changing constitutional structure of the British Empire between the founding of the first English-American colonies at the beginning of the seventeenth century and the American Revolution.[11] Building upon the conceptual scheme of Shils, not Wallerstein, Greene principally focused on the federal nature of constitutional relationships between England, or after 1707 Great Britain, and its colonies in North America and the West Indies. Whereas both Shils and Wallerstein had emphasized the flow of authority outward from center to periphery, Shils had at least raised the possibility that, given the weakness of coercive resources in premodern societies, peripheral areas within state and social structures necessarily enjoyed considerable autonomy from the center, their condition of "approximate independence" from the center evidently serving as the mirror image of the center's nominal authority over the peripheries.

Greene expanded upon and modified this point in several significant ways. He found that in the British Empire the considerable autonomy enjoyed by the peripheries derived not just from the weakness of metropolitan coercive resources and distance from the center, but from settler domination of local authority structures, which, so far from being implanted by the center, emerged internally out of settler efforts to construct European-style polities in the New World.

These structures, routinely established through an adaptive process of trial and error early in the history of every colony, proved extraordinarily resilient, surviving, if sometimes in modified forms, repeated metropolitan efforts to subordinate them to central authority. Indeed, the practical working constitutional structure that developed over time was one in which the several polities of the American peripheries exerted considerable power, the settlers who presided over those polities retained substantial agency, and the imperial constitution was a federal constitution that, presaging the United States Constitution of 1789, was the product not of central imposition upon a weak periphery, but of elaborate and ongoing negotiations between the center and the many peripheral polities that had attached themselves to the center. The British Empire was, thus, a negotiated empire. In a subsequent essay, Greene suggested that these findings could be expanded to all early modern European empires in the Americas. Like the British Empire, he argued, those empires were all polities whose shape was determined by a process of negotiation between on the one hand metropolitan cores, and on the other, colonial peripheries presided over by the dominant elements in the settler populations of those peripheries.[12]

In *Atlantic America, 1492–1800*, volume 1 of *The Shaping of America: A Geographical Perspective on 500 Years of History*, the historical geographer D. W. Meinig also employed the concepts of center and periphery in his quest for "a geographical scheme" that would facilitate a "more refined geographical understanding" of the complex economic, political, and social systems that developed in the Atlantic world during the early modern era. In this scheme, Meinig made a clear distinction between *center* and *core*, the former term applying only to those "European *centers*, the capital cities that served as headquarters for the control of financial resources, commercial intelligence, . . . marketing systems," central political institutions, and arenas in which metropolitan social institutions were most fully developed, and the latter term to the system of hinterlands and ports involved in the production and transmission of articles "specifically in response to American needs."[13]

With similar results, Meinig also deconstructed the term *periphery*, distinguishing among colonial ports, heavily colonized areas, back countries, and Indian countries, the last of which had no centers but often were organized around core areas that had their own hinterlands. He thus conceived of the spatial organization of the peripheries in terms of "a *spectrum* showing gradations in power, intensity of interaction, and social character," in which "imperial power declined with distance from the European capital until it became feeble and indirect in the interior" of the Americas, while the various national versions of Europeanness—Spanishness, Portugeseness, Dutchness, Frenchness, or Englishness "as defined by a social elite" in each capital—passed through "an incremental divergence, area by area, from center to periphery" until it faded "to the faintest evidence of things" European and disappeared entirely in "the still strong 'Indianness' of the American interior." Not only does center-periphery theory help to organize scholarly understanding of the process of cultural divergence within imperial units, but, as Meinig noted, it also aids in the identification of "those systems of spatial interaction binding center and periphery together and thus serving to counter pressures toward separation."[14]

Wallerstein, Greene, and Meinig all used center-periphery concepts to describe relationships between European centers and colonial peripheries. However, together with Greene's discovery of the considerable authority and power enjoyed by the peripheries in the negotiated structure that comprised the British Empire, Meinig's deconstruction of the concept of periphery in the context of early modern European colonization in America strongly suggested the utility of extending the use of those concepts to the analysis of the internal workings of European empires within America. Specifically, these usages raised the possibility of conceiving of those American empires in terms of the construction of a series of *colonial* centers and peripheries, using center-periphery concepts to describe a process of differentiation within the Americas.

Scholars have long recognized that Spanish Mexico and Spanish Peru, places generating enormous wealth, filled with large populations, and characterized by complex economic, political, and cultural forms, functioned as core areas in Spanish America. James Lockhart and Stuart B. Schwartz used the concepts of cores and fringes as a principal organizing device in their synthesis, *Early Latin America: A History of Colonial Spanish America and Brazil*.[15] And historians of the Spanish-American frontier, among others, make explicit use of periphery models.[16] But many colonial scholars have yet to exploit the potential of center-periphery concepts for analyzing the internal organization of Europe's early modern American empires.[17]

This volume represents a step in this direction. It had its origins in a small conference at Michigan State University organized by Jack P. Greene, Amy Turner Bushnell, and Christine Daniels. Entitled "Colonial Centers and Colonial Peripheries: Studies in the Social and Cultural History of the Early Modern Americas," this conference was held in East Lansing, November 21–22, 1997, while Greene and Bushnell were visiting professors at Michigan State. The organizers asked the contributors, each of whom is a recognized specialist on the history of a particular national empire, to write essays addressing or illustrating the utility of center-periphery concepts for the analysis of either the transatlantic relations between European metropolises and their American colonies, or the internal relations between the American colonies and their respective dependencies, or both.

By choosing to leave the conference mandate relatively unstructured and thrown open to a wide array of ideas and approaches, the organizers took the risk that the combined essays would lack the level of intellectual conviction and coherence required for a volume with the audacity to embrace five early modern empires. Fortunately, the contributors have justified this choice through their individual and imaginative responses to the challenge, and the whole is considerably more than the sum of its parts. Nine of the fourteen substantive essays in this volume are revised versions of papers presented at the conference; five, including two by other conference participants, were recruited later. Each of the essays focuses on the developing economic, political, and social organization of one of the European empires in America, under which they have been arranged. The first five essays (by Amy Turner Bushnell, John Jay TePaske, Ida Altman, coauthors Lyman L. Johnson and Susan Migden Socolow, and David J. Weber) are on Spanish America; they are followed by two (by A. J. R. Russell-Wood and Mary Karasch) on Portuguese America; two (by Leslie Choquette and Philip P. Boucher) on French America; one (by Wim Klooster) on Dutch America; and four (by Elizabeth Mancke, Jack P. Greene, Peter S. Onuf, and H. V. Bowen) on British America. Regrettably, Scandinavian and Russian America are unrepresented in the volume.

In the opening essay, "Gates, Patterns, and Peripheries: The Field of Frontier Latin America," Bushnell addresses the problem of how significance is determined in colonial history and presents three paradigms: the paradigm of power, favoring the imperial powers and their colonies destined to merge into nation states; the paradigm of the victim, which fails to subvert the canon; and the paradigm of negotiation, which offers a fresh approach to the study of colonial peripheries and periods long neglected by traditional historians dismissive of marginality and social historians dismissive of narrative. As part of an effort to deconstruct and reconcile frontier and center-periphery terminology, she offers several new definitions and proposes a classification system for the new field of Latin-American frontiers. According to that typology, seventeenth-century Spanish Florida was an external, strategic, maritime periphery where the leaders of the two republics, Spanish and Indian, managed by negotiation to convert royal subsidies into perquisites of local authority.

A periphery is not a periphery when it is a necessary part of an organic whole, objects TePaske in "Integral to Empire: The Vital Peripheries of Colonial Spanish America." With no interval between the reconquest of Spain and the conquest of America in which to develop more modern values and institutions, Spanish colonial society was an extension of medieval Spain in its institutions, economy, religion, culture, social organization, and concepts of an ideal commonwealth. Each of the peripheries was integral to empire. Florida protected the Bahama Channel and maintained a Spanish presence in the Southeast; the Southwest and California extended the empire and solidified Spain's claims; the Moxos and Paraguay protected the Spanish borders against the Portuguese. Chile protected the Pacific coast and served as a breadbasket for Peru. Huancavelica supplied mercury. The Philippines established a Spanish presence in the Orient and provided an outlet for American silver, TePaske continues, expanding the meaning of *empire* to include the interests of settlers; Buenos Aires was an outlet for silver and a transfer point for slaves; the Isthmus of Panama was the legal transfer point for silver and European goods; and Cuba, thanks to tobacco, shipbuilding, and sugar, advanced to become a core region (semiperiphery), and then a significant center. Medieval it may have been, but Spain's empire in America endured well into the nineteenth century.

With the city of Puebla (1550–1650) as her example, Altman challenges the conventional conceptualization of colonial center and core region in her "Reconsidering the Center: Puebla and Mexico City, 1550–1650." She finds no precedent for the hegemonic city model of a single urban center dominating a large region in early modern Spain, where the urban network was more diffused than concentrated, nor yet in the Valley of Mexico, where "the paradigm of the city of the conquerors ruling the countryside of the conquered never really existed." Puebla, a regional center in competition with Mexico City, eighty miles to its west, was a center of trade with the south, an inland port for the Atlantic, an ecclesiastical center, and a center of textile trades. Emphasizing the centrality of the capital skews our understanding of the relative weight of the international economy, Altman cautions. The local and regional economies may well have accounted for a larger proportion of economic activity. Moreover, *core* and *periphery* are defined by perception as well as distance and resources, and perception is subjective. For emigrants from Brihuega, Spain, the frontier was central New Spain, and Puebla was not peripheral, but central.

For Johnson and Socolow, the terms *center* and *periphery* recall the discourse of dependency theory popular with Latin-American economic historians and policymakers in the 1960s and 1970s, according to which the center shifted from Spain and Portugal to Great Britain and then the United States, leaving Latin America a perennial periphery. In the late 1980s, dependency theory began to attract critics, who objected that it ignored regional market relations and denied the agency of local actors. By the early 1990s policymakers had abandoned the theory, and economic history turned numerically dense and arcane. In "Colonial Centers,

Colonial Peripheries, and the Economic Agency of the Spanish State," Johnson and Socolow salvage center-periphery concepts by applying them in a context that is interregional rather than transatlantic or hemispheric. They argue that "an elaborately articulated and hierarchical relationship of center and peripheries existed, not only between the Spanish colonies and the imperial center, but between colonial capitals . . . and colonial dependencies." In the Viceroyalty of Peru, this relationship underwent metamorphosis. In the Andean region, where the peripheries had minimal ties to either viceregal or European centers, state power combined with market forces to create a large, integrated regional economy centered on the silver mines. The system was cumbersome and exploitive. Forced sales to Indians underwrote the textile and mule trades, and a merchant monopoly in Lima drove commerce to take an illegal route through the port of Buenos Aires on the Río de la Plata. In 1776, when the Río de la Plata became a viceroyalty, it shed its role as a colonial periphery and began to tax the neighboring economies. The conflict in the Platine region after 1810 was not with Spanish armies, but with Upper Peru, Chile, Paraguay, and Uruguay, each of which achieved political independence from Buenos Aires, a center that did not hold.

In "Bourbons and Bárbaros: Center and Periphery in the Reshaping of Spanish Indian Policy," Weber examines the "interplay between core and periphery" in Spain's changing policies toward the independent Indian nations. In the mid-eighteenth century the "barbarians," controlling over half of "Spanish" America and less and less susceptible to either military or spiritual conquest, were a growing menace to the peripheries. Bourbon officials adopted new, conciliatory strategies that appealed to enlightened Spaniards. Commercial expansion, on the British model, sought to turn the Indians into dependent consumers and producers; written treaties recognizing them as autonomous sovereign nations, on the French and British models, marked a shift from "pacification" to relations based on the law of nations; while expeditions of reconnaissance appropriated their territories intellectually. All of these policy shifts were products of negotiation, as Indian ideas and initiatives reshaped royal directives.

In "Centers and Peripheries in the Luso-Brazilian World, 1500–1808," Russell-Wood assigns himself the task of applying center-periphery concepts on the one hand to the relations between a metropolis and its colonies, and on the other to the relations between colonial centers and their peripheries, to which he applies the geographical model of *umland*, *hinterland*, and *vorland*. In the case of the Portuguese empire, he finds, inefficiencies of metropolitan government undermined the mercantilist assumption that it was the obligation of the periphery to support the center, leaving opportunities for colonials to coopt and subvert the system through a "culture of evasion," while avoiding confrontation over periphery rights. Well before the royal court arrived in Rio de Janeiro, periphery-periphery linkages had diminished the role of the metropolis and Brazil possessed de facto independence. Imposing a rare order on the Brazilian peripheries, Russell-Wood draws distinctions based upon such factors as distance from the core, topographic insulation, self-sufficiency, military or economic circumstances, and evolution, with the first stage being the frontier of settlement, and the last the point at which the periphery develops its own satellites and becomes a core. The *ultraperipheries*, regions like the *sertão*, associated with disorder and barbarism, were essentially outside of empire.

The failure of center-periphery categories to fit colonial realities is the subject of Karasch's essay, "The Periphery of the Periphery? Vila Boa de Goiás, 1780–1835." Capital of the immense and wealthy captaincy of Goiás, Vila Boa possessed many of the characteristics of a regional core. It answered directly to the Portuguese Crown, it stood at the juncture of east-west and north-south trade networks, and it monopolized an important resource, gold, which plugged central Brazil into the Atlantic economy. But the captaincy also had the characteristics of a periphery. Vila Boa, with its small white and black population, was remote, often lawless, at war with a sea of Indian nations. If Goiás was a periphery, no one port city was its core, for the northern half of the captaincy traded with Salvador de Bahía, the southern half with Rio de Janeiro, and its gold circulated everywhere. When the gold gave out, the Portuguese moved on. Vila Boa de Goiás, Karasch concludes, was at once core, periphery, and an impermanent outpost in a sea of grass.

Klooster's essay, "Other Netherlands beyond the Sea: Dutch America between Metropolitan Control and Divergence, 1600–1795," examines how the Dutch Republic, a highly decentralized state, colonized and attempted to control the neo-Dutch periphery in America. The United Provinces' businesslike solution to the problem of a dispersed metropolitan center was a joint stock company, with Holland contributing four-ninths of the capital and Zeeland two-ninths. The Dutch West India Company, founded in 1621 with a monopoly of trade and navigation in the Atlantic world, had many of the attributes of a state, administering justice, making treaties, maintaining an army, and farming out colonization to patroons, whose efforts were most successful in the Caribbean and on the "Wild Coast." Although colonists were able to achieve a measure of self-government informally, the status of the colonies was commensurate to that of the "Generality" lands captured from Spain in 1648 and never admitted as full members to the republic. Nor was it possible to replicate Dutch culture in colonies that relied on black slavery and feared attack by maroons and Indians. New Holland, in northeast Brazil, and New Netherland, between Virginia and New England, were the only parts of Dutch America substantial enough to offer examples of colonial centers and colonial peripheries. In those colonies, the frontier marked the border between civilization and barbarism, not because Indians were barbarians, but because settlers—like seamen on the maritime frontier, engaging in contraband, forced trade, and piracy—behaved lawlessly when they passed the bounds of civil society.

In her essay, "Center and Periphery in French North America," Choquette challenges the image of France's North American empire as hegemonic, shaped by French absolutism and mercantilism into a state of metropolitan dominance and colonial dependency. New France's distance from Europe and its dual function as frontier and borderland—both a meeting place of peoples and a site of imperial rivalry—gave colonists more room for maneuvering than imperial rhetoric and Anglophilic historiography suggest. Canada, which according to Wallerstein's world system was part of the external area beyond the periphery, took on the characteristics of a semiperiphery. Although subordinate to core interests and power, it emulated metropolitan society, developed a metropolis, and dominated a hinterland. Elsewhere, metropolitan authority was frustrated at every turn: by clandestine commerce in Acadia; an Indian middle ground in the Great Lakes; ungovernable *coureurs* in Indian territory; spontaneous settlement in the Illinois Country; peripheral to both Quebec and New Orleans; and a shortage of free settlers for Lower Louisiana. In French North America, peripheral to empire, absolutism softened into a kind of enlightened despotism, mercantilist policy gave way to free trade, and frontier freedoms persisted.

Boucher's purpose in "The 'Frontier Era' of the French Caribbean, 1620s–1690s" is to identify a frontier model for the French Antilles, distinct from and preceding the more familiar model of a sugar plantation society. The frontier era was a stage in island life characterized by sparse population, relative demographic parity between Europeans and Africans, relatively flexible social relations, an uncertain supply network, weak control by the metropolis, contested leadership in the colony, and relatively better treatment of slaves. Beginning with permanent occupation and ending with the "closing" of the frontier at the end of the seventeenth century, it is divisible into the pioneering phase, characterized by war with the Caribs, tobacco farming, and barter, and, after the Carib peace of 1660, the phase of the opening of the Carib lands, characterized by logging, hunting, and attacks on transfrontier societies of buccaneers and maroons. The evolution of center-periphery relations in the French Antilles, where governors were domesticated, local customs prevailed over royal ordinances, and passive and active resistance limited royal authority, might well be compared to similar developments in Virginia, Carolina, and Louisiana. When it came to overseas colonies, the rhetoric of empire differed more than the reality.

In an oceanic empire the peripheries were commercial; a territorial empire had peripheries of settlement, says Mancke, in "Negotiating an Empire: Britain and Its Overseas Peripheries, c. 1550–1780." England's empire of commerce was early and extensive, with charter or company ties to Newfoundland, West Africa, the Levant, Muscovy, and the East Indies, and contraband connections in Spanish and Portuguese America. Overseas colonies were governed like units of the commercial empire, by delegation and charter. After the Seven Years' War, the metropolitan government, finally beginning "to combine policy initiatives with the funding necessary to make them effective in overseas dominions," tried to change a commercial empire into a territorial one. But the metropole was unprepared for direct governance and, without colonial consultation, made important decisions, not just about taxation, but about naval stores, settlement in Nova Scotia, Indian commissioners, and the reservation of Crown lands in trans-Appalachia. By the time the colonists were numerous enough and wealthy enough to interest the metropole, they were also strong enough to resist it and to seize control over their own backcountry. In a free society, government could not remain at odds with the governed.

Greene criticizes the indiscriminate use of the coercive and centralized model of imperial organization, in which powerful nation-states preside over colonies and authority flows downward from the center to subject populations in distant peripheries, in "Transatlantic Colonization and the Redefinition of Empire in the Early Modern Era: The British-American Experience." Early modern empires, he argues, were composite monarchies in which rule was indirect, sovereignty fragmented, governance consensual, and considerable authority left with the peripheries. The addition of colonial entities did not produce a devolution of authority, but rather the construction of authority in new arenas, followed by the creation of authority through negotiation. The cause did not lie on the one side in a deficient will to power, or on the other, in a desire to sever the connection, but in the limited resources available for coercion, the remoteness of overseas empire, the device of farming out colonization, and the predominantly economic orientation of both colonists and sponsors. Contemporary commentators commonly attributed the British colonies' growth to their spirit of commerce and their attachment to their English "liberties," meaning a representative system of government, with imperial authority prudently distributed between metropolis and colonies. The end of the Seven Years' War offered British ministers an opportunity to implement a *directive* mode of imperial governance and reduce the colonies to subordination, shifting from a focus on commerce to a focus on the control of territory and people. The colonists protested that they were not subject to England, but, like England, subject to the king, but the controversy could not be settled short of war. Having learned nothing from the American Revolution, the British Empire went on to neo-absolutism, creating an imperial version of the centralized nation-state.

Bowen, in "Perceptions from the Periphery: Colonial American Views of Britain's Asiatic Empire, 1756–1783," focuses on interprovincial relationships between peripheries, or on how colonists of the "old" periphery of North America perceived and responded to the globalization of the British Empire after the Seven Years' War and to the "new" periphery in Asia. The Britishness of American colonials became more acute as they rejoiced in the victories over France, but their links to the Oriental empire were indirect, limited to what they read and the goods they consumed (tea and textiles). They feared the insidious "easternizing" influence of the East India Company on the imperial core and suspected the Company of planning to impose on them the same alien form of government as on Bengal. Americans did not reject the material benefits of Asian trade. Emphasizing their British liberties, they looked forward to an empire of trade of their own.

The premise of Onuf's essay, "'Empire for Liberty': Center and Peripheries in Postcolonial America," is that the American Revolution precipitated a controversy over territorial expansion. Federalist antiexpansionists were anti-imperial and in favor of national integration, thus "modern." They feared that an overextended union could not function competitively. Jeffersonian proexpansionists—republican imperialists—looked backward. Rejecting the consolidation of authority, they continued to think and act within an antiquated imperial framework and to believe in an idealized world order in which the expanding American union would be a transformative "empire for liberty," an empire without a center and without peripheries, having neither a dominant metropolis nor—under a liberal regime of free trade, operating through a great system of inland commerce—subject provinces. That vision failed from within. Memories of the old empire, British and monarchical, had ideologically regressive effects on the new empire, American and republican, causing republicans to see themselves as legatees of the revolution and their domestic foes as despots. The consequence of their obsessive focus on provincial liberties against the power of the modern nation-state was nation-breaking sectionalism.

Collectively, these fourteen essays consider the applications of center-periphery concepts for the analysis of the early modern European empires of the Americas. Their treatment of that vast subject is neither comprehensive nor systematic, but they do represent a significant beginning. In particular, they deepen our understanding of the underlying conditions, changing dynamics, and shifting internal organization of those empires and throw light upon the emergence of colonial centers and their association with colonial peripheries. In the process, they stress the importance of metropolitan inheritances, the incredible adaptability of those inheritances, the agency of settlers, and the power of peripheries to shape the negotiated empires of the early modern Americas. We recommend these essays in the hope that those who read them will make their subject the object of further elaboration and refinement.

Notes

1. See Jack P. Greene, "Mastery and the Definition of Cultural Space in Early America: A Perspective," in Greene, *Imperatives, Behaviors, and Identities: Essays in Early American Cultural History* (Charlottesville: University Press of Virginia, 1992), 1–12.
2. Derwent S. Whittlesey, *The Earth and the State: A Study of Political Geography* (New York: Henry Holt, 1944), 2, defines *ecumene* as the core of a political unit, identified by density of settlement and access to transportation. For a concentric model of ecumene, sphere of influence, and continental claim see Amy Turner Bushnell, *Situado and Sabana: Spain's Support System for the Presidio and Mission Provinces of Florida*, Anthropological Papers of the American Museum of Natural History, Number 74 (1994):18, 82, 144, 155–56, 169–70, 206.
3. Edward Shils, "Centre and Periphery," *The Logic of Personal Knowledge: Essays in Honour of Michael Polanyi* (Glencoe, Ill.: Free Press, 1961), 117–30. The quotations are from 117, 120, 122–24. Shils republished this piece as the title essay in his *Center and Periphery: Essays in Macrosociology* (Chicago: University of Chicago Press, 1975), 3–16.
4. Ibid., 123–25.
5. Ibid., 127.
6. Immanuel Wallerstein, *The Modern World-System: Capitalist Agriculture and the Origins of the European World-Economy in the Sixteenth Century* (New York: Academic Press, 1974); *The Modern World-System II: Mercantilism and the Consolidation of the European World-Economy, 1600–1750* (New York: Academic Press, 1980); *The Modern World-System III: The Second Era of Great Expansion of the Capitalist World-Economy, 1730–1840* (New York: Academic Press, 1989).
7. Wallerstein, *The Modern World-System: Capitalist Agriculture and the Origins of the European World-Economy in the Sixteenth Century*, 102–3, 129, 349.
8. See Steve J. Stern's extended, appreciative, and richly bibliographic critique of Immanuel Wallerstein in "Feudalism, Capitalism, and the World-System in the Perspective of Latin America and the Caribbean," *American Historical Review* 93:4 (1988), 829–72, which describes the intellectual antecedents of his schema and assesses its applicability to colonial and national systems of production, and Stern's debate with Wallerstein in the same issue, 873–97. For historical paradigm parallels for Latin America, the Caribbean, and Africa, see Frederick Cooper, Allen F. Isaacman, Florencia E. Mallon, William Roseberry, and Steve J. Stern, *Confronting Historical Paradigms: Peasants, Labor, and the Capitalist World System in Africa and Latin America* (Madison: University of Wisconsin Press, 1993).
9. A sociologist who continues to find the Wallerstein formulation useful for the analysis of these regions is Thomas D. Hall, "The Río de la Plata and the Greater Southwest: A View from World-System Theory," in Donna J. Guy and Thomas E. Sheridan, eds., *Contested Ground: Comparative Frontiers on the Northern and Southern Edges of the Spanish Empire* (Tucson: University of Arizona Press, 1998), 150–66.
10. David J. Weber, *The Mexican Frontier, 1821–1846* (Albuquerque: University of New Mexico Press, 1982), 124, 282; "Turner, the Boltonians, and the Borderlands," *American Historical Review* 91:1 (1986), 66–81, esp. 80–81; and *The Spanish Frontier in North America* (New Haven: Yale University Press, 1992), 11–13, 366–67.

11. Jack P. Greene, *Peripheries and Center: Constitutional Development in the Extended Polities of the British Empire and the United States, 1607–1788* (Athens: University of Georgia Press, 1986).
12. Jack P. Greene, "Negotiated Authorities: The Problem of Governance in the Extended Polities of the Early Modern Atlantic World," in Greene, *Negotiated Authorities: Essays in Colonial Political and Constitutional History* (Charlottesville: University of Virginia Press, 1994), 1–24.
13. D. W. Meinig, *Atlantic America, 1492–1800,* Volume I of *The Shaping of America: A Geographical Perspective on 500 Years of History* (New Haven, Conn.: Yale University Press, 1986), 258–67; emphasis in the original.
14. Ibid., 265–67.
15. James Lockhart and Stuart B. Schwartz, *Early Latin America: A History of Colonial Spanish America and Brazil* (New York: Cambridge University Press, 1983).
16. Examples are David Block, *Mission Culture on the Upper Amazon: Native Tradition, Jesuit Enterprise, and Secular Policy in Moxos, 1660–1880* (Lincoln: University of Nebraska Press, 1994), and Bushnell, *Situado and Sabana.*
17. An exception is Steve Stern, who writes of the emergence in America of a "competing center of gravity in the world marketplace." See Stern, "Feudalism, Capitalism, and the World System," 51.

Gates, Patterns, and Peripheries

The Field of Frontier Latin America

Amy Turner Bushnell

The past is a moving target, and any view of it is parallax and selective. Historians omit most places, periods, and peoples and declare the rest to be significant. But how does the selection process operate? When historians look at scraps of the past, how do they determine what to salvage and what to discard? What are the conditions of significance? The historical profession has a foolproof way of judging the value of any branch of historical knowledge: the Invisible Hand of the job market. Historians who specialize in a particular field are either hired or not. To paraphrase Stephen Crane, the historian says to the historical profession: "Sir, I exist!" "However," the profession shrugs, "the fact has not created in me a sense of obligation."[1] Any historian can identify the handful of viable specialties in her field. In the early modern Americas, each specialty follows the story of a particular group of European settlers as they conquer territory, displacing or appropriating its native inhabitants, then as a charter culture impose their language, religion, laws, and customs on those settlers who follow. What do these stories have in common? Primacy, success, and survival.

Primacy can derive from being either early or normative. When a charter culture splits to form several nations, as did the Viceroyalty of Peru, historians give primacy to the region that contains the original core. When multiple charter cultures unite to form one nation, as did thirteen of the colonies in eastern North America, primacy goes to the region considered normative, and the others are consigned to the ranks of state and local history to await a change in the criteria of anomaly. New England, long held to be normative for British America, has had its position challenged: the Chesapeake appears to offer a more typical settlement model, while the Middle Colonies more accurately prefigure subsequent American development. Historically significant cultures are successful: They increase in population and wealth, win pivotal wars, and expand territorially into nation-states, which use the tools of conquest and colonization to acquire empires. States that lose their empires or their independence retain their historical significance for another generation or two, thanks to the lag factors of institutional inertia, nostalgia, and the intellectual investment of scholars, but as historical specialties they are doomed to dwindle. If primacy is an attribute and success a conditional warranty, survival is what makes the story matter, for history is a consumer item which demands a constituency. Are the people who interest you destined to die out or to move without leaving a forwarding address? Tell them to pick up the bones of their fathers, for history is going to march them off the page. The past is layered. Spanish Jamaica built on Taino sites; British Jamaica let Spanish Jamaica biodegrade and is itself now falling to pieces.

As always, the reigning practice enjoys an elegant rationale. An analysis of historical significance, however, yields three propositions which call for elaboration: (1) the *paradigm of power* has traditionally determined what is significant and what is not; (2) the *paradigm of the victim* is the obverse of the first paradigm and lends it support; and (3) the *paradigm of negotiation* examines the mechanisms other than force that deliver balance to relationships and keep disparate societies in equilibrium.

The paradigm of power, highlighting the hegemony of Western Europeans and their descendants during the early modern and modern eras, is a spinoff of history's absorption with the nation-state.[2] As such it has long served as the gatekeeper of the profession. By favoring the imperial powers of early modern Europe and privileging those colonies which are destined to be both independent and imperial, it has narrowed historical significance down to manageable proportions. For decades, most doctoral candidates have moved along the chute and out the gate confident that any history department in good standing would welcome their specialty.

Within the framework of the nation-state or empire, the paradigm of power concentrates unapologetically on the ideas and acts of the people who possess power and exercise authority. In the radical 1960s, this approach came to be characterized as history from the top down or the inside out. Stung by charges of elitism, historians proclaimed a new social history from the bottom up and the outside in. They borrowed theories from the social sciences to analyze social structures and institutions and developed the imaginative tools and methodologies that permitted them to attend to society's least regarded members.[3] Some, convinced that they held the moral high ground, searched the past for the first signs of ideas consonant with their own, compounding rightmindedness and scholarship.

The new social history was not as revolutionary as it thought. Although universities in the United States moved into the study of the non-Western world, introducing courses on Eastern Europe, Asia, the Middle East, and Africa, the canon of historical significance for the Western world, defined as Western Europe and its settler colonies, was unaffected, its fields still governed by the gatekeeping paradigm of power. Historians played with interpretations that criticized the uses of power—world systems, dependency theory, cultural origins, postmodernism—but they did not question the right of power to determine which countries' histories mattered and which did not. They addressed new subjects, but their regional specialties, the nation-states and empires whose histories were common intellectual property, did not change.

Some scholars responded to the temper of the times by standing the paradigm of power on its head, creating the paradigm of the victim. This too failed to challenge the canon. Far from eliminating the paradigm of power, the substitution of culturalism for nationalism made power indispensable. The history of the Americas was reduced to a neomythology of the good and evil twins, pairing an essentialized victim and victor, conquered and conqueror, American Indian and European/

Eurocreole in a symbiotic relationship, like a doll with a reversible skirt and two heads. (Invert Little Red Riding Hood and she becomes the Wolf in Grandmother's nightgown.) A variant of victimhood is insider history, which holds that certain specialties, defined by race, gender, sexual orientation, or ethnicity, are of a nonintellectual nature, innate, to be known from the inside out, not studied from the outside in and thus subjected to ordinary rules of evidence.

The paradigm of power and its inversion urge us to divide the world into oppressed and oppressors. The paradigm of negotiation supplies an alternative.[4] Those who prefer to express historical phenomena in terms of power may think of it, with apologies to Richard White, as the middle ground that prevails when no one group has the incentive or the wherewithal to dominate the rest.[5] In premodern societies, where the means of coercion were limited, the political pattern was one of consensus. In an empire such as that of the Spanish Habsburgs, scholars uncover what to our modern sensibilities appear to be unseemly levels of bureaucratic flexibility, unlikely pockets of moral tolerance, and untenable disparities between law and practice. If the empowered and the disempowered were present in every premodern society, between them stood the broker. Premodern political authority was negotiable, as were other forms of authority. At every level of the social hierarchy and in every relationship, negotiation was a continuous process, shaping and reshaping the customary.

Historians who apply the paradigm of negotiation to a particular society frequently do so in terms of *agency*. Agency gives voice to society's least articulate members, grants them a modicum of control over their individual and collective fates, and applauds their every step toward self-determination. But the paradigm can also be applied territorially, and I use it to draw distinctions among the early Latin-American peripheries, based on the thesis that, all else being equal, the more remote the periphery, the weaker the grasp of central authority.

On the Latin-American frontier, the premodern European pattern of consensus and negotiated authority encountered an American-Indian pattern of consensus combined with a striking level of individualism. In European terms, the native pattern approached anarchy, yet it proved functional when the time came to construct or dissolve a polity. On both sides of the frontier, institutions existed to create bonds with outsiders and draw them into a relationship of mutual advantage. The Spanish "conquest by contract," which in the Spanish mind committed Indians to Christianity, fealty, and exclusive trade,[6] had its counterpart in equally solemn Indian ceremonies intended to turn Europeans into responsible kinsmen.

The paradigm of negotiation opens a way to approach the subject of Spanish settlement without combatting, once again, the Legends: the Black Legend exaggerating Spanish cruelty and the White Legend minimizing it. One need not be an apologist for Iberians in America to note their commonalities with the English, French, and Dutch. If non-Iberians were responsible for the deaths of fewer Indians, they had fewer to kill, which may explain why historians of the northern colonies tend to treat Indians as proscenium players who slip away as the curtain rises. The Spaniards' early arrival was probably their saving grace, for in their intellectual baggage were remnants of the communal morality, answerability, and paternalism designed to curb man's inhumanity to man. When these medieval concepts faded, many protective institutions went with them, institutions that were inconceivable to later colonizing powers and barely within the ken of modern scholars.

From time to time, historians find it helpful to stand back and take a fresh look at their field's terminology, tracing its development and giving it crisper definition.[7] The uneasiness scholars display over whether to make the language shift from "frontier" to "periphery" suggests that such an exercise would be useful now. We have a few starting points. With David J. Weber, we now commonly define "frontier" in geographical terms as both place and process, a zone of interaction between two cultures.[8] Also, James Lockhart and Stuart B. Schwartz have made a distinction between peripheries, which had some connection to the centers, and fringes, which had little or none, defining the latter as places with "no major export asset," "that portion of the hemisphere in which Iberians at any given time were not very interested."[9]

Historians of British America and the United States have traditionally regarded the frontier as a transitory stage on the continuum between reconnaissance and replication, with a mature polity being one which in population density, political forms, social institutions, economic structure, customs, laws, and values replicates the core from which the first settlers came.[10] Latin-American historians, by contrast, are prone to treat frontiers as places of fear and barbarism, where the advance agents of civilization—*degredados*, *bandeirantes*, *gaochos*, and Indian fighters—are near barbarians themselves. The multiple Latin-American frontiers do not progress along the continuum from reconnaissance to replication with the same sense of inevitability as the Anglo frontier in North America. On the "wild" frontiers, the process may well stall or go into reverse. Using *nation* in the old sense of a group sharing a language and customs, I define the early modern frontier as a geographic area contested by two or more nations, each of which is engaged in a process of polity formation in which control is tenuous and continuously negotiated, and each of which tries to extend its negotiating mechanisms to include the others. This definition is ethnically neutral and allows for various casts of actors. It can be applied to American-Indian confederations, amalgamations, conquests, and migrations just as it can to the ones that Europeans and Eurocreoles set in motion.

Spaces that Europeans represented as under their jurisdiction may be divided into three concentric zones. The *ecumene* was a *zone of mastery*, the immediate area over which an urban settlement of European origin asserted political and economic control. In Spanish America, an ecumene usually consisted of a European settlement and a hinterland of native provinces. Several ecumenes grouped around, and in supporting a *colonial center* they formed a colonial core, or *core region*. The *colonial periphery*, which I define as the most remote area where the authority of a particular colonial center was recognized, was a *zone of marginality*. Such a periphery was also a *frontier* if it was, as Howard Lamar and Leonard Thompson explain, a zone of cultural interaction or interpenetration among previously distinct societies.[11] People of European origin living on a frontier were not so much settlers as agents of settlement, surviving in mixed communities on the edges of empire by negotiating with all sides. Beyond the periphery lay the *sphere of influence*, or transfrontier, an intermediate *zone of exchange*. In terms of central control, the boundary crossers hunting and trading in this zone were transients, temporarily "outside of empire." Beyond the sphere of influence was the *claim*, which was no zone at all but rather the vast cartographic expanse to which an early modern monarch held title under European international law.[12] Over time, French, Dutch, and English interlopers challenged the validity of titles based upon discovery and papal donation and justified by exploration and conquest, and their states were able to enforce the contrasting international norm of effective occupation, with native acquiescence as the tacit condition.

In their relationship to the colonial centers, the Latin-American peripheries may be divided into the categories of internal and external, which roughly correspond to nearer and farther. They may be divided further into contiguous and noncontiguous, or into regions that will eventually be incorporated into a historically significant entity and regions that will not. These are not hard and fast categories; a given periphery may start out in one camp and end up in another. One might say it is a case of *estos y esos*. *These* peripheries are internal/contiguous/to-be-incorporated and *those* peripheries are external/noncontiguous/to-be-dropped.

Latin-American historians have no problem identifying the cores: proud cities adorned by courts of law, cathedrals, palaces, mints, theaters, and (except in Brazil) universities, with their attendant hinterlands and ports. Between James Lockhart's "law of the preservation of energy of historians," which impels scholars to use the easiest sources first,[13] and the paradigm of power, which makes it professionally canny to focus on those colonies that will evolve into nation-states, the Latin-American cores are well known. Less well known, but with a respectable and growing literature, are the *internal peripheries*. Relatively close to the cores geographically, they manifest a high level of central control, coupled with a high level of exploitation of natural resources and high demands on the subject population in the form of taxes and tributary labor. An example of the internal periphery is the Sierra de Oaxaca.[14] The internal peripheries are the places most likely to fit the paradigm of the victim and thus to yield support to the paradigm of power. They are marginal, but in the schema of historical significance, they are significantly marginal, for they orbit a significant center and any work done on them contributes to the historiography of one of the countries in the historical canon. As a result, historians of the internal peripheries such as the Peruvian Montaña, the Sierra de Oaxaca, the Yucatán, the Llanos, or the Pampas take care to associate themselves with a colonial core as card-carrying Peruvianists, Mexicanists, or specialists in Gran Colombia or the Southern Cone.

The *external peripheries* are another matter. Relatively distant and loosely connected to the cores that bear administrative responsibility for them—responsibility that is not sought and may well be divided among several cores—they are the fringes. The tide of empire that once established colonies like Florida, the Philippines, Jamaica, and New Mexico, reached by sea or across great deserts, has ebbed and retreated, leaving the external peripheries stranded, excluded from national or colonial histories, unrepresented in history departments. With their archives damaged and dispersed in riots, Indian wars, revolutions, border conflicts, and changes of sovereignty, the external peripheries are insignificantly marginal.

Historically, the external peripheries enjoyed a lower level of central control and a correspondingly higher level of autonomy. In the words of Susan Migden Socolow, "the frontier developed its own distinct social forms and life-styles, in which the relative distance from centers of viceregal power bred independence, valor, and self-sufficiency."[15] The traditional view of Latin America's lightly controlled external peripheries is that settler autonomy led to Indian abuse and went hand-in-hand with victimization, with more liberty for Europeans and Eurocreoles translating into less liberty for everyone else. For the brutal years of the high conquest, this is no doubt the case. But once the name of the game changes to pacification and old-style conquerors find themselves in disrepute and facing an altogether different kind of American Indian, the old theory of limited liberty, like the peasant concept of limited good, becomes ripe for challenge, for nowhere is the process of negotiation more demonstrable than on the external peripheries, Latin America's true frontiers.

There are many possible ways to subdivide the Latin-American frontiers for analysis. Some of the variables might well be whether a particular frontier is in the *doctrina* stage or has advanced to paying tithes; whether it is tropical or temperate, maritime or landlocked, military or civil. Other variables might be its racial composition, its labor and tribute systems, its settlement patterns, its internal and external trade, its method of naturalizing outsiders, and its wary adaptation to European cultigens and animals, iron tools and firearms.

The categories I find most useful for frontier analysis are *strategic* and *nonstrategic*. Nonstrategic frontiers made their way toward or away from Europeanness unaided. They were virtually independent, the European presence being maintained by persons who owed little to king or kingdom. A nonstrategic frontier could be produced in a number of ways. When a religious order undertook conversions at a remove from European settlement, the polity on Utopian or theocratic lines that they and their native allies created could exist in splendid isolation, at least until its resources and labor pool came to settler notice. An *adelantado* with a personal army could establish the equivalent of a European marchland. If he or his successors tried to recoup their costs by selling captives, the war of conquest and reprisal was apt to last as long as the market for slaves. Sometimes, entrepreneurs of various nationalities swarmed around a wreck or other source of treasure to create a rough and temporary community. Finally, Europeans or Eurocreoles could slip the leash entirely, establishing themselves as buccaneers, smugglers, or wildcat conquerors. Maroon communities and enclaves of exaction-fleeing Indians were their non-European counterparts.

Strategic frontiers were, by contrast, heavily subsidized by the cores, whether the financial support came from the Crown or from a religious order, as was the case with Jesuit missions on the Upper Amazon.[16] The strategic frontier I study is Spanish Florida, which on the scale of historical significance falls into the realm of negative numbers. Years ago, Irene Zimmerman, librarian of the Latin American Collection at the University of Florida, tried to steer me away from the study of colonial failures, specifically from a comparison of France's two mid-sixteenth-century ventures in Brazil and Florida.[17] "There's no future in failed colonies," she warned. "Things go from bad to worse, and then everyone gets up and goes home." It is safe to say that a majority of colonies ended in failure or took a different turn than their founders planned. In many parts of America, Eurocreoles had to choose between accepting a change of flag and moving on. Florida, a pawn on the treaty table, changed hands three times, going from Spain to Great Britain in 1763, from Britain to Spain in 1784, and from Spain to the United States in 1821. In state history textbooks, the two centuries before 1763 suffer from the Sleeping Beauty syndrome. St. Augustine, the castle on the coast, comes to life only when someone appears, sword in hand, to force an entrance. Juan Ponce de León, Pánfilo de Narváez, Hernando de Soto, Jean Ribault, Sir Francis Drake, assorted pirates, James Moore of Carolina, and James Oglethorpe of Georgia—all receive more attention than the colonists themselves.[18]

In terms of the paradigm of power, in which the finale is all that counts, Spanish Florida unquestionably failed. As far as the Crown itself was concerned, Florida's purpose was strategic. It was first a captaincy general, second a mission field, and only by sufferance a colony of settlers. Its garrison town, or *presidio*, was founded by royal command in an enterprise heavily underwritten by royal funds. For strategic reasons the Crown continued to maintain the colony with a *situado*, or annual subvention, as a steady drain upon the royal exchequer. Dependence had its advantages. The important division within the Florida elite was not between peninsulars and Creoles but between royalists and provincials, with the royalists substantially outnumbered. In the Florida branch of the royal treasury, provincials, either born or naturalized, were in office 97 percent of possible time between 1571 and 1702, drawing several royal governors into their family networks. All of the rulers of the Republic of Indians, natural lords of the land, were provincials. These chiefs were paid out of the situado for their role in defense and labor procurement. The laborers, too, were paid. The provinces of Franciscanized Indians served as military buffer zones and sources of provisions and labor for St. Augustine. Had Spain not been concerned about the return route of the silver galleons, Florida, with its semisedentary, demanding Indians, its poor soils and piney woods, and its modest maritime resources, would undoubtedly have been left to itself.[19]

At its largest, Florida was a discoverers' claim stretching from the Pánuco River around the Gulf of Mexico and up the Atlantic coast to Newfoundland. Within that claim, explorers searched for a northern water route to the Orient and sought to open a transcontinental road from Santa Elena to Zacatecas.[20] England challenged Spain's sovereignty with colonies of its own under the principle of effective occupation, an expression of squatter's rights. But in the Southeast, as truly as in New York, the American-Indian nations held the balance of power. Florida's sphere of influence was a fragile one, maintained by treaties of alliance and trade and ratified by gifts. Within that sphere was the smaller ecumene of mission provinces, acting as a hinterland to the presidio in St. Augustine. As Spain trimmed its sails in eastern North America, the area known as Florida contracted. In the mid-1680s Florida lost its sphere of influence to traders from Carolina, and by 1706 its provinces as well. In the eighteenth century, Spanish Florida controlled little more than the fortified ports of St. Augustine, St. Marks, and Pensacola. The territory west of the St. Johns River was in Indian hands and would remain so until the nineteenth-century Seminole Wars. Spain was overextended in eastern North America, and the colony of Florida, an external periphery, was left stranded. Yet, because the outpost of St. Augustine was strategic, the Crown continued to support it, postponing the inevitable for over a hundred years and offering historians a chance to observe a maritime periphery with and without provinces.

One might imagine that the strategic frontiers, receiving a subvention from the defense funds of one of the royal treasuries in the Indies, would be at least as tightly controlled as the internal peripheries those same cores exploited, but in Florida, a "tierra reputada por guerra viva," Indian and non-Indian provincials took advantage of the Crown's preoccupation with distant events to wrest political and economic control from the royalists—all without damage to the empire's two discourses of union, the "divine cult" and the cult of the king. In Florida, a higher level of royal investment did not bring a correspondingly higher level of central control. On the contrary, it offered low-risk financial opportunities. Both royalists and provincials treated the situado as a kind of trust fund. *Floridanos* paid themselves for serving in the militia. Instead of paying tithes to a bishop, they asked for and received royal grants to build and maintain their church and to support their secular priest and his entourage. Mission Indians similarly worked the system. Gifts from the Crown outfitted their doctrinas and paid their *doctrineros'* stipends. True, the Indians planted *sabanas* to support public and religious officials, but they also benefited by them. Unless rationed with corn from the king's sabana, Indians refused to build themselves stockades or to campaign against Spain's enemies, and they expected the convent's sabana to beautify their sanctuaries and support their orphans. The colony survived on give and take, constantly renegotiated.

The reason why, on the frontiers, I would replace the paradigm of power and its inversion with the paradigm of negotiation is that this third paradigm makes it possible to escape on the one hand the teleology of the nation-state and empire and, on the other, the sterilities of economic determinism, politicized multiculturalism, and self-referential postmodernism. Focusing on negotiation allows one to see, on a frontier, two societies surviving side by side, not because the one is economically stagnant, spiritually irresolute, and unable to conclude a conquest and the other is irretrievably ruined and wronged, but because together they have achieved that wonder of human accomplishments, a delicate, constantly negotiated balance.

North Americans in cowboy boots and Stetsons may find it difficult to understand, but Spanish Americans have never shown much interest in their frontiers. The Wars for Independence led them in a different direction altogether than the Revolutionary War took British Americans. Instead of forming a federation, the Spanish-American patriots lost one: Spain's great viceroyalties fractured into their component parts of *audiencias*, presidencies, and captaincies. Interpreting the move from union to disunion, empire to nations, as a decline, historians of Spanish America have shown a tendency to look back upon a Golden Age of Spanish wealth and culture or upon an even more glorious pre-Columbian one. Their colonial picture focuses on the populous centers, not on the disorderly, Indian-bedeviled frontiers, and especially not on the places fated to be overrun by Anglo settlers and engulfed by the brashly expansionist United States. Historians of colonial Brazil have been more cognizant of their peripheries, but no Frederick Jackson Turner has appeared to pull the geographically scattered and temporally disparate Latin-American frontiers into a single conceptual field. Even now, no one historian pretends to encompass them. In the epic of European expansion, Latin-American frontiers and frontiersmen are markedly missing, and without them, the colonial story line goes flat.

Twenty-five years ago, Richard Boyer summarized the historiography of New Spain's so-called "century of depression." The original thesis, set forward by Lesley B. Simpson, Woodrow Borah, and François Chevalier, was that a shortage of labor in Central Mexico, created by a declining Indian population, led to "falling exports of silver and less trade with Seville," and that these in turn "caused an economic dark age" in which "society withdrew for survival into self-sufficient haciendas." This elegant thesis, said Boyer, had not stood up to examination. Historians had come to see New Spain's seventeenth century "not as a century of depression, but as one of transition to capitalism, economic diversification, and vigorous regional economies."[21]

Dramas similar to the Mexican one were being enacted all across Spanish and

Portuguese America. Scholars of colonial Latin America have studied the middle period at length, examining far-flung mission provinces,[22] frontiers of settlement[23] and their environmental consequences,[24] disease and depopulation,[25] the settler capacity to hold office yet resist regulation,[26] the survival of indigenous religion,[27] the sociology of plural societies,[28] and labor systems.[29] The monographs march under a bold banner: Agency to the provincials! Coverage to the peripheries! Action to the seventeenth century!

Yet the general impression of the middle period continues to be one of lethargy and stagnation, devoid of narrative structure.[30] Between the 1550s, when viceroys brought the period of freelance reconnaissance and conquests to an end, and the 1740s, when rapid population growth and increases in commerce brought fresh intrusions into the hemisphere along with higher defense costs, higher taxes, and more controlled economies, periodization is weak, pinned to the reigns of kings or the forays of European rivals. Like writers of romance novels, authors of textbooks on colonial Latin America seem to regard maturity as uneventful. Faced with a long, seemingly warless stretch between the sixteenth-century high conquest and the eighteenth-century wars for empire, and unable to do justice to every place, they retreat into the thematic. A typical text begins with the contrasting heritages brought to the encounter by Iberians and Native Americans but not Africans, then summarizes the early period of discovery, exploration, and conquest. The long middle period is treated in terms of colonial institutions, civil and religious, the society of castes, external trade, and the internal economy. Narrative returns at the close, with the eighteenth century's economic upturns and defense-driven Bourbon and Pombaline reforms.

While a thematic scheme has unquestionable interpretive value, it can obscure the factors of place and time in ways that narrative, with its stubborn particularisms, cannot. Concentrating upon the established colonial centers of population and governance, on which the literature is large and accessible, the thematic approach slights the scattered literature on the peripheries, which has yet to be subjected to synthesis. This omission is unfortunate, for during the long seventeenth century, when Iberian metropolises and colonial centers were hardpressed, the frontiers were exhibiting energy and initiative.

The static view of the long middle period, 1570 to 1715, infers a past blessedly free of wars—a distortion that military historians, concentrating on the professional army created in 1764, have done little to correct. The Pax Hispaña, like the Century of Depression, is a myth. Between the high conquest of the imperial peoples at the start of the colonial period and the mercantilist, absolutist reforms at the close, warfare moved to the frontiers. On the edges of empire, war, declared or undeclared, was a factor in virtually every equation. Fear of the loss of herds and harvests inhibited the development of ranches and farms. Fear of pirates reshaped the settlement pattern and the transportation network. A reversion to the feudal host lay behind the *encomienda* subjecting Indians to tribute and personal service. Missions were located defensively and had the walls of fortresses. In a "tierra reputada por guerra viva," war interrupted communications, interfered with trade, spawned monopoly trading companies, and led to inflation. It offered cover to smuggling, profiteering, and bold experiments in self-government. Every facet of colonial life becomes sharper in the glare of war, yet in the pages of Latin-American colonial history, warfare, like the frontiers, is downplayed. Lives of conquistadors and liberators are as unfashionable and unread as lives of saints and chronicles. Historians gloss over the ravages of conquest and slave raiding, letting European pathogens shoulder all the blame for the massive declines in native populations, or they refashion the past by playing down Indian violence.

When the new social history appeared on the scene, historians of colonial Latin America readily dismantled what was left of the old politico-military framework. Combining theories adapted from the burgeoning new fields of social science, ideas of labor value and class struggle taken from Marxism, and methodologies borrowed from the Annales school of French historians and the Cambridge Group for the History of Population and Social Structure, the new social historians tried to look at past societies from top to bottom, including the inarticulate and powerless. The use of new social and economic sources—visual materials, oral traditions, parish registers, public records, censuses, notary books, price lists, manifests, militia musters, and ledgers—many of them closer to serial data than to literature, made it possible partially to reconstruct vanished communities and neglected groups and recreate structures, processes, and mentalities that contemporaries had neither perceived nor remarked.[31] The civil rights movement in the United States focused much of the new social awareness on the experience of African slaves. A Russian-supported communist regime in Cuba, a new and peasant-centered strain of communism in China, and bitter generational conflict in the Western world over such concerns as university access, nuclear weapons, and the war in Vietnam—all suggested new themes to scholars and exerted new pressures, on the one hand for social relevance and on the other for ideological conformity. The feminist movement created further tensions and demands.

But the new social history was a mixed blessing. While it yielded an impressive number of regional studies to be explored for *conjuncture*, its thrust was to take the historiography even farther from events and narrative. Expanding graduate studies and narrowing dissertation topics—the latter a function of the new history's new sources—brought about a proliferation of local studies. Most historians chose to focus on the microcosm, abandoning the tasks of synthesis and overview. Attent to singularity, they regarded the level of generality necessary for comparison as unacceptable. Narrative history gave way to analytical; comprehensiveness, to the telling moment or the representative place. Subjects that had been significant during the colonial era were denied historical representation as no longer relevant; places that were to end up on the wrong side of a modern border were left unclaimed, along with their historians. Among the many regions which fell from grace and out of historiography were the loyal British colonies; the inconstant French, Dutch, and Spanish Caribbean; French Canada and Louisiana; and the Spanish Borderlands.

When in 1995 the Conference of Latin American Historians (CLAH) added a committee on the Spanish Borderlands to its regional studies committees, scholars working in that field were given a rare opportunity to redefine themselves and chart a new course. At their inaugural meeting, the "Borderlanders" looked resolutely forward. They did not revisit the sixteenth-century Black Legend or the nineteenth-century Hispanophiles, nor rehash the ideas of Frederick Jackson Turner's student Herbert E. Bolton, whom they held responsible for their field's ambiguous name.[32] They did not review the historiography of attempts to identify a common colonial experience, such as Bolton's Greater America or Silvio Zavala's Program for the History of the Americas.[33] They did not survey the recent literature, nor note how large a share of it had been produced by scholars writing in English and living by their wits outside of academe.

Largely early modernists, the Borderlanders were inclined to limit their temporal mandate to the colonial and early national periods, with closure in the 1840s, but they left their territorial mandate open. Borderlanders of both species, Southeastern and southwestern, were comfortable with a Greater Caribbean that took in Florida, a Greater Mexico that included the western borderlands and the Philippines, an early Southeast that started with the mound-building Mississippians, and even with the concept of European expansion and its alter ego, the Atlantic world. Forty years of wandering in the *Handbook for Latin American Studies* and regional CLAH committees had taught them to shelter under any wing.

Historians of the "New West" had rejected the term *frontier*, but Borderlanders came from a separate historical tradition and took pride in its distinctiveness. They did not seek to be recognized as a subset of early American history. The new multicultural climate had made it political for historians of the United States to acknowledge that the past was polycolonial, and, prompted by the Omohundro Institute for Early American History and Culture and the *William and Mary Quarterly*, British-American colonialists were sending forth their graduate students to colonize it. The battle for recognition had been won. Would gaining ground in the United States mean losing ground in Latin America? Borderlanders saw no reason why that should follow. Like a child in joint custody, they planned to play one parent against another.

The first action that the membership of the newly formed Spanish Borderlands committee took was to enlarge their boundaries. Recognizing the need to play in ensemble with their counterparts on Latin America's other historical frontiers, they changed the group's name to Frontiers and Borderlands and invited all historians with parallel interests to join them. Like most new fields, Frontier Latin America faced difficulties of fragmented historiography, idiosyncratic terminology, and insufficient theory. Unlike most scholars in a new field, however, the Frontier/Borderlanders were experienced at comparison. Already, they had launched comparative projects, taught comparative courses,[34] published comparative articles in major journals, and organized sessions, workshops, and conferences to bring themselves face-to-face with their colleagues working not only on northern New Spain, Bolton's "Rim of Christendom," but on Chile, the Yucatan, Argentina, the Peruvian Montaña, the Amazon, and the *islas inútiles* of the Caribbean.

Frontier Latin America is richly comparable, with parameters drawn deliberately wide. The scholars of this new field disregard the watershed of independence to follow their subjects from start to finish. They overlook political boundaries to reach as far west as New Spain's Pacific colonies in the Philippines and as far north as Nootka. They bridge the fearful Spanish-Portuguese language divide. They consider themselves equally free to ask the new questions about marginality, resistance, gender, ethnicity, ecology, encounters, and texts and to revisit the classic questions about institutions, elites, politics, and wars. While many topics remain to be explored, enough studies have now been done to make possible a systematic and comparative synthesis of the Latin-American frontiers, attentive to the unfolding patterns of peace and war. By acting in concert, the historians in this promising new field may find the power to open the gates of historical significance, at last, to the peripheries.

Notes

1. Stephen Crane, "A Man Said to the Universe," in J. Paul Hunter, ed., *Poetry* (New York: W. W. Norton, 1973), 352.
2. See Jack P. Greene, "Beyond Power: Paradigm Subversion and Reformulation and the Re-Creation of the Early Modern Atlantic World," in Greene, *Interpreting Early America: Historiographical Essays* (Charlottesville: University of Virginia Press, 1996), 17–42.
3. Jack P. Greene, "The New History: From 'Top to Bottom'," *The New York Times*, January 8, 1975, 37, reprinted in Greene, *Interpreting Early America*, 3–5; Steve J. Stern, "Africa, Latin America, and the Splintering of Historical Knowledge: From Fragmentation to Reverberation," in Frederick Cooper, Allen F. Isaacman, Florencia E. Mallon, William Roseberry, and Steve J. Stern, *Confronting Historical Paradigms: Peasants, Labor, and the Capitalist World System in Africa and Latin America* (Madison: University of Wisconsin Press, 1993), 3–20.
4. Jack P. Greene, "Negotiated Authorities: The Problem of Governance in the Extended Polities of the Early Modern Atlantic World," in Greene, *Negotiated Authorities: Essays in Colonial Political and Constitutional History* (Charlottesville: University of Virginia Press, 1994), 1–24.
5. The term was introduced by Richard White, *The Middle Ground: Indians, Empires, and Republics in the Great Lakes Region, 1650–1815* (Cambridge: Cambridge University Press, 1991), to refer to a region of Indian refugees so mixed and chaotic that French colonial authorities assumed the role of mediator, being the only parties with the means to make the appropriate gifts. Its adoption was so immediate that Gregory Evans Dowd is concerned that historians of eastern North America have begun to use "middle ground," representing a frontier phenomenon "unusual, isolated, and fleeting," as a synonym for "frontier." See Dowd's "'Insidious Friends': Gift Giving and the Cherokee-British Alliance in the Seven Years' War," in Andrew R. L. Cayton and Fredrika J. Teute, eds., *Contact Points: American Frontiers from the Mohawk Valley to the Mississippi, 1750–1830* (Chapel Hill: University of North Carolina Press, 1998), 114–50, citing 118, n. 3.
6. See Amy Turner Bushnell, "Spain's Conquest by Contract: Pacification and the Mission System in Eastern North America," in Michael V. Kennedy and William G. Shade, eds., *The World Turned Upside Down: The State of Eighteenth-Century American Studies at the Beginning of the Twenty-First Century* (Bethlehem, Penn.: Lehigh University Press, 2001), 289–320.
7. As an example, see the deconstruction of the terms used for evangelism in colonial Spanish America in Amy Turner Bushnell, *Situado and Sabana: Spain's Support System for the Presidio and Mission Provinces of Florida*, Anthropological Papers of the American Museum of Natural History, Number 74 (1994), 20–23.
8. David J. Weber, *The Spanish Frontier in North America* (New Haven, Conn.: Yale University Press, 1992), 11.
9. James Lockhart and Stuart B. Schwartz, *Early Latin America: A History of Colonial Spanish America and Brazil* (New York: Cambridge University Press, 1983), 253–56.
10. For expressions of this position see Jack P. Greene, "Independence, Improvement, and Authority: Toward a Framework for Understanding the Histories of the Southern Backcountry during the Era of the American Revolution," in Greene, *Imperatives, Behaviors, and Identities: Essays in Early American Cultural History* (Charlottesville: University of Virginia Press, 1992), 181–207, and "Social and Cultural Capital in Colonial British America: A Case Study," in Robert I. Rotberg, ed., *Patterns of Social Capital: Stability and Change in Historical Perspective* (Cambridge: Cambridge University Press, 2001), 153–71.
11. For this definition see Howard Lamar and Leonard Thompson, "Introduction," in Lamar and Thompson, eds., *The Frontier in History: North America and Southern Africa Compared* (New Haven, Conn.: Yale University Press, 1981), 7.
12. For a definition of "ecumene" see Derwent S. Whittlesey, in *The Earth and the State: A Study of Political Geography* (New York: Henry Holt, 1944), 2. For a concentric model

of ecumene, sphere of influence, and continental claim see Bushnell, *Situado and Sabana*, 18, 82, 144, 155–56, 169–70, 206.

13. James Lockhart, "The Social History of Colonial Spanish America: Evolution and Potential," *Latin American Research Review* 7:1 (1972), 8.
14. See John K. Chance, *Conquest of the Sierra: Spaniards and Indians in Colonial Oaxaca* (Norman: University of Oklahoma Press, 1989).
15. Susan Migden Socolow, "Introduction to the Rural Past," in Louisa Schell Hoberman and Susan Migden Socolow, eds., *The Countryside in Colonial Latin America* (Albuquerque: University of New Mexico, 1996), 3–18, quoting from 8.
16. David Block, *Mission Culture on the Upper Amazon: Native Tradition, Jesuit Enterprise, and Secular Policy in Moxos, 1660–1880* (Lincoln: University of Nebraska Press, 1994), 174–81.
17. On this subject see Frank Lestringant, "Geneva and America in the Renaissance: The Dream of the Huguenot Refuge 1555–1600," *The Sixteenth Century Journal* 26:2 (1995), 285–95; John Terrence McGrath, *France in America, 1555–1565: A Reevaluation of the Evidence* (Ann Arbor, Mich.: University Microfilms, 1995); and John T. McGrath, *The French in Early Florida: In the Eye of the Hurricane* (Gainesville: University Press of Florida, 2000).
18. Charlton W. Tebeau, *A History of Florida* (Coral Gables: University of Miami Press, 1971).
19. See John Jay TePaske, *The Governorship of Spanish Florida 1700–1763* (Durham, N.C.: Duke University Press, 1964), and these studies by Bushnell: *Situado and Sabana*, 18, 82, 144, 155–56, 169–70, 206; *The King's Coffer: Proprietors of the Spanish Florida Treasury, 1565–1702* (Gainesville: University Presses of Florida, 1981); "How to Fight a Pirate: Provincials, Royalists, and the Defense of Minor Ports during the Age of Buccaneers," *Gulf Coast Historical Review* 5:2 (1990), 18–35; and "Ruling 'the Republic of Indians' in Seventeenth-Century Florida," in Peter H. Wood, Gregory A. Waselkov, and M. Thomas Hatley, eds., *Powhatan's Mantle: Indians in the Colonial Southeast* (Lincoln: University of Nebraska Press, 1989), 134–35.
20. See Paul E. Hoffman, *A New Andalucia and a Way to the Orient. The American Southeast during the Sixteenth Century* (Baton Rouge: Louisiana State University Press, 1990).
21. Richard Boyer, "Mexico in the Seventeenth Century: Transition of a Colonial Society," *Hispanic American Historical Review* 57:3 (1977), 455–78.
22. For examples, see David Block, *Mission Culture on the Upper Amazon: Native Tradition, Jesuit Enterprise, and Secular Policy in Moxos, 1660–1880* (Lincoln: University of Nebraska Press, 1994); Bushnell, *Situado and Sabana*; John H. Hann, *Apalachee: The Land between the Rivers* (Gainesville: University of Florida Press, 1988); John L. Kessell, *Kiva, Cross, and Crown: The Pecos Indians and New Mexico 1540–1840*, 2nd ed. (Albuquerque: University of New Mexico Press, 1987); James Schofield Saeger, *The Chaco Mission Frontier: The Guaycuruan Experience* (Tucson: University of Arizona Press, 2000); and Harry W. Crosby, *Antigua California: Mission and Colony on the Peninsular Frontier, 1697–1768* (Albuquerque: University of New Mexico Press, 1994).
23. See Ramón A. Gutiérrez, *When Jesus Came, the Corn Mothers Went Away: Marriage, Sexuality, and Power in New Mexico, 1500–1846* (Stanford, Calif.: Stanford University Press, 1991); Oakah L. Jones Jr., *Nueva Vizcaya: Heartland of the Spanish Frontier* (Albuquerque: University of New Mexico Press, 1988); James Officer, *Hispanic Arizona, 1536–1845* (Tucson: University of Arizona Press, 1987); and Ida Altman, *Emigrants and Society: Extremadura and Spanish America in the Sixteenth Century* (Berkeley and Los Angeles: University of California Press, 1989).
24. See Warren Dean, *With Broadax and Firebrand: The Destruction of the Brazilian Atlantic Forest* (Berkeley and Los Angeles: University of California Press, 1995); Elinor G. K. Melville, *A Plague of Sheep: Environmental Consequences of the Conquest of Mexico* (Cambridge: Cambridge University Press, 1994); and Cynthia Radding, *Wandering Peoples: Colonialism, Ethnic Spaces, and Ecological Frontiers in Northwestern Mexico, 1700–1850* (Durham, N.C.: Duke University Press, 1997).
25. See Suzanne Austin Alchon, *Native Society and Disease in Colonial Ecuador* (Cam-

bridge: Cambridge University Press, 1991); Daniel T. Reff, *Disease, Depopulation, and Culture Change in Northwestern New Spain, 1518–1764* (Salt Lake City: University of Utah Press, 1991); Ann F. Ramenofsky, *Vectors of Death: The Archaeology of European Contact* (Albuquerque: University of New Mexico Press, 1987); David Henige, *Numbers from Nowhere: The American Indian Contact Population Debate* (Norman: University of Oklahoma Press, 1998); and Noble David Cook, *Born to Die: Disease and New World Conquest, 1492–1650* (Cambridge: Cambridge University Press, 1998).

26. See Bushnell, *The King's Coffer*; Chance, *Conquest of the Sierra*; Eugene Lyon, *The Enterprise of Florida: Pedro Menéndez de Avilés and the Spanish Conquest of 1565–1568* (Gainesville: University Presses of Florida, 1976); Ralph Vigil, *Alonso de Zorita: Royal Judge and Christian Humanist, 1512–1585* (Norman: University of Oklahoma Press, 1987); and Christopher Ward, *Imperial Panama: Commerce and Conflict in Isthmian America 1550–1800* (Albuquerque: University of New Mexico Press, 1993).

27. See Sabine MacCormack, *Religion in the Andes: Vision and Imagination in Early Colonial Peru* (Princeton, N.J.: Princeton University Press, 1991); Kenneth Mills, *Idolatry and Its Enemies: Colonial Andean Religion and Extirpation, 1640–1750* (Princeton, N.J.: Princeton University Press, 1997); Vicente Rafael, *Contracting Colonialism: Translation and Christian Conversion in Tagalog Society under Early Spanish Rule* (Ithaca, N.Y.: Cornell University Press, 1988); and Fernando Cervantes, *The Devil in the New World: The Impact of Diabolism in New Spain* (New Haven, Conn.: Yale University Press, 1994).

28. See John K. Chance, *Race and Class in Colonial Oaxaca* (Stanford, Calif.: Stanford University Press, 1978); Nancy M. Farriss, *Maya Society under Colonial Rule: The Collective Enterprise of Survival* (Princeton, N.J.: Princeton University Press, 1984); Cheryl English Martin, *Rural Society in Colonial Morelos* (Albuquerque: University of New Mexico Press, 1985); Robert Patch, *Maya and Spaniard in Yucatan, 1648–1812* (Stanford, Calif.: Stanford University Press, 1993); and Karen Spalding, *Huarochirí: An Andean Society under Inca and Spanish Rule* (Stanford, Calif.: Stanford University Press, 1984).

29. See Ann M. Wightman, *Indigenous Migration and Social Change: The* Forasteros *of Cuzco, 1520–1720* (Durham, N.C.: Duke University Press, 1990); Ann Zulawski, *They Eat from Their Labor: Work and Social Change in Colonial Bolivia* (Pittsburgh: University of Pittsburgh Press, 1995); Murdo J. MacLeod, *Spanish Central America: A Socioeconomic History, 1520–1720* (Berkeley and Los Angeles: University of California Press, 1973); Jeffrey A. Cole, *The Potosí Mita 1573–1700: Compulsory Indian Labor in the Andes* (Stanford, Calif.: Stanford University Press, 1985); and William Frederick Sharp, *Slavery on the Spanish Frontier: The Colombian Chocó, 1680–1810* (Norman: University of Oklahoma Press, 1976).

30. See Amy Turner Bushnell, "A Peripheral Perspective," *Historical Archaeology* 31:1 (1997), 18–23.

31. Greene, "The New History."

32. David J. Weber, *Myth and the History of the Hispanic Southwest* (Albuquerque: University of New Mexico Press, 1988), and, as editor, *New Spain's Far Northern Frontier: Essays on Spain in the American West, 1540–1821* (Albuquerque: University of New Mexico Press, 1979); Light T. Cummins, "Getting Beyond Bolton: *Columbian Consequences* and the Spanish Borderlands, A Review Essay," *New Mexico Historical Review* 70:2 (1995), 201–15.

33. See Amy Turner Bushnell, "Introduction: Do the Americas Have a Comparable Colonial History?" in Bushnell, ed., *Establishing Exceptionalism: Historiography and the Colonial Americas* (Aldershot, England: Variorum, Ashgate, 1995), xvii-xix.

34. Alistair Hennessy's suggestive *The Frontier in Latin American History* (Albuquerque: University of New Mexico Press, 1978) is still the only text. Three excellent readers are David J. Weber and Jane M. Rausch, eds., *Where Cultures Meet: Frontiers in Latin American History* (Wilmington: Scholarly Resources, 1994); Erick Langer and Robert H. Jackson, eds., *The New Latin American Mission History* (Lincoln: University of Nebraska Press, 1995); and Donna J. Guy and Thomas E. Sheridan, eds., *Contested Ground: Comparative Frontiers on the Northern and Southern Edges of the Spanish Empire* (Tucson: University of Arizona Press, 1998).

Integral to Empire

The Vital Peripheries of Colonial Spanish America

John Jay TePaske

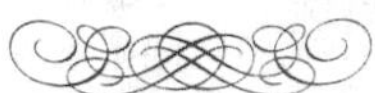

Peripheries and Cores in Colonial Spanish America

Twenty years ago Alistair Hennessy published his thoughtful, schematic, *The Frontiers in Latin American History*,[1] in which he identified various types of frontiers in Latin America from the sixteenth through the nineteenth centuries. For the colonial epoch they included mission frontiers such as New Mexico, California, Florida, Paraguay, and the southern Andes (Moxos). Closely related to these mission frontiers and sometimes synonymous with them were Indian or military frontiers such as the Araucanian frontier in Chile, the Chichimeca and Apache frontiers in northern Mexico, and the Chiriguano frontier in the Tarija region of Upper Peru. Hennessy also singled out frontiers of maroons, runaway black slaves and mulattoes who created their own communities independent of the established colonial order. On Española during the eighteenth century, for example, the maroon community of La Maniel on the border between the French and Spanish portions of the island was never conquered by either European power. The same was true of Esmeraldas on the Ecuadorian coast, which fiercely defended its autonomy. The maroon communities in Mexico near Veracruz and Campeche, the *palenques* in Cuba with *cimarrones* living deep in the mountains of the Oriente, the *cumbe* villages like Ocoyta in Venezuela, and maroon communities near Popayán and Cartagena in Nueva Granada all testified not only to black defiance of the existing order of things but also to the existence of independent black societies away from the mainstream of empire.

Spanish America was replete with mining frontiers. Although silver was mined in Mexico relatively close to Mexico City at Taxco, Pachuca, and Sultepec and in Guanajuato in the Bajío, other rich silver strikes occurred in remote areas far to the north in Zacatecas, Durango, San Luis Potosí, and on the Pacific coast at Rosario/Cosalá/Los Alamos. Early in the sixteenth century in Central America, Nicaragua and the Isthmus of Panama constituted gold frontiers while later Guascarán and Comayagua near Tegucigalpa in Honduras produced silver. In New Granada new gold mining frontiers emerged as rapidly as old veins or placers were exhausted in Antioquia, the Chocó, Magdalena Valley, and the eastern cordillera of the Andes. To the south in Ecuador, Zaruma and Zamora in the presidency of Quito constituted gold mining frontiers. In Peru and Upper Peru, where silver dominated, the *cerro* of Potosí became the richest mine in the Spanish empire if not in the world in the late sixteenth century, with its production being complemented later by the silver mines at nearby Oruro and Chucuito. In Lower Peru the mines of Pasco, Hualgayoc near Trujillo, and Huantajaya and Cailloma near Arequipa emerged as significant silver mining camps in the eighteenth century. Discovered in the barren windswept central Andes of Peru in the last half of the sixteenth century, Huancavelica became a unique New World mercury frontier. Chile, too, had its mining camps in the gold-producing areas in the north at Coquimbo and Quillota and to the south near Valdivia. Significantly, mining frontiers often became metropolises in their own right. Potosí, for example, was estimated to have had 150,000 inhabitants in the early seventeenth century while Zacatecas became the third largest city in New Spain after Mexico City and Puebla de los Angeles. Both Potosí and Zacatecas were characterized, among other things, by the sumptuousness of their churches and the wealth of some of their Spanish or creole inhabitants.

Hennessy also identified livestock and agricultural frontiers. Perhaps one of the Spaniards' greatest contributions to the New World, for good or for ill, was livestock—goats, sheep, pigs, horses, mules, cows, and steers. Northern New Spain, the *pampas* of Argentina, the *llanos* of New Granada in western Venezuela and eastern Colombia, and the island of Cuba, especially in the sixteenth and seventeenth centuries, were good examples of such frontiers. The sugar cane-producing areas of Cuba, Española, and coastal Peru, the cochineal frontiers of southern Mexico and Central America, the cacao plantations of Venezuela, and the wheat-rich central valley of Chile all constituted agricultural frontiers within Hennessy's framework.

Much before Hennessy, Hubert Howe Bancroft (in the nineteenth century[2]) and Herbert Eugene Bolton (in the early twentieth[3]) both reminded us of the Spanish Borderlands on the northern fringes of New Spain in the Southeast, Southwest, and the Pacific Coast. Bolton reminded us too, as Hennessy has done, that the mission was a vital institution in the Spanish Borderlands, particularly important for expanding and solidifying Spain's hold on its empire.[4] A more contemporary reminder of these North American fringe areas has been David Weber's recent brilliant synthesis of borderland history.[5] Weber leaves no doubt that the borderlands were peripheral areas, far removed geographically and in other ways from the large cosmopolitan viceregal capital in Mexico City and its many amenities.

If various peripheries or frontiers abounded in Spanish America, so too did major and regional centers grow up in the Spanish Indies. Two major centers emerged as the vital cores of empire—Mexico City and Lima. After the short-lived ascendancy of Santo Domingo in Española in the Caribbean, Mexico City emerged as one of these vital centers. After only a bit more than a decade after the conquest of Tenochtitlan, Mexico (New Spain) in 1535 became a viceroyalty whose viceroy ruled over virtually all of North America from just north of the Isthmus of Panama ostensibly to the northern reaches of Canada, the "land of the cod." Mexico City gained its eminence by becoming the seat of the pretorial *audiencia* (appeals court and viceregal council), the archdiocese of Mexico, and the inquisition. Its royal treasury became a clearinghouse treasury (*caja matriz*) for the viceregal fisc and after

1605 the site of a royal auditing bureau (*tribunal de cuentas*). Empresarios under viceregal supervision coined specie for the viceroyalty until 1733 when a royal mint staffed by royal officials replaced them. The royal *protomedicato*, a board for examining physicians, surgeons, and other medical practitioners, also sat in Mexico City. Most major orders had convents or monasteries in the city, also schools (*colegios*) and seminaries, while the royal and pontifical university of Mexico gave the city intellectual prestige. Moreover, it was by far the most populous city of the viceroyalty.

To the south, Lima enjoyed the same status as Mexico. After its founding in 1535, the viceroy appointed there governed all of Spanish South America from the Isthmus of Panama to the Straits of Magellan. Like Mexico City it was the seat of the viceroyalty, pretorial audiencia, archdiocese of Lima, inquisition, a caja matriz, protomedicato, mint, and the royal and pontifical university of San Marcos. Unlike Mexico City, however, which was founded on the site of the old Aztec capital of Tenochtitlan, Lima, labeled by Spaniards as the City of Kings, was established as a new capital in 1535, presumably so it could maintain closer links by water with Spain. Although it ultimately became the most populous city of the viceroyalty, in the early seventeenth century silver-rich Potosí had more inhabitants.

In the eighteenth century royal authorities fashioned two new viceroyalties out of the viceroyalty of Peru. In 1739 Philip V created the viceroyalty of Nueva Granada with its capital at Santa Fe de Bogotá, encompassing present-day Colombia, Ecuador, and Venezuela. Thirty-seven years later, in 1776, Charles III established the viceroyalty of the Río de la Plata, which included present-day Argentina, Uruguay, Paraguay, and Bolivia, with its capital at Buenos Aires. Although neither Bogotá nor Buenos Aires ever achieved the eminence of a Lima or Mexico City, both became important centers for their respective regions.

Because royal policy organized the Indies into audiencia or appeals court districts, regional centers arose because the judges of these audiencias heard their cases in that particular city. For New Spain these audiencia districts included Mexico (the pretorial audiencia), Guadalajara, Guatemala, and Santo Domingo in the Caribbean. In Peru prior to the establishment of the two new viceroyalties, these included Panamá, Santa Fe de Bogotá, Caracas, Quito, Charcas or La Plata (present-day Sucre in Bolivia), Buenos Aires, Chile (Santiago), and the pretorial audiencia at Lima. With the exception of Central America and Guadalajara, the audiencia district defined the boundary lines for the new nations of Spanish America that arose after the wars of independence.

Other factors, too, gave various cities or towns significance at a local or regional level. Establishment of bishoprics, usually the site of an audiencia also, gave special status to the city where an archbishop or bishop resided. The implementation of the intendancy system in various areas of the Indies during the last half of the eighteenth century provided a special standing to the city where the intendant governed. The Río de la Plata, for example, was divided into seven intendancies with capitals at Buenos Aires, Asunción in Paraguay, Tucumán, Santa Cruz de la Sierra, La Paz, Mendoza, La Plata or Chuquisaca, and Potosí. Establishment of royal treasuries also provided a much-coveted status for the city where they were established. New Spain, for example, had twenty-three treasuries (cajas) at the end of the eighteenth century, while Peru had nine, including Upper Peru. The Río de la Plata expanded its number to twelve by the end of the eighteenth century, but was eclipsed in its fiscal expansion by Cuba where there were at least twenty-one cajas functioning on the island at the beginning of the nineteenth century. Because inhabitants of these districts visited these treasuries regularly to pay their taxes or tribute or to register silver and gold, the royal caja symbolized a Spanish fiscal presence in the various cities or towns where they were set up and gave them status as regional centers.

For many Spaniards assigned to the Indies, particularly those appointed to colonial offices, the New World itself was a periphery. Such was the case for the distinguished Spanish jurist, Juan de Solórzano Pereira, who, after teaching for a time at the University of Salamanca in Spain won appointment in 1609 as *oidor* of the audiencia of Lima, at that time the most prestigious appeals court in the Spanish colonies. Solórzano was neither flattered by or grateful for the appointment; rather he believed the king had sent him into exile in Peru, perhaps because while serving there he became the viceroy's choice to go to Huancavelica to refurbish and repair the mercury mines. He did, however, marry a Peruvian woman.[6] In fact, Solórzano's experience was true of many Spaniards who came to the Indies, either to seek their fortunes or to serve the king: They wanted to acquire wealth or serve their tour of duty and return to beloved Spain. Others, like Francisco López de Caravantes, a Spaniard from Sigüenza chosen by Philip III in 1606 to head the new auditing bureau in Lima settled in nicely in the City of Kings and enjoyed a distinguished career in Peru as a royal bureaucrat and chronicler.[7]

For Spaniards and Creoles in the royal service, some peripheral regions were more undesirable than others. Florida, for example, had a particularly unpalatable ambience and appointees to the governorship sometimes refused the office, or, if they took the job, complained bitterly about an overly long tenure in that position. Since the law required that governors could not depart Florida until their successor arrived, some had to wait years before they could leave for a more alluring post. Joseph Zúñiga y Cerda, for example, became governor of Florida in 1699 for a three-year term. In 1703, after serving one more year than required, he won appointment as the governor of Cartagena, but had to wait three years until his replacement, Francisco de Córcoles y Martínez, arrived. The new governor met the same fate as his predecessor when his term in office in Florida dragged on for eleven years (1706–1716) before it finally ended. He was especially unhappy in Saint Augustine, where he complained that the humidity aggravated pain from old wounds, making it impossible to mount his horse.[8] Clearly, whether in the view of Solórzano in the City of Kings or of Zúñiga y Cerda and Córcoles y Martínez in the Florida backwater, the sense of being in a periphery depended upon the perception of the individual.

A post in Huancavelica was equally unpalatable. As already noted, Solórzano was terribly unhappy in his stint in that bleak, barren place, supervising repairs on the mercury mine. So, too, was Antonio de Ulloa over one hundred years later. In the 1730s and early 1740s this talented young naval officer had represented Spanish interests in Ecuador with a French scientific expedition under Charles de la Condamine, measuring a degree on the equator. Returning to Europe in the late 1740s, Ulloa engaged in various scientific pursuits and wrote up accounts of his sojourn in Spanish South America. Then, in 1757, he again found himself in the royal service when Ferdinand VI appointed him governor of Huancavelica, a post he viewed as purgatory. While there he made himself terribly unpopular by exposing graft and corruption, but in 1764 a successor relieved him.[9] On his way home to Spain, however, the Crown tapped Ulloa for an equally undesirable position—the governorship of Louisiana, like Florida a backwater for administrators—but even more unpalatable because of its predominantly French population. In Louisiana, though, he was as unpopular with the French as he was with the mercury and silver miners of Huancavelica and was ultimately forced out of the post in 1768, probably to his great relief.[10]

Parenthetically, although the perspective here is imperial, a parallax view, as John Russell-Wood has put it, also prevailed among native peoples within the Spanish empire. Cuzco, for example, the former residence of the Inca emperior and the site of major Inca religious rites and rituals, was a major center for the vestiges of the old Inca nobility in the colonial epoch. For other indigenous peoples, their universe was no bigger than their local *ayllu* or *calpulli*, the basic clan group for the Incas and the Aztecs. The world of the Lower Creeks of the North American Southeast centered on the woods, rivers, and streams of that region, with their perception of their universe defined by the worldview and experience of the individual just as it was for Juan de Solórzano Pereira, Francisco López de Caravantes, Antonio de Ulloa, and the various governors of Florida.

The Spanish Empire in America as a Medieval Construct

The existence of frontiers or peripheries in colonial Spanish America cannot be denied, but these peripheries all had important positions within the Spanish empire in America as component parts of an organic whole that constituted the Spanish enterprise in the Indies. Signficantly, both the institutions and the worldview the Spaniards brought with them to the New World were essentially medieval as noted by the distinguished Mexican philosopher and historian Edmundo O'Gorman, who writes, "Spanish colonization is animated by a medieval spirit; whatever it contains that is modern is a blemish in it."[11] But it was not only a medieval spirit: Spanish colonization of the New World encompassed a host of medieval institutions that held sway throughout virtually the entire colonial epoch.

Eric Wolf has pointed out that Spain was the victim (beneficiary?) of a historical accident: the "discovery" of the New World came in 1492, nine months after the *reconquista* finally ended with the capitulation of Muhammad XII, Abu Abd Allah Bobadilla at Granada. In essence, this meant the easy transfer to the New World of those institutions and values engendered by the seven-hundred-year crusade against the Moors. For Spain there was no interval for development of more modern bourgeois values and institutions to replace those that had proven so useful during the reconquest and which could so conveniently be brought into play in the New World.[12] These included the practice of awarding segnioiries, *mayorazgos*, and titles to the warriors who slowly reconquered and reoccupied territory taken from the infidels, Moors or Indians. These same knights came to enjoy *encomiendas*, guardianships over subjugated Moors, which gave them the right to collect tribute from them and to exploit their labor in *repartimientos*, practices easily extended to natives in the Indies. *Adelantados* in the medieval Visigothic and Leonese traditions were common early in the conquest of Spanish America, with these adelantados gaining titles over the land they conquered, along with special economic and judicial privileges. In the Aragonese portions of late medieval Spain, viceroys emerged when Aragonese monarchs began appointing viceroys to represent them in newly conquered areas where they could not be personally present. *Chancillerías* or royal courts of appeal (audiencias in the Indies) grew up in late medieval Spain to handle judicial disputes. In the Indies they proved useful not only as judicial bodies but also as advisory councils for viceroys, governors, and captains-general. Municipal governance rooted in the *cabildo* or town council, with urban planning based on the grid system and central plazas containing buildings housing political and religious authorities, were the norm in late medieval Spain, and later in the New World. The concept of *policía*, or public order, was a vital principle for those who laid out medieval and New World cities or repopulated old ones.[13] Both civil and religious officials combined to reinforce this concept.

In the economic sphere in the conquered Taifa kingdoms of medieval Spain, it was common practice to reserve for the Crown a fifth (*quinto*) of all precious metals and jewels seized, which was later applied in the Indies to the gold, silver, and precious stones found there. Spanish taxes of the late medieval epoch, such as the import-export tax (*almojarifazgo*) and sales tax (*alcabala*), also made their way to the Indies with their Moorish names intact.

Religion and the clergy played a vital role. During the reconquest (or *reconquista*), Santiago (James, the son of Zebedee), purportedly appeared miraculously thirty-eight times to lead the Christians to victory in battles against the Moors. He thus became the patron saint of the knights doing battle against the infidels, a combination warrior-saint with both a military and religious aura. Not surprisingly, "Santiago" became the battle cry for the *conquistadores* of the New World. In fact, Santiago, riding his white horse, purportedly appeared in a number of battles in the Indies to insure victory for the Spaniards against the Indians as he had against the Moors in Spain. Initially, in the ninth and tenth centuries, as the Christians began to spill over the Cantabrian Mountains southward into Moorish territory, both the regular and secular clergy aided in the repopulation of vacant land, establishing new frontiers with the Moors and giving religious guidance and support to the colonists who moved into these vacant lands.[14] So, too, would the regular clergy lead the way in the Indies in populating new areas and extending the empire at the same time they Christianized the Indians. Although the Jesuit order so instrumental in espousing Christianity in the Indies and worldwide was not founded until the early sixteenth century, in many ways the Society of Jesus was a throwback to medieval times with its military organization and its label as "a spiritual order of knighthood." Medieval belief in miracles, millenarianism, and intense devotion to the Virgin Mary also characterized Spanish religious views in both medieval Spain and the New World. The appearance of the Virgin of Guadalupe atop the hill at Tepeyac very soon after the conquest of Mexico and the existence of at least forty-four different cults of the Virgin Mary in Mexico City during the colonial epoch reaffirm these tendencies.[15]

Culturally, Spaniards also brought their medieval trappings to the New World. Most universities were organized on the Salamancan model; teaching was in Latin; clergymen predominated in the faculty; the chair of theology was the most important in these institutions; and both the principles and curriculum of scholasticism prevailed until the eighteenth century. Romances of chivalry like *Amadis de Gaula* became the most popular literary genre for Spanish colonials.[16] Receptions (*recibimientos*) for new viceroys in Mexico City and Lima manifested all the pomp and panoply of a coronation in late medieval Spain, reinforcing the viceroy's position as a surrogate king in the colonial ambience.[17]

The structure of Spanish colonial society was also medieval. One only has to read a brief description of the ideal medieval commonwealth by John of Salisbury (c. 1115–1180), secretary to Thomas Becket, Archbishop of Canterbury and Bishop of Chartres, to realize how the society which grew up in the Spanish Indies in the colonial epoch resembled his ideal model. In his *Statesman's Book* of the twelfth century he describes the ideal commonwealth in this way:

> The prince is first of all to make a thorough survey of himself, and diligently study the condition of the whole body of the commonwealth, of which he is the representative, and in whose place he stands. A commonwealth, according to Plutarch, is a certain body which is endowed with life by the benefit of divine favor, which acts at the prompting of the highest equity, and is ruled by what may be called the moderating power of reason. Those things which establish and implant in us the practice of religion, and transmit to us the worship of God (here I do not follow Plutarch, who says "of the Gods") fill the place of the soul in the body of the commonwealth. And therefore those who preside over the practice of religion would be looked up to and venerated as the soul of the body. For who doubts that the ministers of God's holiness are His representatives? Furthermore, since the soul is, as it were, the prince of the body, and has rulership over the whole thereof, so those whom our author calls the prefects of religion preside over the entire body. . . . The place of the head in the body of the commonwealth is filled by the prince, who is subject only to God and to those who exercise His office and represent Him on earth, even as in the human body the head is quickened and governed by the soul. The place of the heart is filled by the Senate, from which proceeds the initiation of good works and ill. The duties of eyes, ears, and tongue are claimed by the judges and the governors of provinces. Officials and soldiers correspond to the hands. Those who always attend upon the prince are likened to the sides. Financial officers . . . (keepers of the privy chest) may be compared to the stomach and the intestines, which, if they become congested through excessive avidity, and retain too tenaciously their accumulations, generate innumerable and incurable diseases, so that through their ailment the whole body is threatened with destruction. The husbandmen correspond to the feet, which always cleave to the soil, and need the more especially the care and foresight of the head, since while they walk upon the earth doing service with their bodies, they meet more often with stones of stumbling, and therefore deserve aid and protection all the more justly since it is they who raise, sustain, and move forward the weight of the entire body. Take away the support of the feet from the strongest body and it cannot move forward by its own power, but must creep painfully and shamefully on its hands, or else be moved by means of brute animals.
>
> Those are called the feet who discharge the humbler offices, and by whose services the member of the whole commonwealth walk upon solid earth. Among these are to be counted the husbandmen, who always cleave to the soil, busied about their plough-lands or vineyards or pasture or flower gardens. To these must be added the new species of clothmaking, and the mechanic arts, which work in wood, iron, bronze and the different metals; also the menial occupations, and the manifold forms of getting a livelihood and sustaining life, or increasing household property, all of which, while they do not pertain to the authority of the governing power, are yet in the highest degree useful and profitable to the corporate whole of the commonwealth. All these different occupations are so numerous that the commonwealth in the number of its feet exceeds not only the

> eight-footed crab but even the centipede, and because of their very multitude they cannot be enumerated; for while they are not infinite by nature, they are yet of so many different varieties that no writer on the subject of offices or duties has ever laid down particular precepts for each special variety. But it applies generally to each and all of them that in their exercise they should not transgress the limits of the law, and should in all things observe constant reference to the public utility. For inferiors owe it to their superiors to provide them with service, just as the superiors in their turn owe it to their inferiors to provide them with all things needful for their protection and succor.[18]

John of Salisbury described his ideal twelfth-century commonwealth in organic terms, classifying the various groups in that society hierarchically in their importance for the body politic. He may well have been describing the Spanish colonies five centuries later. He ranked religious teachers at the top of the ladder, as the soul of the commonwealth; the political ruler was the head, the next in importance; other elements of the society were its eyes, ears, hands, sides, arms, stomach, and feet. Explicit in his description was that, despite their hierarchical position, all sectors were important to the proper functioning of an ideal society: Each one had contributions to make. So, too, were Spaniards, Indians, blacks, and castes in the Spanish Indies arranged hierarchically, with those who fought, prayed, and governed at the top; others of the various ranks below them were made to perform more menial tasks. Native peoples were at the bottom of the social hierarchy and constituted the so-called *república de indios* in counterdistinction to the *república de españoles*, or *gente de razón* (rational people). The principle of policía was explicit: The *plebe* was not "to transgress the limits of the law." Despite his belief that all members of the society were integral to its proper functioning, John of Salisbury was not timid in asserting the superiority of some sectors over others. Inferiors were to provide service to their superiors; superiors, in turn, were to provide protection and succor, presumably religious as well as physical. In the Spanish Indies the Spaniard often justified (rationalized?) exploitation of slaves or the native population on this principle; they were the minions playing their ascribed roles as laborers toiling in the cane fields, *haciendas*, and mines in the service of their superiors. Although Spanish colonials believed firmly that in the eyes of God all men and women were equal—hence the strong missionizing urge—within their larger concept of society, each sector or individual had an appropriate, fixed place in the economic, social, and political spheres.

Peripheries as Integral Parts of an Organic Whole

The argument thus far has been that the Spanish empire in the New World was a medieval construct, an extension of medieval Spain in its institutions, worldview, and social organization. Moreover, the so-called peripheries were integral parts of this organic whole and functioned as parts of it. Some of the mission frontiers, for example, had significant roles beside their ostensible purpose of Christianizing and Hispanicizing the native peoples. Florida, for example, was crucial as the outpost protecting treasure fleets plying the Bahama Channel on their way home to Spain, and also in maintaining a Spanish presence in the Southeast against English and French intrusions. After 1763, Louisiana protected Spanish interests against these same two powers in the Mississippi Valley and northern edges of New Spain. In the

Southwest and along the California coast, missions served to solidify Spanish claims on new territory and to extend the empire. Spanish missions of the Moxos in the eastern Andes and jungle on the borders with Brazil served as a religious buffer against the encroachments of the Portuguese, a similar role played by the Jesuit reductions of the Guaraní in Paraguay. Chile, too, had its share of missions, but that periphery also served as the breadbasket for Peru, to the north, and as a defensive outpost on the southwestern flank of the empire.

Huancavelica was another periphery that played a vital role within the Spanish empire. Mined by the Indians in pre-Columbian times and discovered in 1563 by a Spanish *encomendero*, it was formally founded as a colonial city in 1571 as the Villa Rica de Oropesa. A year later it became a Crown district, with royal officials assuming control over the production and sale of mercury. The good fortune for the Spaniards was immeasurable. Throughout the length and breadth of the Spanish Indies, virtually no mercury was available, but the existence of the mine near major silver-producing areas of Peru and Upper Peru became a boon to silver output, enabling producers to replace smelting with the more efficient, cheaper amalgamation method for processing silver ore. New Spain, in turn, relied almost entirely on the mercury coming from the mines of Almadén in Spain, or late in the eighteenth century from Idria in central Europe. Since mercury became a royal monopoly, income from mercury sales helped to fill royal coffers and enabled Spanish authorities to ferret out fraud by correlating mercury sales to individual miners with their registered production. As pointed out earlier, however, Juan de Solórzano Pereira and Antonio de Ulloa viewed Huancavelica as a miserable periphery, a place Spanish bureaucrats hoped to avoid. The city itself was over 12,000 feet in altitude, and the major mine of Santa Bárbara over 14,000 feet. Surprisingly, though, unlike Potosí or Zacatecas, it never developed into a metropolis in its own right, yet it played such a crucial role in the silver economy of Peru and Upper Peru. In fact, the importance of Huancavelica for New World bullion production and the world supply of silver begs for a counterfactual analysis.

Westward, in the Philippines, Imanuel Wallerstein quickly relegated the islands to periphery status in the core-periphery scheme he created for a world system beginning in the sixteenth century,[19] yet these islands, far removed from imperial centers in New Spain or Peru, had a significant place within the Spanish imperial and world systems. Most important, perhaps, besides defending military interests in the region and establishing a Spanish presence in the Orient, the Philippines provided an outlet for Mexican silver to the silver-poor Far East, probably in far greater amounts than generally assumed. At the same time, the Manila *galeones* (galleons) brought back jade, damasks, and other Asian luxury goods for the rich and the powerful in Mexico City. This also occurred in Peru, where, despite efforts to prevent it, daring traders (*peruleros*) chanced the dangerous and illegal Pacific voyage to exchange their silver for the same kinds of luxury goods entering Mexico.

Other peripheries also deserve brief mention. To the mid-eighteenth century, Buenos Aires in the Río de la Plata was a colonial backwater, yet it served, as did the Philippines, as an outlet for illicit silver from Upper Peru and as a transfer point for black slaves being purchased to work in the mines and fields of the interior. The Isthmus of Panama was still another periphery that played a vital role in the Spanish Indies, particularly for the silver economies of Peru and Upper Peru and for the

Spanish commercial system. Panama City, on the west coast of the isthmus, was the transfer point for Peruvian silver shipped northward on the Armada del Sur from Callao and other Peruvian ports. Portobelo, on the east coast became the drop-off point for European goods carried on the galeones, goods to be toted across the isthmus and sold at points south in Spanish South America. Beginning in the 1720s and perhaps earlier, however, both Portobelo and Panama City became more peripheral as lone ships (*registros*) began plying their way to and from the Indies. Meanwhile, in 1739, the long-standing system of galeones ended completely, diminishing the importance of both cities and the isthmus even more.

Cuba presents an interesting case study of a periphery turned metropolis, a dynamic periphery which, like Zacatecas and Potosí, was transformed into a core region. Initially, after a brief gold boom in the early sixteenth century and the ensuing Spanish depopulation of the island by the emigration of colonists to Mexico, Cuba became a cattle frontier with an economy based on the shipment of hides to Spain and the sale of beef jerky to the combined *flota* and galeones which rendezvoused in Havana before sailing on the final leg of their voyage to Spain. Tobacco growing and shipbuilding also became important on the island, and with Guayaquil on the coast of Ecuador, Cuba was one of the two principal shipyards (*astilleros*) in the Indies, both for building new ships and careening and refurbishing old ones.

Yet Cuba lost its semiperipheral status to become a significant center of empire. The increase in both licit and illicit trade after the British took Jamaica in 1655, the repair and revictualing of ships plying the Caribbean or returning to Spain, the sugar boom of the eighteenth century, and the establishment of the Havana trading company in 1740 to promote tobacco and sugar production all contributed to its rapid growth. Cuba also became the Spanish colony where metropolitan authorities first experimented with structural reforms and was the first area in the Indies where an intendancy system was put in place. Cuba also experienced an expanded military and naval presence after the brief British takeover of Havana in 1762–1763. The number of cajas increased markedly in the eighteenth century, so much so that by the end of the last decade, Cuba had nearly as many treasury districts as New Spain. Also at the close of the century, the inability of Spain to supply its own colonies turned Cuba into an entrepôt for inter-American trade, which was never reversed once Spain reestablished firmer commercial ties with the Indies. All these factors transformed Cuba into a vital center of empire, not yet rivaling Lima or Mexico City, but growing and prospering, and assuming an important role within the imperial context.

The increasing importance of Havana as a redistribution point for military subsidies (situados) going to other areas of the Caribbean was also a factor in its growth. The *situados* coming from New Spain to Havana and for other areas of the greater Caribbean, such as Santiago (Cuba) at the eastern end of the island, and Florida, had always passed through Havana, which had often caused problems because Havana merchants used these situados to purchase food and military supplies at exorbitantly high prices, leading to complaints by the recipients. By the 1780s, however, funds coming from Mexico supported Spanish garrisons not only in Havana, St. Augustine, and Santiago but also in Pensacola, Louisiana, Trinidad de Barlovento, Puerto Rico, and Santo Domingo. Later, additional subsidies passing through Havana also supported Spanish diplomats in New York and Philadelphia and provided funds for the Havana tobacco factory and a new Spanish military outpost at Trujillo on the coast of Central America. In 1799, for example, the situado sent from New Spain for Santiago amounted to 152,000 pesos; for Florida 214,000 pesos; Louisiana 301,000 pesos; Trujillo 53,000 pesos; Puerto Rico 750,000 pesos; Santo Domingo—in the throes of a black revolt on the French half of the island—1,103,000 pesos; and Trinidad, in the hands of the English since 1797, only 6,000 pesos. Havana itself received over 2,000,000 pesos, some of which went to smaller garrisons throughout the island with a bit over 900,000 pesos of this situado being allocated to the Havana tobacco factory.[20]

If viewed another way, in the unsettled decade 1791–1800 approximately 45,000,000 pesos left Veracruz for Havana and other military outposts in the greater Caribbean. (Situados for the Isla del Carmén, Campeche, and Tabasco did not go to Havana.) Monies from New Spain reaching Havana during this decade amounted to 43,000,000 pesos with Havana and its satellite garrisons, including Santiago, getting almost 25,000,000 pesos (58 percent), Louisiana 5,740,000 pesos (13 percent); Puerto Rico 3,446,000 pesos (8 percent); Santo Domingo 6,202,000 pesos (15 percent); Trinidad de Barlovento 1,200,000 (3 percent); and Florida (St. Augustine and Pensacola) 1,210,000 pesos (3 percent): By comparison, remissions from New Spain to Castile during the same epoch amounted to 48,000,000 pesos, a bit more finding its way to the Iberian metropolis than to needy American military outposts and Spanish ministers in the United States. In all, Castile and Caribbean defense drained an average of about 10,000,000 pesos annually from Mexico during the last decade of the eighteenth century.[21]

The flows of money out of New Spain for defense of the greater Caribbean and for Spain demonstrate in part the interrelationships of the various components of the Spanish empire and the dependence of one upon the other, particularly peripheries upon metropolises, but also periphery upon periphery. The funds remitted from Veracruz for Caribbean defense and Castile had been generated all over New Spain. Mining areas such as San Luis Potosí, Durango, Zacatecas, Chihuahua, Guadalajara, Guananjuato, and Rosario/Cosalá/Los Alamos continuously poured their surplus tax revenues, produced primarily by the royal tenth (*diezmo*) from silver production, into the matrix treasury in Mexico City. There the viceroy and other royal officials assessed the needs of the viceroyalty and the mother country and decided how much and where these funds should be disbursed. Their priorities for the last decade of the eighteenth century have already been spelled out. Following the course of the redistribution of colonial taxes also establishes the links between the remote mining camps of New Spain to the greater Caribbean outposts of Louisiana, Trinidad, Española, Puerto Rico, Trujillo, and Florida. Bound to these mining centers, the military garri-sons of the greater Caribbean were dependent upon them for sustenance, if not survival.

Conclusion

At the opening of the nineteenth century, with the wars of independence approaching, how did the Spanish empire, this essentially long-standing medieval creation in the New World, endure in a rapidly changing world? Quite nicely, it appears. In retrospect Spain's venture in the Indies lasted over three hundred years, almost a century longer than either the English or French empires in America. At the same time, the Spanish empire remained virtually intact. Jamaica fell to the English in 1655; the western end of Española was lost to the French in 1698; some territory of what had initially constituted La Florida had been given up to thc English and the French in the Southeast, but was reclaimed in 1783. The English had seized Trinidad in 1797, but during the same period, Spain had extended its hold on the Southwest and established a series of mission stations on the California coast in the last half of the eighteenth century. At the end of the eighteenth century, Spanish expeditions were exploring the Canadian and Alaskan coasts with an eye toward obtaining a place in the fur trade and to extending Spanish holdings northward from California.[22] (The place names for harbors, bays, and rivers testify to Spanish activity in this region in the late eighteenth century, and also to the expansive urges of eighteenth-century Spaniards in Mexico.) Somehow the restless, adventurous spirit of the sixteenth century had not been lost, even after two centuries. After 1810, however, it took a little over a decade for wrenching wars pitting Creoles against Spaniards to bring down this grandiose medieval edifice, both for good and for ill. The persistence of so many colonial institutions and attitudes into the nineteenth century and the tortuous process of state building that characterized all of Spanish America in the same epoch demonstrate, perhaps, how ingrained these institutions and attitudes were.

Notes

1. Alistair Hennessy, *The Frontier in Latin American History* (Albuquerque: University of New Mexico Press, 1978).
2. Hubert Howe Bancroft, *California Pastoral, 1769–1848* (San Francisco: History Company, 1888); *History of California*, 7 vols. (San Francisco: History Company, 1884–90); *History of Arizona and New Mexico, 1530–1888* (Albuquerque: Horn and Wallace, 1962).
3. Herbert E. Bolton, *Coronado on the Turquoise Trail: Knight of Pueblos and Plains* (Austin: University of Texas Press, 1949); *Outpost of Empire: The Story of the Founding of San Francisco* (New York: Alfred A. Knopf, 1931); *The Spanish Borderlands: A Chronicle of Old Florida and the Southwest* (New Haven, Conn.: Yale University Press, 1921); *The Colonization of North America* (New York: Macmillan, 1920).
4. Herbert E. Bolton, "The Mission As a Frontier in the Spanish American Colonies," *American Historical Review* 23 (1917), 42–61.
5. David J. Weber, *The Spanish Frontier in North America* (New Haven, Conn.: Yale University Press, 1992).
6. There is an excellent discussion of the life and work of Solórzano by Miguel Angel Ochoa Brun in the Estudio Preliminar of the 1972 edition of the *Política Indiana*, xii–lxvix. *Política Indiana compuesta por el Señor don Juan de Solórzano y Pereyra corregida e ilustrada con notas por el Licenciado don Francisco Ramiro de Valenzuela* 5 tomos. Biblioteca de Autores Españoles, tomos 252–56 (Madrid: Compañía Ibero-Americana de Publicaciones, 1972).
7. Francisco López de Caravantes, *Noticia general del Perú*, 2 tomos. Biblioteca de Autores Españoles, tomos 292–93 (Madrid: Atlas, 1985); see also the excellent analysis of the life and work of López de Caravantes by Guillermo Lohmann Villena in his Estudio Preliminar in this same edition, ix–cxxv.
8. John Jay TePaske, *The Governorship of Spanish Florida, 1700–1763* (Durham, N.C.: Duke University Press, 1964), 12–13.
9. For a brief discussion of Ulloa's career, see the introduction to Jorge Juan and Antonio de Ulloa, *Discourse and Political Reflections on the Kingdoms of Peru* (Norman: University of Oklahoma Press, 1978), 11–16.

10. For a discussion of Ulloa's tenure in Louisiana, see John Preston Moore, *Revolt in Louisiana: The Spanish Occupation, 1766–1770* (Baton Rouge: Louisiana State University Press).
11. Quotation from Edmundo O'Gorman in Lewis Hanke, *Do the Americas Have a Common History?* (New York: Knopf, 1964), 25–26.
12. Eric Wolf, *Sons of the Shaking Earth* (Chicago: University of Chicago Press, 1959), 152–75.
13. The concept of policía as it pertains to architecture is developed in Valerie Fraser, *The Architecture of Conquest: Building in the Viceroyalty of Peru, 1535–1635* (Cambridge: Cambridge University Press, 1990), 21–25, 41–45.
14. Thomas F. Glick, *Islamic and Christian Spain in the Early Middle Ages* (Princeton, N.J.: Princeton University Press, 1979). In this work Glick develops the theme that the reconquest of the Iberian peninsula in its early phases was more a repopulating of vacant land than a military conquest.
15. Luis Weckmann, *The Medieval Heritage of Mexico*, trans. Frances López-Morillas (New York: Fordham University Press, 1992), 281.
16. Irving Leonard, *Books of the Brave: Being an Account of Books and of Men in the Sixteenth-Century New World* (Cambridge, Mass.: Harvard University Press, 1949).
17. Irving Leonard, *Baroque Times in Old Mexico: Seventeenth-Century Persons, Places, and Practices* (Ann Arbor: University of Michigan Press, 1959), 130–44.
18. John of Salisbury, *The Statesman's Book*, trans. John Dickinson (New York, Alfred A. Knopf, 1927), 3, 33–4, 243–44, 258. Reprinted in Franklin Le Van Baumer, *Main Currents of Western Thought*, 4th ed. (New Haven, Conn.: Yale University Press, 1978), 71–74.
19. Immanuel Wallerstein, *The Modern World-System: Capitalist Agriculture and the Origins of the European World Economy in the Sixteenth Century*, Studies in Social Discontinuity (New York: Harcourt, Brace, Jovanovich, 1974), 335–39.
20. Archivo General de Indias, Sevilla, Santo Domingo, Legajo 1859.
21. Archivo General de Indias, México, Legajos 2027, 2920–40.
22. See Warren L. Cook, *Flood Tide of Empire: Spain and the Pacific Northwest, 1543–1819* (New Haven, Conn.: Yale University Press, 1973) and Stephen J. Langdon, "Efforts at Humane Engagement: Indian-Spanish Encounters in Bucareli Bay, 1779" in Stephen Haycox, Caedmon A. Liburd, and James K. Barnett, eds., *Exploration and the Enlightenment in the North Pacific, 1741–1805* (Seattle: University of Washington Press, 1997), 187–97.

Reconsidering the Center

Puebla and Mexico City, 1550–1650

Ida Altman

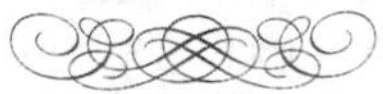

From the moment of its founding on the rubble of the vanquished Aztec city of Tenochtitlan, the dominance of Mexico City over what became the kingdom of New Spain was so indisputable that since that time virtually all other regions and towns to some extent have been discussed in terms of their relationship to the capital. Notwithstanding its disadvantages, the location of Mexico City dictated the development of the key routes that connected the capital to the mining centers of the north, especially Zacatecas, and to ports on the Gulf of Mexico and the Pacific—what James Lockhart has called the "trunk lines"[1]—along which the greatest volume of people, goods, and wealth moved and population and production concentrated. Mexico City's dominance from the time of the conquest has fostered certain tendencies in the historiography on New Spain for the sixteenth and seventeenth centuries. Institutional studies that focused on or included the early decades after the conquest almost by definition concerned Mexico City, but Charles Gibson's great work on the Indians of the central valley was one of the few that examined the city's demographic, economic, and social development as a whole.[2] Perhaps assuming that much of what could or should be understood about the capital was largely known or could be inferred from its relations with and impact on other places, the generation of scholars that followed Gibson turned to regional studies. The articles in the volume *Provinces of Early Mexico*, which included studies by William Taylor on Oaxaca, Marta Hunt on Yucatan, Peter Bakewell on Zacatecas, and John C. Super on Querétaro, exemplify this trend.[3]

The attention paid to regions beyond the central valley certainly has been crucial to the field of colonial Mexican history, yet developments in the capital itself have been relatively neglected, at least in the early years.[4] Mexico City's history from the latter part of the sixteenth century onward has received considerably more attention from scholars. In contrast to the kind of regional studies mentioned above that shed much light on the function of the capital through consideration of its impact on and connections to other regions, more recent works on Mexico City have not necessarily tried to do the reverse—that is, to place the capital in the context of its relations with other parts of the viceroyalty.[5] As a result, it is difficult to go beyond the hegemonic model of the relationship between Mexico City and other places to arrive at some understanding of how other cities and regions might have functioned in conjunction with, rather than just subordinate to, the capital to organize and maintain the economic and political life of the viceroyalty.

The rise of the hegemonic city is a phenomenon commonly associated with Spanish America from the colonial period to the present, but the development of a single urban center dominating a large region was not the inevitable result of the consolidation of Spanish control over its newly conquered territories. The pattern was a departure from the Spanish precedent. Its appearance in the early years of colonization of various parts of the Americas mainly reflected a lack of wealth and personnel and the still primitive state of the economy.[6] The urban network that over time took shape in many parts of Spanish America would be less radically distinct from its peninsular counterpart than is often assumed.[7]

In the late fifteenth and sixteenth centuries Castile had an extensive, complex network of towns and cities, none of which had achieved a position of real dominance, notwithstanding the rise of Seville, which grew to over 100,000 inhabitants by the end of the sixteenth century. Located in a highly productive agricultural region and a center for industry and trade well before the opening of the Americas to settlement and commerce, Seville acted as the hub for all facets of the Indies enterprise, regulating through the House of Trade the movement of people as well as products and precious metals to and from the Americas.[8] The city did not become the administrative capital for the Americas in all senses, however; the supreme governing body for the Crown's American realms, the Council of the Indies, sat at court, not in Seville. Even as a center for the Indies trade and a departure point for migrants, Seville to some extent lost its monopoly and increasingly shared those functions with Cádiz. Seville also shared economic power with other centers with which it was connected, especially the Castilian city of Medina del Campo, whose great trading fairs made it a financial capital of sorts for Castile and linked it to the north-central city of Burgos and and the port of Bilbao on the Cantabrian coast, which together dominated the wool trade.[9] In the first two-thirds of the sixteenth century, Toledo perhaps came closest to acting as an administrative and institutional capital for Castile. As the seat of the archbishopric it was Castile's leading ecclesiastical city as well as a venue of the royal court, in addition to being a thriving center for textile manufacture.[10] The court, however, moved around (Valladolid and Madrid were also frequent sites, the latter increasingly so). Although Toledo remained an important ecclesiastical city, the establishment of the court in Madrid in the late sixteenth century undermined its position, even though at the time Madrid was fairly small—still *villa* rather than *ciudad*—and certainly not an economically significant place.

In general, diffusion rather than concentration of function characterized the Spanish urban network. Medium-sized towns and small cities were the rule, usually acting with a fair degree of autonomy in the sixteenth century even after more than half a century of the centralizing reforms of Ferdinand and Isabella and their grandson Charles V, who sent royal officials to preside over a growing number of municipalities and imposed new ordinances that transformed many of the older, fairly open and elective municipal councils that dated back to the *reconquista* and the Middle Ages into much more closed, aristocratic entities. Notwithstanding such changes the varied origins and historical experiences of towns and cities resulted in continuing distinctiveness and independence, meaning that they frequently replicated the same economic, political, and social functions as one another even when located in close proximity, while at the same time they exhibited local idiosyncrasies and might fulfill some special role, such as serving as the site of a bishopric, university, principal residence of a noble family, regional market town, or manufacturing center. The existence of networks that tied financial and administrative centers (such as Toledo, Medina del Campo, or eventually Madrid) to towns that were headquarters for local and regional economic production and marketing and to port cities like Seville, Bilbao, or Cádiz was a pattern that would recur in the Indies. There was, therefore, more than a little similarity to the peninsular situation in the urban networks that eventually took shape in New Spain, Peru, or New Granada.[11]

The relationship between the communities of the countryside and larger towns and cities in Spanish America also shared many characteristics with rural-urban patterns in Spain, especially in those regions that had dense indigenous populations already settled in towns and smaller places. In central Mexico, Yucatan, Guatemala, and the Andean region newly established Spanish towns and cities from the outset existed in relationship to a rural hinterland filled with population clusters primarily oriented toward agricultural production, just as in Spain. The basis for the rural-urban connection in Spanish America initially was seemingly quite different from that in Castile, as the towns and cities of the conquerors had been superimposed on an indigenous base. Yet in at least some parts of the Iberian peninsula the transfer of political control of cities from Muslims to Christians meant that cities under Christian rule might have jurisdiction over a countryside that still had a substantial population of Muslims or their descendants; this pattern was probably strongest in the east and southeast (Valencia and Murcia).[12] In the Americas, also, an arguably similar pattern could be found in some places before the arrival of the Spaniards, probably most notably in Cuzco, which the Incas deliberately fashioned as an imperial capital, elevating the status of the inhabitants (and thereby distinguishing them from conquered subjects) and requiring nobles of conquered provinces to spend periods of time living in the city.

Regardless of how the postconquest towns and cities originated, over time the physical mobility of all groups (Spaniards, Indians, Africans, and mixed people), drastic reduction of indigenous populations and relative increase of other groups, and economic and institutional development all worked to diminish some of the sharp distinctions between the towns and cities of the conquerors and the communities of the conquered, and to modify the relationship between them. Within the reorganized system of municipal government that Spaniards imposed on Indian towns they functioned with some or even much autonomy,[13] just as did Castilian towns and villages that lay within the jurisdiction of larger cities or under the authority of a great noble or ecclesiastical ruler. The intended segregation of Indians from Spaniards was from the beginning more ideal than real, especially since Spaniards often chose indigenous towns and cities as sites for their municipalities. Spaniards also went to live in Indian towns, and even Spanish towns that were not based on preexisting indigenous entities, like Puebla de los Angeles, attracted substantial Indian populations within a generation or two following their establishment. Relatively early in the sixteenth century Puebla's Indian *barrios* attained formal recognition and had their own officials.[14] Thus, the paradigm of the city of the conquerors ruling the countryside of the conquered never really existed, meaning that something like the complex and fairly diffuse urban network that connected Castilian towns and cities to one another and to smaller rural communities appeared early in many parts of Spanish America as well.

The existence of this pattern clearly has implications for understanding the basis for, and limitations of, centralization of political and economic power. If in the sixteenth and seventeenth centuries Mexico City was headquarters for the highest levels of administration of church and royal government and for many of the most extensive and profitable economic enterprises, as well as being the cultural and intellectual capital of New Spain, it functioned as such by virtue of the existence of a network of exchange and communication that linked it closely with other important centers of population and production (such as the mining town of Zacatecas, to the north) and with smaller places as well. As has frequently been suggested, Mexico City largely replicated the position of the leading city of the preconquest Triple Alliance (Aztec Empire) it had supplanted in the political and economic subordination of the towns and rural communities of the area under its authority. If anything, Mexico City surpassed Tenochtitlan in its definitive eclipse of such formerly important indigenous centers as Texcoco (which became a virtual suburb of the Spanish capital)[15] and the extent of territory under its control. Mexico City's primacy in the viceroyalty can hardly be questioned; in the 1550s its Spanish population was more than twice the size of that of the second largest city, Puebla de los Angeles, and by 1570 it might have been six times as great.[16] Nonetheless, the early development of such cities as Antequera in the south and Guadalajara in the west—which, while closely linked to the capital almost from the beginning acted as significant regional centers—suggests not only the limits of Mexico City's ability to order and subsume the economic and political life of the core of the viceroyalty, but also underscores the continued relevance of traditions of localism characteristic of both Spanish and indigenous society that allowed for some measure of often tempered recognition of superior authority (of the *audiencia*, the viceroy, the Crown) while reserving strongest loyalty for, and primary orientation toward, one's own place.

The most notable example of a regional center in New Spain in the sixteenth and seventeenth centuries that managed to forge and sustain an existence not only in some ways autonomous of the capital but often in competition with it as well was that of Puebla. This "City of the Angels" offers a highly interesting illustration of the sometimes paradoxical relationship between the capital and a secondary city, especially because in contrast to other comparable cities of the period—Antequera, Guadalajara, Zacatecas—Puebla was located geographically very close to Mexico City, meaning that their direct spheres of influence were contiguous and sometimes overlapping or disputed. Examination of Puebla's relationship to the viceregal capital should provide some insight into the significance of centrality in the viceroyalty of New Spain, which was dominated, but by no means defined, by Mexico City. In this context, I will discuss the activities of a large group of immigrant entrepreneurs and artisans who chose Puebla rather than Mexico City as the site for the realization of their economic ambitions. In doing so they played a crucial role in the city's transformation from a moderately prosperous secondary town, mainly dependent on the agricultural productivity of the region, into a thriving center for commerce and industry as well as commercial agriculture that in the late sixteenth and seventeenth centuries challenged the capital's political power and pretensions as well as complementing its economic functions.

Founded a decade after Mexico City, and eighty miles to the east of the capital in a fertile, well-watered site near some important Indian towns (Cholula was the closest),[17] Puebla was conceived as a sort of counterweight to the capital with its incipient aristocracy of *conquistadores* and wealthy *encomenderos* (individuals who received *encomiendas*—grants of Indian tribute and labor). Although no encomiendas were assigned in the area around the new city, not only did the municipality and its citizens (*vecinos*) and clergy gain access to indigenous labor through other means, but a substantial number of individuals who already held encomiendas arrived early to settle in the city, no doubt attracted by its favorable site, access to the rich agricultural lands of the Atlixco Valley, where the vecinos of Puebla received grants, and in most cases proximity to the location of their encomiendas.[18] While the city as such lacked any formal jurisdiction over the Indian towns and villages in its vicinity, from the outset it endeavored with considerable success to extend its unofficial control over the indigenous countryside and its resources through various means. Its vecinos served as administrators of nearby Indian towns, and encomenderos and judges (*corregidores*) occupied seats on the town council. In 1543 Puebla officially became the seat of the diocese of Tlaxcala, making it the headquarters for a bishopric that would be considerably wealthier than the archbishopric of Mexico itself,[19] thus assuring the city not only a considerable degree of influence over a large area in religious matters but also an additional platform for the expression of its political ambitions.[20]

Thus, far from adopting the kind of antiaristocratic lifestyle that the founders hoped would foster the development of a population of farmers and workers who would not depend on their Indian neighbors for support in the form of labor and supplies, the upper echelons of early Spanish society in Puebla instead reproduced the patterns of the capital, as Julia Hirschberg has documented. Indeed, Puebla was so closely connected with Mexico City, not least by virtue of the arrival of both settlers and transients from that source, that in its earliest years the city seemed more an extension of or spillover from the capital rather than a truly distinct entity; some people maintained vecino status in both cities. Nonetheless, certain elements in Mexico City resented the creation of the new city, suspicious of a new potential rival that to many seemed to offer greater attractions than the capital itself. Such suspicions were hardly unfounded, as from early times Puebla's apparent ambition was both to emulate and outshine its rival. Woodrow Borah notes that the city's "sentiments toward the capital may be inferred from the first item in specifications for its town clock: 'that it be of the same height and size as that of Mexico City, and one palm more.'"[21]

Puebla might have aspired to compete with the capital through emulation, but the key to its success and importance lay in its distinctiveness from, not superiority to, Mexico City. Located southeast of Mexico City, Puebla was more closely tied to the south than the capital, which with the rise of mining in the north and subsequent development of the Bajío region increasingly oriented itself northward. Puebla was an important center for long-distance trade with Guatemala, Peru, and the

Philippines as well as for the regional trade in cochineal, and the city and surrounding agricultural region supplied the fleet in Veracruz. Puebla reached a high point of prosperity and influence during what Guy Thomson has called its "golden age," from 1550 to 1650, by which time its early aristocratic pretensions had been tempered by the greatly increased importance of its industrial and commercial sectors. The city's council (*cabildo*), long the stronghold of the remnants of the old conquistador-encomendero founding group, began to incorporate representatives of the rising entrepreneurial group into its ranks, an almost inevitable development as descendants of conquistadors and founders intermarried with families whose wealth came from commerce or industry.[22] Hence, over time Puebla in some senses came more to resemble what its founders had envisioned, although in the reliance of its economy on low-paid or unpaid indigenous and slave labor it actually developed along much the same lines as most of the rest of the colony following the eclipse of the encomienda and loss of that particular source of Indian labor to those who had held such grants, who in any case were always in the minority.

In order to examine Puebla's position in the colony and in relation to Mexico City and thus consider the larger question of the meaning and function of centrality in the Spanish empire we must go beyond generalizations to a more detailed understanding of the city's society, economy, and politics. Rather surprisingly, scholarly work on the city during the period in which it attained its greatest influence and prosperity is still rather sparse.[23] Hirschberg's dissertation treats in considerable detail the origins and changing composition of Puebla's population and the relationship of Spanish society to the indigenous population of the countryside and nearby towns during the first three decades of the city's existence. She suggests the key trends in the city's social and economic development that would become increasingly important in the latter part of the sixteenth century, but her study ends in 1560. Guy Thomson focuses on the period from 1700 to 1850 and is concerned principally with Puebla's decline in importance and affluence rather than its rise, although he does discuss briefly the basis for its early success. He notes that "during its first prosperous century, the city and its immediate region became Spanish America's principal producer of woolen cloth and New Spain's breadbasket. . . . The city possessed a merchant body which rivalled that of the viceregal capital, serving as the inland port of Mexico's Atlantic trade."[24]

Those works that do include fairly detailed treatment of aspects of poblano society in the middle colonial period show that Puebla and Mexico City were closely intertwined, often acting in tandem if not necessarily in concert. José F. de la Peña, whose study of the wealth of the New Spanish upper class includes much material on Puebla, in discussing the characteristic centralization of the economy of New Spain states that "everything flows to, or from, Mexico and, in lesser degree Puebla," even though he emphasizes the capital's role as the distribution point for the viceroyalty. He concludes that Puebla's merchants held a substantial portion of the colony's mercantile capital. In his opinion, "Puebla was the second great city of New Spain, and the first in not just a few things."[25] Jonathan Israel, whose work on seventeenth-century Mexico focuses principally on the colony's complex politics, notes that "the Mexico and Puebla city councils, as the chief representative organs of New Spain, were represented at court in Madrid,"[26] a situation which arguably made Puebla nearly the capital's peer in political influence at court.

The source of this influence is not easily explained. By the standards of contemporary colonial cities Puebla was fairly wealthy and populous, but in neither respect did it come close to Mexico City. In 1612 the assessment for the sales tax (*alcabala*) for the capital was approximately three times that for Puebla (77,000 pesos, compared to 25,000) and three-and-one-half times the amount Puebla paid twenty years later (180,000 pesos, compared to 50,000).[27] Nonetheless, by the early seventeenth century Puebla clearly had carved out a niche that distinguished it from other New Spanish cities and often appeared to place it on a par with the capital itself. Israel writes that "Mexico City claimed a special pre-eminence among the Mexican cabildos, considering itself supreme spokesman and guardian of all Mexican Creoles, a claim hotly contested by Puebla which considered its own effort for the Creole cause to be of comparable worth." Indeed, he notes that "the Puebla city council, the largest and most determined in New Spain was . . . the most difficult to handle."[28] Puebla's geographic remove from the viceroy and the audiencia might have given it some room to maneuver that Mexico City's council lacked when it came to conflicts with royal officials. Furthermore, the local presence of both royal and ecclesiastical officials, such as Don Carlos de Luna y Arellano (brother-in-law of Don Luis de Velasco el mozo[29]), who served more than one term as Puebla's district governor (*alcalde mayor*), and most notably Bishop Palafox, who had real clout and ties at the highest levels and also forged a substantial local base of connections and support, also must have bolstered Puebla's position and pretensions.

As an ecclesiastical center Puebla was nearly the capital's equal, especially in the secular branch of the church. Israel estimates Mexico City's total ecclesiastical personnel at over 2,500 in the middle of the seventeenth century, including 1,000 nuns, compared to Puebla's approximately 1,400, about 600 of whom were nuns. But Puebla's diocese included 700 members of the secular clergy in 1635, their numbers rising to over 1,000 by the end of the century, compared to perhaps half that number in the diocese of Mexico.[30] Construction of Puebla's cathedral began earlier in the sixteenth century than that of the capital, and finally reached completion sooner in the seventeenth century, thanks largely to the impetus provided by Palafox, who presided over the festivities for its consecration in April 1649. Lasting for several days and attended by some 1,200 members of the clergy as well as many lay people, the celebrations included, according to Israel, "a dazzling display of choral music by the Puebla choir, then the best in the Americas, conducted by Juan Gutiérrez Padilla, New Spain's most eminent composer."[31] Those in attendance probably did not doubt Puebla's claim at least to religious preeminence in the colony, a position that had been considerably enhanced by Palafox's activities from the time he arrived in 1639 with appointments as both bishop of Puebla and visitor-general of New Spain and during his stint as interim viceroy as well as archbishop-elect in 1642.

It is tempting to try to account for Puebla's unusual position by assuming that—as a smaller city lacking the viceregal capital's institutional and economic complexity—greater social and demographic stability and coherence might have existed there. Perhaps Puebla was more genuinely American, or creole, than the capital and therefore commanded more strongly the loyalties of its vecinos. Yet Spanish poblano society was not notably closed or stable. Puebla continually received migrants, both from Castile and from other parts of New Spain (including the capital, although over time the percentage of people from Mexico City seems to have decreased in the migrant group as a whole). Immigrants from the peninsula sat on the city council all through the period, even if they were a minority, and normally one of the two annually elected *alcaldes ordinarios* was an immigrant.[32]

The activities of what was doubtless the most important of the immigrant groups to arrive in Puebla in the late sixteenth and early seventeenth centuries, the people from the Castilian town of Brihuega, are instructive.[33] The *briocenses* (as people from Brihuega were called) concentrated their efforts precisely in those economic sectors that made Puebla sufficiently distinctive and independent from Mexico City that, notwithstanding its geographic proximity to the capital, it perhaps could be said to have shared Mexico's centrality rather than remaining economically subordinate. The people from Brihuega contributed significantly to the development of enterprises that although they had gotten their start in the first decades following the city's founding only reached full fruition later in the sixteenth century.

In Puebla, the briocenses became involved above all in the manufacture of woolen cloth. Their hometown of Brihuega had been a center for textile production since the Middle Ages, though in the latter part of the sixteenth century the town seems to have been in economic crisis. Nonetheless, a substantial percentage of the town's working population was still involved in one or another aspect of textile production, and the manufacture of textiles continued to be the single most important commercial activity in Brihuega. When people began to leave the town in substantial numbers, they tried to relocate in a place where they could pursue what they knew best. It is surely no coincidence that around the same time considerable numbers of briocenses began to emigrate to New Spain. In the early 1570s, a large group of people from the town decided to relocate in the Alpujarras. This mountainous region east of Granada had been virtually depopulated following the defeat of a large-scale rebellion of the Morisco inhabitants (descendants of the Muslims) who were subsequently exiled to other parts of the peninsula. The Alpujarras was an important region for silk production, and after the deportation of the Moriscos, officials tried to attract potential settlers by offering them houses in the then-empty towns and lands already planted with mulberry trees for the cultivation of silkworms. Some fifty vecinos of Brihuega went to the Alpujarras where they almost singlehandedly colonized one town, Mecina de Buen Varón, though probably few if any of them had previous experience in sericulture. Brihuega produced woolen cloth almost exclusively, with perhaps a small amount of linen. The transition to an entirely new kind of cloth production in the Alpujarras likely proved difficult despite the assistance that the new colonists received. Some of the people who went there subsequently left, some to move on to New Spain, and there is no indication that the movement from Brihuega south to the Alpujarras continued.

In contrast, New Spain, and specifically the city of Puebla, offered the briocenses almost ideal conditions in which to pursue their familiar trades on a whole new scale. Located near the convergence of the San Francisco and Atoyac Rivers, Puebla had water to power mills, and the region produced wool, dyestuffs, and plentiful and cheap supplies of food. The city also had attracted a substantial indigenous population that could provide labor. Production of woolen cloth in Puebla had started in the 1540s but probably received a major impetus with the arrival of the briocenses, who first began to have an impact in the 1560s. Although perhaps fewer than thirty briocenses were in Puebla before 1570; most of the adult men who arrived in the 1550s and '60s established *obrajes*, or textile shops. A number of them returned or sent back to Brihuega for their families and other relatives and acquaintances, many of whom had skills and experience in the textile trades. By the early 1570s, the movement that over the next fifty years or so would convey perhaps a thousand people from Brihuega to Puebla was well underway. The briocenses set up obrajes all over the city, often in the same houses in which they lived or right next door, and secured sites for fulling mills along the city's rivers. They maintained workforces of as many as one hundred or more Indian men and women, many of whom were literally locked inside the buildings, in addition to owning slaves and employing Spanish or mestizo managers and apprentices.

By the end of the sixteenth century Puebla had become the leading textile manufacturer of New Spain, its *obrajeros* sending their cloth to be sold in the capital or as far away as Peru, and it was the main center for the production of higher quality fabrics.[34] Although there were other obrajeros in the city, at any one time probably the majority of the obraje owners in Puebla were briocense by origin or descent and those who were not were closely associated with them through business interests and marital and fictive kinship (*compadrazgo*) ties. The obrajero group as a whole was strongly commercially oriented. They did not limit their economic interests to textile production, but instead typically invested and participated in a range of activities which included the trade in cacao and indigo (from Guatemala), wine (from Castile) and cochineal, as well as trade with the Philippines, mining, and estate ownership, especially sheep raising. Some of these activities doubtless yielded greater profits than the obrajes, but few gave up obraje ownership altogether, a sure sign that even if the profits were fairly modest they nonetheless continued to be reasonably secure.

The briocense immigrants diversified quite a bit, much along the same lines as did Puebla's economy, and in doing so they contributed significantly to the city's growing economic complexity. One of the best illustrations of how these immigrants were able to tap into the city's economic potential and in turn develop it further can be seen in the careers of the siblings and relatives of the Anzures family.[35] Probably the first briocense to establish himself in Puebla was the second-oldest son of the family, Diego de Anzures (his older brother, Rodrigo, remained in Brihuega). Diego went to New Spain in 1555 while in his early twenties with a family friend, Cristobal Escudero, who had been living in Seville, where he had worked as a merchant for ten years. Escudero decided to stay on in Mexico City, where he became an obrajero. By the early 1560s Diego de Anzures was living in Puebla, where he owned obrajes. At least some of his economic success there hinged on the series of increasingly prestigious offices he held. The first was the relatively modest position of inspector of cloth (*veedor de paños*), an office that a number of his compatriots would hold subsequently. In 1566 he became notary of the city council (*escribano del cabildo*), an influential position that afforded access to the city council (which had authority to grant land and water rights); in 1570 his younger brother Pedro de Anzures succeeded him in that office. Diego de Anzures also served as notary of the registry of cochineal (*escribano de la grana*) in the early 1570s, which probably provided an entrée into the lucrative cochineal trade. Together with a relative of his wife, María de Montoya, Anzures became involved in the sale and shipment of hides and cochineal to Castile. He also served as magistrate appointed by the city council (*alcalde ordinario*) in 1575 and the following year as magistrate of the stockraisers' association (*alcalde de la mesta*); in 1576 he purchased the prestigious office of *alferez mayor* for 8,000 pesos, which conferred a vote on the city council. In 1580 he left Puebla to return to Brihuega, where he lived another thirty years or so, into his eighties.

Diego de Anzures's brothers Pedro and Macario followed him to Puebla, as did his sisters Francisca, with her husband Juan de Roa, and Isabel, with her husband Francisco Barbero. All of these men owned obrajes with the exception of Barbero, who was a farmer (*labrador*) and owned farms or ranches (*estancias*). A number of other relatives and in-laws accompanied or followed these individuals. Pedro de Anzures's career most closely imitated his older brother's; he served as escribano del cabildo for ten years, alcalde de la mesta in 1585, and alcalde ordinario four times. He married into one of Puebla's most distinguished conquistador families, albeit one with mercantile connections.[36] Macario de Anzures did not hold office in Puebla, although quite late in life, in 1613, he served as corregidor of the pueblo of Papaloticpac. His economic activity was considerable, however; in addition to owning obrajes and estancias producing a dyestuff known as *pastel* he also became involved in a mining venture in the 1580s. He was the member of the family who perhaps was most active in encouraging other relatives to come to Puebla, recruiting his oldest brother's son, Diego de Anzures, to come work for him, as well as brother-in-law Francisco Barbero to run his estancias and Barbero's son-in-law Juan de Iñigo, a fuller (*batanero*), whom he also promised to employ.

The family of immigrant Alonso de Ribas and his wife María de Pastrana, who arrived in Puebla in the 1560s, was extensively involved in textile manufacture but diversified to some degree. Alonso de Ribas and his son Juan de Ribas were leading obrajeros, in the early 1580s jointly purchasing an obraje which had 150 workers in addition to obrajes they already owned.[37] Son Lucas de Ribas also owned obrajes, but was plagued with legal and financial problems. Juan and Lucas participated in the trade with Guatemala. Alonso de Ribas served as veedor de paños in 1570 together with his brother-in-law Andrés de Angulo and another briocense, Juan de Pastrana (Alonso's brother Cristóbal had been veedor in 1567 and 1568); Pastrana and Ribas also were veedores in 1580. Alonso de Ribas purchased two cattle ranches (*sitios de estancia de ganado mayor*) for 5,400 pesos in 1571 from his brother Cristóbal de Ribas when the latter departed for Castile with his family; ten years later Ribas owned eighteen sitios de estancia with 15,000 head of cattle and 400 horses, mares, and mules, as well as six slaves. If not exactly wealthy, this family did well enough in Puebla, especially considering that they started out with virtually nothing. According to Ribas's wife María de Pastrana, who made her will in 1577, she had brought little to their marriage and he nothing at all.

More notably successful was the family of Alonso de Ribas's brother-in-law, Andrés de Angulo, another early obrajero who also diversified, in 1573 authorizing his son Juan de Angulo to sell merchandise in Guatemala, Izalcos, and Soconusco and invest the profits in cacao. Juan de Angulo later went to Peru. Andrés de Angulo maintained a shop to sell his cloth in Mexico City with his son-in-law Juan Bautista Ruiz, but he returned to Brihuega with his family in the late 1570s. His sons Pedro, Gabriel, and Andrés went back to live in Puebla in the 1580s, and in this generation the family attained real wealth and prominence. Not much is known of Andrés, but both Pedro and Gabriel de Angulo became leading obrajeros, and Gabriel owned cattle ranches and shipped hides to Castile. Gabriel also held local office and in 1592 purchased a seat on the city council, which he held for ten years.

While for the briocenses textile manufacture clearly remained paramount, some people were primarily involved in trade and transportation and in the operation of bread-baking establishments, supplying biscuit or hardtack (*bizcocho*) and flour for Veracruz and Acapulco as well as bread for the local market. The bakeries (*panaderías*), some of them owned by women, were similar to the obrajes (although not as large) in the use of a labor force ostensibly constrained through the practice of advancing wages. Cases of Indian or mestizo bakers (*panaderos*) who changed places of employment, however, suggest that debt alone was not very effective in binding them to an employer, and the relatively high wages paid the bakers probably meant that their skills were at a premium. It was not uncommon for emigrants to pursue both textile manufacturing and bread baking, as was true in Brihuega also. As was the case for the textile obrajes, Puebla was well suited for the establishment of such integrated agricultural and semi-industrial enterprises, given the availability of fertile land for growing wheat, water power for grist mills, and labor. An immigrant named Cristóbal García de Zúñiga and his sister María García developed this kind of enterprise. Cristóbal went to New Spain in 1583 when he was in his early twenties and lived and worked for some time with a relative named Miguel Angón who had a carting business. In 1608, when Cristóbal decided to leave Puebla for Castile, he sold his estate near the Atoyac River with its lands, grist mill, carts and other equipment, along with three African slaves, for 12,000 pesos to his sister María's second husband, Lorenzo de Pajares (also from Brihuega) and the canon of the cathedral, Alonso Hernández de Santiago. When María García made her will five years later she had been widowed a second time. She owned two houses next to each other, with a panadería in one, doubtless linked to the mill she and her husband had taken over from her brother.

Probably because bizcocho was produced almost exclusively for export rather than the local market, a number of briocenses, like Juan Llorente and the brothers Miguel and Juan Angón, were involved in carting and regional trade in addition to owning panaderías. Cristóbal de Guadajalara, who was called *bizcochero*, invested in the trade in cacao with Guatemala and the sale of salt from Tehuacan in the mines of Pachuca. The briocenses who were active in trade and transport often worked together, lived and maintained their businesses in the same neighborhood (the commercial barrio of San Francisco), and were closely connected by ties of kinship, marriage, and compadrazgo.

The enterprises to which the briocenses in Puebla dedicated themselves underscore the acceleration and diversification of economic activity in the city in the last third of the sixteenth century and into the early decades of the seventeenth. Obrajes and other semi-industrial establishments like the panaderías were growing in size and number. Puebla's textile manufacturers sold their cloth in Mexico City and exported it to Peru. Although the big merchants of Mexico City had representatives in Puebla, the city also had its own merchants and entrepreneurs who, if not nearly as wealthy as the merchants of the capital, nonetheless functioned to a great extent independently and successfully, particularly at the level of regional trade. While less profitable than the transatlantic commerce that hinged on the fleet's arrival in Veracruz or the trade with the Philippines, local and regional trade had the advantage of being ongoing and nonseasonal. Although the route connecting the port of Veracruz to Mexico City that passed through Puebla was not necessarily the one that the merchants of the capital preferred, certainly the existence of an established route to Veracruz played an important part in the city's economy, stimulating the production of bizcocho and sustaining a flourishing transportion business as well as providing opportunities for local merchants.

The city's location on the routes to the south and to the Pacific coast gave it a significant advantage in trade in that direction as well. Puebla was closer to Huatulco, the most important port for New Spain's trade with Peru early in the sixteenth century, than was Mexico City; probably the most commonly used routes from the capital to Huatulco went through Puebla. After the 1570s the increasing importance of trade with the Philippines made Acapulco the main Pacific port, but Puebla was at least as close to Acapulco as was the capital, and some of its merchants participated directly in that trade even if on a relatively modest scale.[38]

In what ways might this consideration of Puebla's economy in the late sixteenth and early seventeeth centuries modify our understanding of the question of centrality in colonial New Spain? Mexico City is often pictured as a monstrous octopus, drawing in the wealth and productivity of much of the rest of New Spain and eclipsing all contenders as it reached out to shape and guide local and regional economic development. Yet we must consider the parameters of this kind of control and concentration. The rapid building and institutionalization that took place in the capital and a few other places in the sixteenth century, the arrival of thousands of voluntary immigrants from Spain and involuntary ones brought as slaves from Africa, and the profits first from gold and then silver mining that fueled transatlantic commerce together have fostered a picture of precocious development and economic maturity in New Spain—much of it centered in Mexico City itself—that may be at odds with the reality of colonial society.

Real wealth was highly concentrated in a few hands and in certain places. Despite the drastic reduction in the size of the indigenous population during the sixteenth century, the great majority of people in New Spain still were Indians who mostly lived in small towns, rural communities, or in the poorest barrios of the Spanish cities. Especially in the first century or two of the colonial era, their participation in a commercialized domestic market was limited by both their traditional lifestyle and relative lack of earning power, although there is much evidence of a significant degree of commercialization of the indigenous economy that undoubtedly predated the conquest and then increased thereafter with the introduction of Spanish commodities and enterprises, fueled at least indirectly by silver production. The rapid growth of mixed groups in colonial society—mestizos and mulattoes who for the most part were basically Hispanic in language, diet, and dress—also meant the expansion of demand for products associated with Spanish society, although again their consumption of such products was limited by relatively low levels of income. Thus, while Mexico City could claim much of New Spain's wealth, regional centers like Puebla—which in many ways probably was more comparable to cities like Antequera and Guadalajara than to the capital, notwithstanding its pretensions—in fact mediated significant portions of the local and regional economy that overall accounted for much of the economic activity of New Spain as a whole. Emphasizing the centrality of the capital and its role in orchestrating the colonial economy skews our understanding of the relative weight of the international economy that hinged on the export of silver and import of goods from Europe and Asia that were mainly destined for the small colonial elite, versus the local and regional economies of New Spain that might well have accounted for a larger proportion of the economic activity in New Spain as a whole, by volume if not value.

Puebla's prosperity and its success (for a while, anyway) in convincing at least some people in both the royal and viceregal courts to take its claims and pretensions seriously foreshadowed the future growth and importance of other cities and regions—the Bajío, Guadalajara, and eventually even Veracruz itself—that during the colonial period achieved a significant degree of wealth and economic independence from Mexico City. Puebla's early ability to challenge the capital really was something of a fluke. Located close to Mexico City, the ports on both coasts, and several leading Indian towns as well as on the routes to the south, rather than being overshadowed by the capital, Puebla in effect shared in Mexico City's centrality, since it combined the human and natural resources needed for diversified economic development with the advantages of location. Puebla, in other words, was an early regional focus of development that happened to be centrally located.

The emigration of the briocenses to Puebla also raises certain questions about the notion of centrality in colonial New Spain. At the time the first emigrants left Brihuega for New Spain the colony had been in existence for nearly forty years and had already achieved a significant degree of stability and institutionalization. Yet the initial phases of the migration movement from Brihuega to New Spain resembled the beginning stages of other movements that started much earlier, when society in the Indies was far less settled and organized. At the outset they were principally movements of men, either young bachelors or married men unaccompanied by their spouses or families. Briocenses, in other words, treated central New Spain—their nearly unanimous choice of destination—as if it were a frontier. Even in the 1570s, by which time a good deal of information on Puebla must have reached people back home in Brihuega through letters and conversations with those who returned, single men continued to form a significant part of the migrant group. The contrast to the movement to the Alpujarras is interesting, since the briocenses who went there in the early 1570s presumably knew considerably less about their destination than did those who contemplated a move to Puebla. Nonetheless, rather than moving there in stages or sending the men first to test the feasibility of settlement, they relocated to the Alpujarras en masse and mainly in family units. Thus, while one might expect the residents of Castile's center to view the remote and little-known Alpujarras as a frontier, they instead treated it more as if it were an extension of their own home region. Comparison of the movements to the two destinations, then, suggests that perception defined core and periphery as much as distance, resources, or the prior migration of compatriots and relatives.

Virtually all transatlantic emigrants from Brihuega settled in Puebla or places nearby, in Indian towns like Cholula and Tlaxcala or the growing Spanish community of the Atlixco Valley. Those who decided to live in Mexico City acted in many ways as an extension of the Puebla immigrant community, maintaining close ties with the briocenses in Puebla, often acting as their agents or as retailers of the cloth that obrajeros sent to the capital. The migrants chose Puebla for its economic potential which, when it became known, made the city central rather than peripheral in the perceptions of briocenses looking for a new home.

Notes

1. See James Lockhart, "Trunk Lines and Feeder Lines: The Spanish Reaction to American Resources," in Kenneth J. Andrien and Rolena Adorno, eds., *Transatlantic Encounters: Europeans and Andeans in the Sixteenth Century* (Berkeley: University of California Press, 1991).
2. Charles Gibson, *The Aztecs under Spanish Rule* (Stanford, Calif.: Stanford University Press, 1964).
3. Ida Altman and James Lockhart, eds., *Provinces of Early Mexico* (Los Angeles: UCLA Latin American Center Publications, 1976).
4. See Ida Altman, "Spanish Society in Mexico City after the Conquest," *Hispanic American Historical Review* 71:3 (1991), 413–45.
5. Louisa Schell Hoberman's book *Mexico's Merchant Elite, 1590–1660* (Durham, N.C.: Duke University Press, 1991) for example, focuses almost exclusively on the merchants of the capital.
6. J. I. Israel, *Race, Class and Politics in Colonial Mexico* (Oxford: Oxford University Press, 1975), 12, comments that "before the big silver strikes had been made, the necessary economic basis for effective urbanization of Spaniards in Mexico did not exist." Similarly many of the early Spanish settlements of Hispaniola established in conjunction with gold mining proved unviable, and Santo Domingo emerged as the one substantial city. Peru was somewhat different; there the rapid development of a network that included the new Spanish capital of Lima, the old Inca capital of Cuzco, and the mining center of Potosí and other towns doubtless reflected the greater wealth in precious metals that Spaniards found virtually from the outset.
7. Richard Morse, "A Prolegomenon to Latin American Urban History," *Hispanic American Historical Review* 52:3 (1972), 359–94 discusses the Iberian precedents of Latin-American urbanization.
8. On Seville, see Ruth Pike, *Aristocrats and Traders: Sevillian Society in the Sixteenth Century* (Ithaca, N.Y.: Cornell University Press, 1972); Antonio Domínguez Ortiz, *Orto y ocaso de Sevilla: Estudio sobre la prosperidad y decadencia en la ciudad durante los siglos XVI y XVII* (Seville: Diputacion Provincial, 1946); and Mary Elizabeth Perry, *Gender and Disorder in Early Modern Seville* (Princeton, N.J.: Princeton University Press, 1990).
9. On urban growth and networks in the late fifteenth and early sixteenth centuries see the discussion in Stephen Haliczer, *The Comuneros of Castile* (Madison: University of Wisconsin Press, 1981), 12–29. On the financial and commercial roles of Medina del Campo, Burgos, and Bilbao, see Carla Rahn Phillips and William D. Phillips Jr., *Spain's Golden Fleece. Wool Production and the Wool Trade from the Middle Ages to the Nineteenth Century* (Baltimore: Johns Hopkins University Press, 1997), chapter 9.
10. See Linda Martz, *Poverty and Welfare in Habsburg Spain. The Example of Toledo* (Cambridge: Cambridge University Press, 1983), especially 93–119, on the city's growth in the sixteenth century.
11. For a succinct discussion of the main characteristics and organization of the urban system in colonial Latin America, see Frédéric Mauro, "Urban Preeminence and the Urban System in Colonial America," in Jorge E. Schaedel, Richard P. Hardoy, and Nora Scott Kinzer, eds., *Urbanization in the Americas* (The Hague: Mouton, 1978), 249–68.
12. See Felipe Fernández-Armesto, *Before Columbus: Exploration and Colonisation from the Mediterranean to the Atlantic, 1229–1492* (London: Macmillan Education, 1987) on Valencia and Murcia after the reconquest.
13. See James Lockhart, *The Nahuas after the Conquest* (Stanford, Calif.: Stanford University Press, 1992), chapter 2, and Robert Haskett, *Indigenous Rulers: An Ethnohistory of Town Government in Colonial Cuernavaca* (Albuquerque: University of New Mexico Press, 1991).
14. Most of the indigenous residents of Puebla came from fairly nearby, but Puebla attracted many people from around Mexico City as well. Julia Hirschberg, "A Social History of Puebla de los Angeles, 1531–60" (Ph.D. diss., University of Michigan,

1976), 416–17, notes that "in 1546 the *cabildo* identified *barrios* for Indians from Cholula, Texcoco, Totimehuacan, Tlaxcala, and Mexico. In later years enough Indians migrated from Huejotzingo, Calpa, Tepeaca, Tlatelolco and Tecali to form communities within Puebla. By the fifties Puebla's Indian barrios had become formalized into the barrios of San Sebastian, San Pablo, San Francisco and Santiago."

15. See Leslie Lewis, "In Mexico City's Shadow: Some Aspects of Economic Activity and Social Processes in Texcoco, 1570–1620" in Altman and Lockhart, *Provinces of Early Mexico.*
16. See Hirschberg, "Social History of Puebla," 209–10.
17. Guy P. C. Thomson, *Puebla de los Angeles: Industry and Society in a Mexican City, 1700–1850* (Boulder, Colo.: Westview Press, 1989), 3, writes that "the Puebla region is . . . the most extensive and meteorologically and ecologically the most varied of the great basins of the Mexican plateau. Here the relation between mountainside and valley bottom is more favorable for agriculture than in any other temperate region of settlement within central and southeastern Mexico. . . . Commentators over the centuries agree that this region has the most benign climate of the entire Mexican plateau."
18. Hirschberg, "Social History of Puebla," 126, states that "by 1534 one of every three Pueblans was an encomendero" and the majority of them held encomiendas "closer to Puebla than to any other major Spanish city. The major exceptions were encomenderos whose towns were in the Oaxacan region—and even these would have been closer to Puebla than to Mexico City."
19. Israel, *Race, Class and Politics*, 291, writes that "the financial strength of the Mexican dioceses was roughly in proportion to their agricultural wealth; thus Puebla, having within its limits the most intensively cultivated land in the viceroyalty, was twice as rich as the archbishopric of Mexico and several times richer than most of the other bishoprics."
20. According to Hirschberg, "Social History of Puebla," 200–201, the 1540s were a decade of considerable progress for Puebla: "In addition to the grant of Indian maize, Puebla received new farmlands in Atlixco, official designation as the seat of the diocese of Tlaxcala, and authority to hold biannual *mestas* for Spanish and Indian estancias within the Tlaxcalan bishopric. Not only were its powers over *comarca* towns thus substantially increased but also its prestige at the colonial level was considerably enhanced. At the same time the city came to function as an unofficial administrative center and regional center for official secular and religious celebrations."
21. Woodrow Borah, *Silk Raising in Colonial Mexico* (Berkeley and Los Angeles: University of California Press, 1943), 34.
22. Hirschberg, "Social History of Puebla," 329, notes that in 1559 "Martin de Mafra Vargas's *regimiento* was disputed by the *cabildo* not only on grounds of youth, but also on the basis of his one-time service in his merchant brother-in-law's *tienda de mercaderes.*" In the 1590s three men from Brihuega obtained regimientos and one became *alférez mayor*, although all of them owned obrajes, which in principle they were forced to give up; the sales they effected were probably mainly fictitious.
23. Guadalupe Albi-Romero's study of Puebla in the sixteenth century ("La sociedad de Puebla del los Angeles en el siglo XVI," *Jahrbuch für Geschichte von Staat, Wirtschaft und Gesellschaft Lateinamerikas* 7 [1970]) is perceptive and suggestive but her research was limited to sources in the Archive of the Indies. Her study complements Enrique Otte's discussion of Puebla that prefaces his transcriptions of letters from migrants in Puebla, "Cartas privadas de Puebla del siglo XVI," *Jahrbuch für Geschichte von Staat, Wirtschaft und Gesellschaft Lateinamerikas* 3 (1966). There has been increasing scholarly interest in Puebla and its region in recent years. On agriculture see, for example, Carlos Salvador Paredes Martínez, *La región de Atlixco, Huaquechula y Tochimilco. La sociedad y la agricultura en el siglo XVI* (Mexico: Fondo de Cultura Económico, 1991) and David J. Weiland, "The Economics of Agriculture: Markets, Production and Finances in the Bishopric of Puebla, 1532–1809" (Ph.D. diss., University of Cambridge, 1995). On aspects of religious life see Michael Destefano, "Miracles and Monasticism in Mid-Colonial Puebla, 1600–1750: Charismatic Religion in a Conservative Society" (Ph.D. diss., University of Florida, 1977).

24. Thomson, *Puebla de los Angeles*, xix-xx. Hoberman, *Mexico's Merchant Elite*, 30–31, states that "Puebla, with New Spain's second-largest merchant class, helped provision the ships and was a source of capital and a way station on one route to the port."
25. José F. de la Peña, *Oligarquía y propiedad en Nueva España 1550–1624* (Mexico City: Fondo de Cultura Económico, 1983), 107, 109, 110, 162.
26. Israel, *Race, Class and Politics*, 98.
27. Hoberman, *Mexico's Merchant Elite*, 22.
28. Israel, *Race, Class and Politics*, 97, 180. In this instance the disputed point was the city's contribution to Olivares's Union of Arms, which would have granted funds to maintain the Castilian army in 1628. Puebla resisted the demand longer than the capital or any other New Spanish city.
29. See Peña, *Oligarquía y propiedad*, 200, 203, 205.
30. Israel, *Race, Class and Politics*, 48 (notes 94 and 95).
31. Ibid., 247.
32. Ibid., 96. Hirschberg, "Social History of Puebla," 311, notes that "by the late fifties, two-thirds of known prior residences were non-Mexican. . . . [The] figures would indicate that Puebla regional ties had become less firmly Mexican and more wide-ranging over the period 1531–60." This trend probably continued with perhaps some particular exceptions, such as the migration that Israel notes (p. 29) of substantial numbers of Spanish vecinos who left Mexico City for Puebla and other cities like Querétaro and Antequera due to the major floods in the capital in the years 1629–34.
33. For a detailed discussion of the immigrants from Brihuega and their experinces in Puebla, see Ida Altman, *Transatlantic Ties in the Spanish Empire: Brihuega, Spain and Puebla Mexico, 1560–1620* (Stanford, Calif.: Stanford University Press, 2000).
34. An excellent study of the first century of textile production in New Spain that includes much material on Puebla is Carmen Viqueira and José I. Urquiola, *Los obrajes en la Nueva España, 1530–1630* (Mexico City: Consejo Nacional para la Cultura y las Artes, 1990). In the late sixteenth century Brihuega apparently produced mainly low-quality woolens ("paños bajos") according to some statements, but large producers manufactured higher quality cloth as well; see Archivo General de Simancas, Expedientes Hacienda leg. 60.
35. Information on members of the Anzures, Ribas, and Angulo families is drawn from a number of sources, including records of the Inquisition of Toledo in the Archivo Histórico Nacional in Madrid and inquisition and other records in the Archivo General de la Nación in Mexico City; notarial records in the Archivo General de Notariás in Puebla (AGNP); the judical and municipal archives of Puebla; and the Archivo General de Indias in Seville.
36. His wife Doña Isabel de Vargas's father, Juan de Formicedo, was one of the city's first obraje owners. He was the brother-in-law of *regidor* Martin de Mafra Vargas (see note 21, above).
37. On the suit in the mid-1580s between Pedro de Alcanadre (the seller) and Alonso and Juan de Ribas over the purchase of this obraje, see AGN Civil 1310, exp. 2.
38. See Woodrow Borah, *Early Colonial Trade and Navigation between Mexico and Peru* (Berkeley and Los Angeles: University of California Press, 1954), 22–29, on the land and water routes to Huatulco. One example of the participation in the Philippines trade was a five-year partnership ("compañía") formed by two vecinos of Puebla, Pedro Alonso Enríquez and Horacio Levanto, with a man from Genoa named Sebastián Rodríguez Bertarde in January 1600. The first two men invested 2,000 pesos each and the third 400 pesos. Sebastián Rodríguez was to travel "personally to the Philippine islands" with the costs of his trip and and a 100 pesos a year to cover his expenses in Manila coming out of their joint profits, which would be shared equally among the three; AGNP Juan de la Parra.

Colonial Centers, Colonial Peripheries, and the Economic Agency of the Spanish State

Lyman L. Johnson and Susan Migden Socolow

The terms *center* and *periphery* have had a contentious and often politicized place in the historical literature devoted to Latin America. During the 1960s and 1970s, these terms were common referents in the discourse of dependency theory. Reduced to its shared core, the literature of dependency theory argued that Latin America (a *periphery*) had had its economic character imposed by the colonial economic policies of Spain and Portugal. With independence, two modern industrial powers, Great Britain and later the United States (consecutively exercising the role of *center*), used interventions and the imposition of exploitative commercial terms to maintain what were essentially colonial relations of dependence. Scholars writing in this determinist tradition produced a literature rich in convincing anecdote. Certainly, there was overwhelming evidence that richer and more powerful nations had consistently worked to pursue their own advantage at significant cost to Latin America. This intellectual exercise not only created lively debate; it also influenced economic policy in Latin America. If foreign investment and foreign direct ownership of Latin-American resources had impeded development in the past, then the creation of effective impediments to foreign investment and ownership of local resources would facilitate autonomous development in the future. For a generation of planners and politicians influenced by dependency theory, import substitution was the logical policy objective.

By the late 1980s, dependency theory had attracted numerous critics among both policymakers and scholars.[1] For policymakers the problem was the demonstrated lack of efficacy when the theory was actively pursued, most commonly in the form of wide-ranging import substitution. Years of slow growth, inflation, and limited technological innovation seemed a telling critique of the underlying assumptions. Why persist with implementation, many asked, if the end result led to scarcities and high-priced, poor-quality consumer goods? Others noted that the region's broad economic crisis of the 1980s had begun with the Organization of Petroleum Exporting Countries, oil price shocks, rather than with the exercise of hegemonic power by Western industrial nations, conditions not easily explained by dependency theory. With socialism stalled at its European center, dependency seemed less convincing in Latin America. For all of Argentina's rough treatment by international capital, the average Argentine was, after all, richer than the average Russian. By the 1990s, policymakers were walking away from this once-dominant theory without a backward glance.[2]

The disaffection of scholars flowed from a different source. For Latin-American economic historians in particular, dependency theory offered only limited illumination and unsteady guidance, for it seemed to deny the agency of Latin-American economic actors and paid little attention to domestic and regional economic activity. Focusing narrowly on international trade relationships and the actions of external agents in the large drama of foreign penetration, scholars in the dependency tradition slighted the market relations of local producers and thus neglected business history, the actual practice and experience of firms, farms, and ranches.

As policymakers and scholars drifted away from dependency theory as an overarching explanation for Latin America's economic history, the terms center and periphery nearly disappeared from discussions of both economic policy and history. One of the great misfortunes associated with the rapid decline in the fortunes of dependency theory, and Marxist history more generally, has been the disengagement of Latin-American economic history from public policy. When looking for guidance from the past, economic planners in Latin America are now more likely to examine the histories of Australia, Canada, or South Korea than those of their neighbors. Today economists, rather than historians, produce most serious Latin-American economic history. The general audience of Latin Americanists is unprepared to evaluate the conclusions generated by modern statistical techniques and reacts by dismissing these studies out of hand as bloodless and apolitical. As a result, colonial economic history, once charged with the political energies of dependency theory, has become an arcane area of scholarship generating numerically dense measures of economic performance, but finding few readers.

The widespread inclination to jettison the broad critique of dependency theory and the nomenclature it spawned may soon be viewed as an overreaction that has slowed our efforts to understand the colonial economies of Latin America. In this essay we attempt a less mechanistic use of these tools than was common a decade ago. We argue that an elaborately articulated and hierarchical relationship of center and peripheries existed, not only between the Spanish colonies and the imperial center, but between colonial capitals like Lima (and, after 1776, Buenos Aires) and colonial dependencies like Bolivia, Chile, and Ecuador. We focus our examination on the Spanish Viceroyalty of Peru and its eighteenth-century stepchild, the Viceroyalty of Río de la Plata. Our discussion develops dialectically, exploring the interaction of colonial production and exchange with the institutionalized economic authority of an international state, the Spanish empire.

We further argue that the combined effects of the Bourbon Reforms of the eighteenth century and the achievement of independence in the 1820s altered the economic trajectory of Spanish South America generally, and Peru and Argentina specifically. These large political events forged new and influential external commercial linkages and reconstituted the vectors of state intervention in the new national economies of Peru, Argentina, and their neighbors. The economic structures that had emerged by 1850 were fundamentally different from those of 1700. Both the new forms and the old were colonial in nature, in the sense of being subordinated to more powerful external centers. Nevertheless, the differences between the reform era and the early national period seem to us to have been more important than the continuities. During this century of upheaval (1750–1850), the articulated economic linkages tying the region's major urban center to its secondary cities and to agricultural and mining production were both weakened and transformed.

Assessing the nature of these changes requires a brief review of our point of origin, the Spanish Viceroyalty of Peru. This vast administrative unit, with Lima as its capital, was the largest and ecologically most varied of the Spanish colonial jurisdictions. Until the second half of the eighteenth century, it encompassed all of Spain's South American colonies. The viceroyalty stretched from the Caribbean coast of present-day Venezuela west across the northern Andes to Colombia (colonial New Granada), south along the length of the Pacific coast, and east across the southern Andes to include what are now the nations of Paraguay, Uruguay, and Argentina. The city of Buenos Aires was its easternmost urban outpost.

The Inca provided the foundation for this vast colonial structure. Long before the Spanish arrived, the indigenous peoples of the Andean region had, despite daunting environmental obstacles, constructed a complex cultural synthesis and economy. A remarkably diverse geography and climate divided the region into three distinct ecological zones: desert along the Pacific coast, high sierra dominated by the soaring peaks of the Andes, and jungle at the headwaters of the Amazon. Each of these zones had been exploited by human populations for millennia before the Spanish arrived. The arid coast was dotted by agricultural oases where the melting snow and seasonal rains of the Andes flowed through river valleys into the Pacific. The forbidding heights of the Andes surrounded fertile valleys strung like an archipelago from Colombia to Chile. Even the hot country of the tramontane interior hosted a diverse, if fragile, agriculture. Yet each of these environments presented significant obstacles to agriculture and to commerce. Human populations succeeded in a limited way under difficult circumstances. Large sections of the coast were arable only with intense irrigation; much of the sierra could not be tamed by terracing; and the jungle was subject to seasonal flooding, high humidity, and scorching temperatures.[3] Only by evolving complex systems of shared labor obligations (*mit'a*) and of verticality, the specialized production and exchange across ecological boundaries, in this case within the native community (*ayllu*), had indigenous peoples gained a conditional victory over the environment.

The Inca state multiplied the economic potential of these long-established systems through military conquest and an expanded bureaucracy, extending their reach and managing their resources more efficiently. By the 1520s, however, the limitations of the Inca state were becoming manifest. An increased number of ethnic uprisings and tensions within the governing elite foreshadowed the destructive civil war that would weaken the Inca cultural synthesis on the eve of the Spanish conquest. Given their limited technological tools, the political and military achievements of the Inca were indeed impressive, but it is important to recall that the Spanish viceroyalty created in the sixteenth century dwarfed the Inca empire in scale and proved its durability over more than two hundred years. The Viceroyalty of the Río de la Plata was created by decree in 1776 out of the mundane concerns of a metropolitan regime desperate for increased fiscal resources and worried about English commercial penetration through Colônia, the Portuguese contraband center on the eastern bank of the Río de la Plata.

Among the many changes that followed the violent disposition of the Inca political order was Francisco Pizarro's decision in 1535 to build a new capital, Lima, rather than to center his enterprise in the Inca capital, Cuzco. Located near the Rimac River's outlet to the Pacific Ocean and thus more easily supplied from Panama, Lima became the capital of the viceroyalty and administrative heart of the entire Andean region. It also quickly developed into a major commercial center. At first it served as the transfer point for the vast booty of conquest. Later, its commercial functions were normalized as its great merchants took control of much of the trade of the viceroyalty. This commercial dominance did not spring from any comparative advantage, but was the result of the Spanish Crown's decision to establish a merchant monopoly (*consulado*) there in 1613. Consulado members alone possessed the right to import European goods legally. From this powerful position, they effectively controlled silver exports.

More important still, Lima became one of the most important American colonial markets due to the power of the colonial state to construct markets, allocate resources, and redistribute wealth. The viceroy and his court resided in Lima, as did the legion of bureaucrats who staffed the head offices of the Royal Treasury and the Audit Bureau (*Tribunal de Cuentas*). The population of Lima and its nearby seaport, Callao, also included large numbers of military, naval, and coast guard personnel. The city hosted the most important and prestigious high court (*audiencia*) in South America. In addition to this dense employment sector, the city government (*ayuntamiento*) employed hundreds more, including clerks, jailers, nightwatchmen, and, periodically, artisans to maintain buildings and construct public works. The viceroyalty's upper ecclesiastical establishment, with its formidable ability to assess taxes in the form of sacramental fees and tithes, was also located in Lima. The city boasted a bishop (later an archbishop), cathedral chapters, houses of the regular orders, nunneries, and a branch of the Holy Office of the Inquisition. As the mineral wealth of the Andean interior was revealed and exploited in the second half of the sixteenth century, Lima's population grew and its economy flourished. This expansion reflected the growing power of the colonial state.

By relocating the region's political and commercial center from the Inca capital of Cuzco in the southern highlands to Lima near the coast, Pizarro helped to determine the future economic development of all South America, including Portuguese Brazil. His decision meant that the Andes' vast mineral wealth would be connected with the Atlantic economy via a slow and difficult Pacific route north to Panama and across the isthmus, rather than down the eastern slope of the Andes and through the Río de la Plata estuary. In the first decades of Spanish occupation, the logic of this route was irrefutable, retracing the route of Pizarro back to the colonial beachhead of Panama, source of resupply and settler recruitment. In the longer term, however, the limitations of the Pacific route became obvious.

The Spanish Crown found it nearly impossible to protect individual vessels from the depredations of pirates and foreign enemies; as a result, by 1550 it imposed a system of annual transatlantic commercial fleets protected by naval convoys.

Although fairly successful in limiting shipping losses, the fleet system impeded the shipping of European goods, especially to Pacific coastal destinations. This bureaucratically induced bottleneck was made worse by the Lima merchant guild's inclination to restrict competition and keep prices high. The combination of the high cost of transportation, monopoly commerce, and Lima's state-subsidized consumption meant that the broad Andean region experienced chronic shortages of imported goods and extremely limited opportunities for export trade. Almost the only commodities capable of overcoming these obstacles were high-value-to-weight mineral exports. State policy pumped the wealth of interior mineral and agricultural sectors toward Lima.

Lima was one of the few major colonial cities in the Andean region that had not been a substantial pre-Colombian city. Its initial growth was hampered by a fifteen-year civil war that broke out between competing groups of *conquistadores* in the 1530s. Once peace was established, however, the city's population growth rate reflected its importance as the capital of the new Viceroyalty of Peru. As early as 1560, Lima's population had reached nearly 8,000; by 1614 it exceeded 25,000, rising to 30,000 by 1640. A major earthquake that devastated the city and the surrounding region in 1687 produced a brief demographic plateau, but the population resumed its growth early in the eighteenth century, increasing from 37,200 in 1700 to about 54,000 in the 1760s and 63,900 in 1812.[4]

After the city's founding, market agriculture developed quickly in the nearby coastal valley oases to feed the burgeoning population of Spaniards and mestizos. A wave of epidemics reduced the indigenous population of the coast, setting the stage for a more focused commercial agriculture organized by Spaniards and dependent on the labor of African slaves. By the end of the seventeenth century, wine, sugar, and wheat production had replaced the corn agriculture of the early colonial period. Because of their proximity to Lima, the Huaura, Ica, and Chili River Valleys became centers of market agriculture.[5] A similar transformation occurred in urban manufacturing, with European artisans training Indians, mestizos, and Africans to produce goods for the emerging colonial consumer market. Within a remarkably short time, everything from furniture and silverware to oil paintings was being produced in Lima and in secondary cities like Cuzco and Potosí. Textile production, which relied on forced labor, remained outside Lima, located in areas of dense indigenous population.

The Viceroyalty of Peru was so vast that its governance was divided into five high court jurisdictions (audiencias) and numerous subunits (captaincies-general). The essential structure was in place in the sixteenth century: the Audiencia of Lima was founded in 1543, that of Santa Fé de Bogotá in 1548, that of Charcas (present-day Sucre, Bolivia) in 1558, and that of Quito in 1562. The Audiencia of Chile was created in 1563 and, after an interval, reestablished in 1606. Buenos Aires, located on the viceroyalty's eastern periphery, was granted an audiencia in 1661, but the weakness of the local economy doomed it after a decade. As part of the general reforms of the eighteenth century, the Audiencia of Buenos Aires was reestablished in 1783, a new Audiencia of Caracas was carved out of the territory of the Audiencia of Santa Fé (colonial New Granada) in 1786, and a new Audiencia of Cuzco out of the Audiencia of Charcas in 1787.[6]

A large portion of the Andean region extending from the Putumayo River to the Quebrada of Humahuaca—a distance of approximately 1,900 miles—was divided into two geographical entities: Lower and Upper Peru. The former corresponded more or less to the present nation of Peru, while the latter included much of present Bolivia. Vast mineral wealth was found in each of the two Perus: the mercury mine of Huancavelica and the silver mines of Pasco and Castrovirreina were in Lower Peru, while Upper Peru was the site of the most important silver mine in South America, Potosí.

All the principal mines of Upper and Lower Peru were located at high altitudes. At more than 13,000 feet above sea level, Potosí was the highest. Discovered in 1545, by 1580 this "mountain of silver" had emerged as the most important mineral center in the Americas. By the end of the sixteenth century the production of silver at Potosí depended on the availability of mercury, used in the amalgamation process, and was linked to supplies of mercury from Huancavelica, 12,000 feet above sea level in Lower Peru. Huancavelica mercury moved in sacks made of hides, first on muleback to the port of Cañete, then by ship to the port of Arica, where it was off-loaded and sent via muleback more than three hundred miles across desert and mountains to the mines of Upper Peru. By the eighteenth century, the output of Huancavelica was being supplemented by mercury from Almadén in Spain and Idrija in modern Slovenia, shipped to Arica via the isthmus of Panama.

The presence of the mines spurred extraordinary demographic growth for such a high altitude; by 1580 the number of people at the *cerro rico* of Potosí reached 120,000. Barren of all but minerals, the mining regions depended on other districts for labor, food, supplies, textiles, and draft animals. Potosí and the other mines were not isolated enclaves; they were strongly tied to regions near and far in a mutually productive relationship.[7] The result was a network of interregional markets, each one specializing in the production of specific goods and closely tied to other markets. In essence, the entire network was a largely self-sufficient unit, a group of peripheral places that could survive with minimal ties to either viceregal or European centers. The achievement of this large, integrated regional economy was dependent on the application of state power.[8]

Unlike Mexico, where agricultural and ranching products tended to be produced solely for local markets, goods produced in the two Perus were often marketed a long distance from their points of origin.[9] The mines of the two Perus drew goods from an area that extended from Quito to Buenos Aires. Each region supplied a specialized product to the mineral axis and participated in an economy that extended over 5,000 miles. As a result, producers on the periphery of the viceroyalty, at Tucumán and Quito, for example, were surprisingly well integrated into the large markets of the mining centers. This integration was only partly the result of market forces; it also arose from the colonial state's coercive authority. The cloth manufactured in Ecuador and the mules raised on the plains of Argentina satisfied the miners' needs for clothing, transportation, and traction in driving machinery, but the forced sale of these and other surplus goods to Indian communities was what made production profitable. Potosí and other mining centers were in turn subordinated to Lima via the agency of state power and monopoly trade. The fact that the urban economy of Lima was more than twice as large as the economy of Potosí in the early eighteenth century is a strong indication of the redistributive power of the colonial state.[10] Although the size and profitability of the viceroyalty's markets waxed and waned with the levels of silver production, the Andean economic system survived into the 1770s. The transforming crisis would come in two waves, provoked by new imperial economic policies and by local indigenous rebellion.[11]

A brief description of several regional economies will illustrate the economic integration of the viceroyalty from colonial periphery to colonial center. By the last decades of the sixteenth century, the high valleys and plains surrounding the city of Quito were renowned for their sheep. Large farms near the Quito region raised these animals and processed their wool into a variety of textiles. These rural processing plants, or *obraje* complexes, employed large numbers of Indian men, women, and children in jobs ranging from textile workers (carders, spinners, dyers, warpers, weavers, fullers, and pressers) to the muleteers who transported the cloth to distant ports.[12] About 80 percent of Quito woolen textile production consisted of dark blue cloth (*paño azul*). Other textiles included coarse frieze (*jerga*), black serge (*estameña negra*), brown serge (*estameña parda*), brown cloth (*paño pardo*), coarse cloth (*jergueta*), ordinary black woolens (*paño negro ordinario*), and fine black woolens (*paño negro fino*). All textiles, coarse and fine, were destined for the market of the two Perus.[13] Although cotton and wool textiles were also produced in obrajes in Tucumán in Argentina, and Cuzco, Trujillo, and Cajamarca in Peru, Quito was by far the largest producer. By 1700 there were 169 textile obrajes in the audiencia, plus hundreds of small cottage producers. Together, they produced more than 650,000 *varas* of cloth a year, worth more than three million pesos, making Quito one of the most important manufacturing centers in the hemisphere.[14] Lima, the redistribution point for this market, lay almost 900 miles away. The textiles moved overland from Quito's hinterland to the port of Guayaquil and then by sea north to Callao, linked by Pacific coastal shipping to Panama City and Acapulco.

The colonial state was involved in nearly every facet of the development of this large and specialized textile industry. First, Peru's indigenous community provided labor through the *mita*, a colonial institution imposed by the viceregal government in the sixteenth century, based on the pre-Columbian rotational labor obligations (mit'a) but more disruptive and exploitative than its antecedent. Colonial courts supplemented this labor supply by sending convicts to the obrajes. Second, while Quito's textiles were sold at the mining centers of Upper and Lower Peru, this market-based consumption was subsidized by forced consumption elsewhere. Mita laborers were compelled to accept a large portion of their legally mandated wages in unsold textiles that obraje laborers had been compelled to produce. Third, indigenous villages were also forced to purchase textiles from the agents of Spanish judges (*corregidores*) at set prices, in the so-called distribution of merchandise (*repartimiento de mercancias*). The system was monetarized by the silver production of the region's mines, but the entire industry was dependent on the coercive authority of the colonial state.

Far to the south lay another regional economy integrated by the viceroyalty's mining sector. Initially, the city of Lima was supplied with wheat from nearby coastal valleys. After the devastation of the 1687 earthquake, Lima's authorities were forced to find new sources of agricultural products, and the rural hinterland of Santiago in the captaincy-general of Chile emerged as a major wheat-producing region for Peru. Grain raised in Chile's central valley was shipped overland to the port of Valparaíso and from there transported by ship to Callao, 1,500 miles to the north. Ships built in

Guayaquil and owned by merchants in Lima connected Chile's distant wheatfields to Peru's urban consumers.[15] The volume of Chile's wheat exports rose from about 10,000 *fanegas* per year before the earthquake to more than 150,000 fanegas after, as the central valley of Chile became Lima's breadbasket.[16] Here again the state's role was crucial. The creation of a consulado in Lima gave the capital city's merchant elite a powerful vehicle for determining the terms of trade, forcing agriculturalists in Chile to subsidize consumers in Peru.

A few highly specialized regional products also entered the Andean circuit and widened its economic impact. Perhaps the most interesting of these goods was *yerba mate*, an herbal tea produced in Paraguay. Although Paraguay also supplied sugar, honey, and tobacco to nearby areas, yerba was its most marketable crop.[17] The tea not only fueled a complex trade route that linked Asunción to Buenos Aires, Santiago de Chile, and Lima, it encouraged the creation of a shipbuilding industry in Asunción, which manufactured boats for the internal river trade.[18] This complex set of market relationships was in some measure a consequence of the Bourbon state's decision to establish a tobacco monopoly in Paraguay in 1779. Prior to this move, the Paraguayan economy had been limited by a chronic shortage of specie, with many transactions arranged in a local paper currency based on bales of yerba. The tobacco monopoly monetarized this dormant economy by paying local producers in silver, the same silver that had flowed into the colonial fiscal system, either in the form of taxes on mining production in Upper and Lower Peru or of revenues generated across the viceroyalty by the tobacco monopoly itself.[19]

Still another distant region integrated into the silver-driven Andean economy was the interior province of Tucumán in the northwest of present Argentina, to the east of the Andean mountain range.[20] At the beginning of the seventeenth century, this large jurisdiction extended from the Jujuy-Salta region to the city of Córdoba. Regions to the south of Potosí had provided raw materials and manufactured goods to the mining region since the end of the sixteenth century. Although Tucumán also exported wooden beams, shoe leather, tallow, grease, soap, cheap textiles, and low-quality spirits, without question its most important export was mules.

The beasts of burden most suited to the difficult Andean terrain, mules carried silver and other goods and also powered the grinding mills essential to the silver-refining process. The breeding and raising of mules for the two Perus became the economic engine that linked a large area to the southeast of the Andes into the Peruvian commercial circuit. The principal market for mules was the mining region of Upper Peru, especially the great silver mines of Potosí and Oruro, but animals were routinely sent as far as Lima. Although the specifics of the trade changed over time, the mule trade stretched across vast distances, joining the hinterland of Buenos Aires, where the mules were bred; to Córdoba, where they were wintered, on through Salta and Jujuy, where they were sold at mule fairs; to their eventual destinations in Upper and Lower Peru. This trade was a going concern as early as 1610; by 1650, roughly 25,000 mules were being driven from the Río de la Plata via Tucumán to the two Perus. Over time the geographic scope of the trade grew; by the end of the seventeenth century mules from the Río de la Plata served in the mining centers of Potosí and Oruro, the city of La Paz, and places such as Cuzco, Coporque, and Jauja in the Peruvian sierra. By 1770, the mule fair of Salta sold as many as 40,000 mules per year to Peru; between 1778 and 1809, Salta exported nearly 810,000 mules northward.[21]

Merchants realized large profits from the mule trade. In the seventeenth century, a pair of mules valued at 12 to 14 *pesos* in Córdoba brought 40 to 50 in Peru, an increase of 333 to 357 percent. By 1770, a mule worth 1 1/2 to 2 pesos in Buenos Aires was valued at 4 1/2 pesos after wintering in Córdoba, 8 to 9 pesos at the Salta and Jujuy fairs, and 16 to 18 pesos at its Upper Peruvian destination. Although the price per mule had fallen, the increase in value between Córdoba and Potosí was constant at 355 to 400 percent.

Mules were sold to the mining towns through regional livestock fairs and local livestock markets. A significant cattle trade to Peru was conducted along the same route. The annual cattle fair in Jujuy supplied between 7,000 and 10,000 head of cattle to the provinces of Chichas, Cinti, Chuquisaca, and Porco.[22] There was also a growing trans-Andean livestock trade from regions close to the city of Buenos Aires to the valleys of central Chile. The Mapuche Indians who in the mid-eighteenth century still controlled most of southern Chile and the western pampas in Argentina were participants in this trade, enabling cattle stolen in Argentina to be sold in Chile with the connivance of colonial officials.

The market mechanisms of the livestock trade, like those in the textile industry, were supplemented by state compulsion. Through the repartimiento de mercancias, corregidores forced indigenous communities throughout the Andes to purchase at inflated prices animals that they in turn were often compelled to resell below cost to neighboring farmers and ranchers in order to secure the cash necessary to pay taxes and religious fees. Indians were similarly compelled through the repartimiento to consume overpriced European textiles and other goods. But mules and textiles produced by mita labor in the Quito region were the two most important products in total value subsidized through the forced consumption of native communities.[23]

The Túpac Amaru Rebellion (1780–82) was provoked in part by these abuses. The resulting property destruction and forced population movements reduced mineral production, seriously disrupted regional trade, and forced a reform of the repartimiento system. The combined effects of the rebellion and of economic reforms, including the abolition of the repartimiento de mercancias, undermined both the textile and the mule trade. But only the deeper disruption of silver mining, caused by the wars of independence that began in 1809, finally brought Salta's mule trade with the high Andean mining centers to an end.

To the southeast of Tucumán lay the Río de la Plata, a sparsely populated flat plain around the fledgling port of Buenos Aires, on a broad estuary flowing into the Atlantic. Despite its distance from the mines of the interior, the Río de la Plata was deeply integrated into the Andean economic zone. Its port, however, was also tied to the Portuguese colony of Brazil through contraband trade. Whereas regions located in the northwest of present Argentina, such as Salta and Córdoba, and districts closer to the Peruvian silver mines were officially integrated into the trade network, sixteenth- and seventeenth-century Spanish imperial policy toward the Río de la Plata was ambivalent. On the one hand, the Spanish Crown, responsive to the needs of Peruvian merchants and aware of the illegal flow of silver out of Buenos Aires, worked to isolate the Río de la Plata region from the rest of the viceroyalty. Lima's consulado systematically opposed all commerce through Buenos Aires because the merchant elite rightly saw the latter port as a threat to their domination of Upper

Peru.[24] The Crown, on the other hand, was conscious of the need to maintain Buenos Aires as a defense against foreign incursion into the vital silver-producing regions. It was therefore willing to authorize minimal direct trade between the port and Spain, leaving to the coast patrol the impossible task of controlling the seepage of silver out of Spanish hands. In an attempt to reconcile its contradictory imperial aims, the Crown created an inland customs house in Córdoba in 1622 to monitor the route between Buenos Aires and Potosí, and other customs houses in Salta and Jujuy in 1685. But all efforts to block the flow and counterflow of goods and silver failed, as local merchants and smugglers (often one and the same) simply avoided these towns.

Only rarely in the sixteenth century did the Spanish Crown allow a merchant ship to sail to Buenos Aires. In the seventeenth century, once every two or three years the city received a licensed ship from Spain bringing military equipment, troops, ecclesiastical personnel, and administrators. Many of these appointees, hiding valuables in their personal baggage, introduced goods for sale in local and Upper Peruvian markets.[25] Under pretext of "emergency landings," foreign ships brought other European goods. Goods entering the port through these subterfuges were purchased with silver extracted from the mines of Upper Peru; precious metals comprised 80 percent of the total value of exports from Buenos Aires.[26] The city also conducted an intense coastal commerce with Brazil, exporting wheat, dried beef, and tallow, and importing slaves for resale in the markets of Upper Peru.[27] Indeed, by the second half of the seventeenth century, the volume of port activity in Buenos Aires roughly equaled that of Portobelo, Spain's principal port for the legal movement of goods to all of Spanish South America.[28] What drove this contraband trade was the price differential between goods imported through Buenos Aires and Lima.[29] A vara of European cloth introduced by way of Lima sold in Upper Peru for twenty to twenty-five pesos; by way of Buenos Aires, the same cloth sold for four pesos. In spite of Crown policy that sought to restrict commercial access to the Río de la Plata, the largely illegal trade of Buenos Aires flourished, proving the advantage of the city's location on the Atlantic Ocean and its proximity to Brazil. By the middle of the seventeenth century, Portugal's deepening commercial relations with England made Brazil a conduit for English commercial penetration of Spanish South America. The critical role of the Río de la Plata as a link between Brazil and the two Perus would continue until the end of the colonial period.

Politics as well as economics shaped the initial framework of trade in the viceroyalty. In 1580, just as Potosí was emerging as the Spanish empire's major silver producer, the Crowns of Spain and Portugal were joined under the Spanish Habsburgs. Although legally the two kingdoms and their respective dominions were to be separately ruled, in reality their South American colonies experienced a general loosening of the mercantilist restrictions that had barred trade between Spanish and Portuguese possessions. One consequence was the rapid establishment of Portuguese merchant communities in the economies of Lima, Potosí, and Buenos Aires.[30] Once established, these rival merchant communities worked to redirect the movement of Potosí's silver toward Brazil, with its supplies of English manufactures, African slaves, and tobacco. New trade links articulated Upper Peru to the Brazilian coastal ports of Bahia and Rio de Janeiro by way of Buenos Aires. When the Spanish rule of Portugal ended in 1654, these fragile commercial connections were threatened. The scale and importance of the trade between Brazil and Upper Peru quickly became evident when the Portuguese established a trading entrepôt, Colônia da Sacramento, directly across the Río de la Plata from Buenos Aires in 1680. Colônia would serve as an illegal market for the exchange of Brazilian slaves and Peruvian silver for almost one hundred years.

The Atlantic location of Buenos Aires made it a natural link between the interior markets of Spanish South America and the African slave trade. Within eight years of its permanent founding in 1580, the city was importing slaves. Because of the severe legal limitations the Crown placed on this trade, enslaved Africans, like most commodities, came into the region illegally. In fact, 94 percent of the approximately 233 slaves introduced via Buenos Aires between 1588 and 1597 were illegal imports.[31] During the seventeenth century, the demand for slaves in Upper Peru increased the average annual number of imported slaves tenfold, with a corresponding increase in smuggling. The illegal slave trade was managed first by the Portuguese and later by the Dutch, both of them in collaboration with local merchants.

In addition to this contraband trade, a tightly controlled legal slave trade was always carried on by individual Spanish merchants who had been granted royal contracts to transport a set number of slaves to Buenos Aires within a set period. The legal trade increased greatly in the first half of the eighteenth century, with the granting of the slave trade monopoly (*asiento*), first to the French Guinea Company (1701–1713) and then to the British South Sea Company (1713–1748). Of the approximately 14,000 slaves who entered Buenos Aires legally during this half century, about 30 percent were absorbed by the local economy; the rest were reshipped to the interior or to Upper Peru.[32] In the second half of the eighteenth century and up to the effective end of the colonial period in 1810, at least 12,000 slaves were shipped legally from Brazil to Upper Peru via the Río de la Plata. For example, Tomás Antonio Romero, a Buenos Aires merchant, received permission in 1784 to import 1,000 slaves from Brazil. Although they were shipped to Buenos Aires, their destination was the distant markets of Chile and Peru.[33] During the 1780s, approximately 280 slaves were imported legally each year. During the era of free trade the legal slave trade peaked, rising to 900 per year in the 1790s and 1,300 per year in the last decade of the colonial period.[34] Meanwhile, thousands of slaves continued to enter the city illegally by both land and sea.

The complex network that developed to move all of these goods, animals, and people over vast distances also created a transportation system that varied from region to region. Yerba mate, for example, was carried on rafts from Asunción and the Misiones region down the Paraguay and Uruguay river systems to Buenos Aires. Products being shipped to Upper Peru were sent by boat to Santa Fé, then loaded onto large carts and moved northwest to Jujuy. In Jujuy, they were reloaded onto mules to negotiate the steep Andean passes to Potosí and other Upper Peruvian markets. Products destined for Lima were sent via Buenos Aires, Mendoza, and Santiago de Chile by cart and on muleback, and then by ship from Valparaíso to Callao. By the end of the eighteenth century, goods were also sent via ship from Buenos Aires to Valparaíso through Cape Horn.[35] By modern standards, travel was slow. The average time on the road from Buenos Aires to Jujuy, a distance of approximately nine hundred miles, was three months. Along the route, cities such as Jujuy developed an infrastructure to house, feed, and equip carters and muleteers.

During the course of the eighteenth century, a series of Spanish administrative and bureaucratic reforms dramatically altered the size and influence of the Viceroyalty of Peru. Between 1717 and 1722, Colombia and Venezuela were split off as the short-lived Viceroyalty of New Granada, reestablished in 1739. The second kingdom to be carved out of Lima's original jurisdiction was the Viceroyalty of Río de la Plata, whose capital was Buenos Aires. Created in 1776, the new viceroyalty included Upper Peru and Chile as well as Paraguay and the "*Otra Banda*" (Uruguay). The scale and importance of Buenos Aires's role in contraband with the Portuguese was acknowledged by the Spanish decision to precede the creation of the new viceroyalty by sending a large military expedition to seize Colônia. Notwithstanding these jurisdictional changes, the economic motor that had driven the entire region since the middle of the sixteenth century, the mineral wealth of the Andes, leveraged and directed by institutions of the Spanish state, continued to hold it together.

Despite the emergence of Buenos Aires as an entrepôt for contraband in the late seventeenth and early eighteenth centuries, the city's elevation into a vital player in the South American silver economy was a product of the Bourbon Reforms. The new imperial role assigned to this peripheral region began when the Crown granted the asiento to Great Britain following the Treaty of Utrecht (1713). The asiento gave the English an excuse to maintain a permanent commercial establishment in the city, thus providing an effective cover for smuggled textiles and other goods for the "maintenance of slaves" prior to sale. The commercial importance of the region was further enhanced in 1721 when Philip V authorized regular trade between Spain and Buenos Aires. In 1778, when free trade within the Spanish empire was extended to the Río de la Plata, Buenos Aires shed its role as a colonial periphery and benefited from the newly established institutions of empire that allowed it to subordinate and exploit the economies of Upper Peru, Chile, Paraguay, and Uruguay.

The demographic growth of Buenos Aires and its immediate environs reflected the increasing importance of the region. For a Spanish-American city, Buenos Aires was a relative latecomer. Founded in 1536, it was abandoned shortly afterward because of harsh conditions and hostile native peoples and not refounded until 1580. On the very edge of empire, the city probably numbered a few hundred inhabitants in 1600, and 4,000 to 5,000 in 1700. By 1744 the population was approximately 11,600; it grew rapidly to 22,000 in 1773, to 26,000 five years later, and to 42,500 in 1810,[36] numbers that suggest that Buenos Aires was the fastest-growing city in the Spanish colonial world. The city was surrounded by its own wheat-producing zone. Locally grown grain fed a growing population and supplied the flour for hardtack to provision a growing naval trade.

Paradoxically, this region of rapid population growth suffered from an endemic shortage of labor. As a result, labor costs were inordinately high in Buenos Aires and its immediate vicinity. The creation of the viceroyalty compounded the problem. One of the hallmarks of viceregal Buenos Aires was a dramatic increase in military expenditures, much of which went to increasing military manpower, expanding the officer corps along with the local garrison and enlarging as well as improving the urban militia. Installing a viceregal infrastructure also swelled the civil bureaucracy. The newly appointed officers and bureaucrats and their households added thousands of relatively affluent consumers to the city's growing number of commercial and professional families.[37] These changes resulted in a long-term building boom and a continuous demand for unskilled and skilled labor. The demand for housing, goods, and services floated urban wages upward, causing a labor shortage in the countryside.

Increasing government expenditures to support both the military establishment and the civilian bureaucracy of Buenos Aires were met in part by taxes on a burgeoning local commerce. More important sources of government revenue, however, were the taxes on Upper Peruvian mining and the tribute paid by Andean indigenous communities.[38] By redirecting Upper Peru's mining taxes and Indian tribute to Buenos Aires, Spain subsidized the rapid development of the new viceroyalty's vastly expanded bureaucracy and defenses. The net result was the forced redistribution of wealth from the miners of Upper Peru to the merchants and bureaucrats of Río de la Plata, or more precisely, a redirection of state funds from Lima to Buenos Aires. It is difficult to estimate the size of the colonial public sector or even to estimate the annual tax flow. As a guideline, government expenditures for eighteenth-century Mexico increased 3 percent per year between 1750 and 1809 as a result of the Bourbon Reforms, to the point, after 1800, of absorbing 25 percent of the Crown's revenues from colonial Mexico.[39] The public sector in Río de la Plata probably exercised a similar influence.

The scarcity and high relative cost of labor retarded the growth of agriculture in the city's hinterland. Despite the growing slave trade and an increasing influx of free immigrants from Europe and the South American interior, farmers were unable to find sufficient labor even for the modest demands of wheat. The colonial government was forced to bring in Guaraní Indians from distant Paraguay to harvest the wheatfields near Buenos Aires. The same labor shortage led to the imposition of harsh vagrancy laws on country people, punishing with prison or conscription those who lacked written proof of employment.

Although Buenos Aires had already emerged as the commercial center of both transatlantic trade and coastal shipping, the creation of the Viceroyalty of Río de la Plata in 1776 and the decreeing of the Free Trade Ordinances two years later legitimized the city's position in the Atlantic economy. After 1790, intermittent European wars forced the city to look beyond its traditional links to Spain and its extralegal ties to Brazil and Portugal and to develop trade with Hamburg, Mauritius, Cuba, and the principal Anglo-American ports.

For merchants, the South American trade was always risky business. Zealous bureaucrats, fresh government regulations, European geopolitics—all could reverse mercantile success, as could changing market conditions and dependence on an overextended credit system. Many of the markets, moreover, were so small that a single ship filled with a competitor's goods could sink a merchant's hopes of profit if it arrived before his shipment did. Good information was essential to commercial ventures; traditionally, this information was conveyed in personal letters and business communications between merchants, supplemented by word-of-mouth market intelligence carried from port to port by ships' crews. The Bourbon state greatly improved the flow of information by creating a transatlantic mail system in the mid-1760s, with regular service between La Coruña and Montevideo and a direct link to Buenos Aires. One could now make the Atlantic crossing in less than three months. Regular overland mail service from Buenos Aires to the northwest was established in 1748 and soon extended to the northeast, and the opening of new overland routes during the late eighteenth century slightly reduced transportation time.

By the end of the eighteenth century regular newspapers improved the level of market intelligence, although personal communications continued to be important. Both conveyed political and economic news, prices, and information on fleet sailings and traffic in other ports. One issue of the *Telégrafo Mercantil*, a Buenos Aires newspaper, contained the following items in its commercial news:

> From the brig Bengador, which entered the port of Montevideo on the 26th of last month sailing from Bahia de Todos los Santos, we have learned that it left the brig belonging to Don Tomas Salas arriving from Cadiz and the ship El Rescate in that port.
>
> From the Spanish Consul resident in Algeria, we have received news that up to 11 privateers were about to leave from that port, destination unknown. Therefore it is advisable that entering and leaving port on the Spanish Peninsula and adjacent islands, ships navigate with great care.
>
> The frigate Cleopatra from Bilbao has opened its register (is currently loading goods) for the port of La Coruña. It still has room for 4000 hides to complete its cargo. Whomever wishes to take advantage of this opportunity, please contact Messieurs Llanos, merchants of this city . . . the ship will sail on 11 October. . . .[40]

The Río de la Plata region achieved political independence from Spain with little of the drama or destructive violence that afflicted Peru, Mexico, or Venezuela. In Buenos Aires, effective independence was accomplished in May, 1810, when the creole elite, constituted as an augmented town council (*cabildo abierto*), decided to remove the viceroy and establish a junta in imitation of the Spanish junta created after the forced abdication of Ferdinand VII. Although claiming to rule in the king's name, the city's new political class never looked back; for them, Spanish authority had ended. The next stages of the regional political story were marked by conflict not with Spanish armies, but with neighbors. The Buenos Aires elite wished to continue dominating the interior provinces. The city had grown accustomed to political preeminence within the boundaries of the old viceroyalty and to the transfers of wealth that had underwritten its growth. But Buenos Aires's new political leadership found this objective both costly and elusive. In less than five years Paraguay had achieved independence, Uruguay had been divided into a royalist city-state (Montevideo) and an insurrectionist countryside, and Upper Peru, alienated by the incompetencies and brutalities of military commanders from Buenos Aires, was moving toward effective independence. When the dust settled in the 1820s, not only had Paraguay, Uruguay, and Bolivia gained their independence, but Buenos Aires had lost effective control of the interior provinces of what is now Argentina. It would take nearly fifty years to construct a single constitutional order for this fragment of the old viceroyalty. The origins of these political disasters could be sought in the actions of the political class brought to power in Buenos Aires after 1810, but for our purposes it is more useful to examine the economic nature of the colonial viceregency.

As we argued earlier in our discussion of the Viceroyalty of Peru prior to the Bourbon Reforms, remarkable economic diversity and commercial integration had been achieved within the Spanish colonial system. The first stage of this process of state-directed economic development focused on the Andes, with Lima as the center, and Potosí, Quito, Santiago, and, to a lesser degree, Buenos Aires as distant, secondary economic nodes, or peripheries. Recall the incredible inefficiencies of the commercial articulation imposed by Lima's political ascendancy. Goods sent from Europe reached the capital city and its monopoly merchants via a transatlantic voyage first to Havana, then to the isthmus of Panama. The goods crossed to the Pacific on muleback, then were reshipped by boat to Lima's port, Callao. The official routes from Lima to Buenos Aires, Asunción, or Santiago subjected them to months of expensive and dangerous travel. Regardless of its designers' intentions, the system could only guarantee scarcity and high prices. Colonial production for the viceroyalty's markets also faced enormous difficulties imposed both by nature and by state policy. Other than the construction of rudimentary bridges, the state initiated almost no internal improvements. Early settlers, in fact, often remarked that the surviving Inca roads were the only improved roads in the colony. And, unlike in British North America, private investors played no role in improving roads or building canals. In speed and carrying capacity, the Spanish system of transportation was an improvement over the pre-Columbian one. Wheeled vehicles, sure-footed mules, and powerful oxen unquestionably allowed for the transportation of heavier burdens over longer distances than indigenous porters and llamas, and sailing vessels extended the reach and reliability of the transportation infrastructure. Nevertheless, every contemporary opinion by a European visitor to the Spanish South American colonies included a contemptuous appraisal of their streets, roads, and harbors. Spain had erected a costly and inconvenient system of commercial controls, and European producers seeking to trade in the Pacific markets of the Viceroyalty of Peru could obtain only limited market intelligence. Even domestic producers located a few hundred miles from potential consumers had little access to reliable market information.

How then can we explain the development of highly specialized production centers like Quito, the Central Valley of Chile, or Salta? The redistributive power of the colonial state can be found everywhere in the articulation and functioning of this complex system, operating directly through its enforcement of trade, tariff, and tax policies and indirectly through its creation of monopolies and other privileged enterprises. Even the unforeseen consequences of corruption and coercion worked to sustain this colonial system of manifest inefficiencies and high costs. The state's toleration of the coercion of Indian labor through the mita made the textile obrajes of Quito possible, and the state's indulgence of corrupt corregidores and their compulsory sales of Salta's mules and Quito's textiles to Indian communities by means of the repartimiento made the broad Andean "market" a reality.

The Bourbon Reforms—smaller political jurisdictions, new administrative offices, new recruitment mechanisms, new taxes more efficiently collected, and the facilitation of direct trade with Spain—eroded the practices and altered the expectations that made this system work. The dramatic reconstitution of colonial jurisdictions, especially the creation of two new South American viceroyalties, consequentially changed the scale of enterprise and undermined the merchant networks that had managed long-distance trade. Indigenous rebellion, most spectacularly the Túpac Amaru Rebellion of 1780–81, forced the end of the repartimiento de mercancias. Free trade loosened the hold of monopoly merchants in both Lima and Buenos Aires. European wars, especially the war with France in the 1790s, forced the Crown to accept neutral trade, legitimizing the long heritage of contraband in the Río de la Plata region. As the tide of European imports rose, the textile producers of Quito and Tucumán were forced to retreat, and the merchants of the two viceregal capitals of Lima and Buenos Aires began to lose their leverage over peripheral regions.

Buenos Aires was at first a major beneficiary of these changes. Its progress in the 1770s and 1780s was won at the cost of Lima. The Bourbons sought to reduce contraband through Buenos Aires by legitimizing the city's contacts with Europe. But the Crown was never able to suppress the preexisting commercial linkages with Brazil, and through Brazil to England. After the creation of the viceroyalty, more silver flowed to Spain and less to Portugal and England, Portugal's patron and protector. But the ties to Portuguese Brazil were too deep and too important to disappear simply because Spanish ships more routinely called at Buenos Aires. First, Portuguese merchants were "rooted" (*radicado*) in the city and accustomed to doing business as far north as Paraguay and Upper Peru, where their goods, mostly reexported English wares, were commonly preferred to Spanish manufactures. Second, the slow decline of Brazil's sugar sector in the eighteenth century led to an oversupply of slaves, which flowed toward the booming labor market in Buenos Aires. And third, Buenos Aires's dried meat became a staple of Brazil plantations, while its hides were quickly reexported to England. In the late seventeenth and early eighteenth century this growing interdependence was monetarized by Brazil's gold boom, coinciding with a low point in Upper Peru's silver production, and then, between the mid-eighteenth century and the rebellion of 1780, by a recovering Potosí.

The quickening cycle of European wars after 1790 undid the limited success of the Spanish reforms and forced the Spanish Crown to open its American empire to free trade. Spanish commercial connections in the Río de la Plata region never recovered from the effects of this expedient. In 1807, the second of two early nineteenth-century English invasions was accompanied by a vast merchant fleet. The unforeseen effect of this flood of merchandise was the permanent destruction of the traditional Spanish price structure on imported goods. By 1810, when the cabildo abierto assumed control, trade with merchants from the United States and other nonbelligerent nations was so well organized and lubricated with bribes that incoming ships bearing contraband were given special flags to identify them to sympathetic customs officials.

Independence, despite its anarchic political character, built on these late colonial forms. Tariffs and taxes were increasingly little more than the means to pay for a much smaller and less intrusive bureaucracy. The city of Buenos Aires trimmed its territorial ambitions in the face of demonstrated military and political incompetence in the interior. By the end of the 1820, little remained of Buenos Aires's traditional economic authority as a Spanish colonial center. Commerce with the exterior was largely in the hands of foreigners. Domestic manufacturing was reduced in scale and commercial reach. Cottage-industry textiles from the interior of Argentina survived until the 1830s, servicing the needs of low-end consumers. But the Spanish colonial structure that had used the state's coercive authority to permit the development of a complex and diversified economy, despite inefficient producers, costly and unpredictable transportation, and impoverished consumers, was washed away by the political changes of the independence era.

In its place, there emerged a new economy rooted in the grazing lands of the pampa. Even before the first conflicts of the independence period, the mines of the southern Andes that had propelled the old system were in decline. Still, the first generation of local political leaders struggled to reimpose some version of the old redistributive state on the territory of the old viceroyalty. Only after twenty years of destructive and costly civil war was this ambition discarded. A new transitional order then emerged during the dictatorship of Juan Manuel de Rosas (1829–1852). Given the region's historic high labor costs and abundant open range, the rapid development of a livestock economy now appears to have been inevitable. By the 1840s the Province of Buenos Aires, especially its capital, was relatively rich. Buenos Aires, which had once controlled distant La Paz, now controlled a compact grazing hinterland dominated by ranches (*estancias*) devoted to cattle and sheep. Government had been reduced to a shadow of the Spanish-era model in fiscal scale and economic influence. Moreover, the commerce of the city and the region had been redirected from the costly and unproductive Spanish metropole to England, the era's most modern economy. If the political ambitions of the independence period were thwarted by the failures of the 1810s and 1820s, the more compact, limited economy and polity that had emerged by 1840, linked to England and other European importers, was a more reliable, more equitable producer of wealth.[41]

Notes

1. This is not the place to provide an overview of this vast literature. Instead we offer a few worthwhile sources by way of introduction. See Tulio Halperin-Donghi, "Dependency Theory and Latin American Historiography," *Latin American Research Review* 17:1 (1982), 115–30; Joseph L. Love, "The Origins of Dependency Analysis," *Journal of Latin American Studies* 22:2 (1989), 143–68; H. C. F. Mansilla, "Crítica a las teorías de la modernización y la dependencia," *Revista Internacional de Sociología* (Madrid) 37:31 (1979), 329–49; Kate Manzo, "Modernist Discourse and the Crisis of Development Theory," *Studies in Comparative International Development* 26:2 (1991), 3–36; D. C. M. Platt, "Dependency in Nineteenth-Century Latin America: An Historian Objects," *Latin American Research Review* 15:1 (1980), 113–30; and Carlos Sempat Assadourian, "Modos de producción, capitalismo y subdesarrollo en América Latina," *Cuadernos de la Realidad Nacional* (Santiago: Universidad Católica de Chile, 1971): 116–42.
2. One of the most interesting scholarly trajectories is that of Fernando Henrique Cardoso, the Brazilian sociologist who was once one of the most important scholars of dependency theory and now serves as the neoliberal president of his country. See his "The Entrepreneurial Elites of Latin America," *Studies in Comparative National Development* (Washington University, Social Science Institute) 2:10 (1966), 147–59; and, with Enzo Faletto, *Dependency and Development in Latin America* (Berkeley and Los Angeles: University of California Press, 1979), one of the most important works of this era. Cardoso was himself critical of some of the mechanistic dependency treatments. See "The Consumption of Dependency Theory in the United States," *Latin American Research Review* 12:3 (1977), 7–24.
3. Noble David Cook, *Demographic Collapse: Indian Peru, 1520–1620* (New York: Cambridge University Press, 1981), 6.
4. Richard E. Boyer and Keith A. Davies, *Urbanization in Nineteenth-Century Latin America: Statistics and Sources* (Berkeley and Los Angeles: University of California Press, 1973), 41, 59.
5. Nicholas P. Cushner, *Lords of the Land: Sugar, Wine and Jesuit Estates of Coastal Peru, 1600–1767* (Albany: State University of New York Press, 1980).
6. Mark A. Burkholder and D. S. Chandler, *From Impotence to Authority: The Spanish Crown and the American Audiencias, 1687–1808* (Columbia: University of Missouri Press, 1977), 2.
7. Zacarías Moutoukias, *Contrabando y control colonial en el siglo XVII: Buenos Aires, el*

Atlántico' y el espacio peruano (Buenos Aires: Centro Editor de América Latina, 1988), 47.

8. Enrique Tandeter, Vilma Milletich, and Roberto Schmit, "Flujos mercantiles en el Potosí tardío," in Jorge Silva Riquer, Juan Carlos Grosso, and Carmen Yuste, eds., *Circuitos mercantiles y mercados en latinoamérica* (México, D.F.: Instituto de Investigaciones Dr. José María Mora, 1995), 13–55.
9. Cushner, *Lords of the Land*, 132.
10. Héctor Omar Noejovich, "La economiá del virreinato del Peru bajo los Habsburgo y la denominada crisis del siglo XVII," Actas del 49 Congreso Internacional de Americanistas, Quito, Ecuador (1997).
11. See Jürgen Golte, *Repartos y rebeliones: Tupac Amaru y las contradicciones de la economía colonial* (Lima: Instituto de Estudios Peruanos, 1980) for the connection of forced sales to rebellion. For the rebellions of the 1770s and 1780s see Scarlett O'Phelan Godoy, *La gran rebelion en los Andes: De Túpac Amaru a Túpac Catari* (Cuzco: Centro de Estudios Regionales Andinos Bartolomé de las Casas, 1995).
12. Nicholas P. Cushner, *Farm and Factory: The Jesuits and the Development of Agrarian Capitalism in Colonial Quito, 1500–1767* (Albany: State University of New York Press, 1982), 100.
13. Ibid., 172.
14. Kenneth J. Andrien, *The Kingdom of Quito, 1690–1830: The State and Regional Development* (Albuquerque: University of New Mexico Press, 1995), 24–27, 55–65.
15. Mark A. Burkholder and Lyman L. Johnson, *Colonial Latin America*, 3d ed. (New York: Oxford University Press, 1998), 162.
16. Marcello Carmagnani, *Les mécanismes de la vie économique dans une société coloniale: Le Chili (1630–1830)* (Paris: S.E.V.P.E.N., 1973). See especially 213–49.
17. Cushner, *Lords of the Land*, 156.
18. For production of yerba mate see Juan Carlos Garavaglia, "Un capítulo del mercado interno colonial: el Paraguay y su región (1537–1682)," *Nova Americana* (Torino, Italy) 1 (1978), 11–55, and "El mercado interno colonial y la yerba mate (siglos XVI-XIX)," *Nova Americana* 4 (1981), 163–210. See also Jerry W. Cooney, "An Ignored Aspect of the Viceroyalty of the Rio de la Plata," *Intercambio Internacional* (Western Kentucky University) 11:1 (1977), 10–12; "Paraguayan *Astilleros* and the Platine Merchant Marine, 1796–1806," *The Historian* 43:1 (1980), 55–74; "A Riverborne Society: Life and Labor on the *Carrera del Paraguay*, 1776–1811," *SECOLAS Annals* 20 (1989), 5–19.
19. Juan Carlos Garavaglia, *Economía, sociedad y regiones* (Buenos Aires: Ediciones de la Flor, 1987).
20. See Carlos Sempat Assadourian, *El sistema de la economia colonial: El mercado interior, regiones y espacio económico* (Mexico [City]: Editorial Nueva Imagen, 1983).
21. Gustavo L. Paz, "Between the Atlantic and the Andes: Trade and Transportation in Late Colonial Argentina," (Harvard Seminar on Atlantic History, Working Paper 14, 1999), 5, 14, 15; Nicolás Sánchez-Albornoz, Patricia Ottolenghi de Frankmann, Manuel Urbina, and Dorothy R. Webb, "La saca de mulas de Salta al Perú, 1778–1808," *Anuario del Instituto de Investigaciones Históricas* (Rosario) 8 (1965), 261–312.
22. Paz, "Between the Atlantic and the Andes," 4.
23. Jürgen Golte, *Repartos y rebeliones*, 87–106.
24. Moutoukias, *Contrabando y control*, 76.
25. Ibid., 62, 77.
26. Zacarías Moutoukias, "Power, Corruption, and Commerce: The Making of the Local Administrative Structure in Seventeenth-Century Buenos Aires," *Hispanic American Historical Review* 68:4 (1988), 782.
27. Moutoukias, *Contrabando y control*, 62–63. See also Carlos Sempat Assadourian, "El trafico de esclavos en Córdoba, 1588–1610," *Instituto de Estudios Americanistas. Cuadernos de historia* 32 (1965), 1–36.
28. Moutoukias, "Power, Corruption, and Commerce," 772–74.
29. Cushner, *Lords of the Land*, 157.
30. See Harry E. Cross, "Commerce and Orthodoxy: A Spanish Response to Portuguese

Commercial Penetration in the Viceroyalty of Peru, 1580–1640," *The Americas* 35:2 (1978), 151–67; Alfonso W. Quiroz, "The Expropriation of Portuguese New Christians in Spanish America, 1635–1649," *Ibero-Amerikanisches Archiv* 11:4 (1985), 407–65; Alice Canabrava Piffer, *O comércio português no Rio da Prata, 1580–1640*, 2d ed. (Belo Horizonte: Editôra Itatiaia/São Paulo: Editôra da Universidade de São Paulo, 1984). See also Eduardo R. Saguier, "The Social Impact of a Middleman Minority in a Divided Host Society: The Case of the Portuguese in Early Seventeenth-Century Buenos Aires," *Hispanic American Historical Review* 65:3 (1985), 467–91.

31. Elena F. S. de Studer, *La trata de negros en el Río de la Plata durante el siglo XVIII* (Buenos Aires: Libros de Hispanoamérica, 1984), 91.
32. Lyman L. Johnson, "The Competition of Slave and Free Labor in Artisanal Production: Buenos Aires, 1770–1815," *International Review of Social History* 40:3 (1995), 409–24.
33. Archivo General de la Nación Argentina (AGNA), División Colonia, Sección Gobierno, Hacienda, 1777–1787, legajo 26, expediente 627, as cited in Studer, *La trata de negros*, 267.
34. Johnson, "The Competition of Slave and Free Labor," 413–16.
35. Juan Carlos Garavaglia, *Mercado interno y economía colonial* (Mexico [City]: Editorial Grijalbo, 1983), 456.
36. Lyman L. Johnson and Susan Migden Socolow, "Population and Space in Eighteenth Century Buenos Aires," in David J. Robinson, ed., *Social Fabric and Spatial Structure in Colonial Latin America* (Syracuse: Dellplain, 1979), 342–43.
37. Lyman L. Johnson, "The Military as Catalyst of Change in Late Colonial Buenos Aires," in Mark D. Szuchman and Jonathan C. Brown, eds., *Revolution and Restoration: The Rearrangement of Power in Argentina, 1776–1860* (Lincoln: University of Nebraska Press, 1994), 46.
38. Herbert S. Klein, "Structure and Profitability of Royal Finance in the Viceroyalty of the Río de la Plata in 1790," *Hispanic American Historical Review* 53:3 (1973), 440–69.
39. John Coatsworth, "The Limits of Colonial Absolutism: The State in Eighteenth Century Mexico," in Karen Spalding, ed., *Essays in the Political, Economic and Social History of Colonial Latin America* (Newark: University of Delaware Press, 1982), 25–41.
40. *Telégrafo Mercantil*, September 10, 1802.
41. See Lyman L. Johnson, "The Frontier as an Arena of Social and Economic Change: Wealth Distribution in Nineteenth-Century Buenos Aires Province," in Donna J. Guy and Thomas E. Sheridan, eds., *Contested Ground: Comparative Frontiers on the Northern and Southern Edges of the Spanish Empire* (Tucson: University of Arizona Press, 1998), 167–81, for an analysis of this changed economy.

Bourbons and Bárbaros

Center and Periphery in the Reshaping of Spanish Indian Policy

David J. Weber

In the mid-eighteenth century, two centuries after the Spanish conquest of Mexico and Peru, independent Indians controlled over *half* of the land mass that we think of today as Spanish America.[1] Clearly, Spain had not completed the conquest of America in the Age of Conquest. Independent Indians still held much of the tropical forests and drylands—northern Mexico, the Central-American lowlands and the Gulf of Darién, the Amazon and Orinoco basins, the Gran Chaco, the pampas, Patagonia, and Tierra del Fuego.[2] From Hispanic perspectives, independent Indians occupied the frontiers of Spain's New World empire and the lands beyond; from the perspectives of independent Indians, Hispanics occupied the frontiers of Indian-controlled lands, and the territory beyond.

In the last half of the eighteenth century, Bourbon officials moved with renewed vigor to win the allegiance of the independent Indians who lived along and beyond the peripheries of the empire. Those officials, products of the Age of Enlightenment,[3] brought new values and sensibilities to the task of controlling "savages," who themselves had acquired new values, skills, and technologies for coping with Spaniards. Out of the dialectic between the program that emanated from the Bourbon centers and the strategies of peoples who lived on Spain's American peripheries, came new ways for Spaniards and "savages" to relate to one another.[4]

For the Habsburgs who ruled Spain until 1700, the benefits of extending the conquest of the mainland beyond the highlands of Mexico, Central America, and South America had not, in the main, seemed worth the cost. With notable exceptions (such as the cacao-producing area of Venezuela, the Cauca and Magdalena River Valleys in present Colombia, parts of Paraguay, and central Chile south to the Biobío River), the climate, accessibility, and an apparent lack of valuable resources in the lowlands had discouraged Spaniards from making them their own. These impediments continued to discourage Bourbon administrators, who replaced the Habsburgs in the eighteenth century.[5] As a viceroy of Peru explained in the mid-1700s, "The unconquered country is jungle and mountains, difficult to traverse, and plains that are humid, swampy, and hot, and so cannot support Spaniards."[6] Native opposition in these regions also deterred Spaniards from permanently occupying them. In general, Spaniards chose to conquer highland farming peoples whose labor they could exploit and whose hierarchical governments they could control rather than waging prolonged wars against nomads or seminomads who tended to live in the lowlands. As the same viceroy of Peru noted, "The nations that inhabit these places are savages. They do not cover their nakedness and their houses are so poor that they lose nothing when they leave them. . . . To conquer them by force always has been impossible, considering that they can move from one place to another."

By the mid-eighteenth century, it became more difficult for Bourbon officials to ignore the Indian country that bordered the empire. Out of those lands came Indians who, more boldly and adeptly than ever before, raided Spanish farms and ranches, destroyed Spanish property, took Spanish lives, and blocked the arteries of commerce that kept the empire alive. Spaniards knew these independent Indians by their local names, but referred to them generically as "savages" (*indios bárbaros* or *salvajes*), as "wild Indians" (*indios bravos*), as heathens (*gentiles*), or as "Indians who had not submitted" (*indios no sometidos*), and so distinguished them from Christian Indians, or Indians who recognized Spanish authority—*indios sometidos*, *reducidos*, *domésticos*, or *tributarios*.

Throughout the world in the modern era, state societies in general have found it difficult to control tribal societies, especially nomadic and seminomadic peoples.[7] For Spaniards in America, the difficulty seemed to increase as "savages" made themselves more effective adversaries. A Jesuit who worked in the Paraguayan Chaco in the mid-1700s described the change, noting, "Seeing those first Spaniards who arrived in America, so impressive astride their horses, covered in metal, with shiny swords, firing weapons, and with great beards and mustaches, the beardless, scarcely clothed, weak natives, armed only with wooden weapons, fled from this new kind of men . . . or, if they could not escape, they surrendered. Now, the savages who declare war on the Spaniards see daily that they are able to defeat and kill these men, mocking their attacks with fast horses and metal lances. . . . They began to consider the thundering barrels of the guns of little danger, knowing that they frequently misfired and that if they did fire they would produce a harmless noise."[8]

Throughout the hemisphere, indios bárbaros had studied the fighting techniques of Spaniards, learned to defend themselves against them, adopted Spanish horses and weapons, and reorganized themselves into new polities or societies. Spaniards had begun to feel the effects of those transformations in the sixteenth century, most famously in the effective resistance of Araucanians in southern Chile, Chichimecas in northern New Spain, and Chiriguanos in southern Peru.[9] Those borderlands where Spaniards encountered "indomitable" Indians had grown more extensive as Spaniards and Indians alike moved onto new frontiers, and as Indians obtained ammunition and firearms from Spain's European rivals.

By the mid-eighteenth century, Spanish policymakers also had to worry that indios bárbaros might ally themselves with Spain's chief European rival, England, and facilitate English expansion into lands long claimed but never occupied by Spain. Writing from Madrid in 1762 at the close of the Seven Years' War, Pedro Rodríguez de Campomanes, one of the leading Bourbon theorists, explained this threat clearly.

In North America, Campomanes saw danger on all sides. Englishmen from the Carolinas and Georgia, together with their Indian allies, threatened Spain's hold over the peninsula of Florida, whose strategic location along the Bahama Channel made it as important to the Spanish Caribbean as Gibraltar was to the Mediterranean.[10] Looking farther west, he feared that England, victorious in the recent war against Spain and France, would become the new owner of Louisiana. If the Englishmen allied themselves with independent Indians in Louisiana, Campomanes warned, "the consequences would be lamentable for Spanish dominion in North America."[11] He also pointed to the Pacific Coast of North America. With nothing more than two war ships and five hundred men, Campomanes reckoned, the English could enter the Pacific, seize Baja California, ally themselves with California Indians, and link their new possessions on the Pacific to Louisiana. From those northern lands, a European rival could easily invade the heartland of New Spain, and make Spain's most valuable colony its own.[12]

In strategic Central America, Campomanes noted that Englishmen had already planted themselves on the Caribbean coast and formed alliances with "Indios Mosquitos-Zambos," whom they had alienated from "Spanish dominion."[13] In South America, European competitors could readily ally themselves with Indians in the enormous stretch from Buenos Aires south to the Strait of Magellan, a region devoid of Spanish colonies. In southern Chile, Spain faced the danger that the Araucanians would abandon the "amnesty in which they live with us," and "would go over to the side of our enemies," the British.[14] Warnings to this effect had come to Madrid from several quarters in Chile, and Campomanes also knew of the boast of the British admiral George Anson, who had calculated that fifteen hundred Englishmen could drive Spaniards out of both Chile and Peru if Britain gained the support of the Araucanians.[15]

Along the margins of the empire, independent Indians also threatened the commercial viability of Spain's colonies. Allied with Englishmen or other foreigners, independent Indians could facilitate the introduction of contraband and retard the growth of Spanish trade. Conversely, independent Indians could trade stolen Spanish property to English merchants in exchange for guns and ammunition, then use their greater firepower to steal still more goods from their Spanish neighbors.

Independent Indians seemed poised to weaken the margins of the empire at the same time that Bourbon reformers hoped to strengthen them.[16] Eager to draw more revenue from America in order to reverse what they saw as Spain's economic decline, the Bourbons sought to streamline public administration, raise productivity and trade, and increase security in America. That project, begun early in the century, reached fruition in the reign of Carlos III (1759–88), the most dynamic, innovative, and America-oriented of Spain's eighteenth-century monarchs. As he and his enlightened advisors, such as Campomanes, looked beyond the empire's profitable cores to the development of its vulnerable but potentially profitable peripheries, it became apparent that they had to bring the "savages," who occupied those peripheries, under control.[17]

The ways that Bourbon administrators sought to achieve that control tell us much about the formulation of policy by the absolutist Bourbon regime, which has seemed to some historians to part from the Habsburg tradition of compromise and to govern instead through "non-negotiable demands" or a "hard line."[18] If Bourbon policies toward indios bárbaros can be taken as exemplary, Bourbon officials compromised as readily as had their Habsburg predecessors.

For Bourbon administrators in search of ways to control indios bravos along the empire's peripheries, Spanish tradition offered two obvious solutions: send fighting men to conquer recalcitrant natives by force or missionaries to conquer them through persuasion. But armed Indians on horseback did not succumb readily to the blandishments of missionaries, whose successes seemed to diminish in the eighteenth century. Similarly, private armies led by *encomenderos* or would-be encomenderos, upon whom Spain had previously relied to advance its frontiers, no longer filled the bill against increasingly mobile bands of Indian raiders. The Bourbons responded, particularly after Britain's humiliating occupation of Havana in 1762, by building up the army and the militia in America, and looking to a more professional army to pacify Indians in areas where missionaries and private armies had failed. Much has been written about that military reform and the employment of troops and fortifications in regions where Indians threatened Spanish control, particularly along the southern borders of the Viceroyalty of Río de la Plata and the Comandancia General de a Provincias Internas of New Spain, both created in 1776 to promote the defense and development of these vast areas.[19]

Enlightened thought and British and French examples, however, offered the Bourbons another strategy: control Indians through commerce rather than by physical or spiritual conquest. Nowhere in Spanish thought was this idea articulated more clearly than in the well-known *Nuevo sistema de gobierno económico para la América*, a master plan for the economic development of Spain's colonies. Scholars disagree about the authorship of the *Nuevo sistema*, first published in 1779, and about its influence on Spanish policy. But if it was not "the reformers' bible, the definitive text which inspired this Bourbon revolution in government," as one historian has argued, it clearly reflected the views of some of the liberal policymakers who redesigned the administrative structure of Spain's American colonies under Carlos III.[20]

The author of the *Nuevo sistema* lamented that Spain had wasted millions of pesos in making war against Indians who, "if treated with tact and friendship, would be of infinite use to us."[21] In the early sixteenth century, he reasoned, Spaniards in America had no alternative to military force "for there were few Spaniards in America and millions of Indians to subject." But Spain made the mistake of "preserving the spirit of conquest beyond its time, and preferring dominion over the advantages and utility of commerce and friendly trade with the savage nations." [22]

Even as the wildest beast can be tamed by kind treatment, the *Nuevo sistema* analogized, "there is no savage who cannot be dominated by industry and made sociable by a ready supply of all the things he likes."[23] Establishing trade with "wild Indians" would take "time, skill, and patience, but it is not impossible."[24] Other nations had already done so.

Spaniards, however, had a handicap: They had earned "the hatred of neighboring Indian nations."[25] But if Spain's missionaries could enter the lands of those Indians by treating them with kindness, he argued, so could Spain's merchants. Indeed, the *Nuevo sistema* suggested that merchants would have an easier time of it. Unlike missionaries who "threaten [Indians] with hell if they become drunk or take more than one woman, harshly condemning all of the vices to which they are naturally very inclined," he said, merchants treat Indians kindly, give them goods that they need and alcohol (*aguardiente*) "that they so esteem" while making no demands on them.[26]

In this enlightened formulation, Indians would become the foundation of Spain's commercial and economic revival in America rather than enemies, and they would play their role in a new way. Where Spaniards of the Renaissance had expected Indians to adopt the Christian faith when missionaries revealed it to them, the *Nuevo sistema* expected Indians to behave like rational European consumers when merchants displayed their wares. Where Spaniards traditionally viewed Indians as vicious or lazy by nature, needing to be forced to work for their own good,[27] the *Nuevo sistema* argued that Indians would respond to profits and self-interest and voluntarily become producers and consumers.[28] In short, Indians could change if the system changed, and the economic benefits for Spain would be enormous. Commercial expansion rather than costly conquest would bring Spain the benefits of trade without the costs of formal political and economic control over Indians.[29]

Spanish administrators concerned with Indian policy need not have read the *Nuevo sistema* to have heard its message. Enlightened Spaniards, who often preferred to look abroad for new ideas, had ample opportunity to learn directly of the French and English practices that inspired the *Nuevo sistema*. Campomanes, for example, became enthusiastic about the English trading system in 1784, when he received a detailed description of it while serving as head of the Council of Castilla. He recommended the British system to José de Gálvez, as the best way to control the indios bravos in the area contiguous to the new United States. "This [British] method can be advantageous to our present situation and an indirect way of maintaining those [Indian] nations free of the dominion of the American Republic, preventing it from populating the banks of the Mississippi or the Ohio rivers."[30]

For his part, José de Gálvez, the powerful and dynamic minister of the Indies from 1776 to 1787, did not need Campomanes to tell him about the policies of his European rivals in North America. He had his own sources of intelligence, including a nephew and protégé whom he had appointed acting governor of Louisiana in 1776. Drawing from his observations in Louisiana, as well as previous experience fighting Apaches, Bernardo de Gálvez had urged his uncle to rely on trade to control Indians rather than fight costly and ineffective wars. Through trade, he argued, "the King would keep [Indians] very contented for ten years with what he now spends in one year in making war upon them."[31]

Apparently persuaded by this argument, and strapped for resources as he prepared for war with Great Britain, José de Gálvez ordered a policy of "kindness, good treatment, and benevolence" toward Indians in Provincias Internas of New Spain in 1779. He instructed his officers to take defensive action only, to avoid bloodshed, and to make Indians dependent on Spaniards for merchandise, including luxury goods and guns, so that "they will not be able to live without our help." The king, he said, preferred a slow and peaceful conquest.[32] Three years later, however, Gálvez ordered a return to offensive warfare when Apaches refused to substitute trading for raiding, and when powerful oligarchs angrily demanded a more aggressive military policy that would protect their dwindling herds from Indian predators.[33]

In 1786, when Bernardo de Gálvez benefited from his uncle's penchant for nepotism to become viceroy of New Spain, he ordered officials in the Provincias Internas to return to the kind of policy that his uncle had enunciated in 1779.

Although he placed greater emphasis on offensive action against Apaches than his uncle had, Bernardo de Gálvez still hoped for the same result: to force Apaches to appeal for peace and to enter into trade with Spaniards. "With time," he suggested in his well-known *Instrucción* of 1786, "trade may make them dependent on us." [34] Like other enlightened thinkers of his day, he believed that "interest in commerce tightens and binds the interests of men." In the case of Apaches, a strategy that made them rely on Spanish foods, clothing, and weapons would also make them "realize the advantages of rational life."[35] In short, military pressure combined with trade would make Apaches, or at least their grandchildren, into what one officer termed "useful subjects."[36]

Not all Spanish officers agreed with Bernardo de Gálvez's preference for "a bad peace" over a "good war."[37] Nonetheless, with various modifications and embellishments, Gálvez's policy, as articulated in his *Instrucción* of 1786, prevailed in the Provincias Internas of New Spain. Spain's ablest officers followed his dictum and offered independent Indians access to trade fairs, gifts, cooperation against mutual enemies, and more equitable and consistent treatment than they had in the past. Conciliation and negotiation, previously subordinate to force, became the hallmark of Bourbon Indian policy in northern New Spain in the late 1780s.[38]

This conciliatory Indian policy included reservations for Apaches who appealed for peace. On these reservations, some Spanish policymakers hoped to turn Apaches into town-dwelling Spanish Catholics who farmed, ranched, and practiced familiar trades. Since the Bourbons needed to populate the empire's vulnerable frontiers with loyal subjects but lacked sufficient colonists to achieve that goal, it made sense to try to turn Apaches into Spaniards.[39] Spain had relied heavily on missionaries to achieve this kind of transformation on earlier frontiers and, despite withering criticism by some enlightened Bourbon administrators, they would continue to do so in places where Indians seemed "docile," as in Alta California. But among peoples whom missionaries had failed to convert, soldiers became the preferred agents of paternalistic cultural change on the late-eighteenth-century reservations in northern New Spain.[40] Bernardo de Gálvez's plan ignored missionaries, whose political and economic power had diminished in northern New Spain during the reign of Carlos III.[41]

For Spain, a conciliatory Indian policy promised more than economic and strategic advantages. It also offered a soothing balm for enlightened Spaniards stung by their forebears' reputation for cruel oppression of Indians during and after the conquest of America. "Humanity is the greatest characteristic of civilization. All the sciences and arts have no value if they serve only to make us cruel and haughty," wrote one Spanish botanist in America, José Mariano Moziño, as he lamented the brutal way that some of his less enlightened countrymen treated independent Indians.[42] Indeed, some Spanish army officers close to the scene also extolled the new Indian policies as humane as well as effective. Writing at El Paso in 1796, for example, Lt. Col. Antonio Cordero y Bustamante, a veteran frontier soldier, noted that the "wise measures" of the Spanish government were bringing the war to a close. Spain did "not aspire to the destruction or slavery of these savages," he noted with pride. Rather, Spain sought "their happiness . . . leaving them in peaceful possession of their homes," while at the same time getting them to recognize "our justice and our power to sustain it" so they would cease raiding Spanish settlements.[43]

The more humane policy that Cordero applauded could not work, however, if Apaches were demonized. Frontier officers like Cordero, Bernardo de Gálvez, and José Cortés needed a new discourse if they were to redeem Apaches—and they found one. These enlightened officers depicted Apaches as fierce, courageous, and skilled warriors, but not as innately indolent, untrustworthy, and thieving, as the previous generation of officers, intent on exterminating Apaches, tended to do.[44] Enlightened officers sought to explain Apaches' behavior as responses to external forces, rather than as innate characteristics. If Apaches possessed "extraordinary robustness" it was because they lived outdoors and ate basic foods; if they moved with a great agility, speed, and endurance it was because of daily exercise and the conditioning of a nomadic life.[45] If Apaches waged "cruel and bloody war" against Spaniards, the cause could be found in the Spaniards' own "trespasses, excesses and avarice," as Cordero put it.[46] If Apaches treated Spaniards cruelly, it was, Gálvez observed, "because he owes us no kindness, and that if he avenges himself it is for just satisfaction of his grievances." "The truth is," Gálvez wrote, "that they are as much grateful as vengeful, and that this latter [quality of vengeance] we ought to forgive in a nation that has not learned philosophy with which to master a natural feeling. . . ."[47]

These were ideas whose time had come, defended on pragmatic grounds and shared by enlightened officials who faced "savages" throughout the frontiers of the hemisphere. In Chile, for example, Ambrosio Higgins, an Irish-born Spanish officer, argued that Spain could not defend its vast Pacific coast from foreigners without the goodwill of Indians. Indians would not support Spaniards, he said, "while we are at every opportunity irritating and beating Indians along the frontiers, making them internal enemies."[48] Alienated from Spain, they would ally themselves with Spain's opportunistic European rivals.

Frontier imperatives, then, forced the Bourbon state to find peaceful ways to win the allegiance of independent Indians and, in the words of one historian, turn them into "frontier soldiers of the Crown."[49] That policy was consistent with Bourbon efforts to draw other native-born Americans, *criollos* and mestizos, into its defensive system after the loss of Havana in the Seven Years' War revealed how badly Spain could be outmanned in one of its own colonies.[50]

Frontier conditions alone, however, do not explain the Bourbons' conciliatory policies toward indios bárbaros. In South America as in North America, reinvigorated European sensibilities about human rights combined with pragmatic considerations to inform Bourbon policies. In 1799, when the governor of Cochabamba sentenced Sacuarao, a leader of the so-called Chiriguano rebellion of 1799 to be baptized and hung, he aroused the ire of the Crown's chief attorney in the Viceroyalty of the Río de la Plata. Victorián de Villava, chief attorney of the Real Audiencia de Charcas, condemned Sacuarao's baptism and hanging as a "return to the times of Atahualpa." In putting Sacuarao to death and taking revenge, he said, Spaniards had acted like savages.[51] Villava criticized the governor, Francisco de Viedma, for treating the Chiriguanos as criminals without reflecting on the nature of crime or criminality. A criminal act, he said, consists of breaking the social compact within a nation by one who belongs to that nation. The Chiriguanos did not belong to Spain. Because they lived beyond Spanish control and were not vassals of the Crown, they had not rebelled. Instead, they had invaded Spanish territory, and "the invasion of another nation," Villava said, "would be an offense against the rights of man that could be vindicated with arms, but not a crime that can be punished under the law."[52] Villava went on to reject force as an effective policy against the Chiriguanos: "The best policy is not to punish them but attract them: by having punished them with whips, they have punished us with arrows, and by not knowing how to negotiate with them and civilize them, we are in continuous war with men who have no place, land, or fixed residence, which makes it impossible to defeat them or subject them."[53]

Independent Indians who forced Spanish leaders to make rhetorical and tactical concessions also pushed Spaniards to relinquish claims to full dominion over them, as the legal opinion of Victorián de Villava suggests. In practice if not in theory, those claims went back to the famous papal donation of 1493 and to the notorious *requerimiento* of 1513, which summoned Indians to submit or face military attack.[54] Spaniards had continued to assert those claims even in pictorial representations that placed "savage" Indians within the Hispanic world rather than beyond it.[55]

During the Bourbon era officials came increasingly to see the practical benefits of recognizing that some Indians had the right to live autonomously beyond the bounds of the empire—a recognition that occurred, ironically, at the same time that the Bourbons extended the effective boundaries of the empire. In the 1700s, Spain's recognition of Indians' rights to autonomy increasingly took the form of written treaties that rose out of formal discussions. In North America, for example, Spanish officers entered into a series of treaties with independent Indians, following Spain's acquisition of Louisiana from France in 1762.[56] In 1784 alone, officials in Mobile signed written agreements with representatives of Alabamas, Chickasaws, and Choctaws, and officials in Pensacola signed an agreement with Creeks.[57] In 1785 and 1786, respectively, the Spanish governors of Texas and New Mexico signed treaties of alliance with Comanches; in 1786, the New Mexico governor also signed a treaty of alliance with Navajos.[58] In 1793, Spanish officials in Louisiana signed a treaty of mutual assistance with Alabamas, Cherokees, Chickasaws, Choctaws, and Creeks, all of whom, on paper if not in fact, had formed a confederation.[59]

In these agreements, Spaniards referred to Indian peoples as "nations" and recognized Indian polities as distinct from their own. Both parties agreed to peace, to make war against common enemies, and to establish commerce.[60] In signing these treaties, Indians usually accepted the "protection" of the Crown, as did Ecueracapa, the leader of the western Comanches in 1786, and the tribes bordering on Louisiana and Florida in 1793. These natives did not, however, become "vassals or subjects" of the Crown, surrender autonomy, or accept missionaries.[61] Nor did Spanish leaders ask these things of them. Rather than attempt to tax these Indians, Spanish officials regularly presented gifts to their leaders, as the French and English had done before. By 1794, gifts to Indians amounted to 10 percent of Spain's cost of supporting Louisiana and west Florida suggesting that, where Spaniards failed to tax Indians, Indians had succeeded in taxing Spaniards.[62]

In the Southeast, Spaniards came to recognize a native "nation" as more than a people of common origin (an ordinary usage of *nation* in that era), but as a sovereign nation-state—inferior, to be sure, but a nation-state nonetheless.[63] Manuel Gayoso de Lemos, governor of Spanish Louisiana's Natchez district, offered that view explicitly in regard to Creeks, Chickasaws, and Choctaws, when he wrote in 1792 that those Indians "are free and independent nations; although they are under His Majesty's protection, we cannot forcibly prevent them from signing a treaty with the

United States."[64] United States Secretary of War Henry Knox had argued similarly in 1789 that "the independent nations and tribes of Indians ought to be considered as foreign nations, not as the subjects of any particular State."[65] The idea that Indians could maintain their sovereignty while under Spanish protection conformed to the usage of the day. "Mere alliances of protection, tribute or vassalage, which a state may contract with another, do not hinder it from continuing perfectly sovereign," one jurist noted in 1788.[66]

By the late eighteenth century, Spanish Indian policy in the Southeast had come to resemble French and British policy, as the *Nuevo sistema* had urged. Traders or interpreters on the Spanish payroll, many of them mestizos who understood Indian languages and customs, with names like Brashears and Thompson, lived among the Indian nations to maintain their friendship and trade, as provided for in the treaties with southeastern tribes (as had a 1786 treaty with Navajos in the Southwest).[67] In this way, Spain tried to control Indians indirectly through trade without exercising dominion.

Circumstances in southeastern North America in particular gave Spain no other practical alternative. As Campomanes warned in 1792, if Spain tried to assert direct control over the "savage Indians" along the Gulf of Mexico or build settlements among them, the Indians would "lose confidence [in us] and . . . call the Americans to their defense."[68] Even as the benevolently despotic Bourbon monarchy reduced the power of its own subjects—Spanish aristocrats, American criollos, and indios domésticos—it paradoxically loosened its claims to dominion over some of North America's independent Indians.[69]

Spanish officials' reliance on written documents that recognized Indian autonomy in North America represented an innovation. In the past, Spaniards had treated with Indians throughout the hemisphere, but usually to specify the terms of the Indians' surrender and to require that Indians put themselves at the service of the Crown. Previously, as one historian has aptly put it, "Spaniards understood Indian peoples to be royal subjects, ready for Christianization and exploitation, but inappropriate for the kinds of bargaining and negotiation that might have resulted in [written] treaties."[70]

The Bourbons' employment of written treaties, however, had precedents in South America that reached back to the Habsburg era. In Chile, Spanish officials had held formal negotiations, or *parlamentos,* with Araucanians as early as 1606 and 1612, and by 1641 Araucanians had forced Spaniards to recognize the Biobío River as a permanent boundary. Beyond the river Indians would be free of obligations to serve individual Spaniards, but would be "under the Royal protection of his Majesty." This written agreement, in which Araucanians also allied themselves with Spain against its enemies, was signed at Quillín in 1641 by the conciliatory governor of Chile, the marqués de Baides, and Araucanian representatives. The Crown itself approved the terms of this treaty, which gave the Araucanian signatories greater rights than those enjoyed by other Indians over whom Spain claimed dominion.[71] According to one version of the treaty, the Araucanians agreed in 1641 to recognize their "vassalage" to the Spanish Crown and to permit missionaries to come among them. Nonetheless, well into the late eighteenth century Spaniards *implicitly* recognized that Araucanian lands, the Estado de Arauco, enjoyed autonomy. Beginning in 1774, Araucanians even sent ambassadors to represent them in the Spanish capital.[72]

The Hispanic-Araucanian frontier did not become permanently peaceful after the Pact of Quillín in 1641, but parlamentos and formal written treaties became a standard mechanism for settling disputes.[73] Moreover, Chilean officials recognized the value of commerce for controlling Araucanian Indians long before *philosophes* or Bourbon officials lauded its virtues. Beyond the Biobío, beginning in the 1600s, Spanish officials placed bilingual, bicultural, and usually biracial agents (*capitanes de amigos*) to live among friendly Araucanians (*indios amigos*). These agents, who drew a salary from the military budget and also engaged in the Indian trade on their own account, played the same influential role in maintaining peace that French and British traders did among North American tribes.[74] One Franciscan in Chile complained in 1783 that "the Indians obey only their captain or lieutenant and no one else."[75]

In the late eighteenth century, influenced by their Chilean counterparts, officials in the Río de la Plata also began to employ capitanes de amigos,[76] and written treaties became commonplace, too, on the pampas and the Gran Chaco. In contrast to those late-eighteenth-century treaties in North America that recognized full Indian autonomy, written treaties in South America usually required Indians to accept missionaries, settle in specified areas, recognize their vassalage to the Crown, and obey royal officials. In the Araucanía, the Chaco, and the pampas, Indians lacked the immediate threat of powerful foreign allies that enabled their North American counterparts to gain greater concessions by playing one side against the other.[77]

South American precedents appear to have had little if any influence on the Spanish policy that evolved in North America in the 1780s and 1790s. Rather, the impetus for change in North America seems to have come from Indians themselves, who demanded the kind of treatment they had received from the French and English, and from officials on the scene like Bernardo de Gálvez, who recognized that Spain needed Indian allies to hold its borders against Americans in the Southeast and Apaches in the Southwest even if it meant taking the radical step of giving Indian allies arms and ammunition.[78] In North America, then, recommendations for change seemed to flow less from the metropolis to the frontiers than from the frontiers to the metropolis, where they met a ready reception by Bourbons schooled in enlightened thought.

Local impetus also characterized peace arrangements with Indians along the Caribbean coast of Central America, where Englishmen exerted strong influence over Miskito Indians. In 1778, Miskitos dictated the terms of a peace treaty that they negotiated with the governor of Panama, Pedro Carbonell. Rejecting Governor Carbonell's idea that he visit them, Miskitos sent an envoy to him. In June, 1778, the son of a Miskito governor, a militia captain named Fara, arrived in Panama City with two sergeants, one corporal, and full powers to sign a treaty of peace. Fara demanded concessions, among them that Spaniards not interfere with the Miskitos' fishing and that they be allowed "free trade in all the [Spanish] ports from the Río de San Juan to the Chagres."[79] Eager to enlist the Miskitos in a campaign to drive English traders from the Miskito coast, Governor Carbonell agreed to Fara's terms so long as the Miskitos not trade with foreigners. When the governor asked Fara if he could count on the Miskitos to participate in an offensive against the English, Fara agreed on the condition that the governor furnish all of the supplies for the expedition. In exchange for signing a treaty of "alliance and friendship" with the Spaniards, the Miskitos gained Spanish protection and the promise that the Crown would send "instructors who would teach them to read and write, and other mechanical and liberal arts," a benefit that Fara suggested the Miskitos had enjoyed from their association with the English. Signed in Panama City on June 16, 1778, the treaty was subsequently approved by Carlos III.[80] A decade later, on the Gulf of Darién, Cunas also used their relationship with English traders to negotiate concessions from the Viceroy of New Granada, Antonio Caballero y Góngora.[81]

If Bourbon officials ignored South American precedents as they considered Indian policy in North and Central America, it may have been because of their tendency to look to the present and the future without deeply consulting their own past. As historian John Lynch has explained, "Charles III and his ministers knew less of Spanish America than do modern historians. The records lay around them.... But they seem not to have read them, or if they read them, not to have understood their meaning. The past was ignored, indeed repudiated."[82]

Spanish officials would have found it particularly easy to ignore the fact that negotiations had led to harmonious relations between Araucanians and Spaniards on the Chilean frontier in much of the eighteenth century. In the Hispanic world, the Araucanía had acquired a reputation as a land of war, and military officials in Chile, eager to maintain their budgets and their privileges, kept that reputation alive with exaggerated reports of Araucanian ferocity.[83] Then, too, homegrown ideas seemed to lack the cachet of foreign varieties for the Bourbons. The Spanish savant and mariner, Alejandro Malaspina, understood this. He had visited Chile in 1790 on his epic reconnaissance of the Pacific and learned that negotiations, trade, and treaties had brought a high level of harmony to Spanish-Araucanian relations. In recommending a more peaceable approach to Spain's Indian relations in northern New Spain, however, he emphasized the English system rather than the Chilean, perhaps supposing it would have greater effect on readers who, like him, tended to look abroad for solutions to Spanish problems. Malaspina did, however, lament the sharp contrast between the northern provinces of New Spain, where "the ground is uselessly darkened with Spanish blood," and Chile, where "our border with the *araucanos* is peaceful, under a system almost identical to that which the English colonies have followed."[84]

Even as Bourbon officials recognized that some Indians had the right to live independently under the "protection" of the Crown, other officials questioned the wisdom of Spain's claims to the very lands those Indians occupied. By the mid-eighteenth century it had become clear to enlightened thinkers in Spain that the papal donation of 1493 would not assure Spanish dominion over most of the hemisphere, from pole to pole.[85] Beginning with the 1750 Treaty of Madrid, in which Spain tried to resolve its long-standing differences with Portugal over the limits of its possessions in Asia and America, Bourbon officials moved vigorously to locate natural boundaries that could be measured, marked, and clearly separate their holdings from those of other powers, even when those new boundaries represented a retreat from earlier claims.[86]

In the late eighteenth century Spain continued to import colonists and to found new towns in strategic areas that it wished to maintain but had not occupied previously, such as Patagonia, the Miskito coast, Louisiana, and California.[87] And Carlos III, in particular, sent a wave of Spanish scientists to America, who intellectually appropriated peripheral territories—along with their flora and fauna, natural resources, and inhabitants—as an integral part of taking actual possession of them in the Age of Enlightenment.[88] Yet amid this continuing expansion and reconnaissance, the idea of pressing Spanish claims to areas that lacked strategic value came to be regarded as anachronistic by some enlightened officials. Theirs was an eminently "rational" response to the reality that Spain could not defend or colonize all of the space that it claimed. In military terms alone, it seemed prudent, as one army officer put it, to try to control only those regions that Spaniards actually occupied—"what should be called the dominion and true possessions of the King."[89]

Some enlightened thinkers went a step further and argued against military expenditures to defend even Spain's "true possessions," when the cost exceeded the benefits. Malaspina, who thought it foolhardy to occupy the California coast, argued that Spain should abandon its effort to defend northern New Spain with soldiers and forts: "a border that consumes a million pesos to defend property worth 100,000 pesos should be avoided."[90] In economic terms, Malaspina seems to have been attracted to the views of philosophes who argued that "in these distant climates, one must trade not conquer."[91] Campomanes and the mysterious author of the *Nuevo sistema* would have agreed, although they probably would not have carried the argument to the extreme that the Conde de Aranda did in famously advising the Crown in 1783 that, with the exception of some ports of call or bases for trade on islands like Cuba and Puerto Rico, "your Majesty should rid himself of all his dominions on the continent of both Americas."[92]

Those Spanish policymakers in administrative centers of the empire who sought to limit Spain's claims to dominion and to emphasize domination through commerce, redefined the use of power on the frontiers of the empire. Their new definition of Spain's relationship to those American lands it had not settled or firmly controlled provided a theoretical and legal rationale for recognizing the autonomy of Indians (who were, of course, autonomous in fact). The new policy also provided ideological space for Spaniards to build relationships with independent Indians based on the law of nations, rather than require Indians to submit as vassals or suffer the consequences of war or "pacification."[93]

The new policies, which were not entirely new, did not entirely replace the old, either in their enactment or in their implementation.[94] Implementation of policies required the initiative of individual officials, many of them career army officers who generally held the highest administrative offices in America under the Bourbons.[95] Some of those army officers, conditioned to distrust indios bravos and trained to fight them, balked at the idea of coexisting with them rather than smashing them.[96] Even one of Bernardo de Gálvez's successors as viceroy of Mexico, Manuel Antonio Flores, repudiated Gálvez's strategy of pursuing peace with Apaches and pressed, instead, for war with no quarter.[97] In the Río de la Plata, Juan José de Vértiz, described as an enlightened viceroy who detested war and opposed expansion into areas that Spain could not effectively control, reported that neither he nor his officers saw any point in treating with Auca chief Lincó, when he asked for peace in 1779. Vértiz regarded the request as a tactic to buy time so that Indians might continue raiding. Moreover, he said, the "savages do not have sufficient principles to comprehend the power of these pacts."[98] Like the long debate over the capacity of Indians to work without coercion, the debate over the merits of using commerce instead of force to pacify "wild Indians" continued until the end of the colonial period.[99]

Whatever ideas informed their actions, Bourbon officials in the colonial centers and on the frontiers responded pragmatically to local circumstances as their Habsburg predecessors had done. Spanish officials made substantial concessions to Indians who forced them to recognize that conquest would cost more than peace, and to Indians who could turn to foreigners for support.[100] In places such as southeastern North America, the Miskito coast, and the Araucanía, Spanish officials, like Europeans on similar frontiers, paid tribute to natives and recognized their autonomy.[101]

Conversely, when Spain expanded into California beginning in 1769, officials saw no need to sign treaties or enter into alliances with small groups of seminomads who lacked horses, firearms, the political organization to offer effective resistance, and had little prospect of aid from foreign powers. In California, as in other remote areas like Tierra del Fuego, or the llanos of today's Colombia, where Indians offered only modest resistance, Bourbons relied on missionaries and small mission guards to establish dominion, much as the Habsburgs had done.[102]

Between these two extremes were places where Spaniards succeeded in isolating Indians from weapons and allies, defeated them, and forced them to surrender. Some Apache prisoners, whom Spaniards regarded as incorrigible, were be put in chains and sent into virtual slavery—a time-honored practice.[103] Others were confined to reservations around military posts, through the formal treaties that Bourbon officers came to rely upon. On May 17, 1787, for example, Spaniards obliged the leaders of two small, bedraggled groups of Mescalero Apaches to enter into an eleven-part agreement at Presidio del Norte. Rather than guarantee their independence, the treaty required the Mescalero bands to live near the fort, not to leave without obtaining a license.[104]

At the level of the individual, Bourbon policies toward indios bárbaros were subverted by "Spaniards" and "savages" who chose to ignore established categories. Individuals from each group moved across the porous boundaries that separated them and resided within the society of the other. Some did so by choice and others as captives. Some moved back and forth with the seasons. "Wild" Indians, for example, entered the Hispanic world to work temporarily in missions or for wages in haciendas, just as Hispanic traders in pursuit of profit ventured into Indian territory and lived among "wild" Indians.[105] Some marginalized individuals—Hispanics, Indians, and mixed bloods—lived together in multiethnic outlaw bands as outcasts from both societies.[106] In such ways, individuals on the frontiers of the empire looked after their own interests, usually preferring commerce and negotiation over war, a preference that they came to independent of the policies or philosophies of enlightened Bourbon officials.[107]

In the Bourbon era, then, policy was not consistent or consistently applied. Directives that originated in the core of the absolutist Spanish state often took local conditions into account, and peripheral peoples—native and European alike—shaped and reshaped royal directives according to their own needs, perceptions, and power. New Indian policies emerged out of the interplay between core and periphery, tradition and innovation, pragmatism and ideology, and venality and idealism. In this respect, then, Spain resembled other early modern empires where, as historian Jack Greene has noted, authority did not merely flow "by imposition from the top down or from the center out but through an elaborate process of negotiation among the parties involved"—even in situations where relationships of power were unequal.[108]

The various ways that Spaniards engaged independent Indians in the late colonial period would seem unremarkable were it not for the tendency of North American scholars to regard Spanish policy toward independent Indians as homogeneous and timeless, fixed in the sixteenth century,[109] and to reduce Spain's multifaceted and pragmatic practices to caricature. Familiar oversimplifications resonate throughout our literature: the idea that the Indian policy of England and France "was based on trade . . . and Spain's was based on the vain hope of mass conversion to Catholicism,"[110] the generalization that all Indians who resisted conquest "were defined [by Spaniards] as barbarians, as natural beings to be conquered and tamed by their betters," the argument that "placelessness" of nomads and seminomads "deprived them of any autonomous right to a frontier territory,"[111] the notion that "there were no Spanish-Indian treaties,"[112] the commonplace distinction that, "While the French sought a consensual 'alliance' with the natives, Spaniards sought submission. Even the most benevolent methods of enacting Spanish authority *never* sought consent from natives. . . ."[113]

Never say never.

Notes

I am currently working on a book-length manuscript, *Spaniards and Their Savages in the Age of Enlightenment*, that elaborates on the themes in this essay. I am indebted once again to my former colleague William B. Taylor for his generous reading and advice. This essay has also benefited from the kindness and insights of James Axtell of the College of William and Mary, Allan J. Kuethe of Texas Technical University, Raúl Mandrini of the Universidad Nacional del Centro, Tandil, Argentina, and Sam Truett, a 1997–98 fellow at Southern Methodist University's Clements Center for Southwest Studies. I also owe thanks to the organizers of a conference of the South Central Society for Eighteenth-Century Studies (Edmond, Oklahoma, March 1, 1997), and to the Sixty-sixth Anglo-American Conference of Historians (London, July 4, 1997), who prompted me to prepare earlier versions of this essay.

Michael Riekenberg, "'Aniquilar hasta su exterminio a estos indios . . .' Un ensayo para repensar la frontera bonaerense (1770–1830)," *Ibero-Americana Pragensia* 30 (1996), 61–75, which came to my attention after I had completed this essay, argues suggestively that in Argentina the colonial center favored extermination of Indians in the 1770s as the Bourbon Reforms reached that area, and that frontier elites opposed such a policy. Recent works on treaties with Indians by Carlos Lázaro Ávila, "Conquista, control y convicción: el papel de los parlamentos indígenas en México, el Chaco y Norteamérica," *Revista de Indias* 69 (Septiembre–Diciembre, 1999), 645–73, and Abelardo Levaggi, *Paz en la frontera. Historia de las relaciones diplomáticas con las comunidades indígenas en la Argentina (Siglos XVI–XIX)* (Buenos Aires: Universidad del Museo Social Argentino, 2000), confirm changes in Bourbon policy that I identified in this essay.

A Spanish version of this essay, translated by Aníbal Minnucci, appeared in Argentina as "Borbones y bárbaros. Centro y periferia en la reformulación de la política de España hacia los indígenas no sometidos." *Anuario del IEHS* 13 (1998), 147–71. Original quotations from Spanish sources, which appear in translation in this English-language essay, can be found in the *Anuario* version.

1. Claudio Esteva-Fabregat, *Mestizaje in Ibero-America*, trans. John Wheat (1st ed., 1988; Tucson: University of Arizona Press, 1995), 232, calculates that they controlled 3.9 million square miles. Figures for continental Latin America, include Mexico (761,601), Central America (188,708), and South America (6,875,000), for a total of 7,825,309 square miles. The actual area under control by independent Indians was much larger; Esteva-Fabregat did not factor in Spain's possessions in what is now the United States.

2. James Lockhart and Stuart B. Schwartz, *Early Latin America: A History of Colonial Spanish America and Brazil* (Cambridge: Cambridge University Press, 1983), chap. 8, offers a cogent overview of these areas.
3. I use the term *Enlightenment* loosely, to suggest that some eighteenth-century Spanish officials reflected the broad sensibilities of *la época de las luces*. Spanish *ilustrados*, like the French *philosophes*, held widely divergent and often contradictory views. Through the crosscurrents of the Spanish Enlightenment, however, ran a strong belief in the power of human observation and reason unaided by either divine revelation or the authority of the ancients. In Spain, particularly under Carlos III (1759–1788), "enlightened" officials attempted to apply reason to public policy and thereby increase trade, industry, agricultural production, and, not incidentally, public revenues. At the same time, rational, scientific approaches to social problems promised to liberate the king's subjects from poverty, ignorance, and oppression, making them more productive taxpayers in the American colonies as in Spain itself. For larger crosscurrents of the age, Peter Gay, *The Enlightenment: An Interpretation*, 2 vols. (New York: Knopf, 1966), offers a sweeping and engaging overview. For Spain's application of these ideas to its American colonies, see Ramón Ezquerra, "La crítica española sobre América en el siglo XVIII," *Revista de Indias* 22 (1962), 159–283.
4. In this essay I employ *frontier, periphery,* and *borderlands* as synonyms, meaning those broad zones of interaction between Hispanic societies and the societies of independent Indians. See David J. Weber and Jane M. Rausch, eds., *Where Cultures Meet: Frontiers in Latin American History* (Wilmington, Del.: Scholarly Resources, 1994), xiii–xiv. The Bourbon "centers" in this essay refer to policymakers in Spain and the high-ranking officials in the New World centers who served as their spokesmen. Daniel R. Brower and Edward J. Lasserini, eds., *Russia's Orient: Imperial Borderlands and Peoples, 1700–1917* (Bloomington: Indiana University Press, 1997), introduction, xiii–xiv, laments that "much of the literature produced about the Russian imperial experience has focused on policy as defined from the center, along with generalizations and conclusions from 'official' statements that pay little heed to, first, the unarguable tension between theory and practice; second, the influence on policy implementation of local circumstances . . . ; and third, the role of regional/local authorities and populations in actual policy formulation and application." This lament would apply as well to our understanding of the history of colonial Latin America. See Michiel Baud and Willem van Schendel, "Toward a Comparative History of Borderlands," *Journal of World History* 8 (Fall 1997), 211–42. See, too, n. 108, below.
5. I focus on the mainland, since Spaniards had largely annihilated Indians on the major Caribbean islands, replacing them with laborers from black Africa.
6. This, and the quotation that follows, are from the Conde de Superunda, quoted by Manuel Lucena Giraldo in his introduction to Francisco de Requena, *Ilustrados y bárbaros. Diario de la exploración de límites al Amazonas (1782)*, ed. Manuel Lucena Giraldo (Madrid: Alianza, 1991), 7–8.
7. Thomas D. Hall, "Civilizational Change: The Role of Nomads," *Comparative Civilization Review* 24 (1991), 48.
8. Martín Dobrizhoffer, *Historia de los Abipones*, ed. Ernesto J. A. Maeder and Guillermo Furlong, 3 vols. (Resistencia: Universidad Nacional del Nordeste, 1967–1970), 2:417. Teodoro de Croix made the same point in an informe general to José de Gálvez, January 23, 1780, Arizpe, oficio #458, Archivo General de Indias (AGI), Guadalajara, leg. 522.
9. For a very able summary and comparison, see Carlos Lázaro Ávila, *Las fronteras de América y los "Flandes indianos"* (Madrid: Consejo Superior de Investigaciones Científicas, 1997). Space limitations do not allow me to describe the process of "ethnogenesis," but see, for example, Neil L. Whitehead, "Tribes Make States and States Make Tribes: Warfare and the Creation of Colonial Tribes and States in Northeastern South America," in *War in the Tribal Zone: Expanding States and Indigenous Warfare*, ed. R. Brian Ferguson and Neil L. Whitehead (Santa Fe: School of American Research, 1992), 127–50.
10. Pedro Rodríguez Conde de Campomanes, *Reflexiones sobre el comercio español a Indias [1762]*, ed. Vicente Llombart Rosa (Madrid: Instituto de Estudios Fiscales, 1988), 28.

11. Ibid., 32.
12. Ibid., 27, 32.
13. Ibid., 53.
14. Ibid., 122.
15. Campomanes had consulted a French translation of George Anson, *A Voyage Round the World, in the Years MDCCXL, I, III, IV* (London: J. and P. Knapton, 1748), published in Geneva in 1750. See Campomanes, *Reflexiones*, 92, n. 33. Anson had attempted to establish a base on the Chilean coast in 1741, Hugo O'Donnell, *España en el descubrimiento, conquista y defensa del mar del sur* (Madrid: Editorial MAPFRE, 1992), 239. For concerns expressed from Chile, see Leonardo León Solis, "Los araucanos y la amenaza de ultramar, 1750–1807," *Revista de Indias* 54 (1994), 313–22.
16. See, for example, the concerns expressed in 1799 by José Cortés, *Views from the Apache Frontier: Report on the Northern Provinces of New Spain by José Cortés, Lieutenant in the Royal Corps of Engineers, 1799*, ed. and trans., Elizabeth A. H. John and John Wheat (Norman: University of Oklahoma Press, 1989), 40.
17. Allan J. Kuethe, "Towards a Periodization of the Reforms of Charles III," in *Iberian Colonies, New World Societies: Essays in Memory of Charles Gibson*, ed. Richard L. Garner and William B. Taylor (University Park, Penn.: Private Printing, 1985), 103–17, provides a good introduction to the period and suggests its different stages.
18. The quotes are, respectively, from John Lynch, "The Institutional Framework of Colonial Spanish America," *Journal of Latin American Studies* 24 (1992), 78; Orlando Fals Borda, *Historia doble de la costa. vol. 4: Retorno a la Tierra* (Bogotá: Carlos Valencia Editores, 1986), 44A.
19. For example, Christon I. Archer, *The Army in Bourbon Mexico, 1760–1810* (Albuquerque: University of New Mexico Press, 1977); Max L. Moorhead, *The Presidio: Bastion of the Spanish Borderlands* (Norman: University of Oklahoma Press, 1975); Norberto Ras, *Crónica de la frontera sur* (Buenos Aires: Academia Nacional de Agronomía y Veterinaria, 1994).
20. The quotation is from D. A. Brading, *Miners and Merchants in Bourbon Mexico, 1763–1810* (Cambridge: Cambridge University Press, 1971), 25. Brading adhered to the view that José del Campillo y Cossío wrote the manuscript version of the *Nuevo sistema* in 1743 when he served as Minister of Finance, of the Navy, of War, of the Indies, and of the State (early in his career Campillo had spent six years in Mexico and the Caribbean), and that the work was highly influential because it circulated in manuscript among Bourbon ministers even though it was not published as a discrete work until 1789: Joseph del Campillo y Cosío, *Nuevo sistema de govierno económico para la América* (Madrid: Imprenta de Benito Cano, 1789). D. A. Brading, *The First America: The Spanish Monarch, Creole Patriots, and the Liberal State, 1492–1867* (Cambridge: Cambridge University Press, 1991), 469–70; 486–87, continues to take that position, and he has been in good scholarly company. See, for example, Miguel Artola, "Campillo y las reformas de Carlos III," *Revista de Indias* 12 (1952), 692, 711–14, Josefina Cintrón Tiryakian, "Campillo's Pragmatic New System: A Mercantile and Utilitarian Approach to Indian Reform in Spanish Colonies of the Eighteenth Century," *History of Political Economy* 10 (1978), 234–35, 254–57, and Anthony Pagden, *Lords of all the World: Ideologies of Empire in Spain, Britain and France c.1500-c.1800* (New Haven, Conn.: Yale University Press, 1995), 121–22. For Campillo's years in America, see José del Campillo y Cossío, *Dos escritos políticos: Lo que hay de más y de menos en España/España despierta [1741]*, ed. Dolores Mateos Dorado (Oviedo: Junta General del Principado de Asturias, 1993), ix–xxi. The *Nuevo sistema* first appeared in print as part 2 of the *Proyecto económico*, which the Spanish ilustrado and economist Bernardo Ward wrote in 1762, but which was not published until 1779. Ward has been accused of plagiarizing the *Nuevo sistema*, and does, indeed, make only modest changes (part 2 of his work, "Sobre la América," included the passages on winning the loyalty of independent Indians through trade). See Bernardo Ward, *Proyecto económico*, ed. Juan Luis Castellano Castellano (Madrid: Instituto de Estudios Fiscales, 1982), 324–30. Other scholars, however, point to internal inconsistencies and errors that suggest that Campillo could not have written the *Nuevo sistema* and that the document did not so much influence as reflect the views of

some Bourbon thinkers. For the arguments and citations to other critical works, see Luis Navarro García, "Campillo y el Nuevo Sistema: una atribución dudosa," *Temas Americanistas* 2 (1983), 22–29, and "El falso campillo y el reformismo borbónico," *Temas Americanistas* 12 (1995), 5–14. The editor of the most recent edition of the *Nuevo sistema*, José del Campillo y Cosío, *Nuevo sistema de gobierno económico para la América*, ed. Manuel Ballesteros Gaibrois (Oviedo: Grupo Editorial Asturiano, 1993), 30, declines to consider the question of attribution.

21. Campillo, *Nuevo sistema*, 16.
22. Ibid., 14.
23. Ibid., 211.
24. Ibid., 210.
25. Ibid., 212.
26. Ibid., 212–13.
27. This was an idea still held by some enlightened Spaniards, such as Antonio de Ulloa, a naval officer, scientist, and philosophe par excellence, who had carried out a remarkable investigation of America with Jorge Juan in 1736–44 and governed Spanish Louisiana in 1766–68. Ulloa remained convinced that Indians were innately lazy, deceitful, and rebellious, and that Spaniards had to force Indians to work for their own good. Antonio de Ulloa, *Noticias Americanas. Edición Facsímil [1772]*, ed. Miguel Molina Martínez (Granada: Universidad de Granada, 1992), xxxvi–xl, 305–34.
28. Tiryakian, "Campillo's Pragmatic New System," 243.
29. This vision of an informal empire held considerable appeal; American expansionists, for example, would champion it in the last decades of the nineteenth century. See Walter LaFeber, *The New Empire: An Interpretation of American Expansion, 1860–1898* (Ithaca, N.Y.: Cornell University Press, 1963).
30. Campomanes to José de Gálvez, reservado, Madrid, September 14, 1784, Archivo Histórico Nacional [Madrid], Estado, leg. 3.885, exped. 17, no. 4.
31. Bernardo de Gálvez to José de Gálvez, [New Orleans], October 24, 1778, quoted in Elizabeth Howard West, "The Indian Policy of Bernardo de Gálvez," *Proceedings of the Mississippi Valley Historical Association* 8 (1914), 100–101.
32. José de Gálvez to Comandante General Teodoro de Croix, El Pardo, February 20, 1779. Photocopy in the University of Texas Library, Archivo de San Francisco el Grande, vol. 33, XI, 1779, 33–39. This copy of Gálvez's orders was called to my attention by Alfred B. Thomas, *Teodoro de Croix and the Northern Frontier of New Spain, 1776–1783* (Norman: University of Oklahoma Press, 1941), 43.
33. Juan Lucas de Lassaga and el Marqués de San Miguel de Aguayo to [the king], Mexico, February 20, 1782, and [Gálvez] to Croix, San Ildefonso, June 27, 1782, AGI, Guadalajara 519. For the context, see David J. Weber, *The Spanish Frontier in North America* (New Haven, Conn.: Yale University Press, 1992), 224–30.
34. Bernardo de Gálvez, *Instructions for Governing the Interior Provinces of New Spain, 1786*, ed. and trans., Donald E. Worcester (Berkeley: Quivira Society, 1951), article 24 (*con el tiempo los ponga bajo de nuestra dependencia*). Worcester includes the Spanish-language version, too. I have cited articles rather than pages, for ready reference to the text in either language.
35. The quotations are respectively in ibid., article 47 and article 52.
36. Cortés, *Views from the Apache Frontier*, 31.
37. Gálvez, *Instructions for Governing*, article 29.
38. Kuethe, "Towards a Periodization," 115–17.
39. Cortés, *Views from the Apache Frontier*, 34.
40. The details of governing the Apache peace establishments were spelled out by Pedro de Nava in Instructions of 1791. Nava emphasized gifts over trade and dictated policies left unaddressed by Bernardo de Gálvez in 1786. Moorhead, *The Presidio*, 260–65, summarized Nava's Instructions. For a case study, see William B. Griffen, *Apaches at War and Peace: The Janos Presidio, 1750–1858* (Albuquerque: University of New Mexico Press, 1988).
41. Luis Navarro García, "El ilustrado y el bárbaro: la guerra apache vista por Bernardo de Gálvez," *Temas Americanistas* 6 (1986), 15, makes this point in a lengthy gloss on Gálvez's *Instructions for Governing*. There is a large if fragmentary literature on this

subject. For an especially interesting analysis of the northern frontier of New Spain, see Luis Navarro García, "Política indígena de España en el Noroeste," *Culturas de la costa noroeste de América*, ed. José Luis Peset (Madrid: Turner Libros, 1989), whose subject is larger than his title suggests.

42. José Mariano Moziño, *Noticias de Nutka: An Account of Nootka Sound in 1792*, ed. and trans., Iris Wilson (Seattle: University of Washington Press, 1970), 84.
43. Antonio Cordero y Bustamante, "Noticias relativas a la nación apache, que en el año de 1796 extendió en el Paso del Norte, el Teniente Coronel D. Antonio Cordero, por encargo del Sr. Comandate general Mariscal de Campo D. Pedro Nava," *Geografía de las lenguas y carta etnográfica de México*; ed. Manuel Orozco y Berra (Mexico: Impr. de J. M. Andrade y F. Escalante, 1864), 379. For a translation, see Antonio Cordero y Bustamante, "Cordero's Description of the Apache—1796," *New Mexico Historical Review*, ed. and trans., Daniel S. Matson and Albert H. Schroeder 32 (1957), 350.
44. See, for example, Nicolás de Lafora, *The Frontiers of New Spain: Nicolás de Lafora's Description, 1766–68*, ed. and trans., Lawrence Kinnaird (Berkeley: Quivira Society, 1958), 79. For an introduction to the large literature on discourse as rationalization, and an application of it in an earlier era in northern Mexico, see Charlotte M. Gradie, "Discovering the Chichimecas," *The Americas* 51 (1994), 67–88.
45. Cordero, "Noticias relativas," 370. Similarly, see Elizabeth A. H. John, ed. and trans., "A Cautionary Exercise in Apache Historiography ['Notes and Reflections on the War with the Apache Indians in the Provinces of New Spain,' by Bernardo de Gálvez, ca. 1785–86]," *Journal of Arizona History* 25 (1984), 303–4.
46. Cordero, "Noticias relativas," 379.
47. Quoted in John, "A Cautionary Excercise," 304.
48. Ambrosio Higgins, "Descripción del Reyno de Chile. . . . con algunas prosposiciones relativas a la reducción de los indios infieles, y adelantamiento de aquellos dominios de Su Magestad, 2 de septiembre de 1767," *El Gobernador Ambrosio O'Higgins*, ed. Aurelio González Santis (Santiago: Editorial Salesiana, 1980), 37, called to my attention in León Solis, "Los Araucanos y la Amenaza," 326.
49. The phrase "frontier soldiers of the Crown" is that of Carlos Lázaro Ávila, "El reformismo borbónico y los indígenas fronterizos americanos," *El reformismo borbónico*, ed. Agustín Guimerá (Madrid: Alianza, 1996), 286.
50. Allan J. Kuethe and Lowell Blaisdell, "The Esquilache Government and the Reforms of Charles III in Cuba," *Jahrbuch Für Geschichte von Staat, Wirtshaft und Gesellshaft Lateinamerickas* 19 (1982), 119.
51. The opinion of Villava, Plata, June 29, 1800, in the "Expediente obrado a representación del señor Governador Intendente de Cochabamba sobre haber mandado ahorcar al indio rebelde Sacuarao." Archivo General de la Nación, Buenos Aires, IX, Guerra y marina, 1800, legajo no. 24.3.6. Transcript courtesy of Silvia Ratto.
52. *"Asi la invasión de otra Nacion podría ser un atentado contra el derecho de gentes que podrá vindicarse con las armas pero no un delito que pueda castigarse con las leyes."* Significantly, Viedma and his followers did not dispute the argument that the rebels were not part of the social compact Viedma to the Viceroy of Buenos Aires, October 15, 1800, in ibid. For an able analysis of this episode, see José María Mariluz Urquijo, "El levantamiento chiriguano de 1799 y la controversia sobre la legitimidad de la guerra," *Investigaciones y ensayos* [Academia Nacional de la Historia, Argentina] 1 (1966), 309–30.
53. Ibid.
54. Patricia Seed, *Ceremonies of Possession in Europe's Conquest of the New World, 1492–1640* (Cambridge: Cambridge University Press, 1995), 69–97, offers a fine analysis of the famous *requerimiento* and a brief introduction to its successor, the "Royal Orders for New Discoveries," of 1573, which spelled out Spanish expectations that Indians must become vassals of the Spanish Crown and instructed in Catholicism. For a different reading of the 1573 orders, see Abelardo Levaggi, "Los tratados entre la Corona y los indios, y la plan de conquista pacífica," *Revista Complutense de Historia de América* 19 (1993), 85.
55. Elena Isabel Estrada de Gerlero, "The Representation of 'Heathen Indians' in Mexican Casta Painting," in *New World Orders: Casta Painting and Colonial Latin America*, ed. Ilona Katzew (New York: Americas Society, 1996), 42–54.

56. The first attempts at treaties with the "Nations of the North" and Comanches along the Texas-Louisiana frontier, negotiated in 1771 and 1774 by a former French trader, Athanase de Mézières, met opposition from Viceroy Bucareli and the leading officer in northern New Spain, Hugo Oconor, largely because traders furnished guns and ammunition to these new Indian allies. Herbert Eugene Bolton, ed. and trans., *Athanase de Mézières and the Louisiana-Texas Frontier, 1768–1780*, 2 vols. (Cleveland: Arthur H. Clark, 1914), I:93–108, and docs. 83, 120, and 123.
57. The Spanish texts of these treaties appear in Miguel Gómez del Campillo, *Relaciones diplomáticos entre España y los Estados Unidos según los documentos del Archivo Histórico Nacional*, 2 vols. (Madrid: Consejo Superior de Investigaciones Científicas, 1944), 1:412–30.
58. Odie Faulk, ed. and trans., "Spanish-Comanche Relations and the Treaty of 1785," *Texana* 2 (1964), 44–53, includes the terms of the treaty, as described in Pedro de Nava to the viceroy, Chihuahua, July 23, 1799; much of this same document is reproduced in Marc Simmons, ed. and trans., *Border Comanches: Seven Spanish Colonial Documents, 1785–1819* (Santa Fe: Stagecoach Press, 1967), 21–22. Alfred B. Thomas, ed. and trans., *Forgotten Frontiers: A Study of the Spanish Indian Policy of Don Juan Bautista de Anza, Governor of New Mexico, 1777–1787* (Norman: University of Oklahoma Press, 1932), contains translations of key documents for New Mexico, including Gov. Juan Bautista de Anza's own remarkable account of the forging of the Comanche peace (294–321) and his treaties with Comanche leaders (329–31), and Navajos (346–48).
59. The text in Spanish of this Treaty of Nogales, October 28, 1793, is in Manuel Serrano y Sanz, *España y los Indios Cherokis y Chactas en la segunda mitad del siglo XVIII* (Seville: Tip. de la Guía Oficial, 1916), 91–92. This followed on the heels of treaties of 1792, with Creeks, Chickasaws, and Choctaws. For a detailed account written from Spanish sources, see José Antonio Armillas Vicente, "La gran confederación india. Interacción hispano-angloamericana con las naciones indias del sudeste norteamericano a fines del siglo XVIII," *Estudios sobre política indigenista española en América* (3 vols.; Valladolid: Seminario de Historia de América, Universidad de Valladolid, 1975–77), 225–66.
60. Anza also negotiated an eleven-point agreement with some Navajos in 1786, which resembled these other treaties, but whether representatives of both nations signed it is not clear from the summary that remains. The summary is translated in Thomas, *Forgotten Frontiers*, 347–48.
61. The 1784 treaty has Creek leaders refer to "nuestro Soberano, el Gran Rey de las Españas" (article 4), but the treaty also made it clear that Creeks were making peace with the king's "súbditos y vasallos," a category that did not include them (Gómez del Campillo, *Relaciones*, 1:414–15).
62. Jack D. L. Holmes, *Gayoso: The Life of a Spanish Governor in the Mississippi Valley, 1789–1799* (Baton Rouge: LSU Press for the Louisiana Historical Association, 1965), 154.
63. Pedro Álvarez de Miranda, *Palabras e ideas: El léxico de la ilustración temprana en España (1680–1760)* (Madrid: Anejos del Boletín de la Real Academia Española, 1992), 211–26, who suggests the importance of context in determining the meaning of *nación* in this era, when it was used interchangeably with words like *patria*, *país*, *estado*, and *reino* (217).
64. Gayoso de Lemos to Carondelet, Natchez, March 24, 1792, quoted in Holmes, *Gayoso*, 157.
65. Quoted in Dorothy V. Jones, *License for Empire: Colonialism by Treaty in Early America* (Chicago: University of Chicago Press, 1982), 166.
66. Georg Friederich von Martens, *Summary of the Law of Nations*, trans. William Cobbett (1st ed., 1788; Philadelphia: Thomas Bradford, 1795), 23–24. See also Felix S. Cohen, *Handbook of Federal Indian Law* (Washington, D.C.: Government Printing Office, 1942), 34. For Iberian antecedents, see Charles Gibson, "Conquest, Capitulation, and Indian Treaties," *American Historical Review* 83 (1978), 5.
67. Frank Defina, "Mestizos y blancos en la política india de la Luisiana y Florida del siglo XVIII," *Revista de Indias* (1966), 61.

68. Campomanes, "Dictamen sobre los medios de asegurar el dominio de España en la Florida y Luisiana y sobre el proyecto para aumentar su comercio," San Lorenzo, November 11, 1792, in Pedro Rodríguez Conde de Campomanes, *Inéditos políticos*, ed. Santos M. Coronas González (Oviedo: Junta General del Principado de Asturias, 1996), 311–12. Campomanes wrote this from his position on the Consejo del Estado at the end of his distinguished career. Earlier in his career he advocated expanding Spanish dominion in the Floridas through trade. Campomanes, *Reflexiones*, 1988, 29–30.
69. For the tightening of controls, see for example, D. A. Brading, "Bourbon Spain and Its American Empire," in *The Cambridge History of Latin America, vol. 1: Colonial Latin America*, ed. Leslie Bethell (Cambridge: Cambridge University Press, 1984), 389–439; Nancy M. Farriss, *Maya Society under Colonial Rule: The Collective Enterprise of Survival* (Princeton, N.J.: Princeton University Press, 1984), 355–65.
70. Gibson, "Conquest, Capitulation, and Indian Treaties," 2, seeks to explain why Spaniards throughout America generally did not negotiate formal, written treaties as did the English and French. See also Lawrence Kinnaird, "Spanish Treaties with Indian Tribes," *Western Historical Quarterly* 10 (1979), 39–48, and, Levaggi, "Los tratados," 88–89, both of whom address Gibson directly. Levaggi suggests that the Bourbon treaties of peace did not represent an innovation but rather the more consistent application of much violated royal intent as expressed in the Royal Orders for New Discoveries of 1573. The goal of the 1573 laws, it seems to me, however, was to persuade the natives to become "vassals" of the Crown, to reduce them to tribute-paying Christians, not to treat Indians as distinct nations with the right to retain their autonomy. "Ordenanzas de su Magestad hechas para los nuevos descubimientos, conquistas y pacificaciones [July 13, 1573]," *Colección de documentos inéditos relativos al descubrimiento, conquista y organización de las antiguas posesiones españolas de América y Oceanía* (42 vols.; Madrid, 1864), 16:181–87. See also Seed, *Ceremonies of Possession*, 95–96. Levaggi makes light of the distinction between written and unwritten treaties, arguing that "the custom of entering into treaties of peace occurred on all the Indian frontiers, and for the entire Spanish period" (90). The content and spirit of most of those early agreements, however, seem qualitatively different from those of the late eighteenth century in southeastern North America.
71. For the 1616 and 1612 antecedents, which also gave Araucanians a special juridical status, see Andrea Ruiz-Esquide Figueroa, *Los indios amigos en la frontera araucana* (Santiago: Dirección de Bibliotecas Archivos y Museos, 1993), 25–28, and Horacio Zapater, "Parlamentos de paz en la guerra de Arauco, 1612–1626," *La Araucanía. Temas de historia fronteriza*, eds. Sergio Villalobos R. and Jorge Pinto (Temuco: Ediciones de la Universidad de la Frontera, 1985). Several versions of the language of the Treaty of 1641 have come down to us, including that of Diego de Rosales, *Historia general del reyno de Chile, Flandes indiano*, ed. Benjamin Vicuña Mackenna, 3 vols. (Valparaíso: Imprenta del Mercurio, 1877), 3:184–85, an eyewitness to the proceedings. The versions vary in particulars, and are analyzed in a forthcoming article: Carlos Lázaro Ávila, "La diplomacia fronteriza en la araucanía: el precedente del Marqués de Baides (1641)," *Mar Océano*. I have taken the quote, "Que no han de ser encomendados a los Españoles, sino que han de estar en cabeça de su Magestad; y debaxo de su Real amparo, reconocerle vassalage como a su señor," from the version of the Pact that appears in José Antonio Abreu y Bertodano, *Colección de tratados de paz, alianza, neutralidad, garantia . . . hechos por los pueblos, reyes y principes, republicas y demas potencias de Espana . . . hasta el feliz reynado del rey N.S. don Felipe V* (12 vols.; Madrid: Antonio Morin, Juan de Zúñiga, y la Viuda de Peralta, 1740), 4:416. The idea of an alliance appears in Felipe Gómez de Vidaurre, "Historia geográfica, natural y civil del reino de Chile. " *Colección de historiadores de Chile y documentos relativos a la historia nacional* (vols. 14 and 15), ed. J. T. Medina (Santiago: Imprenta Ercilla, 1889), 15:240. Eugene H. Korth, *Spanish Policy in Colonial Chile: The Struggle for Social Justice, 1535–1700* (Stanford, Calif.: Stanford University Press, 1968), 175–76, mistakenly asserted that Araucanians achieved independence on this occasion.
72. Mariano José Campos Menchaca, *Nahuelbuta* (Santiago: Editorial Francisco de Aguirre, 1972), 152–54.

73. Luz María Méndez Beltrán, "La organización de los parlamentos de indios en el siglo XVIII," *Relaciones fronterizas en la Araucanía*, ed. Sergio Villalobos R. et al. (Santiago de Chile: Ediciones Universidad Católica de Chile, 1982), 107–73.
74. Sergio Villalobos R., *La vida fronteriza en Chile* (Madrid: Editorial MAPFRE, 1992), 363–82.
75. A Franciscan missionary of Río Bueno to his superior, April 22, 1783, quoted in Claudio Gay, *Historia física y política de Chile . . . Documentos sobre la historia, la estadística y la geografía* 1 (Santiago: Museo de Historia Natural, 1846), 384: called to my attention in Villalobos, *La vida fronteriza*, 376.
76. Abelardo Levaggi, "Una institución chilena trasplantada al Río de la Plata: El 'Capitán de Amigos,'" *Revista de Estudios Histórico-Jurídicos* 13 (1989), 99–107.
77. A good sample of these treaties is in Abelardo Levaggi, "Tratados entre la Corona y los indios del Chaco," *Homenaje a Ismael Sánchez Bella*, ed. Joaquín Salcedo Izu (Pamplona: Biblioteca Jurídica, Universidad de Navarra, 1992), 291–323. He quotes liberally from them and suggests that they may not have become more common in the eighteenth century, but rather that the sources better preserved. See also Guillermo Furlong, *Entre los pampas de Buenos Aires, según noticias de los misioneros jesuítas Matías Strobel, José Cardiel, Tomás Falkner, Jerónimo Rejón, Joaquín Camaño, Manuel Querini, Manuel García, Pedro Lozano y José Sánchez Labrador* (Buenos Aires: Talleres Gráficos San Pablo, 1938), 77–80, 124. Guillame Boccara, "Notas acerca de los dispositivos de poder en la sociedad colonial-fronteriza, la resistencia y la transculturación de los reche-mapuche del centro-sur de Chile (XVI–XVIIII)," *Revista de Indias* 56 (1996), 682–90, rightly notes that from the Spanish viewpoint, control of Indians was the goal of all trade and treaties.
78. As viceroy, Bernardo de Gálvez approved the idea of arming Indians in both the interior provinces of New Spain and in the Southeast, as scholars observed long ago; West, "The Indian Policy of Bernardo de Gálvez," 96–98; Jane M. Berry, "The Indian Policy of Spain in the Southwest, 1783–1795," *Mississippi Valley Historical Review* 3 (1917), 466. See Weber, *The Spanish Frontier*, 271–85, for context and guidance to the large literature on Spanish-Indian relations in the Southeast in this era.
79. Pedro Carbonell y Pinto, Governor of Panama, to José de Gálvez, August 4, 1778 (reservado no. 4), AGI, Estado, Audiencia de Guatemala, contains a description of the "tratados de paz, que verificaron en esta plaza." For the context, see Troy S. Floyd, *The Anglo-Spanish Struggle for Mosquitia* (Albuquerque: University of New Mexico Press, 1967), 127.
80. Conde de Floridablanca to Gálvez, January 4, 1779, in AGI, Estado, Audiencia de Guatemala.
81. The text of this treaty of Turbaco is published in "Pacificación general de los indios de Darién, celebrada en 21 de julio de 1787," *Boletín de historia y antigüedades* 13 (1920), 197–202. Its language in Spanish suggests that the Cunas had surrendered, declaring themselves vassals of the Crown and agreeing not to trade with foreigners. It seems unlikely, however, that the Cunas saw it as a surrender. They received permission to travel throughout Spanish territory, including major urban centers, and to market their products wherever they chose. If they failed to sell their produce at the prices they would have received from the English, the treaty guaranteed that the *comandante* of military posts would buy them on the king's account. For the context, see Allan J. Kuethe, *Military Reform and Society in New Granada, 1773–1808* (Gainesville: University Presses of Florida, 1978), 143. Other examples abound. The concessions made to Guajiros, for example, are well explained in Allan J. Kuethe, "The Pacification Campaign on the Riohacha Frontier, 1772–1779," *Hispanic American Historical Review* 50 (1970), 467–81, and Lance R. Grahn, "Guajiro Culture and Capuchin Evangelization: Missionary Failure on the Riohacha Frontier," in *The New Latin American Mission History*, ed. Erick Langer and Robert Jackson (Lincoln: University of Nebraska Press, 1995), 130–56.
82. Lynch, "Institutional Framework," 80.
83. José Perfecto Salas, Informe sobre el Reino de Chile, 1750 in Ricardo Donoso, *Un letrado del siglo XVIII. El doctor José Perfecto de Salas*, 2 vols. (Buenos Aires: Universi-

dad de Buenos Aires, 1963), 1: 119 (called to my attention in Villalobos, *La vida fronteriza*, 263, 293).

84. Alejandro Malaspina, "Reflexiones políticas sobre las Costas Occidentales de la América al S. del Cabo Blanco de Martín de Aguilar y sobre los ocho Provincias Internas de Oriente, y Occidente," *La expedición Malaspina, 1789–1794: vol. 7: Descripciones y reflexiones políticas*, ed. Juan Pimentel Igea (Madrid: Ministerio de Defensa, Museo Naval, and Lunwerg Editores, 1995), 146 ("se halla tranquila nuestra frontera con los araucanos, bajo de un sistema casi semejante al que han seguido las colonias inglesas"); see also 147. Malaspina based his judgments about northern New Spain on written sources, and his conclusions were somewhat out of date when he wrote this in the 1790s, upon his return home. In suggesting the Bourbons' enchantment with things French, I do not mean to validate the old idea that Spanish reforms were entirely French inspired, and I am mindful of the caveats in Allan J. Kuethe and Lowell Blaisdell, "French Influence and the Origins of the Bourbon Colonial Reorganization," *Hispanic American Historical Review* 71 (1991), 579–607.

85. Demetrio Ramos Pérez, "'Linea' y 'Frontera': De Tordesillas a la borbonización delimitadora," *Boletín de la Real Academia de la Historia* 191 (1994), 197–214. Patricia Seed, "Taking Possession and Reading Texts: Establishing the Authority of Overseas Empires," *William and Mary Quarterly* 94 (1992), 207, suggests that Spaniards stopped asserting their rights under the papal donation in the late sixteenth century "with the end of papal universality," but some Spaniards still invoked the papal bull in the late seventeenth and early eighteenth centuries. See Weber, *The Spanish Frontier*, 152, 158. Spanish jurists distinguished between the right to possess lands and the right to sovereignty over peoples who occupied the land. In the last half of the sixteenth century, Spanish officials under Felipe II came to understand the papal concession of 1493 as applying only to territory, and not to Indians who occupied it. Hence, they reasoned, Spain had the right to take territory without the natives' permission. Levaggi, "Los tratados," 85. For the continuing debate in Spain, see James Muldoon, *The Americas in the Spanish World Order: The Justification for Conquest in the Seventeenth Century* (Philadelphia: University of Pennsylvania Press, 1994), 29–30, 62–75.

86. Manuel Lucena Giraldo, "El reformismo de frontera," *El reformismo borbónico: una visión interdisciplinar*, ed. Agustín Guimerá (Madrid: Alianza, 1996), 265–75.

87. Luis Navarro García, "Fundación de poblaciones en las indias españoles en el siglo XVIII." *Las nuevas poblaciones de España y América. Congreso Histórico sobre Nuevas Poblaciones. V. 1992* (Seville: Junta de Andalucía, Consejería de Cultura, 1994), 37–52. Navarro García, "Fundación de poblaciones," 37–52.

88. The literature on this era of rediscovery is vast, but see, for example, Robert S. Weddle, *Changing Tides: Twilight and Dawn in the Spanish Sea, 1763–1803* (College Station: Texas A&M University Press, 1995), and Requena, *Ilustrados y bárbaros*.

89. Marqués de Rubí, "Dictámenes que de orden del exmo. sor. marqués de Croix, virrey de este reino, expone el mariscal de campo marqués de Rubí en orden a la mejor situación de los presidios . . . 1768," *La frontera norte y la experiencia colonial*, ed. María del Carmen Velázquez (Mexico: Secretaría de Relaciones Exteriores, 1982), 30 ("lo que debe llamarse dominio y verdaderas posesiones de Rey").

90. Malaspina, "Reflexiones políticas," 144, and 113–15 for his views on California. See also Angel Guirao de Vierna, "Notas para una comparación entre las expediciones a la Patagonia y a las del Noroeste americano," in *Culturas de la Costa Noroeste de América*, ed. José Luis Peset (Madrid: Turner Libros, 1989), 265–76.

91. Charles de Brosse, *Histoire des navigations aux Terres australes* (Paris: Durand, 1756); Pagden, *Lords of all the World*, 151.

92. Joaquín Oltra and María Angeles Pérez Samper, *El conde de Aranda y los Estados Unidos* (Barcelona: PPU, 1987), 237–38. See also Pagden, *Lords of all the World*, 118–25, 194; Ezquerra, "La crítica española," 212–25; Campomanes, *Reflexiones*, 355.

93. I refer here, of course, to the famous requerimiento and its successor, the Royal Orders for New Discoveries of 1573, which emphasized peaceful "pacification."

94. Carlos Lázaro Ávila, "Los tratados de paz con los indígenas fronterizos de América: evolución histórica y estado de a cuestión," *Estudios de Historia Social y Económica de América* 13 (1996), 15–24, emphasizes continuities over discontinuities in Spanish

pactismo, which he traces back to Columbus, but in so doing I think he glosses over the innovative nature of Spanish written treaties that recognize Indian autonomy in North America. Lázaro Ávila, "El reformismo borbónico," 277–92, contains much of the same argument and prose.

95. In general, army officers had supplanted the clerics and lawyers upon whom the Habsburgs depended. In provinces threatened by Indians or foreigners, such as the La Plata, soldiers dominated key positions in the government. Lockhart and Schwartz, *Early Latin America*, 361, and John Lynch, *Spanish Colonial Administration, 1782–1810: The Intendant System in the Viceroyalty of the Río de la Plata* (London: Athlone Press of the University of London, 1958), 36–37.

96. Officers' failures to implement policy can be discerned on many levels. Although the Crown mandated that Apache prisoners sent to Mexico City be treated well, for example, officials responsible for transporting them feared they would escape and do still greater harm. The Apaches' journey from the frontier to the viceregal capital became a "hideous punishment," in the words of one historian, where death rather than benevolence awaited them. Max L. Moorhead, "The Spanish Deportation of Hostile Apaches: The Policy and the Practice," *Arizona and the West* 17 (1975), 210.

97. See Luis Navarro García, *Don José de Gálvez y la Comandancia General de las provincias internas del norte de Nueva España* (Sevilla: Escuela de Estudios Hispanoamericanos, 1964), 464, and Max L. Moorhead, *The Apache Frontier: Jacobo Ugarte and Spanish-Indian Relations in Northern New Spain, 1769–1791* (Norman: University of Oklahoma Press, 1968), 135–42. Also an officer, Flores was a lieutenant general in the Royal Armada.

98. Vértiz to José de Gálvez, Buenos Aires, October 24, 1780, AGI, AB, leg. 60, transcript in the Museo Etnográfico, Universidad de Buenos Aires, carpeta J25 ("Que no teniendo estos bárbaros principios bastantes para discernir la fuerza de estos pactos"). For Vértiz, see Ras, *Crónica de la frontera*, 468–69.

99. See, for example, Feliciano Antonio Chiclana to the king, Buenos Aires, December 29, 1804, in Feliciano Antonio Chiclana, "Actuación pública de Feliciano Antonio Chiclana [1804]," *Revista de la biblioteca nacional* 13 (1945), called to my attention by Alfred J. Tapson, "Indian Warfare on the Pampa during the Colonial Period," *Hispanic American Historical Review* 42 (1962), 26, and the debate of the mid-1790s between Victorián de Villava and Paula Sanz, in Ricardo Levene, ed., *Vida y escritos de Victorián de Villava* (Buenos Aires: Peuser, S.A., 1946).

100. León Solis, "Los Araucanos y la Amenaza," 328–29; the debates of the Cortes de Cádiz on Indian questions, examined in Marie Laure Rieu-Millan, *Los diputados americanos en las cortes de Cádiz* (Madrid: Consejo Superior de Investigaciones Científicas, 1990), 107–46.

101. Whatever Spaniards thought of the gifts they offered, some Indian beneficiaries of Spanish largesse probably understood Spanish payment as tribute. Rolf Foerster G., "Guerra y aculturación en la araucanía," *Misticismo y violencia en la temprana evangelización de Chile*, ed. Jorge Pinto, Maximiliano Salinas, and Rolf Foerster G. (Temuco: Ediciones Universidad de la Frontera, 1991), 200–1. Hall, "Civilizational Change," 49. On the Miskitos, whose relations with Spaniards I have not developed in this essay, see José Moñino y Redondo Conde de Floridablanca, "Instrucción reservada que la junta de estado, creada formalmente por mi decreto de este día, 8 de julio de 1787, deberá observar en todos los puntos y ramos encargados á su conocimiento y exámen," in *Obras originales del Conde de Floridablanca*, ed. Antonio Ferrer del Río (Madrid: M. Rivadeneyra, 1867), 230, who emphasizes gifts and kind treatment; for a brief summary and guidance to secondary literature, see Craig L. Dozier, *Nicaragua's Mosquito Shore: The Years of British and American Presence* (University: University of Alabama Press, 1985), 18, who rightly notes that following the Seven Years' War, Spain "attempted to win over the interior tribes and the Mosquitos, not by missionary endeavors but by adopting the methods that had been used successfully by the British."

102. Weber, *The Spanish Frontier*, chap. 9; Fernando Casanueva, "La evangelización periférica en el reino de Chile, 1667–1796," *Nueva Historia: Revista de Historia de Chile* 5

(1982), 20–22; Jane M. Rausch, *A Tropical Plains Frontier: The Llanos of Colombia, 1531–1831* (Albuquerque : University of New Mexico Press, 1984), chap. 5.

103. Max L. Moorhead, "The Spanish Deportation of Hostile Apaches: The Policy and the Practice," *Arizona and the West* 17 (1975), 205–20.

104. The text of the "Capitulaciones" signed by two mescaleros, Patule and Quemado, "alias Inddafindilchi y Yl-lydé," May 17, 1787, is in the report of Joseph Antonio Rengel, apparently extracting a report by Capt. Domingo Díaz, in a lengthy *carpeta* on the mescaleros, copied at Arizpe 15 October 1787 by Pedro Garrido y Durán, in AGN, Provincias Internas, tomo 112, exped. 1, microfilm at University of Texas, Austin. For the context, see Moorhead, *The Apache Frontier*, 209–10, 212. Misunderstood by Anglophone writers, the word *capitulación* was used interchangeably with *treaty*. Gibson, "Conquest, Capitulation, and Indian Treaties," 1, 3–4, 9.

105. See, for example, Carlos A. Mayo, "El cautiverio y sus funciones en una sociedad de frontera. El caso de Buenos Aires, 1750–1810," *Revista de Indias* 45 (1985), 235–43; Carlos A. Mayo and Amalia Latrubesse, *Terratenientes, soldados y cautivos: La frontera, 1736–1815* (1st ed., 1986; Mar del Plata: Universidad Nacional de Mar del Plata and Grupo Estado y Sociedad, 1993), 87–93; Cynthia Radding, *Wandering Peoples: Colonialism, Ethnic Spaces, and Ecological Frontiers in Northwestern Mexico, 1700–1850* (Durham, N.C.: Duke University Press, 1997), 109–12; Thierry Saignes, "Entre 'bárbaros' y 'cristianos': el desafío mestizo en la frontera chiriguano," *Anuario IEHS* 4 (1989), 13–51; Peter Stern, "The White Indians of the Southwest," *Journal of the Southwest* 33 (1991), 262–81; Silvio Zavala, *Los escalvos indios en Nueva España* (1st ed., 1968; Mexico: El Colegio Nacional Luis González Obregón, 1981), 179–309; Ana A. Teruel, "Zenta y San Ignacio de los Tobas. El trabajo en dos misiones del Chaco occidental a fines de la colonia," *Anuario del IEHS* 9 (1994), 236–39.

106. William L. Merrill, "Cultural Creativity and Raiding Bands in Eighteenth-Century Northern New Spain," in *Violence, Resistance, and Survival in the Americas: Native Americans and the Legacy of Conquest*, ed. William B. Taylor and Franklin Pease G.Y. (Washington, D.C.: Smithsonian Institution Press, 1994).

107. Daniel J. Santamaría, "La iglesia en el Jujuy colonial, siglos XVII y XVIII," *Jujuy en la historia: avances de investigación II*, ed. Marcelo Lagos (Jujuy: Facultad de Humanidades y Ciencias Sociales, Universidad Nacional de Juyuy, 1995), 36, makes the point that in the Chaco "la guerra no fue lo normal, pero sí el comercio y la negociación permanente entre europeos y aborígenes," and I think that generalization applies to all of the frontiers of Spanish America. See, too, Daniel J. Santamaría and Jaime A. Peire, "¿Guerra o comercio pacífico? La problemática interétnica del Chaco centro-occidental en el siglo XVIII," *Anuario de Estudios Americanos* 50 (1993), 93–127.

108. Jack P. Greene, "Negotiated Authorities: The Problem of Governance in the Extended Polities of the Early Modern Atlantic World," *Negotiated Authorities: Essays in Colonial Political and Constitutional History* (Charlottesville: University of Virginia Press, 1994), 4, who applies this model to Spain "at least down to the Bourbon reforms" (18). The idea that frontier peoples helped shape policy may seem self-evident, yet it bears noting since Wallerstein's world-systems theory focused heavily on the core and slighted the ways that peripheral nonstate societies prevented the core from unilaterally imposing policies on them. See, for example, the critiques of Wilma A. Dunaway, "Incorporation as an Interactive Process: Cherokee Resistance to Expansion of the Capitalist World-System, 1560–1763," *Sociological Inquiry* 66 (1996), 455–70, and Thomas D. Hall, *Social Change in the Southwest, 1350–1880* (Lawrence: University Press of Kansas, 1989). I agree with the position that the Bourbons took into account "the realities and needs of the individual colonies" and did not abandon "the Spanish habit of advancing change piecemeal, proceeding by trial and error," as argued by Allan J. Kuethe and G. Douglas Inglis, "Absolutism and Enlightened Reform: Charles III, the Establishment of the *Alcabala*, and Commercial Reorganization in Cuba," *Past and Present: A Journal of Historical Studies* (November 1985), 119, 137. See, too, Allan J. Kuethe, "La desregulación comercial y la reforma imperial en la época de Carlos III: Los casos de Nueva España y Cuba," *Historia mexicana* 162 (1991), 288; Lockhart and Schwartz, *Early Latin America*, 315; Felipe Castro Gutiérrez, "De paternalismo autoritario al autoritarismo burocrático: Los éxitos y fracasos de

José de Gálvez, 1764–1767," in *Mexico in the Age of Democratic Revolutions, 1750–1850*, ed. Jaime E. Rodríguez O. (Boulder: Lynne Rienner, 1994), 32, who finds similar flexibility in the application of policy in the established colony. On the interplay between the periphery and the core in the shaping of policy, see Robert W. Patch, *Maya and Spaniard in Yucatan, 1648–1812* (Stanford, Calif.: Stanford University Press, 1993), 167, who argues that "the Bourbon Reforms in Yucatan, in short, were possible only because of social and economic changes that were fundamentally internal in origin." See also n. 4, above.

109. The sophisticated anthropologist Edward Spicer articulated the conventional wisdom that "to a large extent, the major outlines of the Spanish program for civilizing the Indians remained the same from the early 1600s to the early 1800s." He did recognize what he called "adjustments of program" following the expulsion of the Jesuits, including Bernardo de Gálvez's 1786 *Instrucción*, which he misreads as a pessimistic document built on the assumption that "Apaches could never be civilized." Edward H. Spicer, *Cycles of Conquest: The Impact of Spain, Mexico, and the United States on the Indians of the Southwest, 1533–1960* (Tucson: University of Arizona Press, 1962), 332.
110. Nicholas Lemann, "A Failed Dominion," *Atlantic Monthly* (November 1992), 151–52.
111. Ana María Alonso, *Thread of Blood: Colonialism, Revolution, and Gender on Mexico's Northern Frontier* (Tucson: University of Arizona Press, 1995), 63. Alonso also asserts that "during the eighteenth and nineteenth centuries, a logic of territorial conquest rather than economic exploitation underpinned the subjection of frontier indigenes and posited their social exclusion, that is, their extermination or segregation" (56).
112. Gibson, "Conquest, Capitulation, and Indian Treaties," 13, offers this statement, but concludes his essay by noting two exceptions from North America.
113. Seed, *Ceremonies of Possession*, 97–98. Emphasis added. Seed's study encompasses the years 1492–1640, yet her usage, especially the word *never*, implies a timeless quality to her portrayal of Spanish practice and policy.

Centers and Peripheries in the Luso-Brazilian World, 1500–1808

A. J. R. Russell-Wood

News of the landfall on the coast of Brazil by the fleet of Pedro Álvares Cabral in 1500 did not resonate loudly in the streets of Lisbon or at the royal court. Symptomatic of this indifference was the royal decision (1502) to farm out the contract for cutting brazilwood (the only discernible resource other than parrots and monkeys) and that the contractors should be New Christians, a group already marginalized in Portuguese society. Only the threat of French occupation spurred Dom João III to establish a formal Portuguese presence in the New World. This occurred in 1532, with extension to Brazil of an administrative recourse already practiced in the fifteenth century in Madeira and the Azores and extended to the Cape Verde Islands: namely, the donatory system.[1] Other than this insular experience, there was no precedent or policy in Africa or the Estado da India for colonization other than to secure key locations essential to trade. In Brazil the crown preserved its suzerainty but granted broad rights to individuals in exchange for their assuming specific responsibilities. Under-capitalization and inadequate support from the royal treasury, coupled with hostile Indians and apparent absence of mineral wealth or commercial potential, did not make Brazil an attractive location for potential migrants or investors. Crown government was established in Brazil only in 1549, but for the next half century Brazil remained peripheral to royal attentions. That it was gaining royal attention in the seventeenth century may have been as much attributable to signs of erosion in the hitherto unblemished aura of richness surrounding Portuguese India and distress at the Dutch presence in the northeast of Brazil as to the intrinsic merits of the colony. Discovery of alluvial gold in the 1690s, subsequent gold rushes, the arrival in Lisbon of bullion in such quantities as to enable Dom João V to realize his absolutist ambitions to emulate Louis XIV, and the discovery of diamonds in the 1720s placed Brazil at center stage for the king. The shift from periphery to center, already manifest in economic terms, gained political recognition with the arrival of the royal family in Brazil in 1808. That a royal court should be located in America was not unique to Brazil (compare the experience of Ferdinand Maximilian Joseph, emperor of Mexico,

1864–67, whose rise and fall involved Napoleon III) but Brazil was unique in two regards. First, such a move had been mooted centuries earlier, and secondly, Brazil became host to a royal court that had been established in the Old World and transferred to the New.

What constitutes a center and a periphery is subjective, depending on the person making the assessment. Moreover, it is parallax—the apparent change in the position of what constitutes *center* and what *periphery* resulting from a change in the viewer's position—be this in spatial or chronological terms, or even of social or financial circumstances, that demands that the parameters and limitations of this essay be clearly stated. It will examine center-periphery relationships under two headings. First, by taking Portugal as center and Brazil as periphery, metropolitan policies and attitudes toward the colony and the dynamic of this relationship between 1500 and 1822 will be discussed. The term *metropolitan* encompasses the king, ministers, councils of state, and interests of Lisbon that politically, demographically, socially, commercially and as the major urban nucleus, were preeminent for the period under discussion. Whether *Lisboeta* interests represented those of Portugal as a whole is beyond the scope of this essay. The second part of the esay will examine three facets of center-periphery relations in Brazil: settlement, administration, and commerce.

Center and Periphery: Portugal and Brazil

That Brazil was peripheral to metropolitan interests in the sixteenth century, was never in question. In the course of the seventeenth century, there was metropolitan acknowledgment that Brazil was critical to the mother country's economic well-being. In the eighteenth century, the dependency on Brazil of the mother country for its economic survival was never doubted. With full justification, an official referred to Brazil as the "prime jewel" in the royal Crown. Remarkably, this centrality of Brazil to the national interests was only grudgingly acknowledged. More remarkable is that the Crown and metropolitan officialdom remained resolutely and stubbornly unbowed and uncowered in some of their attitudes and policies toward Brazil.

My object is to examine the rigidity of such policies and attitudes and then turn to how, centralization and royal and conciliar edicts notwithstanding, there was the potential for flexibility and negotiation. Policies applicable to Brazil were conceived and formulated in Lisbon. While Portuguese with Brazilian experience served on the Overseas Council (the major policymaking body for overseas matters), and other councils of state in Lisbon, rarely did a Brazilian-born person serve on such councils. Alexandre de Guzmão (1695–1753) was arguably the most distinguished Brazilian-born person to gain the royal ear as statesman, private secretary to Dom João V, diplomat, and architect of the Treaty of Madrid. Yet, he was passed over by Dom José I to be secretary of state and his views on the collection of the fifth (*quinto*) due to the king on all gold extracted in Brazil were ignored by the Marquis of Pombal.[2] Metropolitan decisions were not the results of extensive exchanges even with royal representatives in the colony, let alone of broader consultation with colonists. Here a distinction can be drawn between Portuguese America and Portuguese India. Whereas only in the eighteenth century did it become commonplace for the senior Crown representative in Brazil to be accorded the title of viceroy, this had been the case for India from the sixteenth century. Moreover, viceroys in India exercised greater authority than did governors-general and viceroys in Brazil whose authority in practice was limited to the captaincy-general in which they resided. Viceroys had advisory councils, but the Conselho do Estado in Goa was more formally constituted and more powerful than its counterpart in Salvador or, as of 1763, in Rio de Janeiro. In both hemispheres there were forums for viceroys and governors-general to consult more broadly, but this practice appears to have been more prevalent in Goa than in Salvador or Rio de Janeiro.[3]

At first blush the administration of the Portuguese empire appears highly centralized and hegemonic. Absolute authority was centralized in the person of the monarch. Final decisions on appointments (civil, ecclesiastical, and military) were taken in Lisbon and subject to royal confirmation. All councils were advisory to the king and were in Lisbon. Final sentencing in major legal cases was referred to the Casa da Suplicação in Lisbon because appellate courts in Brazil lacked full jurisdiction. Agencies of government with primary jurisdiction over overseas matters—the Overseas Council, Desembargo do Paço, and Mesa da Consciência e Ordens—were in Lisbon. Unlike English, French, or Spanish America, no slave code was created for Brazil. Nor was there a corpus of laws that was colony-specific: codifications of Portuguese laws—Ordenações Manuelinas and Ordenações Filipinas—were equally applicable to the colony and were supplemented by laws known as "leis extravagantes." Administrative bodies and personnel structure in the colony were closely modeled on their metropolitan counterparts. This applied to fiscal and judicial matters, but not to inquisitorial courts that were not formally established in the colony. Municipal government in Brazil was modeled on its metropolitan counterparts. Municipal councils (Senados da Câmara) in Brazil vied for privileges granted to the councils of Lisbon, Oporto, or Évora.[4] Statutes of third orders and of brotherhoods of lay men and women in Brazil were modeled on their metropolitan counterparts and subject to royal confirmation. The Crown refused to create an administrative structure for Brazil that reflected colonial priorities and interests. When the Crown faced the challenge of administering the extraction and regulation of gold, the code (*regimento*) approved by the king in 1702 was not a new document but a revision of an earlier code of 1652 that had had its genesis in a mining code (1603) ordered by Philip III of Spain and amplified in 1618. The Intendancy of Mines in each captaincy reflected metropolitan and royal goals. Intendants of gold were appointed by the king and answerable to the king or his councils in Lisbon. When the glut of Brazilian diamonds on the European market was such as to threaten revenues to the royal treasury because of lower prices, the Crown acted by restricting diamond extraction to northern Minas Gerais, by creating a Distrito Diamantino and appointing an intendant answerable to Lisbon (1734). Diamond production became a royal monopoly and was farmed out to Portuguese-born contractors (1740–71). In 1771 the contract system was abolished and replaced by direct Crown administration from Lisbon. The administration of diamond extraction was a blatant example of Crown and metropolitan disregard for colonial interests. Movement in and out of the district was controlled; legal redress against confiscations ordered by the intendant was denied; local economies were sacrificed to the extraction of diamonds; dragoons patrolled to curb illicit extraction or smuggling; denunciations were encouraged; protests by individuals or town councils were ignored; and not even the governor of Minas Gerais had jurisdiction over this district within the captaincy.[5] The Crown preferred to exercise direct metropolitan control over extractive industries rather than create a system geared to colonial realities or entrusted to Brazilians.

At the heart of metropolitan policies was the unswerving belief that the raison d'être of Brazil was to serve as a source of raw materials and bullion and to generate revenues for the metropolis. Portuguese policies toward Brazil constituted a textbook case of mercantilism and bullionism. The corollary was that no colonial initiative was permitted if it might impinge negatively on the metropolitan economy or interests. Prohibitions on exploitation of iron deposits and restrictions on establishment of smelteries in the colony were intended to protect this important Portuguese export. That the cultivation of grapes or olives, refining of sugar, manufacture of better-quality cloth, or tanning of hides were forbidden reflected this desire to avoid competition between colonial and metropolitan production. Protoindustrialization in Brazil was prohibited; private entrepreneurial initiatives were squelched; and inventions were not encouraged. Even when Portugal itself was not the producer of items essential to domestic use or colonial production, Lisbon was the major port for transshipment for goods bound for Brazil but of European provenance from nations other than Portugal. Such goods were taxed heavily and repeatedly. No less so was the case of Portuguese Asia, where much of the revenues flowing into the royal coffers were derived from dues and taxes. Royal monopolies were imposed, at different times, on such items as brazilwood, salt, wine, olive oil, and on the practice of whaling. The Crown not only invested as little as possible in the colony, but even misappropriated funds designated for colonial ends. The classic case was the tithe (*dízimo*) levied initially on agricultural products and later extended to a broader range of commodities but whose designated purpose—as stipulated by the Padroado Real—was for support of the church and maintenance of churches in Brazil. Some funds were used for this purpose, but others were misappropriated and siphoned off for wholly secular (and even metropolitan) purposes. Payment and collection of church tithes was a long-standing source of colonial grievances and protests.

Given this mercantilist perspective, it is surprising that until 1580 there was unrestricted access to Brazilian ports by vessels of all nations. During the union of the Crowns of Spain and Portugal (1580–1640), trade to Brazil by nationals whose countries were at war with the Iberian nations was restricted. Succeeding decades saw measures imposed for commercial and military reasons on Atlantic commerce and on vessels engaged in this trade. These included launching of monopolistic overseas trading companies (Brazil Company, 1649; Maranhão Company, 1679; Pombaline companies for Grão Pará and Maranhão, 1755, and for Pernambuco and Paraíba, 1759), regulation of annual fleets and convoys, and measures to curb foreign dominance of commerce and contraband.[6]

Brazil was viewed by metropolitans, both secular and religious, as a bottomless pit whose financial resources or reserves could be tapped for metropolitan ends. It was to Brazil that Portuguese monarchs turned at times of perceived crisis or need: rebuilding of Lisbon after the 1755 earthquake; underwriting the costs of an embassy to Rome; construction of the royal palace at Mafra; or contributing to the expenses of royal marriages or dowries. In no case could these be interpreted other than as benefiting the center in terms of prestige, self-aggrandizement, or material gain, at the financial cost of the periphery. Such "voluntary" levies reflected the assumption that the obligation of the periphery was to support the center. In the eighteenth century, Brazilian wealth and riches led Dom João V to be revered by his fellow European monarchs, and Brazilian material resources—fine woods, gold, and diamonds—permitted culture and promotion of the arts to be part of the Portuguese foreign policy portfolio. The period from the 1720s to the 1750s especially witnessed the dispatch to Brazil by priors of religious houses in Portugal of friars in search of alms for metropolitan institutions precisely at a time when there were complaints by municipal councils in Brazil that unrestrained building of monasteries in the colony was a drain on local and regional economies. Moreover, that such friars frequently absconded with the alms they did collect and remained in the colony where they became disruptive influences occasioned protests from town councils, especially in the gold mining regions of Minas Gerais and Goiás.

The Crown pursued a policy of cultural imperialism. Repeated requests for a university in the colony were rejected. Outside of the Jesuit colleges there was no opportunity for higher education in the colony and the sons of Brazil were dispatched to European universities to obtain degrees.[7] There was close scrutiny of the book trade and the dissemination of ideas, notably in the later eighteenth century with fears verging on paranoia concerning "Jacobinic thoughts." This was especially distressing to Brazilian intellectuals because of the prohibition on printing presses in the colony. Works—be they technical treatises, humanistic scholarship, or even catechisms—written in Brazil, had to be submitted to censors in Portugal prior to publication. A press in Recife in the early eighteenth century was destroyed on the orders of the Lisbon authorities when its existence came to their attention in 1706.[8] The fate of another press is instructive. Gomes Freire de Andrada, a product of the Colégio das Artes in Coimbra in the early eighteenth century, and who wrote excellent Spanish and spoke fluent French, was appointed governor of Rio de Janeiro in 1733. At his encouragement, in 1746 António Isidoro da Fonseca moved his publishing house from Lisbon to Rio de Janeiro. In short order the press published a small book describing the entry of the bishop into Rio, thirteen poems, and a short essay. But even such a powerful protector as the governor could not prevail against the order from Lisbon in 1747 to close the press.[9]

Throughout the colonial period an underlying, but none the less pervasive, subtext to metropolitan correspondence with Crown representatives in Brazil is the theme of degeneracy associated with the "sons of the earth" (*filhos da terra*). There was a peripheralization of Brazil in mental, spiritual, physical, and human terms. If Portugal was seen as the hallmark of religious orthodoxy, civility, civilization, proper interpersonal relations, political stability, and refinement, comments on Brazil and its inhabitants reflected attitudes that saw land and peoples as marginalized and on the periphery, or even beyond what was acceptable. Sporadically, charges of physical degeneracy and moral turpitude were leveled against its inhabitants. Their loyalty, courage, physical stamina, moral fortitude, and integrity were questioned. Doubts were cast on the orthodoxy of their religious beliefs and degree of adherence to the canon of Catholicism. As seen from the center, there was gradation of the population of Brazil and increasing peripheralization as these deviated from the metropolitan ideal. This was based on a combination of birth, race, and whether a person counted slave ancestry. A person whose parents were Portuguese-born and who was also born in Portugal was viewed as closest to this ideal. Persons born in Brazil but of Portuguese descent on both sides were somewhat removed. There then occurred rapid peripheralization. In the case of mixed bloods, those of Amerindian-Portuguese ancestry, and thus free of the stigma of slavery, were preferred over those of Portuguese-African, Afro-Brazilian, or African-Amerindian ancestry. Amerindians were preferred over Africans. New Christians were persecuted on religious grounds, but were not as marginalized as persons of mixed race. Gypsies were excluded from society. The social marginalization of New Christians and gypsies took concrete form, namely that these ethnic groups were systematically sentenced to exile (*degredo*) from the metropolis to the Atlantic islands, Brazil, and Africa and there was a hierarchy among places for exile that reflected the negative connotations associated with such extra-European regions in the metropolitan mind-set.[10] Inquisitorial courts looked on Brazil as a purgatory where a purifying process could occur.[11] At least this did hold out the possibility for redemption. Observations by persons who accompanied the royal court to Rio de Janeiro were less positive. Rio was referred to as an "inferno"; a Babylon corrupted by the pernicious effects of slavery; a land of perdition; a Godless land whose peoples were libertines, listless, physically and morally weak, and degenerate.[12]

From the sixteenth century onward, continental Portuguese Brazil was a stage on which was played out a struggle between good and evil, virtue and vice, and God and the devil. The descent from whatever grace might have accompanied the early years of Portuguese America had been described by the "Portuguese Livy," João de Barros who, in his *Décadas* had excoriated those who had permitted the name first given by the Portuguese to the newfound land, which they called Terra da Santa Cruz, to be replaced by the name Brasil, and the evocation of Christ on the cross by a dyewood associated with commerce. The legacy of Barros's juxtaposition was to resonate three centuries later in the writings of Sebastião da Rocha Pitta and Nuno Marques Pereira.[13] If Christianity had triumphed over the devil in Europe, there was the question: To where had the devil been expelled? The vast expanses of the Americas provided a ready answer. Unlike Hernán Cortés or Francisco Pizarro and their priestly advisers or followers who readily identified alleged works of the devil in Mesoamerican or Andean religious practices and places of worship and extirpated them, in Brazil men of the cloth and lay men were less specific and went beyond demonization of the exclusively human or (in their eyes) subhuman and their mores. Meteorological phenomena, chaos implicit in climatological excesses, irregularity of the seasons, unpredictability of droughts and torrential rains, extremes of feast or famine, the apparent disorder of a topography unfamiliar and thus suspect to European eyes, all were seen as evidence of the works of the devil. These negative attitudes may also have been the product of a European mind-set incapable of coming to grips with the reality of the vast expanses of the Americas. Inhabitants of one of the smaller countries of Europe in demographic and territorial terms, and despite sparse population south of the Tagus River, Portuguese were accustomed to regimented space and to the allocation of space for specific purposes. The *terras sem fim* (literally, "infinite lands") of Angola and Brazil, by their vastness and impenetrability, created unease and even fear in Europeans. No region of Brazil and its inhabitants was so offensive to the metropolitan mind-set as was the backlands known as the *sertão*. If, for many metropolitans, Brazil represented the periphery, the sertão, whose plural form sertões was also used, was ultraperipheral. The picture of Brazil derived from metropolitan correspondence can be depressing—a hostile land of excesses of climate and topography—and contrasts with the enthusiastic comments in the treatises of Fernão Cardim, S.J., the *Diálogos das grandezas do Brasil* (1618) attributed to Ambrósio Fernandes Brandão, and the *Relação sumária das coisas do Maranhão* (1624) of Simão Estácio da Silveira, all authors who had firsthand knowledge of Brazil. Finally, the correlation between greater spatial distance from the metropolis and the attribution of greater infernalization of the land and people of that region, so apparent in the Portuguese Atlantic world, was not applicable to peoples and lands of Asia with whom the Portuguese came into contact.

This attitude may have been at the root of the reluctance on the part of the Crown to countenance Brazilian-born people holding high public office. This attitude found resonance among the religious orders. As well, the Crown was resolute in forbidding persons of "impure blood," be this measured in racial (persons of African descent) or in religious (persons of Jewish origin) terms, from holding public office. Most telling, especially compared to Portuguese Asia, was a failure tantamount to refusal on the part of the Crown adequately to recognize public service or acknowledge positions of respect held by Brazilian-born people in their communities. No black person (*prêto*) in seventeenth century Brazil gained admission into the Portuguese military Orders of Christ, Santiago, or Avis: Henrique Dias, although awarded a *hábito*, received only a medal with the king's effigy. But others of African birth or descent not born in Brazil, such as the Prince of Warri and João Fernandes Vieira, did become members of the Order of Christ. The Bahian-born mulatto Manuel Gonçalves Doria was the first and only known Afro-Brazilian to be awarded and to receive the "habit" of the Order of Santiago.[14] More surprising was the failure of Portuguese kings to grant knighthoods to the Brazilian-born (or even Portuguese-born residents in Brazil) in recognition of being pioneers in exploration and settlement, contributions to the economy by planters, merchants, and mining entrepreneurs, and those who saw long and loyal service to the Crown. In Goiás, the king did use the instrument of the royal gift (*mercê*) of a habit of the Order of Christ to reward miners who delivered their gold to foundry houses,[15] but further research is necessary to verify if this strategy was also employed in Minas Gerais and Mato Grosso. If there was one social group in the colony that was identified with the ethos and trappings of nobility and identified itself as such, it was the sugar planters (*senhores de engenho*) of the northeast, notably of Bahia and Olinda. Despite their social preeminence and economic clout they were not as much in evidence as might have been expected among those honored as knight-commanders and by other gifts that constituted royal patronage.[16]

Another clear indication of Crown and metropolitan reticence to provide any instrument whereby colonists in Brazil might emulate their metropolitan counterparts were sumptuary laws (1742, 1749) that prohibited colonists from using silks, velvets, gold, and silver in their dress, curbed ostentation in the use of gold and silver in furniture and carriages, and limited those who could carry sidearms or firearms or other symbols of elevated status.[17] When the targets of such sumptuary laws or even municipal edicts were persons of African descent, the rationale was that it was inappropriate or indecorous for such persons to adorn themselves in a manner that might lead them to exceed their social state. But, when the objects of such rulings were predominantly white, the Crown and metropolitan officials took a different tack: Expenditures on dress, carriages, palanquins, servants, and lackeys were a drain on the local economies, and such displays exacerbated underlying social tensions in the colony where social and economic inequities were rampant. Such metropolitan measures may be seen in the context of emphasizing that Brazilian-born people, who were perceived as being on the peripheries of what for the Portuguese was "society," should not be encouraged to indulge—no matter how fleetingly—in the notion that they were on a par with citizens of Lisbon or courtiers.

The above recitation reveals the extent to which the center dominated the periphery in Portugal-Brazil and metropolis-colony relationships. This dominance included the financial and commercial sectors, administration and policymaking, suppression of a colonial "voice," be this through the instrument of appointments and limited career advancement or by the absence of adequate mechanisms for colonial "input," and a form of cultural imperialism which controlled—or better, denied—a free intellectual life to the colony. Interesting is the extent to which Brazilians apparently accepted this situation; there were few outbreaks against such oppression or suppression. Was this attributable to colonial apathy, fear of reprisals, or to lack of organizational skills, of leadership and of collective conviction, or did it reflect one of two opposing sentiments—first, that expression of outrage was pointless in the face of metropolitan obduracy, or second, that there was enough porosity, elasticity, or potential for evasion in the system to make confrontation unnecessary except in cases of extreme hardship? If the latter, this represented a crucial "safety valve" that defused otherwise potentially destabilizing situations. Even more prominent uprisings—Maranhão (1684), Vila Rica (1720), Inconfidência mineira (1789), "revolt of the tailors" in Salvador (1798) and in Pernambuco (1801, 1817) were of limited duration, lacked broad-based support, and rarely had repercussions beyond the immediate locality or region. In fact, few came to full term but were betrayed or revealed prematurely. The salt monopoly and high prices provoked attacks on the salt warehouse in Santos (1710, 1734) and against the house of the salt contractor in Salvador (1710). Periodically, there were local outbreaks of protest against taxes—notably, in the sertão of Minas Gerais in the eighteenth century. Major uprisings met with draconic exemplary punishment and execution of the ringleaders: Manuel Beckman, Felipe dos Santos, and Joaquim José da Silva Xavier; in the tailors' conspiracy four were executed, and in Pernambuco in 1817 twelve were executed. This was followed by the granting of a general amnesty by the governor or the king, as in the "war of the *emboabas*," the "war of the *mascates*," Vila Rica (1720), and Pernambuco (1818) inter alia. The use of amnesty and pardons merits further study. Not only was it a strategy to bring closure to unstable situations, it also was tacit recognition of the inability of the authorities to control sustained and concerted opposition or to suppress a major uprising.

No less interesting, and indicative of a collective psychology prevailing in the colony even into the eighteenth century, is that despite resentment of metropolitan exploitation, colonists looked to the metropolis as the yardstick against which the mental, moral, or spiritual health of the colony was measured. Much in the same way as an independent Brazil during the empire turned to Europe, and especially to France, as the epitome of civilization and came up short because of the continuing presence of the institution of slavery,[18] so too did the Brazilian-born in the colony turn to Lisbon and the court. If the municipal worthies of Salvador, São Paulo, or Vila Rica petitioned for extension to them of privileges enjoyed by their counterparts in Lisbon, Évora, or Oporto; if the Misericórdia of Salvador took pride in enjoying the same privileges as the mother house in Lisbon; if sugar planters and mill owners were assiduous in their quest for honorific titles (*mestre de campo* was highly coveted); if even the inhabitants of São Paulo (*paulistas*) could be tamed by concession of royal favors and benefices; and if citizens of Rio de Janeiro, Vila Rica, or Salvador sought to adopt metropolitan styles of dress or behaviors, how are we to interpret this? Was it a craven deference to the metropolis? A desire to emulate what was, from a colonial peripheral perspective, seen as desirable? Or was the flood of requests for titles and privileges indicative of colonial insecurity and the hope that such privileges would bestow legitimacy on colonial recipients (individually or corporatively) and parity with their metropolitan peers? Or was this indicative of a more aggressive and proactive stance on the part of colonists? Were they seeking, nay demanding, metropolitan recognition, or at least validation, both as individuals and collectively? Or did such petitions reveal resentment at the fact that what was long overdue was recognition of multigenerational struggles by colonists to overcome hostile Indians, tame and settle the land, work and exploit surface and subterraneous resources, and build towns and cities? Or was it that established white elites in the colony sought privileges and titles so avidly, the more to distinguish themselves from *arrivistes* and also to disassociate themselves from the majority of the population of Brazil, which was poor and enslaved?

I do not have a ready answer, but would insist on a distinction being drawn between center-periphery relations as illustrated by our case study of metropolis and colony and the relationship between subject and sovereign. Whatever the vicissitudes on the often rocky road of relations between the Portuguese and the Brazilians, between metropolis and colony, between center and periphery, Brazilians were unswerving in their loyalty to the Crown. Petitions by colonists were often couched in language that regarded the king as fictive kin. What the colonists sought by such requests was royal recognition of their worth, of their services and of their sacrifices. Such requests were made and granted in the highly personal context of a vassal-sovereign relationship. This was summed up in the words of Cipriano Borges de Santa Ana Barros, a free black man who traveled from his native Bahia to Portugal in the waning years of the eighteenth century to conduct business, and with the express object of kissing the hand of the prince-regent: "Having successfully concluded that business which had brought him to Lisbon, there still remained for him as a loyal and humble servant the most important purpose of his visit: namely, to have the good fortune to kiss the hand of His Royal Highness and thus come face to face with Him in whose service he has the bounden duty to give the last drop of his blood."[19] Vicissitudes of center-periphery relations had no bearing on the binding nature of this social contract between kin.

The notion of a centralized metropolitan government, of the formulation of policies impervious to colonial input and implemented to the letter by Crown agents, of an unresponsive Crown, and of rigid metropolitan attitudes toward Brazil demands revision. Whereas the structure of government was highly centralized in the metropolis—indeed, this was the rationale for creation (1642) of the Overseas Council—this was paralleled by decentralization: convergence of jurisdiction and authority over multiple functions of government in a single individual or single branch of government and, on the other hand, multiple branches of government and several individuals exercising jurisdiction and authority over a single function of government. Unstated, ill-defined, or blurred areas of jurisdiction led to diffusion of authority, and rivalries and tensions between individuals and between branches of government.

Centrifugal forces attributable to multiple points of decision making and lack of coordination between individual administrators and between branches of government undermined the effectiveness of government. This opened the door for colonials to participate in government and contribute to the formulation or implementation of Crown policies.

That there existed in the administration of an empire with prescribed channels for communication there existed a mechanism whereby petitions by individuals who might be categorized generically as the "voiceless" (Amerindians and persons of African and Asian descent—notably women) could be directed directly to the king appears to be a case of Brazilian exceptionalism. Such people sought redress against cruelty by owners, illegal captivity, or denial of letters of freedom despite a reasonable offer by a slave. That such individuals were familiar enough with the appropriate strategies and channels to use an extrajudicial appellate mechanism to bring their cases directly to the king suggests that non-Europeans were not as unversed in the legal system and its mechanisms as is suggested in the historiography. The Crown was also responsive to petitions of a nonjudicial nature made by corporate groups who felt their services to be devalued by their peers or by officialdom in the colony, or that they were demeaned by the denial of that status accorded to whites in identical circumstances. These have been discussed elsewhere,[20] and may be summarized here. Militia regiments of free blacks and mulattoes received no remuneration. Petitions to the king by officers of black regiments of the Henriques of Pernambuco and Salvador for basic monthly pay and annual uniform allowances, as was the case of officers of the white militia regiments, were successful. Later, Dom João VI (prince-regent, 1792–1816; succeeded to the throne in 1816 as Dom João and ruled until 1826) extended this equality of pay to all free black officers of the Henriques throughout Brazil.[21] Officers of African descent also sought equality of privileges, namely respect for their rank, eligibility for positions in the regular paid troops, the right to wear certain insignia, and the privilege that they be tried in military courts (*foro militar*). In 1802 the prince-regent supported a resolution (1800) of the Overseas Council that mulatto regiments be commanded by officers of their own color. In this, Dom João and the council rejected the precipitate action of the governor in Salvador who had relieved such officers of their commands and replaced them with white officers of lower rank.[22] The degree to which such petitions were region specific, reflecting local demography and racial composition, was illustrated by the fact that Mary Karasch has found that already in the 1780s in Goiás the pattern was well established for mulatto regiments to be commanded by pardo officers—often the sons of prominent white fathers. Also in the eighteenth century, the governing bodies of brotherhoods of blacks and mulattoes were successful in petitions to the Crown for equality of privileges and the right to self-governance. More specifically, the brotherhood of Our Lady of the Rosary sought the privilege to have a bier for funerals of its brothers, as was the case of the white Santa Casa da Misericórdia; and certain brotherhoods of blacks secured the royal approval that the offices of treasurer and scribe be occupied by blacks and not by whites.[23] In 1759, the king acceded to the petition made on behalf of the better educated mulattoes of Rio de Janeiro and Minas Gerais that they be permitted to carry sidearms.[24]

It is tempting to see successful petitions as indicators of a softening of metropolitan policies toward the colony, and concessions to individuals or special interest groups as paving the way for greater access to public office than had hitherto existed for persons of African descent despite there remaining in force orders excluding persons of African descent from eligibility to hold public office. But the documentation suggests that these were isolated instances where the Crown responded to specific requests by specific groups for specific privileges. That these were granted was not indicative of greater egalitarianism in royal attitudes toward persons of African descent. However, demographic factors in the colony did result in local interpretations that directly contravened the letter and the intent of royal decrees concerning eligibility for public office. Persons of African descent did come to hold elective and public office in the course of the eighteenth century and were members of the priesthood and possibly of some regular orders, albeit not of the Society of Jesus. This porosity was dictated by local circumstances and did not reflect a change in center-periphery or metropolis-colony relationships.

While Brazilian-born people were eligible for public office, few reached the upper echelons of church or state. Opportunities for further promotion, as in the case of magistrates for whom the apex of their careers in the Portuguese-influenced world was appointment to the Relação of Oporto, the Casa de Suplicação or exceptionally to the Desembargo do Paço in Lisbon, were very limited other than for those born in Portugal and who had the advantages of kinship, personal networks, and the protection of powerful people in the metropolis. This extended to the religious sector. In 1736 the city councilors of Salvador complained that in the 145 years of the existence of the Benedictine Order in Brazil, few Brazilian-born people had held high office and that the order refused to admit the "sons of Brazil." In Olinda, the Discalced Carmelites allegedly refused to admit native-born Pernambucans, and sought novices exclusively from Portugal.[25]

The eighteenth century saw larger numbers of Brazilian-born people holding office in church and state. In 1730, the Bahian-born and Coimbra-educated Sebastião da Rocha Pitta wrote with pride of his fellow Brazilians who had held high office in church and state in Brazil, in Portugal, and elsewhere in the Portuguese empire, and who had achieved distinction as men of letters.[26] Even the councilors of Salvador conceded that between 1720 and 1780, three Brazilian-born men had been elected provincials of the Franciscan Order.[27] This was attributable in part to an increase in Brazilian-born people who studied at the university of Coimbra and returned to Brazil to pursue careers in the civil service; Brazilian-born persons served as colonial governors and as senior officials in the royal treasury, and on boards of inspection. It was also attributable to the increasing practice of the sale of public office, which had broader ramifications. By putting public offices on sale, the Crown opened the gate for colonists to bid and secure such offices: some were comparatively minor, such as that of clerk (*escrivão*) of a town or city; others were of considerable import, such as secretary of state, head of the royal treasury (*provedor da fazenda*) in Brazil, and even judge (*desembargador*) on the Relação of Bahia. Not only was an instrument created whereby regional landowning elites could become involved in governance at a level other than that of municipal councils, but merchants and businessmen also had access to public office. Greater participation in the decision-making process by colonists at the local and regional levels could translate into increased autonomy. Those involved in this creolization of government were motivated more by the prospect of self-enrichment than of providing additional revenues to the royal exchequer, by loyalties to kin or to the intricate web of special local interests rather than to a distant monarch, or by regional or sectoral rather than metropolitan interests. The coldly financial instrument of the contract in a way absolved contractors and purchasers of public office from their loyalties to the king or to Portugal. Purchase of office also spurred creation of local oligarchies that achieved exclusive domain over certain posts passed from father to son or given as dowries, intending to secure a marriage but equally to strengthen colonial kinship networks, reinforce the authority of colonial oligarchies, and buttress preservation of colonial capital assets. Creolization and centrifugal tendencies resulting from the sale of public offices modified center-periphery relations by giving colonists greater participation in the governing of the colony.

The Marquis of Pombal recognized this potential pool and, in the context of his efforts to nationalize the Luso-Brazilian economy, encouraged Brazilian-born people to share in colonial administration. But the available evidence casts doubt on whether such people were able to rise above the constraints and pressures at local or regional levels and gain a colony-wide perspective. If the example of business interest groups as represented in chambers of commerce in the late eighteenth and nineteenth centuries is indicative, this was not the case: They did contribute to economic and urban integration, and to improving communications, port facilities, and harbors in their respective jurisdictions but their actions and behavior reflected inter-city rivalries and exacerbated and perpetuated regionalism.[28]

Without the lubricant presented by subject-sovereign fictive kinship ties, the changing demography of the colony, and Pombaline policies that more directly sought to engage colonists in the promotion of what by then was being referred to in metropolitan correspondence as "empire"—by which was meant a bonding between metropolis and colonies in a joint endeavor for the betterment of both—the history of colonial Brazil provides numerous examples of how colonists were able to exert enough pressure to lead metropolitan authorities totally to eschew or modify a policy, delay implementation of a prescribed course of action, or negotiate a settlement less offensive to colonial interests. In its most extreme form, there was physical confrontation. Even governors were forced to flee. Under threat of attack by the planters of Olinda, in 1710, Sebastião Castro e Caldas, governor of Pernambuco, took a boat from Recife to find safety in Salvador. The governor of the captaincy of Goiás was apparently driven out of the city of Goiás in 1805 by local political elites against his will, though he later returned.[29] Other governors were rebuffed by colonists and forced to return to their home bases. These included the governor of Rio de Janeiro, Dom Fernando Martins mascarenhas de Lencastre, forced (1709) by the emboabas to leave Rio das Mortes and return to Rio; identical treatment was meted out his successor António de Albuquerque by the paulistas. Colonial pressure groups exerted enough muscle to force the ouster of governors. In Rio, merchants were behind the recall of governor Luís Vahia Monteiro in 1732.[30]

There was also the potential for negotiation, the classic illustration being negotiations over payment of the fifths (quintos) on gold production. The preferred method for collecting quintos due to the Crown pitted miners against successive to governors of Minas Gerais and the Crown. The king's initial proposal of a tax levied on *bateias* (the wooden bowls used to pan for gold) was opposed by miners. Through their town councils, miners made a counterproposal, namely that of an annual quota. This was accepted by the governor in the interests of stability and expediency, but rejected by the king who told him (in 1715) to impose the bateia method. The governor was placed in the difficult position of risking the charge of committing lèse majesté because compliance would have meant disruption. The citizenry prevailed. His successor as governor, the count of Assumar, was charged (1719) by the king to introduce smelting houses for extraction of the quintos. An uprising was brutally suppressed by the governor, but he did accept the colonists' proposal of an annual quota. The town councils negotiated an increase in the annual contribution to further delay building of a smelting house. This was a Pyrrhic victory for the miners. The first smelting house was opened in 1725. The returns were not adequate, and the king ordered that it be replaced in 1733 by a capitation tax payable by owners on slaves over the age of twelve, by free persons of color on themselves, by artisans, and by owners of shops, stores, and taverns. There were further negotiations between town councils and the governor and implementation of the royal order was delayed until 1735. As this method did not provide adequate returns, smelting houses were reintroduced in 1750. At every stage of this saga, town meetings were convoked. Seeing their interests threatened, councillors of the different towns conferred, proposals were presented to governors, and negotiations were held between governors and municipal councillors to achieve a mutually acceptable resolution of the problem.[31]

Such negotiations point out the interesting fact that Crown officials in Brazil not only negotiated with colonists but on occasion sided with colonists against the Crown. The count of Sabugosa (viceroy, 1720–35) supported the Bahian business community in its efforts to preserve its monopoly of the slave trade to West Africa and the Gulf of Benin against efforts by the merchants of Lisbon who, with the backing of Dom João V, tried to horn in on this trade. In 1734, the newly appointed governor of Minas Gerais, André de Mello de Castro, count of Galvêas joined the miners in opposing the introduction of a capitation tax. The governor also supported the local proposal of an annual quota of 100 *arrobas* (1 arroba = approximately 14.75 kilos) of gold payable to the Crown. In a protest against the royal salt monopoly and exorbitant prices, a low-ranking member of the magistracy, the *juiz de fora*, led an attack in 1734 on the salt warehouse in Santos and placed the salt on sale at the legal price. Ironically, the office of juiz de fora had been created in Brazil specifically to preside over, and thereby curb, the excesses of Senados da Câmara.

The negotiating agency representing Brazilian interests was often the Senado da Câmara. Eligibility for election to such public office, coupled with eligibility to vote being limited to *homens bons* (literally, "good men") who met stringent criteria, meant that not only were the major families of a town, city, or region represented on a council, but that inevitably the council advocated, articulated, and protected the interests of local elites. Such municipal councils enjoyed greater autonomy and were more powerful than their counterparts in Spanish America, and had extensive jurisdiction. Viceroys and governors disregarded them at their own peril, aware that influential colonials had direct lines of communication to the court and could readily gain the ear of powerful ministers or the king. Failure by a governor to negotiate or accommodate local interests might provoke a royal reprimand or lead to recall as in the case of the unpopular and mentally unstable governor Luís Vahia Monteiro from Rio de Janeiro in 1732.[32] Or it might lead to negative evaluations at the judicial enquiry at the end of an incumbent's term of office, which could decide whether or not he would be selected for higher office and a royal pension or rusticated to the provinces in Portugal. In the sixteenth and seventeenth centuries, its location enabled the Senado of São Paulo—whose royal charter as a municipality dated back to 1554—to act independently of rulings by governors in Rio de Janeiro. While no Senado in colonial Brazil rivaled that of Macao, which totally dominated the governor, such was their power and influence that they often challenged or ignored Crown authority as vested in viceroys or governors-general.

Viceroys, governors-general, and governors were subject to pressure from powerful groups such as planters, landowners, merchants, colonists, bishops, Jesuits, and members of religious orders. The mixture was particularly volatile in the Maranhão, where governors had to navigate between the Scylla of settler demand for Amerindian labor and the Charybdis of the forceful presence of the Jesuits and the Crown's desire to protect Native Americans from exploitation. Nor could they count on the support of bishops, over whom governors exercised no jurisdiction. That Crown policies vacillated between protection of Amerindians and the favoring of settlers further weakened the position of governors. The state of Maranhão provided an extreme example of competing interests but governors elsewhere found that triennial terms of office placed them at a disadvantage vis-à-vis settlers and that they lacked the human resources to force through the royal will. All too often governors-general and governors were forced to compromise, accede, or turn a blind eye to flagrant abuses ranging from forced enslavement of Amerindians to unauthorized land grabs in defiance of royal edicts.

In the seventeenth century the Atlantic economy equaled, and then surpassed, that of the route to the east via the Cape of Good Hope and revenues derived by the Portuguese Crown from fiscal controls on trade in the Arabian Sea and points further east. If most of the seventeenth century represented the apex of the prestige and political clout of sugar planters as a class, the late seventeenth and eighteenth centuries saw the emergence in Brazil of merchant communities that forcefully pursued their own agendas and challenged the hitherto indomitable supremacy of metropolitan merchants. Salvador and Recife still maintained their preeminence, but Rio de Janeiro was establishing itself as a commercial emporium for trade to the northern captaincies as well as to Río de la Plata and Angola. In the course of the century, Belém, São Luís, and Santos gained in commercial prominence. In 1618 the author of the *Diálogos das Grandezas do Brasil*, already referred to Brazil as being at the crossroads of global trade routes. The eighteenth century witnessed a number of developments that were testimony to the swing from the metropolis to the periphery in the commercial sector. First, merchants became a collective group with political ambitions. In Salvador this was acknowledged by the viceroy, who responded to requests by merchants to create a Mesa do Comércio or Mesa do Bem Comum in 1726.[33] Although the term *pressure group* was associated in the northeast with sugar planters, there was sufficient cohesion among merchants of Salvador to thwart Pombal's efforts to create a monopolistic trading company for Bahia, whereas the marquis prevailed in Pernambuco and in Pará and Maranhão. Second, whereas in the first half of the century Brazilians had primarily been commission agents for metropolitan commercial houses, by the second half more Brazilians were acting on their own behalf in Atlantic trade. This was taking place at precisely that time when the marquis of Pombal as minister of state was attempting to "nationalize the Luso-Brazilian economy."[34] Third, capital accumulation within Brazil was the driving force behind the emergence of the colony as a proactive commercial presence that was achieving a degree of independence from the metropolitan commercial hegemony. This applied to sugar planters in the northeast, whom we find diversifying and engaging in trade; to gold miners in Minas Gerais, Mato Grosso, and Goiás, who also engaged in trade and agriculture; but most especially to the burgeoning merchant community of Rio de Janeiro and its environs. Capital accumulation within the colony was critical in laying the foundation for an independent Brazil.

The ultimate irony for Portugal, a country for which mercantilism was central to its attitudes and policies toward Brazil, was that it was unable to enforce such policies. Given the multicontinental and multioceanic nature of the Portuguese presence, without a metropolitan component commerce between colonies of Brazil and Angola, Brazil and Goa or Mozambique, Diu and east Africa, and Macao and Goa—not only undermined mercantilist policies and deprived Portugal of potential revenues but also insured that profits remained extrametropolitan, thereby strengthening peripheries. The Crown remained intractable on the matter of having universities and printing presses in Brazil and tried to control the book trade to the colony both through the Atlantic ports and to the interior of Brazil via the Paraguay River to Mato Grosso, but it could not stem the flow of ideas and books from Europe to Brazil as evidenced by libraries in the colony. So too was it powerless to stop foreign participation in oceanic commerce and contraband. Soon after the restoration (1640) the Crown introduced the first measure to curb participation by foreign shipping in the Brazil trade. For the remainder of the colonial period until the opening of the ports of Brazil in 1808, measures were promulgated to restrict foreign traders and foreign vessels, or even to deny non-Portuguese access to Brazil. The goals were strategic, namely to defend the colony against intruders, but primarily to ensure that the colony was dependent—this is "periphery dependence" in the words of Jack P. Greene—on the metropolis for imports and that exports on vessels from Brazil had Lisbon or Oporto as their first European port of call.

In this the Crown was thwarted by forces beyond its control, forces that were natural (vast expanses of ocean, presence of Atlantic archipelagos, a 4,603-mile-long Brazilian coastline, and secluded harbors), human (inadequate enforcement power and foreign interlopers—notably the British), and material (shortage of Portuguese vessels). Powerful, too, was the strength shown by Brazilians (and some Portuguese) in resisting control mechanisms and regulations put in place by metropolitan authorities. A "culture of evasion" was so prevalent as to be inalienable from the colonial ethos and ultimately contributed to undermining metropolitan control. This took many forms: refusal to pay taxes and duties, circumvention of check points on trails in Brazil, dodging of military service, avoidance of being listed on municipal rolls, clandestine movement of tobacco of lower grades by night to regions associated with a higher-quality yield, or the mixture of particles of tin with gold dust. Contraband was rife on land and on the high seas. Smuggling to Africa (gold and tobacco), to Europe (gold, diamonds, tobacco, and brazilwood), and to other parts of the Americas such as the Guianas and Peru, and the clandestine exchange in the Río de la Plata of Brazilian slaves and sugar for Spanish silver and for hides. Porosity was endemic. The financial loss to metropolitan merchants and to the royal treasury was serious. So too was the unconcealable and well-publicized inability of the Crown or metropolitan authorities to control or even curb this illicit siphoning off of revenues. On the other hand, the success of such practices bolstered colonial morale, bred a sense of self-sufficiency and control, and increased access to capital, products, human resources, and the means to assert this independence of action.

There were two groups in the seventeenth century that remained largely untouched by metropolitan or colonial government. The first were some owners of cattle ranches in the sertão whose lifestyles earned them the title of *poderosos do sertão* (literally, "powerful men of the backlands"). They lived and operated for the most part beyond what to metropolitan authorities was the frontier between civilization and barbarism and beyond the limits of effective enforcement of royal edicts or Portuguese laws. Their methods of operation placed them at odds with the Crown and its representatives in the colony. Often they had armies of henchmen to act as enforcers. Such powerful men of the backlands could afford to ignore a succession of royal decrees in the 1690s limiting the size of land grants (*sesmarias*). Self-sufficiency, remoteness, and inaccessability made them impervious to Crown control. The second group were the paulistas who, from São Paulo penetrated westward, northward, and southward. São Paulo was geographically isolated by the Serra do Mar, and the plateau of Piratininga afforded few comforts. The settlement was multinational (Portuguese, Spanish, Italian, and Northern European) and multicultural (Amerindian, African, and European). The predominant language was not Portuguese but the *língua geral*, a mixture of Portuguese and Tupi Guarani. São Paulo itself had a small resident population, serving rather as a staging point for expeditions known as *bandeiras*. A self-sufficiency bred an independence of spirit, and the paulistas rejected or ignored Crown authorities. These two groups contributed in their very different ways to the colonial economy and played an important role in opening up the interior of Brazil, but they remained peripheral to, or even beyond, colonial society. At least they were not regarded as pariahs, as were the sons and daughters of Romany, exiled to Brazil and Angola as a cancer on Portuguese metropolitan society and held by colonists and governors alike as threats to law and order. That such groups remained untouched by Crown rule was attributable to their peripheral location and to their diffusion and absence of a center. That peripheralization was in itself no protection, unless accompanied by decentralization, had been graphically and tragically illustrated by the vulnerability of Native Americans to paulista attacks on mission villages in Guairá, in what today is Paraguay.

The absence of open revolt on the part of Brazilian-born people against high-handed metropolitan measures, and accommodations referred to above that reveal how Brazilians negotiated settlements with authorities in the metropolis or Crown representatives in the colony, should not lull the reader into the belief that all was well in the relationship between Portuguese-born and Brazilian-born people. At the most visceral level, there remained deep-rooted mutual distrust by many Brazilians toward the Portuguese-born, especially when they were in representative capacities but also as private individuals. The most cited outbreak of hostilities is the Guerra dos Emboabas (1707) in which the "sons of the soil" (filhos da terra) were at odds with "outsiders" (emboabas). This example of Brazilian-born versus Portuguese-born antagonisms is acceptable only with the caveat that to paulistas, anybody who was not a paulista was an "outsider." While this embraced Portuguese people from the European mainland and Atlantic islands, it also included Brazilian-born people from Maranhão, Pernambuco, or Bahia, and underlines the degree to which paulistas saw themselves—and were so identified by others—as an ethnic group, and the strength of interregional rivalries within the colony. Closer scrutiny of other disturbances, such as the Guerra dos Mascates (1711), portrayed in the historiography as a struggle between merchants of Recife and sugar planters of Olinda, may also reveal a strong component of colonial and metropolitan interpersonal distrust. Admissions registers for third orders and brotherhoods at the end of the colonial period continued to contain expressions of antipathy to Portuguese-born people.

Finally, there is the vexed question of a colonial identity. The paulistas were not alone in having a strong identification with the land. Cattle ranchers of the sertões of Pernambuco, Ceará, Piauí, Maranhão, Minas Gerais, and Bahia, and sugar planters (*lavradores de cana*) and sugar mill owners (*senhores de engenho*) of the coastal regions of the northeast must have felt a degree of identity with the land although some of the latter preferred to spend substantial periods in urban mansions (*solares*) and, even when resident on their estates, delegated to others the day-to-day management of mills and cane production. Identification between man and land was expressed in the designation poderoso do sertão. Longtime overseas residence did not necessarily mean a transfer of allegiance from metropolis to colony, but there are well-documented instances of Brazilian-born people clearly identifying themselves not as Portuguese or Portuguese Americans, but as Brazilians.

Center-Periphery: Intra-Brazil

Examination of center-periphery relations in Portuguese America opens up a Pandora's box of tantalizing opportunities for historians. The human dimension is the most intriguing but also the most elusive, namely to view the face of Brazil as measured by race and/or gender in the framework of center-periphery relations. Persons of European origin or descent dominated colonial administration and were regarded, and regarded themselves, as being at the apex of Brazilian society. Nevertheless, they remained a demographic minority throughout the colonial period. Sugar planters and merchants, at different times and in different places, constituted groups central to the formation not merely of their region but of Brazil as a whole. Writing in the early eighteenth century, the Italian Jesuit Antonio Giovanni Andreoni, better known by his Portuguese name of André João Antonil, pointed out that slaves of African descent were "the hands and feet of the *senhor do engenho*" (a dictum equally applicable to miners), and there is no doubt that slaves were central to the economic survival of the colony.[35] As shown so tellingly in the seventeenth century during the Dutch occupation (1630–54) of Pernambuco and northwards to Maranhão, the survival of Portuguese America depended on non-Europeans militarily as well as for labor and procreation. Gender also may be studied in the center-periphery framework. Only now is the historiography, so accepting of the passive role attributed in 1728 by "a pilgrim" in Minas Gerais to women of European descent in the colony,[36] being revised in the light of evidence that women of Portuguese descent acted independently, were instigators of legal cases, administered mines and plantations, managed estates, and ran their own businesses. Women of African descent were central to local commercial networks. The center-periphery framework can serve the historian well in studies of society, race, gender, occupation, culture, and language as well as administration, economies, and commerce, and stimulates a new set of questions. Given the multilingual skills of persons of African descent, was Portuguese the core language of Brazil? Was Catholicism in Portugal of such orthodoxy and uniformity, when brought to Brazil at the time of initial transmittal (let alone within the colony), that it constituted the core religion of the colony? What was the impact on Catholicism in Brazil of the dichotomy between centralization of the secular church in cities and geographical peripheralization of missionary activities? My examination of center-periphery relations in Portuguese America will be limited to the following: settlement and demography, administration, and commerce. Each had its own dynamic, although all three were interrelated at certain times and in certain regions.

A remarkable aspect of the 322 years of Brazil's existence as a colony is how patterns of settlement in place by 1600 were still present two centuries later. The preponderance of population and of cities and towns was on the littoral. Even on this littoral, there was grossly unequal distribution as the northeast and the greater Guanabara region comprised the major demographic nuclei. In general, core regions in the sixteenth century remained cores—demographically, economically, and politically—in the nineteenth century.[37] Still valid was the comment by Father Vicente do Salvador in the seventeenth century that the Portuguese were like crabs, so attached were they to the coast. While true in the broad sweep, this and similar statements conceal changing center-periphery relationships as regards settlement patterns.

At the outset I should say what I mean by *center* or *core.* For king and colonist, a center was associated with an urban nucleus. In the Portuguese world this fell into the category of *vila* (town) or *cidade* (city). Whereas Salvador had been created as a city, vilas were created as vilas, and might later be accorded the coveted status of city. Creation of such entities was the royal prerogative. The granting of a municipal charter was a royal response to a situation resulting from prior and spontaneous settlement by individual colonists that grew to the point that the Crown deemed it necessary to provide municipal government. This was the Senado da Câmara. The royal intent was to bring administrative, social, and economic stability. Not all vilas became cores other than in the local or regional sense. But for a vila which grew to assume a multifunctional role, there was the real likelihood that it would be accorded the status of city. Correlation between city and core was not automatic. Some cities never fully achieved the status of core in the context of colony-wide interests. For others, their importance waxed and waned, whereas still others retained their status undiminished throughout the colonial period. This last instance was attributable to their multifunctional roles as centers of civil government and commerce, and as bishoprics; their strategic importance for defense; their population growth; and their ability to adapt. Not surprisingly, the few urban nuclei in the colony that enjoyed city status were sited in those captaincies which, in the colony-wide context, constituted core regions: the northeast (Pernambuco, Bahia), southeast (Rio de Janeiro), and the center-west (São Paulo and Minas Gerais).

A distinction must be drawn between towns or cities with multifunctional roles and those whose prominence was attributable to a single facet. The town of Ribeirão do Carmo in Minas Gerais illustrates the latter. It was elevated to the status of city and renamed Mariana on the creation (1745) of an episcopal see. Other than in this ecclesiastical role, Mariana did not constitute a core. But its neighbor Vila Rica do Ouro Prêto, with a population of 20,000 in the 1740s, was not raised to the status of city despite the fact that it was the seat of the governor of the captaincy-general of

Minas Gerais, home to a smelting house and mint, and residence of senior fiscal officials and magistracy, and was celebrated for the wealth and elegance of its public buildings and a rich lifestyle for some built on gold.[38] There were also towns that were important points of articulation for intracolonial commerce, or centers for collection of taxes and tithes, but whose importance was never such as to make them cores.

By definition, a periphery must have a point of reference—namely, a center. Our purpose is to examine the nature of this relationship. Although distance may be a factor, this is not a sine qua non. Brazil provides numerous examples of regions that were peripheral in that they were separated from their cores not by distance but by topographical features. The Serra do Mar, impenetrable forests, or raging rivers made access difficult and transportation or communication all but impossible. There were also regions whose economic profile was so low in terms of exports, whose location vis-à-vis other regions or urban centers was such that they remained isolated, or whose administrative or military importance was so negligible on the broader canvas of the colony or to the mother country that they remained peripheral albeit self-sustaining (e.g., Espírito Santo). Some regions enjoyed a blaze of short-lived glory, attributable to economic or military circumstances. Goiás and Mato Grosso were prominent during a short golden age, but never transcended their peripheral status in the colony. The southern subordinate captaincies that, during periods of conflict with Spain, were a central preoccupation of authorities in Rio de Janeiro, but otherwise remained peripheral to the colony's interests. In their most extreme form, peripheries were associated with a term used in Angola and Brazil: *o sertão*. This was the arid and semiarid crescent extending from the interiors of Minas Gerais, Bahia, and Pernambuco to Piauí, Ceará, and Maranhão, subject to their extremes of temperature and climate, long droughts, violent storms, and flash floods. Coupled with vicious undergrowth and scrub of cacti and thorn bushes, these were a deterrent to intruders. In the minds of kings, metropolitan councillors, colonial administrators, and many colonists, the sertão or sertões were associated with disorder, deviance, and instability. They were seen as being populated by persons (according to rumor, some of whom were grotesque) who were marginalized at best or totally beyond the pale as set against metropolitan-imposed standards of religious orthodoxy, mores, morality, culture, and interpersonal relations. Civility was absent; barbarism reigned. When the word *sertão* appeared on colonial maps, it was invariably accompanied by an ethnographic qualifier, such as *sertão dos tapuias*. Given the constraints on Portuguese administration, the sertão might be beyond the reach of government or, indeed, so far removed as to be effectively outside of empire. As such, it had a high degree of autonomy. For all but the resident *sertanejos*, the sertão was a state of mind and of perceptions: to describe it merely as a periphery ignores the multiplicity of connotations that the word and the region evoked.[39]

While the term *periphery* possesses the flexibility to be applied to nonspatial relationships, it is precisely in the geographical or spatial context that it is least satisfactory and can become synonymous with frontier. In my treatment of "peripheries" I will resort to three terms used by geographers: *Umland*, *Hinterland*, and *Vorland*.[40] By *Umland*, I mean a region immediately contiguous to a core. For coastal colonial Brazil, an Umland is usually characterized by moderate climate, soils of differing composition suitable for a variety of crops, adequate and predictable rainfall, access to labor and, most importantly, proximity to markets and to a port. An Umland has close cultural, political, economic, and social links to a core/center. The region comprising a *Hinterland* is more distant from a core/center, but there is territorial continuity between the core point of reference and the Hinterland, and there exists a definable relationship, ranging from tenuous to strong, between the two. For my purpose, Hinterland does not include the region I designate as Umland nor do the two necessarily share a common boundary. *Vorland* refers to locations that do not have territorial continuity to the core, but with which the core has connections of such intensity as to constitute a significant relationship. Ports often come into this category. For colonial Brazil two examples of such close relationships between core and Vorland are those between Salvador and ports of the Gulf of Benin, or between Rio de Janeiro and Luanda or even Mozambique. What constituted an Umland, Hinterland, and Vorland was subjective, depending on the perspective or perceptions of an individual or group. The strength of the relationship was determined less by space or geography than by such factors as common gene pools; shared or strongly derivative artistic, cultural, and linguistic traits; close approximation of belief systems, values, and mores; and connections that might be political, commercial, or based on the ebb and flow of persons. All or some of these criteria could be present at any given time, but were subject to change.

The relationship between the center and its Umland, Hinterland, or Vorland was also susceptible to change. For example, a one-dimensional relationship based on an Umland or Hinterland being the prime provider of foodstuffs to a core might evolve into a more complex commercial relationship and take on social, strategic, or administrative importance: In short, it might become multidimensional. By its contiguity to a core, an Umland was unlikely to be other than the Umland for a specific core, but a Hinterland or Vorland might have this relationship to a single or multiple cores, concurrently or *in seriatum*. Conversely, time and circumstances could mean that a core did not maintain the same Hinterland or Vorland, or that two cores might share the same Hinterland or Vorland. In short, there were variants and combinations attendant on such relationships involving a core. A Hinterland could develop a relationship with another Hinterland in the absence of a core, or a Hinterland could evolve into a core. The market was the single most important factor effecting change. Such terms bring to the discussion a specificity absent in the term *periphery* while preserving the core or center as the point of reference.

The questions that must be posed are: What are the circumstances that lead to a region being designated as peripheral in spatial terms? At what stage does contiguity merge into the peripheral? For example, is the Recôncavo contiguous or peripheral to Salvador? Answers may be in spatial terms, but may also depend on the period under discussion. In the sixteenth century, sugar plantations and mills of the Recôncavo were remote enough from Salvador in terms of distance—but more importantly, in terms of accessibility and communications—that they could be considered peripheral.[41] By the seventeenth century, this was no longer the case. Greater accessibility by land and water and creation of townships in the Recôncavo made this region contiguous to Salvador. Some parishes (*freguesias*) of the Recôncavo could by then be considered part of a "greater Salvador." In the first decade of the eighteenth century-mining encampments in the westerly part of what was still the captaincy of Rio de Janeiro were peripheral to the city of Rio de Janeiro and, indeed, constituted a western frontier of the captaincy. By the 1730s, mining townships in what by then had become Minas Gerais had a different relationship with the city of

Rio de Janeiro. Regular connections and shared commercial interests made such townships more accessible to Rio de Janeiro and thus less peripheral. In both cases what had occurred was that a peripheral location, be it of plantations or mining communities, constituted a frontier of settlement initially. In a second phase, more settlement, greater accessibility to the erstwhile or current core, and a degree of administrative autonomy by such settlements not only provided a nexus to the core but also moved them from the category of peripheral to one that might be described as contiguous regardless of whether this is measured in spatial terms. They had moved within the sphere of influence of Rio de Janeiro. Complementary or converging interests between cores and erstwhile peripheries bred a sense, or perception, of contiguity. In some cases what had been peripheries were transformed into cores that developed their own network of satellites that might or might not spin off their own peripheries, or they became incorporated into what had been the periphery of the first generation core that became more powerful.

Vilas had been created in Brazil prior to the establishment of Crown government in 1549. These included São Vicente, Santos (1532), Vitória (1535), and Olinda (1537). As centers of wealth and social grace, Olinda and Salvador were preeminent prior to 1600, testimony to the importance of sugar in the formation of the colony. They were to be joined by Rio de Janeiro (1565) as core cities of Brazil. They were the only cities in the colony before 1700. To the south of Rio de Janeiro the captaincy of São Vicente included settlements at Santos and São Vicente, and inland was the small settlement of São Paulo. If, in this period there was little development in terms of cores, there was considerable development as regards peripheries. The last two decades of the sixteenth century and the early seventeenth century saw the opening up to the Portuguese of regions in Brazil hitherto inaccessible because of hostile Indians, distance from population centers, and a Dutch presence that extended (1630–54) from Pernambuco to Maranhão. The impetus to move beyond core settlements came not from Crown authorities but from three groups, none of whom were central to metropolitan or colonial society. These were Jesuits and men of the cloth in search of souls; paulistas in search of Indians and precious metals or stones; and cattle ranchers in search of pasturage. The Crown's interests, which did not amount to a policy, were colonization of strategically sensitive regions, defense against European powers, settlement of newly revealed regions, and rapid growth of a population of European origins to provide soldiers for defense. This population would also provide the basis for production of agricultural products which could sustain nuclei of settlement and for export. In reality, the Crown's contribution was negligible in financial terms and was limited to allocation of land grants (*sesmarias*), giving fiscal exemptions to selected colonists, and granting privileges to those investing in cane production. Orders were given to the crown magistrate (*corregedor*) in Lisbon to commute sentences of exile for those destined for Africa or the Estado da Índia to serve their time instead in Brazil with the express object of providing soldiers for garrisons and potential colonists. The late sixteenth century saw sustained Portuguese migration northward from Salvador/Bahia to Sergipe and northward from Pernambuco. Before century's end, Sergipe and Paraíba were colonized. The subsequent eradication of Indians, the expulsion of the Dutch, and the incentive to oust the French from north of Paraíba—coupled with the search for new lands to colonize—led to expansion by colonists both westward and northward in the seventeenth century. From Bahia and Pernambuco future settlers traveled westward and then bifurcated to the northwest and northeast through the sertão or headed southward. There was settler movement into Rio Grande do Norte, Ceará, Piauí, and Maranhão (after expulsion of the French), and sporadic entries into (rather than sustained settlement in) the delta and basin of the Amazon River. The establishment of vilas reflected these changes: São Luís, 1615; Belém, 1616; Paraíba, c. 1646–49; Fortaleza, 1699; Recife, 1709). But, for the seventeenth century these new vilas—all of which were maritime ports—cannot be regarded as being more than local or regional centers each with its own umland rather than a periphery. Small settlements came into being along cattle routes of the sertão. Belém was sui generis. The peculiarities of Atlantic current and wind systems placed Belém in a pivotal role between Lisbon and the east-west coast of Brazil and the Amazon. It was the port for exports from the north of Brazil as far as the middle and upper Amazon and the primary port for imports from Portugal that would be transshipped. As such, Belém had a hinterland but, more exceptionally for a vila of its limited size, also a vorland, namely Lisbon. In contrast, Santos, whose hinterland embraced São Paulo, remained subordinate to the port of Rio de Janeiro and did not develop transatlantic trade to such a degree as to merit consideration of an African or Portuguese port as a vorland. However, such was the legal trade to ports to the south and illicit trade to Buenos Aires that a case could be made for Buenos Aires as a one-dimensional (viz, commercial) vorland for Santos. What set Salvador and to a lesser degree at this time Rio de Janeiro and Olinda/Recife apart was that they were multifunctional, and that each had an established umland, hinterland, and vorland.

Concurrently, in the seventeenth century there was movement to the south from Rio de Janeiro and São Paulo. In the 1640s Salvador Correia de Sá e Benevides advocated, for economic and strategic reasons, settlement of the southern part of Brazil and establishment of a Portuguese presence in the Río de la Plata. In the 1650s there were settlements in Curitiba, Paranaguá (vila, c. 1646–49) and São Francisco do Sul. In 1680, the Portuguese constructed their first fort in Colônia do Sacramento.[42] Of these, only Curitiba was not situated on the sea and none of these vilas merit the name *core*. This was also the case with São Paulo. Although among the earliest vilas to be created in Brazil, São Paulo continued to be a frontier settlement with a growing population and satellite communities, but was less a core than a launching place for raiding and exploring parties (*bandeiras*) to the west, north, and south of Brazil. Such expeditions (often *razzias* against Jesuit missions to capture Amerindians whom the Paulistas would sell as slaves) were so unstructured, uncoordinated, and sporadic that they did not establish a nuclei of settlements peripheral to São Paulo, though they did extend their travels to the boundaries (and beyond) of Portuguese America as specified by the Treaty of Tordesillas (1494).[43] The seventeenth century also witnessed movement inland from coastal Rio de Janeiro into Campos dos Goitacazes, whose lands were ideal for cattle raising. But the relationship between Campos dos Goitacazes and Rio de Janeiro was that of an umland for provision of foodstuffs to the core and for providing raw materials for export. There was mutual dependency on a single level, not a multidimensional core-periphery relationship.

The eighteenth century was the age of change. Discovery of placer gold in paying quantities in the 1690s in the Rio das Velhas region set in motion a series of major gold rushes through to the 1730s, primarily in central and western regions of Brazil

(Minas Gerais, Goiás, and Mato Grosso). Places of origin of persons caught up in this fever were Portugal, Portuguese Atlantic islands and, in the case of slaves, from west and central Africa and, to a lesser degree, east Africa. The Jesuit Antonil described the broad racial spectrum: "Das cidades, vilas, recôncavos e sertões do Brasil, vão brancos, pardos e prêtos, e muitos índios, de que os paulistas se servem."[44] This was a new departure for Brazil in five regards. First, for the first time Brazil experienced migratory waves *in seriatum*. Second, this was a major mass demographic move from ports and the littoral to the interior. Third, this represented the most intensive migration to date exclusively between regions of the interior: Migrants and speculators bound for mining areas originated from Maranhão, Pará, Ceará, Piauí, Pernambuco, Bahia, São Paulo, and Curitiba. Fourth, while the river São Francisco had been an important conduit for migrants to Minas Gerais, fluvial transportation was to be a major factor in migration to the extreme west of Brazil, notably those regions that were to become Mato Grosso, Mato Grosso do Sul, and what is now Rondônia. So important was the maritime dimension that Rolim de Moura, first governor (1748) of Mato Grosso, ordered gun-carrying canoes and drew up a strategic plan for the naval defense of Mato Grosso.[45] Fifth, numbers in the interregional slave trade probably exceeded migration by whites and by free persons of African descent. This coincided with continuing migratory movements leading to settlement in the south and in Amazonas. The former was motivated by political and strategic concerns, namely to have a Portuguese presence in regions ("the debatable lands") whose ownership was contested by Spain; the latter represented the search for new lands, for labor, and for trading opportunities. Unlike the seventeenth century, the eighteenth saw Crown-sponsored migration from the Azores specifically to settle and populate southern lands. Colônia do Sacramento and Santa Catarina failed to meet expectations, but fertile soils and healthy climate, coupled with a good port and ownerless wild cattle, attracted settlers from Portugal and from as far away as Bahia and Minas Gerais to Rio Grande de São Pedro. By 1780 the population was 18,000, including 5,102 black slaves.[46] In an interesting initiative, after 1808 funds from the Intendência Geral da Polícia in Rio de Janeiro were used to bring Azorean immigrants to settle in Rio de Janeiro, São Paulo, Porto Seguro, and Espírito Santo.[47] In Amazonas, here taken to be the captaincies of Grão Pará and Maranhão, the white population probably did not exceed 2,000 in 1700.[48] Cacao and indigenous *drogas do sertão* in the Amazon basin, and cultivation of cotton on the coast stimulated by the creation by Pombal of the Companhia do Comércio do Grão Pará e do Maranhão in 1755, and cultivation of rice, cacao, and coffee in Grão Pará were not such as to induce major settlement other than an increase in the numbers of black slaves. Although this region gained in economic importance because of exports, it remained demographically and administratively peripheral to the colony. Also, because of wind systems and currents, the east-west coast of Brazil from São Roque to the island of Marajó was isolated from the rest of Brazil and could be reached more easily from Lisbon than from Salvador.[49]

The eighteenth century brought a period of incessant movement throughout the colony. This mobility reflected a pervasive and dynamic entrepreneurial spirit that opened up new opportunities and frontiers but also led to instability and civil unrest. For the first time, groups of intellectuals existed in Brazil other than in the easy-to-monitor port cities. Although there was greater spatial distribution of the population of Brazil in 1800 than in 1700, only in Minas Gerais can we talk of a significant new core population that for the third quarter of the eighteenth century not only outnumbered any other region but remained consistently at about 20 percent of the colony-wide population: 319,769 around 1776, and 407,004 in 1805. Ceará showed a remarkable growth spurt from 61,408 (3.9 percent) in 1776 to 125,764 (6.1 percent) in 1808. The captaincy of São Paulo saw a twofold increase between 1776 and 1810 but remained in fifth place: slightly more than half of that of Pernambuco and less than a third of Bahia. Persons of African descent were the majority in all captaincies (and over 78 percent in Bahia, 74 percent in Minas Gerais, and 82 percent in Goiás) by the end of the colonial period with the exception of São Paulo and Rio Grande do Sul, which maintained a white majority. Despite transoceanic and intra-Brazilian migration, for the period 1700–1820, Paraíba, Pernambuco, Bahia, and Rio de Janeiro remained the demographic core of the colony, with about half of the colony's population. At the end of the colonial period probably as much as 70 percent of the population still lived on the coast or within access of the coast.[50]

The eighteenth century witnessed increases in the population of already established coastal towns and cities and of São Paulo. Porto Alegre in Rio Grande do Sul was the only additional port town or city of any size and by 1810 was comparable to Belém and São Luís in population.[51] The eighteenth century also saw creation of townships inland; these were established haphazardly in response to local or regional needs and often associated with the supply of foodstuffs or commerce, but did not take on great importance beyond their immediate localities. The exception was the nucleus of eight townships established in Minas Gerais (1711–18), which formed an archipelago of urban growth in an area hitherto virtually uninhabited by Europeans that was transformed demographically by gold strikes. Vila Rica's population grew to some 20,000 in the 1740s. Its newly acquired status as a core was attributable primarily to its role in the production and administration of gold. The status of other townships was based solely on the relative importance of gold production in their immediate vicinity and to the degree of complexity of the fiscal and regulatory apparatus housed in them. None achieved the multidimensional stature of Vila Rica. The importance of two other towns created by gold—Cuiabá (1727) and Vila Bela (1752) in Mato Grosso—was never such as to make them colony-wide core towns. Indeed, they remained peripheral to the city of São Paulo. More perplexing and unresolved pending research is the case of Vila Boa in Goiás. A census of 1804 puts the population of the *julgado* of Goiás at 9,474; presumably the population of Vila Boa was smaller.[52] While Vila Boa's population did remain small, Mary Karasch makes a strong case for considering it a significant core. She notes that officials at the Tribunal de Contas in Lisbon were concerned about Goiás, which in 1775 was the fifth wealthiest captaincy in Brazil; that Vila Boa was an administrative center with jurisdiction over a vast region; that it was a vital entrepôt for commerce to Vila Bela and—via the Araguaia/Tocantins river system—to Belém; and that it was a hub for mining through to the 1790s. While not an episcopal see, Vila Boa also played a significant role as a religious center.

The case of Vila Rica is instructive. Despite economic decline with the exhaustion of mineral resources and a vertiginous drop in population to some 7,000 by 1804, Vila Rica remained the capital of Minas Gerais until superceded by Belo Horizonte in 1897. But it was an administrative capital only: Politically and economically it increasingly became of marginal importance. It bears out the maxim that, to be a core city, it was essential to be multifunctional. Creations of the extractive industries—the vilas of Sabará, São João del Rei, São José del Rei, Ribeirão do Carmo (Later city of Mariana), Vila do Príncipe, Vila Bela, and Vila Boa—never attained that combination of commercial, administrative, economic, and social functions such as to become core towns in the colony-wide context. The same applied to townships of the Recôncavo. The prominence of Santo Amaro was attributable to the wealth and social prestige of some of its inhabitants derived from sugar production but, for that very same reason, it did not constitute a core even among townships of the region. Once again, São Paulo is sui generis: Its location made it the launching point for exploratory expeditions by water and overland to the west in the first half of the eighteenth century, to which can be added its change of status with elevation to the rank of city in 1712. But it was passed over to be capital of the newly created (and short-lived) captaincy of São Paulo and Minas Gerais in 1710. Only with the administrative dismemberment of this vast region in 1721 did it become the capital of the captaincy of the same name. But neither this nor a population (24,311) that rivaled that of Recife (25,000) in the first decade of the nineteenth century could make it more than a regional capital with limited resonance beyond its own borders.[53]

Turning from settlement to administration, the seventeenth and eighteenth centuries witnessed three trends that have a bearing on center-periphery relations. The first was a concerted effort by the Crown to remove the anomaly of some captaincies being owned by individuals and others by the Crown. The Crown sought to regain control of captaincies granted to donatories in the 1530s and private captaincies created subsequently. This was finally accomplished in 1761 with the annexation of Ilhéus to Bahia.[54] The second trend was the fragmentation and reformulation of the administrative structure of the colony in attempts to assert greater Crown control. This occurred in the sixteenth century and early seventeenth century (1572–78; 1608–12) with an administratively divided Portuguese America. From 1621 to 1772 (except for the years 1652–54) the captaincies of Ceará, Maranhão, and Pará formed the Estado do Maranhão e Grão Pará and were not under the jurisdiction of the governor-general or viceroy in Salvador and later in Rio de Janeiro. From 1658 to 1662 the captaincies of Espírito Santo, Rio de Janeiro, and those to the south were detached from the authority of governors-general in Bahia and formed a unit known as the Repartição do Sul under the governorship of Salvador Correia de Sá e Benevides. This arrangement was ad hoc as well as ad hominem, in recognition of his services to king and country. After his death they reverted to the jurisdiction of the governor-general in Salvador. The third trend was that, in the eighteenth century, the Crown responded to new demographic, social, economic, and strategic developments by creating new captaincies-general and subordinate captaincies. This was a dynamic process. Initially the captaincy of São Paulo and Minas Gerais extended to Mato Grosso, Paraná, and Rio Grande do Sul. Later, Mato Grosso and Rio Grande do Sul were separated from São Paulo, which itself became subordinate to the captaincy of Rio de Janeiro before regaining its autonomy as a captaincy in 1765. The territory of Goiás, initially part of the captaincy of São Paulo, became a captaincy in its own right. New captaincies were São Paulo and Minas do Ouro (1709–20), Minas Gerais (1720), São Paulo (1720), Goiás (1748), and Mato Grosso (1748). These were in addition to the older captaincies-general of Pernambuco, Bahia, Rio de Janeiro and, after 1772, Maranhão and Grão Pará. By 1800 there were ten captaincies-general and seven subordinate captaincies.[55] Attempts to centralize control over the captaincies under the Crown and concurrently to exert greater Crown control by dividing vast territories into manageable administrative entities under governors, *capitães gerais* and *capitães mores* were largely thwarted by an administrative fragmentation stemming from the continuation of a captaincy structure. Not only did this place considerable power in the hands of the "man on the spot," but undermined the unity of the whole by pitting governors against each other. The result was decentralization of metropolitan authority and increasing authority being embodied in governors on what had hitherto been the peripheries of Brazil.

New administrative units such as the short-lived Repartição do Sul and the more enduring Estado do Maranhão e Grão Pará also undermined what had hitherto been at least the perception of a single entity called Brazil. In the case of the Estado do Maranhão e Grão Pará it could be argued that, because of its location and difficulty of communications between the east-west coast and the north-south coast, this was, and always would be, peripheral to the administrative center of Brazil, be this in Salvador or Rio de Janeiro. But the administrative link forged between this new state and the metropolis undermined the hitherto exclusive nature of a single colony-metropolis relationship. The Repartição do Sul, although short-lived, was more serious because the captaincies that constituted the new entity were integral to what had hitherto been Brazil. From Espírito Santo southward, these coastal captaincies were parts of the network of cabotage along the north-south coast of the colony. In terms of agricultural production, coastal defense, and population, these captaincies were important to the integrity of the colony. Finally, Rio de Janeiro was already beginning to emerge as a major port with a growing population, its own mercantile community, development of the *Baixada fluminense* (the lands abutting the Bay of Guanabara), and as a gateway to São Paulo. That this Repartição was created in recognition of service by an individual and in expectation that he would provide more dynamic leadership than would otherwise have been the case was an affront to the governor-general in Salvador. Such fragmentation diffused what had been a direct line of authority from the king or his councils to the governor-general in Salvador. In the colony, centralization of authority in the persona of the governor-general was weakened correspondingly.

If governors-general and viceroys were, hierarchically speaking, at the center of the colonial administrative structure, and governors subordinate to them, distance and problems of communication combined to undermine their effective authority. Regional differences also militated against the colony-wide applicability of a single policy. The eighteenth century saw such problems becoming more acute with the move to the west and creation of new judicial districts (*comarcas*), captaincies-general, and subordinate captaincies. This century saw the emergence of governors of captaincies-general as the dominant forces in colonial administration. There was increased erosion of the authority and prerogatives of the governor-general or viceroy. In part, this was attributable to the continuing practice of exempting some areas from his jurisdiction, or merely giving him nominal but not effective authority over others. Into the former category came the archbishop and bishops, who were exempt from his jurisdiction; into the latter came his role merely as presiding officer over the two *relações* (high courts of appeals) and financial juntas. It was also attributable less to any curtailment of viceregal authority but to the fact that his jurisdiction, privileges, and prerogatives were extended to governors who made appointments, issued land titles, and exercised jurisdiction over matters (including military matters) internal to their respective captaincies-general. The governor-general or viceroy had explicit instructions not to leave the seat of government without royal written authorization. He had supervisory authority over a slew of tribunals in Salvador or Rio de Janeiro, but effectively his jurisdiction was limited to that captaincy-general in which he resided and was the seat of colonial government.[56] Although they were exhorted to keep the viceroy posted on breaking developments in their captaincies-general, often governors failed to do so and corresponded directly with the king and Overseas Council in Lisbon.[57] Governors of Minas Gerais of the stature of Dom Pedro de Almeida e Portugal and Dom Lourenço de Almeida—the former who would go on to be viceroy (1744–50) in India and the latter who had served in that capacity prior to coming to Brazil—were well enough connected at court to forgo the niceties of informing a viceroy in Salvador of their actions. But there was also the problem of ill-defined areas of jurisdiction: The Count of Assumar alleged that he was given no regimento establishing his own special responsibilities and relations with other organs of government. Governors of captaincies-general often fitted the same profile as viceroys—of noble birth, military service, and prior administrative experience—but incumbents of such offices in the eighteenth century often had better-honed organizational, managerial, and logistical skills than their predecessors. Gomes Freire de Andrada, appointed governor of Rio de Janeiro in 1733 but who over the next thirty years came to exercise jurisdiction over more of Brazil than the viceroy, exemplified this new breed of executive governor-general.[58] Exceptional in terms of ability, dynamicism, and independence of thought was Luís António de Sousa Botelho e Mourão, governor of São Paulo from 1765 to 1775.[59]

The result was increasing decentralization of authority and attenuation of links between center and periphery at two levels: center as represented by the king and Overseas Council and periphery as represented by the viceroy; and center in the person of viceroy and periphery as represented by governors of captaincies-general. What had been defined and respected lines of command became blurred. Whether the emergence of what might be described as executive ("systems-oriented," in current idiom) governors was attributable to the vacuum in authority stemming from this change or whether they were the agents of change is unclear.

Three other related circumstances are relevant. The first is the exceptionally important role in the Portuguese overseas empire exercised by the magistracy. There was a symbiotic relationship between the Crown and the magistracy: creatures of the king, to whom they owed their appointments and the authority delegated to them, magistrates as a collectivity were strong and consistent upholders of royal authority. As such, they were the king's eyes and ears. It was to this group that kings turned to fulfill extrajudicial duties of a social, economic, and administrative nature and for special assignments. For the seventeenth and eighteenth centuries no group in colonial Brazil constituted such a powerful professional class. While they reinforced Crown authority, *desembargadores* of the Relação (the highest appellate court in the colony) could constitute a challenge to viceregal authority. At a lower level, regional judges (*ouvidores da comarca*) could be a threat to the authority vested by the king in a governor: The count of Assumar was overruled by Crown judges whom he had convoked to implement royal policy. At the lowest level, Crown judges known as *juízes de fora*, introduced into Brazil in 1696, had multiple responsibilities—both judicial and administrative—within a municipality, which caused tensions with locally elected officers.[60] Crown authority was reinforced, but at the expense of the authority delegated by the king to viceroys, governors, or holders of elected municipal offices.

The second development, primarily in the eighteenth century, was the introduction of groups of skilled and specialized civil servants into Brazil to meet specific needs. Some were linked to the extractive industries: the smelting and assaying of gold; the minting of colonial currency; the regulation of the extraction of gold and diamonds; and the collection of the royal fifths. Others were attributable to Pombaline fiscal reorganization: the quality control of agricultural exports; the introduction of a double-entry system of bookkeeping. While under the jurisdiction of viceroys or governors, such skilled personnel had their own institutional and occupational cultures. Some, the *provedor* of the mint and minters being the most flagrant examples, claimed privileges exempting them from the full authority of a governor. As was noted earlier, the intendant of the Diamond District had virtually absolute authority and acted independently of both the governor of Minas Gerais and the viceroy.[61] The result was twofold: There came into being a group who, by virtue of their occupations, were not part of established administrative agencies; nor were they answerable to officials of the royal treasury or judiciary but to the intendant of the mint, who himself enjoyed a degree of autonomy. The presence of such specialist cadres weakened the centralization of government in certain regions of the colony but also constituted a challenge to the authority of a viceroy or governor.

The late seventeenth and eighteenth centuries saw another trend that weakened metropolitan control and eroded the authority of a governor-general or viceroy. Longevity in a posting far exceeding the initial triennial appointment became more prevalent not only among senior officers of the fisc and magistracy but to an even higher degree among middle-level bureaucrats in the treasury and judiciary. Many Portuguese-born people became so enamored of Brazil that they were unwilling to leave their postings. For the Brazilian-born, the pressures to remain in a colonial posting in excess of the first term were overwhelming. One judge served on the Relação of Salvador from 1678 to 1702. Some civil servants sought multiple renewals of their appointments; others left the royal service but remained in Brazil. Royal attempts to insulate Crown appointees from colonial pressures were thwarted by powerful colonial social mechanisms to which they became subject. Some were insidious: choice of place of residence; social prestige associated with election to the Santa Casa da Misericórdia or a third order; invitation to be the godparent of a newborn. Others were more blatant, such as marriage to a local woman or entering into joint commercial enterprises. While there could be advantages, such as better appreciation of a colonial perspective, disadvantages included the potential for blackmail, embezzlement, or deflection (*desvio*) of public funds, abuse of office, or sale of judicial favors. A 1799 governor-general's report for Brazil referred to magisterial influence peddling, amorous trysts, and socializing with planters and merchants whose cases were *sub judice*.[62] When taken in conjunction with the sale of public office, and increasing numbers of Brazilian-born people assuming administrative roles in the governance of the colony, there was great potential for the attenuation of the centralizing and centripetal force exerted by Crown and metropolis, and of the authority vested in governors-general and viceroys by the king.

The eighteenth century brought to a head systemic shortcomings in Portuguese overseas administration that revealed the tensions between centralization and decentralization of administrative authority. In the regulation of the extractive industries, the Crown sent a strong and unambiguous message. Elsewhere, the messages were ambivalent, ambiguous, contradictory, and lacking in consistency. By granting authority to intendants and provedores of the mint, by exempting certain officers of church and state from viceregal or gubernatorial authority, and by fragmenting the administrative structure of the territory, the Crown undermined its own efforts to assert metropolitan control. By attempting to micromanage sectors of the economy and administration, the king and the Overseas Council came to reinforce the authority and legitimize the role of members of the magistracy and governors at the expense of viceroys or governors-general. Regional variations in the enforcement of policies, notably as regarded use of gold as legal tender, distribution of coins, and in the methods for collection of the fifths, were highly disruptive. The peripheralization and dilution of authority reached its peak with the delegation to prominent but nevertheless private citizens of responsibilities such as raising auxiliary troops, collecting taxes, enforcing law and order, curbing revolts, or attacking communities of runaway slaves (*quilombos*). But even they could not conceal the fact that at the end of the colonial period much of the vastnesses of Brazil remained outside of empire in administrative terms.

Colonial commerce provides particularly striking examples of the dynamic of center-periphery relationships. The sixteenth and seventeenth centuries saw the consolidation of already existing commercial relationships. Via the ocean these were between Lisbon and Brazil, Brazil and west and central Africa, and to a lesser degree Brazil and southeast Africa and Asia. These reflected supply and demand factors that remained mostly unchanged as regards their composition: simply put, American raw materials in exchange for European manufactured goods and specific food stuffs; American demand for African labor. Oceanic legs were complemented by coastal trade that grew in the sixteenth and seventeenth centuries and whose expanding network reflected new settlements, new ports, and new markets in Brazil. While there was an increase in the intensity of oceanic and coastal trade, less evident is that this led to changes in center-periphery relationships. Demand for the supply of foodstuffs to port cities and towns was met (excepting meat) by small holdings (*roças*) in a region (umland) contiguous to the markets. For Salvador this was the Recôncavo. This was a mutually beneficial and reciprocal relationship. Salvador was not only a market for foodstuffs from the umland, but it was also the source of supply for imported goods from Europe and Africa. By the mid-seventeenth century a relationship had developed between Salvador and a hinterland. Hitherto, although Salvador had derived its supply of meat from the sertão, the relationship between center and periphery had been tenuous, virtually limited to the supply of meat on the hoof. By mid-century, the region beyond the Recôncavo had become sufficiently colonized to become a market for goods imported through Salvador. Social links were being established between hinterland and city. The connections between merchants of Salvador and these areas that were both supply areas and markets was very important.[63] This model of development from center-periphery (center-umland) to center-umland-hinterland may be applicable to other port towns. But as cattlemen moved further into the sertão, the combination of topography, distance, climate, and lack of grazing meant that they were ever more removed from their coastal markets. This led to a switch from meat on the hoof to trade in hides or dried meat. It also meant that for an area such as the sertão that was peripheral to colonial markets, if it was to gain access to metropolitan markets for its surplus production it was dependent on Brazilian ports.

In the eighteenth century, these linkages continued. With more settlers moving up the Amazon, and coastal communities growing from the mouth of the Amazon southward as far as Ceará, Belém and São Luís grew as markets and export ports for foodstuffs and other commodities, but also as way-stations for imports from Europe and Africa. Salvador and Recife continued as major centers for imports and exports, and as markets for food supplies from as far south as Espírito Santo, as far north as Rio Grande do Norte, and from the Recôncavo and Várzea and their hinterlands. Rio de Janeiro was the third major center whose "catchment area" for foodstuffs extended north to Espírito Santo, and southward, but also to the interior. More importantly, suddenly there was a hitherto unparalleled opportunity for Brazilian ports. The catalyst that created new relationships between centers and peripheries in general and between center-umlands and hinterlands in particular was discovery of gold in Rio das Velhas in the 1690s and gold rushes—primary, secondary, and tertiary—over the next fifty years. New markets in Minas Gerais and other mining areas proved the salvation of cattlemen. The São Francisco valley provided an easy route for herds of meat on the hoof. Subsequently a cattle industry, hitherto associated with the north and northeast, grew in Minas Gerais, Mato Grosso, Goiás, and São Paulo, and later in Rio Grande do Sul, for the inland markets, primarily São Paulo and Minas Gerais. Discoveries of gold deposits had an impact on all ports. Salvador and Recife acted not only as ports of entry for those inflicted with gold rush fever, but also expanded their range of internal markets for European-made goods and African slaves. They also became export ports for gold from southern Bahia and Minas Gerais. The Rio São Francisco and its valley was an important artery for people and commodities. With settlement in Mato Grosso and northern Goiás, fluvial navigation made possible the establishment of commercial links to the northerly port of Belém. To the south, Paranaguá took on greater importance because of its location as an access point to the escarpment and the plateau that included Curitiba and other settlements. All ports developed an umland that provided them with foodstuffs, primarily, and hinterlands based on supply and demand factors. Ports also became intermediary way-stations for imported goods destined for markets in a contiguous umland and more distant hinterland(s).

Nowhere was exploitation of mineral resources, population moves away from the coast, colonization, and urbanization in the interior to have such an impact as on the port city of Rio de Janeiro. Rio became a major player in Atlantic trade, cabotage, and intra-Brazilian trade. In the seventeenth century merchants had developed considerable prominence; their position became unassailable in the eighteenth century. The primary destination in Brazil for slaves directly from Africa moved from Bahia and Pernambuco to Rio de Janeiro. Furthermore, large numbers of slaves arriving in the northeast were transshipped to Rio de Janeiro. It has been estimated that one-half of all slaves imported into Brazil in the eighteenth century passed through Rio de Janeiro.[64] Rio replaced northeastern ports as the major distribution point for slaves within Brazil. In the eighteenth century, Rio de Janeiro was also the major Brazilian port in the clandestine trade to Río de la Plata exchanging slaves and sugar for Spanish silver. Only in 1763, with the transfer of the colonial capital from

Salvador to Rio de Janeiro, was the political importance of Rio to receive tacit recognition; but already Rio de Janeiro had supplanted Salvador and Pernambuco as the commercial center of Brazil and the process of Balkanization—which was to reach its height in the nineteenth century—was under way.

The emergence of Rio had a ripple effect on the creation of new intra-Brazilian relationships. In 1700, the umland of Rio de Janeiro was the Baixada fluminense. While the governor of the captaincy-general of Rio de Janeiro had administrative jurisdiction over a broad swath of territory extending north, south, and west, these regions were peripheral rather than constituting a hinterland. The relationship to São Paulo and Santos likewise was center-peripheral rather than center-hinterland. Seventy years later, Rio was a major center with multiple vorlands, umlands, and hinterlands. As regards vorlands, these were in Angola and (a new development for Rio) in East Africa; the former was unifaceted and was virtually exclusively driven by the slave trade, but there were multidimensional relations to the latter that saw commodity exchange in addition to the slave trade and human and financial investment in Mozambique by Brazilian merchants and traders who took up residence, owned shops, and married or cohabited with local women.[65] By 1770, Rio de Janeiro was also the center of a coastal trade in foodstuffs for the city that radiated as far north as Bahia for manioc flour and as far south as Rio Grande do Sul for jerked beef (*charque*) and wheat.[66]

If Rio developed as a center and an entrepôt for blue water and coastal trade, it was also the center of an extensive supply and trade network in foodstuffs, embracing much of central and southern Brazil. The network's livelihood was based on Rio as "the most important entrepôt and urban consumption center in the southern half of Brazil."[67] For merchants who lacked the capital required to invest in oceanic trade, intracolonial trade offered considerable financial advantages.[68] The city of Rio de Janeiro was the center for an umland and multiple hinterlands. The immediate umland was the Baixada fluminense. Larissa Brown has described as a "little hinterland" the coastal region roughly from Cabo Frio to Angra dos Reis, which includes the Baixada and its many rivers flowing into the Bay of Guanabara: It provided the city with staple foodstuffs and exported sugar.[69] What is revealing is how visitors described rings of cultivation around the city. Within an immediate radius of approximately twelve miles, moving away from the center the rings were forage and horticulture, cows and sugar cane, and mixed agriculture. In the course of the century, Campos dos Goitacazes also developed a relationship sufficiently intensive as to constitute an umland. Brown describes as "coastal hinterlands" the region from Espírito Santo southward to Rio Grande do Sul, in distinction to what I would call "an interior hinterland," which comprised Minas Gerais and the interiors of São Paulo and Rio Grande do Sul.[70] Mato Grosso and Goiás remained peripheral to Rio de Janeiro, although their connection to the outside world was through the entrepôt of Rio de Janeiro and thus might be included in this hinterland. Concurrently, Goiás was part of the hinterland of Bahia. Trade in cattle and the legal and illegal transportation of gold occurred between Goiás and Salvador, and Mary Karasch has suggested that Goiás was the place of origin of inferior-quality tobacco shipped from Salvador to Africa for the purchase of slaves.[71] Whereas in the early gold rush decades, mining regions had siphoned off foodstuffs, tools, and slaves from coastal regions, later the tide changed and they became suppliers of foodstuffs to Rio especially and for export. In the case of Minas Gerais the relationship had two phases, partly overlapping. The first was attributable to the importance of Rio as the prime export port for Brazilian gold and entrepôt for imports from Europe and slaves from Africa in great demand in mining areas. With increasing affluence in Minas Gerais, the nouveaux riches were consumers of luxury goods from Asia and Europe. Diversification of the economy in Minas Gerais enabled the captaincy to survive the decline in gold production. In this second phase, Rio was again the beneficiary as the major market for farming and cattle products from Minas Gerais. Rio de Janeiro also became the hub for a supply network in foodstuffs that extended to Minas Gerais and the southeast and included mules and cattle. The arrival in 1808 of the court provided the incentive to further develop the central-southern internal economy to meet a surge in demand for foodstuffs as well as stimulating foreign trade by opening the ports: Rio was the prime beneficiary again. In short, there was no city of the Portuguese overseas empire in the late eighteenth and nineteenth centuries that so merited the title of *center* (of colony and empire) as did Rio de Janeiro.[72]

That Rio de Janeiro should have achieved this central role was attributable to the vitality of a burgeoning merchant community. This community merits closer scrutiny because it was to play a decisive role in altering center-periphery relations between Portugal and Brazil and within the colony. Unlike Salvador, where merchants shared affluence, social prestige, and political power with planters and sugar mill owners, in Rio de Janeiro merchants had a virtual lock on political power, the economy, and social prestige. Before century's end, most of the capital accumulation was in the hands of the merchant sector. As in Bahia, there was a hierarchy among members of the merchant community of Rio de Janeiro.[73] An elite included merchants engaged in oceanic and intra-Brazilian trade. The former included long-haul merchants (*comerciantes de longo curso*) who owned vessels in which they traded within the Atlantic basin,[74] but also with Goa, Malabar ports, and Macao. This elite dominated the Atlantic trade and internal trade. One characteristic was that its members engaged concurrently in a broad spectrum of business activities: export and import trade; trade on their own account; and as insurers of consignments. The financial demands of oceanic or transoceanic trade—high initial investment and high risks—demanded high liquidity. Because of this, a select group of the very wealthy also dominated the slave trade and made smaller traders dependent on them for credit, loans, vessels and commodities for exchange.[75] But there was also ample opportunity for capital accumulation by merchants engaged solely in internal markets and who created a power base through their control of intra-Brazilian regional commerce in central and southern Brazil. The most successful merchants built a portfolio based on asset allocation: commerce, financial sector, coins and precious stones, slaves, and urban and rural properties.[76] In a region that had hitherto lacked a landed aristocracy, members of the merchant community—by transforming liquid capital into land—created and reinforced a social aristocracy based on ownership of land, production of an export crop, and slave labor.

This community played a major role in altering the balance between Portugal and Brazil. Portuguese policy was quintessentially mercantilist. Recent research suggests that not only was metropolitan control over colonial production incomplete but that, no less importantly, the Portuguese Crown was not able to control either intercolonial commerce (between Rio de Janeiro and Angola; Rio and Mozambique; or Rio and Goa) or intra-Brazilian trade. This was attributable in part to lack of personnel, in part to a colony-wide regulatory system that imposed its own criteria as to what was legal or illegal and thus condoned or condemned,[77] and in part to a pervasive culture of evasion, that raises the question as to whether this is culturally inherent to peripheral regions or the result of inadequate metropolitan control. This was apparent in illegal extraction of diamonds, circumvention of gold registers on roads between production areas and smelting houses or between mining areas and ports, refusal to pay the royal fifths, or trading in other than third-grade tobacco to Africa. There was extensive contraband trade from Rio de Janeiro to Río de la Plata, from Brazilian ports to the Atlantic islands, Africa, and Portugal, in addition to collusion with non-Portuguese ships' captains that led to Brazilian diamonds, gold, and precious stones having Amsterdam and London rather than Lisbon as their final destination.

This also raises the question of the degree to which merchants in Brazil acted autonomously of, or merely as agents for, metropolitan commercial houses, as alleged by the marquis of Lavradio in reference to the *comerciantes* of Rio de Janeiro.[78] Data from registers of bullion consignments from Brazil to Portugal suggest that by the mid-eighteenth century merchants in Brazil were acting on their own behalf rather than at the express bequest of metropolitan merchant houses. It was they who increasingly were the consignors and insurers of remittances of bullion and precious stones.[79] Moreover, they were gaining access to colonial credit networks. The Bahian and carioca experiences reinforce this impression. In both, the major sources of credit were colonial, not metropolitan, an important indicator of the potential for capital accumulation within the colony from agricultural activities as well as from the export sector. This capital remained in the colony and was critical in the creation of further opportunities and stimulating growth in the commercial and agricultural sectors by the availability of credit and liquid capital for investment within the colony. Capital accumulation within Brazil served as a cushion against fluctuations resulting from conditions (political, dynastic, or economic) external to Brazil that would otherwise have been deleterious to the colonial economy. In short, merchant communities in Salvador and Rio de Janeiro had weaned themselves from dependency on metropolitan sources for credit and dependency on metropolitan merchant houses and increasingly in the course of the eighteenth century moved toward achieving a high degree of autonomy from metropolitan control.

Conclusion

The overall theme of this essay is the divergence between what has been seen in the historiography as metropolitan hegemony and a highly centralized administration and the reality of what Jack P. Greene has described as "negotiated authorities" and decentralization.[80] A metropolitan statement of principles vis-à-vis the periphery, namely Brazil, was unambiguous: The center exerted full control over the periphery; the periphery should exist without infusion of funds from the center; the periphery existed to support and advance the center; and any relationship entered into by the periphery other than exclusively with the center was illegal. Systemic flaws in metropolitan administration, ill-conceived and inconsistent Crown policies for the colony, inflexibility in implementation of orders, and failure to acknowledge the uniqueness of Brazil contributed to undermining the authority of metropolitan councils. Indeed—and here an increase in the incidence of crime might be an indicator—it may well have been that within Portugal itself, the eighteenth century witnessed an attenuation in the degree of control exercised by the central government over regional matters.

In Brazil, colonists were quick to recognize this vulnerability and the administrative lacunae, breaks in the chain of authority, and the indecisiveness that resulted. In their quest for participation in policy and decision making, colonists were further aided by natural circumstances: distance from center to periphery, defective communications, demography, human failings on the part of the king's representatives, and the sheer size and diversity of the many Brazils. The history of the colony is a trajectory toward increasing erosion of the mercantilist principles on which the metropolis had built a colonial compact, and the progressive assertion of participation by the periphery without this necessarily being synonymous with the acquisition of "periphery rights."[81] Herein may lie a distinction between the British and Portuguese empires in the Americas. Whereas in the former the colonists fought for "rights," in the latter the colonists sought to exploit fissures and weaknesses in the system to achieve their goals but without, for the most part, risking confrontation by directly and overtly challenging the authority of the king or the metropolis. Thus it is that in the course of the seventeenth and eighteenth centuries Crown positions concerning appointments, taxation, and monopolies were subverted by colonial pressure groups and by strategies that included negotiation, resistance, evasion, and simple disregard. The one area where colonists failed was in their quest for a university.

These accommodations in favor of the periphery in center-periphery relations were echoed within the colony by changes in settlement patterns, governance, and patterns of trade that occurred without orchestration but that, when taken together, represented assertions of collective thought and actions in a Brazilian rather than an imperial or even colonial context. The dispersal of population radiating out from the Portuguese-dominated major port cities into regions hitherto unpopulated by Europeans and increasingly distanced from seats of metropolitan government in the colony was the most evident example of this centrifugal urge. Metropolitan contortions to assert administrative control were of limited effectiveness. The metropolitan institution of the Senado da Câmara was co-opted to colonial ends. Concurrently, there was greater Brazilianization of the personnel in Crown agencies of government in the colony, attributable as much to metropolitan decisions as to any self-assertion on the part of Brazilian-born people. This progressive wresting away of control from hitherto exclusively metropolitan-dominated decision making and governance finds its parallel in the commercial sector, where not only merchants but planters were accumulating enough capital to diversify their asset allocation with a view to what was in their own best interests rather than in response to metropolitan orders or compliance with policies to support or enhance the metropolitan economy.

Within the eighteenth century, and well before either the arrival of the royal court let alone the unilateral declaration of Brazilian independence, the periphery possessed leadership cadres, a sense of "Brazilianness," commodities for exchange, networks of informal communication, webs of trade, capital, an appreciation of the territory of Brazil, and ideas. Furthermore, there was social and commercial interaction not only between peripheries within Brazil but, in the broader sense from the metropolitan perspective, between Brazil as a periphery and other peripheries of empire as represented by Portuguese holdings in west, central, and east Africa; India; and east and southeast Asia. The development of such periphery-periphery linkages not only diminished the role of the metropolis as a commercial partner but enhanced Brazil as the leader among Portuguese overseas colonies. Many of these linkages occurred parallel to, in interaction with, or independent of, metropolitan-inspired or -controlled principles, assumptions, or practices. Even before 1808, condoned or condemned illegal trade had seen the forging of links from Brazil to North America, the Caribbean, and Northern Europe. When the prince-regent chose Rio de Janeiro as the seat of his court, with great enthusiasm he went about embellishing and modernizing the city and promoting commerce and scholarship. But he was no less diligent in providing the entrepôts with vorlands through opening up the ports of Brazil to international trade, to establishing and enhancing fluvial and land-based transportation and communications to break down obstacles between centers and peripheries and between peripheries themselves, to promoting domestic industries and agriculture, and to giving attention to the peripheries such as Goiás and Pará. For the first time, a future king of Portugal was to see Brazil on Brazilian rather than on Portuguese terms.

Notes

1. António Vasconcelos de Saldanha, *As Capitanias: O regime senhorial na expansão ultramarina portuguesa* (Funchal: Secretaria Regional do Turismo, Cultura a Emigração: Centro de Estudos de Historiado Atlãntico, 1992).
2. Marcello Caetano, *O Conselho Ultramarino, Esboço da sua história* (Lisbon: Agência-Geral do Ultramar, 1967), 51–52; Ross Little Bardwell, "The Governors of Portugal's South Atlantic Empire in the Seventeenth Century" (Ph.D. diss., University of California, Santa Barbara, 1974), 95–103.
3. Stuart B. Schwartz, *Sovereignty and Society in Colonial Brazil: The High Court of Bahia and Its Judges, 1609–1751* (Berkeley and Los Angeles: University of California Press, 1973), 273.
4. C. R. Boxer, *Portuguese Society in the Tropics: The Municipal Councils of Goa, Macao, Bahia, and Luanda, 1510–1800* (Madison: University of Wisconsin Press, 1965), 74, 108–109.
5. C. R. Boxer, *The Golden Age of Brazil, 1695–1750: Growing Pains of a Colonial Society* (Berkeley and Los Angeles: University of California Press, 1962), 204–5; Júnia Ferreira Furtado, *O Livro da Capa Verde: O Regimento Diamantino de 1771 e a Vida no Distrito Diamantino no período da real extração* (São Paulo: Annablume, 1996).
6. Kenneth Maxwell, "Pombal and the Nationalization of the Luso-Brazilian Economy," *Hispanic American Historical Review* 48 (1968), 608–31.
7. Francisco Morais, *Estudantes da Universidade de Coimbra nascidos no Brasil* (Coimbra: Faculdade le Letras da Universidade de Cormbra, Instituto de Estudios Brasileros, 1949); Luiza da Fonseca, "Bacharéis brasileiros-elementos biográficos (1635–1830)," *Anais, IV Congresso de história nacional* 2 (Rio de Janeiro: Imprensa Nacional, 1951): 109–405.
8. Boxer, *The Golden Age of Brazil*, 301–2.
9. Rubens Borba de Moraes, *Bibliografia Brasiliana 1* (Rio de Janeiro: Livraria Kosmos Editôra, University of California at Los Angeles, 1983), 25–26, 42, 239–40, 303. That the prospect of official suppression of what were considered strategically sensitive publications was overcome by subterfuge was illustrated in Francisco Tavares de Brito, *Itinerario geografico com verdadeira descripção dos caminhos, estradas, rossas, citios, povoacoens, lugares, villas, rios, montes e serras, que ha da Cidade de S. Sebastião do Rio de Janeiro até ás Minas do Ouro*. Although the printer's office is listed as that of "Antonio da Sylva" and the place of publication as "Sevilha," the former was fictitious and the latter concealed the fact that this itinerary was published clandestinely in Lisbon in 1732.
10. Timothy J. Coates, *Degredados e orfãs. Colonização dirigida pela coroa no império português, 1550–1755* (Lisbon: Comissão Nacional para as Comemoracões dos Descobri-

mentos Portugueses, 1998); Elisa Maria da Costa, *O povo cigano entre Portugual e terras de além-mar* (Lisbon: Grupo de Trabalho do Ministerio da educação, 1997).

11. Laura de Mello e Souza, *Inferno Atlântico: Demonologia e colonização, séculos XVI-XVIII* (São Paulo: Companhia das Letras, 1993), 89–101. See also Geraldo Pieroni, "No purgatório mas o olhar no paraíso: o degredo inquistorial para o Brasil-Colônia," 115–141, and other essays in *Textos história: Revista de pós-graduação em história da UNB* [Universidade de Brasília], 6:1–2 (1998, actual publication date 1999).
12. Kirsten Schultz, *Tropical Versailles: Empire, Monarchy, and the Portuguese Royal Court in Rio de Janeiro 1808–1821* (New York and London: Routledge, 2001), 69–70.
13. Mello e Souza, *Inferno Atlântico,* 21–46.
14. Francis A. Dutra, "Membership in the Order of Christ in the Seventeenth Century: Its Rights, Privileges, and Obligations," *The Americas* 27 (1970), 3–25; "Blacks and the Search for Rewards and Status in Seventeenth-Century Brazil," *Proceedings of the Pacific Coast Council on Latin American Studies* 6 (1979), 25–35; "A Hard-Fought-Struggle: Manuel Gonçalves Doria, First Afro-Brazilian to Become a Knight of Santiago," *The Americas* 56 (1999), 91–113.
15. Mary Karasch, personal communication with the author.
16. Stuart B. Schwartz, *Sugar Plantations in the Formation of Brazilian Society: Bahia, 1550–1835* (Cambridge: Cambridge University Press, 1985), 272–77, 284–85; Boxer, *Portuguese Society in the Tropics*, 105–6.
17. Public Archives of the State of Bahia: Collection of Royal Orders (hereafter APBOR) v. 40, doc. 25a; v. 50, fols. 28–35; Eduardo de Castro e Almeida, *Inventário dos documentos relativos ao Brasil existentes no Archivo de Marinha e Ultramar de Lisboa* 2 (Rio de Janeiro: Officinas Graphicas da Bibliotheca Nacional, 1914), doc. 10907.
18. Joaquim Nabuco, *O abolicionismo* (São Paulo: Instituto Progresso Editorial, 1949).
19. ". . . a concluzão de vários negócios que finalmente decidio, so lhe restava o mais importante objecto como fiel e humilde vassalo, que he o de ter a fortuna de beijar a Mão de V.R. Alt. para que ficasse conhecendo aquele por quem tem de obrigação dar a ultima gota de sangue, e para queficasse de tudo gravado na sua alma, esta mesma obrigação . . ." APBOR v.89, fols. 177r–178r.
20. A. J. R. Russell-Wood, *Slavery and Freedom in Colonial Brazil* (Oxford, U.K.: Oneworld, 2002), 90–94, 154–56; "'Acts of Grace': Portuguese Monarchs and Their Subjects of African Descent in Eighteenth-Century Brazil," *Journal of Latin American Studies* 32:2 (2000), 307–32.
21. APBOR v.8, doc. 106; v.42, docs. 98–98a; v.91, fols. 228–35v; José António Caldas, *Notícia geral de toda esta capitania da Bahia desde o seu descobrimento até o presente ano de 1759* (Salvador: Beneditina, 1951), 342.
22. APBOR v.21, doc. 39; v.75, fol. 89; v.91, fols. 228–235v; Castro e Almeida, *Inventário* 5, doc. 25053; Public Archives of the State of Bahia, collection: Cartas do governo a Sua Magestade (hereafter APB), v.142, fols. 386–88.
23. National Library, Rio de Janeiro (hereafter BNRJ): Seção de manuscritos, 11–33, 32, 12, index #166; APBOR v.75, fols. 312, 317.
24. National Archive, Rio de Janeiro (hereafter ANRJ): codex 952, v.37, fols. 129, 131–32; C. R. Boxer, *Race Relations in the Portuguese Colonial Empire, 1415–1825* (Oxford: Clarendon Press, 1963), 117; Ibid., *The Golden Age of Brazil*, 166.
25. A. J. R. Russell-Wood, *Fidalgos and Philanthropists: The Santa Casa da Misericórdia of Bahia, 1550–1755* (London: Macmillan, 1968), 329; F. A. Pereira de Costa, *Anais Pernambucanas* 2 (Recife: Arquivo Publico Estadual, 1951), 283; "Ambivalent Authorities: The African and Afro-Brazilian Contribution to Local Governance in Colonial Brazil," *The Americas* 57 (2000), 13–36; Dauril Alden, The making of an Enterprise: The Society of Jesus in Portugal, Its Empire, and Beyond, 1540–1750 (Stanford, Calif.: Stanford University Press, 1996), 258–66.
26. Sebastião da Rocha Pitta, *História da América Portugueza*, 2nd ed. (Lisbon: Editor Francisco Arthur da Silva, 1880): livro segundo, 8114–18; and addendum titled "Pessoas naturaes do Brazil, que exerceram dignidades e governos ecclesiasticos e seculares na patria e fóra d'ella," livro decimo, 334–36.
27. Afonso Ruy, *Historia da Câmara Municipal da Cidade do Salvador* (Salvador: Camara Municipal, 1953), 157–58.

28. Eugene Ridings, *Business and Interest Groups in Nineteenth-Century Brazil* (Cambridge: Cambridge University Press, 1994), 234–310.
29. Boxer, *The Golden Age of Brazil*, 111–12; and Mary Karasch, personal communication.
30. A. J. R.Russell-Wood, "Identidade, etnia e autoridade nas Minas Gerais do século xviii: leituras do Códice Costa Matoso," *Vária Historia* 21(July 1999; published 2000), 100–118, esp. 107–11; Charles Joseph Dorenkott Jr., *José de Silva Pais: The Defense and Expansion of Southern Brazil, 1735–1749* (Ph.D. diss.: University of New Mexico, 1972), 55.
31. Boxer, *The Golden Age of Brazil*, 191–200.
32. Dorenkott, *José de Silva Pais*, 55; Dauril Alden, *Royal Government in Colonial Brazil: With Special Reference to the Administration of the Marquis of Lavradio, Viceroy, 1769–1779* (Berkeley and Los Angeles: University of California Press, 1968), 426.
33. Castro e Almeida, *Inventário* 1, 71–72, #2573–2579; John K. Kennedy, "Bahian Elites, 1750–1822," *Hispanic American Historical Review* 53(1973), 415–39.
34. Maxwell, "Pombal and the Nationalization of the Luso-Brazilian Economy," 608–31.
35. André João Antonil, *Cultura e opulência do Brasil por suas drogas e minas*, introduction by A. P. Canabrava, Liv. 1, cap. 9 (São Paulo: Companhia Editoria Nacional, 1967), emphasis. Thomas Nelson, *Remarks on the Slavery and Slave Trade of the Brazils* (London, 1846), 23–24.
36. Nuno Marques Pereira, *Compendio narrativo do peregrino da América* (Lisbon, 1728); A. J. R. Russell-Wood, "Female and Family in the Economy and Society of Colonial Brazil, in Asuncion Lavrin, ed., *Latin American Women: Historical Perspectives* (Westport: Greenwood Press, 1978), 60–100.
37. Caio Prado Jr., *Formação do Brasil contemporâneo: Colônia*, 7th ed. (São Paulo: Editora Brasiliense, 1963), 29–78.
38. Dauril Alden, "Late Colonial Brazil," in Leslie Bethell, ed., *The Cambridge History of Latin America* 2 (Cambridge: Cambridge University Press, 1984), 605; Simão Ferreira Machado, *Triunfo Eucharistico. Exemplar da Christandade Lusitana* (Lisbon, 1734): Facsimilé edition in Affonso Avila, ed., *Residuos seiscentistas em Minas, Textos do seculo do ouro e as projecões do mundo Barroco* (Belo Horizonte: Centro de Estudos Mineiros, 1967), V. 1.
39. Euclides da Cunha, *Os Sertões*, trans. Samuel Putnam as *Rebellion in the Backlands* (Chicago: University of Chicago Press, 1944); João Capistrano de Abreu, *Caminhos antigos e povoamento do Brasil* (Rio de Janeiro, 1889).
40. Audrey N. Clark, *Longman Dictionary of Geography: Human and Physical* (Harlow, Essex, UK: Longman, 1985).
41. Schwartz, *Sugar Plantations*, 94–95.
42. Alden, *Royal Government*, 66–72; Joaquim Veríssimo Serrão, *História de Portugal* 5 (Lisbon: Editorial Verbo, 1977), 304–5.
43. Prado, *Formação do Brasil*, 29–48.
44. Antonil, *Cultura e opulência*, parte III, cap. VI.
45. Carlos Francisco Moura, *A contribuição naval à formação territorial do extremo oeste*, Monografias no. 8 (Lisbon: Museu da Marinha, 1986).
46. Alden, *Royal Government*, 71–80.
47. Larissa V. Brown, *Internal Commerce in a Colonial Economy: Rio de Janeiro and Its Hinterland, 1790–1822* (Ph.D. diss., University of Virginia, 1986), 98–99.
48. Boxer, *The Golden Age of Brazil*, 275.
49. A. J. R. Russell-Wood, *The Portuguese Empire, 1415–1808* (Baltimore: The Johns Hopkins University Press, 1998), 33–36.
50. Alden, "Late Colonial Brazil," 603–7. Alden's estimates for Minas Gerais may have to be revised. See Laird W. Bergad, *Slavery and the Demographic and Economic History of Minas Gerais, Brazil, 1720–1788* (Cambridge: Cambridge University Press, 1999), 81–159.
51. Ibid., 605.
52. Mary Karasch, personal communication, compared to the figure of 9,477 for Vila Boa in 1804 as cited by Alden, "Late Colonial Brazil," 605, based on *Revista do Instituto Historico e Geografico Brasileiro 12*, 2nd ed. (1874), 482f.
53. Alden, "Late Colonial Brazil," 605.

54. Francis A. Dutra, "Centralization vs. Donatarial Privilege: Pernambuco, 1602–1630," in Dauril Alden, ed., *Colonial Roots of Modern Brazil* (Berkeley and Los Angeles: University of California Press, 1973), 19–60; Saldanha, *As capitanias*, 86–88, 259–91.
55. Francisco Adolfo de Varnhagen, *História geral do Brasil* 5 (São Paulo: Edições Melhoramentos, 1975), 243–96.
56. Caldas, *Notícia geral*, 73–88; Luís dos Santos Vilhena, *Recopilação de notícias soteropolitanas e brasílicas* 2 (Salvador: Imprensa Oficial do Estado, 1921–22)2, carta nona.
57. Alden, *Royal Government*, 30–44, 452–72.
58. Robert Allan White, *Gomes Freire de Andrada: Life and Times of a Brazilian Colonial Governor, 1688–1763* (Ph.D. diss., University of Texas at Austin, 1972), 98, 183–84, 240–49; Varnhagen, *História geral do Brasil* 5, 258.
59. Alden, *Royal Government*, 459–71.
60. Schwartz, *Sovereignty and Society*, 268.
61. Boxer, *The Golden Age of Brazil*, 208.
62. Ignacio Accioli de Cerqueira e Silva, *Memórias históricas e políticas da Provincia da Bahia do Coronel Ignacio Accioli de Cerqueira e Silva: Anotador Dr. Braz do Amaral* 3 (Bahia: Imprensa Official do Estado, 1919), 221–22; Schwartz, *Sovereignty and Society*, 306, 314–56.
63. Joâo Luís Ribeiro Fragoso and Manolo Garcia Florentino, *O arcaísmo como projeto: Mercado Atlântico, sociedade agrária e elite mercantil no Rio de Janeiro, c.1790–c.1840*, 2nd ed. (Rio de Janeiro: Livaria Sette Letras, Ltda., 1996), 61.
64. Fragoso and Florentino, *O arcaísmo*, 34–35; João Luís Ribeiro Fragoso, *Homens de grossa aventura: acumulação e hierarquia na praça mercantil do Rio de Janeiro, 1790–1830* (Rio de Janeiro: Arquivo Nacional, Ministério da Justiça, 1992), 144–147.
65. A. J. R. Russell-Wood, "A Brazilian Commercial Presence beyond the Cape of Good Hope, 16th-19th Centuries," in Pius Malekandathil and T. Jamal Mohammed, eds., *The Portuguese Indian Ocean and European Beachheads: Festschrift in Honour of Professor K. S. Mathew* (Goa: Fundaçao Oriente, 2001), 191–211; and " A Projeção da Bahia no Imperio Ultra Marino Português," IV Congresso de História da Bahia, Anais Vol. 1 (Salvador: Instituto Geográfico e Histórico da Bahia/Fundaçao Gregório de Matos, 2001), 81–122.
66. Fragoso and Florentino, *O arcaísmo*, 41–42, 62–66; Fragoso, *Homens de grossa aventura*, 86–91.
67. Brown, *Internal Commerce*, 46–91.
68. Fragoso, *Homens de grossa aventura*, 212–16.
69. Brown, *Internal Commerce*, 147–192.
70. Ibid., 292–524.
71. Mary Karasch, personal communication.
72. Rudolph W. Bauss, *Rio de Janeiro: The Rise of Late Colonial Brazil's Dominant Emporium, 1777–1808* (Ph.D. diss., Tulane University, 1977).
73. Fragoso and Florentino, *O arcaísmo*, 71–100; Fragoso, *Homens de grossa aventura*, 174–92, 262–83.
74. Corcino M. dos Santos, *Relações comerciais do Rio de Janeiro com Lisboa, 1763–1808* (Rio de Janeiro: Tempo Brasileiro, 1980).
75. Manolo Garcia Florentino, *Em costas negras: Uma história do tráfico de escravos entre a Africa e o Rio de Janeiro, séculos XVIII e XIX* (São Paulo: Campanhia das Letras, 1997), 183–94.
76. Fragoso, *Homens de grossa aventura*, 254–55.
77. Ernst Pijning, *Controlling Contraband: Mentality, Economy and Society in Eighteenth-Century Rio de Janeiro* (Ph.D. diss., The Johns Hopkins University, 1997).
78. Fragoso and Florentino, *O arcaísmo*, 36–37.
79. A. J. R. Russell-Wood, "As frotas do ouro do Brasil, 1710–1750," *Estudos Econômicos* 13 (1983), 707–8.
80. Jack P. Greene, *Negotiated Authorities: Essays in Colonial Political and Constitutional History* (Charlottesville, Va.: University Press of Virginia, 1994).
81. Jack P. Greene, *Peripheries and Center: Constitutional Development in the Extended Polities of the British Empire and the United States, 1607–1788* (Athens, Ga.: University of Georgia Press, 1986), 19–42.

The Periphery of the Periphery?

Vila Boa de Goiás, 1780–1835

Mary Karasch

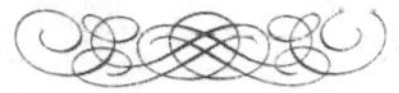

The Captaincy of Goiás and its capital, Vila Boa de Goiás, pose the following questions. Was it a regional center, or merely an unimportant periphery of the periphery? From the perspective of its governor João Manoel de Mello, writing from Vila Boa in 1760, Goiás was "the center of Portuguese America."[1] If a highborn Portuguese bureaucrat viewed Goiás as central, where then do we fit the region that now includes the modern states of Goiás and Tocantins in the late colonial period?

This case study will respond to issues raised by A. J. R. Russell-Wood in his "Centers and Peripheries in the Luso-Brazilian World, 1500–1808," and will illustrate the ways in which Vila Boa functioned as a regional center administratively dependent on Lisbon but linked commercially to other Brazilian captaincies as well as to Portugal and its empire. In order to clarify how Vila Boa became a core or center for its vast region, we will consider the following topics: its geographical location and population size, administrative and military structures, ecclesiastical structures, and late colonial trade patterns. Our central hypothesis is that Vila Boa played the role of a regional core subject to the Overseas Council and Lisbon rather than to the viceroys resident in Salvador da Bahia or Rio de Janeiro (after 1763). The overall objective of this study is to explain how a remote administrative center of the Portuguese empire that had less than 1,500 resident whites in 1783 maintained Portuguese authority and presence on the frontier in a period of economic decadence.

To understand the role of Vila Boa de Goiás in the late colonial period, we must begin with its location near where Brasília was later constructed from 1957 to 1960. Now known as the City of Goiás, the small town no longer functions as an administrative capital or economic center of the State of Goiás. Since the 1930s Goiânia has been the capital of the State of Goiás, and the former Vila Boa is now a historic city that attracts tourists, especially during Holy Week. The widespread idea held by foreigners that Brasília was built in a uninhabited region is negated by the City of Goiás, which has been continuously inhabited since the 1720s.

The growth of Brasília and Goiânia obscure, however, the past significance of the small town of Vila Boa de Goiás under the Portuguese. During the eighteenth century Vila Boa was the capital of the Captaincy of Goiás until independence in 1822. Renamed City of Goiás, it then served as the capital of the Province of Goiás (1822–89) during the empire, and of the State of Goiás until the creation of Goiânia in 1933.

The colonial Captaincy of Goiás, governed from Vila Boa, was an immense region that should not be equated with the modern State of Goiás. In the eighteenth century, the Portuguese governors based in Vila Boa ruled a much larger region than does the current governor of the State of Goiás. Their administrative authority extended over what is now the State of Tocantins, about 289,000 square kilometers separated from Goiás in 1989; Araxá, Desemboque, and Rio das Velhas, which became part of Minas Gerais; and lands to the west and south of the Araguaia River that now belong to Mato Grosso. In effect, the Captaincy of Goiás was larger in area than many sovereign European nations—about 900,000 square kilometers in size.[2]

In addition to enormous size, the captaincy also possessed gold, a major resource of significance to Portugal, and Vila Boa stood at the juncture of central Brazil's trade networks in gold and other commodities. In the 1720s Bartolomeu Bueno da Silva and a expedition (*bandeira*) from São Paulo discovered gold along the Vermelho River, where the first mining camps were constructed.[3] The first chapels and churches appeared in the 1720s and '30s, the most important of which was dedicated to Saint Ann. Thus, Vila Boa's initial reason for existence was gold mining; but as miners grew rich, they donated gold to construct the chapels and churches to meet the religious needs of those living in the mining camps and on small farms or large ranches in the countryside around the mining town. Only in 1734 did the Portuguese send an superior magistrate (*ouvidor*) to impose their bureaucratic controls on the chaotic town, which they raised to town (*vila*) status in 1736–39, and developed the administrative structures to collect taxes and export the king's fifth of gold, the *quinto*, to Lisbon.[4]

While the vila's location was based on mining, Vila Boa escaped ghost-town abandonment, which happened to so many other eighteenth-century mining towns, because of its propitious location between two great river systems, the Amazon in the north and the Paraguay/Paraná in the south. A short distance to the west of Vila Boa, merchants loaded goods on canoes for the journey via the Vermelho and Araguaia Rivers to the Tocantins River and Belém do Pará, at the mouth of the Amazon River. Or, other merchants moved their goods directly via the Tocantins River to Belém after transporting them via muleback to the river; but the direct trade via the Tocantins River to Belém was generally controlled from towns in the north, especially Porto Real (now Porto Nacional), Carmo, and Natividade, which were also subject to the governor of Goiás.

From Vila Boa merchants could also send commodities to the south connecting with the Paranaíba River, which flows into the Paraná River, and empties into the estuary of the Río de la Plata. Thus, the small town of Vila Boa stood near the juncture of two great river systems. Merchants based in Vila Boa could command trade with the eastern Amazon or as far south as Buenos Aires, or at the very least the trade that flowed to and from São Paulo via the Paranaíba, Paraná, and Tietê Rivers.[5]

The next important characteristic of the location of Goiás is that it was well situated for the East-West trade routes that ran from Salvador da Bahia to Vila Boa and then from there to Cuiabá and on to Vila Bela, whose merchants controlled the gold trade of the far western frontier of Mato Grosso via the Guaporé, Madeira, and Amazon Rivers. Other trade routes connected the neighboring northeastern captaincies, such as Maranhão, Piauí, and Pernambuco, which bordered the Captaincy of Goiás, and the southeastern routes through Minas Gerais to Rio de Janeiro. Principal port cities that received the gold of Goiás were Salvador, Brazil's first colonial capital, and Rio de Janeiro, the second capital (after 1763). Contraband trade, especially in gold, flourished along the Amazonian routes to Belém and across the backlands (*sertão*) of Bahia.[6]

Finally, the City of Goiás was located not in dense tropical rain forest but in a hilly river valley near the Serra Dourada in the midst of the savannah lands of central Brazil known as the *cerrado*.[7] Trade and communications were possible because merchants and mule teams did not have to traverse dense tropical rain forests or high mountains, but they could move convoys of mules and enslaved Africans across open savannahs or via the great rivers. Great areas of grasslands could also serve as pasture for cattle, horses, and mules, which were essential for food and land transport throughout the captaincy.

Vila Boa's location proved to be advantageous for the merchants who ran the interior trades, but the town also monopolized an essential resource to the Portuguese, and that was gold. What was lacking, however, was population, that is, Luso-Brazilians and enslaved Africans. The indigenous populations, most of whom were Gê speakers, lived seminomadic lifestyles and pursued hunting, fishing, and farming, and usually refused to settle in Christian missions and labor for the Portuguese. Those that did were subject to coerced labor under abusive secular administrators, but the vast majority lived apart from Portuguese settlements. Only a few chose to reside in Christian missions, such as Duro, Carretão, São José de Mossâmedes, and Maria II.[8] After the initial gold rush that attracted so many adventurers and their slaves before the 1750s, the Portuguese complained of the difficulty of attracting settlers and their slaves from coastal Brazil, where they still "clung like crabs." Or, if they participated in a gold rush, the Portuguese who made their fortunes left the region to claim rewards (*mercês*) in Portugal for their services in delivering gold to the Crown. Others returned to families in São Paulo or Minas Gerais, or moved on to other parts of the empire such as Angola.

What is obvious from surviving census records is that the white men who governed the captaincy and dominated the economy formed a small percentage of the population. Table 1 clarifies just how few whites (*brancos*) lived in Vila Boa in 1779. The census total of 1,460 *brancos* and *brancas* included men, women, and presumably some children. Thus, only about one-fifth (21 percent) of the population was defined as white; the remainder of 1,003 were classified as mulattoes (*pardos* and *pardas*) at 14.4 percent, with 4,491 blacks (*prêtos* and *pretas*) at 64.6 percent. The total population of Vila Boa and its surrounding district (*julgado*) numbered 6,954. It is unclear from this census how many people actually lived within the urban perimeter of the mining town.

The next census of 1783 (table 1) recorded a slight drop in Vila Boa's white population to 1,416 but increases in its nonwhite population: pardos to 1,250, while prêtos (804 freed persons; 4,689 captives) added 1,000 to reach 5,493, or 67.3 percent.

Table 1: Population of Vila Boa de Goiás and Its District, 1779–1832

Year	Whites	Pardos	Blacks	Total
1779	1,460	1,003	4,491	6,954
1783	1,416	1,250	5,493[a]	8,159
1784	—	—	4,721[b]	8,111
1785	—	—	—	8,005
1789	2,293	2,810	7,857	13,250[c]
1791	2,279	2,806	7,848	12,933
1792	2,233	2,776	8,029	13,312[d]
1799	—	—	—	8,000
1804	1,219	2,811[e]	1,012[f]	9,474[g]
1825	2,527	8,366[h]	3,274[b]	14,167
1832	2,527	8,331	3,309	14,251[i]

Sources: Rio de Janeiro, Instituto Histórico e Geographico Brasileiro (hereafter IHGB), Arq. 1.2.7, Estatística, Ofício de Luiz da Cunha Menezes á Martinho de Mello e Castro, remetendo o Mapa da população da Capitania de Goiáz, com distinção de classes, Vila Boa, 8 July 1780, f. 246; Rio de Janeiro, Biblioteca Nacional (hereafter RJBN), manuscript section, Cod. 16.3.2, Notícia Geral da Capitania de Goiás, 1783; Lisbon, Arquivo Histórico Ultramarino (hereafter AHU), Goiás, caixa 4, 2 March 1804, Processo no. 11, Pelos Mappas de População se mostra, que no anno de 1784 tinha Vila Boa de Pessoas Livres 3,390 e de Escravos 4,721; Lisbon, Biblioteca de Ajuda, 54-V-12, no. 5, Notícia de todos os Governadores e população das provincias do Brasil, 1782, ff. 33–34; AHU, Goiás, caixa 35, Mappa em que Tristão da Cunha Menezes . . . apresenta ao Real Ministerio pela extração das rellaçoens dos Parrochos o numero existente dos habitantes da dita Capitania . . . até o prezente ano de 1789, Vila Boa, 19 October 1790; IHGB, Arq. 1.2.8, vol. 37, Relação em que Tristão da Cunha Menezes . . . apresenta ao Real Ministerio pela extração das relações dos Parrochos dos seus respectivos julgados abaixo declarados até o prezente anno de 1791, f. 7; Lisbon, AHU, Goiás, caixa 35, Mappa em que o Governador, e Capitão General da Capitania de Goyaz Tristão da Cunha Menezes aprezenta ao Real Ministerio . . . até o prezente anno de 1792, Vila Boa, 29 July 1792; City of Goiás, Arquivo do Museu das Bandeiras, vol. 353, no. 15, letter from João Pereira Pinto Bravo, Vigario, to Tristão da Cunha Menezes, Vila Boa, 22 May 1799; Lisbon, AHU, Cod. 2109, Reflexoens Economicas sobre as Tabellas Statisticas da Capitania de Goyaz Pertencentes ao anno de 1804 e feitas no de 1806; RJBN, 11,4,2, Estatistica da Provincia de Goyáz remettida á Secretaria de Estado dos Negocios do Imperio . . . , 1825; and Rio de Janeiro, Arquivo Nacional, Cod. 808, vol. 1, Goiás, Censo da População da Provincia de Goyaz, 30 May 1832, f. 96.

[a] Includes 4,689 slaves.

[b] Slaves

[c] Includes 290 newborns.

[d] Includes 274 newborns.

[e] *Mulatos* and *mulatas* (mulattoes).

[f] Free blacks.

[g] Also includes 4,432 slaves.

[h] *Ingenuos* and *Libertos de Cor* (Free persons and freedpersons of color).

[i] Includes 84 Indians.

The total population of the julgado was 8,159, presumably reflecting increased mining activity in the region. Subsequent reports on Vila Boa's total population establish that it remained stable in the low 8,000s with 3,390 *livres* (free) and 4,721 slaves (58.2 percent) in 1784 (8,111) and 8,005 in 1785.[9] Significant increases in population occurred after 1785, although the numbers may only reflect a more accurate census conducted in 1789. What is notable is that the population of the julgado of Vila Boa had soared to 13,250 with a significant increase in the number of blacks (7,857), a doubling of pardos to 2,810—up from 1,250 in 1783—and a rise in the number of whites to 2,293. Slaves numbered 9,200. The question these figures pose is this: Why had the population grown in a period of economic decadence when the Portuguese were less able to collect and ship the quinto back to Lisbon? The answer to this question may lie in changing trade patterns as well as bureaucratic corruption, both of which are to be addressed shortly. The Portuguese discourse on decadence in the captaincy runs counter to the fact that the slave population almost doubled in five years. Traditionally, the Portuguese had counted the slave population to measure mining productivity.

The next census of 1791 recorded slight drops in all population groups in the vila. In 1791 Vila Boa had 2,279 whites, 2,806 pardos, and 7,848 blacks for a total of 12,933. The census of 1792, however, recorded another increase in the black population to 8,029, suggesting that mining was still going on, but with slight declines in the number of whites to 2,233 and pardos (2,776). Seven years later in 1799 a parish priest reported that the parish of Vila Boa had only 8,000 inhabitants, of which 3,000 were *forros* (ex-slaves) and livres. He did not give the source of his information, which was probably based on church records, since he reported that 6,000 were "of confession."[10]

Between 1786 and 1802, the quinto delivered to the smelting houses plummeted (table 3), and people left Vila Boa to seek greater opportunities elsewhere. The drop in the number of whites was especially significant—a loss of 1,014. By 1,804 only 1,219 whites continued to live in the vila, and only 4,432 slaves still labored for them or nonwhite slaveowners. By that year, free blacks were almost equal in number to whites (at 1,012), while free mulattoes (at 2,811) comprised 55.8 percent of the free population. Slaves (4,432), however, formed almost half of the vila's total population of 9,474 at 46.8 percent. Obviously, slavery still played an important role in Vila Boa's society and economy, although the number of slaves had dropped by almost one-half from the 9,200 of the 1789 census.

After independence in 1822, the first national census of 1825 recorded a historic transformation in the social structure of the City of Goiás, as it was now known: the rise of a free population of color to 8,366 and a further decline in the slave population to 3,274, or 23.1 percent. In other words, the free and freed people of color formed 59.1 percent of the total population (14,167) and far outnumbered both slaves and whites (2,527), who had slipped to less than 17.8 percent. Their numbers had risen slightly, however, possibly reflecting the new administrative position of the City of Goiás as the capital of the province of Goiás, thus requiring the bureaucrats of the new capital city to reside there at least part of the year. Apparently, there was no significant in-migration of whites, since the census of 1832 recorded the same number of whites (2,527) living in the city, along with 84 Indians, 8,331 pardos, and 3,309 blacks for a total population of 14,251.

What the censuses establish is that Vila Boa was a small town rather than a large city for more than fifty years from 1779 to 1832. Furthermore, many of its people actually lived in the surrounding rural district where they worked at mining gold, raising cattle, or in food production on the small plots of land (*roças*). One indication of just how few lived in the town comes from a map, Planta de Villa Boa Capital da Capitania de Goyas levantado no ano de 1782, which recorded only 554 dwellings (*moradas de cazas*) or households in the capital, which were inhabited by 3,000 persons (about 5.42 per household). At that time, most households in the captaincy included slaves and dependents (*agregados*), thus increasing household size beyond that of a nuclear family. It is unclear, however, if slaves and dependents were included in this count of the population. By the early nineteenth century, however, the number of households had increased to 699.[11]

The population statistics for the capital of Goiás reveal that a few whites governed an immense region of 900,000 square kilometers in the late colonial period. Thinly populated with Luso-Brazilians and enslaved Africans, the captaincy also encompassed diverse autonomous Amerindian nations, such as the Kayapó, Xavante, Xerente, Karajá, and Canoeiro, who were ignored by the census takers unless they lived in mission villages in 1825 and 1832.[12] We do not know how many Amerindians lived in the captaincy outside of the missions. Table 2 records the total population of the captaincy of Goiás between 1779 and 1804 and for the province of Goiás in 1825 and 1832. During the late colonial period, this vast region had less than 100,000 people. In 1779, only 54,489 were reported, the majority of whom lived in the administrative unit (*comarca*) of the south. In general, the population grew slowly to 60,428 in 1792, but then suffered a precipitous drop related to the decline in gold production by about 10,000 to 50,365 in 1804. That year seems to have been the low point in population, because the first national census of 1825 recorded growth and recovery to 62,478 and yet another increase, to 68,497, by 1832. To put such totals in perspective, we should note that one city in Brazil, Rio de Janeiro, had about 54,000 people in 1808 and almost 80,000 in 1821.[13] The entire region of central Brazil counted fewer people than the capital city of Brazil.

Sparse population spread out over 900,000 square kilometers, much of which was held by autonomous Amerindian nations, posed special problems of administration, military occupation, and social control. The few Portuguese bureaucrats, military officers, and priests could not govern such an immense region and extract its gold

Table 2: Total Population of the Captaincy of Goiás, 1779–1832

Year	Comarca of the South	Comarca of the North	Total
1779	30,395	24,094	54,489
1781	—	—	58,829[a]
1783	—	—	59,287
1785/89	41,931[b]	15,867[c]	57,798
1786	—	—	56,303
1789	36,992	21,512	58,504
1791	35,972	20,932	56,904
1792	39,807	20,621	60,428
1798	—	—	55,000
1804	36,399	13,966	50,365
1825	39,824	22,654	62,478
1832	42,406	26,091	68,497

Sources: See table 1; and Rio de Janeiro, Instituto Histórico e Geographico Brasileiro, Arq. 1.2.7, Ofício de Luiz da Cunha Menezes to Martinho de Mello e Castro, Vila Boa, 9 August 1781, ff. 263–65; Ibid., 15 February 1783, ff. 273–78; Ibid., Arq. 1.2.8, Relação da população atual da Capitania de Goiás no ano de 1786, 28 August 1787, f. 4; and Lisbon, Goiás, caixa 36, João Manoel de Menezes to Rodrigo de Souza Coutinho, Vila Boa, 3 June 1800.

[a] Includes 12,000 blacks.

[b] Comarcas of Vila Boa and Meia Ponte in 1785.

[c] Comarca of Natividade in 1789.

without the aid of nonwhites—pardos, blacks, mestizos (also termed *bastardos* in eighteenth-century Goiás), and mission Indians. They had to delegate, share, and negotiate power; nonetheless, they aimed to establish a Portuguese system of governance over the huge region. Following is a brief survey of the administrative structures imposed from Lisbon.

The Captaincy of Goiás was created in 1748, when it was separated from the Captaincy of São Paulo. Up to that date, the region had been subject to the governor of São Paulo. Its first Portuguese governor, Dom Marcos de Noronha, took office in 1749. Henceforth, the captaincy would be governed by a governor captain–general who was responsible for the delivery of the quinto (from 1752 on) and the defense of the king's share of gold in spite of *contrabandistas* and thieves. His authority came directly from the king or queen of Portugal, and he corresponded regularly with the Overseas Council and other councils in Lisbon rather than with the viceroys resident in Salvador and Rio de Janeiro (after 1763). In the decentralized administrative system of the late colonial period, the governor of Goiás was the personal representative of the Crown in this remote part of the Portuguese empire. His authority was equal to that of other governors in Brazil, but the gold of Goiás made his captaincy rank among the five richest captaincies of Brazil in the 1770s,[14] which gave him considerable influence—as long as the gold lasted. Because of his responsibility and access to gold, the governor was expected to be a nobleman "of quality" and honor and above corruption, who would serve his king or queen before moving on in royal service to more prestigious postings. Moreover, he came alone, without wife or children, but with ambitious retainers and faithful servants who were less honest and alienated Goianos as they enriched themselves from the gold of Goiás.[15]

One of the governor's principal and "noble" obligations was to see to the spread of Christianity to the pagan Amerindian nations (*gentios*) and provide funds for the Christian missions (*aldeias*). In order to accomplish these duties imposed from Lisbon, each governor mounted bandeiras to conquer the "obstreperous" nations who refused to settle down in mission villages and work for the Portuguese. The most famous conquests were of the Karajá in 1775 and the Xavante in 1788. After forcibly expelling the Jesuits from their missions in the Tocantins region in 1759, the governors saw to the support of the new secular missions and took pride in their Christianization efforts, although most Amerindians fled the forced labor imposed on them in the missions and resumed raids on mines and settlements, killing slaves and stealing cattle and horses. The governors also sent the troops to attack the settlements of fugitive slaves (*quilombos*), and to discover new gold mines.[16]

Since the Amerindians would not work for them, the governors expended much effort in making economic proposals and needed reforms to resolve the labor shortages and economic decadence of the early nineteenth century. They also enforced the king's justice when the gold of Goiás proved too tempting to men of "lesser quality." What is remarkable about the governors of Goiás is that such highborn men, some of whom were able administrators, governed a frontier outpost. In effect, both they and the Portuguese bureaucrats in Lisbon regarded Vila Boa as significant enough to merit governors of "quality."

Various sources help to explain why men of such stature endured the isolation of central Brazil. Wilhelm Ludwig Von Eschwege, who visited Vila Boa in the 1820s, narrated the custom of the miners (of Minas Gerais?) in which they gained the "benevolence" of the Portuguese governor when he first visited the mining region. They preserved intact a vein of "extraordinary concentration" of gold. They then invited each governor who visited the region to give "the first bateada" (i.e., to pan for gold with a large wood or metal basin).[17] Whether this custom was followed in all of the mining captaincies is unclear, but there is no doubt that Portuguese governors, bureaucrats, military officers, and priests notably enriched themselves while serving in Goiás. In fact, the Conde de São Miguel, who was governor from 1755 to 1759, was imprisoned for malfeasance in office after he returned to Lisbon along with twenty-nine high functionaries, such as judges, intendants, and treasurers; but most corruption went unreported and unpunished, which makes it difficult to track in official records.[18]

Rivals to the governors in status and position were the intendants of the smelting houses, which were established in Vila Boa in 1752 and São Félix in the north in 1754 (until 1796, when it was moved to Cavalcante). The intendants were appointed from Lisbon, expected to be incorruptible, and able to supervise the registering, assaying, and shipment of the quinto to Lisbon. Each intendant supervised many men, including four fiscal agents (*fiscais*), a treasurer, a smelter (*fundidor*), two scribes to record receipts and expenditures, and slaves. With so many men having access to gold, it is understandable why the Portuguese complained of corruption at the smelting houses. Official correspondence from Goiás clarifies that the intendants were powerful men in their own right who could and did challenge the governor, as did Manuel Pinto Coelho in 1805. Four years later, the intendants were replaced with fiscais.[19]

In comparison to the powerful governors and autonomous intendants of gold, judges could also be powerful if they were an *ouvidor* of the comarca. The *ouvidores* (superior magistrates) and local judges, such as *juízes ordinários*, were essential to the legal system. The first ouvidor arrived in Goiás in 1734, and his responsibility was to reestablish the king's authority after "disorders" in the nearby mining town of Meia Ponte (now Pirenópolis). Henceforth, educated men trained in the law at the University of Coimbra in Portugal were few in number and never sufficient to meet the demands for justice on a violent frontier. Only those who committed serious crimes, such as murder, or significant tax evasion involving large sums of money were sent for trial at the high court, the *relação* in Salvador or Rio de Janeiro. While waiting for transport to the coast, criminals as well as the innocent languished in the great jail located on the ground floor of the Senado da Câmara building; men died in jail before their cases were resolved.[20] One of the principal judicial institutions seems to have been the *devassa*, or judicial inquiry, in which deponents gave testimony regarding a crime, which was then forwarded to Salvador, Rio de Janeiro, and/or Lisbon. Present were the scribe (*tabelião*) to record the testimony and an ouvidor to preside at the hearing. Men and women of all social classes, including slaves, could tell what they knew about a crime.[21]

Such devassas took place wherever there were the appropriate officials, but most commonly in the capitals of the comarcas (administrative units). In 1809 the Captaincy of Goiás was divided into two enormous comarcas: the comarca of the south, with its capital of Vila Boa de Goiás and the comarca of the north, created in 1809 with its capital of São João.[22] The ouvidor of the comarca of the south, resident in Vila Boa, exercised both judicial and administrative functions, having the ability to arrest, sentence, and punish criminals. As the *corregedor,* he was in charge of the police; but he also supervised the notaries (*tabeliões*), scribes, and justice officials. Moreover, he was the superintendant of mineral lands, president of the Tribunal de Ausentes, which was charged with the administration of the property of absentees, and superintendent of the property of the lay religious brotherhoods (*irmandades*). Until Joaquim Theotonio Segurado assumed the position of ouvidor in the north in 1805, only one ouvidor served in the Captaincy of Goiás.[23]

As of 1809, Vila Boa also had a municipal judge (*juiz de fóra*), who sat on the Senado da Câmara. As so many public officials in Goiás, he also had other responsibilities as probate judge (*juiz dos órfãos*) and Crown's attorney (*procurador da coroa*). More common were the juízes ordinários. A juíz ordinário presided over the Senado da Câmara of Vila Boa in the eighteenth century. There were two judges assigned to each of the julgados, which were administrative subdivisions of the comarcas. In the early nineteenth century, the comarca of the south had eight julgados, and presumably sixteen juízes ordinários. The vast comarca of the north also had eight julgados, but rarely sixteen judges. Since these judges were elected by the "good men"—men of property and status—of the julgado, they were often "ignorant of the law." They owed their power to local political position or family connections rather than their knowledge of the law acquired at the University of Coimbra.[24]

Judges detained prisoners or sentenced them to serve time for lesser crimes in local jails, which in the nineteenth century became a ubiquitous argument advanced by petitioners to elevate a village's status to that of a vila. The construction of a jail was equated with progress and development. The most famous jail of the eighteenth century, however, was the heavily barred lower half of the city council building. The meetings of the Senado da Câmara were held on the upper floor, while the ground floor held prisoners, including slaves, such as fugitives captured in quilombos. Women were also sentenced to prison there. Before the baroque building once stood the pillory (*pelourinho*), symbol of vila status, which was a whipping post where criminals and slaves were publicly flogged. Is it any accident that the câmara/jail structure is the most grandiose public building constructed in eighteenth-century Vila Boa? It visibly demonstrated not only the power of the town council in making laws, but also in enforcing them and maintaining social control in the captaincy. Prisoners from all over the captaincy were housed there.[25]

The correspondence on justice, or rather the lack of it, in late colonial Goiás demonstrates that most judicial positions went unfilled, especially after the decadence of the mining economy, and most communities lacked even a minimum of security (i.e., a jail) to protect its citizens from criminals. In contrast to other parts of Brazil, the magistracy was comparatively weak and ineffectual. Only a powerful military officer and/or wealthy miner or landowner could protect the local citizens from the lawless. Vigilante justice enforced by a powerful man with a military title was the norm rather than the king's justice as applied by trained lawyers, especially in the northern comarca.

In contrast to the weak magistracy in late eighteenth-century Goiás, the financial arm of the state could be strong, imposing jail time, confiscation of properties, and even deportation from the captaincy for fiscal malfessance—nonpayment of the quinto and other taxes. The Tribunal of the Royal Treasury board and the Tribunal of Accounts (*Contas*) in Lisbon exercised clout over Goianos under the authority of the treasurer-general (*provedor-mor*). Given the importance of gold in Goiás, the governor served as the president of Vila Boa's treasury board (*Junta da Fazenda*), established in 1761. Its other members included a Judge, the Crown's attorney, a treasurer, and a scribe. Officials of the Junta da Fazenda in Vila Boa were feared, and their "unjust" taxes widely evaded.[26]

Goianos had to pay burdensome taxes. Gold miners were subject to the quinto. They had to send all their gold dust and bars to the smelting houses to be weighed, assayed, and the royal tax recorded. Once a year at the beginning of the dry season, the quinto was transported in bags bearing the king's arms on the backs of mules in a convoy under military escort through the neighboring Captaincy of Minas Gerais to Rio de Janeiro for export to Lisbon. The journey easily took three months. This tax, however, only affected those with access to gold, since it was only imposed on mineral production. Table 3 tracks the amount of the quinto delivered between 1752 and 1803.[27]

The hated taxes that affected most Goianos, however, were the *entradas* and the *dízimos*. The *entradas* were the taxes imposed on merchants that had to be paid in registers (*registros*) when commodities were imported into the captaincy. Taxes were paid based on weight rather than value. Thus, a merchant paid more to import necessities, such as salt, than luxury goods, such as jewelry or fine silks. Bribes to officers at the registers led to lower royal revenues as military officers and merchants evaded the required taxes. Once a church tithe, the dízimo was a tax imposed on the value of each year's crops and animals. Since it was collected from both small farmers and wealthy landowners, it imposed great burdens on the agropastoral economy and led to rural revolts, resistance, and tax evasion in Goiás. It was also responsible for inciting small farmers and ranchers to migrate to frontier lands to avoid the tax contractors, who did not always have a reputation for honesty. Others who remained in more settled areas did not pay the dízimo but remained on the debtor's lists year after year. Apparently, the fiscal authorities either chose not to collect or could not collect dízimos from many small farmers and ranchers.[28]

But these were not the only taxes—only the most onerous. Other taxes were imposed to cross rivers (the *passagens*). Specific donations were also levied, in particular for the rebuilding of Lisbon after the earthquake of 1755.[29] What is obvious from a study of income generated by the Captaincy of Goiás in 1774 is that the dízimos and entradas generated significant income in gold for Portugal. In the period of 1772–1774, the total income for the captaincy was 109:344$305, of which the dízimo contributed 24:913$332 and the entradas yielded 12:120$000. In contrast, the quinto from Vila Boa amounted to 22:361$850, while the yield from that of São Félix was 30:559$266. In other words, the quinto accounted for less than half the income of the captaincy in the early 1770s. Obviously, the Portuguese had other means of capturing the gold of Goiás than through the quinto. Needless to say, revenues then extracted from Goiás amounted to far more than expenditures in the captaincy. In that same period, Portugal spent in Goiás only 57:084$187.[30] The Captaincy of Goiás generated a substantial surplus for Portugal in the 1770s, which helps to explain Portugal's concerns about this remote region.

Not too surprisingly, one major area of expenditure was on the military. Since the captaincy was still in a state of war with various Amerindian nations, in particular the Kayapó in the south and the Xavante in the north, military forces were essential to

TABLE 3: THE INCOME OF THE ROYAL FIFTH OF THE TWO SMELTING HOUSES OF THE CAPTAINCY OF GOIÁS, 1752–1803[a]

Year	Vila Boa	North	Total	Year	Vila Boa	North	Total
				1781	434	224	658
1752	1:094	—	1:094	1782	502	173	675
1753	2:641	—	2:641	1783	474	178	652
1754	1:732	517	2:249	1784	449	163	612
1755	1:497	931	2:428	1785	470	136	606
1756	1:341	688	2:029	1786	543	143	686
1757	1:423	732	2:155	1787	487	144	631
1758	1:322	837	2:159	1788	414	115	529
1759	1:307	703	2:010	1789	382	147	529
1760	1:366	736	2:102	1790	395	163	558
1761	1:045	532	1:577	1791	445	104	549
1762	1:085	737	1:822	1792	431	115	546
1763	1:114	587	1:701	1793	317	119	436
1764	1:030	514	1:544	1794	376	109	485
1765	1:017	576	1:593	1795	350	120	470
1766	842	487	1:329	1796	289	132	421
1767	1:003	527	1:530	1797	287	140	427
1768	932	506	1:438	1798	255	143	398
1769	982	424	1:406	1799	330	94	424
1770	920	456	1:376	1800	273	97	370
1771	839	429	1:268	1801	204	71	275
1772	879	445	1:324	1802	186	94	280
1773	693	320	1:013	1803	192	107	299
1774	748	357	1:105	1804	285	54	339
1775	677	314	991	1805	208	52	260
1776	669	336	1:005				
1777	700	255	955				
1778	585	365	950				
1779	548	263	811				
1780	620	251	871				

Source: Lisbon, Arquivo Histórico Ultramarino, Goiás, caixa 40, Mappa do rendimento do Real Quinto das duas Cazas de Fundição da Capitania de Goyaz desde que principiarão alaborar thé o anno de 1803, Contadoria de Vila Boa, 5 March 1805. A complete printed copy of the *quintos* is in Gilka V. F. de Salles, *Economia e Escravidão na Capitania de Goiás* (Goiânia: CEGRAF/UFG, 1992), 184–86. She also has data for the quintos from Vila Boa only, 1806–1822.

[a] In *marcos* of gold. The numbers have been rounded off. The more complete figures in *marcos*, *onças*, and *oitavas* are reproduced in Salles, 184–86. John Jay TePaske has also converted these amounts into silver pesos (personal communication with the author).

the survival and protection of Luso-Brazilian towns and mines. The first military forces to enter Goiás were the bandeiras organized by men from São Paulo, who raided the region for slaves, thus exterminating the original indigenous population known as Goiases of the Vila Boa region. From the seventeenth century onward, bandeiras from São Paulo continued to explore the region, searching for gold, emeralds, and Amerindian slaves; but once the Portuguese governors took up residence in Vila Boa, they too organized official bandeiras to fight the Kayapó. Their usual practice was to appoint an experienced military officer to lead an expedition composed of lower-ranked troops, local citizens organized in militias, and their slaves, and agregados. Recently conquered Indians from nearby aldeias (mission villages) also participated. When bandeiras were formed to seek out and destroy quilombos, black troops even joined up, fighting together with professional slave hunters led by a bush captain (*capitão do mato*). Part of Portuguese practice was to utilize the recently conquered and loyal ex-slaves to fight the frontier wars.[31]

The reason the Portuguese employed the conquered and enslaved is that few soldiers and officers from Portugal served in the vast region. Their small numbers gave them an elevated social status, and those that lived for decades in the captaincy often married local women and acquired property, slaves, and extended families of white and racially mixed children. Those that left the captaincy continued in the king's service in other parts of the empire, most notably in Angola, where one suspects that they exchanged the gold of Goiás for enslaved Africans. The military unit that employed men from Portugal as professional soldiers was the cavalry force, the regiment of dragoons. The first regiment of dragoons arrived in Goiás in 1736. Composed of less than fifty men, it was headed by a captain and a lieutenant. As late as 1801, the dragoons had only eighty soldiers; seven years later in 1808 only sixty remained. So few men had an extraordinary variety of responsibilites: to guard the Pilões and Claro Rivers, which were reputed to be rich in gold and diamonds; to protect the registers and the intendant's safe where the gold was safeguarded; to conduct the quinto to Rio de Janeiro; to lead bandeiras to discover new gold mines, conquer Amerindian nations, and destroy quilombos; to patrol the roads in search of contraband; and to accompany the governor on his visits of inspection.[32]

Because the dragoons focused on Portuguese concerns regarding gold and service to the Crown and governors, more prosaic matters of public safety and frontier warfare were left to less prestigious military units. Obviously of inferior social status in the Portuguese view were the barefooted *pedestres*, a paid troop (organized in 1743) that earned minimal salaries—if they were paid at all. Led by a captain, two *alferes*, a *furriel*, and two *cabos* (1777–1780), the pedestres of Vila Boa were composed of racially mixed men—mestizos, bastardos, and pardos—and mission Indians, most notably the Akroá from the old Jesuit mission of Duro. Other mission Indians were recruited from the aldeia (missions) of São José de Mossâmedes and Maria II, and many of them were the Kayapó that the Portuguese had fought for decades. The men of color and the Indian men thus did the "drudge work" in bandeiras, fighting as foot soldiers in the frontier wars. They were also used like a police force to keep peace in the missions or to patrol more remote regions of the captaincy to capture common criminals or hunt down and reenslave quilombolas. Their basic job was to protect and defend the mining towns from any threat. Registers of the men who joined the pedestres document their few numbers in the eighteenth century as well as their frequent desertions and disciminatory pay. Indians received half of what non-Indians were paid in salary.[33]

Since the paid troops—the dragoons and pedestres—were based in Vila Boa and the region of their responsibilities was enormous, most of the military duties were fulfilled by the unpaid militia units of the Companies of Ordenanças [of white and pardo men], the auxiliary regiments of the Terços dos Pardos, and the black regiments known as the Henriques, after Henrique Dias, the black hero of the war against the Dutch in the seventeenth century. In sharp contrast to the few Portuguese officers resident in the captaincy, the officers in the militias were numerous; so too were their honorific titles. As the historian Luis Palacin has observed, the Ordenanças were "always affected by macrocefalismo, [a] great head without any body." The officers' patents were given to men who had no military experience, who were of advanced age, and who sought the social status linked to a military title with the right to carry a large staff (*bengala*) in public processions. The Portuguese governors, in particular, Tristão da Cunha Menezes, used this hunger for social status to increase revenues by exchanging military patents for small gifts of gold—gold dust was preferred.[34]

The mulatto men of the captaincy, often the sons of Portuguese officers and African women, served under their own mulatto officers in the Terços dos Pardos. The duties of these militia regiments are well summed up in a petition to the Crown by the leading pardo officers then resident in the captaincy. In their petition, they protested against their treatment by the city council of Vila Boa and recorded their services as "humble and faithful vassals" of the Crown in the bandeiras that conquered the Kayapó and Xavante. They also staffed the garrisons of the missions and defended the captaincy from its enemies. In spite of their exalted titles granted in patents and signed by the king in Lisbon, the pardos actually provided many of the same services as the troops in the pedestres. Perhaps the difference is that some of the pardos fought in cavalry units, but their much higher ranking than the pedestres is revealed by an episode that challenged racial hierarchies in the captaincy. In the 1780s, when the post of governor fell vacant, the highest ranking and most senior military officer, who held the oldest patent and who should have assumed his duties until the Crown appointed a new governor, was a mulatto coronel. The white men on the Senado da Câmara, however, protested and refused to allow him to become interim governor. In defending this violation of past practice, the members of the council justified their decision in these words: "by his quality [of being a mulatto], he ought not to be admitted to the interim government." The Portuguese authorities in Lisbon agreed in 1790.[35] Obviously, the pardos could fight for the Portuguese, but they would not be permitted to hold a public office in which they would command white men.

Of less stature than the pardo regiments was the third militia regiment, the Henriques, named for the black hero of the seventeenth century. Formed of ex-slaves and free black men of color, they performed similar duties to the pedestres and pardo regiments, that is, serving in bandeiras that attacked Amerindian nations and quilombos; defending their families and slaves from Indian attacks; and in general providing an additional force with which to defend the mining towns of the frontier. As one regimental list clarifies, they were Africans by birth or the sons of African parents in the mining town of São José de Tocantins in 1799. By the 1820s, however, other regimental lists document that those who belonged to the Henriques were largely Brazilian-born blacks (*crioulos*) who were miners, small farmers, and artisans and craftsmen. Many were also small slaveholders, owning one to three slaves. In 1782 the captaincy had seven companies of Henriques, but in the early nineteenth century, their number had increased to at least twelve Henriques regiments headed by black officers (see table 4). As the pardo and white men prized their titles, so too did the officers in the black regiments.[36]

The Portuguese depended on the men of color and local white men to guard and protect their colony. They rewarded those who served them with military patents that raised their social status.[37] "Selling" such patents also helped compensate Portuguese bureaucrats for their services on a violent frontier. Officerships also gave them access to remunerative bureaucratic positions, especially if they had been born in Portugal. Since there were so few white men "of quality" throughout the captaincy, the

Table 4: Number of Military Units in the Captaincy of Goiás, c. 1812

Town	Cavalry	Infantry	Ordenanças	Henriques
		Comarca of the South		
Vila Boa	4	4	2	1
Barra	—	—	1	—
Anta	1	1	1	—
Santa Rita	—	1	—	—
Ouro Fino	—	—	1	—
Meia Ponte	3	2	2	1
Jaraguá	1	2	1	—
Santa Luzia	2	2	2	1
Santa Cruz	1	1	1	—
Bonfim	1	1	1	—
Pilar	2	2	2	1
Crixá	1	1	1	1
Dezemboque	1	—	1	—
Araxá	—	—	1	—
		Comarca of the North		
Pontal	—	1	1	—
Natividade	2	1	1	1
Carmo	1	1	—	1
Conceição	1	1	1	1
Arraias	1	2	1	—
Cavalcante	1	1	2	1
Traíras	1	1	1	1
Aguaquente	1	1	—	—
São José de Tocantins	—	2	—	1
Amaro Leite	—	1	2	—
São Félix	1	1	—	1

Source: Biblioteca Nacional Rio de Janeiro, manuscript section, 9,2,10, [Luiz Antônio da Silva e Souza], Memoria sobre o Descobrimento, Governo, População, e cousas mais notaveis da Capitania de Goyaz, Vila Boa, 13[?] August 1786 [1812], ff. 37–42. This table was compiled based on information contained in this Memoria.

Portuguese relied on military and militia officers and priests to perform the functions that minor bureaucrats did on the coast. Hence, one of the major characteristics of the military and the clergy was that many of them also exercised political power, being noted for their involvement in affairs of state and use of public office to gain additional wealth.

While it is understandable that military men would transfer leadership skills from the battlefield to the public arena, it is more of a surprise that the clergy of Goiás were also politically powerful. After the Jesuits were forcibly expelled in 1759, they were replaced with secular priests from nearby mining towns, which meant that henceforth mission Indians often lacked resident clerics; but after gold production declined, even settled towns of some size had difficulty obtaining priests. Correspondence from Goiás reveals a neglected Catholic Church, unable to meet the religious needs of parishioners or engage in significant missionary work among the Indians. As an institution, the church was comparatively weak in late colonial Goiás.[38]

First, Vila Boa had no resident bishop in the colonial period. At various times, the people of the Captaincy of Goiás were subject to the bishops of Rio de Janeiro, Recife, Pernambuco, or in the north of Belém do Pará. The authority of the Inquisition also stretched to this remote region, but those accused of heresy or grave sins against morality were sent all the way to Lisbon until tried by the Holy Office. The highest ecclesiastical official resident in Vila Boa in 1804 was the prelado and vigario (prelate and vicar), who was attached to the church of Santa Anna.[39] In the absence of a bishop, priests had to be ordained in Rio de Janeiro or Lisbon, and only a few were appointed to serve in Goiás. In 1782, for example, only one priest out of fifty ordained in Rio de Janeiro was assigned to Goiás.[40] Those that did take up their duties in Goiás were often incapacitated with fevers due to malaria or died untimely deaths on the frontier, while many of those who escaped illness or death neglected their religious duties in order to support themselves and their households. Many priests did not observe clerical celibacy, and openly lived with the mothers of their children.[41] They also had children by their slave women. Even if celibate, census records reveal that priests did not live alone. Their households often included a widowed mother, unmarried sisters, nephews, and agregadas. Moreover, they owned slaves who labored to support them all, since priests could not depend on clerical incomes.[42]

In addition to their clerical and familial responsibilities, Catholic priests also acted as merchants or at least as partners (*socios*) in economic ventures. In 1816, for example, the Vigario da Vara of Traíras, Manoel de Silva Alvares, petitioned for the Order of Christ for performing his clerical duties as well as promoting a mercantile society between the Captaincy of Goiás and Pará. Although he was one of the richest priests in the captaincy, his petition was denied because he had already received an exemption for the entradas, which he did not have to pay for ten years. Priests also served in local political offices or undertook secular responsiblities for the governor of Goiás. They often acted as scribes in the absence of a notary, and collected census data from the parish registers. Such secular and familial responsibilities made it difficult to perform their clerical duties, and parishioners complained to Rio de Janeiro and Lisbon of local priests who did not say Mass or administer the sacraments.[43]

Since priests were often negligent or missing altogether, lay Catholics formed lay brotherhoods (*irmandades*) to meet the religious and social needs of the people who lived so far from coastal churches. The lay brotherhoods were also essential to the construction of chapels and churches, where each brotherhood buried the dead. As society was divided by color, so too were these brotherhoods. Their charters (*compromissos*) reveal that whites formed the brotherhood devoted to the Blessed Sacrament (*Santissimo Sacramento*), one of the most prestigious in the captaincy, which banned men and women of color from membership. Portuguese military officers joined the brotherhood devoted to Saint Anthony, while pardo officers honored Our Lady of the Immaculate Conception in the church of Boa Morte. The blacks of the captaincy built churches for Our Lady of the Rosary or Our Lady of Mercies. They also constructed chapels dedicated to the black saint Benedict.[44] The presence of these lay Catholic institutions in the mining towns helps to explain how many people remained Catholic in spite of the decline of the mines and a weak institutional church. As in the case of the military, the lay brotherhoods composed of lay Catholics of all colors ensured the continued practice of essential rituals that expressed religious values. Contemporary folk traditions that celebrate the festivals of the Holy Spirit, honor Our Lady of the Rosary, and organize processions during Holy Week and Pentecost are heirs of eighteenth-century religious traditions.[45]

Although we can easily describe Portuguese institutional structures by which they maintained control in the Captaincy of Goiás, it is more difficult to determine the town's economic role. Obviously, the Crown, the Overseas Council, the royal treasury, and financial councils, such as the Tribunal de Contas, imposed a command or state-directed economy over the captaincy. The governor was the key person assigned to execute the economic policies set in Rio de Janeiro and/or Lisbon, but he too evolved solutions to economic problems (i.e., the decline of gold export), and proposed them to Lisbon for consideration. Thus, the governors attempted to direct the economy to ensure the delivery of gold to Lisbon; but in spite of their efforts, they failed to effect economic transformations because of underlying structural weaknesses in the economy, as well as Goiano evasion of taxes, refusal to send gold to the smelting houses, and widespread contraband activities devoted to gold and cattle. In effect, much of the economy escaped gobernatorial fiat, in part because the captaincy was so large and the Portuguese so few. The following section will describe briefly the legal and illegal trades in gold. As I hope to document, Goiás was a region in which there was "a pervasive culture of evasion" that led to an internal economy in which the gold of Goiás slipped from the king's hands into Luso-Brazilian hands: white, mulatto, and black.[46] Everyone from the governor of Goiás to pious priests and black slaves accumulated gold, hiding it in sacred statues, while others used it to buy letters of liberty if enslaved or to build churches or to acquire mercês and other honors in Lisbon. How much of the gold of Goiás circulated in Brazil is unknown, but here we will trace out the general trade networks. We cannot establish, however, how much gold flowed along those routes; what we can document is what was delivered to Lisbon as the quinto (see table 3).

To understand the trade networks of the Captaincy of Goiás, it helps to view Vila Boa as the center of a large tree with branches to the east (Bahia) and the west (Mato Grosso) as well as to the north (Pará), and deep roots in the south (São Paulo and Rio de Janeiro). Commodities, except in the case of small luxury items, did not travel entirely along these routes, but only along segments to reach interior towns or coastal ports. Thus, we will explain the east-west trade first, followed by the north-south trade in order to document the economic role of the small town of Vila Boa.

The description begins with Salvador da Bahia, Brazil's first colonial capital, which was also a port city in contact with the world. Here were unloaded European textiles and Asian silks, enslaved Africans from west and central Africa; silver from Potosí via the Río de la Plata region; ritual objects from Africa and statues of saints from Portugal; olive oil and wines from Portugal; and tools and weapons from Europe. These were loaded on horses and mules or on the heads of new Africans, who followed the convoys to central Brazil. They traversed a well-worn road from Salvador to Cachoeira, then across the *sertão* of Bahia to the Rio São Francisco, then to the towns of Barreiras and Duro, and on to Natividade and São Félix in the northern comarca, and from São Félix to Vila Boa. A second Bahian route crossed the sertão of Bahia via São Domingos, or Lagôa Feia, to Meia Ponte (now Pirenópolis), and Vila Boa. When Salvador was the colonial capital of Brazil (to 1763), much gold followed similar routes for the return trip to Salvador for export to Lisbon. While the governor controlled the quinto trade, Portuguese merchants residing in northern towns and Vila Boa organized the contraband and legal trades between Salvador and the Captaincy of Goiás. They imported slaves, luxury goods, and dry goods, and exported gold to Salvador. After the decline of the mines, they forwarded cattle and cotton to Bahia.[47]

Continuing on west from Vila Boa, trade goods went via mule teams across eastern Mato Grosso through Kayapó lands to Cuiabá, the center of the gold mining region of Mato Grosso. Since Mato Grosso was strategically important to the Portuguese after the Treaty of Madrid in 1750, the governor of Goiás legally sent gold to the governor of Mato Grosso to strengthen the military defenses of the border captaincy with Spanish territory. Merchants based in Vila Boa, however, also forwarded gold to merchants based in Cuiabá, as well as other trade goods that were "indispensable to the provisioning of the far west." In exchange, the merchants of Cuiabá returned salt, quinine used in treating fevers (malaria), and other drugs of the sertão, as they were called, to treat illnesses. Cattle were also driven from ranches in Mato Grosso to meet the demand for meat by miners in Goiás. Trade between Vila Boa and Mato Grosso streched, however, as far west as Vila Bela, whose merchants accessed the trade of the Amazon River via the Guaporé and Madeira Rivers and the Jesuit missions of the Moxos in what is now Bolivia.[48] We suspect that the gold of Goiás also slipped from Portuguese hands into the Spanish territories via merchants in Mato Grosso, who engaged in contraband. Did some of that gold buy the "Herva de Paraguai" (*mate*, or tea) that was sold in Desemboque in the south of the captaincy? In brief, one could travel overland from Salvador to Vila Bela and then by river to Belém do Pará. It is uncertain, however, if any one merchant did so given the time and distances involved, not to mention deadly diseases and raiding Amerindian nations. Most merchants handled only one portion of that trip: Salvador to Vila Boa or Natividade; Vila Boa to and from Cuiabá; or Cuiabá to and from Vila Bela.

Another branch of the east-west trade routes was that across the sertão of the northeastern states of Maranhão, Piauí, and Pernambuco, principally exchanging cattle, horses, meats (salted/dried), tallow, salt, fish, leather, and sugar bricks (*rapaduras*) for gold. The merchants from these states traded, however, principally with the mining towns of the northern comarca, in particular with Natividade. Documents from the register at Duro (once a Jesuit mission), located to the east of Natividade, establish that both legal trades and contraband gold passed through Duro and contraband gold via Bocaina, near the register of Santa Maria to the south. In particular, the trade from Pernambuco went via Duro, Taguatinga, and São Domingos. Through Duro were imported gunpowder, dry goods, agricultural implements, tobacco, salt, fish, cattle, wine, and dried beef. In the 1820s, the merchants were dealing in salt,[49] and gold was no longer a significant commodity in official registers. The significance of the northern comarca's sertão trade to the São Francisco River was recognized by the governor of Goiás, when he had the imports of the captaincy tabulated. It was larger in value than trade with either Rio de Janeiro or São Paulo (see table 5).

How important the northeastern routes were for the gold trade of the eighteenth century is uncertain, except for Portuguese complaints about the amount of contraband gold that exited the captaincy via the sertão. In the eighteenth century, the mining regions depended on the Captaincy of Maranhão for Portuguese manufactures, foodstuffs, and African slaves, which were exchanged for gold, cattle, and horses. Almost all commerce of the port city of São Luis with Piauí and the towns of Natividade and São Félix went via the small town of Aldeas Altas, located near Caxias in eastern Maranhão. Another gold route from the mines of Goiás was northward via the Tocantins River. The merchants then traveled east to the Mearim River, which took them almost to São Luís. A second river route was via the Parnaíba River of Maranhão to the headwaters of the Itapicuru River and then to the ocean at São Luís. Presumably, enslaved Africans and European trade goods followed the same river routes to the mining towns of Goiás.[50]

Related to the trade of the Tocantins River and the Northeast was that of eastern Amazonia, dominated by merchants resident in Belém do Pará. After 1782 they outfitted the riverboat expeditions that made annual trips down the Tocantins River to connect with the mining towns of what the Portuguese then called the Maranhão River (i.e., the upper Tocantins River). They sent European manufactures, foodstuffs, and salt to exchange for gold and leather. The opening of the Tocantins River route in the early 1780s apparently played a key role in increasing the volume of contraband gold trade in the late colonial period. Previously, Portuguese interdiction of trade on the Tocantins between 1737 and 1782 in a vain attempt to stop the contraband gold trade, combined with Indian attacks on river expeditions, had slowed trade on the

Table 5: Monetary Value of Imports into the Captaincy of Goiás, 1804

Region	Comarca of the South	Comarca of the North
Bahia	3:577$369	42:968$000
Pará	5:326$100	5:000$000
Rio de Janeiro	51:035$091	644$000
São Francisco River	—	2:008$057
São Paulo	25:555$597	995$200
Total:	85:494$157	51:615$257

Source: Lisbon, Arquivo Histórico Ultramarino, Cod. 2109, Reflexoens Economicas sobre as Tabellas Statisticas da Capitania de Goyaz Pertencentes ao anno de 1804 e feitas no de 1806.

great river. With Indian removals in the 1790s and government encouragement of trade to counteract mining declines, trade rebounded once again, and by 1804 trade with Pará was once more significant (see table 5). By 1806 the ouvidor Joaquim Theotonio Segurado had organized a company of commerce to trade with Pará in the town of Traíras.[51]

To the west of the Tocantins River is the other great river of central Brazil, the Araguaia River, which flows north to join the Tocantins on its way to emptying into the delta of the Amazon River. Thus, this river's trade was also linked to the port of Belém do Pará, but additionally to Mato Grosso. Portuguese merchants in Vila Boa or Cuiabá sent goods via the Araguaia River—if the Karajá, who controlled the river, permitted it. In fact, the Karajá traded directly with the merchants of Belém. Because so much of the river was still in Indian control, the Araguaia was not as important for the legal trades dominated by Portuguese merchants. In the 1790s Francisco de Souza Coutinho referred to the "poor Comboyeiros" who traded up river to Belém transporting sugar, leather, shoe leather (*sola*), and tobacco, as well as bars of gold. However, in 1806 Segurado left gold off of his list of commodities traded in ten canoes via the Araguaia River to Belém: sugar, tobacco, *toucinho* (bacon or pork fat), and shoe leather.[52]

The Belém merchants were also involved in the slave trades of eastern Amazonia; they imported enslaved Africans into Belém and sent them down the Tocantins River to the mining towns. After the decline of the mines and the collapse of the demand for enslaved African men, some may have been involved in the trade of captive Amerindian women and children from the Tocantins River region, who were branded and traded north as slaves to Belém.[53] How large or significant this trade in human beings was is unknown.

In general, the merchants of the northern comarca traded with northeast ports and Belém. Apparently, much of this northern trade was independent of the trade conducted in the southern comarca. In contrast, Vila Boa not only looked to Salvador but also to the Southeast since the great majority of its imports came from Rio de Janeiro or São Paulo (see table 5). After 1783 the legal quinto trade followed the road from Vila Boa to Meia Ponte, south to Santa Cruz, Paracatú, and to Vila Rica (now Ouro Prêto) in Minas Gerais, and then overland through Minas Gerais to the port of Rio de Janeiro. European goods loaded on mules, and enslaved Africans, followed the same route overland to Vila Boa. The merchants of Minas Gerais, however, also sent live goods (*viveres*) raised in their own captaincy through the register at Desemboque for sale there or in Araxá. Peddlers also brought the luxury European imports that they had purchased from merchants resident in Vila Rica and São João del Rei. By 1804 Rio de Janeiro provided the greatest volume of imported goods to the southern comarca; and such items as textiles, hats, wine, codfish, paper, gunpowder, and iron all followed the overland route via Minas Gerais to Vila Boa.[54]

The other major southern routes were by river, and the men of São Paulo traded with the Captaincy of Goiás via the Tietê and Paranaíba Rivers. Their journeys took less time and were less hazardous than the much longer Amazonian routes. Others traveled overland to Goiás with pack animals laden with salt, ironwares, and foodstuffs. Upon arrival in Vila Boa, they sold everything, including the mules and horses, and returned to São Paulo with gold.[55] It is likely that much contraband gold as well as other trade goods followed the trade routes to and from São Paulo. Notably, many Paulistas returned with the gold of Goiás to build family fortunes in Santa Anna de Panaíba and elsewhere in São Paulo. Some measure of the relative significance of the São Paulo trade with the southern comarca comes from 1804. By then São Paulo was second to Rio de Janeiro in imports into the southern comarca (see table 5).

Two other important routes of the South were the Paraná River, which connected Goiás to the trade of the Río de la Plata region—and to Spanish silver. The Paraguay River that originates in Mato Grosso was another trade artery that connected Mato Grosso to the Paraná river system. In other words, the gold of Goiás was also traded west to Cuiabá, and then south via the Paraguay River and into Spanish hands. Perhaps this was the return route by which Spanish silver and Paraguayan mate entered the Captaincy of Goiás.[56]

The rivers of the interior of South America thus facilitated the trade of late colonial Brazil. Only one small leg of a vast interior trade network was under the effective authority of the Portuguese governor in Vila Boa—the delivery of the quinto to Rio de Janeiro. Vila Boa's remoteness from the coast made possible an extensive internal trade, including contraband gold, that resembled a free market responsive to the forces of supply and demand rather than a command economy dominated by the Portuguese governors of Goiás, Mato Grosso, or Pará. The interior of Brazil may even have been more integrated into and linked with Spanish America than the Portuguese authorities desired.

Merchant identities—in particular, the names of those who were involved in gold contraband—and their ties with coastal entrepôts are more difficult to determine than trade routes. According to the historian Luis Palacin, however, those responsible for contraband and for trade to the ports were one and the same.[57] In other words, the wealthiest merchants controlled both legitimate and contraband trades between Vila Boa and the coast, and they bribed guards and scribes at the registers or the soldiers who guarded the quinto convoys to the coast. Much of the contraband was actually in gold dust, but they utilized gold bars for more valuable trade. In official records, especially those of the Tribunal de Contas, those customarily accused of contraband, however, were nonwhites (pardos, prêtos, and mestizos), especially those involved in the trade across the sertão to Salvador.[58] What can be teased from the sparse documentation is the following picture of some of the merchants involved in trade in the captaincy.

The first type of merchant was the long-distance trader who imported both dry goods and slaves to Vila Boa and Natividade.[59] One of the wealthiest of these merchants, who was resident in Vila Boa, was João Botelho da Cunha, born in São Miguel in the Azores, who had been a businessman for forty years at the time of his petition in 1765. In his petition to become a familiar or agent of the Inquisition in Vila Boa, he revealed that he and his brother João Antônio Botelho da Cunha did more than sixteen thousand *cruzados* (a monetary unit equal to 400 *réis*) of business. According to one testimony, his fortune was thirty thousand cruzados in size. He customarily traveled between Vila Boa and Bahia, and on one occasion had brought a large convoy of 170 slaves and horses along with dry goods. Other merchants who traded in slaves and dry goods testified on his behalf, suggesting that the Bahian traders commonly dealt in both dry goods and slaves.[60]

The next merchant is of interest because of his educational background at the University of Coimbra. In the 1790s, Antônio de Souza Telles e Menezes was resident in Vila Boa and held the title of *captitão mor* (great captain) of the Ordenanças. He was also professed in the Order of Christ, another marker of high social status in the Portuguese value system. He was a merchant with thirty-three years of experience in the mines, in recognition of which he had served as administrator of the contract for the entradas for six years. Three of his letters establish that he had brought salt-laden beasts from São Paulo to Vila Boa in 1794 as well as ironware from the City of Rio de Janeiro. Thus, he seems to have been important in the trade among Vila Boa, and São Paulo, and Rio de Janeiro.[61] His career, however, illustrates a number of characteristics of the merchants resident in Vila Boa: They did not limit themselves only to trade with one coastal port, and they also combined economic, military, and political roles, in this case serving as a captain in the Ordenanças as well as a tax contractor. If typical of other merchants, he was probably involved in mining—as an investor in a mine and its enslaved labor force—and land ownership, both for status and food production. In many cases, wealthy merchants acquired their vast properties through the bankruptcy of miners who were indebted to them for the purchase of slaves or imported goods.

In 1807 the petition of a third merchant, Lieutenant Manoel José Tavares da Cunha, for the Habit of Christ reveals a variety of roles as a merchant in the Captaincy of Goiás (since 1775). Not only had he managed "a high degree of commerce" in dry goods in Goiás, but he had also worked in São Paulo. After residing in Goiás, he then went to Cuiabá, where he also did business. He bragged that he had sent "many arrobas" of gold to the smelting houses of Goiás and Mato Grosso. In 1776, at his own expense, he had equipped a convoy of forty horses and his own slaves to transport weapons and foodstuffs to supply the garrison on Bananal Island in the Araguaia River, where the Karajá had been pacified in 1775. After his service to the military, he and his two partners (*socios*) received the contract for the entradas of 1782–1787, which indicates that he had also been a tax contractor. Furthermore, he had acted as a lawyer in the causes of the Real Fazenda, administered the mail service, served as Promotor no juizo da Provedoria Geral dos Auzentes, and as Curador Geral of the Orphãos of the Comarca, thus exercising administrative roles. In the previous ten years, he had been a resident of Pilar and Crixás, two wealthy mining towns of Goiás.[62]

The São Paulo/Mato Grosso/Goiás connections of Tavares da Cunha were duplicated by a less able merchant, Antônio Navarro de Abreu, who petitioned for membership in the Order of Christ in 1816. His petition is especially valuable because it clarifies that he dealt in both slaves and agricultural commodities. In 1816 he too had a military title as captain in the first cavalry militia regiment of Goiás, in which he had served for fifteen years, but, as the governor noted when he refused to support the petition, the only military duty he had in Goiás was to walk in processions. He claimed to be one of the best established (wealthiest?) inhabitants of Goiás, with "a great establishment" in Mato Grosso, having sent to one and the other "great caravans of trade goods and slaves." In Mato Grosso, he had supplied the Real Fazenda with supplies needed for the troops. Furthermore, under the previous governor, he had been one of the first to transport goods to Grão Pará as part of the first expedition funded by the Real Fazenda. In other words, he had conducted both private and public trades, and the governor concluded that his services were typical of most merchants in the captaincy and not exceptional enough to merit the special recognition of the Order of Christ.[63]

An examination of the multiple roles of merchants and the diverse trade routes of the Captaincy of Goiás suggests that the vast region of Central Brazil was plugged into the Atlantic economy of the late eighteenth century via the export of gold. Although the ability of the Portuguese to find gold and collect the quinto had declined, population statistics, especially those for slaves, suggest that an internal trade utilizing gold dust mined by blacks was flourishing and that the agro-pastoral economy was beginning to strengthen as many mines were abandoned. By 1800 the Portuguese were complaining about a contraband trade in cattle leaving the captaincy, suggesting that evasion of taxes at the registers was still significant, as it would be in the nineteenth century.[64] The "culture of evasion" was then being transferred to contraband animals.

The first question is this: If the population were increasing in numbers, especially the free population of color, then how were they supporting themselves? Obviously, the answer is by planting foodstuffs, tobacco, cotton, and coffee trees, and raising cattle and pigs. An astute observer, however, Antônio Luis de Souza Leal, argued that the true reasons for the decline of the quinto (see table 3) were not due to lack of gold but rather due to administrative inefficiency in Vila Boa and the societies of black miners who kept the gold for themselves. As he reported, a society of sixty freed (*liberto*) men organized themselves into two groups: forty who mined and twenty who raised foodstuffs to sustain them. Afterward, they divided the gold equally among themselves, thus depriving the king of his royal fifth.[65] That blacks had gold is reflected in the brotherhood records in which they donated gold to support their brotherhoods and build churches and chapels.

The second question is this: If the gold of Goiás circulated so widely in the interior and among so many captaincies, to which port city was the captaincy peripheral? Only Vila Boa was so closely linked to Rio de Janeiro, the second colonial capital; the comarca of the north traded mainly with Brazil's first capital, Salvador; but the gold of Goiás circulated everywhere, and products were introduced from all surrounding captaincies to exchange for that gold. The place of Vila Boa within the context of centers and peripheries continues to be ambiguous. It seems to have been both core and periphery, although in some ways it seems more reminiscent of a trading post (*feitoria*) on an island in an archipelago at sea,[66] in this case a sea of grass (the *cerrado*). Portuguese merchants made their homes in the trading post and established ties with merchants resident in others, such as Cuiabá and Natividade, importing trade goods, animals, and slaves and exporting legal and contraband gold to coastal ports, and on from there. The problem, however, is that Vila Boa was also a mining town with a retail complex of stores and taverns, as well as an administrative center for both church and state. It had at least three major functions, but in spite of these multiple functions, it remained a small town. Its gold had made it important to the Portuguese, but once gold no longer reached Lisbon in the quantities of the past, many of the Portuguese moved on to other more lucrative postings and left Vila Boa to decline as a Portuguese center. Those born in the captaincy, men and women of all colors, continued to pan for gold, plant their crops, raise cattle, and trade with other captaincies. The internal economy established by the mining economy did not completely collapse. Gold, tobacco, leather, cattle, cotton, coffee, and quince marmalades found their way via the old trade routes to neighboring captaincies, while Goianos continued to import salt and European luxury goods. By the time Brasília was inaugurated in 1960, the nation's new capital in the State of Goiás was once again perceived to be the "heart" or center of Brazil, as Vila Boa had been in 1760.

Notes

1. Rio de Janeiro, Instituto Histórico e Geographico Brasileiro (henceforth IHGB), Arq. 1.2.7, vol. 36, Ofício de João Manoel de Mello to the Conde d'Oeiras, Vila Boa, 29 May 1760.
2. Horieste Gomes and Antônio Teixeira Neto, *Geografia Goiás-Tocantins* (Goiânia: Editora UFG, 1993), 59.
3. Discovery: José Maria Pereira de Alencastre, *Anais da Província de Goiás* (1st ed., 1864; repr. ed., Brasília: Editora Gráfica Ipiranga, 1979), 32–47; and Luis Palacin, *Goiás 1772–1822: Estrutura e Conjuntura numa Capitania de Minas*, 2d ed. (Goiânia: Oriente, 1976), 23–26.
4. Palacin, *Goiás*, 48–51. The *vila* (town) status defined the largest populated urban centers. The captaincy had no *cidades* (cities) in the colonial period. At that time, however, Vila Boa was either a village or small town. Its exact population is unknown for its early history.
5. River routes: David Michael Davidson, "Rivers and Empire: The Madeira Route and the Incorporation of the Brazilian Far West, 1737–1808" (Ph.D. diss., Yale University, 1970); see the map before xi, and xvii–xxii.
6. Descriptions of roads traversed and distances in leagues are in Rio de Janeiro, Biblioteca Nacional, manuscript section (hereafter RJBN), 9,2,10, [Luiz Antônio da Silva e Souza], Memoria sobre o Descobrimento, Governo, População e cousas mais notaveis da Capitania de Goyaz, Vila Boa, 13 August 1786, ff. 49–50. A published version, which is dated 30 September 1812, is in *Revista Trimensal de História e Geographia* 16 (1849; reprint edition, Goiânia: UFG, 1967), 136–39.
7. Cerrado: Gomes and Teixeira Neto, *Geografia*, 96–98.
8. Indian policy: Mary Karasch, "Catequese e cativeiro: Política indigenista em Goiás, 1780–1889," trans. Beatriz Perrone-Moisés in *História dos Índios no Brasil*, ed. Manuela Carneiro da Cunha (São Paulo: Companhia das Letras, 1992), 397–412. Indian resistance: Mary Karasch, "Interethnic Conflict and Resistance on the Brazilian Frontier of Goiás, 1750–1890," in Donna J. Guy and Thomas E. Sheridan, eds., *Contested Ground* (Tucson: University of Arizona, 1998), 128–34.
9. Population, 1784: Lisbon, Arquivo Histórico Ultramarino (henceforth AHU), formerly caixa 4 (henceforth the caixas indicated are from the old system before the reorganization of the Goiás documents), Processo no. 11; e ultimo, "He relatorio este Processo ao estado das Rendas Reaes no tempo prezente . . . Pelos Mappas de População se mostra, que no anno de 1784 tinha Vila Boa . . . ," 2 March 1804; Population, 1785: Lisbon, Biblioteca da Ajuda, 54-V-12, no. 5, Noticia de todos os Governadores e população das provincias do Brasil, 1782, ff. 33–34.
10. City of Goiás, Arquivo Municipal das Bandeiras (henceforth AMB), vol. 353, no. 15, letter to Governor Tristão da Cunha Menezes from João Pereira Pinto Bravo, Vigario, Vila Boa, 22 May 1799.
11. Lisbon, Gabinete de Estudos Arqueológicos de Engenharia Militar, Arquivo de Desenhos (and maps), #3890, 6-82-117, "Planta de Villa Boa Capital da Capitania de Goyas Levantado no ano de 1782 pelo Ill.mo e Ex.mo Snr. Luis da Cunha Menezes. . . . It was drawn by dragoon Manoel Ribeiro Guimarães. Besides the number of 554 households with 3,000 persons, the number of military units was noted. The total of 699 households is in Silva e Souza, Memoria, f. 37.

12. A summary of major indigenous groups in Goiás is in Karasch, "Interethnic Conflict," 128–34.
13. Mary C. Karasch, *Slave Life in Rio de Janeiro, 1808–1850* (Princeton, N.J.: Princeton University Press, 1987), 61–62.
14. Lisbon, Arquivo Nacional da Torre do Tombo (henceforth ANTT), Conselho de Guerra, Secretaria de Estado da Guerra, Relação das freguesias de Portugal, 1798, numero de ordem 279.
15. Governors of Goiás: Palacin, *Goiás*, 140–44.
16. Karasch, "Catequese e cativeiro," 397–412; and Mary Karasch, "Os quilombos do ouro na capitania de Goiás," trans. João José Reis in *Liberdade por um fio: História dos quilombos no Brasil*, ed. João José Reis and Flávio dos Santos Gomes (São Paulo: Companhia das Letras, 1996), 253–54.
17. Wilhelm Ludwig von Eschwege, *Pluto Brasiliensis*, 2 vols., trans. Domício de Figueiredo Murta (Belo Horizonte: Editora Itatiaia, 1979), vol. 2: 12; note 245, p. 279. The sources for the statement about the governor's giving the first bateada are on p. 12 and in note 245 on p. 279.
18. Corruption: Ibid., vol. 2: 61. Conde de São Miguel: Alencastre, *Anais*, 125–58; and RJBN, manuscript section, 3,1,25, Goiás (Capitania), Prospecto da Capitania de Goyáz no anno de mil outocentos [*sic*] e trez [1803], em que tomou pósse de Secretario do Governo della o Bacharel Manoel Joaquim da Silveira Felis (a strong denunciation of all that was wrong with the captaincy, including corruption).
19. Intendents: Von Eschwege, *Pluto*, vol. 1: 61. The conflict between Governor Dom Manuel de Meneses and the Intendant of gold, Manuel Pinto Coelho, in which it was affirmed that "the intendant did not have to obey him," is narrated in Hernani Cidade, "Um Dramático Episódio da História de Goiás," in *Anais do Congresso Comemorativo* of the Instituto Histórico e Geographico Brasileiro (1963), vol. 1 (Rio de Janeiro: Imprensa Nacional, 1967), 417–28. A list of the twelve intendants who served in Goiás are in Francisco Ferreira dos Santos Azevedo, *Annuario Histórico, Geographico e Descriptivo do Estado de Goyaz para 1910* (Brasília: reprint edition; SPHAN/8a DR, 1987), 102.
20. Judges and slowness of justice: Palacin, *Goiás*, 147–52.
21. Devassas: Stuart B. Schwartz, *Sovereignty and Society in Colonial Brazil* (Berkeley and Los Angeles: University of California Press, 1973), 164.
22. Division into comarcas: Manuel Aires de Casal, *Corografia Brasílica* (1st ed. 1817; Belo Horizonte: Ed. Itatiaia, 1976), 150–51.
23. Ouvidores: Dauril Alden, *Royal Government in Colonial Brazil* (Berkeley and Los Angeles: University of California Press, 1968), 423–24; Schwartz, *Sovereignty and Society*, 25–26, 149–50. List of colonial ouvidores: Azevedo, *Annuario Histórico*, 101.
24. Judges (de Fóra and ordinários): Casal, *Corografia*, 150–52. Lists of the juízes de fóra are in Azevedo, *Annuario Histórico*, 101. See also Palacin, *Goiás*, 149.
25. The Casa da Câmara was built in 1763. A picture of it and the jail is in Ana Maria Borges and Luiz Palacin, *Patrimônio Histórico de Goiás*, 2d ed. (Brasília: SPHAN/próMemória, 1987), 20.
26. Real Fazenda: Casal, *Corografia*, 153; and Palacin, *Goiás*, 152–53.
27. Quinto: Palacin, *Goiás*, 152–53 (table of income from the quintos, 1753–1822); and Gilka V. F. de Salles, *Economia e Escravidão na Capitania de Goiás* (Goiânia: CEGRAF/UFG, 1992), 184–89 (tables). The Casa de Fundição (variously translated as foundry house or smelting house), which guarded the king's fifth, is described in C. R. Boxer, *The Golden Age of Brazil, 1695–1750* (New York: St. Martins Press, 1995), 56.
28. Entradas, dízimos, and other taxes: Palacin, *Goiás*, 153–56, 215 (table of income from the entradas).
29. An example of the custom of collecting donations in Goiás is from a letter written to the ouvidor da comarca from the Provincial of Francisco of the Observance of Portugal regarding a brother friar, José de Nossa Senhora dos Anjos, who had gone to Goiás ten years earlier to ask for alms to rebuild the Convent of Belém in Lisbon. The problem was that he had not yet sent any money back, and so the provincial

asked the ouvidor's assistance in finding the gold and sending it to a coastal seaport for export to Lisbon. The letter is in Lisbon at AHU, caixa 2, 11 September 1755.

30. Lisbon, ANTT, Conselho de Guerra, Relação das freguesias, 1798, numero 279. These are Portuguese monetary notations for millions of réis.
31. Bandeiras: Karasch, "Interethnic Conflict," 124–25. For correspondence on bandeiras of the 1770s, see Lisbon, AHU, Cod. 1657, Livro primeiro para registo de Portarias, Bandos, Edictáes, Instrucções, e Regimentos para as Bandeiras, . . . da Capitania de Goyaz, e Minas. . . .
32. Portuguese military units, paid: Palacin, *Goiás*, 156–58. Report on the services of José Maria Pinto Peixoto, alferes of the company of dragoons, who served with eight soldiers of the pedestres preventing Xavante attacks on Carmo and Pontal in the northern comarca. He arrived in Goiás in 1799 and left about 1805, when the governor ordered him to follow his father to Angola. Lisbon, AHU, caixas 40, 50, Requerimentos of José Maria Pinto Peixoto, 11 September 1805 and 23 September 1805 with attached letter of Governor Dom Francisco de Assis Mascarenhas, Vila Boa, 30 September 1805(?).
33. Pedestres: Ibid. On racial mixture, see Rio de Janeiro, Instituto Histórico e Geographico Brasileiro, Arq. 1.2.7, vol. 36, "Ofício" of João Manuel de Mello to Francisco Xavier de Mendonça Furtado, Vila Boa, 4 July 1766, f. 147; Lisbon, Arquivo Histórico do Tribunal de Contas, Livro de registo das representações da Capitania de Goyaz . . . , #4076, 3 Prejuizo, 26 April 1785, f. 8 (indios mansos); and City of Goiás, AMB, #444, Praça de Militares, Pedestres [lists of troops], 1777–94.
34. Ordenanças: Palacin, *Goiás*, 129; Silva e Souza, Memoria, *Revista* 16 (1849), 94; and "Lista da Companhia das Ordenanças do Distrito do Arrayal de Santa Cruz da provincia de Goiás creada no anno de 1773 . . . , Goiânia, Arquivo Histórico de Goiás (hereafter AHG), Doc. Diversa, 1823–1824, Correspondencia dirigida do Comandante das Armas, which reveals that one man was age eighty, others seventy and sixty-five, while many others were in their forties and fifties.
35. Pardo protest: "Os homens pardos nacionais e habitantes da Capitania de Villa boa de Goyaz, . . ." Lisbon, AHU, caixa 41, 5 February 1803 and 7 January 1804. See also Lisbon, AHU, caixa 25, letter of the Câmara of Vila Boa, 31 September 1785; letter of Governor Tristão da Cunha, 20 May 1789; and his note of 5 July 1790 that *mulatos* who had the patent of a colonel did not have any right to be interim governor.
36. Henriques: AHU, caixa 7, Ofício de Luis da Cunha Meneses, Vila Boa, 16 May 1783; table 4; and Goiânia, Archive of the Cúria, Diocese de Goyaz, Registros, Lançamento das cargas, lista da Companhia de Infantaria, Capitão Luis Gonçalves dos Santos and his men, 1799.
37. The original copies of the signed military patents for Goiás are in Lisbon at the Arquivo Histórico Ultramarino. When I consulted them, they were scattered throughout the uncataloged boxes of Goiás documents, which have since been reorganized by date.
38. Weak church due to economic decadence: AHU, Goiás, letter of Filippe Neri Monteiro e Mendonça to Bispo de Titopoli, 5 June 1805.
39. The first resident bishop was Dom Francisco Ferreira de Azevedo, who was confirmed as bishop in 1844 and died in 1854. Azevedo, *Annuário Histórico*, 123. Luiz Mott identifies those who worked for the Inquisition in Goiás, as well as victims who were deported to Portugal, in "Inquisição em Goiás—Fontes e Pistas," *Revista do Instituto Histórico de Goiás* 13 (1993), 33–76.
40. Of fifty priests ordained in Rio, only one was sent to Santa Anna in Vila Boa de Goiás: Rio de Janeiro, Arquivo da Cúria Metropolitana, Livro 2, Ordens, Relação das igrejas aqui se aderão os 50 Ecclezasticos que se admittirão a ordens em virtude do avizo de 16 de 7bro de 1780, 27 August 1782, f. 104.
41. Auguste de Saint-Hilaire, *Viagem à Província de Goiás*, trans. Regina Regis Junqueira (Belo Horizonte: Editora Itatiaia, 1975), 53.
42. The large households of priests are evident from household lists of 1783 and 1820, which also recorded the women and children living in their households: RJBN, manuscript section, 16,3,2, Notícia Geral da Capitania de Goiás, 1783; and Goiânia,

AHG, Doc. Div., no. 68, Correspondência, Raymundo José da Cunha Mattos, 1823–1824.

43. Secular duties and complaints: AHG, uncataloged document in restoration, Ofício of Governor Fernando Delgado Freire de Castilho to the Marquez d'Aguiar, Vila Boa, 31 May 1816 (Manoel da Silva Alvares); and complaint against the priest Joaquim Liandro da Silva for nonperformance of his religious duties is at Rio de Janeiro, Arquivo Nacional (henceforth RJAN), caixa 315, pacote 2, doc. 7, queixas, Goiás, without a date but attached to documents dated 1821.
44. Various *Irmandade compromissos* for Goiás are archived in Lisbon at the AHU, codices 1812–1815 and other codices. Another collection is in the City of Goiás at the Biblioteca da Fundação Educacional de Goiás (henceforth BFEG), which are uncataloged.
45. For contemporary religious traditions, see the publications of Carlos Rodrigues Brandão, such as, *O Divino, O Santo e a Senhora* (Rio de Janeiro: Campanha da Defesa do Folclore Brasileiro, 1978).
46. The culture of evasion: A. J. R. Russell-Wood, "Centers and Peripheries in the Luso-Brazilian World, 1500–1808," in this volume. One of the famous cases of successful smuggling was that of Friar Ignacio de Santa Teresa, a Carmelite, who took three hundred *oitavas* of gold through the register of São Domingos. He hid the gold in a statue of Our Lady and passed undetected. The Portuguese learned of what he had done only because he confessed his "sin" on his deathbed. Lisbon, AHU, cod. 1657, Livro primeiro para registo de Portarias . . . , Capitania de Goyaz, e Minas . . . , f. 17.
47. The Salvador–Vila Boa trade: Lisbon, AHU, caixa 35, Vila Boa em Câmara, 28 July 1792, which concerns the decline in trade in slaves and foodstuffs; RJBN, manuscript section, 11,2,4, Roteiro do Maranhão á Goyaz pela Capitania do Piauhy, 1800 (copy).
48. Mato Grosso trade: Davidson, "Rivers and Empire," xxii, 37 (opening of the Goiás-Cuiabá route in 1736), and 48 (Moxos); on the amount of gold sent from Goiás to Mato Grosso, see 105–6 and 362–64 (table).
49. Maranhão, Piauí, Pernambuco trades: Lisbon, AHU, Cod. 1657, Livro primeiro para registo de Portarias, f. 29 (contraband gold via Bocaina). Commodities traded: AHU, caixa 2, letter of Captain Mor Antônio de Souza Telles Menezes, 16 November 1793, 24 December 1793; AHG, Doc. Div. #69, Origenais dos Comandantes dos Registros e Présidios da Província, 1823–1825, ff. 58, 60, 62–63, 255, 317–18; Salles, *Economia e Escravidão*, 161–62. Gold trade: AHU, caixa 11, Manoel Gomez da Costa, Intendant of Gold, São Félix, 15 March 1766.
50. Trade routes in Maranhão: RJBN, manuscript section, Roteiro do Maranhão á Goyaz pela Capitania do Piauhy, 1800, copy, ff. 7, 12, note 40.
51. Tocantins-Belém trade: Dalísia E. Martins Doles, *As Comunicações Fluviais pelo Tocantins e Araguaia no Século XIX* (Goiânia: Editora Oriente, 1973), 17–21, 27–30, 39–44, 47–50. Gold smuggling due to the opening of the Tocantins River is in Lisbon, Arquivo Histórico do Tribunal de Contas (henceforth ATC), #4076, Contadoria Geral, 21 April 1801, ff. 139–41. Other documentation of trade is in RJAN, Cod. 807, vol. 10, Joaquim Teotonio Segurado, Memoria sobre o Commercio da Capitania de Goyaz, 1806, ff. 11–14; RJBN, 11,2,4, Roteiro do Maranhão á Goyaz pela Capitania do Piauhy; and RJBN, I-31,21,9, Copia da Memoria oferecida pelo Capitam d'ordenanças Francisco Jozé Pinto de Mangalhens em 3 de Janr.o de 1813.
52. Araguaia and Karajá trades: Doles, *Comunicações Fluviais*, 21–23, 44–47; and AHG, Seção de Municípios, Niquelândia, letter of Alex.e de Souza Von Ar.o J., São José de Tocantins, 5 February 1776, to Rmo. Snr. Vig.ro José Pires dos Santos e Sousa; IHGB, lata 281, pasta 4, doc. 10, Ofício de Francisco de Souza Coutinho to Dom Rodrigo de Souza Coutinho, Pará, 24 June 1797; and RJAN, Cod. 807, vol. 10, Segurado, Memoria, 1806, ff. 13–14.
53. Africans imported into Belém (1757–1804); Davidson, "Rivers and Empire," 477–84. On the trade in Indian women to Belém see RJBN, I-31,21,9, Cópia da Memória oferecida pelo Capitam d'ordenanças Francisco José Pinto de Mangalhens [*sic*] em 3 de janeiro de 1813; with notes dated 1815.
54. Vila Boa—Minas Gerais to Rio trade: Lisbon, AHU, caixa 43, Letter of José de Aguirre do Amaral, Cabo de Esquadra da Companhia de Dragões, Registo de

Dezemboque, 19 April 1806. In 1791–1799, 1,208 new slaves were brought to Goiás, mostly from Rio. See Salles, *Economia e Escravidão*, 162.

55. São Paulo to Vila Boa trade: IHGB, lata 48, doc. 3, "Digressão que fez João Caetano da Silva, natural de Meia Ponte, em 1817, para descobrir como com eff..o descobrio, a nova Navegação entre a Capitania de Goiáz, e a de São Paulo, pelo Rio dos Bois até ao Rio Grande, . . . On the attached map, he shows that the traditional overland route ran from Vila Boa to Meia Ponte, Bomfim, and Santa Cruz; then across the rivers Corumbá, Parnaíba, Rio Grande, Rio Pardo, and Rio Jagua-rimirim; to Vila de Mojimirim, Vila de São Carlos,Vila de Jundiahy, and finally São Paulo. On the salt trade from São Paulo, see AHU, Goiás, Relatorio de Antônio Luis de Souza Leal sobre o estado geral da capitania, Vila Boa, 2 March 1805; and Arquivo do Estado de São Paulo, #334, lata 88, 1802–1803, petition of Dona Anna Rita Mascarenhas e Silva with attached document dated 1 June 1803, Vila Boa, regarding the trade goods her husband imported into Vila Boa from São Paulo via the register of Rio das Velhas. Alida C. Metcalf, in her *Family and Frontier in Colonial Brazil: Santana de Parnaíba, 1580–1822* (Berkeley and Los Angeles: University of California Press, 1992), 57–60, describes the links between wealthy families in Santana and Goiás.
56. Silver trade via Mato Grosso: Davidson, "Rivers and Empire," 198–200.
57. Contraband by merchants: Palacin, *Goiás*, 65; and Von Eschwege, *Pluto Brasiliensis*, vol. 2: 155–60 (contraband by *comboieiros* and tavern owners).
58. Contraband by nonwhites: Lisbon, AHU, caixa 2, 16 November 1793; and ATC #4076, Contadoria Geral do Rio de Janeiro, 9 August 1787.
59. Trade in new Africans from Bahia: Goiás, BFEG, unclassified Paracatú documents, attached to *escrituras* of July 1781, which record the sale of four slaves of the Mina nation for nine hundred *oitavas* of gold. They had been brought to the captaincy by a comboieiro from the City of Bahia. Merchants who traded large convoys of slaves and dry goods from Bahia are identified in Mott, "Inquisição," 170. See also note 60.
60. João Botelho da Cunha: Mott, "Inquisição, 70–72.
61. Antônio de Souza Telles e Menezes: Lisbon, AHU, caixa 2, 16 November 1793; 24 December 1793; 12 April 1794; 2 May 1794; and 10 May 1794. A protest signed by him is in caixa 44, 28 December 1800.
62. Tenente Manoel José Tavares da Cunha: Lisbon, AHU, caixa 43, Requerimento of 22 December 1807; and caixa 36, Ouvedoria Geral, Autto Civeis, Vila Boa, 1800.
63. Antônio Navarro de Abreu: Rio de Janeiro, Arquivo Nacional, IJJ9-193, Ministério do Reino, Goiás, doc. 2, Fernando Delgado Freire de Castilho, Vila Boa, 31 May 1816.
64. Contraband trade in cattle: Lisbon, AHU, caixa 4, Manoel Joaquim de Aguiar Mourão, Meia Ponte, 29 December 1800. David J. McCreery is currently studying the contraband cattle trades of nineteenth-century Goiás.
65. Lisbon, AHU, Goiás, 1805, Relatorio de Antônio Luis de Souza Leal sobre o estado geral da capitania, Vila Boa, 2 March 1805.
66. Concept of archipelago: Davidson, "Rivers and Empires," xvii.

Other Netherlands beyond the Sea

Dutch America between Metropolitan Control and Divergence, 1600–1795

Wim Klooster

In 1655, Adriaen van der Donck, the founder of a small Dutch colony just north of Manhattan, passed away prematurely. In the year he died, Van der Donck published a book on New Netherland (the area in North America governed by the Dutch) that featured a dialogue between a Dutch patriot and a New Netherlander. The latter enumerated a variety of ways in which the Dutch state could benefit from a flourishing province in North America. The first advantage he listed brought out how fresh the war with the House of Habsburg was in the Dutch collective memory. If hostilities with Spain erupted again, no place in the world would be better situated to hit the Spanish hard than New Netherland. The colony also offered iron, timber, and wheat, should the home country ever lack these items. In due course, the colony would boast a sizable population,[1] which could stand by the Netherlands in their hour of need. Finally, the settler argued, those people who had been unemployed since the end of the war would find work in the colony and "erect another Netherland, as an anchor and buttress of the Dutch state."[2]

In the seventeenth century, the Dutch founded other Netherlands at many different places in the Western Hemisphere: in the Caribbean, in Brazil, and on the "Wild Coast" (or Guiana), that vast and thinly populated area between Venezuela and Brazil. This essay is intended to shed some light on the relationship between the Dutch Republic and the neo-Dutch world across the Atlantic. What connective features were there, and to what extent did the center impose its will on the periphery?

The center, the republic—also known as the United Provinces—is often considered a maverick state in early modern Europe. Its domestic authority is said to have been modest compared to the surrounding states, all of them monarchies, who succeeded in strengthening their positions by concentrating their instruments of power and eliminating local rights and privileges. The Dutch case contrasted sharply with the centralizing tendencies of state formation elsewhere. The Union of Utrecht, the constitutive charter of the Dutch Republic, obliged the signing provinces to maintain the privileges and liberties of all the signatories. Since the republic's government continued to be based on provincial assemblies and town councils, power and authority were heavily decentralized.[3]

The great statesman Johan de Witt once aptly called the Dutch polity a confederation of sovereign republics rather than a single sovereign state. It was, indeed, the provinces rather than the States General—the general assembly of provincial delegations—that in the final analysis wielded supreme power. The justice system was still more fragmented. More than three hundred urban and rural courts dealt with criminal cases in the provinces of Holland, Zeeland, and Brabant alone. Persons convicted on account of minor offenses were banished from only the jurisdiction in question.[4] The Dutch state consequently lacked a distinct center, as was borne out in the era of revolutionary agitation that marked the 1780s. The conflict was not fought out on a national stage, but on local and provincial levels. It was "essentially diffuse and episodic."[5]

How did this decentralized state deal with its overseas provinces? Colonial rule was mostly left to two companies, whose combined domains encompassed the entire world: the East and West India Companies (VOC and WIC). The WIC was founded as a joint-stock enterprise in 1621 to coordinate Dutch activities in the Atlantic world. A private company, the WIC also had the attributes of a state. The States General not only granted the company a monopoly of trade and navigation in its domain, they officially allowed the WIC to administer justice, make treaties with foreign princes, and maintain an army.[6]

The company came to display the features of the federal system from which it stemmed. Formally, all provinces might be equal within the Dutch Republic, but in practice some were more equal than others. Although each of the seven United Provinces had one vote in the States General, the economic, fiscal, and demographic significance of Holland was often the deciding factor. Holland therefore viewed most other provinces as dependencies rather than as equal partners in an alliance.[7]

In the same vein, Holland, or more precisely Amsterdam, dominated WIC affairs, although initially sharing many responsibilities with Zeeland, its partner in Dutch expansion. Their primacy was laid down in a distributive code, which underlined both the balance of power between the provinces and the contributions expected from each of the five regional company boards or "chambers." By virtue of the large share of capital they had invested in it, and in keeping with the prevailing tax system, Amsterdam's contribution to company activities was set at four-ninths, Zeeland's at two-ninths, and the other three chambers at one-ninth apiece. Similarly, Amsterdam supplied eight directors and Zeeland four to the so-called Board of Nineteen, which exercised the highest authority.[8]

The day-to-day activities were left to the individual chambers, which kept their own books and managed their own shipping. The chamber system had its flaws. It was hard for the Board of Nineteen to organize tasks, since their authority was circumscribed by the chambers that appointed them—just like the States General were tied to the provincial governments (the Provincial States). Furthermore, the rule limiting company directors to a three-year term was not conducive to administrative continuity.[9]

Apart from an occasional windfall, the financial performance of the West India Company was miserable. The war in Brazil, first with Habsburg Spain and then with local and Portuguese forces, was very costly, and the supplying of African slaves on credit to Portuguese planters did nothing to improve company finances. When the WIC finally went bankrupt in 1674, an organization replaced it that had little in common with its predecessor except the name. Having already lost most of its commercial monopolies in previous decades, the company was now dismantled as a military machine.[10]

Unlike the VOC in its domain, the WIC did not govern all Dutch colonies in the Atlantic world. As emigration was slow at best, and in an effort to economize on the expensive task of colonization, the company after 1628 encouraged private initiatives. It assigned patroonships to applicants, so-called patroons who were granted land in fief, that they were expected to utilize, provided that they transferred fifty colonists within three years' time.[11] It also entrusted patroons with certain administrative and judicial powers.

The WIC delegated the Caribbean islands of St. Martin, St. Eustatius, and Saba to patroons shortly after the Dutch took possession in the 1630s, while Tobago for some time functioned as a patroonship under the name New Walcheren. On the Wild Coast, Berbice was the private domain since 1627 of the Van Pere family from Zeeland. The second WIC gained control of all three Dutch Leeward Islands in 1680, but the patroonship of Berbice survived until 1720, when the colony passed to a joint-stock company, the Society of Berbice.[12] In North America the patroonships had only a short life, with one noteworthy exception: Rensselaerswijck, developed by the Van Rensselaer family along the Hudson River in New York.[13]

The West India Company might have been in charge of Dutch America, but its position was not that of a sovereign. That is to say, it remained accountable to the States General, which interfered more in Atlantic matters than it did in the affairs of the VOC. It was possible, for example, to seek a review in The Hague of a sentence passed in Suriname. In such a case, the States General refrained from serving as a tribunal, but preferred to be guided by advice from the Supreme Court of Holland and Zeeland or the tribunal of government attorneys.[14]

That Amsterdam and Zeeland were the metropolitan bases of the Dutch Atlantic world is well established. Amsterdam in particular played an important role in the migration to the New World. The Dutch entrepôt and New Netherland were part of a single labor market, similar to what has been suggested for Great Britain and its American colonies.[15] Large numbers of Dutch and foreign job seekers were constantly on the move to Amsterdam. The United Provinces in general held a great attraction for numerous foreigners. Half of the soldiers in the Dutch army were born abroad, and Germans, Poles, and Scandinavians lent their weight in a similar measure to the Dutch merchant marine, admiralty, whaling industry, and both the VOC and WIC.[16]

For many of them Amsterdam was not the finishing point of their wanderings, but rather the stepping stone to a new world. A breakdown of available data on both the Amsterdam labor market and migration to New Netherland according to place of origin reveals the degree to which immigration to Amsterdam resembled that to New Netherland.[17] In either case, just over half were Dutchmen (Amsterdam: 53.9 percent, New Netherland: 51.0 percent), one-third of all persons were from Germany or Scandinavia (Amsterdam: 33.9 percent, New Netherland: 34.2 percent), one-seventh from the German coastal area, including Schleswig-Holstein (Amsterdam:

13.5 percent, New Netherland: 14.2 percent), and one-ninth from the inland parts of Germany (Amsterdam: 11.1 percent, New Netherland: 11.0 percent).

Amsterdam's ties were particularly close with Delaware, where it briefly ruled the colony of New Amstel. An expedition led from New Amsterdam, New Netherland's capital, by director-general Petrus Stuyvesant captured New Amstel from Sweden in 1655, but the West India Company was unable to bear the costs of colonization it therefore transferred the colony to Amsterdam, not the chamber but the town, which named it after a village and country district adjoining Amsterdam. In 1657, Amsterdam tried to develop New Amstel as an alternative granary for the Baltic, but the English conquest of the Dutch settlements in North America cut this effort short just seven years later.[18]

Amsterdam also maintained strong ties with Curaçao. Shortly after its conquest, the WIC board delegated the administration of Curaçao to the Amsterdam Chamber.[19] Commercially, the island "belonged" to Amsterdam. In some cases, Amsterdam firms even carried the risk of intra-Caribbean trade by Curaçaoan vessels. Likewise, the merchants of the Amsterdam oceangoing trade sometimes provided financial help to their less substantial colleagues in Curaçao when they found themselves short of cash, by granting short-term loans.[20] Seven in every eight ships sailing from Curaçao to the metropolis in the first half of the eighteenth century left port for Amsterdam, and only one anchored in Flushing, Middelburg, or another Zeeland port. In the same period, Dutch shipping to St. Eustatius was also firmly in the hands of Amsterdam merchants.[21]

There was more to Curaçao's and St. Eustatius's relationship with Amsterdam. Not only did Amsterdam maintain a regular sea link with both islands, it even set them up in its own likeness. Neither Curaçao nor Statia derived its economic significance from crop production. Rather, they developed as entrepôts, emporia, where commercial exchange took place; ships were repaired, fitted out, and bought and sold; and several financial facilities were available. Curaçao was initially out of bounds for non-Dutch vessels, but in 1675, at the outset of the activities of the second WIC, the company declared the island a free port. This action meant that private traders from all countries could come to the port of Willemstad and purchase slaves and West Indian produce.[22] From then on, the island of Curaçao became important far beyond its small size, both as an entrepôt that attracted merchants from all parts of the Caribbean, and a transit point for trade with the United Provinces.

Amsterdam's concentration on New Netherland and the Caribbean islands was matched by Zeeland's focus on the Wild Coast, which went back to the early days of Dutch expansion. In the mid-1590s, Zeelanders set up two trading posts along the Amazon River, and erected another one at the Essequibo River. A contemporary legend may have lured some of them, including Mayor Geleyn ten Haeff of Middelburg; in 1599, he fitted out a large ship "to visit the river called Dorado, situated in America."[23]

Although the economic value of the region fell short of expectations, Zeeland interests never waned. It is telling that when Amsterdam acquired a colony of its own in Delaware, the WIC almost simultaneously transferred the job of colonizing and governing the small Wild Coast colonies of Essequibo and Pomeroon to three Zeeland towns: Middelburg, Veere, and Flushing.[24] Nor was it accidental that the Zeelanders conquered Suriname, an English colony in Guiana, during the second Anglo-Dutch war (1665–67); when the Provincial States of Zeeland found their plan for an attack on the English colonies in the Caribbean blocked by the other provinces, they dispatched a fleet of their own, which captured the English fort at the mouth of the Suriname River.[25] However, when they found out that colonization entailed considerable expenses, the states sold their "conquest" to the West India Company. The WIC, for its part, entrusted Suriname to a new joint-stock company, the Society of Suriname.

Abandoning Suriname closed an important chapter in Zeeland history and underscored the decline of the province's contributions to overseas economic projects. At the root of the problem was the downward turn its economy took soon after the founding of the WIC. After the Peace of Münster, privateering, once a Zeeland specialty, was no longer the important source of revenue it had been during the war. While Holland benefited from the restructuring of the national economy, Zeeland did not share in the postwar boom of trade and industry. Its role in inter-European and transatlantic trade diminished rapidly.[26] To stem the tide, the VOC and WIC directors from Zeeland frequently argued for a fixed ratio between the annual number of Zeeland- and Amsterdam-based voyages outside Europe as laid down in the charters of both companies. Staunch defenders of the various WIC monopolies, they also opposed all pleas of Amsterdam merchants for private trade within the domain of the WIC.[27]

The Zeelanders were fighting a losing battle. Even when they ruled Suriname, they were faced with the ubiquitous Amsterdammers investing in the plantations, shipping sugar to Amsterdam refineries, and before long dominating the commerce between colony and metropolis. By 1682, the city of Amsterdam became the co-owner of Suriname.[28] Still, Zeeland did not completely abandon the Wild Coast. Its WIC chamber continued to administer the small colony on the Essequibo River, and throughout the eighteenth century sought in vain to block the trade of other chambers with the planters. The real rivals, meanwhile, were the North Americans who came to dominate Essequibo's trade.[29]

While the bonds between Essequibo and the metropolis eventually became tenuous, those between old Holland and "New Holland" (Dutch Brazil) remained strong. Few colonies anywhere were so completely reliant on the homeland for their most basic needs. Dutch Brazil's food supply was precarious from the very beginning. Following the invasion of 1630, the troops in Recife subsisted on provisions sent from the Netherlands, despite the presence of orange, lemon, and coconut trees in the neighboring town of Olinda. Afraid of being ambushed by the Portuguese, the Dutch refrained from going inland.[30] The problem did not go away after their colony obtained a firm footing. Before long, its economy revolved around sugar, to the detriment of manioc production. Planters systematically ignored ordinances that called for the cultivation of between two hundred and one thousand manioc beds per slave.[31] Monoculture led to such a dependence on food supplies from the homeland that even the Portuguese residents of New Holland came to prefer Dutch lard, butter, and oil. That the only surviving Dutch word in northeastern Brazil is *brote*, a corruption of the Dutch *brood* (bread), is telling.[32]

The transport of victuals from Dutch metropolitan ports was very expensive, yet vital, for the hinterland of New Holland could not sustain the 11,000 people living on Recife's spit of land. With the Dutch struggling to control even their own Brazilian ports, the Portuguese rebellion of 1645 had a disastrous effect on the food stock. During the siege of Recife, a soldier in the service of the WIC wrote in his diary that horses, dogs, cats, and rats were his best fare.[33] Trying to find a way out of this situation, the WIC encouraged the settlers of New Netherland to start sending fish, flour, and other local produce to New Holland, but to no avail.[34]

Residents of Dutch America considered the United Provinces their native soil. Their home country provided a model to emulate and a source of legitimacy, expressed in the names of overseas provinces: New Holland, New Netherland, New Walcheren.[35] The metropolis also left its imprint on the landscape of the colonies. A medical doctor accompanying the British forces that conquered Demerara (Guiana) in 1796 detected a striking physical resemblance to the Netherlands: "I could have fancied myself in Holland," he noted. "The land appeared as one wide flat intersected with dykes and canals—the roads mere banks of mud and clay, thrown from the ditches as their sides—and the houses bedaubed and painted in tawdry colors, like Dutch toys, giving the whole a striking resemblance to the mother country."[36]

The colonies came to resemble the republic in less tangible ways as well. Residents of Friesland, Overijssel, or any other province, shared a myriad of folkways with people in the overseas settlements. Arriving colonists were addressed in the Dutch language and encountered the same dishes and forms of entertainment they had grown up with. Weights and measures were familiar, as was the calendar: the main church holidays were Easter, Ascension Day, Pentecost, and Christmas, just as they were in the homeland. Moreover, colonial authorities saw to it that memorable events in the Netherlands received public attention. In 1646, for instance, the surrender of Hulst, a Spanish stronghold in the Netherlands, was celebrated with cannon shots in all the forts of New Holland.[37] A less joyful occasion prompted the Provincial States of Zeeland in 1673 to order a day of prayer and fasting in Suriname. It seemed that the final hour had come for the fatherland, overrun by troops from France, Münster, and Cologne, and embroiled in naval warfare with England.

The appointment of a new *stadholder* was the Dutch equivalent of a coronation.[38] The news of William IV's elevation in 1747 was celebrated exuberantly in Suriname. Everybody, including the slaves, dressed in orange cockades or ribbons. The stadholder's birthday was marked with gunshots, salutes, and festivities with balls and suppers throughout Dutch America, as were other national days of commemoration. In 1779, services were held in all churches of Paramaribo in celebration of the bicentenary of the Union of Utrecht, the original alliance of the United Provinces.[39]

In the Dutch Republic, days of prayer were proclaimed on special occasions to implore divine blessing or to thank God for grace.[40] Colonial days of prayer were sometimes proclaimed in the wake of a local event, as happened in New Netherland after the annexation of New Sweden. Local anniversaries sprang up as well, such as that of the Dutch invasion in Brazil.[41] On Curaçao, an annual day of prayer, fasting, and thanksgiving celebrated the destruction of an impressive French naval expedition in 1678, which miraculously ran aground on a coral reef just as it was ready to attack the island.[42]

Sunday may have been the day of the week when the colonies looked most like the Netherlands. Its significance went beyond the preaching of God's word. In New Netherland, the church was "the chief cultural institution. It regularly brought together the population, guarded the language and cultural heritage, defended

European values, and fostered the community spirit."[43] Colonial authorities therefore set great store by churchgoing. In the patroonship Rensselaerswijck (New Netherland), weekly church attendance was compulsory, and persons staying away were fined according to their means and gender.[44]

While the church of New Netherland was created ex nihilo, in northeastern Brazil the Dutch found a well-entrenched Catholic church. They left the institution untouched, but confiscated several church buildings and adapted their interiors. The changes amounted to a mini-Reformation, as the altar and all images were removed in accordance with the Heidelberg Catechism. In keeping with Dutch practices, a Bible was then placed in the middle of the sanctuary on a high pulpit, and the liturgy could begin.[45]

The WIC introduced the ecclesiastical organization of the United Provinces, based on parishes, each of which had a consistory, throughout New Holland and New Netherland. A conspicuous difference between the two was that New Netherland never had a classis (a subdivision of the Dutch Reformed Church) of its own, whereas all consistories of New Holland were joined under a single classis in 1636. After the example of the homeland, where the classes of each province formed a synod, the classes of Pernambuco and Paraíba constituted a Brazilian synod from 1642 through 1646, a unique episode in the history of Dutch colonialism. Remarkably, the synod was organized on the initiative of the local church hierarchy, despite protests from the churches in Zeeland and Amsterdam.[46]

Although fewer than half of New Netherland's residents were members of the congregation, the reformed church remained the cornerstone of Dutch culture long after the English takeover. Not until 1772 did the Dutch Reformed Church in America acquire its independence from Amsterdam.[47] Nor was the Dutch tongue easily silenced in North America. The language, which, as Joyce Goodfriend has argued, was "at the heart of Dutch culture, the link to memory and the means of communicating with God,"[48] survived well into the eighteenth, and in some rural areas even into the nineteenth century. Ironically, it may have eroded faster in two colonies that remained within the Dutch empire: St. Martin and St. Eustatius. By the early eighteenth century, these Caribbean islands were culturally overshadowed by their English neighbors. Barely one in ten residents of Dutch St. Martin—the other half of the island was and is French—understood Dutch in 1722; most of them were actually Englishmen or Frenchmen who used English as their language of communication.[49] Half a century later, a Dutch fleet commander visiting St. Eustatius remarked that the colony had virtually nothing in common with the metropolis: "The inhabitants' way of life, with regard to morals, manners, clothing, and the design of houses, is so perfectly English, that only a flag is needed to make the Dutch island of St. Eustatius completely English."[50]

The prevalence of metropolitan culture is hardly surprising given that most migrants intended to make their stay a temporary one. The ideal these transients shared was to strike it rich and then retire to the homeland. A governor of Suriname once described this leitmotiv of the Dutch colonial enterprise as the *animus revertendi*. Like the English settlers of early Virginia, the Dutch preferred conquest to agriculture. "We rule the land and the inhabitants, but the Portuguese rule our property," an official in New Holland observed.[51] This conquistador mentality was typical of both planters and officials. During the days of Johan Maurits's regime in

New Holland, virtually all members of the ruling political council tried to cash in on their overseas sojourn. One after another asked to be dismissed, only to go into sugar planting with abandon. Even the judge advocate and several clergymen were accused of neglecting their duties for the sake of sugar production.[52] In Suriname, sometimes referred to as a "new Brazil," sugar planting set off a kind of gold fever in the late seventeenth century. The earnings offered a handsome and often indispensable addition to the functionaries' incomes, since their usual wages were often low and payment tardy at best. The situation was similar in eighteenth-century Berbice, where various governors used their positions to amass wealth from planting.[53]

This mentality helps explain why the WIC directors were disappointed in their hopes of a massive immigration of farmers and farm hands from the Netherlands, which caused problems for Dutch Brazil in particular. Contemporary economic logic dictated a solution that the Portuguese had discovered much earlier: African slavery. The institution of slavery constituted an obvious difference with metropolitan society. When a slave ship anchored in the Zeeland port of Middelburg, for example, all African passengers were freed upon disembarkation. Neither Middelburg nor any other town in the Dutch Republic condoned slavery. There were blacks in the country, including servants at the stadholder's court, but they were free.[54]

Black slavery, therefore, made it impossible to reproduce the metropolitan universe on distant shores. The replication of Dutch customs and practices was further tempered by differences in natural conditions and confrontations with indigenous worlds, both of which required improvisation.[55] In all colonies, misunderstanding and distrust marked Dutch relations with Indians from the outset. Soon after the Dutch acquired Suriname, the WIC ordered its planters to construct their houses on a hill or on a high bank and install palisades as protection from Indian attacks.[56] The main danger the planters faced, however, was not the natives but the so-called maroon frontier. The number of permanent runaway communities grew as the eighteenth century advanced, and the dangers of life on a sugar or coffee estate induced many planters to settle in Paramaribo.

In D. W. Meinig's characterization of center and periphery, imperial power and "Europeanness" was weakest in the American interior.[57] From a European vantage point, the frontier accordingly was the borderline between civilization and barbarism. This notion, widely accepted at the time, could lead settlers to behave lawlessly when they found themselves beyond the bounds of colonial society. This happened, for instance, when the magistrates of Beverwijck passed an ambiguous judgment on the permissibility of trade with natives inside Fort Orange and inside the town. Residents immediately seized the opportunity to go into the forest in order to trick the Indians out of their merchandise.[58]

Violent acts were also a feature of the *maritime* frontier. In the Caribbean, where trade had been paired with warfare ever since the days of John Hawkins, if not earlier, the WIC's connivance with Curaçao's Caribbean contraband trade opened the door to the settlers' use of violence vis-à-vis merchants from Spanish America. The Curaçaoans engaged in the forced exchange of goods whenever it suited them, seizing the cargoes of Venezuelan craft on the high seas and leaving behind assortments of Dutch articles in exchange.[59]

Antisocial behavior seems not to have been confined to the frontier. Clergymen often questioned the settlers' very morality. Complaints about godlessness, religious ignorance, and drunkenness abounded throughout the history of Curaçao.[60] Colonial officials in different parts of Dutch America shared the concerns of the ministers and lamented the lack of culture they encountered. Pointing out that in a three-year period the number of colonists dying a natural death had been surpassed by those landing drunk in the water and drowning, the first governor of Suriname stressed the yawning gap with the metropolis, ruled by "a long-polished and established government."[61] The difference should not come as a surprise, argued the Council of Curaçao, as every colony was initially inhabited by all sorts of people, except for noblemen and rich folks: "Rarely if ever do they leave their land and station unless pressed to do so."[62]

On the other hand, the metropolitan Dutch deemed overseas provinces a suitable temporary destination for paupers. In the WIC's early days, it sometimes depicted America as an *asylum pauperum* that could bring relief for the mother country. In time, the poor emigrants were expected to return home as wealthy men.[63] A colonial sojourn might even have a cleansing effect on criminals. The States of Holland in 1648 seriously considered peopling New Holland with vagabonds and beggars, but ultimately decided against the proposal.[64]

The WIC put more work into plans to send orphans to the New World, especially those dwelling in the charity orphanages. Although schemes drawn up in the mid-seventeenth century called for the migration of hundreds of orphans to Curaçao and New Netherland, in actual fact only a few dozen were shipped. Suriname was slightly more successful in attracting orphans, on whose own consent migration usually hinged.[65]

The administration of law in the overseas provinces emanated from the dispensation of justice on board the ships sailing across the Atlantic from Dutch ports. As long as a maritime expedition lasted, specific instructions sought to maintain discipline at sea and on land.[66] A gradual change set in once a settlement had been founded. WIC employees soon began to introduce major elements of Dutch jurisprudence. They adopted the written and customary laws covering inheritance and matrimony in Holland and Zeeland, and in civil cases and commercial disputes used Roman law, as was done in the Republic.[67] Because these laws suited a society revolving around commerce, the decision to transplant them to the colonies was a judicious one. The laws greatly helped the effectiveness of Dutch colonial governance, especially in those places where the raison d'être was trade.[68]

Here and there, elements of maritime law lingered on beyond the stage of exploration. In Berbice, it was customary that the first ship's captain to arrive after the death of the colonial commander should act as his temporary successor. Maritime law was in effect during the interregnum.[69] Likewise, the captains of WIC ships lying in the harbors of New Amsterdam and Curaçao were allowed to sit on the colonial councils. There was something unfinished about this arrangement, which—as we will see below—formed a marked contrast with the well-thought-out government structure of New Holland.

Because of the size and settlement patterns of the Dutch colonies, New Holland and New Netherland were the only colonies that possessed colonial centers and peripheries. In its mature form, New Holland was made up of two very different areas: the twin cities of Recife and Mauritsstad, on the one hand, and the interior settlements, where Luso-Brazilians predominated. The turmoil of war made communication between the various Dutch-held settlements hazardous, as the inaccessible hinterland provided the enemy with a good operational base. Although it was in the former Portuguese captaincy of Pernambuco where the Dutch established their base, its principal city of Olinda was unfit for a capital. Its sprawling size and scattered houses made it very difficult to fortify; nearby Recife was more suitable for the seat of government.[70]

The WIC intended Recife to be another type of center as well. The Dutch wanted to centralize their operations in the Atlantic world on a single capital and decided upon Recife. The VOC had set up Batavia on the island of Java as the nerve center of its Asian empire. Batavia was connected with an intricate network of "factories," fortified trading posts defended by garrisons. Recife was to be Batavia's Atlantic counterpart.

The government of New Holland in Recife, therefore, received a solid foundation. Once again, the WIC invoked the distributive code when it set up the supreme Political Council in the wake of the invasion of 1630. The Chamber of Amsterdam elected four of nine councilors, Zeeland two, and the three remaining chambers one apiece. Although the council was transformed six years later into a court for civil and criminal cases, the same code remained operative.[71]

By then, the WIC had introduced another type of government, fashioned after the one in Batavia. It appointed Johan Maurits as governor-, captain-, and admiral-general of Dutch Brazil. He assumed supreme command of the army and navy, and a three-member High and Secret Council, nominated by the WIC and approved by the stadholder, assisted him in determining colonial policies.[72]

Compared to New Holland, New Netherland was of secondary importance in the grand scheme of Dutch colonization. Dutch presence in the area ensued from the famous voyage of the Englishman Henry Hudson, whom the Dutch East India Company (VOC) had instructed to find a northwestern route to Asia. Instead, in 1609 he reached the river that still bears his name. When the WIC embarked on a colonization program, it first tried to make the Albany region the focus of Dutch colonization. Some emigrants settled there, while others went to the "Southern Colony" on the Delaware River, near present-day Philadelphia. These two locations were more or less the northern and southern poles of New Netherland, while New Amsterdam on Manhattan Island, acquired in 1626, became the company headquarters.

The government of New Netherland was made up of a director, vice-director, and fiscal (the prosecuting attorney who was also in charge of finances), but in criminal cases two residents were added from the districts where the crime was committed.[73] Apart from that, settlers had no say in government. Yet the need for increased settler participation in colonial government surfaced every time the governor established a committee patterned after the *gemeenslieden*, a time-honored administrative council in the east of the Dutch Republic. The difference with its metropolitan counterpart was that the colonial committee could offer advice only on a specific problem. Discontent with their status as ad hoc bodies, the committees unvaryingly aspired to be a permanent feature.[74]

The WIC created no such body in New Holland. But Johan Maurits and his High and Secret Council did convene a diet in 1640, to listen to the complaints of delegates from towns and villages in the three captaincies of Pernambuco, Itamaracá, and

Paraíba. Fifty-six Luso-Brazilians, for the most part sugar lords, owners of sugar warehouses, and merchants, gathered.[75]

The legal system created in both colonies resembled that of the homeland. Inferior courts operated in eighteen towns in New Netherland and at least seven in New Holland. The magistrates of Recife and New Amsterdam enjoyed wider powers than their colleagues in smaller settlements. The courts in these two colonies comprised a minimum of three magistrates, initially chosen by the colonial council from lists of nominees submitted by the settlers, and later co-opted by the incumbent magistrates.[76] In the districts of New Holland, where Lusophones outnumbered the Dutch, the courts of justice were composed of three Luso-Brazilians and two Dutchmen.[77]

These local courts made law and administered justice. They tried minor criminal cases, while adultery, blasphemy, theft, and other felonies were outside their jurisdiction. Inhabitants of New Netherland accused of such offenses were arrested and sent to the capital. If wrongfully convicted of a minor offense, they could take their case to the colonial council in Manhattan; New Hollanders could appeal in Recife. Keeping a close watch on the inferior courts, the councils regularly intervened when local magistrates called in their help, or when mistakes were made. In practice, distant towns enjoyed most independence from the capital.[78]

In the major towns of Dutch America, settlers could lay claim to the *burgerrecht*. A key ingredient of urban life in the metropolis, the burgerrecht reached back to medieval times. It was reserved to natives of the town or those who had worked their way up to the burgher ranks through marriage or capital. Attached to it were certain privileges, including political rights and the exercise of public office. The burgher's oath set the burghers apart from other residents and strangers, who were all merely inhabitants. Those taking the oath committed themselves to maintaining law and order within the town walls. [79]

The Europeans in the Dutch colonies originally belonged to one of two types of colonists: Either they served the West India Company as soldiers, mariners, and officials, or they were "free" settlers, some of them former company employees themselves. The latter could aspire to become burghers. When old Amsterdam introduced a so-called great burgerrecht, New Amsterdam followed suit in 1657. Those purchasing a common certificate obtained the right to have an open retail shop or practice a trade, whereas the burghers given a hereditary great burgerrecht were entitled to hold office on the town council.[80]

The WIC expected every able-bodied burgher in the Netherlands who could afford his own flintlock and kit to serve as a militiaman (*schutter*). The colonies copied this arrangement. Like their metropolitan colleagues, the schutters of Curaçao performed sporadic guard duties in peacetime, going on patrol at regular intervals and standing guard at night at the town gate of Willemstad. More intensive duties were required in times of war or unrest. In Suriname, the civic militia's main task was to patrol swamps and forests for several consecutive days in search of maroons.[81] The government of New Holland, a colony in a permanent state of war, could count on the male residents of Recife to do their bit in defending the town as members of the four civilian companies. In 1641, the WIC board decided that the welfare of the company depended on peopling New Holland, and began trying to attract soldier-settlers. Thus, many of the male burghers "were time-expired soldiers who had married and settled down as shopkeepers, retail-traders, or smallholders who worked plots of sugar-cane with the aid of a few slaves."[82]

However close Dutch institutions were replicated, an ocean divided the Old World and the New. Colonial officials were aware of the distance and the resulting slow correspondence with their superiors at WIC headquarters, or the boards of the Suriname and Berbice Societies. Choosing to ignore metropolitan orders, some invariably used their own discretion in dealing with colonial affairs. Director Willem Kieft of New Netherland went so far as to compare his position to that of the stadholder in the fatherland.[83]

This attitude could have unpleasant consequences if the official failed to take notice of pressing local demands or grievances. The vice-commander of St. Martin learned to his peril in 1736 how ill-advised it was to go against the population's wishes and levy a new tax. A rebellion broke out, which drove him off the island. Upon his return, he found that "his house had been destroyed by an angry mob, much of his cattle and many of his slaves had been killed, his plantations and warehouses ruined."[84]

Despite the animus revertendi, officials in eighteenth-century Suriname and Curaçao had to come to grips with colonial elites that became increasingly creolized. A defining moment in the relations between the Society of Suriname and its colonists was the arrival of French privateer Jacques Cassard in October 1712, during the last stages of the War of the Spanish Succession. With an impressive fleet and three thousand soldiers, Cassard attacked the capital of Paramaribo, but failed to conquer it. As the hinterland lay unprotected, Cassard sailed up the Suriname River and exacted a levy of over 600,000 guilders under threat of pillage.[85]

This incident put a great distance between the colonists and the Society of Suriname after Cassard's departure, as the burden fell upon the planters, who for their part held the society responsible. While some planters even flirted with the idea of forming a government of their own, the Society was unyielding, arguing that it had invested three times as much in the colony as the settlers over the previous thirty years.[86]

Four months elapsed before Cassard turned up in Curaçao and exacted a ransom of 115,000 pesos—less than half the amount paid in Suriname. Contrary to the Surinamese elite, the Curaçaoans proved very cooperative when it came to shouldering the burden. But they would never forget their contribution. Many years later, in 1770, a resident upset about his tax assessment wrote to the West India Company, wondering, "What right do you have to this land, did you ransom it from the French in the year 13, wasn't it our blood and sweat?"[87]

The colonies' subordination to the metropolis might suggest that their political leverage was commensurable to that of the so-called generality lands in the republic. These areas in the south and east, by 1648 comprising one-third of Dutch territory, had been captured by the Dutch troops from Habsburg Spain during the war.[88] The generality lands were never admitted as full members to the Republic and were governed from The Hague by the States General.[89] In the colonies, the governor (or director) and his council occupied a position comparable to that of the States General in the generality lands.

That does not mean that local participation in government was ruled out. First of all, settlers were included in the administration of most colonies, even though company personnel always outnumbered them. The Council of Curaçao usually comprised of six WIC officials and three "civilian" members, who were allowed to attend only when legal cases were tried, and had to absent themselves when company or administrative affairs were discussed.[90] As the *primus inter pares*, the governor had the privilege of a double vote when the votes were equally divided on a motion. Moreover, it was to the governor that the settlers submitted lists of candidates for approval.[91]

The settlers, at least, had a vote in government meetings. The importance of that practice may be gathered from events rocking the Dutch colony in South Africa. As the Council of Policy at the Cape did not have a single civilian member, local grievances could not be properly channeled. The VOC, which governed the colony, was faced with the consequences in the 1770s and 1780s, when displeasure with the government's economic policies led to great turmoil.[92]

What therefore prevented estrangement between center and periphery was the habit to man the governing councils of the Dutch colonies with local people—with the notable exception of New Holland. Not only were settlers admitted to the governing bodies to advocate local viewpoints, they acted as representatives of metropolitan power as well. Usually, the only imperial appointee was the governor, and even that "rule" was broken increasingly. The local roots of councillors and the tendency of metropolitan officials to go into planting or trade made it relatively easy for colonial elites to co-opt them. So while officials in the homeland tried to keep a tight rein on colonial life, their own agents, normally members of the planter and/or commercial elites, checked their policies. Indeed, local interests often won out over metropolitan ones.[93]

The elimination of a mercantilist article of faith in Suriname is a case in point. Dutch colonial trade was bound by strict rules, just like that of other Atlantic powers. Ships returning from any of the Dutch colonies in the domain of the WIC were only allowed to put into ports of company chambers. They were expressly forbidden to sell the colonial produce they carried before disembarkation in the Netherlands.[94] Once Suriname had achieved a certain measure of self-sufficiency, the economic bonds with the mother country became galling. Planters routinely violated mercantilist laws by engaging in a lively trade with ships from British North America, exchanging molasses for provisions and horses. However, authorities suddenly legalized the trade in 1704, not only because the Society of Suriname was unable to root out existing commercial practices, but because it came to realize that colonial interests were served by lifting the ban.[95]

This was an exceptional case. It rarely happened that the victory of colonial interests was legalized. The normal way in which Dutch authorities accepted practices that could not stand up to examination was by turning a blind eye to them. The Dutch were experts in connivance. This was no feature specific to colonial government; it was practiced at a local level in the home country as well, and with good reason. Strict adherence to the law might prove incompatible with the interests of commerce. Likewise, enforcing the law was on occasion considered a greater threat to communal peace than connivance.[96] Peace and quiet were sometimes of greater importance than law and order.

For West India Company officials, the difficulty in luring Dutch settlers to America was an additional factor in the equation. Their concern about the viability of individual colonies goes a long way to explain why they tended to be so forbearing as regards the admission of dissenting (i.e., non-Calvinist) Protestant groups. Not only were the Englishmen moving from New England to New Netherland granted the same rights as Dutch immigrants, they were allowed to build their own forts and churches and elect their own officials.[97] The residents of New Sweden, who found themselves "trapped" in Dutch territory after Petrus Stuyvesant's conquest of the colony in 1655, also received lenient treatment. These Swedes and Finns did not have to renounce their Lutheranism, a handsome gesture of the Dutch government, given that the 150 Lutheran families of New Amsterdam could not openly profess their religion.[98]

Tolerance was never a matter of policy, either at home or in America. It was a result of discussions between a colony's political and religious authorities, who were alive to the local context, but often had competing perspectives on the role of the Calvinist church or the economic weight of the dissenters. That explains why the actual treatment of individual groups of settlers varied. The Jews who received an unfriendly welcome in New Netherland lived in New Holland under very favorable conditions, enjoying freedom of conscience and state protection.[99]

More remarkable still than the tolerance of Jews was the WIC's policy vis-à-vis the Luso-Brazilian Roman Catholics in New Holland. Because Roman Catholics were seen as the natural allies of Habsburg Spain, Catholic worship in the Netherlands was illegal, as were baptism by a Catholic priest, wearing rosaries, and singing Catholic hymns. In Brazil, however, the WIC made elaborate concessions to facilitate the transition to Dutch rule. The conditions for the capitulation presented in 1645 to the inhabitants of Paraíba included freedom of conscience and further use of churches and divine sacrifices. Priests and images would not be molested.[100] This was no idle talk. In spite of the resistance of some Dutch settlers, the government fulfilled the agreement. Subsequently, processions were held in New Holland and priests came to the Dutch-owned sugar mills once a year to give their blessing to the start of the cane-crushing season.[101]

The cumulative effect of decades of connivance in Curaçao was a wide variety of unwritten laws, which tended to deviate substantially from those upheld in the metropolis. Thus, to accommodate the poor of the island, marriage services could be performed in private houses.[102] Furthermore, the distinction between burghers and others became blurred. True, each man—Dutch-born or not—who took up his abode on the island, was registered with the civic guard after a stay of one year and six weeks.[103] But beyond military obligations, "citizenship" lost its rationale. In the Netherlands, criminal cases against burghers were settled in ordinary procedures, in which the defendant had the right to counsel. Former sailors, vagabonds, and beggars, however, were tried in extraordinary procedures, which implied that they could be apprehended without difficulty and, if convicted, they awaited corporal rather than financial punishment.[104] In Willemstad, however, no distinction was made between ordinary and extraordinary procedures. What is more, a resident suspected of a crime but failing to appear in court did not have to be afraid of being arrested. If he did turn up and lost the lawsuit, he would be wise to enter an appeal, since it meant that the case would be shelved.[105] The same sluggishness, incidentally, surfaced in Suriname, as one governor noticed shortly after his arrival. Over four hundred legal cases were still undecided, many of them postponed indefinitely by the Court of Justice.[106]

Sometimes the WIC got up on its high horse, as in the case of the import duties. The company did not levy taxes on products imported on Dutch vessels from Spanish colonies. This regulation, which was never formalized, compensated for the losses that shipowners were often forced to sustain. The provision fell into abeyance in wartime. The neutral stance maintained by the Dutch Republic throughout most eighteenth-century wars allowed Dutch vessels free run of the coasts of the Spanish Caribbean, but as Curaçaoan shipping no longer ran any risk in buying Spanish articles, import duties were now levied.[107] By the 1780s, however, Curaçaoan traders were convinced that Spanish American crops by definition were exempt from import duties. The WIC directors eventually had their way, and judged that all types of commerce were subject to customs duties. Local pressure, however, forced the company shortly afterward to decide that a wide range of products—coffee, hides, indigo, dyewood, and tobacco—would be exempt from export duty.[108]

Divisive issues were often settled in favor of Curaçao's settlers, as WIC officials chose the line of least resistance. A serious problem, for instance, was the encroachment of private planters on company land. For dozens of years, no governor dared take the matter in hand, until it was too late to turn back the clock and reclaim the land.[109] In the same vein, numerous islanders successfully evaded the slave poll tax, as company officials were afraid to collect the money.[110] Backing out of the political arena might have the salutary effect of placating the settlers, but it was certainly no panacea. The absence of a strong government could even backfire. When the government of St. Eustatius failed to take active measures in the first half of the eighteenth century, it perpetuated the feuds between the island's leading families.[111]

The late eighteenth century saw a different approach in Demerara and Essequibo, the Guiana colonies that were then jointly governed. Upon his arrival, the new governor-general, Jan Lespinasse, discharged all company officials as well as the members of the political and judicial councils. He thereby antagonized the colonial elite, which had elected the officials, for a long time to come. Curaçao showed that systematic lenience did not necessarily result in a more cooperative attitude from the colonists. When it came to a crunch, the company was in charge, much to the dismay of the settlers. As radical Enlightenment ideas added fuel to the flames in Guiana and Curaçao, and political authority was undermined in increasingly brazen ways, the WIC was at its wits' end.[112] Arguing that the colonial governments were no longer able to maintain order, the company board made an emotional appeal to the States General to assume the government of the overseas provinces.[113] This request was not granted immediately, but in 1791 the states gave in. Four years later, the curtain dropped for the Dutch Republic, and the Societies of Berbice and Suriname were dissolved as well. A new era had begun for the Netherlands on either side of the ocean.

The seventeenth and eighteenth centuries, then, can be considered a distinct stage in Dutch colonial history. This period saw the replication of metropolitan weights, measures, dishes, and holidays in the American settlements. Likewise, the metropolis and the colonies shared both the dominant religion and ecclestiastical organization. In other ways, the colonies were obviously different, particularly regarding the presence of African slaves and Native Americans. The cultural impact of the United Provinces contrasted sharply with the home country's limited political leverage. As connivance became a prominent feature of colonial government, metropolitan agents frequently had to give in to local pressure.

Notes

1. In this essay, *colony* denotes any overseas settlement, although the contemporary meaning was a different one. A colony used to be a group of settlers who planned to or were ordered to establish themselves in a territory belonging to the States General. In regulations issued in view of the peopling of Brazil, such a gathering was supposed to consist of at least twenty-five families or fifty persons. José Antônio Gonsalves de Mello, ed., *Fontes para a história do Brasil holandês* (Recife: MinC—Secretaria da Cultura, 1985) II, n. 7.
2. Adriaen van der Donck, *Beschryvinge van Nieuvv-Nederlant, (Ghelijck het tegenwoordigh in Staet is) Begrijpende de Nature, Aert, gelegentheyt en vruchtbaerheyt van het selve Lant; mitsgaders de proffijtelijcke ende gewenste toevallen, die aldaer tot onderhout der Menschen, (soo uyt haer selven als van buyten ingebracht) gevonden worden* (Amsterdam: Evert Nieuwenhof, 1655), 91.
3. G. de Bruin, "Het politiek bestel van de Republiek: een anomalie in het vroegmodern Europa?" *Bijdragen en Mededelingen betreffende de Geschiedenis der Nederlanden* 114 (1999), 16–38. A.Th. van Deursen, "Tussen eenheid en zelfstandigheid. De toepassing van de Unie als fundamentele wet," in *De hartslag van het leven: Studies over de Republiek der Verenigde Nederlanden* (Amsterdam: Bert Bakker, 1996), 307–21.
4. Florike Egmond, *Underworlds: Organized Crime in the Netherlands 1650–1800* (Cambridge: Polity Press, 1993), 12, 34.
5. Wayne Ph. te Brake, "Provincial Histories and National Revolution in the Dutch Republic," in Margaret C. Jacob and Wijnand W. Mijnhardt, eds., *The Dutch Republic in the Eighteenth Century: Decline, Enlightenment, and Revolution* (Ithaca, N.Y.: Cornell University Press, 1992), 60–90, esp., 86.
6. Henk den Heijer, *De geschiedenis van de WIC* (Zutphen: Walburg Pers, 1994), 28–34; The VOC (Verenigde Oostindische Compagnie) refers to the Dutch East India Company.
7. E. H. Kossmann, "The Dutch Republic in the Eighteenth Century," in Jacob and Mijnhardt, eds., *The Dutch Republic in the Eighteenth Century*, 19–31.
8. Heijer, *Geschiedenis van de WIC*, 31.
9. C. R. Boxer, *The Dutch in Brazil 1624–1654* (Oxford: Clarendon Press, 1957), 175.
10. P. C. Emmer, "The West India Company, 1621–1791: Dutch or Atlantic?" in L. Blussé and F. Gaastra, eds., *Companies and Trade: Essays on Overseas Trading Companies during the Ancien Régime* (Leiden: Leiden University Press, 1981), 71–95.
11. Cf. the Charter of Freedom and Exemptions of June 7, 1629, in A.J.F. van Laer, *Van Rensselaer Bowier Manuscripts. Being the Letters of Kiliaen van Rensselaer, 1630–1643, and Other Documents Relating to the Colony of Rensselaerswyck* (Albany: University of the State of New York, 1908), 136–52.
12. Cornelis Ch. Goslinga, *The Dutch in the Caribbean and in the Guianas 1680–1791* (Assen: Van Gorcum, 1985), 128, 440.
13. In addition, Fernando de Noronha, a group of islands off the coast of Brazil, was for a while a patroonship of Michiel Pauw.
14. G. W. van der Meiden, *Betwist Bestuur: Een eeuw strijd om de macht in Suriname 1651–1753* (Amsterdam: De Bataafsche Leeuw, 1987), 11–12.
15. John J. McCusker and Russell R. Menard, *The Economy of British America 1607–1789* (Chapel Hill: The University of North Carolina Press, 1985), 225.
16. Around 1770, 80 percent of the soldiers employed by the VOC were foreign born. Femme S. Gaastra, *De geschiedenis van de VOC* (Zutphen: Walburg Pers, 1991), 81. Roelof van Gelder, *Het Oost-Indisch avontuur: Duitsers in dienst van de VOC* (Nijmegen: SUN, 1997), 53.
17. What follows is a comparison of data presented in Ad Knotter and Jan Luiten van Zanden, "Immigratie en arbeids markt in Amsterdam in de 17e eeuw," *Tijdschrift voor Sociale Geschiedenis* 13 (1987), 403–31, esp. table 3, and those supplied by David Steven Cohen, "How Dutch Were the Dutch of New Netherland?" *New York History* 62:1 (1981), 43–60, table 2.
18. S. Hart, "De stadskolonie Nieuwer-Amstel aan de Delaware River in Noord-Amerika," *Amstelodamum* 38 (1951), 89–94. C. A. Weslager, "The City of Amster-

dam's Colony on the Delaware, 1656–1664; With Unpublished Dutch Notarial Abstracts." *Delaware History* 20 (1982), 1–26, 73–97.

19. It was not until the foundation of the second WIC that the board itself stepped in. Johannes Hartog, *Curaçao van kolonie tot autonomie*, 2 vols. (Aruba: D. J. de Wit, 1961), 1:162–63.
20. Wim Klooster, *Illicit Riches: Dutch Trade in the Caribbean, 1648–1795* (Leiden: KITLV Press, 1998), 69.
21. Out of 206 vessels leaving St. Eustatius for the United Provinces in 1738–1751, 196 sailed to Amsterdam, 4 to Flushing, 2 to Rotterdam, and 1 to Middelburg. No destination was listed for the 3 remaining ships. Algemeen Rijksarchief (ARA) Nieuwe West-Indische Compagnie (NWIC), 621–24.
22. J. A. Schiltkamp, *Bestuur en rechtspraak in de Nederlandse Antillen ten tijde van de West-Indische Compagnie* (Willemstad: Uitgaven van de Rechtshogeschool van de Nederlandse Antillen, 1972), 13–14. A. J. M. Kunst, *Recht, commercie en kolonialisme in West-Indië vanaf de zestiende tot in de negentiende eeuw* (Zutphen: De Walburg Pers, 1981), 115.
23. George Edmundson, "The Dutch on the Amazon and Negro in the Seventeenth Century," *English Historical Review* 18 (1903), 642–63, esp. 644, 651. Cornelis Ch. Goslinga, *The Dutch in the Caribbean and on the Wild Coast, 1580–1680* (Assen: Van Gorcum, 1971), 56–58. Victor Enthoven, "Zeeland en de opkomst van de Republiek: Handel en strijd in de Scheldedelta, c. 1550–1621" (Ph.D. diss., Rijksuniversiteit Leiden, 1996), 260–62.
24. In spite of the arrival of refugees from Dutch Brazil, the attempts to develop both colonies were a failure.
25. Victor Enthoven, "Suriname and Zeeland: Fifteen Years of Dutch Misery on the Wild Coast, 1667–1682," in J. Everaert and J. Parmentier, eds., *International Conference on Shipping, Factories and Colonization* (Brussels: Académie Royale des Sciences d'Outre-Mer, 1996), 249–60.
26. Jonathan Israel, *The Dutch Republic: Its Rise, Greatness, and Fall 1477–1806* (Oxford: Clarendon Press, 1995), 611–12.
27. Pieter Emmer and Wim Klooster, "The Dutch Atlantic, 1600–1800: Expansion without Empire." *Itinerario: European Journal of Overseas History* 23 (1999), 48–69.
28. Goslinga, *Dutch in Caribbean and Guianas*, 306, 320, 321. Enthoven, "Fifteen Years," 259.
29. Goslinga, *Dutch in the Caribbean and the Guianas*, 449–50, 584.
30. José Antônio Gonsalves de Mello, *Tempo dos flamengos: Influência da Ocupação Holandesa na Vida e Na Cultura do Norte do Brasil*, 2nd ed. (Recife: Governo do Estado de Pernambuco, 1978), 41–44.
31. Governor and Council of Dutch Brazil to the Board of Nineteen; Recife, March 5, 1639. ARA Oude West-Indische Compagnie 54, no. 9. Mello, *Tempo dos flamengos*, 150–51.
32. Mello, *Tempo dos flamengos*, 156.
33. Frank Ibold, Jens Jäger, and Detlev Kraack, eds., *Das Memorial und Jurenal des Peter Hansen Hajstrup (1624–1672)* (Neumünster: Wachholtz, 1995), 76.
34. D. J. Maika, "Commerce and Community: Manhattan Merchants in the Seventeenth Century" (Ph.D. diss., New York University, 1995), 35. At an earlier stage, in 1633, the company had suggested that New Netherland grain or animals could be exported to the Netherlands, Cape Verde, Guinea, and Brazil; Van Cleaf Bachman, *Peltries or Plantations: The Economic Policies of the Dutch West India Company in New Netherland 1623–1639* (Baltimore: Johns Hopkins Press, 1969), n. 70. Cf. Oliver A. Rink, *Holland on the Hudson: An Economic and Social History of Dutch New York* (Ithaca, N.Y.: Cornell University Press/Cooperstown: New York State Historical Association, 1986), 196.
35. Anthony Pagden, *European Encounters with the New World: From Renaissance to Romanticism* (New Haven, Conn.: Yale University Press, 1993), 3. Joyce D. Goodfriend, "Writing/Righting Dutch Colonial History," *New York History* 80 (1999), 5–28. For Dutch cartographic nomenclature, see Benjamin Schmidt, "Mapping an Empire: Cartographic and Colonial Rivalry in Seventeenth-Century Dutch and English North America," *William and Mary Quarterly*, 3rd series, 54:3 (1997), 549–78.

36. George Pinckard, *Notes on the West Indies: Written during the Expedition under the Command of the late General Sir Ralph Abercomby*, 3 vols. (London: Longman, Hurst, Rees and Orme, 1806), 2:171.
37. Ibold, Jäger, and Kraack, *Memorial und Jurenal*, 75.
38. Originally the representative of the Habsburg king, the stadholder was both the servant and master of the Provincial States. In several provinces, he had the right to appoint members of town councils.
39. Van der Meiden, *Betwist Bestuur*, 13, 100. L. Bosman, *Nieuw Amsterdam in Berbice (Guyana): De planning en bouw van een koloniale stad, 1764–1800* (Hilversum: Verloren, 1994), 33. Pinckard, *Notes on the West Indies*, III, 349–50. J. M. van der Linde, *Surinaamse suikerheren en Thun Kerk* (Wageningen: H. Veenman, 1966), 108.
40. Peter van Rooden, "Dissenters en bededagen: Civil religion ten tijde van de Republiek," *Bijdragen en Mededelingen betreffende de Geschiedenis der Nederlanden* 107 (1992), 703–12.
41. Frans Leonard Schalkwijk, *Igreja e estado no Brasil holandês, 1630–1654* (Recife: Governo de Pernambuco, Secretaria de Turismo, Cultura e Esportes, Fundação do Patrimônio Histórico Artístico de Pernambuco, Diretoria de Assuntos Culturais, 1986), 119. Jaap Jacobs, *een zegenrijk Gewest: Nieuw-Nederland in de zeventiende eeuw* (Amsterdam: Prometheus, Bert Bakker, 1999), 384–85.
42. J. A. Schiltkamp, and J. Th. de Smidt, eds., *West Indisch plakkaatboek: Publikaties en andere wetten alsmede de oudste resoluties betrekking hebbende op Curaçao Aruba Bonaire*, 2 vols. (Amsterdam: Emmering, 1978), 140–41.
43. Willem Frijhoff, *Wegen van Evert Willemsz: Een Hollands weeskind op zoek naar zichzelf, 1607–1674* (Nijmegen: SUN, 1995), 581.
44. Leonie van Nierop, "Rensselaerswyck, 1629–1704," *Tijdschrift voor Geschiedenis* 60 (1947), 1–39, 187–219, esp. 217.
45. Schalkwijk, *Igreja e estado*, 108–9.
46. Ibid., 121–22, 129, 137.
47. J. Tanis, "The American Dutch, Their Church, and the Revolution," *Bijdragen en Mededelingen betreffende de Geschiedenis der Nederlanden* 97 (1982), 505–16. A religious Dutch identity persisted well beyond that date: Firth Haring Fabend, "The Synod of Dort and the Persistence of Dutchness in Nineteenth-Century New York and New Jersey," *New York History* 77 (1996), 273–300.
48. Joyce D. Goodfriend, *Before the Melting Pot: Society and Culture in Colonial New York City, 1664–1730* (Princeton, N.J.: Princeton University Press, 1992), 196.
49. Jan de Wint to the Council of St. Eustatius, Saba, and St. Martin; St. Eustatius, April 8, 1722. ARA Nieuwe West-Indische Compagnie (NWIC) 1181, fol. 139.
50. Cornelius de Jong, *Reize naar de Caribische eilanden, in de jaren 1780 en 1781* (Haarlem: François Bohn, 1807), 108.
51. Jack P. Greene, *Pursuits of Happiness: The Social Development of Early Modern British Colonies and the Formation of American Culture* (Chapel Hill: University of North Carolina Press, 1988), 9. Mello, *Tempo dos flamengos*, 132.
52. Hermann Wätjen, *Das holländische Kolonialreich in Brasilien. Ein Kapitel aus der Kolonialgeschichte des 17. Jahrhunderts* (The Hague: Martinus Nijhoff/Gotha: F. A. Perthes A.-G., 1921), 187. Mello, *Fontes para a história*, 20. Mello, *Tempo dos flamengos*, 131, 133.
53. Linde, *Surinaamse suikerheren*, 63. Bosman, *Nieuw Amsterdam in Berbice*, 16–17, 19.
54. Allison Blakely, *Blacks in the Dutch World: The Evolution of Racial Imagery in a Modern Society* (Bloomington: Indiana University Press, 1993), 225–30.
55. Cf. D. W. Meinig, *The Shaping of America: A Geographical Perspective on 500 Years of History. Volume I: Atlantic America, 1492–1800* (New Haven, Conn.: Yale University Press, 1986), 215.
56. Van der Linde, *Surinaamse suikerheren*, 41.
57. Meinig, *Shaping of America*, 265–66.
58. Donna Merwick, *Possessing Albany, 1630–1710: The Dutch and English Experiences* (Cambridge: Cambridge University Press, 1990), 90–91.
59. Contraband trade carried risks for the Curaçaoans as well. Spanish Americans some-

times posed as merchants to launch a covert attack, or had them waylaid by privateers. Klooster, *Illicit Riches*, 152–53.

60. A. Eekhof, *De Hervormde Kerk in Noord-Amerika (1624–1664)*, 2 vols. (The Hague: Martinus Nijhoff, 1913), 1:84. Nicolaas van Beeck and Ferdinand van Collen to Director Bastiaan Bernagie; Amsterdam, November 4, 1694. ARA NWIC 469, fol. 174. Pieter de Senilh to the WIC, Chamber of Zeeland; Curaçao, January 2, 1712. ARA NWIC 1150. R. Wildrik to the WIC, Chamber of Amsterdam; Curaçao, July 30, 1764. ARA NWIC 318. Church Council of Curaçao to the WIC; Curaçao, May 24, 1770. ARA NWIC 608, fol. 287.
61. Van der Linde, *Surinaamse suikerheren*, 65.
62. Council of Curaçao to WIC, Chamber of Amsterdam; Curaçao, December 30, 1766. ARA NWIC 318.
63. Goslinga, *Dutch in Caribbean and on Wild Coast*, 40. O. van Rees, *Geschiedenis der Staathuishoudkunde in Nederland tot het einde der achttiende eeuw*, 2 vols. (Utrecht: Kemink en Zoon, 1865–1868), 2:76.
64. A. Th. Van Deursen, *Mensen van klein vermogen: Het kopergeld van de Gouden Eeuw* (Amsterdam: Bert Bakker, 1991), 66.
65. Bernard R. Buddingh', *Van Punt en Snoa: Ontstaan en groei van Willemstad, Curaçao vanaf 1634, De Willemstad tussen 1700 en 1732 en de bouwgeschiedenis van de synagoge Mikvé Israël-Emanuel 1730–1732* ('s-Hertogenbosch: Aldus Uitgevers, 1994), 34. Eekhof, *Hervormde Kerk in Noord-Amerika*, 2:93–94. Van der Linde, *Surinaamse suikerheren*, 56.
66. Martha Dickinson Shattuck, "A Civil Society: Court and Community in Beverwijck, New Netherland, 1652–1664" (Ph.D. diss., Boston University, 1993), 26–28. W. R. Menkman, *De Nederlanders in het Caraibische zeegebied waarin vervat de geschiedenis der Nederlandsche Antillen* (Amsterdam: Van Kampen and Zoon, 1942), 50–51.
67. Mello, *Fontes para a história*, 10. Shattuck, "A Civil Society," 23–25.
68. Shattuck, "A Civil Society," 33–34.
69. "The Representation of New Netherland, 1650," in J. Franklin Jameson, ed., *Narratives of New Netherland 1609–1664* (New York: Charles Scribner's Sons, 1909), 285–353. Jacobs, Zegenrijk gewest 110. Hartog, *Curaçao*, vol. 1, 221. Goslinga, *Dutch in Caribbean and Guianas*, 433.
70. Johannes de Laet, *Jaerlyck Verhael van de Verrichtinghen der Gheoctroyeerde West-Indische Compagnie in derthien Boecken*, ed. S. P. L'Honoré Naber; 4 vols. (The Hague: Martinus Nijhoff, 1931–1937; original ed. 1644), 2:137. Mello, *Tempo dos flamengos*, 46.
71. Mello, *Fontes para a história*, 2:9–10. Wätjen, *Das holländische Kolonialreich*, 186.
72. Wätjen, *Das holländische Kolonialreich*, 184–85.
73. Shattuck, "A Civil Society," 44.
74. Langdon G. Wright, "Local Government and Central Authority in New Netherland," *New-York Historical Society Quarterly* 57 (1973), 7–29, esp. 9, 17–18. Jacobs, *Zegenrijk gewest*, 134–35.
75. Mello, *Fontes para a história*, 2:301–6. Starting in 1649, at least four diets were held in New Netherland, where delegates of Dutch and English settlements advised the director-general and council. Jacobs, *Zegenrijk gewest*, 156–57.
76. Shattuck, "A Civil Society," 47–48. Wätjen, *Das holländische Kolonialreich*, 188–90.
77. Conversely, practicing members of Catholic churches in the Dutch Republic were excluded from public office.
78. Wright, "Local Government," 13. Jacobs, *Zegenrijk gewest*, 151, 155. Dennis Sullivan, *The Punishment of Crime in Colonial New York: The Dutch Experience in Albany during the Seventeenth Century* (New York: Peter Lang, 1997), 43.
79. Paul Knevel, *Burgers in het geweer: De schutterijen in Holland, 1550–1700* (Hilversum: Verloren, 1994), 45.
80. Shattuck, "A Civil Society," 212. Maika, "Commerce and Community," 204–5. Jacobs, *Zegenrijk gewest*, 306–7, 318–19. Wätjen, *Das holländische Kolonialreich*, 298.
81. C. Stuijlingh, I. O. van Brandt, and Michiel Römer, minutes of the meeting of the Council of Curaçao, September 16, 1789. ARA NWIC 1176, fol. 341. Wim Hoogbergen, "*De Bosnegers zijn gekomen!*" *Slavernij en Rebellie in Suriname* (Amsterdam: Prometheus, 1992), 9.

82. Boxer, *Dutch in Brazil*, 132, 145. Mello, *Fontes para a história*, 1:218. See, for New Netherland, Jacobs, *Zegenrijk gewest*, 310–15.
83. Remonstrance of the Deputies from New Netherland, July 28, 1649, In E. B. O'Callaghan, ed., *Documents Relative to the Colonial History of the State of New-York; Procured in Holland, England and France, by John Romeyn Brodhead* (Albany: Weed, Parsons, 1856), vol. 1, 298. Augustus van Quelen, *Kort Verhael Vanden staet van Fernanbuc, Toe-ge-eygent de E. Heeren Gecommitteerde ter Vergaderinghe vande Negenthiene, inde Geoctroyeerde West-Indische Compagnie, ter Camere van Amstelredam* (Amsterdam: n.p. 1640). Cf. Johan Maurits's political testament: "Memória e Instrução de João Maurício, Conde de Nassau, acerca do seu governo do Brasil (1644)" in Mello, *Fontes para a história*, 2:403.
84. Goslinga, *Dutch in Caribbean and Guianas* 2:133–35.
85. The levy was paid in sugar, slaves, and bills of exchange.
86. Van der Meiden, *Betwist bestuur*, 74–75. Goslinga, *Dutch in Caribbean and Guianas*, 282–83.
87. Anonymous resident of Curaçao to the WIC. Read June 12, 1770. ARA NWIC 607, ff. 556–57.
88. They included States Brabant, States Flanders, Maastricht and the Overmaas, and Wedde-Westerwolde. In 1713, States Upper Gelderland was added.
89. Israel, *Dutch Republic*, 297–300, 710–11.
90. The Board of the WIC to the States General, October 19, 1786. ARA Collectie G. K. van Hogendorp 155, fol. 187. The composition of the ruling council of the cape colony was almost identical; Gerrit Schutte, "Company and Colonists at the Cape, 1652–1795," in Richard Elphick and Hermann Giliomee, eds., *The Shaping of South African Society, 1652–1840* (Middletown, Conn.: Wesleyan University Press), 283–323.
91. After 1764, the governor of Curaçao no longer had a double vote in judicial affairs. J. A. Schiltkamp, *Bestuur en rechtspraak in de Nederlandse Antillen ten tijde van de West-Indische Compagnie* (Willemstad: Uitgaven van de Rechtshogeschool van de Nederlandse Antillen, 1972), 24. Van der Linde, *Surinaamse suikerheren*, 65, 67. *Een Vertoogh van de considerabele Colonie, By de Edele Groot Mog. Heeren Staten van Hollandt ende West-Vrieslant, uytgeset op de vaste Kust van America* (The Hague: Jacobus Scheltus, 1676), 5–6.
92. Schutte, "Company and Colonists," 283–323. G. J. Schutte, *De Nederlandse Patriotten en de koloniën. Een onderzoek naar hun denkbeelden en optreden, 1770–1800* (Groningen: Tjeenk Willink, 1974), 78–81.
93. Jan Marten Schalkwijk, "Colonial State Formation in Caribbean Plantation Societies: Structural Analysis and Changing Elite Networks in Suriname, 1650–1920" (Ph.D. diss., Cornell University, 1994), 705–6.
94. A negligible number of the Dutch merchantmen returning from Curaçao violated this provision and sold their cargoes abroad. Between 1695 and 1723 only six such ships were recorded. The illegal destinations were Bilbao, Leghorn, Muscovy, Archangelsk, and Hamburg (twice). Jan Noach du Fay to the WIC Board of Ten. Curaçao, February 26, 1723. ARA NWIC 577, ff. 317–21.
95. Van der Meiden, *Betwist bestuur*, 71–72.
96. Jaap Jacobs, "Between Repression and Approval: Connivance and Tolerance in the Dutch Republic and in New Netherland," *de Halve Maen* 71 (1998), 51–58. Shattuck, "A Civil Society," 65–66.
97. Wright, "Local Government," 10–11.
98. Hans Norman, "The New Sweden Colony and the Continued Existence of Swedish and Finnish Ethnicity," in Carol E. Hoffecker, Richard Waldron, Lorraine E. Williams, and Barbara E. Benson, eds., *New Sweden in America* (Newark: University of Delaware Press/London: Associated University Presses, 1995), 188–214. The Reformed Church in New Holland also successfully blocked attempts to set up a Lutheran congregation in Recife; Schalkwijk, *Igreja e estado*, 387.
99. By 1641, Dutch Jews constituted the single most important group of immigrants into New Holland. They were joined by New Christians from Portuguese Brazil, many of whom reverted to Judaism. An estimated 1,450 Jews lived in the town of Recife alone

in 1645, a substantial number, considering that in 1655, after the return of Jews from New Holland, the entire Jewish population of Amsterdam was 1,800. Other Jewish families lived in Mauritsstad, Igaraçu, Paraíba, Porto Calvo, and Rio São Francisco. Their overall number was probably quite modest. Schalkwijk, *Igreja e estado*, 369–70.

100. De Laet, *Iaerlyck Verhael*, 4:132.
101. Mello, *Tempo dos flamengos*, 135.
102. J. de Veer Abz. and Council of Curaçao to the WIC board; Curaçao, February 13, 1789. ARA NWIC 324.
103. C. Stuijlingh, I. O. van Brandt, and Michiel Römer, minutes of the meeting of the Council of Raad Curaçao, September 16, 1789. ARA NWIC 1176, ff. 333–34. Originally, a new burgher had to promise to observe the colonial laws and defend the land; I. Faesch to WIC, Curaçao, February 2, 1745. ARA NWIC 591, ff. 714–15.
104. Florike Egmond, "Onderwerelden: Marginaliteit en misdaad in de Republiek," in Peter te Boekhorst, Peter Burke, and Willem Frijhoff, eds., *Cultuur en maatschappij in Nederland 1500–1850: Een historisch-antropologisch perspectief* (Meppel: Boom/Amsterdam: Open Universiteit, 1992), 153.
105. W.A.S. Grovestins, and W. C. Boey, "Rapport betreffende het eiland Curaçao (1791)," in Maritza Coomans-Eustatia, Henny E. Coomans, and To van der Lee, eds., *Breekbare banden: Feiten en visies over Aruba, Bonaire en Curaçao na de Vrede van Munster 1648–1998* (Bloemendaal: Stichting Libri Antilliani, 1998), 109–26, esp. 115. See also the letters from fiscal Hubertus Coerman, governor J. Rodier, J. Lixraven, and C. Stuijlingh, to the WIC. Curaçao, August 23, 1765, and December 30, 1766. ARA NWIC 604, ff. 1423 and 605, ff. 496–97.
106. Van der Meiden, *Betwist Bestuur*, 86.
107. Jean Rodier and Council of Curaçao to the WIC; Curaçao, June 26, 1770. ARA NWIC 670 fols. 606–7. Johannes de Veer Abz. to the WIC; Curaçao, August 11, 1783. ARA NWIC 612, ff. 747–48.
108. Cacao was exempted from import tax; Cause against Hubertus Coerman, Curaçao, 1782. Customs collector C. A. Roelans and bookkeeper Michiel Römer to the WIC; Curaçao, April 4, 1783. C. A. Roelans to the WIC; Curaçao, March 26, 1784. ARA NWIC 612 ff. 460–70, 645–46, 1054.
109. Goslinga, *Dutch in Caribbean and Guianas*, 91–92, 101.
110. Grovestins and Boey, "Rapport betreffende het eiland Curaçao," 121. Cf. Klooster, *Illicit Riches*, 65.
111. Goslinga, *Dutch in Caribbean and Guianas*, 129.
112. Wim Klooster, "Economische malaise, politieke onrust en misdaad op Curaçao in de Patriottentijd," in Coomans-Eustatia, Coomans, and Lee, eds., *Breekbare Banden*, 101–8. Goslinga, *Dutch in Caribbean and Guianas*, 457.
113. WIC, Chamber of Amsterdam, to the States General; Amsterdam, April 1, 1788. ARA Staten-Generaal 5809.

Center and Periphery in French North America

Leslie Choquette

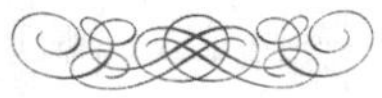

European colonization of North America has often been viewed through the lens of mercantilist doctrine. From this vantage point, the relationship between metropolitan center and colonial periphery is unambiguous. The function of a colony is to provide raw materials, foodstuffs, and revenues for the metropolis. The political, economic, and cultural subordination of periphery to center is never in doubt; however, the power differential is particularly pronounced when the metropolis in question is a bastion of absolutism.

France's North American empire certainly corresponds to this schema in many ways. According to the influential staples theory of Harold Innis, New France was founded on the exploitation of primary resources—cod and furs—for the benefit of the mother country.[1] Extending this argument to the eighteenth century, tobacco and indigo played an analagous, if more limited, role in French Louisiana. The hegemonic character of colonial governance, shaped as it was by those architects of French absolutism, Cardinale Richelieu, Louis XIV, and Jean-Baptiste Colbert, has been a leitmotif of New France's historians since Francis Parkman.[2] The hypercentralization of the New French state was inscribed "in the logic of an authoriarian power that nothing prevented from giving way to its natural penchants, in Tocqueville's phrase, and that could freely pursue its own objectives." In Canada, according to Louise De chêne, "the arbitrary was more than a practice, it was a principle."[3]

Yet truisms about metropolitan dominance and colonial dependency fail to convey the full complexity of center/periphery relationships in New France. As Cornelius Jaenen has reminded us recently, "It is a commonplace that dominant core societies impose their ideology and culture on peripheral societies, especially on colonies. The impact of cultural penetration is greatly modified, however, by such factors as the sophistication and power of the institutions of diffusion, the integrity of existing cultures in the periphery, and accessibility to the hinterland."[4] What historians have sometimes forgotten is that New France, for much of its history, was also a frontier, "a meeting place of peoples in which geographic and cultural borders were not clearly defined." It was, at the same time, a borderland, "a site of imperial rivalry" and "contested boundaries between colonial domains."[5] These geographical realities meant that the peoples of New France, whether Native, European, or African, had more room for maneuvering than was acknowledged in imperial rhetoric. In Canada (the contemporary term for the St. Lawrence Valley), frontier conditions prevailed only until the 1660s, when the Crown took direct control of the colony. But elsewhere in New France—in Acadia (present-day Nova Scotia), the Great Lakes, the Illinois Country, and the Lower Mississippi Valley—frontiers and borderlands persisted to the end of the French regime.

Nor was Canada, after the 1660s, in all respects a model Ancien Régime society subject to metropolitan rule. As in Portuguese Brazil, metropolitan control was limited in practice by distance. Colonial officials often needed to act on their own initiative because poor communications made prior consultation impossible. To limit their authority, the Crown relied on a system of overlapping jurisdictions, most notably between the governors and intendants. This system, however, could backfire if rival officials sought allies among the population and thereby acquired a local base.

That locals would have their own interests, distinct from those of the metropolis, was guaranteed by the gradual but steady development of the colony. As a result, Canada "took on some of the characteristics of a semi-peripheral society. Although it was still subordinate to core interests and power, it did emulate some of the policies and processes of the metropolitan core society."[6] The late historian W. J. Eccles went even further in his assessment of the shift, writing that Canada "can be said to have been a metropolis, dominating the hinterland around it."[7]

Canada's *habitants* and merchants, as members of a dynamic colonial society, did not always behave in sanctioned, deferential ways. Throughout the seventeenth and eighteenth centuries, administrators charged with representing the French state either complained of the recalcitrance of the Canadian population or urged that metropolitan policies be adapted to colonial realities. An official of the latter persuasion, Intendant Jacques Duchesneau, warned the minister in 1681 that "we should not consider the cultivation of land and the raising of livestock . . . as solid means to establish this country, since it is only commerce that will make them pay, and the number of inhabitants, who will never be drawn here except by profit, gentle government, and the hope of living more comfortably than in France."[8]

Interestingly, this relatively enlightened attitude was not merely the product of colonial circumstance. As Eccles has noted, the administrative framework of Canada was "modeled on that of a French province but with significant differences."[9] Specifically, "reforms that the government could not make in France owing to the resistance of powerful vested interests were made in Canada."[10]

This observation accords with François Furet's nuanced portrait of the French Ancien Régime as an unstable compromise between the construction of a modern administrative state and the persistence of a corporatist society based on privilege. As a modern force, the absolute monarchy worked "slyly to subvert the traditional social fabric by levelling its ranks under general submission to a sole authority, and breaking up the hierarchies of birth and tradition"; it was thus "one of the foremost agents of change and progress—a permanent building-ground for 'enlightened' reform." At the same time, however, its fiscal policies "separated the orders of society into castes, by converting them into cash, weighing each privilege at its highest price, and creating out of an *esprit de corps* a passion for separateness." The tensions within this mixed system were very great, as monarchs were constantly torn between the rationalist demands of state building and their solidarity, born of necessity as well as sentiment, with "aristocratic society."[11]

The monarchy, however, was less ambivalent or less constrained where colonial matters were concerned. By the end of the seventeenth century, obedient *commissaires* from the naval bureaucracy had transformed Canada, in many respects, into a kind of laboratory of state-of-the-art social practices. To the extent that metropolitan absolutism was untrammeled, therefore, it could work against rather than for the construction of a traditional Ancien Régime society. This same phenomenon was also seen in New France's other important colonial center, the eighteenth-century colony of Ile Royale.

Acadia, the site of France's first permanent outpost in North America (Port Royal, founded by Samuel de Champlain in 1605), as described by Eccles, served "as a border march in the defensive system of Canada, as a base for the French and Anglo-American fishing industries, as a French agricultural settlement, as a base for missionary and fur trade activities, and as a hinterland of rival metropolises, Canada and New England," also noting that it was "also an area of overlapping imperial systems."[12] As a source of fish, furs, and eventually wheat, Acadia appeared to fulfill the economic functions assigned to a colonial periphery. The very importance of the fur trade, however, brought the few French settlers into close contact with the Mi'kmaq majority, resulting in the creation of a relatively fluid frontier society. Mi'kmaq and French interests would eventually diverge, as agriculture replaced the fur trade as the linchpin of the colonial economy. But Acadia's status as a disputed borderland would continue to guarantee the relative independence of the French colonists until the middle of the eighteenth century.

Port Royal, at the time of its founding, was nothing more than "a base for exploration, with fish and fur paying the costs."[13] Briefly abandoned from 1607 to 1610, when Champlain refocused French efforts on the St. Lawrence, it survived—barely—as an undercapitalized trading post. In the 1620s, the colony had just twenty year-round residents, none of them women, and they were "reputed to be living like savage beasts."[14] The 1630s brought little improvement, as "rival claimants to the trade of the region fought savagely for control, raiding each other's posts, seizing everything that could be carried off, and destroying what could not." The metropolis "exerted little influence and less control over individuals and events in this distant overseas wilderness."[15] Even at mid-century, when the French population (which now included women) had swelled to some three hundred, "the real rulers of Acadia were the Abenaquis, Micmac and Malecite tribesmen."[16] The Native population, although much reduced by epidemics at the time of French colonization, still numbered between 3,000 and 3,500.[17]

The relations between the French and Mi'kmaq were cordial in the early decades. Individual French and Mi'kmaq families established close trading ties, some of them cemented by intermarriage, and thanks to French missionary efforts, the two communities worshiped together as Catholics. "These economic, social, and cultural ties," historian William Wicken notes, "made possible a peaceful co-occupation of adjoining lands."[18]

This multicultural frontier was not to last, disproving the myth that the French, unlike their English rivals, had some sort of ontological affinity for Indians. As the French abandoned the declining fur trade for farming, they lived increasingly apart from the Mi'kmaq. Tensions between the growing, sedentary farm population and the migratory hunting and fishing society were further exacerbated by the struggle between France and England for sovereignty over this borderland. Ironically, the Mi'kmaq proved more steadfast opponents of the English than the French settlers, whose agricultural exports to New England made them anxious to maintain the peace.[19]

Yet the borderland situation that alienated the Acadian French from the Mi'kmaq also preserved them from metropolitan control. Political authority in early Acadia was nothing if not mutable. From the founding of Port Royal to the formal cession of the colony to Great Britain in 1713, the Acadians experienced English occupation several times, once for well over a decade.[20] Metropolitan supervision, as a result, was very weak. In particular, mercantilist policies were virtually impossible to implement when what was legal trade one year was smuggling the next, and vice versa.

The Acadians took advantage of this situation to develop a prosperous economy based on sea-dependent agriculture, fishing, and trading.[21] French census records portray "an agriculture that provided a good standard of nutrition for the settlers." It must, however, have done much more, for "trade made the Acadians the very reverse of an isolated peasantry."[22] Statistics are lacking owing to the smuggling problem, but it is clear that surplus grains, cattle, sheep, poultry, pigs, and furs made their way regularly from Acadian farms to Boston.[23] In 1679, Governor Frontenac of Canada complained that the Acadians were reluctant to obey orders, either from lack of habit, "or the divisions among them, or else a certain English and Parliamentary Inclination, which is inspired by the frequent contact and Commerce they have with those from Baston [*sic*]."[24]

Acadian independence continued after the transfer to British rule, culminating in an official form of self-government and a deliberate policy of neutrality in Franco-British imperial struggles. By 1721, British authorities recognized the right of Acadian communities to elect representatives annually. These representatives, however, became the spokesmen for a political stance that never satisfied the British Crown. Neutrality, despite its failure, was a conscious strategy rooted in a view of the English as *nos amis les ennemis* and articulated in the language of the Enlightenment.[25] Indeed, it was taken so seriously that after the deportation, Acadians who had escaped to the islands of St. Pierre and Miquelon preferred to move on rather than swear allegiance to France, the price of remaining on the periphery of French North America.[26]

With the founding of Quebec in 1608 and Ville-Marie in 1642, French colonization shifted westward to center in the St. Lawrence Valley. The economy of the new Canadian settlements, like those of Acadia, revolved around the fur trade, while agriculture developed slowly.[27] The existence of even a small number of true settlers, however, made it impossible for a company to monopolize all aspects of the fur trade. Throughout most of Canada's pioneer period, there was a monopoly over exporting furs to France, but not over trading with the Indians, the more lucrative of the two operations. Even the Jesuits, who loathed the moral disorders associated with the fur trade, accepted the settlers' "natural right" to engage in it.[28]

The intercultural realities of the fur trade wreaked havoc on the best laid metropolitan plans. Ville-Marie was founded by the Paris-based Société Notre-Dame as a missionary community, but it soon became a fur trading center by virtue of its location on the frontier. By mid-century the Société Notre-Dame was virtually bankrupt, and the settlement now known as Montreal (the name change came about because the habitants refused to say Ville-Marie), was a rough-and-ready marketplace for Indian furs and illegal alcohol.[29]

Up until the 1660s, much of the trading took place at Montreal's annual trade fairs, which in good years featured the arrival of large convoys of Great Lakes Algonquians and Iroquoians. On first sight, these fairs conformed closely to Native cultural norms. The visitors began by setting up their birch-bark wigwams and laying out their merchandise some five or six hundred paces from town. The next day they proceeded to speeches, councils, and ceremonies of pipe smoking and gift giving, suggesting that diplomacy, not exchange, was their primary goal. Only on the third day did the trading, often accompanied by feasting, begin.[30]

An alternative interpretation of the fairs emphasizes not their Indianness but their Frenchness. They brought out the entire settler population, female and male, poor and rich, united in pursuit of profit. As one observer noted, "during this time everyone becomes a Merchant."[31] Transactions were well lubricated with alcohol, despite the prohibitions—the better to fleece the Natives. Thanks to the fairs, Montreal acquired something of a reputation as a place to get rich quick. Ambitious young people trickled in from major metropolitan centers—Paris, Amiens, Rouen, La Rochelle, Bordeaux—lured by the prospect of easy money.[32]

A means to reconcile these conflicting readings is provided by Richard White, who points out that "whether a particular practice or way of doing things was French or Indian was, after a time, not so clear." On the frontier, after all, the two distinct societies "had to arrive at some common conception of suitable ways of acting"; they had to create a "middle ground" where "those who created it" could "justify their own actions in terms of what they perceived to be their partner's cultural premises."[33] Participants on the middle ground "acted for interests derived from their own culture, but they had to convince people of another culture that some mutual action was fair and legitimate."[34]

It goes without saying that the invention of the middle ground was fraught with conflict. At the Montreal trade fairs, for instance, the French used gift giving as a pretext for extortion, and brawls erupted, leading to violence on both sides.[35] But even when the process went smoothly, it was a threat to metropolitan hegemony, a frightening indication that French and Indian worlds had "melted at the edges and merged."[36]

There is a prevalent misconception that Indians grew quickly dependent upon European trade goods for their subsistence. In fact, "the material day-to-day existence of Indian peoples showed remarkable continuity during the seventeenth and early eighteenth centuries," and of the two trading partners, the French were generally the more eager.[37] Beginning in the 1660s, impatient young French trappers and traders known as *coureurs de bois* started taking their merchandise directly to Indian villages in the hinterland. The fur trade frontier thus expanded westward to the Great Lakes, leaving Montreal to supply the capital and coordinate the activities.

The coureurs de bois, who numbered in the hundreds by the 1680s, were Frenchmen who voluntarily adopted an Indian way of life. During their voyages they relied upon Native technologies, Native languages, and the services (sexual as well as economic) of Native women. Unsurprisingly, they were soon a focal point for French "anxieties about order and authority and the difficulties of preserving them in a colonial setting."[38] The Canadian governor lamented to his metropolitan superior in 1685, "They have to pass their lives in the woods, where there are neither priests to trouble them, nor fathers nor Governors to constrain them."[39]

What was at issue here was the collapse of deference on the colonial periphery, as no less a man than Cavelier de La Salle had already learned, to his chagrin, in 1680. Returning to Lake Ontario that year from a voyage of exploration, he discovered that his men had deserted, demolished his fort, stolen his goods, and left him a mocking note reading, "Nous sommes touts Sauvages" (We are all savages). He recognized the handwriting as that of Le Parisien, a Parisian who apparently found in imperialism not reinforced hegemony but an escape from subordination.[40]

Worse still, the coureurs de bois continued to flaunt French mores upon their return to town. "They plunge up to the neck into voluptuousness," one Montreal observer wrote. "Good living, women, gaming, drink, everything goes."[41] The spread of such behavior from colonial periphery to colonial center was particularly unnerving to the governor, who in fact opened his 1685 letter with the observation that "we have to take into account the disorders which occur not only in the woods but also in our settlements."[42]

But while the coureurs de bois were dangerous renegades, they survived into the eighteenth century as their status regularized as *voyageurs*. They succeeded primarily because the Great Lakes frontier was also a borderland and indeed, after 1713, the critical borderland on which the Franco-British struggle for empire was waged. Yet while the strategic importance of these western marches of New France increased, they remained in essence Native-controlled territory. French sovereignty was represented only by widely scattered trading, missionary, and military outposts, together with a fledgling agricultural settlement at Detroit, dating from 1701. Under these circumstances, the fate of the French empire depended on the success of the Indian alliance, a fragile construction requiring constant vigilance and compromise. The coureurs de bois, by virtue of their position on the middle ground, were critical intermediaries.

It was the coureurs de bois who initiated French settlement in the Illinois Country, a southward extension of the Great Lakes via the Mississippi and Illinois Rivers. The distinctiveness of this periphery of New France made it unique. Indeed, the Illinois Country "was the only French colony in North America which was not born from the expansionist will of the home country, but which arose from the free choice of its first colonists."[43]

Although the first trading post in the region (Fort Crèvecoeur) was established in 1680, true settlement began only in the 1690s, when Canadian coureurs de bois married local Indian women. Formal marriages between Frenchmen and Indians had previously been rare, and they were probably born of the coureurs de bois' resistance to the colonial center. But during the 1690s, Canadian officials tried to put the coureurs de bois out of business. Through marriage, therefore, the traders "may have been attempting to establish the necessary kin connections with Indians that would be vital to the ability of any Frenchman to remain safely in the West."[44] According to parish records, nineteen interracial marriages were celebrated between 1699 and 1718, and in one village, eighteen of the twenty-one baptisms recorded from 1704 to 1713 concerned mixed-race babies.[45]

This distant hinterland of Canada went its own way until 1717, when intervention by the metropolis changed the course of its development. In that year it was joined administratively to Louisiana, the Lower Mississippi colony founded in 1699. For strategic reasons, a major project was underway to develop Louisiana, and the Illinois Country was included in it owing to rumors about gold and silver mines. In 1718 the Illinois Country formally became the province of Upper Louisiana, and the next year its officials arrived from New Orleans, together with a hundred or so soldiers and immigrants.[46]

The administrative shift was accompanied by an economic reorientation toward the south, although connections to Canada were maintained. There was also a change in economic activity. Since Lower Louisiana had a greater demand for food than furs, Upper Louisiana's habitants, like the Acadians before them, increasingly abandoned the fur trade for the trade in agricultural products.[47]

The conversion to commercial agriculture brought the independent settlers into conflict with colonial authorities once again. "Because of the limited agricultural techniques and tools," as one historian notes, "the production of a surplus for the Lower Louisiana market could not be obtained without resorting to an additional work force."[48] In the eyes of the habitants, the solution lay in the importation of African slaves.

Although African slaves were brought into Upper Louisiana in the early 1720s, they were intended primarily for the mines. (The only other notable slaveholders at this time were the missionaries, especially the Jesuits.) When the mines failed to pan out, the importations stopped, and Illinois habitants were refused credit to purchase Africans in New Orleans.[49] For metropolitan officials, African labor was too valuable to squander on goods for colonial consumption. If it could not provide gold and silver, it could at least produce tobacco and indigo for export on Lower Louisiana plantations.

In 1726, the year that the *habitants'* credit was withdrawn, Upper Louisiana had a population of 319 whites (including the Indian wives and their *métis* children), 130 African slaves, and 66 Indian slaves, mostly Missouri war captives purchased from their Illinois enemies. The African slaves were preferred for agriculture, the Indian slaves for domestic work.[50] In the ensuing decades, the prohibition against importing African slaves was honored largely in the breach. When Governor Vaudreuil of Louisiana felt obliged to renew it in 1747, in deference to metropolitan interests, Governor La Jonquière of Canada protested, out of concern for Canada's wheat supply. In this contest between colonial centers, which also pitted metropolis against colony, Canada and colonial interests prevailed. Yet the real victors were the Illinois habitants, thanks to their position on the periphery of both Quebec and New Orleans. A few years later, though they numbered only 789, they were exploiting the labor of no fewer than 446 African and 150 Indian slaves.[51]

Despite the efforts of officials like Vaudreuil, Lower Louisiana also defied metropolitan expectations. Simply put, major initial investment in settling this borderland failed to bring anticipated returns. At least half of the 7,000 Europeans and 7,000 Africans transported to the colony between 1717 and 1731 either died or departed, making for a population at mid-century of no more than 4,000 whites and 5,000 blacks. In contrast, there were still some 70,000 Indians living in the Lower Mississippi Valley in the eighteenth century.[52]

Due to slow population growth, the colony's position in the Atlantic economy remained marginal. Tobacco and indigo were produced for export in limited quantities, but as in the French Caribbean of the previous century, large-scale plantation agriculture emerged only gradually. Lower Louisiana's other main export commodity, deerskins, had to be obtained through trade with the Indians. Here, as elsewhere, that exchange took place upon the middle ground, even calling into being a new language. Mobilian, a trade jargon based largely on western Muskhogean but incorporating European elements, facilitated interactions between Louisianans of every ethnic background.[53]

Left largely to their own devices by a discouraged metropolis, Louisiana's diverse inhabitants "pieced subsistence and commercial endeavors together into a patchwork of farming, herding, hunting, gathering, trade, and transportation activities" that Daniel Usner calls the "frontier exchange economy."[54] Within this feebly regulated economy, scope for intercultural relations was significant, and racial roles were less rigid than they would later become. African slaves, for instance, engaged in food selling, craft work, and even military service, activities that were all potential avenues of emancipation.[55]

Thus, from Acadia to Louisiana, the frontiers and borderlands of New France were more likely to frustrate metropolitan designs than to fulfill them. Neither mercantilism nor absolutism flourished on the colonial periphery, clichés about imperialism notwithstanding. Indeed, it was "a world system in which minor agents, allies, and even subjects at the periphery often guide the course of empires. This is an odd imperialism and a complicated world system."[56] Oddity and complexity, furthermore, were not confined to the periphery.

By the late seventeenth century, Canada was emerging from the frontier age. Like Portuguese Brazil, this colonial periphery was becoming a colonial center in its own right. That does not mean, however, that it was transformed into an exact replica of France's Ancien Régime. Despite the familiar image of Canada as a backward feudal society under tight metropolitan control, new social realities persisted beyond the frontier period. Government, of course, remained absolute, but metropolitan rule was at once more limited and less constrained than in France. As for Ile Royale, the maritime colony founded to replace Acadia in 1713, it evolved rapidly into a colonial center bearing even less resemblance to the traditional society of the metropolis.

Canada never ceased to be a multicultural society.[57] Indeed, there were reserves for Christian Indians right in the heart of the colony, at Kahnawaké and Oka outside Montreal, Lorette outside Quebec, and St. Francis in between. From the 1660s to the end of the French regime, domiciled Indians made up about 10 percent of the colonial population.

Although mission Indians were theoretically subject to the Crown, in practice they were "largely self-governing, economically independent, culturally autonomous." The Kahnawaké Mohawks even "explicitly refused to acknowledge the sovereignty of the king of France" yet succeeded in retaining their independence.[58] Indians continued to manage their own affairs because they were necessary to the fur trade, had no formal empire for the French to grab hold of, and were central to Canada's defense against the English. Laws relating to Indian indebtedness were not strictly enforced, and Indian crimes involving alcohol were resolved by punishing the tavern keeper instead of the perpetrator.[59] Since Canada remained a borderland beyond the frontier period, this colonial center was forced to tolerate not only cultural but juridical difference.

The French *habitants* themselves were distinct, in appearance and behavior, from their counterparts in rural France. Peter Kalm, a Swedish naturalist who toured the colony in 1749, noted that "the French in Canada in many respects follow the customs of the Indians, with whom they have constant relations. They use the tobacco pipes, shoes, garters, and belts of the Indians. They follow the Indian way of waging war exactly; they mix the same things with tobacco; they make use of the Indian bark boats and row them in the Indian way; they wrap a square piece of cloth round their feet, instead of stockings, and have adopted many other Indian fashions."[60]

Like the dreaded *coureurs de bois*, the *habitants* were individualistic and, as one intendant put it, "avid for gain."[61] As in the French Caribbean, the very term *habitant* reflects a changed reality, having been coined by independent farmers to distinguish themselves from peasants. According to the baron de Lahontan, a French officer who served in Canada in the late seventeenth century, "the peasants here are very comfortable, and I would wish such a good cuisine on our whole petty nobility of France. What am I saying: peasants! my excuses to these good sirs. The word, taken in its ordinary sense, would put our Canadians in the fields. A Spaniard, if one called him a villager, would not frown more deeply, or bristle his mustache more proudly. These people are not wrong after all; they do not pay the salt tax or the *taille*; they hunt and fish freely; in a word, they are rich. Would you want to compare them with our raggedy peasants?"[62]

Canada did, to be sure, have a seigneurial system, which siphoned off a larger part of the agricultural surplus as time went on.[63] *Habitants* nonetheless managed to speculate in land, practice a highly individualistic agriculture, and even occasionally achieve upward social mobility.[64] In fact, "the prefabricated society" of New France, "which had been envisioned as an organization where each would have his place, appeared more and more as a shattered society [*société éclatée*] that escaped regulatory control and deviated from original plans."[65]

And where was the French state in all of this? More often than not, it accepted the new social and economic arrangements, albeit not without anxiety in some cases. Adaptations to colonial realities included, but were not restricted to, the tacit recognition of Indian autonomy out of military exigency. Where French colonists were concerned, there was also a gradual abandonment of mercantilist policy in favor of free trade, and a general dismantling of corporatist social regulation. The export trade, as Jacques Mathieu shows, was marked by sincere, if sometimes heavy-handed, efforts at liberalization in the first half of the eighteenth century.[66] Internal markets were less regulated from the beginning, since the elaborate mechanisms that controlled provisioning in French towns were never established in Canada.[67] In the artisanal trades, guilds were out of the question, and corporatist association was strictly limited.[68]

It is interesting to consider whether the state, in pursuing such policies, was merely bowing to circumstances beyond its control. With regard to the Indians, this was certainly the case, but the metropolitan attitude toward the colonists was more complicated. If the *coureurs de bois* needed to be left alone for the sake of the Indian alliance, the same could not be said of ordinary townsfolk and habitants. There were, of course, limits to metropolitan control imposed by distance. Colonial officials frequently had to act on their own initiative, as one Canadian governor acknowledged openly in a dispatch to the minister. The newly appointed intendant, he complained, "has a lot to learn about many things here, in time he will come to understand that there is a great difference between Rochefort and Quebec; at Rochefort one receives your orders every week and here only annually, which means that often something is begun and finished before we have had the time to inform you about it."[69]

Nonetheless, Canadian officials were ultimately responsible to the Crown, which continued to oversee colonial policy. If the minister disapproved of a local decision, he had no qualms about reversing it after the fact. In 1674, for example, Governor Frontenac earned a stinging rebuke for having established a watered-down version of tradesmen's guilds the previous year. "His Majesty orders me to tell you that you have . . . exceeded the limits of the power he has given you," Colbert fumed.[70] Simply put, there were to be no associations of any kind in the colony, "it being good that each speak for himself, and that none speak for all."[71]

Of course, this high-handed response confirms the commonplace view of Canada as a domain of unrestrained absolutism. Still, it is noteworthy how often arbitrary power, as in the case just mentioned, worked to level the traditional orders of the Ancien Régime. From the time of Louis XIV, Canada's metropolitan administrators took advantage of the tabula rasa of colonial society to promote a more streamlined version of absolutism. Indeed, many of their policies exhibit the almost physiocratic repugnance for intermediary bodies and paternalist regulation that historians associate with Enlightened despotism. They tacitly agreed that "[c]ommerce cannot be too free and everything that tends to restrain it tends directly to destroy it."[72]

The reality behind this belief was made evident in the Canadians' response to the Crown's imposition of wartime controls during the final struggle with Great Britain. A year after the colony's capitulation, Montreal merchant Jacques Hervieux wrote to a French correspondent, "Cease, sir, to have this compassion for us. Our fate is less unhappy than it was formerly. We no longer groan under that insupportable tyranny occasioned by an immoderate desire to invade all commerce . . . Commerce is now free and open to everyone and is no longer in a single hand as it was formerly. In short, to be completely happy we want for nothing but to return under the domination of our Sovereign with generals and masters that he would choose as decent folk as our English general and the leaders that are under his orders. You are aware, sir, that this is a pardonnable and natural wish for any good citizen, for you know that it is tyranny and avarice that have caused the loss of Canada, our fatherland."[73] Even after the frontier period, Canada was a distinct colonial society, not a harmonious replica of the metropolitan Ancien Régime.

The situation on Ile Royale (today's Cape Breton Island) was even less traditional. In this colonial center, there were no seigneurs, few farmers, and very little agriculture. Settlement was largely confined to coastal communities, especially the largest of them, Louisbourg. Originally intended as a garrison town, Louisbourg rapidly became both a major base for the North Atlantic fishery and a busy entrepôt in the triangular trade among Europe, North America, and the West Indies. By the mid-eighteenth century, it was a bustling town of some eight thousand inhabitants, fewer than half of whom were soldiers.[74]

The fishing industry, which made Ile Royale the largest per capita exporter of any North American colony except British Newfoundland, was highly efficient and progressive in its reliance on resident fleets, local capital, and regional supply. The latter included not only Canadian wheat but New England ships, building materials, and livestock, which were exchanged for sugar and rum from Saint Domingue.[75] So important was the trade with New England, and so successful the lobbying efforts of Louisbourg's merchants, that "legislation hardly interfered with the incentives of the market."[76] Ile Royale's trade "fell within the regulations, and it was supervised by local officials who supplied regular statistical reports about it to the ministry in France."[77] Far from being Ancien Régime peasants, the inhabitants of Ile Royale were fishermen and traders who proved that "capital accumulation and entrepreneurial enterprise could thrive within the legal and political structures of New France, given the right economic conditions."[78]

In conclusion, an examination of center and periphery in New France calls into question overly simplified notions of the relationship between metropolis and colony in the early modern period. Mercantilism was certainly a motivation for colonization, but it was stymied on the periphery by frontier and borderland conditions and at the center by colonial economic development. Absolutism, although marginal on the periphery, had a powerful if remote hold on the center. Still, the examples of Canada and Ile Royale suggest that colonial absolutism was less constrained by traditional vested interests than the French version and more in tune with modern commercial society. Of course, that did not make it more successful in the long run, a lesson apparently lost on both Louis XV and his hapless successor.

Notes

1. Harold Innis, *The Fur Trade in Canada: An Introduction to Canadian Economic History* (1930; reprt. Toronto: University of Toronto Press, 1970); Harold Innis, *The Cod Fisheries: The History of an International Economy* (1940, rprt. Toronto: University of Toronto Press, 1978).
2. Francis Parkman, *France and England in North America,* 12 vols. (Boston: Little, Brown and Co., 1851–92).
3. Louise Dechêne, *Le Partage des subsistances au Canada sous le Régime français* (Montreal: Boréal, 1994), 10, 188. All translations mine unless otherwise stated.
4. Cornelius Jaenen, *The French Regime in the Upper Country of Canada during the Seventeenth Century* (Toronto: Champlain Society, 1996), 7.
5. Jeremy Adelman and Stephen Aron, "From Borderlands to Borders: Empires, Nation-States, and the Peoples in Between in North American History," *The American Historical Review,* 104 (June 1999), 815–16.
6. Jaenen, *Regime*, p. 4. The concepts of core, periphery, and semiperiphery were developed by Immanuel Wallerstein in *The Modern World-System: Capitalist Agriculture and the Origins of the European World-Economy in the Sixteenth Century* (New York: Academic Press, 1974) and *The Modern World-System II: Mercantilism and the Consolidation of the European World-Economy, 1600–1750* (New York: Academic Press, 1980). Wallerstein, however, considered "the North American fur-trading areas, largely Canada," as part of the external arena beyond the periphery. See *The Modern World-System II*, 273 ff.
7. W. J. Eccles, *The Canadian Frontier, 1534–1760* (Albuquerque: University of New Mexico Press, 1969, rev. ed. 1983), 3.
8. Cited in Leslie Choquette, *Frenchmen into Peasants: Modernity and Tradition in the Peopling of French Canada* (Cambridge, Mass.: Harvard University Press, 1997), 281.
9. Eccles, *Frontier*, 71.

10. Ibid., 10.
11. François Furet, *Revolutionary France, 1770–1880,* trans. Antonia Nevill (Oxford: Blackwell, 1992), 3–14.
12. Eccles, *Frontier*, 3.
13. W. J. Eccles, *France in America* (New York: Harper and Row, 1972), 15.
14. Eccles, *France in America,* 28; Marcel Trudel, *Histoire de la Nouvelle-France,* 3 vols. (Montreal: Fides, 1963–1983), vol. 2, 423, 440.
15. Eccles, *France in America,* 29.
16. Eccles, *France in America,* 66; Marcel Trudel, *Initiation à la Nouvelle-France: histoire et institutions* (Montreal: Holt, Rinehart, and Winston, 1968), 54.
17. Allan Greer, *The People of New France* (Toronto: University of Toronto Press, 1997), 92.
18. William Wicken, "Re-examining Mi'kmaq-Acadian Relations, 1635–1755," in *Habitants et Marchands Twenty Years Later: Reading the History of Seventeenth- and Eighteenth-Century Canada*, Sylvie Dépatie, Catherine Desbarats, et al., (Montreal: McGill-Queen's University Press, 1998), 95, 102.
19. Ibid., 98–108.
20. The British controlled Acadia from 1654 to 1667, and the French did not actually retake possession of the colony until 1670.
21. Naomi Griffiths, "Perceptions of Acadians: The Importance of Tradition," *British Journal of Canadian Studies* 5 (1990), 105; Naomi Griffiths, "Acadian Identity on the Eve of the Deportation: Distinct and Particular Communities," paper presented at the Biennial Meeting of the Association for Canadian Studies in the United States, New Orleans, 1993.
22. Naomi Griffiths, *The Contexts of Acadian History, 1686–1784* (Montreal: McGill-Queen's University Press, 1992), 25. That the census declarations were the work of tax evaders is clear from the archaeological evidence. For instance, the Melanson farm in Port Royal actually contained nine times more arable land in 1707 than was claimed in the census of the same year. See Andrée Crépeau and Brenda Dunn, "A Cultural Landscape: Archaeological and Historical Perspectives on the Settlement Pattern at the Melanson Site," paper presented at the Annual Meeting of the French Colonial Historical Society, Louisbourg, 1994. It should also be noted that seigneurialism was virtually meaningless in Acadia. What little there was of the system to begin with was destroyed by extended British occupation. See Jean Daigle, ed., *The Acadians of the Maritimes: Thematic Studies* (Moncton: Centre d'études acadiennes, 1982), 32; Griffiths, *The Contexts of Acadian History*, 20; John Reid, *Acadia, Maine, and New Scotland: Marginal Colonies in the Seventeenth Century* (Toronto: University of Toronto Press, 1981), 160.
23. Daigle, *Acadians*, 28, 39.
24. Cited in Reid, *Acadia*, 160.
25. Griffiths, *The Contexts of Acadian History*, 42; Naomi Griffiths, "The Golden Age: Acadian Life, 1713–1748," *Histoire sociale/Social History* 17 (1984), 23–24. The Acadian representatives included members of the Melanson family, prosperous farmers with mercantile connections. Of mixed Huguenot, Catholic, and English origins, they had close family ties in Boston.
26. Current research of Donald Desserud at the University of New Brunswick in St. John. St. Pierre and Miquelon were, of course, the only North American colonies remaining to France after 1763.
27. Louise Dechêne, in her classic study of seventeenth-century Montrealers, emphasized the primacy of commerce to their existence: "In a primarily peasant France, wrote Goubert, I tried to get to know the peasants. . . . We would gladly write, in a primarily mercantile Canada, we must get to know the merchants." Dechêne, *Habitants et marchands de Montréal au XVIIe siècle* (Paris: Plon, 1974), 125.
28. Dechêne, *Habitants et marchands*, 163; Trudel, *Histoire de la Nouvelle-France,* vol. 3, part 2, 298–99.
29. Dechêne, *Habitants et marchands*, 158–59; Trudel, *Histoire de la Nouvelle-France,* vol. 3, part 1, 320–21, 360.

30. For an eyewitness account, see Lahontan, *Oeuvres complètes*, 2 vols., ed. Réal Ouellet (Montreal: Les Presses de l'Université de Montréal, 1990), vol. 1, 316–18.
31. Lahontan, *Oeuvres*, 318.
32. Dechêne, *Habitants et marchands*, 171–72. The paradox of immigrants coming to a peripheral colony from the least peripheral parts of the metropolis is true not only for Montreal, but for French North America in general. On immigration to Canada and Acadia, see Choquette, *Frenchmen into Peasants.*
33. Richard White, *The Middle Ground: Indians, Empires, and Republics in the Great Lakes Region, 1650–1815* (Cambridge: Cambridge University Press, 1991), 50, 52.
34. Ibid., 52.
35. Ibid., 107–8.
36. Ibid., 50.
37. Ibid.,132.
38. Greer, *New Frame*, 85.
39. Marquis Denonville, "The Governor's Verdict," in J. M. Bumsted, ed., *Documentary Problems in Canadian History*, vol. 1 (Georgetown, Ont.: Irwin-Dorsey, 1969), 23. Translation by Cornelius Jaenen.
40. White, *Middle Ground*, 58.
41. Cited in Choquette, *Frenchmen into Peasants*, 143.
42. Cited in Bumsted, *Problems*, 23. Jaenen's translation.
43. Cécile Vidal, "The Original Peopling of the Illinois Country, 1699–1765: A Colony of 'Peasants' Not Tied to Their Land," working paper no. 96-29, International Seminar on the History of the Atlantic World, 1500–1800, Harvard University, 1996, 2. This paper summarizes Vidal's two-volume dissertation on the Illinois Country. See "Les Implantations françaises au pays des Illinois au XVIIIe siècle (1699–1765)," Paris, École des Hautes Études en Sciences Sociales, 1995.
44. White, *Middle Ground*, 68.
45. Renald Lessard, Jacques Mathieu, and Lina Gouger, "Peuplement colonisateur au pays des Illinois," in Philip Boucher and Serge Courville, eds., *Proceedings of the French Colonial Historical Society* (Lanham, Md.: University Press of America, 1988), 62; White, *Middle Ground*, 70. These ceremonies were Christian because of the founding of two missions in the region, Cahokia in 1699 and Kaskaskia in 1703.
46. Lessard et al., "Peuplement," 59.
47. Ibid., 61; Vidal, "Peopling," 2.
48. Vidal, "Peopling," 7.
49. Ibid., 5.
50. Ibid., 4–5, 12, table II.
51. Ibid., 6, table V.
52. Daniel Usner, *Indians, Settlers, and Slaves in a Frontier Exchange Economy: The Lower Mississippi Valley before 1783* (Chapel Hill: University of North Carolina Press, 1992), 17, 33–34; Greer, *New France*, 106.
53. Usner, *Indians*, 4–5, 28, 81, 256–59.
54. Ibid., 277.
55. Ibid., 55, 86, 202.
56. Ibid., XI.
57. *New France*, 76.
58. Ibid., 79, 80.
59. Denys Delâge, "The Indians before Justice during the French Regime in the Government of Quebec," paper presented at the Annual Meeting of the French Colonial Historical Society, New Orleans, 1999. See also Cornelius Jaenen, "Some Unresolved Issues: Lorette Hurons in the Colonial Context," in A. J. B. Johnston, ed., *Essays in French Colonial History: Proceedings of the Twenty-First Annual Meeting of the French Colonial Historical Society* (East Lansing: Michigan State University Press, 1997), 111–25.
60. Cited in Greer, *New France*, 84.
61. Cited in Choquette, *Frenchmen into Peasants*, 282.
62. Ibid.
63. Dechêne, *Habitants et marchands,* 247–58.

64. On land speculation and individualistic agriculture, see Choquette, *Frenchmen into Peasants*, 284. The current research of Alain Laberge focuses on social promotion, for example, his "Que dis-je, paisans? l'habitant canadien et la société rurale de la vallée du Saint-Laurent (XVIIe-XIXe siècles), de l'homogénéité à la différenciation," paper presented at the Annual Meeting of the French Colonial Historical Society, New Orleans, 1999.
65. Gilles Paquet and Jean-Pierre Wallot, "Sur quelques discontinuités dans l'expérience socio-économique du Québec: une hypothèse," *Revue d'histoire de l'Amérique française* 35 (1982), 495. The term *prefabricated society* was coined by Sigmund Diamond in "Le Canada français au XVIIe siècle: une société préfabriquée," *Annales: économies, sociétés, civilisations* 16 (1961), 317–54.
66. Jacques Mathieu, *Le Commerce entre la Nouvelle-France et les Antilles au XVIIIe siècle* (Montreal: Fides, 1981), 33–72.
67. Louis Dechêne, *Le Partage des subsistances,* 39–54. A loosening of commercial regulation could also be seen in the treatment of the *coureurs de bois,* as mentioned above.
68. Peter Moogk, "In the Darkness of a Basement: Craftsmen's Associations in Early French Canada," *Canadian Historical Review* 57 (1976), 399–439.
69. Cited in Eccles, *The Canadian Frontier*, 72; his translation.
70. "Lettre du Ministre Colbert au Gouverneur de Frontenac (17 mai 1674)," *Rapport de l'archiviste de la province du Québec* (1926–27), 56.
71. "Lettre du Ministre au Gouverneur de Frontenac (13 juin 1673)," *Rapport de l'archiviste de la province du Québec* (1926–27), 25.
72. Dechêne, *Le Partage des subsistances*, 107, citing ministerial instructions to the intendant from 1733.
73. Cited in Dechêne, *Le Partage des subsistances*, 184–85.
74. For broad-based descriptions of life on Ile Royale, see Eric Krause, Carol Corbin, and William O'Shea, eds., *Aspects of Louisbourg: Essays on the History of an Eighteenth-Century French Community in North America* (Sydney: University College of Cape Breton Press, 1995), and Christopher Moore, *Louisbourg Portraits: Life in an Eighteenth-Century Garrison Town* (Toronto: Macmillan, 1982).
75. Christopher Moore, "Cape Breton and the North Atlantic World in the Eighteenth Century," in Kenneth Donovan, ed., *The Island: New Perspectives on Cape Breton's History, 1713–1900* (Fredericton: Acadiensis, 1990), 32, 38–39, 42.
76. John R. McNeill, *Atlantic Empires of France and Spain: Louisbourg and Havana, 1700–1763* (Chapel Hill: University of North Carolina Press, 1985), 178.
77. Moore, "Cape Breton," 42.
78. Christopher Moore, "The Other Louisbourg: Trade and Merchant Enterprise in Ile Royale, 1713–58," *Histoire sociale/Social History* 12 (1979), 96.

The "Frontier Era" of the French Caribbean, 1620s–1690s

Philip P. Boucher

Raconteur, bon vivant, gourmand *à l'outrance*, the Dominican "missionary" Jean-Baptiste Labat published a long and lively account of his adventures in the French Antilles during the war-torn years, 1693–1705. Consciously, sometimes, and other times not, Labat testified to the denouement of what will be called here the "frontier era" of the French Caribbean. He lived through and, more than once, fought in Louis XIV's late wars, which would both increase the state's presence in the Caribbean and simultaneously legalize for the final time the activities of his freebooter (*flibustier*) friends.[1] He disembarked in the islands during the decade that suffered the outbreak of the *maladie du Siam*, or yellow fever, and the author's survival despite periodic severe ill health was, if not unique among fellow priests, unusual.[2] Skilled, or claiming to be, in all of natural philosophy (and rather immodestly proud of it), the Dominican carefully noted the properties and utility of many plants and animals while pointing out the senseless destruction of so many valuable resources. Colonists had overcut mahogany and other valuable woods and had hunted manatees, sea turtles, water and land fowl, and feral pigs to near extinction.[3] Labat describes at length his participation in a pig hunt far into the mountainous interior of Guadeloupe, the last safe haven for the beasts, and rewards the reader's patience with a succulent account of the stuffing of the victim's cavity with other meats and fruits prior to barbequeing.[4] But clearly neither colonists nor their slaves could any longer depend on easy pickings in times of drought or when supply routes from Europe suffered disruption.

Compared to his predecessors, the Dominicans Raymond Breton and Jean-Baptiste du Tertre, Labat devotes less space to the (in)famous Island Caribs, no doubt because these "cannibals" were less frequently seen anymore in Martinique or Guadeloupe. The intelligent pages about them in his book result in part from a storm-driven landing on to the Carib reservation island of Dominica, whereupon this insatiably curious friar trekked into deep jungle to visit a Carib village. Labat the anthropologist and *littérateur* does not even pretend to talk Jesus to peoples who had long resisted the religion of those who dispossessed them. He is very certain that they could not be converted without deculturation (*dépaïsé*), a process these proud warriors had and would resist to the death.[5] Just as the U.S. frontier "closed" concurrently with the relegation of remaining Indians to reservations, so was the case with the French Antilles.

Labat was interested, however, in the souls of African and African-American (creole) slaves, as well as their bodies. Charged by his order to correct the problems plaguing its island holdings, Labat moved with gusto into the role of sugar plantation manager.[6] His long and lucid descriptions of sugar planting and manufacturing, and of how to employ and manage slaves, are of great interest.[7] Without a hint of either doubt or cynicism, Labat espouses an attitude of religious and social paternalism toward slaves.[8] He believes that the French community, guided by its priests, must make certain of the universal baptism and the gradual conversion of all slaves for the sake of their souls, and to guarantee social order in a slave society. He severely chastises the English for neglecting their slaves' souls, and ridicules their excuse questioning the validity of enslaving fellow Christians. It is tempting to a twentieth-century reader to rush to the conclusion that Labat was more interested in social control than in souls, but *qui sait* (who knows or who can say)? In his own parish of 307 Europeans and 690 African slaves, 64 of the latter had "progressed" enough to receive communion, whereas 58 had not been baptized, a fact Labat notes he is determined to change. Lamenting that many, and occasionally most, planters were not always "rational" in their treatment of slaves, Labat gives "sensible" advice about how to manage these people to ensure their cooperation and loyalty: They should receive adequate nourishment, be allowed to have and accrue possessions "to buy into the system," and always should be treated "fairly" if firmly.[9] He constantly appeals to the planters' self-interest in protecting their investments, even if short-term profits should occasionally suffer. His confidence in his order's slaves is demonstrated by his references to their hunting excursions; indeed, he armed ten to thirty on different occasions when the English threatened. He was very far from alone in this practice: He notes that many slaves of the French repeatedly demonstrated strong resistance to forcible transfer to the English or Spaniards. Today, of course, we do not have to accept Labat's religious and patriotic assumptions about why that was the case.[10]

Labat's specific descriptions of important planter families portray their growing dominance in island life, at least in the "large" islands of Martinique and Guadeloupe in the Lesser Antilles,[11] and the concomitant if very gradual decline of subsistence and tobacco farmers. The transformation was by far most dramatic at tiny St. Christopher (St. Kitts),[12] where displaced tobacco farmers moved on, usually to Saint Domingue (Haiti) in the "wild" west. Although the "mature" stage of the sugar islands, characterized by the dominance of one crop and the ready availability of slave labor, was still one or two generations in the future, the Dominican's book attests to the decline of the frontier era economy at Guadeloupe and Martinique. Nevertheless, he also makes very clear that sugar's triumph was a slow process indeed—unlike, for example, the case of English Barbados or Jamaica.[13] In his own parish, with a population of about one thousand (of whom two-thirds were slaves, which was about the average for Martinique as a whole), only five sugar plantations were established. Making the probably rash assumption that these five contained on average fifty slaves, five indentured servants, and five family members each, then some three hundred of the one thousand people were connected to a product "made from blood." Mixed agriculture, composed of some combination of one or more small-scale cash crops—sugar, indigo, cacao, and ginger—with pastoral pursuits, provision and tobacco farming, and lumber industry, occupied most inhabitants and probably most slaves. Labat frankly and unapologetically makes clear that big sugar works placed gravest pressure on slaves due to the technology and work pace during the harvest season. He describes, too calmly, terrifying "accidents" that primarily involved women "feeding" cane into the crushing mill. The Dominican could only advise fellow planters to give slaves working eighteen-hour days during the long processing months more food, more sugar syrup, more cheap rum, and more tobacco. The fact therefore that the frontier era economy only gradually gave way to the period of monoculture benefited, at least marginally, many African slaves.

Although he visited all French islands, Labat had less familiarity with less developed French settlements, and especially with the burgeoning but still very "frontier" society of Saint Domingue, the future colossus of European sugar islands. This alerts us to the difficulty of defining "frontier" status for any single colony, and a fortiori for a group of island colonies. In a geographic and topographical sense, some islands remained frontiers far longer than others. Islands containing significant Island Carib populations had a very different frontier experience than those that did not, for example, Saint Domingue. But *frontier* is also employed here in a broad cultural sense; the frontier condition lasted until uncertainties in relations among Island Caribs, Europeans, and African slaves were resolved.[14] This essay will test the possibility and utility of identifying such a stage of island life whose economic, social, political, and cultural characteristics were clearly differentiated from those of the classic, "mature" plantation society almost too familiar to scholars. Called "frontier era" here, this stage of social evolution, differently timed on each island, must be conceived as clearly distinct from the more familiar model of a sugar/slave society. In the frontier economy, sugar steadily assumed increasing importance from the 1650s, but it was far from its haughty eighteenth-century status. Among French islands, only Martinique and Guadeloupe had at least two Africans for every European in 1700, whereas contemporary, more "developed" Barbados "boasted" three slaves to every free man.[15] In the "mature" eighteenth-century phase, African and African-American (creole) slaves would outnumber Europeans six, eight, and even ten to one in 1789 Saint Domingue. "Frontier era" French islands still had room for European drivers, professionals, and artisans, many of whom would in the course of the eighteenth century be replaced by trained creole slaves. Social relations, it will be argued here, were somewhat more flexible and elastic in the frontier era than later. For a variety of reasons, perhaps most obviously the relative demographic parity between Europeans and Africans, relations between masters and slaves were probably less horrible than those of the "mature" era, especially in the nonsugar sectors of the economy.

Politically, the frontier eras of colonies imply less control from the center. Thus, if the French islands had such a distinct phase, it would call into question the received opinion about the character of French colonial centralization under Cardinal Richelieu, Louis XIV, and Jean-Baptiste Colbert. This essay intends to challenge such traditional assessments, and in doing so will mirror the current deflating of hallowed notions of French absolutism.[16] French islanders held some aces and some wild cards in the stud game played with Versailles. After all, the colonial militia provided the main defense of the king's possessions at least until the 1690s. The colonists believed, correctly enough, that they and their ancestors had fought for their islands and had made them valuable without significant metropolitan help. In fact, before the mid-1660s, kings and ministers had been a hindrance. All evidence suggests that mandates from Paris that contradicted island customs and beliefs were not well enforced, or at all. For example, Labat makes clear that some parts of the comprehensive 1685 French Code governing master-slave relations (Code Noir), especially those relating to food requirements for slaves, were unfortunately but understandably little obeyed, especially in times of disruptions of supplies during war. Even less obeyed was the repeated demand that big land concessions that had not been improved after three years be returned for redistribution.[17] Despite his strong patriotic and "mercantilist" proclivities, Labat remarks, almost with nonchalance, about the ubiquity and brazenness of colonists' smuggling with the English, the Dutch, and even the Danish at St. Thomas—as if it is something impossible to stop.[18] But if the colonists won many—not all—victories in the tug of war with royal officials, then how can it be argued here that relations with slaves were slightly less disastrous than later? Presumably, planters with a relatively free hand would be little restrained in their treatment of their slaves. Orlando Patterson argues that what is called here the "frontier era" was the worst period of master-slave relations, at least in Jamaica.[19] Were there, therefore, other restraints on French planters' conduct in the seventeenth century?

Should readers be persuaded by what follows that the concept of the frontier era possesses merit, and that Father Labat would be apoplectic to hear of this categorization given his intense efforts to persuade his readers that a polished society had replaced the rough early era, then they will demand answers to the proper questions. Most importantly, if it is claimed that the evolution of "mature" plantation society was not somehow so historically inevitable as to obviate the need for analysis of its evolution, what forces and factors promoted its eighteenth-century emergence in many, but not all, French settlements, and in some but not all areas of "sugar islands," and in ways similar to but not exactly like the British sugar islands? Any short, if unsatisfactory, answer would cite international wars and the concomitant growth of state power, the expansion and "rationalization" of the African slave trade, and the island elite's insatiable need or desire for metropolitan capital and luxuries. I am currently working on a book-length discussion of these relationships.[20]

Next, some readers might grant that the 1620s to the 1660s could be labeled "frontier decades" but would argue that it is a stretch to so characterize the subsequent era, to 1700 or 1713. Of course, they have a point, and in fact, demographic and economic gains accelerated after 1650, and the uncultivated areas diminished, if gradually. The Caribs were at most an annoyance after 1660, not a threat to colonial survival, and the state made its presence increasingly felt. The reader will see that this essay in fact distinguishes the decades of the 1670s, '80s, and '90s from those that preceded. Yet below it is argued that the concept of frontier era to characterize all of the seventeenth century is useful on two accounts: First, it emphasizes the French islands' long period of transition to the classic "plantation complex,"[21] much slower than a Barbados or a Jamaica but certainly much more quickly than a Santo Domingo or Cuba and second, the long frontier allows a more legitimate comparison to those of relatively similar length in Virginia (c. 1610 to 1690s), low country Carolina (c. 1670s to 1730s) and Louisiana (c. 1700 to 1780s). Historians of these colonies have recently asserted that master-slave relations in those frontier eras were less oppressive and more flexible than in later phases of plantation society because of, among other things, the relatively low ratio of slaves to free people, the variegated tasks assigned to Africans (e.g., herding, fishing, lumber industry, and provisions farming) that permitted wider areas of de facto freedoms, and shortages of European women. The examination below of such issues in the context of the French Caribbean should be of some interest to scholars of the Atlantic world.[22]

It is important, however, to reiterate from the outset that French colonies did not develop synchronically, and thus frontier eras of particular colonies occurred at different times. St. Christopher, the initial French colony, emerged first from its frontier phase as early as the 1660s. The Caribs had early on been expelled (massacred, in truth), nature had been thoroughly "tamed," and the tobacco men and other small farmers were already being squeezed out. Thus, according to Labat, the militia had decreased to one-tenth its former size by the 1690s.[23] At the other end of the spectrum, islands such as Cayenne (Guiana, but here treated as a Caribbean island), Marie-Galante, St. Croix, St. Lucia (Ste. Lucie) and Grenada were very sparsely populated and thus true ecological frontiers. Saint Domingue, rich in potential, was filling up quickly with refugees from France and other Caribbean islands, as well as transfrontiersmen of all nationalities. However, it was having problems finding its economic niche given its difficulty in procuring adequate labor to clear its forests. As noted above, Martinique and Guadeloupe were on the threshold of the transition to a "mature" sugar stage, but both were held back by the uncertainties of war, the vagaries of acquiring slaves illegally made necessary by the backwardness of the French supply network, and royal resistance to changes that might overly weaken white settlement and thus "defense." In truth, this issue was a "catch-22" for Versailles by the close of the seventeenth century. Big plantations provided wealth to the metropolis and taxes to the king even as they emasculated the islands' defenses against outsiders and, potentially, against the rebellions of slaves, increasingly greater in numbers.

Of the two phases of the frontier era, the 1620s–60s was that most deserving of the name "pioneering." Colonial propagandists of the 1650s and 1660s, notably Charles de Rochefort and the great Dominican predecessor of Labat, Jean-Baptiste du Tertre, discussed the difficulties of the first twenty or so years of settlement, only to note how much life had since improved.[24] The French experience in the Antilles was thus little different from the troubled times of so many early European colonies in the Americas.

In the Caribbean, a number of factors determined the length of the frontier period but none more so than the "Indian problem." Untroubled by the Indians' presence, Barbados swiftly moved into the age of sugar whereas the tormented English Leewards Islands (e.g., St. Kitts, Nevis, Antigua, Montserrat) struggled painfully for the first half century.[25] In the 1630s French colonists invaded the strategic heart of the Caribs' world, the islands of Martinique and Guadeloupe. As I have shown elsewhere, Norman and Poitevin settlers threatened Carib communications and their peripatetic economy based on gathering resources from all islands, even "uninhabited" ones.[26] Although these aborigines and earlier, temporary French visitors had conducted remarkably amicable relations, permanent occupation generated multiple episodes of cultural misunderstanding and made war all but inevitable.[27] With English assistance, colonists at St. Christopher conducted a "preventive attack" on the tiny Carib march there. These Stone Age warriors had had some successes against Spanish *entradas* in the sixteenth century,[28] and once French hostility was thus announced, were prepared for European military techniques. In the 1650s, in alliance with some maroons, they very nearly booted the French out of Martinique, and without the arrival of Dutch ships and sailors, would probably have done so. Their guerrilla tactics kept the colonists cooped up on about one-half of Guadeloupe and Martinique, and prevented or delayed settlement on Ste. Lucie, Grenada, and Dominica (among others) until after 1660 when they were accorded "permanent" reservations on Dominica and St. Vincent. Obviously, frontier conditions remained as long as these proud warriors silently rowed their dugout canoes (*pirogues*) to unprotected parts of "French" islands. Step by painful step, French settlers carved out small farms (*habitations*) in areas contiguous to earlier occupied lands. Without the Caribs, settlers would have claimed all the best lands very quickly, just as they would do from the 1660s on.

The interethnic conflicts from 1626 to 1659 were sporadic, but both the years of war and those of truce profoundly shaped the character of French colonization in the frontier era, and of course that of a declining Carib culture. Because neither king nor colonial companies provided significant support to besieged colonists, they were forced to acquire the martial skills and toughness to withstand and pursue the fierce and stealthy enemy. For the most part, these settlers had had less experience with weapons and war in France, unlike the *caballeros* of New Spain, but now they forged themselves into a remarkable colonial militia, one that stands comparison with that of their rough-hewn cousins on the St. Lawrence River, to the north. These experiences made the survivors very confident and proud. They called themselves *habitants* and refused to answer to the despised epithets *paysans* (peasants), or worse *roturiers* (common, lowlifes). They strolled about armed with pistols and swords. No wonder that when royal officials determined to impose "order" on these rambunctious frontiersmen, and "reduce" their "licentious" ways, they responded with violence, sometimes, and noncompliance at others. The royal bluff and theater employed so effectively to gain obedience in France had a less respectful audience far out of eye- and earshot across the Atlantic. They, also, of course, had to steel *habitants* to live among peoples whose labor they coerced, often with harshness. What little evidence is available suggests they harbored few fears of uprisings of their indentured servants or from African slaves. Eighteenth-century colonists, however, grew anxious about the appearance of a black Spartacus.

The Carib question dictated the pace of land clearing for agriculture, at least in the Lesser Antilles. St. Christopher, the least threatened colony, had exhausted its timber by the 1650s and had planted all of its arable land.[29] Growing population at Martinique and Guadeloupe by the 1650s spurred both the attempted colonization of St. Lucia and the French pressures that produced the final cataclysm of war with the Caribs. But it was only after the 1660 peace treaty that a land rush made a significant dent on the remaining wilderness areas of the "big" islands. Meanwhile the pig and cattle hunters (*boucaniers*) of the north coast of Saint Domingue slaughtered animals with wasteful abandon to obtain hides and choice strips of meat for smoking, leaving the remainder as carrion. By the last decades of the century, the post-

Columbian wild run of these animals in a predatorless garden of Eden was ending with a bang.

The term *frontier era* ordinarily connotes a stage of colonial development in which the central, metropolitan authority is very weak and leadership in the colony itself contested. Such a situation might arguably characterize the first half century (at least) of Portuguese Brazil, the Spanish-American empire, English continental North America, and the Caribbean. Such was also the case for French America. Traditional categorizations of France's efforts as *colonisation d'état* (state-controled colonization) are grossly exaggerated, at least for the seventeenth century. The story of the evolution of center/periphery relations in both the English and French American colonies is far more similar than is ordinarily thought. Just as the early Stuarts exercised a fitful suzerainty over their transatlantic settlements, so did Louis XIII and the youthful Louis XIV. For the Caribbean, the Norman adventurer Pierre Belain d'Esnambuc did persuade newly appointed grand master of navigation, Armand Jean du Plessis, Cardinal de Richelieu, to obtain royal approval to colonize St. Christopher in 1626, and the first minister even invested personal funds in the enterprise. Iron Armand, like Elizabeth I of England, wanted to tweak the Spaniards without provoking war. Because he had not read K. R. Andrews's books on how privateering was a losing long-term investment, Richelieu may well have dreamed of the capture of a Spanish treasure ship or two.[30] After all, French privateers had grown fat trolling the Atlantic and Caribbean sea-lanes in the 1540s and 1550s. As grand master, he would receive a share of all prizes from American waters.

The first company theoretically controlling French interests in the Antilles hardly got off the ground. By 1635 the cardinal had prepared France for the final showdown with Spain, and thus there remained no further reason for secrecy about Caribbean undertakings. In that year he reorganized the company, now called the Company of the Islands of America (CIA), and appointed Parisian directors led by his *homme de confiance* François Fouquet. For a few years the company vigorously promoted colonial expansion to other islands and attempted to send agents and judicial officials to control the embryonic settlements. Richelieu did his part by persuading the francophile Pope Urban VIII to sanction the sending of French Capuchins, Dominicans, and Jesuits to the "Spanish Caribbean," an explicit rebuff to now bombastic Castilian pretensions of monopoly. The grand master also selected a tough and troublesome knight of Malta, Philippe Lonvilliers de Poincy, to govern St. Christopher and act as the king's lieutenant general for all of the French islands. By 1640 it appeared that the center might realize its efforts to control colonial development.[31]

The 1640s turned out almost as sour for Bourbon absolutist and imperial dreams as it did for their Spanish Habsburg and Stuart cousins. Mired in the endless and difficult wars with Spain, and soon to be torn apart in the civil conflict known as the Fronde (1648–53), France under the regency of Anne of Austria and tutelage of the Italian landlubber and aesthete Jules, Cardinal de Mazarin, allowed naval expenditures to plummet. Sending of ships and troops to the Antilles was out of the question. So when in 1645–46 the CIA, aggrieved that island officials and colonists quite openly flouted its claims to exclusive control of commerce, attempted to replace the worst offender, Poincy, it had no weapons to contest his refusal to accept his delegated replacement. This colonial Fronde ended only when the company sold these now albatross-like possessions to the island governors including the renegade Poincy, who bought St. Christopher for the knights of Malta. Anne and Mazarin (quite the couple now) soon accepted the inevitable, and officially "rehabilitated" the strongman Poincy.

During the 1650s a well-nigh desperate, Mazarin, conceded the Atlantic sphere to the lumbering but dangerous Oliver Cromwell as the price for Commonwealth support against the Spaniard in the lowlands. Thus did Poincy, this astonishing warrior monk with the avaricious instincts of an Amsterdam merchant, survive as unchallenged king of the Antillean hill until his death in 1661. This ignominious debacle was hardly the last time Paris would be compelled to swallow brazen disobedience in these faraway islands.

As the government struggled simultaneously to defeat the Habsburgs and to control rebellion at home, the islands grew rapidly under strong proprietors. The economic centers were Holland and Zeeland, whose reliable merchants provided cheap imports and paid good prices for colonial produce. Dutch and Portuguese Jewish refugees from Brazil, along with their slaves, launched the sugar industry.[32] Dutch arms even played a major role in turning back a Carib and maroon guerrilla war against the French. Even though a number of powerful French officials and nobles, no doubt hearing of the striking prosperity of Barbados and the incipient good times in the French islands, expressed interest in buying some or all of these islands, Paris and the king must have seemed very remote to the *habitants*.[33]

The proprietors themselves were not immune from the natural centrifugal forces of a colonial frontier. To be sure, the multiple dangers of the Caribbean cockpit, from other Europeans, Caribs, and discontented coerced laborers, promoted self-interested support of strong local government. At St. Christopher, the immediate threat of the more numerous, if pusillanimous, English provided Poincy with a plausible excuse to build his heavily fortified, Italianate villa overlooking the French capital, Basseterre.[34] Epitomizing the Machiavellian preference of being feared more than loved, be it necessary to choose, he ruled with an arrogant sangfroid and iron discipline. But even he could not prevent a former lieutenant from creating an independent buccaneer satrapy at Tortuga, adjacent to northwest Hispaniola. At Martinique, the respected and beloved nephew of d'Esnambuc, Jacques Dyel du Parquet, led the colony through the difficult years of the Carib Wars without internal turmoil. After his death in 1657, however, his Parisian widow and a clique of her hangers-on provoked much discontent, then rebellion, among the Norman *confrères* and clients of her virtuous husband. A cold-war tension continued in the colony until the eve of Louis XIV's symbolic *entrée* there in the person of his emissary, Alexandre Prouville de Tracy in 1664. At Guadeloupe, the two proprietors and brothers-in-law Charles Houel and one Jean Boisseret d'Herblay squabbled incessantly, but the former being in situ in the island incessantly tormented the supporters of his sister's husband. Of parasitic *officier* corps that fattened on the emaciated corpses of the peasant masses at home, Houel exhibited the skills of patient fraudulence and fait accompli financial machinations that would make present-day Wall Street freebooters smile with recognition. A segment of the population did not weep when the Sun King (Louis XIV) dispossessed this little-loved figure.[35]

The first phase of the French Antilles frontier-era economy and society cannot easily be described as a slave-based monoculture plantation complex—far from it. As in early stages of other Atlantic settlements, colonists extracted, prepared, and sold wild products, ranging from ornamental parrots, to precious woods, to dried pig meat. They planted potatoes and bitter manioc, as well as European fruits and vegetables. Much time and tears were devoted to clearing land and building palm-frond-roofed huts. But the point of all of this beyond sheer survival, for most *habitants* at least, was to prepare and market a tobacco crop. The first decade or so witnessed the relatively rapid clearing of terrain at St. Christopher and parts of the "big islands" in order to cash in on the growing craze. If this demand had continued apace, then the soil-depleting sot weed would indeed have caused a much quicker closing of the "frontier." But an Atlantic-wide collapse of prices occurred in the late 1630s and early 1640s. Desperate, Poincy received CIA approval to uproot current plantings, although with the less-than-total compliance of hard-pressed colonists.[36]

Alternate sources of income to procure European foods and manufactures had to be discovered. Some colonists, at least in times of truce, occupied themselves with the Indian trade. Caribs supplied fish and foodstuffs, but more importantly tortoiseshell (*caret*, from a particular species), and cotton hammocks for export directly to the French or through itinerant French traders (*coureurs des îles*). These Indians had also found out that the Europeans would pay heavily for African slaves that Caribs had stolen or captured.[37] But these marginal trades were like fingers in the dike, and a cash-crop alternative to tobacco had to be found: cotton, and especially indigo, saved some colonists. Islanders with resources, however acquired, attempted to emulate the emerging Barbadian sugar magnates, but with little success in the 1640s. The Dutch, although troubled by rebellions in their Brazilian sugar holdings, were still ambivalent about fostering competition. The following decade witnessed a dramatic change in their attitude, and with the collapse of Carib resistance by 1660 fewer obstacles to the expansion of sugar acreage existed. Island proprietors, militia captains, Brazilian refugees, and religious orders rushed to take advantage of new conditions. Island governors and Dutch capitalist godfathers shepherded the transition. Only the big planters could, however, afford the land, credit, slaves, and machinery mandatory for sugar production, and so we must avoid overstating the pace of change.

Social relations forged in the first phase of the frontier era may be characterized as diverse and in flux—hardly a surprise given the newness of the environment and the unfamiliarity of peoples living in close quarters on Indian-"infested" islands. Who would expect the congealed and hoary customary interactions of Europe to persist in a wild, multiethnic frontier. And so, although the missionaries expressed horror at the manner in which free settlers treated their fellow Christian indentured servants (*engagés)*, historians do not. People who crossed oceans to settle in disease and Carib-ridden habitats came to gain a quick fortune and return home in triumph. The least literate of them had probably heard of Atalhualpa and Potosí, and perhaps dreamed of some marquisate in a Caribbean *vallée*. Relatively free from customary restraints, they presumably felt few inhibitions to working these servants as hard as possible for three years.[38] Although the chroniclers supply enough specific examples to support with plausibility their indictment of the system, a few caveats may be in order. The missionary writers probably had little experience with the miserable treatment of at least some metropolitan workers, such as textile apprentices and journeymen in general. Furthermore, the engagés were for the most part French, as compared to the large number of Irish indentured servants in the English islands. Many if not all of this era's French servants knew their patrons, and presumably the families at home were familiar. Missionaries themselves professed to be protectors of mistreated servants, a situation not to be found in the English islands. French officials did not express explicit worry about arming these engagés in times of crisis. A more nuanced understanding of such relations may be in order.

Unlike the situation in early Virginia, the legal and social status of African slaves in the French Antilles was less ambiguous. There, from the start of the St. Christopher colony, Africans were treated as permanent slaves, albeit in tiny numbers.[39] In a seeming paradox, the failure to question this practice occurred despite the prohibitions against such restriction of freedom in France itself.[40] In part, the colonists' unquestioning acceptance of the practice resulted from the probability that these privateers turned colonists "liberated" these Africans from their erstwhile Iberian owners. No evidence exists supporting direct importation from Africa before the later 1630s, when the infant Company of Senegal (chartered 1633) may have sent some. Not until the Dutch started importing Africans into the French islands was there anything akin to a regular, if always insufficient, supply. By the 1650s the apparent islands' consensus was that the colonies' prosperity depended on acquiring more of these alien laborers. In any case, no obvious contradiction existed in contemporary minds between African slavery and American (i.e., European) freedom. By 1660, the number of Africans probably at least equaled the number of Europeans in the big French islands.

Any attempt at characterizing the treatment of Africans in this era is fraught with pitfalls given the quantity and nature of the sources. Chroniclers were much less interested in these vaguely known people than in the novel and thought-provoking American Indians. Rochefort devotes hundreds of pages to the Caribs and a very few to Africans.[41] Father du Tertre is more balanced, but only marginally so. All are agreed that French masters worked their slave charges very hard. Du Tertre wrote, with perhaps a hint of unease, "They are sold as slaves, they are fed haphazardly, they are forced to work like beasts and their owners get from them by force or otherwise all their services until their death."[42] Bleak as this assessment is, writers often expressed outrage that *nègres* received better treatment than indentured servants, yet this is doubtful. The range of tasks in which jack-of-all-trade slaves were employed may tell us something, if certain scholars are correct.[43] Although most slaved in fields and sheds working tobacco or indigo (often alongside owners), such crops were not as all-consuming and exhaustive as sugar. Africans cleared land, cut lumber, built shacks or *cases*, farmed provision crops, served as domestic servants, among other tasks. Some slave women became companions and "wives."[44] Africans hunted and fished on behalf of their masters and themselves, and became very proficient in these arts. Slaveholders in snake-infested Martinique and Ste. Lucie must have been very supportive of slaves who searched out these reptiles as food.

Given the wild resources of the frontier islands, and the cheapness of Dutch imports in the 1640s and '50s, it seems likely that slaves' dietary deficiencies may have been less than at the height of the plantation complex in the later eighteenth century. Neither colonist nor slave had yet become as dependent on foreign food supplies as was the case later. Before we wax too lyrical, however, it must be noted that Du Parquet and the Sovereign Council of Martinique had to pass ordinances requiring owners to plant adequate provision crops to feed their slaves, an admission that such was not always the case.[45] In a memoir to Colbert, de Tracy blamed growing food shortages on the colonists' rush to plant sugar.[46] But in the eighteenth century, most arable land had been planted with cane, leaving little available to provision vastly more numerous slaves. And the globalization of war then meant periodic, serious interference with supplies.[47]

Other slight, and possibly debatable, evidence points to marginally better "race" relations in the frontier-era French Caribbean. There were few if any absentee owners in this era, and historians generally equate eighteenth-century absenteeism with impersonal, brutal treatment. Given the uncertainties of the slave trade in the early era, "rational" owners had less incentive to choose to overwork slaves since replacements were not always easily available and could be costly if they were. Not overwhelmed in numbers, and hardened by the struggle for survival in these early years, colonists displayed little overt fear of their bondsmen. Indeed, the occasions of rebellion were few and relatively unthreatening. Such confidence, perhaps attested to by the willingness to put slaves under arms against the English, would have minimized the impulse to use terror to keep slave masses in line.[48] Finally, and most problematically, the influence of the priests and their supporters in "converting" slaves may have produced a minimal human bonding between some slaves and their owners. The universal practice of baptizing slaves and, less frequently, formally marrying and burying them, may arguably be viewed as improving human relations, at least as compared to this era's Protestant policy of totally ignoring the religious practices of slaves. Who knows what Poincy had in mind when he marched two hundred of his "Angolan" youths off to catechism practice every day, but the minimum result was that this was time off from slaving tasks. At least on paper, the Sovereign Council of Martinique passed an ordinance reaffirming the prohibition against working slaves on Sunday and holy days, rather numerous in the old church.[49] Barbadian planters would have been appalled by all of this official and ecclesiastical interference on how they ran their operations.

How did Africans respond to such conditions? We have few clues. Unlike a later period, the majority of slaves were most likely "Angolans," given the Dutch usurpation of Portuguese slaving factories in the 1630s and '40s, and the relocation of many mostly Angolan Brazilian slaves in the 1650s.[50] But it is impossible to know what exactly was meant by "Angolan" and whether these people had much affinity for one another. As far as *overt* protest is mentioned by chroniclers, one hears of "marauding" maroons at St. Christopher in 1639, of armed maroons assisting, even leading, Carib guerrillas at Martinique in 1656, and in that same difficult year of a minor rebellion of "Angolan" slaves led by Jean Le Blanc and a certain Pedro at Guadeloupe.[51] In the latter case Cape Verde slaves purportedly told on the Angolans. It is certainly tempting to believe that the 1656 upheavals resulted from the typical discontent of slaves wrenched from a known environment, in this case Brazil. Certainly, the French did not experience the problems the English would soon have in Jamaica, a much larger and rugged island with more terrain for the support of maroon bands.[52]

The last four decades of the seventeenth century witnessed a gradual transformation of the ecological, political, and economic conditions that had emerged during the first phase. Even these changes, however, compared with the more rapid changes at

English Barbados and Jamaica, will highlight the moderate pace of change in the French Caribbean.

Population growth and environmental alterations moved in tandem in the French Antilles as elsewhere. Unfortunately, the islands' population in 1660, a potential benchmark, is far from certainly known. Various chroniclers estimate between ten and fifteen thousand of each "race."[53] The numbers for Martinique are reasonably well established—approximately 2,800 Europeans and 2,500 Africans.[54] Guadeloupe, it is thought, had a slightly higher figure, and St. Christopher boasted the largest number despite its tiny size. By 1687, according to a supposedly rigorous official count, the islands supported 18,888 *blancs* and 27,000 *nègres*. Of these settlements, fast-growing Saint Domingue, still not de jure French until the Treaty of Ryswick in 1697, numbered some 5,500 whites, with 2,500 of their African slaves.[55] Such figures—although one swallows hard before offering any conclusions—would, if accurate, indicate that overall the white population of the Lesser Antilles had grown modestly while that of Africans and African Americans had perhaps doubled. But Saint Domingue's gains can probably be explained in part by significant reductions at St. Christopher. A growth in the number of *habitants* at Martinique and Guadeloupe is very probable given the opening of Carib lands. One source estimates an increase at Martinique from about 2,800 in 1660 to about 5,000 in 1687; clearly immigration played an important part here. The rate of natural increase is simply not known, but was no doubt closer to the stagnant European rates than those of continental North America. By the 1680s, the white population at sugar-raising Barbados was already stagnant.[56]

Such demographic gains naturally brought ecological tolls. As noted above, little of "pristine" nature survived at St. Christopher.[57] By the end of the seventeenth century, Martinique reported shortages of easily available lumber, as had plagued Barbados as early as the 1660s. Logging outposts were established at Ste. Lucie, St. Vincent, and Dominica, much to the annoyance of some Caribs. And so the frontier very slowly receded on these "neutral islands."[58] The most dramatic changes occurred at Saint Domingue. Relating events of the 1660s, Alexander Exquemeling entertained his readers with blood-spattered tales of buccaneer hunts. Where once Taino villages and conucos had restrained the forests, seemingly millions of animals roamed.[59] But thirty years after Exquemeling's experiences, Labat and others complained about the scarcity of wild cattle and pigs, attributable to the ravages of men and wild dog packs.[60] Though Labat could not have known it, this ecological disaster promoted the settling down of the freebooters, or their eviction if they could not tame their roving urges. The ax replaced the famous buccaneer long rifle as Saint Domingue's chief tool.

When in 1661 Cardinal de Mazarin gave up the ghost, but not before happily securing the disposition of an ill-gained fortune to his heirs, young Louis XIV determined to rouse his state from its mud-encrusted lethargy. He would not be called a *roi fainéant* (do-nothing king), as some of his predecessors had been. In matters of finance, commerce, and colonies, Mazarin's "domestic," Jean-Baptiste Colbert, emerged as chief adviser and paper creator.[61] The state of the French colonies, insofar as he had knowledge of them, galled Colbert. He recognized that in all but name the French islands were Dutch appendages, and his vitriolic hatred of those burgher kings is well known. Memoirs reaching him complained of political squabbles in the islands.

His great strength having been indefatigable pursuit of policy once determined, the minister moved to rid the Antilles of the Dutch and to "reduce" the truculent colonials to dutiful obedience to their right and admirable king. Up to a point these two goals meshed well, because as long as the Dutch supplied the islands and marketed their produce, what was the point of colonists' obedience to a distant Louis?[62]

Louis XIV's and Colbert's sustained efforts to assert royal control over the Caribbean colonies had some success. First, they dispatched the incorruptible, no-nonsense sexagenarian de Tracy as de facto viceroy (more accurately, *visitador*) to survey conditions in the islands, resolve any problems, and announce the king's determination to rein in colonial independence. A man of great gravity, de Tracy possessed the advantages of novelty as the king's emissary and benefited from factional disputes in the islands. Moving quickly and with the gusto of certain authority, he sent some proprietors packing to Paris where they would come under strong pressure either to sell their islands or sit a spell in the Bastille. Colbert organized the giant French West India Company (WIC; 1664–74) and had the royal treasury contribute a significant amount of the capital. Soon a large fleet arrived in the islands bearing new officials and company agents to collect taxes and customs duties. This impressive show of energy and force notwithstanding, the struggle to eliminate the Dutch and bring the *habitants* to the obedience of Louis's majesty would be long, difficult and, in the latter case, less than a complete success. These settlers proved to be poor clay for the royalist potters.

Many factors made the implementation of the goal of one god, one king, and one law frustrating. During the wars of 1666–67 (War of Devolution) and 1672–78 (the Dutch War), Louis lacked the will and thus resources to project significant and consistent power in the Caribbean at the same time as in the main theater, Europe. Colbert's famous work as restorer of the French navy could not produce results overnight. Dutch interlopers had managed to retain significant links with the French colonials, often with the winking knowledge of high officials. With the exception of the last two years of the Dutch War, 1676 and 1677, the colonists were basically on their own. Given these circumstances, the colonial militias performed quite well, thus once again reaffirming their manly self-confidence. On the other hand, French naval campaigns of 1676 and 1677 finally damaged Dutch power in the Caribbean and realized to some extent Colbert's determination to clear these "shopkeepers" from French islands. But even so, upset at the high cost of the squandering of a royal fleet off Curaçao in 1677, the king rejected expensive plans to build a naval station in the Caribbean capable of supplying and overhauling vessels whose hulls rotted quickly in the worm-infested region. Without such, royal fleets could at most stay in the islands four to six months.[63] Colonial smugglers did not have much trouble evading what in the books look like impressive "mercantilist" regulations.

The disappointments with the outcome of the 1666–67 conflict in the Caribbean, in which the lack of a unified command appeared to have snatched defeat from the jaws of victory, persuaded Louis and Colbert to appoint a governor-general of the French islands. The experienced military officer Jean Charles de Baas arrived in the islands at the war's end. He did not bring significant royal troops, and neither he nor the distant new governor of Saint Domingue, Bertrand d'Ogeron, were able to suppress by force a tumult on that island.[64] In 1674 de Baas found himself powerless to retaliate against even Carib "insults" to France.[65] He must have felt great pressure to accommodate the *habitants'* interests, as they constituted his sole military support. They were, however, from the beginning disenchanted with the rule of the WIC, and staged passive yet strong resistance to its implementation. De Baas apparently turned a half-blind eye to their illicit trades. Because the French company had barely begun to supply colonial needs, it might be argued that his "I obey but choose not to enforce" attitude helped smooth the difficult transition to royal rule. Overall, his was an exceptionally difficult position, and in the long run his "flexibility" probably preserved royal rule in the islands.

The West India Company was all but comatose when the Dutch War delivered the coup de grâce. The legal winding-down process was a typically long French one. The upshot of it was that elite investors, and primarily the king, unwillingly covered some of the costs of *habitants'* transition to sugar by their inability to collect only a fraction of what was owed to the bankrupt company. It is not known exactly how much remained unpaid, but the king's fulminations and his concurrent establishment of the tobacco monopoly in 1674 in return for cash during these hard-pressed war years no doubt indicate both royal need and exasperation. The monopoly was a clear example of preference of metropolitan over colonial interests, but its origins in the king's inability to collect monies owed him gives it an ironic nuance.[66]

Honest officials able and willing to implement the orders of Louis and Colbert were not easily found. The attitude that crossing the oceans in royal service constituted a great sacrifice, an opinion shared by Colbert, meant that too many appointees thought first of how to feather their nests; an impulse, to be sure, not entirely foreign to those who toiled in France itself. A relative of the minister such as Michel Bégon might be persuaded, with difficulty, to sacrifice comforts of family and perhaps his health and still act honorably, but even a clan head such as Colbert did not have an unlimited supply of cousins and in-laws.[67] Very few colonial officials would emulate the impeccably honest though impoverished de Tracy, and Colbert found it necessary to tolerate under protest the dissimulations of his strongmen, military governors-general of the French empire, like de Baas (1667–77) of the Antilles, or the comte Louis de Buade de Frontenac at Québec (first term, 1672–82). One has only to read the correspondence between the *nouveau noble* Colbert and such haughty *noblesse d'épée* (nobles of the sword) officials to be amazed at the minister's Job-like patience with their highly selective obedience and to realize the hollowness of such oft-repeated formulas as that of French colonisation d'état. If these plumed proconsuls could not be counted on for honest and full obedience, it is easy to imagine the climate of corruption encompassing lesser officials. *Ça explique mais ça n'excuse pas* is the adage that Colbert must have repeatedly wished to scream at self-excusing officials, but instead he put up with the crusty Frontenac for ten years and the old soldier de Baas died in office.[68]

It was these repeated frustrations that pushed Versailles, at the death of de Baas, to appoint an intendant-general of the islands. After 1677, Jean-Baptiste Patoulet joined the new governor, the comte de Blénac as the twin towers of island administration. The intendant had authority over "internal" affairs—justice, finance, building, and so on—whereas the governor was commander-in-chief and head of the sovereign council. These roles meant that in these dangerous, frontier outposts governors often had the upper hand, which was somewhat different from the situation in the peaceful French provinces. The division of authority worked well in one sense, which means it usually produced suspicion, jealousy, and lavishly communicated backbiting between the sword and robe aristocrats. At least Colbert and his successors could be certain that the most flagrant cases of nonimplementation of ministerial orders would become quickly known. Naturally, these officials appealed to island factions for support in their quarrels and thus assured the latter a larger say in policy. Dependent on the island militia in defense and matters of internal security, royal officials had every reason to get along with island elites. Although it is true that (unlike the English colonies) the administrators' salaries were not paid by colonial legislators, the meagerness of the pay (and more importantly its unreliable disbursement) meant that most of these officials looked for other sources of income. This necessary collaboration of officials and colonial elites resulted in what, in the English context, Jack Greene calls the "domestication of governors."[69]

Although they did not have formal representation in a colonial parliament (the only condition differentiating the English and French systems),[70] French islanders possessed many means of protecting their interests, and their record of noncompliance and outright rebellion when their voices were ignored was on a par with English colonials. They sometimes outright refused to accept alterations to revered island customs, for example, the three-year length of tenure for indentured servants. When he tried to reduce servants' terms to eighteen months, Colbert ran up against a wall of silent dissent. Both de Tracy and de Baas moreover had attempted to reverse the island practice that slaves and beasts of burden, as well as land, were immune from seizure by creditors. Ultimately however, royal ordinances passed in 1679 and 1681 sanctioned island customs in these matters.[71] Clearly, the habitants won a huge victory; creditors had little else to seize. Once again, metropolitan capital unwillingly subsidized colonials who were second to none, not even Virginians, in debt and tax evasion.

Other weapons wielded by "don't tread on me" colonists were the threat (more than once acted upon) to move to non-French islands, their inveterate smuggling of essential goods, and outright resistance.[72] Tumults at Martinique in 1665–66 and at Saint Domingue in 1670 signaled the WIC and Colbert that these musket-toting settlers could not be treated like peasants in Picardy. Although quelled, the leaders of these colonial upheavals usually received mild punishments. Thus, passive and active resistance limited the extent of the imposition of royal rule in this frontier era. Louis XIV never dared to act the royal fool, as did James II, and the results of such actions would have been similar. All that the Sun King could do was to increase gradually the royal grip by strengthening the bonds of affection for his rule, and to do so he often acted as benevolent *père en famille* and not as the overawing figure of freshmen Western civilization courses. When Jack Greene asserts that "pronouncements from the centers of early modern extended polities like the British Empire acquired constitutional legitimacy for the whole only through implicit or explicit ratification by the peripheries,"[73] he could with only slight modifications be describing the workings of the Ancien Régime French colonial empire. The haughty rhetoric of official decrees was accompanied by the reality of "flexible" implementation.

As noted above, significant economic changes characterized this second phase of the "frontier era," even if the classic plantation complex still remained in the relatively distant future. During the last four decades of the century, surely fewer colonists survived by exploiting the diminishing wild products of the islands or, possibly, by the

Carib trade. The number of *habitants* making tobacco their cash crop gradually diminished in the Lesser Antilles, although such was not the case for late-blooming Saint Domingue. In the former islands, some tobacco men emigrated, turned to provisions farming, worked for the emerging sugar planters, or managed to make the transition to sugar themselves. Already by the 1660s, according to one estimate, twice the tonnage of sugar to tobacco was exported from these islands, and by 1671 the value of the sugar produced was fifteen times greater.[74] Sugar occupied two-thirds of arable land compared to one-fifth for tobacco.[75] The government continued to support the transition by granting three-year tax exemptions to habitants attempting to switch to sugar. In 1669, in an important symbolic step, fines no longer were levied in tobacco, but sugar.[76] However, the Dutch Wars and the resulting disruption of the slave trade slowed growth. In Martinique, the number of slaves increased from 6,183 to only 8,039 between 1671 and 1682.[77] As late as 1685 in this most "advanced" colony, 1,048 *habitations* included 172 sugar plantations, of which only 4 or 5 worked more than 100 slaves, the standard size during sugar's heyday.[78] Of course, these large sugar planters acted like tuna swimming through a school of sardines. Despite the wars of the 1690s, by 1700 Martinique contained 242 sugar works.[79] At least this island was rapidly leaving its frontier era, and significant pockets of it had already reached "maturity."

Tobacco made its last stand at Saint Domingue. By 1674, freebooters turned farmers and their motley crew of coerced laborers produced almost three million pounds. However, because of the tobacco monopoly and the growing European preference for Virginia leaf, Saint Domingue production declined rapidly in the last decades of the century.[80] Some planters moved to indigo or returned to their freebooting roots. With the fabulous capture of Cartagéna in 1698, a number of the latter obtained the capital to attempt sugar growing.

The above, brief assessment of changes in the second phase of the frontier era would suggest that conditions worsened for many, even perhaps for the majority of islanders. Clearly, the successful minority of planters lived much better and perhaps longer. They acquired wives, had children, and led a "normal" life.[81] They do seem to have spent inordinately much on consumer goods—food, spirits, clothes—and less on long-term capital improvements. Despite this successful minority's domestication, European society barely reproduced itself, and the slight population gains of these decades probably resulted from immigration. Thus, the white demographic picture resembled that of France itself rather than that of feverishly fertile New France or New England.

Life in Martinique for whites, especially married ones, may have reached a certain level of stability and even contentedness; and this was even more so for the relatively small number of free women.[82] Typical of frontier females, they married early and, some, often. Widows normally inherited habitations (homes) from deceased spouses. The large number of bachelors meant a constant supply of eager suitors for these propertied widows, should the latter express interest. Given the lack of convents, the isolation of habitations as well as managerial responsibilities, most widows remarried after a more or less appropriate interlude.[83]

Perhaps a majority of Europeans, however, and certainly a large majority of slaves found their conditions deteriorating. The majority of French emigrants still came as indentured servants, and unless one possessed a special skill such as that of an artisan or surgeon/barber, one still received miserable treatment, according to chroniclers and government officials.[84] According to an intendant's report of 1681, only fifty of some six hundred recent arrivals had survived their thirty-six month contract. The governor-general at the time was beside himself with anger at their treatment. "The manner of treating the engagés is enough to make one tremble. . . . I could not get angry enough to treat my dog the same."[85] Officials complained that masters were not reporting but rather hiding the deaths of their servants.[86] No evidence exists to suggest that island officials did much to rectify this ugly situation. Population growth meant that survivors, should they wish to remain, had small hope of acquiring a habitation, unless they traveled west to Saint Domingue.[87]

By the 1660s island habitants had reached a clear consensus that African coerced labor was far preferable to that of "insolent," short-term, and often short-lived French indentured servants. The latter would or could not do the grueling tasks associated with sugar planting, according to contemporary opinion. While valued for artisan tasks, the workers responded badly to labor conditions so foreign to their experiences in France, and to such terrible treatment, almost always at the hands of fellow commoners no less. African slaves had fewer choices or means to resist the brutal conditions of sugar. In the 1660s, slaves directly from different parts of Africa, or displaced from Brazil, probably constituted a large majority of the total, and the resulting weakness of their communities inhibited effective responses to the emerging plantation system.[88]

To the extent that sugar planters increased their economic and political power in the last decades of the century, the conditions of a growing number of slaves doubtlessly deteriorated. The French islands gradually evolved from a society with slaves to a slave society, although at a much slower pace than did Barbados or Jamaica. In classic plantation regimes, a fairly clear correlation exists between estate size and slave mortality rates. In eighteenth-century Jamaica, mortality rates on large sugar plantations were fifty percent higher than on coffee plantations. Later in the sugar cycle, death rates for men at Trinidad were three times higher in sugar than cotton.[89] All things being equal, the increasing dominance of sugar at Martinique and Guadeloupe must have brought growing misery to larger numbers of slaves. In 1664 in Martinique, 1,605 out of 2,750 slaves worked on habitations possessing fewer than 15 Africans, and just 245 worked on what might be reasonably called plantations, with more than 40 slaves. By 1680, 2,275 Africans of a total of 6,279 worked on small spreads manned by fewer than 15 slaves, and thus they probably labored on farms producing an assortment of crops.[90] Nineteen hundred of the 6,279, or just under one-third, slaved on plantations of more than 470 bondsmen, surely almost all on burgeoning sugar plantations.[91] Although this percentage was still small compared to that of a century later, such changes in tasks for increasing numbers of Africans had large, mostly nefarious consequences for those affected. The era of the jack-of-all trades drew gradually to a close in these pockets of "maturity."

In these rough equations, however, all things were not always equal. The relatively small size of these sugar plantations and the fact that almost all owners resided on them may have made social relations less inhumane and less impersonal than in a later, more "mature" era. This is not to say that cases of the most horrific kinds of brutality are at all difficult to document—far from it.[92] The expense of slave replacements may also have promoted policies less wasteful of human life than in a later era when slaves were imported in ever-increasing numbers.[93] Perhaps owners resorted more often to rationing sugar crops given the small size of their labor force, and thus lessening the grueling tasks associated with grubbing up the roots and replanting. Although conditions for many slaves no doubt deteriorated, perhaps the rate of change can be exaggerated. But the argument depends less on solid evidence than on identifying differences from the "mature" sugar and slave regime, a risky procedure.

As mentioned previously, the last four decades of the century witnessed somewhere between a doubling and tripling of African peoples in the French islands, although it is worth noting that Barbados in 1700 with 40,000 slaves and Jamaica in 1713 with 55,000 each possessed more than all the French Antilles combined.[94] A number of consequences of this relatively gradual growth ensued. Obviously the major islands of the Lesser Antilles were losing their frontier character. If, as argued above, frontier-era social relations had a marginally less-oppressive character, then the incremental closing of the frontier in some islands had consequences—mostly negative—for the enslaved. Food production from the opening of what had previously been wilderness areas probably did not match the increase in numbers of people to be fed. It is probable that more and more land originally devoted to provisions now was used for cash crops. Other factors put pressure on food supplies. The Dutch War meant a dramatic drop in cheap imports from the United Provinces, and the moribund WIC was of no help. Even if there is only the impressionistic evidence of a Father Labat, it would appear that wild products, previously so critical to slave diets, declined proportionally to the growth of population. Given this conjunction of factors, and remembering Father du Tertre's perhaps too simplistic connection of food supplies for slaves to the amount of rain in any year, any period of drought, especially in wartime, would have produced serious difficulties for the enslaved. Perhaps some such combination of reasons, along with the disruption of the slave trade, explains the miniscule growth in slave numbers at Martinique during and immediately after the Dutch War.

Because the French slave trade in this era was so ineffective, and because the extent of slave smuggling cannot be documented, historians can only guess at the source of the relatively rapid increases in Africans. It is, of course, tempting to suggest that natural increases occurred in this "frontier era," as that proposition would support the thesis that social relations then were marginally better than they would come to be later. Anecdotal and some statistical evidence suggests a surprisingly high birth rate for Africans in the later seventeenth century. In the first case, du Tertre marvels at the fecundity of enslaved women, comparing it felicitously if unconvincingly to that of Jewish wives during their captivity in Egypt. He cites the case of Poincy's estates, which boasted 160 children between the ages of four and ten of a total of perhaps seven to eight hundred "Angolans."[95] The slave birth rate at Guadeloupe and Martinique between 1669 and 1685 was fifty-one per thousand per year, a rate far higher than in Europe and similar to that of the North American continent,[96] although a high mortality rate offset it. The tepid growth rates of slaves at Martinique between 1672 and 1682 would seem to argue against natural increases in favor of legal and illegal imports as explanations for increases at other times, although these years of war and the precipitous decrease of Dutch trade could be viewed as anomalous. What may be safe to say is that the staggering superiority of mortality over birth rates of the "mature" plantation era did not characterize the frontier era.[97]

Even if slave numbers grew fitfully in this era, habitants could never get enough. However, Labat's conclusion that any rational owner in such a situation would preserve and protect such valuable property was not one so obvious to all masters. Unlike Labat who managed his Dominican order's estates for long-term sustenance of its members, many masters probably were aware they were in a dangerous race to acquire fortune before the insalubrious climate cut short their lives, or hurricanes, pests, wars, or other unforeseen causes destroyed their investment. In such calculations, working slaves to or even beyond the limits might make "sense." Consciously or not, each owner was caught in a tug-of-war between maximizing profits and the expense of replacing dead or debilitated slaves. Labat's seemingly sensible prescriptions may have meant little to entrepreneurs hustling to stay a few steps ahead of the grim reaper and return in triumph to their villages and towns in France. The fact that one-fourth to one-third of them were bachelors without much prospect of acquiring a European wife may well have promoted the live-for-the-day psychology.[98] Saint Pierre, Martinique was not Québec, where a man might persist until seventy and have a dozen children on whom to bequeath his "few acres of snow." Far from it.

The increasing presence of the French state inevitably affected living conditions of the enslaved, both positively and negatively. Some officials newly arrived from the metropolis expressed some shock at the treatment of Africans. Governor-general de Baas lamented to Colbert, "The slaves are forced to work twenty out of twenty-four hours. If then, these miserable wretches do not have beef to eat, how is it possible for them to endure so much work . . . slaves are human beings and human beings should not be reduced to a state worse than beasts."[99] The context for this oft-quoted passage, however, reduces its humanitarian aspect. Clearly, the governor engaged in hyperbolic assertions about the length of slaves' workdays in order to persuade the minister to allow the import of foreign meats in which he may have had a personal interest. In any case, there is little evidence to suggest that he or other officials undertook strong actions to limit exploitation of slaves.

Harsh and effective sanctions against masters would have met strong resistance. Instead, punishments were of the slap-on-the-wrist character for odious offenses. For example, in 1671 one master received a fine of five hundred pounds of sugar for burning a female slave's "shameful parts," and he was threatened with corporal punishment in case of recidivism.[100] Patoulet promoted the incorporation of minimum levels of food and clothes, as well as a number of other protective measures, into the Code Noir of 1685.[101] Whether such officials were able to enforce those provisions, especially in times of war, was another matter. The reader will recall Labat's frank statement that masters could not in wartime afford to give slaves the prescribed ration of meat.

Unlike most planters, royal officials expressed much concern about the emerging "racial" imbalance in the islands and what they considered the overly lax attitude of the *habitants* toward possible revolts by the slaves in their midst. Masters too often overlooked crimes committed by their slaves, especially those perpetrated outside plantation limits, so an official fund was established to compensate them for any losses resulting from judicial procedures. Stiff fines were decreed against masters who did not report thefts by their charges. On the other hand, the record is replete with examples of private and public punishment of slaves, and, typically of slave systems, these had a bone-chilling character. For noncapital offenses, slaves lost appendages or had to bear the humiliation of the iron collar accompanied by a vice "sweetened" with red hot pepper propping the mouth wide open.[102] By the 1680s for a second offense of stealing goods of a value less than one hundred pounds of sugar, a slave lost an ear. For one caught stealing a horse or cow one leg was removed, and for leaving the plantation for four to six months a hamstring was cut. Masters were to report implementation of the punishment to local militia leaders, which may indicate some measure of noncompliance.[103] Still, by 1682, enough mutilated slaves existed that Patoulet ruled that their masters be free of the capitation tax on them. The record does not make clear the source of the mutilation—punishment or industrial accident—but one may presume the former was more frequently the cause. The capstone of this legal system was death for striking a white person, and a vicious execution via breaking on the wheel for murdering one.[104]

Amazed that bondsmen were allowed to carry offensive weapons and even wear swords, royal officials passed local ordinances against the practice, while the Code Noir outlawed it unless the owner gave written permission. Officials at Versailles were also perplexed at the ways in which slaves could sell their produce at market when legally they could not own property of any sort. Prohibitions enacted to prevent this practice were retracted when islanders pointed out the material and psychological benefits involved, as well as the fact that they needed these foodstuffs.

Island officials, particularly the intendant-general Patoulet, convinced Versailles to contravene the islands' custom of freeing at twenty-one the mulatto offspring of European men and African women.[105] Although colonists believed that the child should not be punished for the sin of the father (quite often the slaveholders themselves), Patoulet and his ilk believed that such a practice encouraged slave women to "seduce" whites in order to see their children set free and gain other privileges.[106] Although evidence is lacking to prove the point, the fairly rapid growth of numbers of white women in the islands may have been a factor in this attempted crackdown on the "licentious stratagems" of "lascivious" African women. At least legally, mulattoes would now remain slaves unless formally freed in an act requiring government consent, and fathers of such bastards were required to report the fact to local militia captains. As the first censuses counting mulattoes give suspiciously low numbers, however, one may wonder about implementation.[107]

The Code Noir mandated other regulations that, to the extent they were enforced, attenuated at least slightly the comparative harshness of the system. The absolute prohibition of slaves working on Sundays and holy days, for example, meant a significant reduction in a slave's annual labor. Given the relative vitality of the Catholic church in the seventeenth century, this provision was probably enforced at most times and in most parishes. Perhaps those slave owners of little religious inclination went along because they knew slaves used this time to provide food and "luxuries" for themselves and for the market. One can hardly be so confident about articles protecting African women against sexual aggression or the requirement to report mulatto offspring, among many others.

It is far from easy to judge the role of the church and missionaries in the possible amelioration of slave conditions. In 1671, the king certainly removed one of the possible excuses of masters' negligence in this matter by decreeing no fees be placed on them for religious services to slaves. That put the burden on the religious orders, especially the Dominicans and the growing number of Jesuits. But these had multiple duties including regular parish work as there were few secular clergy in the islands and, in the case of Labat, for example, a great need to manage plantations that provided their livelihood. Eventually, the more successful Jesuit effort hinged on assigning certain members whose only duties consisted of evangelizing slaves. To the extent that they enforced laws prohibiting labor on Sundays and holy days; saw to the baptism, catechism, and marriage of significant numbers of bondsmen; and acted as intermediaries between repentant, short-term *marrons* and their masters, the missionaries promoted more humane relations.[108] The problem is that although evidence supports the existence of such activities, to what extent they existed is questionable. Despite growing numbers of priests, especially Jesuits, there were never nearly enough to compensate for the relatively rapid increase of Africans and a slighter gain in European population. Then in the 1690s struck the dreaded *maladie du Siam*, or yellow fever, and the missionaries were hard hit. So whereas the church, not yet infected with the malaise of the eighteenth century, had good intentions concerning slave evangelism, personnel shortages meant that realization of that goal was not achieved. Father Labat, torn between the Nazarene and Epicurus, relates to his reader with a melange of self-pity and Christian selflessness the incredible fatigues occasioned by a missionary's duties. No doubt his reader would not thus protest the occasional delights of the table and libations that eased the suffering.[109]

In compensation for the gradually deteriorating conditions adumbrated above, were the slaves able to foster stronger communities to help cope with the changes? Once again the evidence is mixed and loaded with uncertainties. Insofar as conditions made it possible, slaves lived in family units and the priests nagged masters to formalize relationships. Island consensus seems to have been that married slaves were more content and productive. According to the chroniclers, many planters made an effort to accommodate African choices of mates, even exchanging slaves across plantation lines for that purpose.[110] Obviously, such efforts would reduce slaves leaving the plantation for nocturnal visits. Newly arrived slaves were placed under the care of "seasoned" hands for the socialization process, which included baptism attended by French godparents. Labat provides a "humane" formula for gradually introducing new arrivals to their strange new world, but it is unclear whether many masters followed the prescriptions. If Richard Dunn's chilling characterization of master-slave relations in the English Caribbean is accepted, however, then the French system with all its glaring brutalities probably generated more and stronger strands of personal ties.[111]

Slaves of one *habitation* met those of others at church and market on Sundays and holy days and at informal nightly dances and gatherings. Those of the same "nation" consorted together for a variety of reasons, but certainly one of them is that pidgin French had not yet apparently evolved into the distinctive creole language of the "mature" plantation era.[112] A divisive force, therefore, was the growing variety of African peoples in the French slave community. The percentage of "Angolans" no doubt dropped and that of Senegambians and those exported from the Slave Coast probably increased as the Dutch slavers were gradually restricted, and as political turbulence in Angola reduced its relative share.[113]

Slaves who survived the horrors of the passage and the shock of the new adapted relatively well to conditions puzzling and beyond their control. Island "wisdom" suggested that the enslaved were content if treated "well," which meant that they were given adequate food, allowed to have gardens and market the produce, and were never punished without "cause." Stripped of the proslavery discourse couching this position, there was probably a measure of truth in it. Living in often isolated habitations among other Africans at that time far from considered as "brothers," and without realistic hopes of altering basic conditions short of the desperate acts of *marronage* or overt resistance, slaves attempted to get along as best as possible. As Sidney Mintz posits, "Why need we assume that living better under slavery meant accepting slavery?"[114]

Perhaps we can say that within every slave was contained some combination of the heart of a Spartacus, the soul of a Sisyphus, and the wiliness of the self-deprecating but mocking Molierean valet. Slaves tried to carve out small, private spaces, establish customary "rights" to gardens and to control the product of their labor in their "spare" time. Had not European serfs and then peasants so adjusted to the "feudal" system? African slaves apparently worked the system as effectively as they could. They "accepted" baptism, which was accompanied by alcoholic libations provided by the godparents. Some requested repeated baptisms. They got away with as much "laziness," petty theft, and the "insolence" of declaring themselves better people than whites as their masters would tolerate. Some whites, like the jesting Labat, apparently loved the banter. No doubt intending to amaze his readers, du Tertre writes that Africans believed that "black is beautiful," and actually preferred their "flattened" noses and "frizzy" hair, which he compared to that of Medusa![115]

Giving rein to the impulses of the heart, that of Spartacus, in such circumstances would have occurred only as an act of desperation. The fact that no major upheavals characterized this later stage of the frontier era is open to multiple interpretations, but one of them is that conditions were less than desperate for slaves. Short of rebellion, but indicative of profound unhappiness caused by any number of things—inability to be with a loved one, "unjust" punishments, threat of removal to another island—slaves could without severe consequences engage in *petit marronage*, or short-term flight. A priest would be called upon to plead ritually with the master for forgiveness and at the same time explain the reasons for the flight. Prudent masters, after "appropriate" if minor punishment, might consider some ameliorative measures. Except at large, undeveloped Saint Domingue, long-term flight was a losing proposition in this later period of the frontier and surely experienced slaves must have so warned newcomers. The "capitulation" of Francisque Fabulé's band of maroons at Martinique in 1665, with freedom for the chief and no physical punishment for the rest, was the last important example of organized resistance in the Lesser Antilles, even though small groups survived in high ground.[116] A possible exit was to flee to another island, and the fact that in the 1670s the Sovereign Council of Martinique ordered that all small boats be chained indicates that some did so.[117] Only rarely employing violent means of resistance, African and African-American slaves used every means possible to expand areas of practical freedom and to improve material conditions. They showed great ingenuity at supplementing their meager rations. Some even willingly fought for their masters against foreign enemies, and perhaps a few of these earned acts of manumission as promised for specific heroic acts.

The frontier era did not, of course, come to any rapid or synchronic end in the French Caribbean. In the first three decades of the eighteenth century, the pace of evolution toward a "mature" sugar regime accelerated. Especially at Saint Domingue, the years of the War of the Spanish Succession (1702–13) witnessed rapid growth in the numbers of slaves, presumably the result of war booty and intensified legal and illegal imports. The Spanish alliance generated all kinds of possibilities. After the Treaty of Utrecht and the return of peace, the French slave trade became far better organized and efficient. By the 1730s, the French islands as a whole may be said to have arrived at a "mature" plantation stage even if the system's zenith would not be attained until the years 1763–90.

On the whole, this transformation had primarily detrimental impacts on most French slaves in most places.[118] Glaring and rapidly expanding demographic imbalances combined with a trend toward absentee ownership led to harsher, more paranoid controls over slaves. In 1789, officially, the islands contained 55,000 whites, 36,000 people of color, and 639,000 slaves (an undercount, almost certainly).[119] Practices terrorizing black helots became more typical in the eighteenth century, especially at Saint Domingue. The availability of larger pools of African laborers, the growing ease of credit from French mercantile firms and the addictive European demand for sugar (and, increasingly, coffee) promoted a drive to expand production and to "rationalize" labor costs. Economic calculations that the working of slaves to or beyond their limit and replacing those who could not maintain the demonic pace militated against any humane considerations still alive in the master class. To a rapidly diminishing extent, government officials and clerics were less inclined or able to prick planters' consciences. The burgeoning importance to France of plantation agriculture made officials increasingly loath to kill the goose laying golden eggs by over-zealousness in enforcing the relatively humanitarian provisions of the Code Noir, still on the books. In fact, many had become planters themselves. Overwhelmed ecclesiastics found it difficult to cope with massive arrivals of Africans, and those who tried hardest, the Jesuits, found themselves reviled by island elites, and then evicted after 1764. Managers on the increasing number of absentee plantations were especially noted for their indifference to Christianizing slaves.[120] The secular and materialist values of so-called Enlightenment culture, accompanied on both sides of the Atlantic by a lessening of the value of common, unskilled labor, may have infected the emerging *grand blanc* oligarchs. Nearer the end of the century, the emerging hard, pseudoscientific racism of Atlantic intellectuals that replaced the older hierarchical models of the Christian and classical world may have had an impact, albeit intangible, on masters. These political, economic, and cultural changes were harbingers of increasingly difficult times for African bondsmen of the French.[121]

On the other hand, conditions for a minority of slaves may have marginally improved in this "mature" era, or at least not deteriorated. Those slaves still residing in frontier areas, such as the coffee frontier of south Saint Domingue, lived markedly better lives than the those on the huge sugar plantations of the northern plain or the Artibonite Valley.[122] Even within the monstrous sugar works, those male slaves who took over the skilled occupations of slave drivers, sugar boilers, or teamsters, and those women attached to prosperous owners as domestic help were better off materially. Most of these were Creoles and mulattoes who likely lived longer and better than the masses of "saltwater" Africans (*bossales*) brought into the killing fields of cane labor. And finally, a caste of de jure and de facto free blacks and mulattoes became more and more important as the century waned. These improvements in the life of a minority of African Americans cannot and should not conceal the horrifying existence of a majority almost certainly doomed to a brief life of brutally exhausting labor in an alien environment. Almost certainly, the lives of Africans and African Americans of the frontier era was less intolerable.

In 1693, the French Antilles did not have a Frederick Jackson Turner to announce the closing of its frontier, and such a pronouncement would have been premature given the primitive conditions of that future giant Saint Domingue. Still, the volumes of Father Labat contained much that, at least with the benefit of hindsight, augured the emergence of a new order. But we do not have to agree with the Dominican that this emerging plantation complex promised a more polished, advanced society; clearly it did not for the large majority of Africans and African Americans, and even for a significant slice of European society on the islands.

Notes

1. Jean Baptiste Labat, *Nouveau voyage aux isles de l'Amérique*, 6 vols. (Paris: P. F. Gittant, 1722) 1:216–18, 225.
2. Ibid., 1:72, 435. References to sick, dying, and dead priests occur throughout his volumes.
3. Ibid., 2:200, 394; 3:6.
4. Ibid., 4:214–23.
5. Ibid., 2:8–95 on these peoples. For details of this visit and the broader topic, see Philip P. Boucher, *Cannibal Encounters: Europeans and Island Caribs, 1492–1763* (Baltimore: Johns Hopkins University Press, 1992).
6. Labat, *Nouveau voyage* 1:106–18.
7. Ibid.; see primarily 3:120–465, but many other locations.
8. It is difficult to agree with Gordon K. Lewis that Labat is the "epitome of racial bigotry," given his commitment to the slaves' spiritual equality. His racism is of the soft, pre- (pseudo) scientific sort. Lewis, *Main Currents in Caribbean Thought: The Historical Evolution of Caribbean Society in Its Ideological Aspects, 1492–1900* (Baltimore: Johns Hopkins University Press, 1983), 66.
9. Ibid., 3:312–16, 426–43.
10. Ibid., 2:290, 356–57; 3:166; 4:67, 184.
11. These islands are three to four hundred square miles each in area. *Hammond World Atlas* (Maplewood, N.J.: Hammond, 1987), 156–61.
12. Ibid.; the French portions covered about fifty square miles.
13. For these see Richard S. Dunn's now classic *Sugar and Slaves: The Rise of the Planter Class in the English West Indies, 1624–1713* (New York: W. W. Norton, 1973).
14. See David J. Weber on frontiers in *The Spanish Frontier in North America* (New Haven, Conn.: Yale University Press, 1992), 11–12; see also Howard Lamar and Leonard Thompson, eds. *The Frontier in History: North America and Southern Africa Compared* (New Haven, Conn.: Yale University Press, 1981), Introduction.
15. Dunn, *Sugar and Slaves*, 87.
16. See, e.g., Roger Mettam, introduction to *Power and Faction in Louis XIV's France* (Oxford: Blackwell, 1988), of the introduction in Raymond Kierstead, ed., *State and Society in Seventeenth Century France* (New York: Franklin Watts, 1975).
17. Labat, *Nouveau voyage* 3:440, 444–45.
18. Ibid., 4:114–15.
19. Orlando Patterson, *The Sociology of Slavery : An Analysis of the Origins, Development and Structure of Slave Society in Jamaica* (Rutherford, N.J.: Farleigh Dickinson University Press, 1969), 70ff.
20. The book is tentatively entitled "The French Caribbean, Sixteenth to Eighteenth Centuries: Islands of Discontent?"
21. The phrase comes from Philip Curtin, *The Rise and Fall of the Plantation Complex* (New York: Cambridge, 1990).

22. For Carolina, see Peter H. Wood, *Black Majority: Negroes in Colonial South Carolina from 1670 to the Stono Rebellion* (New York, 1974); for Virginia, Edmund Morgan, *American Freedom, American Slavery: The Ordeal of Colonial Virginia* (New York, 1975); for Louisiana, Daniel H. Usner, *Indians, Settlers and Slaves in a Frontier Exchange Economy: The Lower Mississippi Valley before 1783* (Chapel Hill: University of North Carolina Press, 1992); and Gwendolyn M. Hall, *Africans in Colonial Louisiana: The Development of Afro-Creole Culture in the Eighteenth Century* (Baton Rouge: Louisiana State University Press, 1992).
23. Labat, *Nouveau voyage* 4:284.
24. Charles de Rochefort, *Histoire naturelle et morale des Antilles de l'Amerique* (Rotterdam: A. Leers, 1665), Preface, 338–42; Jean Baptiste du Tertre, *Histoire générale des Antilles,* 4 vols. (Paris: Jolly, 1667–71), 2:420, 447, 463, 472. A recent volume by Ira Berlin, *Many Thousand Gone: The First Two Centuries of Slavery in North America* (Cambridge, Mass.: Harvard University Press, 1998) also argues for the hardening of slave systems over time.
25. See chs. 2 and 3 of Boucher, *Cannibal Encounters.* Historians of the English Caribbean have overlooked this crucial distinction.
26. Ibid., ch. 2.
27. See Jean-Pierre Moreau's edition of the remarkable manuscript account of a long visit on Martinique by the crew of a damaged French ship in 1619–20. *Un Flibustier français dans la mer des Antilles, 1618–1620* (Paris: Seghers, 1990). This document deserves wide attention from ethnohistorians.
28. Joseph Boromé, "Spain and Dominica, 1493–1647," *Caribbean Quarterly* 12 (1966), 30–46.
29. Du Tertre, *Histoire générale* 2:10; Rochefort, *Histoire naturelle,* 99.
30. Among other sources, see Kenneth Andrews, *The Spanish Caribbean: Trade and Plunder, 1530–1630* (New Haven, Conn.: Yale University Press, 1978).
31. Among other sources, see Philip P. Boucher, *Les Nouvelles Frances: France in America, 1500–1815, an Imperial Perspective* (Providence: John Carter Brown Library, 1989); Jean Pierre Moreau, *Les Petites Antilles de Christophe Colomb à Richelieu* (Paris: Karthala, 1992); for Fouquet, see Philip P. Boucher, "Reflections on the 'Crime' of Nicholas Foucquet: The Foucquets and the French Colonial Empire, 1626–1661," *Revue française d'histoire d'Outre-mer* 72 (1985), 5–20.
32. Robert C. Batie, "Why Sugar? Economic Cycles and the Changing of Staples in the English and French Antilles, 1624–1654," *Journal of Caribbean History* 8–9 (1976), 1–41.
33. See, e.g., Cosimo Brunetti, "Cosimo Brunetti, Three Relations of the West Indies, 1659, 1660," ed. Susan Heller Anderson, *Transactions of the American Philosophical Society*, vol. 59, pt. 6 (1969).
34. I used Rochefort's wonderful picture of it as the frontispiece for Boucher, *Les Nouvelles Frances.*
35. One can follow these events in vol. 1 of du Tertre's great *Histoire générale*; Stewart Mims, *Colbert's West India Policy* (New Haven, Conn.: Yale University Press, 1912); and Philip P. Boucher, " Comment se forme un ministre colonial: L'initiation de Colbert, 1651–1664," *Revue d'histoire de l'Amérique française* 37 (1982), 431–51.
36. For Poincy's rule at St. Christopher, see Prosper Cultru, "La Colonisation d'autrefois: Le Commandeur Poincy à St. Christophe," *Revue d'histoire des colonies français* 3 (1915), 289–354; also of interest is David Allen, "The Social and Religious World of a Knight of Malta in the Caribbean, c. 1632–1660," *Libraries and Culture* 25:2 (1990), 147–57.
37. See ch. 1 of Boucher, *Cannibal Encounters.*
38. The essential source remains Gabriel Debien, "Les Engagés pour les Antilles," *Revue d'histoire des colonies* 38 (1951), 1–280. English language readers may consult Christian Huetz de Lemps, "Indentured Servants Bound for the French Antilles in the Seventeenth and Eighteenth Centuries," in Ida Altman and James Horn, eds., *"To Make America": European Emigration in the Early Modern Period* (Berkeley and Los Angeles: University of California Press, 1991), 172–203.

39. Du Tertre, *Histoire générale*, 1:19. He gives the text of a 1627 accord with the English that mentions slaves held by both parties.
40. See Sue Peabody's *"There Are No Slaves in France": The Political Culture of Race and Slavery in the Ancien Régime* (New York: Oxford University Press, 1996).
41. See Rochefort, *Histoire naturelle*, 340–43 for his stereotypical comments.
42. Du Tertre, *Histoire générale*, 2:493; yet he claimed that those treated well preferred their new home to their supposedly miserable lives in Africa, 2:534–35.
43. Wood, *Black Majority*, 104.
44. See, e.g., F. Maurile de Saint Michel, *Voyage des isles Camercames en Amérique* (Mans, 1652), 36.
45. Médéric Moreau de Saint Méry, *Loix et constitutions des colonies françaises de l'Amérique sous le vent* 6 vols. (Paris: Saint Méry, 1785–1790), 1:61.
46. Cited in Jules Saintoyant, *La Colonisation française sous l'ancien régime,* 2 vols. (Paris: La Renaissance du livre, 1935), 1:224.
47. It is true that British North American merchants increasingly supplied foodstuffs to the French islands. A book on this trade is badly needed.
48. See, e.g., du Tertre, *Histoire générale* 1:61.
49. Moreau de Saint Méry, *Loix et constitutions* 1:83.
50. John Thornton, *Africa and Africans in the Making of the Atlantic World* (Cambridge: Cambridge University Press, 1992), 116–20, 137; A. J. R. Russell-Wood, *Slavery and Freedom in Colonial Brazil* (New York: St. Martin's Press, 1982), 27.
51. Du Tertre, *Histoire générale* 1:151, 500–3; Moreau de Saint Méry, *Loix et constitutions* 1:83.
52. Dunn, *Sugar and Slaves*, 242. He points out that after 1670 the problems diminished as each side warily avoided contacts.
53. One scholar arrives at a figure of thirteen thousand French and sixteen thousand Africans by splitting the differences between the lowest and highest estimates of the chroniclers. Batie, "Why Sugar?" 40.
54. Jacques Petitjean Roget, *La Société d'habitation à la Martinique: Un demi-siècle de formation, 1635–1685*, 2 vols. (Paris: Champion, 1980), 2:1376.
55. Some scholars estimate about four thousand Europeans lived in Saint Domingue, in 1687. Jean-Pierre Poussou, "L'Immigration européene dans les îles d'Amérique," in the catalog *Voyage aux îles d'Amérique* (Paris: Archives nationales, 1992), 46.
56. For Martinique, see Roget, *La Société* 2: 1376; Barbadian white population peaked at about twenty thousand in 1689 and then declined. At the same time Jamaica's peaked at ten thousand and then declined to seven. Dunn, *Sugar and Slaves*, 87–88, 164.
57. Of course, it was not "pristine" in 1620, either, because a small population of Island Caribs lived there. For a general perspective see William Denevan, "The Pristine Myth: The Landscape of the Americas in 1492," *Annals of the Association of American Geographers* 82:3 (1992), 369–85.
58. For all this see ch. 4 of Boucher, *Cannibal Encounters.*
59. Alexandre Exquemelin, *Histoire des avanturiers*, 2 vols. (Paris: Le Febvre, 1686), 1:162 for example; for early Hispaniola, see Carl O. Sauer, *The Early Spanish Main* (Berkeley and Los Angeles: University of California Press, 1966).
60. For restrictions on hunting at the turn of the century, see Moreau de Saint Méry, *Loix et constitutions* 1:700, 715.
61. For details see Boucher, "L'Initiation de Colbert."
62. For this and the following paragraphs see ibid., and Mims, *Colbert's West India Policy,* still the most valuable work on Colbert as colonial minister, at least until Alisa Petrovich publishes her recently completed University of Houston dissertation, "Revisioning Colbert: Jean-Baptiste Colbert and the Origins of French Global Colonial Policy, 1661–1683."
63. For the importance of the naval battles of 1676–77, I am indebted to James Pritchard for allowing me to see a chapter on the Dutch War in a work in progress on the French colonial empire, c. 1670–1730. This work will be much anticipated because this period is a black hole in the field.
64. For details, see the important work of Charles Frostin, *Les Révoltes blanches à Saint Domingue aux xviie et xviiie siècles* (Paris: Ecole, 1975).

65. Boucher, *Cannibal Encounters*, 77.
66. Jacob M. Price, *France and the Chesapeake: A History of the French Tobacco Monopoly, 1674–1791, and Its Relationship to the British and American Tobacco Trades*, 2 vols. (Ann Arbor: University of Michigan Press, 1973), 1:19–21.
67. Yvonne Bézard, *Fonctionnaires maritimes et coloniaux sous Louis XIV: Les Bégon* (Paris, 1932).
68. The adage is, "That explains it but does not excuse it," the old favorite of parents.
69. Jack P. Greene, *Peripheries and Center: Constitutional Development in the Extended Polities of the British Empire and the United States 1607–1788* (New York: W. W. Norton, 1990), 47.
70. Ibid., 44.
71. Moreau de Saint Méry, *Loix et constitutions* 1:221–23, 324–25.
72. See ibid., 1:307–8 for an example of how they smuggled.
73. Greene, *Peripheries and Center*, ix.
74. Mims, *Colbert's West India Policy*, 45.
75. Jacques de Cauna, "La Création des grands domains de l'Amérique," in the catalog *Voyage aux îles d'Amérique*, 180.
76. Moreau de Saint Méry, *Loix et constitutions* 1:203, 324–25.
77. Roget, *La Société*, 1376. Two years of peace later, the count was 10,656.
78. Ibid., 1382.
79. Cauna, "La Création," 179–80.
80. Price, *France and the Chesapeake*, 1:85–89.
81. Roget, *La Société*, 1401–3.
82. Arlette Gautier shows that by the 1680s the huge gap between men and women had been reduced to 2–2.5 to 1. *Les Soeurs de Solitude: La Condition féminine dans l'esclavage aux Antilles du xviie au xixe siècles* (Paris: Editions caribéenes, 1985), 83.
83. See Roget, *La Société*, 1409–15.
84. Besides Debien, "Les Engagés: pour les Antilles," see Peter Moogk, "Reluctant Exiles: Emigrants from France in Canada before 1760," *William and Mary Quarterly*, 3d ser. (1989): 463–505.
85. Blénac to the minister, Archives nationales, Fonds des colonies, C8 A3, folio 21. Hereafter, A.N. Col., C8 A3, f.21.
86. Moreau de Saint Méry, *Loix et constitutions* 1:543–44.
87. Peter Moogk, "Manon's Fellow Exiles: Emigration from France to North America before 1763," *Proceedings of the Sixteenth Meeting of the French Colonial Historical Society*, ed. Patricia Galloway (1990), 253.
88. Among the many works on sugar, see Dunn, *Sugar and Slaves*, ch. 6; Sydney Mintz, *Sweetness and Power: The Place of Sugar in Modern History* (New York: Penguin Books, 1985), ch. 2; and Robert L. Stein, *The French Sugar Business in the Eighteenth Century* (Baton Rouge: Louisiana State University Press, 1988), chs. 2–4.
89. Robert Fogel, *Without Consent or Contract: The Rise and Fall of American Slavery* (New York: W. W. Norton, 1989), 127.
90. I have not been able to determine if some of these grew cane to be milled at larger plantations, and thus were akin in some respects to *lavradores de caña*, or as the dependents small cane farmers of Brazil are called.
91. Roget, *La Société*, 1381.
92. It has been argued that social conditions of Brazilian slaves living on the small cane feeder estates were better than those working for the large planters (*senghor de engenho*). See, e.g., James Lockhart and Stuart Schwartz, *Early Latin America: A History of Colonial Spanish America and Brazil* (Cambridge: Cambridge University Press, 1983), 210.
93. A convenient reference work for the French slave trade is Robert L. Stein, *The French Slave Trade in the Eighteenth Century: An Old Regime Business* (Madison: University of Wisconsin Press, 1979).
94. Dunn, *Sugar and Slaves*, 312.
95. Du Tertre, *Histoire générale* 2:505, 518. Their village, arranged with Cartesian precision, was called the ville d'Angole.

96. Gautier, *Les Soeurs de Solitude*, 76; for English North America, see Jerome Reich, *Colonial America* (Englewood Cliffs, N.J.: Prentice Hall, 1984), 187.
97. Among other sources, see Gabriel Debien, *Les Esclaves aux Antilles françaises* (Basse Terre, Guadeloupe: Société d'histoire de la Guadeloupe, 1974), 339–52.
98. Roget, *La Société*, 1401–3.
99. A.N.Col., C8 A1, f. 33.
100. Moreau de Saint Méry, *Loix et constitutions* 1:224–25.
101. Although there are many recent studies of it, I prefer the classic of Lucien Peytraud, *L'Esclavage aux Antilles françaises avant 1789* (Paris: Hachette, 1897). He reprints the entire code.
102. Du Tertre, *Histoire générale* 2:531.
103. Moreau de Saint Méry, *Loix et constitutions* 1:306–7.
104. Ibid., 1:365, 306–7.
105. Du Tertre, *Histoire générale* 2:512–13.
106. Yves Debbasch, *Couleur et liberté: Le Jeu de critère ethnique dans un ordre juridique esclavagiste* (Paris: Dalloz, 1967), 26.
107. There were 1,534 freedmen, presumably mostly mulattoes, out of 47,321. Labat reports that parish priests often did not tell officials of these "bastards" out of fear of angering the offending parishioners. *Nouveau voyage* 2: 121–25.
108. In one Guadeloupe parish in 1680, of 1,480 slaves of marriageable age 17.6 percent were not baptized, 499 were baptized but not married, and 48.6 percent were baptized and married. Gautier, *Les Soeurs de Solitude*, 73.
109. Other than reading the du Tertres and Labats there is no easy access to the issues discussed in this paragraph. An overview is Joseph Rennard, *Histoire religieuse des Antilles françaises des origines à 1914* (Paris: Larose, 1954).
110. Du Tertre, *Histoire générale* 2:504. It was gospel among masters that male slaves worked better when they had sexual outlets. Remember, these were French masters.
111. Dunn, *Sugar and Slaves*, ch. 7. I cite him in preference to many other possibilities because of his seventeenth-century focus.
112. Jonathan Wylie, "The Origin of Lesser Antillean French Creole: Some Literary and Lexical Evidence," *Journal of Pidgin and Creole Languages* 10:1 (1995), 77–126.
113. Lovejoy, *Transformations in Slavery*, 44–53.
114. Sidney Mintz, "Slave Life on Caribbean Sugar Plantations: Some Unanswered Questions," in Stephen Palmié, ed., *Slave Cultures and the Cultures of Slavery* (Knoxville: University of Tennessee Press, 1995), 18.
115. Du Tertre, *Histoire générale* 2:496–97. Arlette Gautier has a relatively favorable impression of master-slave relations in this period in *Les Soeurs de Solitude*, 73–79.
116. Moreau de Saint Méry, *Loix et constitutions* 1:136. Notice the name *Francisque* and thus the probable Brazilian background. Labat did complain about harassment from maroons in the mountains. *Nouveau voyage* 1:132.
117. Ibid., 1:327.
118. Some scholars assert that mortality rates for slaves were highest in the earlier stages of a sugar boom. See e.g., B. W. Higman, *Slave Populations of the British Caribbean, 1807–1834* (Baltimore: Johns Hopkins University Press, 1984), 72.
119. Pierre Pluchon, "Les Blancs des îles," in the catalog *Voyages aux îles d'Amérique*, 189.
120. Gabriel Debien, " La Christianisation des esclaves aux Antilles françaises aux 17e et 18e siècles," *Revue d'histoire de l'Amérique française* 20:4 (1967), 543–44.
121. Scholarship on the eighteenth-century "mature" plantation system is far more extensive than for the previous era. Useful introductions are Michel Devèze, *Antilles, Guyanes, la mer des Caraïbes de 1492 à 1789* (Paris: S.E.D.E.S., 1977) and Pierre Pluchon, ed., *Histoire des Antilles et de la Guyane* (Paris: Privat, 1982).
122. John Garrigus, "Sons of the Same Father: Free People of Color and Whites in French Saint Domingue, 1760–1792," revised manuscript of his Ph.D dissertation, Johns Hopkins University, 1988.

Negotiating an Empire

Britain and Its Overseas Peripheries, c. 1550–1780

Elizabeth Mancke

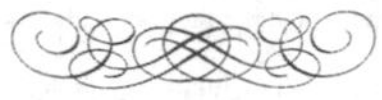

The Seven Years' War, with its territorial acquisitions in the Americas, Africa, and Asia, forced Britain to reassess the kind of empire it governed.[1] For a century and a half, the government had pursued a policy of oceanic empire, emphasizing commercial regulation and the growth of a navy to defend shipping.[2] While the shift from a blue-water empire to a territorial empire may characterize the perspective of the metropolitan government, as well as the East India Company, it was less true for British colonists in North America, for whom stability and growth had long been associated with territorial control, if not expansion. For many colonists, the conquests of Canada and the trans-Appalachian west fulfilled aspirations set in train decades before, albeit with a massive deployment of British troops and matériel that had little morc than a shadow of precedent in the Americas.[3] Thus the question of an oceanic or a territorial empire was not just temporal, dividing the period before the Treaty of Paris from the years afterward, or the rhetorical construction of an increasingly bellicose British public.[4] It was also a perceptual difference among visions of empire, which, this essay argues, reflected long-standing divides in the organization and institutionalization of the early modern British Empire.

The first divide is a spatial one between the oceanic and territorial peripheries. Beginning in the sixteenth century, the new spaces that Europeans competed to dominate included not just land in the Americas, Africa, and Asia, but also the oceans that linked them.[5] These new oceanic peripheries were intrinsically international arenas. The French, English, and Dutch challenges to the Iberian definition of oceans as sovereign spaces had, by the early seventeenth century, made oceanic governance, especially of the Atlantic, a matter of international negotiation and metropolitan regulation. Cash-strapped and absorbed with European politics, the English government delegated the governance of new territorial peripheries to colonial and commercial interests, thereby inexpensively challenging the Iberians overseas while conserving financial resources for European affairs.[6] A major consequence was a division of governance within the emergent empire between oceanic and territorial peripheries, particularly in North America.

Reinforcing this spatial divide was the extension of two distinct expressions of authority, *imperium* and *dominium*, into the non-European world.[7] Imperium implied the extent of a ruler's jurisdiction over which no other power had jurisdiction. Not all rulers had imperium. Henry VIII established English imperium when he rejected papal authority and asserted English sovereignty. The German princes, in contrast, were under the imperium of the Holy Roman Emperor. Dominium implied possession of territory and the attendant right to govern it, though a higher authority might have imperium.[8] The two need not be linked, and indeed one of the characteristics of early modern state formation was the attempt to make the control of territory coterminous with the purported extent of a monarch's jurisdictional authority.[9] Domestic and international definitions of maritime space also turned on the relationship between the two. Elizabeth I did not claim dominium, or property rights, over the waters surrounding England, although she did claim imperium, or the right of jurisdiction, over actions in coastal waters. In contrast, her Stuart cousins claimed both imperium and dominium over Scottish waters, which James I extended to English waters upon his accession to the English throne in 1603.[10]

The Spanish and Portuguese had linked dominium and imperium at the end of the fifteenth century by claiming sovereignty over extra-European waters and lands. Subsequent challenges by the French and English depended, to a great extent, on parsing the two. On the one hand, a subject did not necessarily leave a monarch's jurisdictional authority, or imperium, upon leaving the realm. The French and English Crowns' claims to the extension of their authority overseas through the agency of their subjects was critical to weakening Iberian claims without great governmental expense or direct military challenges. The French and English Crowns asserted diplomatically, and then practically through colonization by their subjects, that transoceanic dominium had to be established through occupation or conquest of an area. Discovery, papal sanction, or royal fiat was not sufficient. Thus the negotiation and manipulation of issues concerning imperium and dominium by England's Tudor-Stuart monarchs, both internationally and domestically, shaped the spatial division of power within the emergent British Empire.

This essay elaborates on the theory that early modern European monarchs lacked the financial resources and coercive power to create overseas empires through the extension of authority from a metropolitan center to colonial peripheries. Rather, these overseas empires were products of transatlantic negotiations and authority constructed on the colonial margins rather than transplanted from Europe.[11] While previous scholars have focused on the British Empire and the negotiations between colonial peripheries and the metropolitan center, this essay contends that there were at least two further patterns of negotiation that sometimes overlapped and sometimes conflicted. First, European powers negotiated among themselves on how to define the extra-European world. Second, governments often mediated among rival interest groups engaged in overseas commerce, which did not claim overseas territory, such as among British traders to Africa. This second arena of negotiation is particularly important, for the British government saw itself as governing an empire of commerce as much as an empire of colonization, and the modes of negotiation for each were quite different.[12]

This essay explores these three patterns of negotiation in an attempt to conceptualize the problems of the early modern British Empire that are inclusive of all its parts. It begins by briefly tracing the sixteenth-century negotiations over the redefinition of extra-European space when the English and French challenged Iberian claims to hegemony. Separate sketches of British interests in Newfoundland, Africa, Asia, the Caribbean, and North America follow. Each region developed distinctive practices of negotiation. By the mid-eighteenth century, imperial growth, both commercial and colonial, coupled with global-scale war and territorial expansion precipitated destabilizing convergences. The metropolitan government's attempts at imperial reform globalized erstwhile regional patterns of negotiation, and the result was the revolution of thirteen colonies.[13]

When the English sponsored their first recorded venture across the Atlantic in 1497, the extra-European world had already been divided between the Iberians with the 1493 papal bulls and the 1494 Treaty of Tordesillas.[14] The Spanish and Portuguese considered all overseas activities by non-Iberians, whether exploration, trade, or piracy, as encroachments on their territories. Not coincidentally, then, it was the English, French, and later the Dutch who produced a number of notorious pirates, seadogs, and interloping merchants while the Spanish and Portuguese, vis-à-vis Europeans, did not. Piracy, of course, is political as well as economic and arises "from the conflict between two political entities, one an established trading power and the other a newcomer."[15]

For the English, French, and Dutch, various forms of plunder were critical to challenging exclusive Iberian claims in Africa, Asia, and the Americas. During the sixteenth century, Spanish and Portuguese diplomats repeatedly delivered requests to the governments of England and France to restrain their subjects, who preyed on Iberian shipping or traded in Africa or the Caribbean. These diplomatic missives, as well as treaty negotiations, seldom elicited the desired contrition, providing instead formal occasions for the English and French governments to challenge the legitimacy of Iberian hegemony in the extra-European world and to assert their right to participate in defining it. In turn, these diplomatic negotiations shaped an international discussion of the political definition of the oceanic and territorial peripheries. By the late 1550s, the English and French quite consistently argued for freedom of the seas (a position they reversed during the seventeenth century and returned to in the eighteenth century). They further asserted that European claims to sovereignty in the Americas, Africa, and Asia had to be accompanied by occupation of territory by European subjects.[16]

By the end of the sixteenth century, wars in Europe and increasing depredations around the Atlantic basin had emboldened France and England to increase the diplomatic leverage on Spain. Henri IV, in the negotiations leading to the Treaty of Vervins (1598), pressed Spain to acknowledge French rights to colonize unoccupied territory in the Americas. Six years later, in the Treaty of London, which ended England's war with Spain and support of the United Provinces, James I sought a similar concession.[17] While the Spanish conceded nothing, the political effect of this diplomatic pressure by the French and English governments weakened Iberian claims and legitimized the commerce, exploration, and colonization of their own subjects in Africa, Asia, and the Americas.

The French, English, and later Dutch challenges to the Iberians depended on a redefinition of overseas territory from Iberian space to extra-European space that could only be made a dependency of European polities through the settlement of European peoples or conquest. This negotiated formula of legitimate expansion made national identity, rooted in being natural-born subjects, critically important to extra-European claims.[18] It challenged the Spanish contention that the indigenous peoples of the Americas were subjects of the Castilian Crown by royal decree.[19] Instead, the French, English, and Dutch argued that American lands without Spanish settlers were not Castilian territory and therefore could be claimed by rival powers with the appropriate settlement of subjects.[20]

The diversity of sixteenth-century English overseas enterprises diffused energies and worked against the planting of permanent settlements.[21] When the English finally deployed the necessary resources to establish sustainable ventures, they created a remarkable range and variety of enterprises, from fishing outports in Newfoundland to plantations in the West Indies to cloth markets in India. We can group early modern British expansion into six regional categories: Newfoundland and the North Atlantic fishery; West Africa; Asia and the Indian Ocean basin; the Caribbean; the eastern seaboard of North America; and Rupert's Land or the Hudson's Bay Company territory. Colonial and commercial enterprises in the first four regions built on sixteenth-century European, if not English, expertise and practices, and consequently encountered, if not conflicted with, existing interests. But along the North American coast between Georgia and the Gulf of Maine, Europeans had neither regular commerce nor persisting settlements before the establishment of Jamestown in 1607, and thus seventeenth-century developments are tangentially rather than directly related to earlier developments. Similarly, even though sixteenth-century English explorers had charted the eastern arctic coast of North America, no Europeans had continual contact in the area before the establishment of the Hudson's Bay Company in 1670.[22]

In negotiating overseas interests the British metropolitan government played one of two roles, which in turn profoundly influenced perceptions of its function in defining the empire. Often it acted as an adjudicator among rival interests, whether they were proprietors in the Lesser Antilles, settlers and fishermen in Newfoundland, competing companies in India, or merchants trading in Africa. While the government's interest in these situations was never far from sight, it was usually indirectly expressed. In other instances, the metropolitan government was the second party in negotiations, in which its interests were directly at issue, as happened in the Caribbean, North America, and after 1765 in India. The qualitative factor in shaping the negotiating role of the metropolitan government was most often dominium, because its establishment legitimized the foundation of a new locus of authority that conflicted with the imperium of the metropolitan government. In short, negotiating a territorial empire had long deviated substantively from negotiating an oceanic empire.

Those deviations had implications for the way in which peripheries were connected to the metropole. The oversight of commercial organizations based in England, including the East India Company, merchants trading to Africa, West Country fishing merchants, and the Hudson's Bay Company had been institutionally integrated with the metropole by the end of the seventeenth century, and generally included regulation by a diverse range of governing bodies, including the Privy Council, Parliament, the treasury, and the navy. In contrast, the institutional integration of the territorial empire occurred far more slowly; it was an eighteenth- rather than seventeenth-century development, and confronted powerful colonial resistance.[23]

From the perspective of Britain, Newfoundland's prospects for colonization were auspicious. English participation in the North American fishery dated back a century. During the privateering wars of the 1580s and 1590s, the English and French had driven out the Portuguese and Spanish, who had dominated the fishery for much of the sixteenth century.[24] A viable commodity, fish, supplemented with furs, minerals, and timber, would provide the money to support settlements. Lying at latitudes almost due west of Britain, Newfoundland, it was believed, would have a climate sufficiently temperate to grow food for the settlers. In the 1580s it figured in the colonization plans of Sir Humphrey Gilbert. Anticipating better success than he met, between 1610 and 1638 seven groups of promoters or individual proprietors, beginning with the Newfoundland Company, attempted to plant settlements on the island. All failed as organized enterprises, although continuous English residence on the island dates from these early plantings.[25] The constraints of the physical environment, alone, could explain these ventures' failure. Newfoundland winters are too long and the ground too barren for most farming, and provisions had to be shipped in from England or later from New England, the mid-Atlantic colonies, and Ireland.[26] As one discouraged colonial organizer reported back to his father in England, "if ever you look for money again in this country, you must send fishermen."[27]

The physical environment, however, does not explain the uniqueness of the extension of English imperium and dominium into Newfoundland. Attempts at organized settlements, initially justified as providing protection against "anie forraine Prince or State," were perceived by West Country merchants and fishermen, who for decades had prosecuted the fishery through seasonal voyages, as attempts to monopolize their livelihood.[28] Chartered settlements carried rights to establish governments, premised on successful occupation of land. The most valuable property in Newfoundland was the shore necessary for the fishery and the nearby woods that provided timber for wharves, buildings, and fuel. As West Country interests recognized, island-based governments with claims of dominium might well restrict migratory crews from the shore rights necessary for the fishery.

Politicized West Countrymen, therefore, lobbied Parliament and the king for legislation or a charter to protect their ancient rights to fish in Newfoundland waters and to cure their catch on shore. In the 1630s, the Privy Council considered solutions to the conflicts. In response to questions about the king's right to legislate for Newfoundland, the attorney general, William Noye, opined that the monarch could effectively legislate through a charter. In January 1634, Charles I issued the Western Charter to provide "Regulations for the Newfoundland Fishery." Its preamble stated the Crown's dominion over the island, its right to intervene in the interests of the native peoples and the fishery, and the need to protect migratory fishermen from planters. It guaranteed the right of all English subjects to fish off Newfoundland, and legitimated the tradition that the master of the first ship to a harbor in the spring would be that harbor's admiral with the first choice of shore rights for stages and boat rooms, as well as the responsibility for maintaining order. Civil or criminal disputes arising among the migratory fishermen in Newfoundland were to be tried in West Country courts, making the island an administrative extension of England. This "charter," whose origins and terms were precipitated by charters for colonization, was not cataloged in the patent rolls, as were its competitors', but in the chancery warrants, indicating its legal ambiguity—and, by extension, Newfoundland's.[29]

Undeterred by the Western Charter, in 1637 Sir David Kirke and his associates, some with West Indian connections, sought a grant to control all the fishery from Newfoundland to Nova Scotia. The king's receptivity put the West Country merchants in common cause with earlier adversaries such as Lord Baltimore, who still claimed proprietary rights on the Avalon Peninsula. Unable to block this seventh and last attempt to colonize Newfoundland, Kirke's charter stipulated that settlements be six miles back from the shore, a prohibitive distance for successful prosecution of the fishery. It restricted the cutting of wood, barred the monopolization of shore rights, proscribed the destruction of fishermen's property, and exempted migratory fishermen from the jurisdiction of any government Kirke might establish. Kirke flagrantly disregarded all of these restrictions and the relative success of his settlement elicited vociferous protests from West Country merchants, fishermen, and planters remaining from earlier ventures.[30]

Civil war in England, followed by the first Anglo-Dutch War, forced the metropolitan government under Parliament and then the Protectorate to become actively involved in the fishery. The Protectorate government sent commissioners to Newfoundland to investigate complaints against Kirke. To protect the fishing fleet against reprisals by the royalist navy under Prince Rupert, Parliament provided naval escorts. The convoy commodore's commission charged him to remain in Newfoundland as the season's governor and to serve as an appellate judge in local disputes. For West Country merchants, the depredations of war, the decline in their share of the provisioning trade due to the increasing trade from New England, and their hostility to Kirke made them receptive to establishing permanent settlements along the coast, yet opposed to island-based government. The land on which people had been settling, however, was not surveyed or deeded; hence, ownership was tenuous and dependent on local legitimation. The metropolitan government, however, became more hardened against both settlement and island-based government, and committed to maintaining Newfoundland as a nursery for seamen.[31]

A half century of international threats eventually tipped the balance on metropolitan acknowledgment of settlement. In 1652 the French had established a fortified settlement at Placentia (Plaisance) on the west side of the Avalon Peninsula and quickly extended their fishing outports along the south shore of Newfoundland. Initially the English government believed that the migratory fishery and naval patrols would maintain English claims to the island. The Nine Years War's (1689–97) ended that pretension when the French attacked and destroyed most English settlements in Newfoundland. The royal navy and soldiers reclaimed St. John's and fortified its harbor. The Treaty of Ryswick (1697) returned conquests to status quo antebellum. In 1699, Parliament passed the Newfoundland Act, terminating the Western Charter, permitting land grants to settlers with claims that predated 1685, not coincidentally the year before James II and Louis XIV agreed in the Treaty of Westminster to honor the extra-European claims of their respective subjects.[32]

In the Treaty of Utrecht (1713) the French acknowledged British claims to Newfoundland and agreed to vacate Placentia, but negotiated seasonal shore rights from Cape Bonavista on the north of the island around to Port Riche on the west coast. These French rights persisted until 1904, with adjustments made in 1763, 1783, and 1815, baroque embellishments to an already peculiar configuration of British imperium and dominium in Newfoundland. In this instance, dominium was internationally recognized as British, but the British government had virtually no jurisdictional authority over French subjects who fished annually from its territory.[33]

The circumstances surrounding the establishment and practices of British dominium in Newfoundland are at one end of the imperial spectrum. Initially, the territorial periphery was only valuable insofar as it facilitated access to and the processing of fish from the oceanic periphery. The vested interests of West Country merchants and fishermen that predated formal attempts at colonization and their vehement and long resistance to colonial government gave the Crown dominium that was largely unqualified by either an island-based government or severalty landownership. Even had intra-English conflicts not drawn in the metropolitan government, international pressure to negotiate the relationship between the oceanic and territorial peripheries would have forced metropolitan involvement. When Newfoundlanders began negotiating their rights within the British Empire in the early nineteenth century, they had to contend with an array of vested interests, from metropolitan-based merchants to the French and American governments, many with greater property rights on the island and to its territorial waters than had the residents themselves.

While no part of the extra-European world had a greater diversity of European participants than West Africa, few had colonial claims on the continent. Britain had no claims to dominium until the late eighteenth century. France ceded Senegambia at the end of the Seven Years' War, but Britain returned it in 1783. In 1787, the British began settling free blacks in Sierra Leone under the auspices of the Sierra Leone Company, which turned the colony over to the Crown in 1808. In 1795, the British conquered the Cape Colony from the Dutch, who briefly repossessed it from 1803 to 1806.[34]

The Portuguese had been commercially active on the West African coast from the late fifteenth century to the early seventeenth century when the Dutch drove them out and assumed dominance in the slave trade until eclipsed by the English at the end of the century.[35] While the Portuguese asserted sovereignty in the area, their claims vis-à-vis West African powers were tenuous, except on the offshore Cape Verde Islands and São Tomé. Angola, in southwest Africa, remained a Portuguese colony, as did Mozambique in southeast Africa, but in East Africa north of Cape Delgado port cities held by the Portuguese fell to Omani raids in the late seventeenth and eighteenth centuries.[36] In short, early modern European involvement in Africa was heavily commercial, not colonial, with most trading factories on land leased from Africans.[37]

Without colonies, British merchants leased bases in Africa from local leaders to facilitate trade. In a number of respects, the West African trades had structural constraints similar to those in the Newfoundland fishery. English commerce along the Guinea coast dated from the mid-sixteenth century, and while more episodic than the exploitation of the fishery, African trade had nonetheless entered merchants' calculus. Even before the mid-seventeenth century when the English became vigorous slave traders, the demand for dyewoods, hides, and gold made attempts at monopoly control attractive. West Africa's proximity to Europe, widely available navigational knowledge, and numerous commercial sites made entering the trade relatively feasible and maintaining a monopoly difficult. Merchants with long-standing African connections, interlopers, and political interests in Whitehall and Westminster posed formidable challenges to monopoly trade. Consequently, regulation of British activities in Africa, like those in Newfoundland, became centralized in the metropole.

Attempts to monopolize the West African trade first received sanction in 1618 when merchants received a charter for the Guinea Company giving them exclusive English trading privileges on the Guinea and Benin coasts. Interloping and parliamentary hostility to the company's royalist leanings undermined its commercial viability. An aggressive London merchant, Nicholas Crispe, bought a controlling interest and in 1631 rechartered the firm. Under his leadership, it built trading forts on the Gold Coast at Komenda and Kormantin, establishing continuous centers of English trade. As with many overseas ventures, the Guinea Company became entangled in the politics of civil war, and in 1644 Parliament divested Crispe of his shares in the company, ostensibly to discharge a state debt he owed, and parliamentary loyalists assumed management of the company. Privateering by the royalist navy, followed by Dutch depredations during the first Anglo-Dutch War, brought the company to the point of collapse, and in 1657 it leased its trading rights and forts to the East India Company.[38]

Restoration courtiers, led by Prince Rupert and James, Duke of York, organized the Royal African Company (RAC), marking England's serious entry into the slave trade. Challenges to its monopoly privileges immediately beset the RAC in Africa and England. In 1698 Parliament, in response to the RAC's inability to protect its monopoly rights, formally revoked them and officially opened the trade to all English merchants. The English, however, needed to maintain forts along the West African coast and diplomatic relations with African kings on whose land the forts were built. Rather than the government providing them directly, Parliament also passed legislation to levy a duty on imports from and exports to Africa for the RAC to use to maintain its forts for all English traders. The act expired after thirteen years, Parliament voted not to continue it, and the company asserted that its monopoly rights had been restored. Less rhetorically, the material reality was that the RAC had to maintain forts for the general benefit of British trade without financial support. After fifteen years of deterioration and decay, Parliament voted the RAC a subsidy of £10,000 to maintain its factories. It continued from 1730 to 1744; in 1744 it was doubled, in 1745 halved, and in 1746 eliminated. In 1750 Parliament revoked the RAC charter and chartered the Company of Merchants Trading to Africa, a regulated company to which all traders to Africa paid a fee for maintaining forts and intergovernmental relations in West Africa in the interests of all British merchants.[39]

Considered spatially, trade with Africa was strongly oriented toward the oceanic periphery and metropolitan governance, and illustrates two structural developments related to British overseas commerce. First, free trade diversified the number of

British ports with merchants trading to Africa; in particular it generated a shift away from London and the merchants who controlled the RAC to ports such as Bristol and Liverpool, as well as colonial ports such as Newport, Rhode Island.[40] Second, the large number of British traders participating in African trades and the complex and diverse international arena made delegated governance of the trade impossible. No one firm could regulate and protect British interests, as did the East India Company in Asia. The Royal African Company and later the Company of Merchants Trading to Africa provided some governmental services at the forts and factories along the African coast, but they could not regulate or protect traders once they left Africa. The transatlantic sectors of the slave trade, whether factories in Africa, markets in the Caribbean and North America, or financial services in Britain, required an integrated infrastructure that the metropolitan state slowly and reactively came to regulate, often in response to pressure groups in Westminster or Whitehall. In this respect, the African trades illustrate how the commercial expansion of Europe engendered a growing government involvement in the regulation of the economy, and in particular overseas trade.[41]

English merchants investing in the Asian trades had long tried to avoid direct confrontation with their European competitors and except in a few instances had elicited little interest in territorial acquisitions in Asia before the conquests of the 1750s and 1760s.[42] In the sixteenth century they financed exploratory expeditions along the arctic coasts of Europe and North America, hoping to find a northern water route to Asia so as to avoid the South Atlantic route dominated by the Iberians. The Muscovy Company (1555) had the dual purpose of opening Russian markets and connecting with the overland trade from Persia. When that avenue did not deliver the desired access to Asian goods, many of the same merchants established the Turkey Company in 1581 (the Levant Company after 1592) for trade into the eastern Mediterranean where many overland routes terminated. While profitable, this trade could not meet the commercial challenge the Dutch posed when they sailed to India in the 1590s; in response, English merchants organized the East India Company (EIC), chartered by Elizabeth I in 1600.[43]

Of all branches of early modern commerce, trade into the Indian Ocean basin posed the greatest logistical challenges for Europeans. Voyages could take over six months one way, and tied up operating capital for eighteen to twenty-four months. Warehouses had to be acquired or built at both ends to store goods headed to and from markets. Successful trade required diplomatic negotiations with Asian rulers to acquire or build permanent factories in their cities. Intense competition required that merchants arm vessels and forts against Europeans rivals, and at times Asians.[44]

In this environment, the EIC did not attempt to acquire territory through conquest, except in the 1680s under the aggrandizing leadership of Sir Josiah Childs. Those military forays, thwarted by Mughal forces, suggested the folly of adventures of conquest and the wisdom of negotiated trade. Rather than govern extensive territory, the company maintained merchant enclaves within Asian-governed cities. In the seventeenth century it acquired jurisdiction over three entrepôts: Madras, Bombay, and Calcutta. In 1652 the company negotiated with a local ruler in southeast India for a grant for Madras. The Portuguese gave Bombay to Charles II in 1661 as part of the dowry of Catherine of Braganza, and he transferred it to the EIC after seven years. In 1696, the company received a long-term lease from a local Mughal prince to build a factory on the Bengal coast that became Calcutta, the presidency of Bengal and one of the largest cities in the eighteenth-century empire. Residents of all three cities, both Asians and Europeans were governed by the EIC, though its writ in Madras and Calcutta was at the sufferance of local Asian rulers.[45]

Over the seventeenth century, the East India Company faced challenges ranging from the nonrenewal of the charter, to competition from rival companies, and to Crown demands for money.[46] Despite these threats to its survival, a number of factors contributed to the continuation of monopoly trade in Asia, rather than a more open system such as was developed in the Atlantic trades. The sheer distance from England to Asia and the dispersed markets in the Indian Ocean and the South China Sea precluded a government presence, such as the navy provided in the fishery, the slave trade, or the Caribbean. Rarely were royal naval vessels or government troops sent beyond the Cape of Good Hope in the seventeenth century. The first major involvement of the British navy in Asian waters was during the wars from 1739 to 1748.[47] Consequently, in the Indian Ocean basin, the British division between territorial and oceanic peripheries did not begin to develop until the mid-eighteenth century. Rather, the EIC represented the British in both arenas.

Distance complicated challenges by rival merchants. Successful trade required permanent facilities, achieved through diplomatic arrangements with Asian rulers and long-term investments in fixed capital. Without these arrangements, trade could drift toward piracy. In 1637 Charles I granted a group of merchants led by William Courteen and Endymion Porter the right to trade in areas of the Indian Ocean and the South China Sea where the EIC did not trade. When legal and profitable trade eluded the Courteen-Porter associates they turned to piracy, and their Asian victims sought indemnity from, and engaged in reprisals against, the EIC.[48] Oliver Cromwell decided not to renew the EIC charter in 1653, but the volatile instability of free trade prompted an about-face and the issuance of a new charter in 1657. When William and Mary chartered a rival East India Company in 1698, the old EIC curbed access to Asian markets by barring the new traders from EIC facilities. The financial losses on both sides led to the formation of a United East India Company in 1709, chartered this time and henceforth by Parliament, not the Crown.[49]

The EIC's role as a major source for government borrowing repeatedly deterred the Crown and Parliament from ending the monopoly. James I wheedled £20,000 out of the company in 1618 in exchange for revoking the grant of a charter for a Scottish East India Company. When Charles II regranted the EIC charter in 1661, the company responded with a series of financial gifts and "loans" that totaled £170,000. In 1698 William and Mary chartered a rival East India Company in exchange for a £2 million loan at 8 percent interest; the old company had offered a loan of only £700,000, at 4 percent interest. The resulting commercial instability threatened not just the viability of British trade in India but the solvency of the state, both in terms of the customs revenues collected and the huge loans lent to the government. The arrangement for the companies' merger in 1709 included a government loan of £3,200,000. Parliament's subsequent willingness to protect the EIC's monopoly privileges and accord it great autonomy in managing its affairs rested on the knowledge that the company's financial health affected the financial health of the government and thousands of investors. After 1765, even staunch antimonopolists abandoned their cause against the EIC's privileges given its new role as a revenue collector in India.[50]

The East India Company's long-standing autonomy in managing British affairs in Asia shifted in the 1740s, when both the British and French navies sent ships into the Indian Ocean. Despite mercantile sentiment to keep the Asian seas neutral, naval battles ensued after the declaration of war in 1744. In 1746 a French naval squadron seized Madras, confirming the military debacle that the War of the Austrian Succession had become for the British. Having performed poorly in Europe, the only bargaining chip the British had at the negotiating table was Louisbourg in North America, taken by New England troops in 1745, and swapped for Madras in the 1748 Treaty of Aix-la-Chapelle.[51] That exchange of territory created tangible linkages between affairs in the Atlantic and Indian Oceans that decades before had become indirectly linked in the account books of the treasury, in parliamentary legislation, and in tons of merchant cargo.

While Anglo-French military engagements mark the beginning of war in India that lasted until 1764, war between two territory-poor European trading rivals cannot account for the emergence of the EIC as a territorial power in India after 1757. The causal linkages between the intra-European wars and the Anglo-Indian wars are contested scholarly terrain.[52] Certainly, however, Anglo-French conflicts coincided with Asian power struggles in Arcot, Hyderabad, and Bengal, areas with a strong British or French commercial presence. The multiple and overlapping mobilizations of troops, including an unprecedented deployment of state, rather than just company, troops from Britain and France, allowed the British to exploit Indian political transitions. By 1765, the EIC had a client state in the territories of the Nawab of Arcot, and in Bengal the Mughal emperor had conceded it the right to collect the *diwani* in Bengal, Bihar, and Orissa, and to provide civil administration.[53]

The transformation of the East India Company from a commercial concern to a territorial power with surplus tax revenues estimated at £1,600,000 per year coincided with a financial crisis in Britain at the end of the Seven Years' War.[54] The enormous state debt had been partially accrued through military support of the EIC, and many Britons thought the government deserved a portion of the surplus revenues. At one level, this issue could be seen as a continuation of the long-standing financial connection between company and state. The larger and more consequential question, however, was who had dominium over the newly acquired territory in India, the East India Company or the Crown? If the EIC owned the territory, then any portion of the revenues granted to the government would essentially be for services rendered. If the Crown owned the territory, then it had a clear right to revenues, even if it farmed their collection to the EIC.

In 1766–67, the ministry convened Parliament's first inquiry of the East India Company. Lord Chatham, who presided, had a narrow focus of getting the newly acquired lands declared Crown territory with revenue collection farmed to the EIC. The metropolitan government would derive a financial return without the difficulty of direct governance of such distant domains. Indeed, Chatham had little interest in investigating the way in which the company conducted its affairs in Asia. The legal and constitutional resolution to the question of Crown claims to Asian territorial revenues, however, was fraught with ambiguities, which in turn became political fodder for opposition in Parliament, the press, and the company.[55]

The charter of 1698, the basis of the 1709 charter, reserved to the Crown in perpetuity the "sovereign right, power and dominion" over EIC "forts, places, and plantations."[56] A 1757 legal opinion by the attorney- and solicitor-general determined that the Crown had sovereignty (or imperium) over all the company's land. Who possessed dominium depended on the mode of territorial acquisition. Lands acquired by company treaty or negotiation with Asians—such as Bombay, Madras, and Calcutta—were EIC possessions. Acquisitions by conquest were the Crown's. By 1767, the authors of the opinion, Charles Yorke and Charles Pratt, were representing the company and the Ministry, respectively, and disagreed on whether the right to the territorial revenues had been acquired by a grant from the Mughal emperor and was therefore company property, or had been a spoil of war and was therefore Crown property. EIC supporters noted that the EIC "acknowledged the Emperor as *de jure* sovereign in Bengal." Could the British Crown be sovereign, as well? Supporters of the Crown's claim pointed to the royal navy's critical role in preserving the company's interest, thereby emphasizing conquest. This legal and constitutional impasse was breached with an interim compromise to leave the property right undetermined and £400,000 per year in the treasury.[57]

By 1772, a ballooning debt was the most glaring and troubling sign of the inadequacies of the company's commercial and administrative structures for managing its post-1765 status as a major territorial power in Asia. In Bengal, revenues declined after the first year the EIC had the diwan. Ignoring the region's weakening economy and the consequences of severe famines in 1769–70, the EIC implemented procedures to rationalize and maximize revenue collection, believing that with care and industry great improvements could be made in the diwani collections. The sharp economic decline, however, reduced revenues from £1.82 to £1.25 million from 1766 to 1771. Of the collected revenues, the EIC used much of them to purchase teas in China, thus draining increasingly precious circulating currency from the Bengali economy rather than investing in it.[58]

The company's directors thought expanding tea markets would boost its war-battered commercial revenues. Beginning in the late 1760s, they increased tea imports, which temporarily boosted sales in Britain and America before glutting the market. To lower tea prices in Britain, Ireland, and America, they negotiated reductions and rebates on tea taxes, codified in the 1767 Indemnity Act, whereby the company would indemnify the government for lost revenues through increased tea sales. That same year, however, Parliament passed the Townshend Revenue Acts, putting a three-pence-per-pound duty on tea imported into the American colonies, thus eliminating the price reduction the Indemnity Act created, as well as angering colonists for whom tea symbolized parliamentary tyranny. Rather than generating sales and boosting revenues, it sparked colonial boycotts and resistance; by 1772, £2 million of tea sat unsold in company warehouses.[59]

When Parliament convened in November 1772, it immediately prepared another inquiry into the EIC, this time undertaken by an elected secret committee. The previous spring, it established a select committee under John Burgoyne to investigate the reputed crimes that EIC servants inflicted upon Indians. By June 1773, despite enormous resistance by the East India Company, Parliament passed the Loan Act and the Regulating Act. The first provided the company a loan and the government suspended any claim to territorial revenues until the EIC's finances were again sound.

The second act reformed the company's executive management and shareholder governance in London. For India, it attempted to separate commercial and civilian affairs through the Crown appointment of a governor-general, Crown-company joint appointment of four councillors, and the establishment of a supreme court in Calcutta, with Crown-appointed judges, to hear all cases involving British subjects. The governance of Indians remained largely unaddressed. The question of the legal possessor of Asian territory remained undetermined, though Parliament passed a resolution introduced by Burgoyne supporting Crown claims to the lands. Not until the Charter Act of 1813 did the Crown's claim receive statutory expression.[60]

The relationships among the economy of Bengal, the purchase of tea in China, its sale in Atlantic markets, the increasing tensions in the American colonies, and the 1772 financial crisis in the East India Company graphically illustrate how interconnected parts of the empire had become. Members of Parliament and the Ministry recognized that the interests of the East India Company were being played off against American colonies. In the 1760s, in response to pressure to repeal the tax on tea imported into the colonies, Lord North said that "if he were disposed to repeal the law he had rather do it at the desire of the India company than that of America."[61] As is well known, the passage of the 1773 Tea Act, designed to relieve the EIC's financial crisis, triggered escalating incidents of colonial rebel action and parliamentary reaction beginning with the Boston Tea Party in December 1773, the passage of the Coercive Acts in 1774, the calling of the first Continental Congress in September 1774, the reinforcement of troops in Boston, and armed conflict in April 1775.[62]

When the EIC had lobbied against the passage of the 1773 Regulating Act, it used language that evoked the rhetoric of resistance in the colonies. The duke of Richmond told a meeting of EIC shareholders in May 1773 that the government had left them with two options. They could "lie at the mercy of the administration," or "resist, like Englishmen, every illegal attack upon their chartered rights and privileges." They chose the latter.[63] In the cases of both the North American colonies and the East India Company, events forced the metropolitan government simultaneously to restructure its relationships with the two most autonomous parts of the empire. The rapid and destabilizing transformations wrought by becoming a territorial power in India had jeopardized the East India Company's autonomy by making its affairs too dangerous for the government to ignore and its structure too weak for a fuller defense of itself against ministerial and parliamentary regulation and oversight. By contrast, the much longer legacy of territorial control in North America had engendered colonial institutional stability and strength that was dangerous for the government to ignore, but too strong to restrain easily.

When the English finally established permanent West Indian settlements they succeeded by planting on islands peripheral to Spanish concerns. St. Christopher (1623), Barbados (1627), Nevis (1628), and Antigua and Montserrat (1632) in the Lesser Antilles have a combined land surface of 417 square miles. Jamaica, conquered from the Spanish in 1655, has 4,411 square miles.[64] None of the Lesser Antilles had Spanish settlers. Caribs, who inhabited many, but not all, of the islands, had militantly resisted Spanish colonization and eschewed regular trade with Europeans. English settlement on this eastern fringe of the Caribbean posed an indirect threat to the Spanish, of less danger than previous settlement ventures in the region or the 1630

Puritan settlement of Providence Island off the coast of Nicaragua, which the Spanish destroyed in 1641. As well, James I's policy of appeasing the Spanish by restraining English settlement ventures in the Caribbean had largely ceased with his death in 1625. Implicitly, though, English colonization still challenged the more sweeping Spanish contention that only the Iberians had legitimate claims to American territory.[65]

Despite these tiny islands' marginality on the Caribbean's eastern edge, they provided the territorial footholds for developing the most lucrative agricultural colonies in the early modern British Empire, as well as serving as commercial entrepôts on the crossroads of the Atlantic world. French colonies lay within sight of the Leeward Islands; until 1713, the French and English shared St. Christopher. New England traders supplied provisions and stores to West Indian planters of all nationalities. African slaves ate cod caught by West Country, Irish, and New England fishermen on the North Atlantic banks. Port Royal served as both the capital of Jamaica and the West Indian headquarters for British merchant houses that sold slaves and manufactures throughout the Caribbean. Britain's first colonial trade war began there in 1739 over tensions with Spain regarding freedom of navigation.

Much of the last three decades of scholarship has conceptualized the British West Indies as part of the empire of colonization more than as the empire of commerce. While studies of sixteenth-century English activity in the Caribbean stress the continuities among "trade, plunder, and settlement," many studies of West Indian colonization begin with the settlement of St. Christopher in 1624.[66] Yet the mercantile interests that predated settlement, and were reinforced by it, distinguished the seventeenth-century Caribbean colonies from their North American counterparts, even before the former became overwhelmingly slave societies. Indeed mercantile interests made possible the earlier, more rapid, and more thorough transition to slavery in the West Indies than in the mainland colonies.[67]

The Caribbean differed from other overseas arenas of commerce, because the competition was not over control of a sector of overseas trade. Rather, it was the location for the convergence of numerous sectors of the Atlantic economy, including the trades in sugar, slaves, provisions, and manufactures, as well as competition among the British, French, Dutch, and Spanish.[68] The diversity of colonial, commercial, and military ventures that became sited in the Caribbean made the negotiation of empire in this region complex and multifaceted. Relations among states, between the metropole and colonial peripheries, and among rival commercial interests were all negotiated over the seventeenth and eighteenth centuries, repeatedly and often simultaneously.

The English occupation of land and the creation of colonies was, however, critical in shaping all three patterns of negotiation. Permanent settlements domesticated critical aspects of English involvement in the extra-European world, making possible economic circuits that could place production, investment, marketing, shipping, and consumption of American goods under English control.[69] Agricultural colonies settled and worked, at least initially, by English labor created territorial peripheries that put the ownership of land, a critical element in the English construction of power and authority, into the hands of overseas subjects. Colonial governments became necessary for the distribution and registration of land, the regulation of labor relations, and the provision of dispute resolution for criminal and civil cases.

Colonial governments always raised metropolitan concern, if not ire, because of the autonomy they exhibited. The decision of planters in Barbados, Antigua, Bermuda, and Virginia to support the royalists in the Civil War provoked Parliament to pass legislation in October 1650 to prohibit all trade with them. Persistent flaunting of parliamentary authority resulted in the deployment of a naval expedition to force their allegiance. The reliance of West Indian colonists on Dutch shipping and finance contributed to the initial passage of the Navigation Acts in 1651, which they routinely violated during the seventeenth century. The claim of Jamaica's assembly to be but a small version of the House of Commons elicited a futile attempt by the Lords of Trade to apply Poyning's Law, written for Ireland (a conquered society), to Jamaica. Jamaicans persistently rejected this constitutional interpretation of themselves as a conquered people, asserting instead that they had all the rights and privileges of freeborn Englishmen. For fifty years the assembly refused to vote a permanent revenue until the metropolitan government acknowledged this contention. Governors who believed that their authority was based on a royal commission rather than local legitimation, and who endeavored to enforce parliamentary legislation or Crown policy too stringently, found their efforts rebuffed. Daniel Parke, governor of the Leeward Islands from 1706 to 1710, exercised his power too fervently and was killed in an uprising of angry planters. An investigation turned up only mute participants and witnesses unwilling to provide evidence for a prosecution.[70]

Authority in the colonies, therefore, did not trickle down from the center to the peripheries but was negotiated between the regions. These negotiations occurred repeatedly. In most cases, the metropolitan government opposed a colony rather than adjudicated between rival interests. The most critical factor engendering the more adversarial metropolitan-colonial pattern of negotiating empire was the establishment of dominium. During Jamaica's privilege controversy in the 1760s, assembly members articulated the belief that their rights had not come from the Crown, but were their inheritance as Britons that they had not relinquished just because they lived in a colony.[71] In this respect, the territorial or colonial empire, even if it comprised just a few hundred square miles of land in the Caribbean Sea, had long distinguished itself from the commercial or oceanic empire. Territorial empire, moreover, always intersected with commercial empire, though the reverse was not true, as in the case of African trade. Finally, the colonial and commercial empires intersected quite differently in the Caribbean from in North America.

From the early seventeenth century, promoters of and investors in Caribbean settlement knew how to exploit existing commercial outlets in Europe for the tropical products that could be grown on the islands, and these products quickly dominated the colonial trades. Customs figures from London for 1686 show imports from the West Indies valued at £674,518, over three times the value of imports (£207,131) from North America. That year, total exports from London were comparable—£111,326 to the Caribbean and £100,541 to North America. White per-capita consumption, on the other hand, was much higher in the West Indies; planters in Barbados and Jamaica consumed an average of £3.46 and £3.87 worth of imported goods, while colonists in New England and the Chesapeake purchased only £.59 and £.63, respectively. White wealth in the West Indies was six times greater than in North America; conversely, the white population in North America was six times greater than in the West Indies. On the eve of the American Revolution, 65.5 percent of all imports from Britain's Atlantic empire came from the West Indies, and they consumed 45.7 percent of all exports from Britain. These "consumption" figures do not include purchases of slaves. Of the 279,100 Africans landed in British America between 1766 and 1775, 55.5 percent were sold in Barbados, Jamaica, and the Leeward Islands, 31.3 percent in the newly acquired Ceded Islands, and 13.2 percent in the North American colonies.[72]

In this inordinately wealthy colonial environment, all the factors of production became subject to scrutiny. By the early eighteenth century, most British-produced sugar was consumed in Britain, with little destined for foreign markets. British sugar also cost more than French sugar, due partly to high demand at home, but which provoked many observers to question the relationship between cultivated land and sugar prices. Critics of high sugar prices suggested that West Indian planters, especially those on Jamaica, intentionally kept land out of production to keep sugar supplies low and demand high. Concentrated landownership on all the islands and the engrossment of much of the uncultivated land in Jamaica by large planters lent substance to the charge. In the 1730s, as hostilities with Spain engendered calls for war, advocates of increased sugar production pressed for British conquests of French or Spanish territories in the Caribbean. West Indian planters, in turn, lobbied against territorial conquest for fear of overproduction.[73]

By the 1720s, the growing population in the mainland colonies produced agricultural and timber products beyond what British West Indian planters needed, and North American traders sought French, Dutch, and Spanish markets in the Caribbean. Irate British sugar planters lobbied Parliament for special duties on foreign sugar products purchased by North American colonists, a policy that found expression in the unenforceable 1733 Molasses Act.[74] Through the 1730s, West Indian planters held political sway in the metropole against both the North Americans engaged in the provisioning trade and the advocates for the territorial expansion of sugar cultivation. During Spain and Britain's war that broke out in 1739 and merged with the War of the Austrian Succession, the government decided to concentrate on commercial objectives rather than territorial conquests in the Caribbean.

Its commercial objectives, in this instance, were not immediately sugar, but the trade in slaves and manufactured goods between British merchants and Spanish colonists. Spain, contending that the line of demarcation defined in the Treaty of Tordesillas was still valid, did not license its own merchants to trade in Africa, but sought slaves in negotiation with other nations. Spain also continued to claim sovereign rights in the western Atlantic and contended that other nations merely had rights of transit between their home societies and colonies.

In 1713 the British had received the asiento, the contract to sell 4,800 slaves per year to Spain's colonies, as well as to provide an annual shipment of manufactured goods. Most slaves and manufactured goods destined for foreign colonies were transshipped through Port Royal, Jamaica, the West Indian headquarters for the Royal African Company, the South Sea Company, and numerous merchant houses. Many slave traders included manufactures in their cargoes, making them subject, often legitimately, to Spanish charges of smuggling. Traders who sailed near Spanish ports, or on routes the Spanish deemed nonessential for British right of transit, were often seized by the *guarda costas.* Festering Anglo-Spanish aggravations finally erupted in war in 1739. The resolution of tensions, however, eventually arose not from military engagements but bilateral interstate negotiations. In January 1750, the Spanish and Portuguese signed a treaty that officially voided the line of demarcation defined in the Treaty of Tordesillas. In the fall of 1750, the British agreed with the Spanish to give up the asiento, thereby ending three decades of commercial hostilities.[75]

The increasing convergence and volatility of commercial and international tensions in the Caribbean in the first half of the eighteenth century reflected structural tensions within the British Empire, and between it and other European empires. The metropolitan government recognized these problems when the Seven Years' War commenced, and thought it could use the conflict to resolve both inter- and intra-empire tensions. The decline of Anglo-Spanish difficulties allowed the British to focus their efforts upon the French threat. During the War of the Austrian Succession Britain directed its military strategy toward commercial rather than territorial objectives. It shifted its focus during the Seven Years' War to the conquest of French territory. In the Caribbean, territorial conquest would reduce French and increase British sugar cultivation, and thereby enlarge the market for provisions from the mainland colonies and reduce the price of sugar in Britain. New territory, therefore, might have rebalanced relations among the existing territorial peripheries and with the metropole.[76]

This strategy reflected an increasingly prevalent metropolitan belief that problems in the empire should and could be resolved through centrally designed policy. The intensifying points of friction with Spanish and French imperial interests was one cause. But within the British world, a perception had emerged that different regions of the empire, such as the Caribbean and North American colonies, were out of alignment with each other, and that problems in one region of the empire could be resolved through adjusting relations with another. The British government attempted such a realignment, with disastrous effects, during the East India Company's financial crisis in the 1770s and its oversupply of tea. The magnitude of these intra-empire tensions had increased over the eighteenth century, and the existing practices of negotiation could not resolve them. Long-standing tensions between the metropolitan government and the North American colonies, which many observers believed had never been properly integrated into the empire, did not dispose the Ministry to consulting them in the realigning of imperial relations. Their large populations and growing wealth, however, made them central to any consumption- or revenue-driven plans to coordinate and integrate the empire.[77]

In 1774 Thomas Jefferson justified the colonists' resistance to parliamentary legislation on the grounds that British settlers in America, like the ancient Saxons of England, had left their homeland to establish colonies. The Saxons' "mother country" on the continent had not pretended that its power extended to England. Likewise, the British government could not assume that its writ extended across the Atlantic. The colonists had continued "their union with . . . [Britain] by submitting themselves to the same common sovereign."[78] Jefferson's argument was a sophisticated rendering of a long-standing interpretation by colonial British Americans of their history in both North America and the Caribbean. The importance they placed on private initiative in planting settlements in the Americas led them to coin the term *colonize*, a word David Hume admonished Benjamin Franklin for using in 1760.[79] However selective this interpretation of their history, colonists essentially argued that there was no British imperium in the Americas except that which developed out of the dominium established and legitimated by the colonists. In the decade leading up to the American Revolution, they elaborated their contention that Parliament's jurisdiction extended only to the shore of North America, articulating as constitutional principle the division between the territorial and oceanic peripheries, between the jurisdiction of the Crown-in-Parliament and the jurisdiction of colonial governments.

The initial establishment of English dominium in seventeenth-century North America occurred where there was no preexisting European, much less English, presence, either commercial or colonial. Nor did commercial and colonial interests intersect in North America as they did in the Caribbean, where merchants could reasonably hope to realize a return on their investments in settlements. The cost of settling mainland colonies quickly exhausted the working capital of organized ventures such as the Virginia Company, discouraged further investors, shifted the cost of colonial development onto the colonists themselves, and justified the core of Jefferson's claim that "their own fortunes [were] expended in making that settlement effectual."[80] After the debacle of the first two years at Jamestown (1607–9) the Virginia Company's promoters abandoned the Elizabethan emphasis on honor and profit as the rewards for overseas colonization. Rather, they launched a propaganda campaign that emphasized the establishment of a commonwealth founded on sacrifice, duty, courage, and virtue and a need "to contemne riches," a theme subsequently mimicked in the promotional literature for Newfoundland, Nova Scotia, and New England, though not in the behavior of most colonists.[81]

The atrophied, if not severed, commercial linkages between metropolitan promoters and colonists were replaced with a diverse range of economic ties. Labor contractors transported thousands of indentured servants to the colonies. Tobacco linked the Chesapeake settlements to European markets. New England merchants shipped provisions into the West Indies by the 1640s, supplemented later with grains from the mid-Atlantic colonies. New England fishermen trolled on the banks off Newfoundland and sold provisions to people who overwintered there. Furs traded down the Hudson and Connecticut Rivers found their way to hatmakers in England. Rice from South Carolina and Georgia found markets in southern Europe and the Caribbean. Indigo supplied a growing demand for textile dyes. Tobacco dominated mainland colonial trade, but on the eve of the Revolution it accounted for only 29.5 percent of British North American exports. The average annual value of tobacco shipped from the Chesapeake from 1768 to 1772 was £756,128; the comparable value of sugar was £3,910,600.[82] The fragmentation of interests that scholars have found difficult to conceptualize had a material reality in the seventeenth-century roots of these colonies.[83]

This economic diversification politically marginalized the North American colonies in Britain. Commercial interests that represented the fishery, the slave trade, West Indian planters, and the East India Company, in contrast, retained more status and influence. Not until the end of the seventeenth century did North American colonies begin to utilize London interests to lobby for them.[84] The metropole, conversely, had a weak presence in the colonies during the seventeenth century. In the Caribbean, the acquisition of colonies solidified and elaborated an existing, though still protean, commercial system. In North America, however, the colonies' greatest strengths were not immediately transportable wealth, but the establishment of extensive dominium, population growth, institutional development, the emergence of a creole elite, and the steady accretion of widely distributed wealth found in farms, houses, barns, slaves, ships, and warehouses.[85]

All of these strengths supported the internal elaboration and consolidation of colonial societies.[86] From a metropolitan perspective, however, they caused power to bleed from the center to the periphery, and were interpreted as creating a dangerous independency.[87] During the first century of colonization in North America, moreover, few structural or institutional forces could stem this flow of power. The oceanic or commercial empire, on the other hand, could be managed largely through the elaboration and extension of existing English governmental institutions, supporting the colonists' contention that the metropole's governing authority reached to the shores of the colonies. A territorial empire, however, required new institutions within colonies, thus engendering questions of constitutional structure and the nature of governance in these distant polities.[88]

In the early seventeenth century, neither the king nor his ministers foresaw that these settlements in the Americas would develop as discrete societies with separate institutional developments rather than as commercial settlements tangential to the home society. Crown officials believed that colonies should have an institutional presence in England, and initially they did, whether as proprietors or as a company's general court.[89] The presence of the Virginia Company's general court in London facilitated the revocation of its charter in 1624. Rather, than regrant it "to anie Companie or Corporation, to whom it maie be proper to trust Matters of Trade and Commerce," Charles I decided it should remain a royal colony, governed by two appointed councils, one in Virginia and one in England. The latter was never appointed, though for six years the Mandeville Commission provided metropolitan oversight.[90]

The Massachusetts Bay Company removed its government and charter to New England, leaving no institutional presence in England, and prompting the King's Bench to revoke the charter in 1637. The court decided, however, that it needed the physical document for revocation to be complete. Massachusetts' governor John Winthrop procrastinated so long that when Charles I was forced to call Parliament in 1640 a sympathetic House of Commons (and subsequent civil war) effectively removed the threat to the colony and nullified the order to return the charter to England.[91] During the 1680s the Privy Council tried to revoke all the colonial company and proprietary charters and establish royal governments. In the proceedings against the Massachusetts Bay Company, however, the absence of a company presence in London meant that the court could not serve a quo warranto writ to appear in court without it expiring before it was delivered. It chose instead to issue a writ of scire facias ordering the Bay Colony to respond to the charges. When the colony ignored the writ, the king's court revoked the charter in 1684. Despite nearly five decades between 1637 and 1684, the proceedings in both instances stalled due to the lack of an institutional presence for the Bay Colony in England.[92]

Over the seventeenth century, institutions, policies, and practices for governing the empire slowly emerged, including the expansion of the navy, the passage of the Navigation Acts, and the elaboration of customs collections, though most were geared toward domestic government in England or European affairs rather than transoceanic interests.[93] These developments were sufficient to integrate the commercial or oceanic empire into the metropolitan order, but they were insufficient for the territorial empire where distinct institutions emerged.

The office of the royal governor is a case in point. Though royal staff, governors were not paid from the monarch's permanent revenue, nor did the Crown's ministers devise a consistent policy for paying them, except the principle that the monies should come from colonial sources. For Virginia, the first royal colony, the governor's salary initially came from tobacco duties until the outbreak of Civil War. After 1660, it was paid from a two-shilling-per-hogshead export duty on tobacco, which the House of Burgesses made permanent in 1680 in exchange for a pardon for Nathaniel Bacon. Virginia was the only continental colony with a permanent revenue. In the 1660s, the assemblies of Barbados and the Leeward Islands agreed to a permanent 4-percent duty on all exports in exchange for freehold tenure of land. That duty produced enough revenues that it helped fund the salaries of governors in Bermuda, North Carolina, South Carolina, and the Bahamas. At different times, part of the salaries for the governors of Bermuda and South Carolina came from captaincies of independent companies of foot (infantry), and thus drew from military funds. The Jamaican assembly did not vote a permanent revenue until 1728, and then only in exchange for recognizing that its constitutional rights were the same as the nonconquered colonies. In North Carolina, New Jersey, and New York, governors attempted to raise part of their salaries from quitrents. Only in the royal colonies of New York, New Jersey, New Hampshire, and Massachusetts was the funding of governors' salaries highly politicized. In 1770 the Ministry ordered that the governors of New York and Massachusetts be paid out of tea duties legislated in the Townshend Revenue Acts (1767), thus linking tea with the contentious issue of salaries.[94]

The funding of governors' salaries provides a graphic example of the kind of institutional innovations that territorial peripheries generated, arrangements that were negotiated colony-by-colony and that resulted in great variation. Diverse institutional arrangements also defined land granting, the calling of assemblies and the voting of taxes, the selection and appointment of colonial officials, and the structure of local government. These developments took decades to refine and provoked contention and negotiation between colonists and metropolitan officials. Colonists, however, generally prevailed in defining administrative arrangements because they financed and staffed most colonial institutions. In the particularities of day-to-day administrative practices, colonists rooted many of their arguments that their constitutions were separate and distinct from England's and Scotland's.

The scope for institutional innovation, and hence metropolitan-colonial friction, was much greater in the North American colonies than in the Atlantic and Caribbean island colonies. Most continental colonies had imprecise, contested, and shifting boundaries, and the vast extent of territory allowed for the creation of new colonies, such as Georgia, or the conquest of others, such as Nova Scotia. These North American borderlands, whether the Carolina and Virginia backcountry, or Georgia, Maine, and Nova Scotia, were zones in which the metropole attempted policy innovations with increasing frequency beginning in the late seventeenth century.[95] Innovations on these colonial peripheries often produced a concatenation of effects that, coupled with rapidly growing colonial populations, became volatile by the mid-eighteenth century. To illustrate the ways in which metropolitan-designed innovations fed into other patterns of convergence in the empire, this section will conclude with a brief look at the shifting and broadening definition of Crown lands.

In the seventeenth century the Stuart kings had staunchly defended their royal prerogative to treat American lands as their own to grant to clients and to govern as they saw fit. When the King's Bench revoked the Virginia charter in 1624, James I and then Charles I rebuffed Parliament's attempts to become involved in the colony.[96] In 1649 the exiled Charles II granted the Northern Neck of Virginia between the Rappahannock and Potomac Rivers to supporters, giving them rights "to hold courts baron, to have markets and fairs, collect tolls, customs, fines and other perquisites including quitrents." After 1660, the grantees pressed their claims, joined in 1674 by Lord Arlington and Thomas Culpepper, to whom Charles II had granted similar rights in the southern portion of Virginia. These manorial and property rights, the latter of which conflicted with settlers' rights, contributed to Bacon's Rebellion in 1676.[97]

After the Restoration, the Privy Council gradually asserted more control over land in the Americas, attempting to revoke all colonial charters and to keep Charles II from granting more.[98] The grant of Pennsylvania to William Penn, a personal friend of the king, in 1681 was the last proprietary or company colony created in the Americas. The Privy Council also scrutinized landholding practices in New England, particularly the "corporate" ownership of land by towns. To resolve the problem, the colonies of Plymouth and Connecticut passed legislation in 1682 and 1685, respectively, to issue patents for common lands to named groups of proprietors. After James II created the Dominion of New England in 1685, all undivided lands technically became Crown lands. Edmund Andros, the governor, declared town commons in Massachusetts to be wild and vacant, therefore Crown lands, and he could grant them to others in his capacity as the king's agent. After the overthrow of the dominion government in 1689 and the regranting of the Massachusetts charter in 1691, the Bay Colony followed the lead of its smaller neighbors and granted land to groups of proprietors rather than to towns.[99]

The 1691 royal charter of Massachusetts instituted a major change in the definition of Crown lands. It reserved all trees twenty-four inches in diameter or larger for the British navy. In 1705 Parliament passed "An Act for the Encouraging of Importation of Naval Stores" that is most commonly seen as an addition to the Navigation Acts. But its larger importance is the way it redefined property rights by giving the Crown preeminent claims to "Pitch, Pine, or Tar Trees" twelve inches or less in diameter from New Jersey through Maine. Further legislation in 1711 expanded the 1705 act to include all white pine trees for the masting of the royal navy. When the French ceded Nova Scotia to the British in 1713, the terms of the Massachusetts charter and subsequent parliamentary legislation were interpreted to include this newest colony.[100] The 1691 Massachusetts charter and the 1705 and 1711 legislation mark a shift from American lands and their resources being treated by Britain's monarchs as a vast reserve of patronage to be given to worthy clients to being defined in terms of state needs.

These preeminent royal claims, whether through charter clauses or parliamentary legislation, were defiantly violated by New England timbermen. In 1685, the first colonial surveyor of pines and timber had been appointed, subsequently upgraded in 1691 to surveyor general of all Crown forests in America. Men from New England or posted there always held this office, which eventually became part of the office of the governor of New Hampshire. When the surveyor general did lay charges against timbermen for cutting the Crown's timber, the charges were not upheld by the colonial courts, which had judges and juries sympathetic to local interests.[101] In the 1760s, the Board of Trade held up royal approval of land grants in eastern Maine in an attempt both to wrest control of that area from Boston and to protect naval reserves. That conflict encouraged patriot sentiment among settlers downeast who could not get clear title to the land they claimed.[102]

In New England, the Board of Trade had difficulty enforcing these policy initiatives because most of the administrative apparatuses to enforce them, particularly the courts, were controlled by colonists. In newly acquired jurisdictions such as Nova Scotia, the Board of Trade could enforce these changes, but the weakness of collateral institutions thwarted smooth implementation. The royally appointed governor in Nova Scotia could grant land, but only after surveying for naval stores, an enormous task that required considerable financial resources. The colony had no money, and the metropole provided almost none. Until the French-speaking Catholic settlers swore oaths of allegiance between 1727 and 1730, they were technically not the king's subjects, did not have their lands titled, and did not pay even paltry quitrents. More significantly, they could not participate in government, and thus there was no assembly to vote taxes, nor did the governor have the authority to levy them. Without money to survey the land, it could not be granted to Protestant settlers who could participate in government. Until 1748, when Parliament provided money to build Halifax as a naval port, the settlement of Nova Scotia was largely paralyzed by a combination of a restrictive land policy, no money, and a non-British, non-Protestant population.[103]

The inadequacy of imperial institutions to manage these circumstances reflected the extent to which the metropole was unprepared for direct, rather than delegated, governance of a territorial empire. Naval reserves were the extension of a discrete metropolitan need with the assumption that colonial institutions could or would implement and administer the policy. In New England, the solidity of settlement and colonist control made naval stores policies ineffective. In Nova Scotia, the lack of money and English-speaking, Protestant settlers made the policies ineffective. In the latter colony, and then throughout post-1783 British North America, new institutions eventually matured that supported greater Crown control of land.

Shifting metropolitan concern with Indian relations also precipitated land policy changes. In the 1740s, the growing international competition among imperial powers, particularly between France and Britain, enhanced the need of the British metropolitan government to control extra-European territory. In North America, that need depended on more direct relations with Native peoples, and the metropolitan government made steps toward removing Indian relations from colonial to imperial jurisdiction; in 1755 it appointed two Indian commissioners, William Johnson for the territory north of the Ohio River and John Stuart for the south. The Seven Years' War elevated the problems of land, money, and non-British subjects to continent-wide issues that could not be delegated back to individual colonies. The Proclamation of

1763 attempted a partial resolution when it declared lands west of the Appalachian Mountains to be Crown lands, gave the first right of occupancy to Indians, and declared that their rights could only be extinguished through an agent of the Crown.[104]

The reservation of naval stores, the building of Halifax, the appointment of Indian commissioners, and the Proclamation of 1763 were decisions made in Westminster and Whitehall with little or no colonial consultation. From Maine to South Carolina colonists responded with various degrees of resentment, resistance, and concern at the expansion of metropolitan influence in North America. Few New England timbermen honored the Naval Stores Act; North American colonists worried about the broader implications of Nova Scotia being governed without an assembly; and settlers ignored the strictures on westward expansion as they pushed across the Appalachian Mountains. Parliament's legislation to tax the colonists, beginning with the Sugar Act in 1764, marked a rapid acceleration of institutional integration that had begun at the end of the seventeenth century. But this time it struck at the core of the old territorial empire rather than on its newer peripheries, and the result was rebellion and independence.[105]

Until the early decades of the eighteenth century, the oceanic and territorial empires had quite particularistic chronologies of institutional development and integration with the metropole. The institutions that coordinated the oceanic empire were largely extensions of metropolitan institutions and by the end of the seventeenth century included, in most cases, both Whitehall and Westminster. The political connections of metropolitan-based commercial interests had helped to shape the involvement of both the Ministry and Parliament in the development and regulation of the oceanic empire. Parliament ended the Royal African Company's monopoly on the slave trade in 1698, passed legislation in 1699 to regulate the fishery, and issued the charter for the United East India Company in 1709.

In contrast, seventeenth-century institutional developments in the territorial empire were separate from, rather than extensions of, the metropole's institutions. Measures that linked the interests of the metropolitan center with the internal organization of colonies began to occur at the end of the seventeenth century with measures such as the Crown claims to naval stores. But without the financial resources to enforce the policies or create the necessary related institutions, the policies had little impact in the colonies established in the seventeenth century. Not until the mid-eighteenth century did the metropolitan government begin to combine policy initiatives with the funding necessary to make them effective in overseas dominions. In short, the relatively complete integration of the oceanic periphery into an imperial system occurred a half century before the integration of the territorial peripheries was systematically undertaken, and occurred as an outcome of political maneuvering and negotiation within Britain.

The attempts to integrate institutionally the territorial empire with both the oceanic empire and the metropole coincided with and were propelled by structural stresses in various British overseas arenas and between empires. The Ministry and Parliament sought to resolve problems with one compensatory measure after another, often formulated without adequate information from or sufficient negotiation with the peripheries. Quite often these measures involved the North American colonies, for by the mid-eighteenth century population growth had made them a vast consumer market, a reserve of military manpower, a source of settlers for new colonies such as Nova Scotia and Quebec, and a trove of potential revenues for a seriously indebted government. As a consequence, these circumstances had made the North American colonies structurally critical within the empire in ways they had not previously been. But population growth and the steady accretion of colonial wealth had also made resistance and independence a viable proposition. Without a metropolitan willingness to negotiate rather than dictate resolutions to imperial problems, these colonists would resist.

The loss of thirteen colonies, the cession of the trans-Appalachian west to the United States, and the return of the Floridas to Spain represented an enormous loss that left many wondering if the British Empire would survive. But the new United States had been only part of the empire and international struggles over empire in the long eighteenth century would not expend themselves until the end of the Napoleonic Wars.[106] Britain may have lost against its own colonies, but against its European competitors it triumphed, and by 1820 its empire had both stabilized and expanded. In the last decades of the early modern contest for empire, the new United States emerged as a vigorous competitor. Hundreds of American ships penetrated the Pacific arena and benefited from the Anglo-Spanish standoff in 1789–90 at Nootka Sound on Vancouver Island. Thomas Jefferson commissioned Meriwether Lewis and William Clark to lead an expedition across French and Spanish territory to the Pacific. By the time they left, the United States had purchased Louisiana from France, and British, Russian, and American intrusions had weakened Spanish claims to the Oregon Country.[107]

Much of the resilience of the British Empire after the American Revolution can be explained by the degree to which the oceanic peripheries and the newer territorial peripheries had been successfully integrated with and linked to the metropole. The extensive merchant networks remained,[108] and the American consumer market was reinvigorated. The remaining colonies of British North America—Nova Scotia, New Brunswick, Prince Edward Island, and Upper and Lower Canada—accepted institutional integration with the metropole, largely because in them the authority of metropolitan imperium had never been separated from the authority derived from dominium, as it had been in the colonies settled in the seventeenth century. And British subjects at home and in the colonies had come to accept the prerogative of the metropolitan government to use overseas territories to realign the British world, as manifested in the recolonization of free blacks from Nova Scotia and Britain to Sierra Leone, the transportation of convicts to Australia, and the incarceration of Napoleon on St. Helena.

Notes

When writing this essay, I benefited enormously from exchanges with Stephen Hornsby, who is working on a book-length analysis of British America from Hudson Bay to the Caribbean Basin. David Armitage, Mike Braddick, Jack Greene, Dick Nelson, and Steve Whitman served as responsive and critical sounding boards for different parts of the argument. Each has a right to claim credit for discrete merits within the essay, while I alone am responsible for the entire package.

1. H. V. Bowen, "British Conceptions of Global Empire, 1756–83," *Journal of Imperial and Commonwealth History* 26 (1998), 1–27; and P. J. Marshall, "Britain and the World in the Eighteenth Century, I: Reshaping the Empire," *Transactions of the Royal Historical Society*, 6th ser., 8 (1998), 1–18.
2. Daniel A. Baugh, "Maritime Strength and Atlantic Commerce: The Uses of a 'Grand Marine Empire,'" in Lawrence Stone, ed., *An Imperial State at War: Britain from 1689 to 1815* (London: Routledge, 1994), 185–223; and N. A. M. Rodger, "Sea-Power and Empire, 1688–1793," in P. J. Marshall, ed., *The Oxford History of the British Empire* (hereafter *OHBE*), vol. 2, *The Eighteenth Century* (Oxford: Oxford University Press, 1998), 169–83.
3. Thomas Perkins Abernethy, *Western Lands and the American Revolution* (New York: Russell and Russell, 1959); and Marc Egnal, *A Mighty Empire: The Origins of the American Revolution* (Ithaca, N.Y.: Cornell University Press, 1988).
4. Linda Colley, *Britons: Forging the Nation 1707–1837* (New Haven, Conn.: Yale University Press, 1992), 101–45; Kathleen Wilson, *The Sense of the People: Politics, Culture and Imperialism in England, 1715–1785* (New York: Cambridge University Press, 1995), 137–205; and Peter N. Miller, *Defining the Common Good: Empire, Religion and Philosophy in Eighteenth-Century Britain* (New York: Cambridge University Press, 1994), 150–213.
5. Elizabeth Mancke, "Early Modern Expansion and the Politicization of Oceanic Space," *Geographical Review* 89 (1999), 225–36.
6. Kenneth R. Andrews, *Trade, Plunder and Settlement: Maritime Enterprise and the Genesis of the British Empire, 1480–1630* (Cambridge: Cambridge University Press, 1984), 10–17; John C. Appleby, "War, Politics, and Colonization, 1558–1625," in Nicholas Canny, ed., *OHBE* vol. 1, *The Origins of Empire: British Overseas Enterprise to the Close of the Seventeenth Century* (Oxford: Oxford University Press, 1998), 55–78; and Michael J. Braddick, "The English Government, War, Trade, and Settlement, 1625–1688," in *OHBE* 1:286–308.
7. David Armitage, *The Ideological Origins of the British Empire* (Cambridge: Cambridge University Press, 2000).
8. For further discussions of the medieval and early modern contexts of *imperium* and *dominium* see James Muldoon, *Empire and Order: The Concept of Empire, 800–1800* (New York: St. Martin's Press, 1999); Anthony Pagden, *Lords of All the World: Ideologies of Empire in Spain, Britain and France c.1500-c.1800* (New Haven, Conn.: Yale University Press, 1995), 11–62; and John Robertson, "Empire and Union: Two Concepts of the Early Modern European Political Order," in Robertson, ed., *A Union for Empire: Political Thought and the British Union of 1707* (Cambridge: Cambridge University Press, 1995), 3–36.
9. Charles Tilly, "Reflections on the History of European State-Making," in Tilly, ed., *The Formation of National States in Western Europe* (Princeton, N.J.: Princeton University Press, 1975), 70–71; Mark Greengrass, "Conquest and Coalescence," in Greengrass, ed., *Conquest and Coalescence: The Shaping of the State in Early Modern Europe* (London: Edward Arnold, 1991), 1–24.
10. Armitage, *The Ideological Origins of the British Empire*, 100–24. That redefinition voided traditional Dutch fishing rights in English waters, engendering hostility between erstwhile allies.
11. Jack P. Greene, "Negotiated Authorities: The Problem of Governance in the Extended Polities of the Early Modern Atlantic World," in Greene, *Negotiated Authorities: Essays on Colonial Political and Constitutional History* (Charlottesville: University Press of Virginia, 1994), 1–24.
12. A fourth arena of negotiation, that this essay can mention only in passing, was between Europeans and their non-European hosts.
13. P. J. Marshall, "Britain without America—A Second Empire?" in *OHBE* 2:576–95.
14. Frances Gardiner Davenport, ed., *European Treaties Bearing on the History of the United States and Its Dependencies to 1648* (1917; reprt. Gloucester, Mass.: P. Smith, 1967), 56–100.

15. Anne Pérotin-Dumon, "The Pirate and the Emperor: Power and the Law on the Seas, 1450–1850," in James D. Tracy, ed., *The Political Economy of Merchant Empires* (Cambridge: Cambridge University Press, 1991), 197–98.
16. W. J. Eccles, *France in America*, rev. ed. (Markham, Ont.: Fitzhenry and Whiteside, 1990), 3; Davenport, *European Treaties to 1648*, 2–3; Philip P. Boucher, *Les Nouvelles Frances: France in America, 1500–1815, An Imperial Perspective* (Providence, R.I.: John Carter Brown Library, 1989), 5–9; Andrews, *Trade, Plunder and Settlement*, 106–12, 223–55; Appleby, "War, Politics, and Colonization, 1558–1625," in *OHBE* 1:56; and C. R. Boxer, *The Dutch Seaborne Empire: 1600–1800* (New York: Alfred A. Knopf, 1965), 22–30.
17. David B. Quinn, "James I and the Beginnings of Empire in America," *Journal of Imperial and Commonwealth History* 2 (1974), 235–52.
18. On the nature of subjecthood in British America see James H. Kettner, *The Development of American Citizenship, 1608–1870* (Chapel Hill: University of North Carolina Press, 1978), 3–128.
19. J. H. Elliott, *Imperial Spain 1496–1716* (New York: St. Martin's Press, 1964), 58–59, 62–64. Exceptions for enslaving Indians were made in the remote regions of the empire; see Ramón A. Gutiérrez, *When Jesus Came, the Corn Mothers Went Away: Marriage, Sexuality, and Power in New Mexico, 1500–1846* (Stanford, Calif.: Stanford University Press, 1991), 150–51.
20. While the implications of this point are too broad to pursue here, it is reasonable to suggest that English colonists emphasized their Englishness and were wary of "going native" in part because the competitive international politics of expansion had placed a premium on European identities to legitimate claims to dominium. For discussions of this issue, see J. H. Elliott, *Britain and Spain in America: Colonists and Colonized* (Reading, U.K.: University of Reading, 1994); James Muldoon, "The Indian as Irishman," *Essex Institute Historical Collections* 111 (1975), 267–89; and Nicholas Canny, "The Permissive Frontier: The Problem of Social Control in English Settlements in Ireland and Virginia 1550–1650," in K. R. Andrews, N. P. Canny, and P. E. H. Hair, eds., *The Westward Enterprise: English Activities in Ireland, the Atlantic, and America 1480–1650* (Detroit: Wayne State University Press, 1979), 17–44.
21. Andrews, *Trade, Plunder and Settlement*, 356–64.
22. Not until the mid-eighteenth century did the British penetrate the Pacific basin; see Glyndyr Williams, "The Pacific: Exploration and Exploitation," in *OHBE* 2:552–75.
23. Distinguishing between the oceanic and territorial peripheries would help in sorting out the question of how much Parliament legislated for the empire. On this scholary controversy see Ian K. Steele, "The British Parliament and the Atlantic Colonies to 1760: New Approaches to Enduring Questions," 29–46, and Jack P. Greene, "Competing Authorities: The Debate Over Parliamentary Imperial Jurisdiction, 1763–1776," 46–64, both in Philip Lawson, ed., *Parliament and the Atlantic Empire* (Edinburgh: Edinburgh University Press, 1995).
24. Gillian T. Cell, *English Enterprise in Newfoundland 1577–1660* (Toronto: University of Toronto Press, 1969), 47–51; Ralph Greenlee Lounsbury, *The British Fishery at Newfoundland 1634–1763* (New Haven, Conn.: Yale University Press, 1934), 28, 31; and Andrews, *Trade, Plunder and Settlement*, 304–7. On the shift in control of the fishery from the Iberians to the French and English see John Mannion and Selma Barkham, "The 16th Century Fishery," in R. Cole Harris, ed., *The Historical Atlas of Canada* (hereafter *HAC*), vol. 1, *From the Beginning to 1800* (Toronto: University of Toronto Press, 1987), Plate 22; and John Mannion and Gordon Handcock, "The 17th Century Fishery," Ibid., Plate 23. The extent of the Portuguese involvement is hard to substantiate; see Darlene Abreu-Ferreira, "Terra Nova through the Iberian Looking Glass: The Portuguese-Newfoundland Cod Fishery in the Sixteenth Century," *Canadian Historical Review* 79 (1998), 100–15.
25. Cell, *English Enterprise in Newfoundland*, 53–81; and N. E. S. Griffiths, "1600–1650: Fish, Fur, and Folk," in Phillip A. Buckner and John G. Reid, eds., *The Atlantic Region to Confederation: A History* (Toronto: University of Toronto Press, 1994), 55–56.
26. Lounsbury, *The British Fishery*, 109, 190–203; and C. Grant Head, *Eighteenth Century Newfoundland: A Geographer's Perspective* (Toronto: McClelland and Stewart, 1976),

100–37. For an analysis of the role of agriculture in Newfoundland see Sean T. Cadigan, *Hope and Deception in Conception Bay: Merchant-Settler Relations in Newfoundland, 1785–1855* (Toronto: University of Toronto Press, 1995).

27. Quoted in "The Atlantic Realm," *HAC* 1:48.
28. Quoted in Cell, *English Enterprise in Newfoundland*, 56.
29. Lounsbury, *The British Fishery at Newfoundland*, 55–91.
30. Lounsbury, *The British Fishery at Newfoundland*, 77–91; and Cell, *English Enterprise in Newfoundland*, 114–25.
31. Lounsbury, *The British Fishery in Newfoundland*, 92–148; and Cell, *English Enterprise in Newfoundland*, 119–25.
32. Lounsbury, *The British Fishery in Newfoundland*, 149–203; John G. Reid, "1686–1720: Imperial Intrusions," in Buckner and Reid, eds., *The Atlantic Region to Confederation*, 78–103; and Alan F. Williams, *Father Baudoin's War: D'Iberville's Campaign in Acadia and Newfoundland, 1696, 1697* (St. John's: Department of Geography, Memorial University of Newfoundland, 1987).
33. Peter Neary, "The French and American Shore Questions as Factors in Newfoundland History," in James Hiller and Peter Neary, eds., *Newfoundland in the Nineteenth and Twentieth Centuries: Essays in Interpretation* (Toronto: University of Toronto Press, 1980), 95–122; and Frederic F. Thompson, *The French Shore Problem in Newfoundland: An Imperial Study* (Toronto: University of Toronto Press, 1961). The practical restraints on sovereignty became a political grievance between Newfoundlanders and the metropolitan government after the island received a year-round governor in 1824 and an assembly in 1832, exacerbated by the existence of similar rights granted to the Americans in 1783 and 1814. The international complications were largely resolved in the early twentieth century, when the French agreed in 1904 to relinquish their shore privileges in exchange for concessions in Africa; in 1910, the international court in The Hague adjudicated the Newfoundland-American dispute.
34. David Richardson, "The British Empire and the Atlantic Slave Trade, 1660–1807," in *OHBE* 2:444–45; Philip D. Morgan, "The Black Experience in the British Empire, 1680–1810," in *OHBE* 2:465–66; Philip D. Curtin, *The Image of Africa: British Ideas and Action, 1780–1850* (Madison: University of Wisconsin Press, 1964), 97–139, 157–59; and James W. St. G. Walker, *The Black Loyalists: The Search for a Promised Land in Nova Scotia and Sierra Leone 1783–1870* (New York: Africana, 1976), 94–114, 258–63.
35. Jonathan I. Israel, *Dutch Primacy in World Trade, 1585–1740* (Oxford: Clarendon Press, 1989), 161–70, 236–44, 319–29; and Richardson, "The British Empire and the Atlantic Slave Trade, 1660–1870," in *OHBE* 2:440.
36. David Birmingham, *The Portuguese Conquest of Angola* (London: Oxford University Press, 1965); M. D. D. Newitt, *A History of Mozambique* (Bloomington: Indiana University Press, 1995); and Newitt, "East Africa and the Indian Ocean Trade: 1500–1800," in Ashin Das Gupta and M. N. Pearson, eds., *India and the Indian Ocean, 1500–1800* (Calcutta: Oxford University Press, 1987), 201–23.
37. John Kelly Thornton, *Africa and Africans in the Making of the Atlantic World, 1400–1800*, 2d ed. (Cambridge: Cambridge University Press, 1998); and Robin Law, *The Slave Coast of West Africa 1550–1750: The Impact of the Atlantic Slave Trade on an African Society* (Oxford: Clarendon Press, 1991).
38. P. E. H. Hair and Robin Law, "The English in Western Africa to 1700," in *OHBE* 1:251–55.
39. Ibid., 255–59; Kenneth Gordon Davies, *The Royal African Company* (New York: Longmans, Green, 1960), 344–45; and Richardson, "The British Empire and the Atlantic Slave Trade," in *OHBE* 2:444–45; and W. R. Scott, *The Constitution and Finance of English, Scottish and Irish Joint-Stock Companies to 1720*, vol. 2, *Companies for Foreign Trade, Colonization, Fishing and Mining* (1912; reprt. New York: P. Smith, 1951), 20–25.
40. Richardson, "The British Empire and the Atlantic Slave Trade," in *OHBE* 446–47; Richardson, "Cape Verde, Madeira and Britain's Trade to Africa, 1698–1740," *JICH* 22 (1994), 11–15; and Paul G. E. Clemens, "The Rise of Liverpool, 1665–1750," *Economic History Review*, 2d ser., no. 29 (1976), 211–25.

41. Pagden, *Lords of All the World*, 178–200; and Nancy F. Koehn, *The Power of Commerce: Economy and Governance in the First British Empire* (Ithaca, N.Y.: Cornell University Press, 1994).
42. D. K. Bassett, "Early English Trade and Settlement in Asia, 1602–1690," in J. S. Bromley and E. H. Kossmann, eds., *Britain and the Netherlands in Europe and Asia* (London: Macmillan, 1968), 83–109; reprinted in Anthony Disney, ed., *Historiography of Europeans in Africa and Asia, 1450–1800* (Brookfield, Vt.: Variorum, 1995), 127–53.
43. Andrews, *Trade, Plunder and Settlement*, 64–115, 167–82, 256–79; and P. J. Marshall, "The English in Asia to 1700," in *OHBE* 1:264–68.
44. Marshall, "The English in Asia," in *OHBE* 1:265–67; and Philip Lawson, *The East India Company: A History* (London: Longmans, 1993), 24–30.
45. Lawson, *The East India Company*, 46–48.
46. Holden Furber, *Rival Empires of Trade in the Orient 1600–1800* (Minneapolis: University of Minnesota Press, 1976), 89–103.
47. Bruce P. Lenman, "Colonial Wars and Imperial Instability, 1688–1793," in *OHBE* 2:157–60; and Williams, "The Pacific: Exploration and Exploitation," in *OHBE* 2:553–55.
48. Lawson, *The East India Company*, 33–34.
49. Ibid., 38–40; and Marshall, "The English in Asia," in *OHBE* 1:276–77.
50. Lawson, *The East India Company*, 33, 44, 55–57, 74–77; John Brewer, *The Sinews of Power: War, Money and the English State, 1688–1783* (London: Unwin Hyman, 1989), 120, 124; H. V. Bowen, *Revenue and Reform: The Indian Problem in British Politics 1757–1773* (Cambridge: Cambridge University Press, 1991), 18–21; and Bruce G. Carruthers, *City of Capital: Politics and Markets in the English Financial Revolution* (Princeton, N.J.: Princeton University Press, 1996), 137–59.
51. Furber, *Rival Empires*, 146–50.
52. P. J. Marshall, "British Expansion in India in the Eighteenth Century: A Historical Revision," *History* 49 (1964), 28–43; and C. A. Bayly, *Imperial Meridian: The British Empire and the World 1780–1830* (London: Longman, 1989), 16–74.
53. Marshall, "The British in India," in *OHBE* 2:485–507, provides a useful overview of the issues. See also Lawson, *The East India Company*, 86–102; and Furber, *Rival Empires*, 146–84.
54. Bowen, *Revenue and Reform*, 15.
55. Ibid., 48–50; and Marie Peters, "The Myth of William Pitt, Earl of Chatham, Great Imperialist, part II: Chatham and Imperial Reorganization 1763–78," *JICH* 22 (1994), 399–404.
56. Quoted in Bowen, *Revenue and Reform*, 53.
57. Ibid., 54–66.
58. Ibid., 103–6.
59. Ibid., 107–10, 117, 124–25; and Bowen, "Tea, Tribute and the East India Company c.1750-c.1775," in Stephen Taylor, Richard Connors, and Clyve Jones, eds., *Hanoverian Britain and Empire: Essays in Memory of Philip Lawson* (Woodbridge, U.K.: Boydell Press, 1998), 158–76.
60. Bowen, *Revenue and Reform*, 169–86; and Bowen, "British India, 1765–1813: The Metropolitan Context," in *OHBE* 2:530–51.
61. Quoted in Bowen, *Revenue and Reform*, 124.
62. Benjamin W. Labaree, *The Boston Tea Party* (New York: Oxford University Press, 1964); Philip Lawson, "Sources, Schools and Separation: The Many Faces of Parliament's Role in Anglo-American History to 1783," in Lawson, ed., *Parliament and the Atlantic Empire*, 18–27; and T. H. Breen, "'The Baubles of Britain': The American and Consumer Revolutions of the Eighteenth Century," *Past and Present*, No. 119 (1988): 97–102.
63. Quoted in Bowen, *Revenue and Reform*, 175–76. On the importance of rights to the English conception of themselves, see Jack P. Greene, "Empire and Identity from the Glorious Revolution to the American Revolution," in *OHBE* 2:208–30.
64. Richard B. Sheridan, *Sugar and Slavery: An Economic History of the British West Indies 1623–1775* (Baltimore: Johns Hopkins University Press, 1973), 123.

65. Andrews, *Trade, Plunder and Settlement*, 280–303; Andrews, *The Spanish Caribbean: Trade and Plunder, 1530–1630* (New Haven, Conn.: Yale University Press, 1978), 224–55; Hilary McD. Beckles, "The 'Hub of Empire': The Caribbean and Britain in the Seventeenth Century," in *OHBE* 1:221; Philip P. Boucher, *Cannibal Encounters: Europeans and Island Caribs, 1492–1763* (Baltimore: Johns Hopkins University Press, 1992); Karen Ordahl Kupperman, *Providence Island, 1630–1641: The Other Puritan Colony* (Cambridge: Cambridge University Press, 1993); and Joyce Lorimer, "The Failure of the English Guiana Ventures 1595–1667 and James I's Foreign Policy," *JICH* 21 (1993), 1–30.
66. Andrews, *Trade, Plunder and Settlement*, 280–303; Andrews, *The Spanish Caribbean*, 224–55; and John C. Appleby, "English Settlement in the Lesser Antilles during War and Peace, 1603–1660," in Robert L. Paquette and Stanley L. Engerman, eds., *The Lesser Antilles in the Age of European Expansion* (Gainesville: University Press of Florida, 1996), 86–104. Examples of studies modeled on the North American colonies are Carl and Roberta Bridenbaugh, *No Peace Beyond the Line: The English in the Caribbean, 1624–1690* (New York: Oxford University Press, 1972); Kupperman, *Providence Island, 1630–1641*; and Richard S. Dunn, *Sugar and Slaves: The Rise of the Planter Class in the English West Indies, 1624–1713* (Chapel Hill: University of North Carolina Press, 1972).
67. Sheridan, *Sugar and Slavery*, 80–95, 262–81.
68. Ibid., 308–19.
69. Ibid., 306–8. For a recent case study of this issue see David Hancock, "'A World of Business to Do': William Freeman and the Foundations of England's Commercial Empire, 1645–1707," *William and Mary Quarterly* 3rd ser., 58 (2000), 3–34.
70. Dunn, *Sugar and Slaves*, 144–47; Sheridan, *Sugar and Slavery*, 44–8; and Michael Craton, "Property and Propriety: Land Tenure and Slave Property in the Creation of a British West Indian Plantocracy, 1612–1740," in John Brewer and Susan Staves, eds., *Early Modern Conceptions of Property* (London: Routledge, 1996), 497–511.
71. Jack P. Greene, "The Jamaica Privilege Controversy, 1764–66: An Episode in the Process of Constitutional Definition in the Early Modern British Empire," *JICH* 22 (1994), 16–53.
72. Nuala Zahedieh, "Overseas Expansion and Trade in the Seventeenth Century," in *OHBE* 1:410, 415; Sheridan, *Sugar and Slavery*, 309; and Richardson, "The British Empire and the Atlantic Slave Trade, 1660–1807," in *OHBE* 2:456.
73. Sheridan, *Sugar and Slavery*, 218–22; and Richard Pares, *War and Trade in the West Indies 1739–1763* (Oxford: Oxford University Press, 1936), 77–85, 475–82.
74. Sheridan, *Sugar and Slavery*, 314–16, 322–23, 352–56, 445–46; and Pares, *War and Trade in the West Indies*, 394–403.
75. Sheridan, *Sugar and Slavery*, 218–19, 249–25, 316–19; Pares, *War and Trade in the West Indies*, 1–64, 517–40; and Peggy K. Liss, *Atlantic Empires: The Network of Trade and Revolution, 1713–1826* (Baltimore: Johns Hopkins University Press, 1983), 9–14.
76. Pares, *War and Trade in the West Indies*, 221–23; and D. H. Murdoch, "Land Policy in the Eighteenth-Century British Empire: The Sale of Crown Lands in the Ceded Islands, 1763–1783," *Historical Journal* 27 (1984), 549–74.
77. Jack P. Greene, "'A Posture of Hostility': A Reconsideration of Some Aspects of the Origins of the American Revolution," *Proceedings of the American Antiquarian Society* 87 (1977), 27–68; Greene, "The Seven Years' War and the American Revolution: The Causal Relationship Reconsidered," in P. J. Marshall and Glyn Williams, eds., *The British Atlantic Empire before the American Revolution* (London: Frank Cass, 1980), 85–105; J. M. Bumsted, "'Things in the Womb of Time': Ideas of American Independence, 1633 to 1763," *William and Mary Quarterly* 3rd ser., vol. 31 (1974), 533–64; and T. H. Breen, "An Empire of Goods: The Anglicization of Colonial America, 1690–1776," *Journal of British Studies* 25 (1986), 467–99.
78. Thomas Jefferson, "A Summary View of the Rights of British-America," in Jack P. Greene, ed., *Colonies to Nation 1763–1789: A Documentary History of the American Revolution* (New York: W. W. Norton, 1975), 227–38, quote on 229.
79. Michael Kammen, "The Meaning of Colonization in American Revolutionary

Thought," *Journal of the History of Ideas* 31 (1970), 337–58. For similar arguments in the Caribbean see Greene, "The Jamaica Privilege Controversy," passim.

80. Jefferson, "A Summary View of the Rights of British-America," 228.
81. Andrew Fitzmaurice,"The Civic Solution to the Crisis of English Colonization, 1609–1625," *Historical Journal* 42 (1999), 25–51; and Robert M. Bliss, *Revolution and Empire: English Politics and the American Colonies in the Seventeenth Century* (Manchester, U.K.: Manchester University Press, 1990), 11–3, 15–16.
82. John J. McCusker and Russell R. Menard, *The Economy of British America, 1607–1789* (Chapel Hill: University of North Carolina Press, 1985), 108, 130, 160, 174, 199.
83. Jack P. Greene and J. R. Pole, "Reconstructing British-American Colonial History: An Introduction," in Greene and Pole, eds., *Colonial British America; Essays in the New History of the Early Modern Era* (Baltimore: Johns Hopkins University Press, 1984), 1–17; and Jack P. Greene, "Interpretive Frameworks: The Quest for Intellectual Order in Early American History," *William and Mary Quarterly* 3rd ser., vol. 48 (1991), 515–30.
84. Alison Gilbert Olson, *Making the Empire Work: London and American Interest Groups 1690–1790* (Cambridge, Mass.: Harvard University Press, 1992), 1–50.
85. McCusker and Menard, *The Economy of British America, 1607–1789*, 211–348.
86. Greene and Pole, "Reconstructing British-American Colonial History," in *Colonial British America*, 14–15; and Jack P. Greene, *Pursuits of Happiness: The Social Development of Early Modern British Colonies and the Formation of American Culture* (Chapel Hill: University of North Carolina Press, 1988).
87. Bumsted, "Things in the Womb of Time," 533–64.
88. Jack P. Greene, *Peripheries and Center: Constitutional Development in the Extended Polities of the British Empire and the United States 1607–1788* (Athens: University of Georgia Press, 1986).
89. Charles M. Andrews, *The Colonial Period of American History* (New Haven, Conn.: Yale University Press, 1934), 371.
90. Wesley Frank Craven, *The Dissolution of the Virginia Company: The Failure of a Colonial Experiment* (1932; reprt., Gloucester, Mass.: P. Smith, 1964), 251–336, quote on 330; and Bliss, *Revolution and Empire*, 13–15, 18–23.
91. Andrews, *The Colonial Period of American History*, 419–24; and Edmund S. Morgan, *The Puritan Dilemma: The Story of John Winthrop* (Boston: Little, Brown, 1958), 195–96.
92. Philip S. Haffenden, "The Crown and the Colonial Charters, 1675–1688," *William and Mary Quarterly* 3rd ser., vol. 15 (1958), 297–311, 452–66.
93. Braddick, "The English Government, War, Trade, and Settlement, 1625–1688," in *OHBE* 1:286–308.
94. Leonard Woods Labaree, *Royal Government in America: A Study of the British Colonial System before 1783* (New Haven, Conn.: Yale University Press, 1930), 312–72; Jack P. Greene, *The Quest for Power: The Lower Houses of Assembly in the Southern Royal Colonies, 1689–1776* (Chapel Hill: University of North Carolina Press, 1963), 129–47; and Craton, "Property and Propriety," 506–7, 510–11.
95. Elizabeth Mancke, "Another British America: A Canadian Model for the Early Modern British Empire," *JICH* 25 (1997), 1–36.
96. Bliss, *Revolution and Empire*, 13–23.
97. David S. Lovejoy, *The Glorious Revolution in America* (New York: Harper and Row, 1972), 36–40.
98. Haffenden, "The Crown and the Colonial Charters, 1675–1688," 297–311, 452–66.
99. Roy Hidemichi Akagi, *The Town Proprietors of the New England Colonies: A Study of Their Development, Organization, Activities and Controversies, 1620–1770* (1924, reprt. Gloucester, Mass.: P. Smith, 1963), 50–58, 115–24; and John Frederick Martin, *Profits in the Wilderness: Entrepreneurship and the Founding of New England Towns in the Seventeenth Century* (Chapel Hill: University of North Carolina Press, 1991), 257–80.
100. Joseph J. Malone, *Pine Trees and Politics: The Naval Stores and Forest Policy in Colonial New England* (Seattle: University of Washington Press, 1964), 10–27; and Robert Greenhalgh Albion, *Forests and Sea Power: The Timber Problem of the Royal Navy, 1652–1862* (1926; reprt., Hamden, Conn.: Archon Books, 1965), 238–55.

101. Albion, *Forests and Sea Power*, 231–80; and Malone, *Pine Trees and Politics*, passim.
102. Elizabeth Mancke, "Corporate Structure and Private Interest: The Mid-Eighteenth Century Expansion of New England," in Margaret Conrad, ed., *They Planted Well: New England Planters in Maritime Canada* (Fredericton, N.B.: Acadiensis Press, 1988), 161–77.
103. John Bartlet Brebner, *New England's Outpost: Acadia before the Conquest of Canada* (1927; reprt; Hamden, Conn.: Archon Books, 1965).
104. Jack M. Sosin, *Whitehall and the Wilderness: The Middle West in British Colonial Policy, 1760–1775* (Lincoln: University of Nebraska Press, 1961), 52–78.
105. Elizabeth Mancke, "Another British America", 1–36; and Mancke, "Early Modern Imperial Governance and the Origins of Canadian Political Culture," *Canadian Journal of Political Science/Revue canadienne de science politique* 32 (1999), 3–20.
106. For the impact of wars of empire on Britain see Stone, ed., *An Imperial State at War*, passim.
107. James P. Ronda, *Astoria and Empire* (Lincoln: University of Nebraska Press, 1990), 1–86; Ronda, "Jefferson and the Imperial West," *Journal of the West* 31:3 (1992), 13–19; James R. Gibson, *Otter Skins, Boston Ships, and China Goods: The Maritime Fur Trade of the Northwest Coast, 1785–1841* (Seattle: University of Washington Press, 1992), 12–61; Barry Gough, *The Northwest Coast: British Navigation, Trade, and Discoveries to 1812* (Vancouver: University of British Columbia Press, 1992); and Daniel W. Clayton, *Islands of Truth: The Imperial Fashioning of Vancouver Island* (Vancouver: University of British Columbia Press, 2000).
108. H. V. Bowen, *Elites, Enterprise and the Making of the British Overseas Empire 1688–1775* (New York: St. Martin's Press, 1996), 194–96.

Transatlantic Colonization and the Redefinition of Empire in the Early Modern Era

The British-American Experience

Jack P. Greene

"For more than a century past," Adam Smith remarked in 1776 in the conclusion to *An Inquiry into the Nature and Causes of the Wealth of Nations*, the "rulers of Great Britain have . . . amused the people with the imagination that they possessed a great empire on the west side of the Atlantic. This empire, however, has hitherto," Smith lamented, "existed in imagination only. It has hitherto been but the project of an empire; not a gold mine, but the project of a gold mine." By this passage, Smith was not suggesting that the colonies that composed the British Empire had not been successful. Indeed, the *Wealth of Nations* included a long section on the "Causes of the Prosperity of new Colonies," in which he revealed an informed appreciation of the extraordinary growth and development of many of those colonies. Rather, Smith's remarks, written nearly three hundred years after Columbus's first encounter with America and at a moment when the British government had already had nearly 175 years, experience with overseas empire, expressed the continuing frustration of metropolitan observers and representatives at the inability of metropolitan governments to impose their definitions of empire upon the extended transatlantic polities created by Europeans during the early modern era.[1]

By no means new, such frustrations had been present from the beginning. Throughout the early modern era, what might be called the centrifugal forces of imperial construction had repeatedly prevented metropolitan states from bringing the many transatlantic polities established in and across the Atlantic under levels of supervision that would enable them to realize what Smith called "this golden dream" of empire.[2] The fragmented and loose character of these polities did not conform to metropolitan visions of imperial organization, and the resulting disparity between structure and theory stimulated periodic demands on the part of metropolitan agents and exponents for the redefinition and reconstruction of empire. The recurrence of such demands registered a deep and abiding unease about the ultimate consequences of the failure of metropolitan efforts at centralization and betrayed a mounting conviction that the future viability of empire depended on tighter metropolitan controls. Without such controls, valuable colonies might fall into the hands of rival powers or confederate together and set up for themselves. Using the British Empire as an example, this essay examines the extended transatlantic polities of the early modern era. It analyzes the major variables that affected their structure and definition and explores the pattern and timing of the recurring conflicts over their shape and character.

Until relatively recently, most historians of early modern empire used the coercive and centralized model of imperial organization derived from late-nineteenth- and early-twentieth-century empires. In this conception, empires were political entities in which colonies were presided over by powerful nation-states with vast administrative and coercive resources to enforce their claims to sovereignty. In these coherent entities, authority did not flow upward from colonial populations, most of which, even in colonies with substantial numbers of European settlers, were disenfranchised subject populations, but downward from distant centers. The very concepts of *colony* and *colonial* were freighted with powerful overtones of subjection, subordination, dependence, domination, inferiority, incapacity, and alterity. Colonies were places and colonials were peoples over whom national states exercised hegemonic control.

But early modern transatlantic empires do not fit this model. Rather, they were very much reflections or logical extensions of the states to which they were symbolically attached. Those states were not modern states. As Charles Tilly and other contributors to recent literature on state formation have shown, the organization of Europe into "a small number of unitary and integrated nations states" is relatively recent. "It took a long time," Tilly writes, "for national states—relatively centralized, differentiated, and autonomous organizations successfully claiming priority in the use of force within large, contiguous, and clearly defined territories—to dominate the European map."[3] In 1490, on the eve of Europe's expansion across the Atlantic, "Europe's political structure," as Mark Greengrass has noted, was still "dominated by a multiplicity of regional political entities," just under five hundred in all, with "a rich variety of [political and constitutional] traditions." These included "large old-established states, new principalities, dynastic empires, city states, confederations," the Holy Roman Empire, representing "the ideal of universal world monarchy," and the papacy, with its claims to worldwide spiritual and temporal jurisdiction.[4]

The process of state building during the early modern era resulted in the creation of the first large nation-states, in Portugal, England, Spain, France, Sweden, and the Netherlands. It proceeded in two ways—either through *voluntary agreements* such as dynastic marriages or defensive confederations or, much more rarely, through *conquest*—and it took two principal forms—either *amalgamation*, as happened with Spain, or *incorporation*, as was the case in England (with regard to Cornwall and Wales) and France (with regard to Toulouse, Champagne, Brittany, Gascony, Burgundy, and Flanders). As yet monarchs lacked the fiscal, administrative, and coercive resources necessary to achieve centralized and integrated polities through either coercive or administrative means; for that reason, coalescence, however it happened and whatever its form, invariably involved negotiation, or what Tilly has called bargaining, "between the crown and the ruling class[es] of their different provinces." As J. H. Elliott has explained, the arrangements worked out through these negotiations almost always, even in cases of conquest, "allowed for a high degree of continuing local self-government" and left considerable authority in the hands of local magnates.[5] The result was a system of "composite monarchies" in which the "constituent parts . . . always antedated their union" and "therefore had different laws, rights, privileges, and traditions." By this system, as H. G. Koenigsberger has noted, "a prince could add province after province, kingdom after kingdom to his realm and rule each as its own prince under different laws, and with varying powers."[6]

These new national entities involved some concentration of power in agencies of the central state but also left considerable authority with the principal holders of power in the peripheries. "Peaceful coexistence . . . depended on the king, who resided in the bigger kingdom, governing [each] . . . smaller one in the way it had been used to, that is respecting the rights of its ruling elite, especially in the matter of religion, and, in the absence of an effective civil service," acknowledging the country's privilege of *jus indigenatus*, by which only natives of the province could be appointed to public office, and "running the country with that elite's advice and cooperation."[7] In the absence of a well-developed conception of unitary sovereignty before the middle of the seventeenth century, composite monarchies were thus characterized by indirect rule, consultation, and, at least initially, fragmented sovereignty.

The nature of these composite monarchies was one of the principal variables in determining the character of the extended transatlantic polities constructed under their sponsorship beginning at the end of the fifteenth century. Unlike the respective parts of any composite European monarchy, the many colonial entities Europeans established in the New World were new polities, even when, as in the case of Mexico and Peru, they arose out of conquests of places that were, in European terms, recognizably states at the time they were conquered. Yet the actual process by which these new politics took shape effectively replicated, in very brief compass, that by which composite monarchies had formed in Europe.

Traditionally, historians have depicted the establishment of early modern European empires in America as the result of a devolution of authority outward from old European centers to new American peripheries. As I have argued elsewhere, however,[8] even a casual inspection of the subject reveals that this conception seriously distorts the process by which authority was created in these new entities. Far from having been carried by would-be colonizers from Europe to America, authority in these empires seems rather to have been constructed in a process characterized by two phases. The first involved the creation in America, through the activities of the participants in the colonizing process, of new arenas of individual and local power. The second involved the actual creation of authority through negotiation between those new arenas and the European centers that aspired to bring them under their jurisdiction and to which those arenas desired to be attached.

Four major factors affected this process. First were the limited resources available to the several states involved in the colonizing process. Just as no prince had the administrative and fiscal resources necessary to hold a composite monarchy together in Europe, so too did no early modern European government have either the coercive resources necessary to establish its hegemony over portions of the New World or the financial resources to pay the high costs of creating them. Second were the enormous distances involved. In Europe, the various parts of each composite monarchy did not always directly adjoin each other: Some were even separated by sea. As Adam Smith noted, however, the "European colonies in America" were considerably "more remote" from the seat of government "than the most distant provinces of the greatest empires, which had ever been known before."[9] Third was the economic orientation of the colonizing process. Although the saving of Amerindian souls became a major objective of both Spanish and French colonization and the goal of establishing the New Jerusalem in America was a prominent aspiration for the settlers of the orthodox Puritan colonies of Massachusetts and Connecticut, economic motives—on the part of sponsors and participants—always predominated, except in missionary enclaves. Fourth, participants in colonial enterprises everywhere revealed a profound desire to retain a connection to their respective metropolitan heritages.

As a consequence of their limited resources, all the nation-states that participated in the colonization of America farmed out, during the early stages of European expansion, the task of colonization to private groups organized into chartered trading companies or to individuals known, in the case of the Spanish, as *adelantados,* and as *donatarios,* proprietors, patroons, and *seigneurs* respectively, in the cases of the Portuguese, English, Dutch, and French.[10] In return for authorization from the ruler and in the hope of realizing extensive economic or social advantages for themselves, such people agreed to assume the heavy financial burdens of founding, defending, and succoring beachheads of European occupation in America. In effect, European rulers gave these private agents licenses with wide discretion to undertake activities in areas that were often extensive and contained aboriginal populations of varying numbers, areas to which those rulers had only a highly tenuous claim and over which they had no effective control, much less authority. In this way European rulers sought to secure at least nominal jurisdiction over American territories and peoples at minimal cost to royal treasuries.

Some of these early private agents of European imperialism, especially the trading companies operating under the aegis of the Portuguese and Dutch, enjoyed considerable success in establishing trading entrepôts to tap the economic potential of the new worlds they encountered not just in America but in Africa and Asia as well. However, unless they encountered wealthy Native empires to plunder, rich mineral deposits to exploit, or vast pools of Native labor that relatively quickly could be turned to profit—something that during the early modern era in America happened on a large scale only in Mexico and Peru—few private adventurers could marshal the resources to sustain for long the high costs of settlement, administration, and development of colonies. Lack of resources to finance such activities early on forced those who presided over them to seek cooperation and contributions from settlers, traders, and other individual participants in the colonizing process.

These efforts to enlist such cooperation acknowledged the fact that the actual process of establishing effective centers of European power in America was often less the result of the activities of colonial organizers or licensees than of the many groups and individuals who took actual possession of land, built estates and businesses, turned wholly aboriginal landscapes into partly European ones, constructed and presided over a viable system of economic arrangements, created towns or other political units, and subjugated, reduced to profitable labor, killed off, or expelled the former inhabitants. Making up for their scarcity of economic resources, thousands of Europeans—including large numbers of Spaniards and English, substantial numbers of Portuguese and French, and significant numbers of Dutch and others—created, by dint of their initiative and the industry and expertise of whatever laborers they could command, social spaces for themselves and their families in America and thereby acquired or, one might better say, *manufactured* for themselves status, capital, and power.

Throughout the new European Americas during the early modern era, independent individual participants in the colonizing process were thus engaged in what can only be described as a deep and widespread process of individual self-empowerment. In contemporary Europe only a tiny fraction of the male population ever managed to rise out of a state of socioeconomic dependency to achieve the civic competence, the full right to have a voice in political decisions, that was the preserve of independent property holders. By contrast, as a consequence of the easy availability of land or other resources and high wages for labor, a very large proportion of the white adult male colonists acquired land or other resources, built estates, and achieved individual independence or competence.

This development gave rise to strong demands on the part of the large empowered settler populations for the extension to the colonies of the same rights to security of property and civic participation that appertained to the empowered, high-status, and independent property holders in the polities from which they came. They regarded such rights as an essential mark of their Spanishness or Englishness, an acknowledgment of their continuing connection to the principal elements of the specific European inheritance of which they professed themselves to be the agents. In their view, colonial government, like metropolitan government, should guarantee that people of their standing should not be governed without consultation or in ways that were patently against their interests. Along with continuing limitations on fiscal resources and the vast distance of the colonies from Europe, these circumstances nudged those who were nominally in charge of the colonies toward the establishment and toleration of political structures that involved active consultation with, if not the formal consent of, local settlers. Consultation meant that local populations would more willingly acknowledge the legitimacy of the authority of private agencies of colonization and contribute to local costs. The earliest stages of colonization thus resulted in the emergence in new colonial peripheries in America of many new and relatively autonomous centers of European power effectively under local control.

Once these local centers of power became established, agents of metropolitan centralization found it exceedingly difficult to bring them under regulation. The discovery of precious metals and other riches in Hispanic America during the first half of the sixteenth century provided the Spanish monarchy with the resources slowly to reduce the several enclaves of private power earlier established by its agents in America to some semblance of effective control. Thenceforth, Spain's rulers could purchase and man the ships needed to defend its colonies and shipping against foreign interlopers, pay for troops and missionaries to bring new areas under its hegemony, and support a growing bureaucracy of royal officials from Spain to oversee the colonies and manifest in them the royal presence. Although private initiatives continued to characterize the first stages of Spanish activity in any new area of occupation, the Crown rarely delayed long in extending its authority over such enterprises.

By contrast, in the case of the English or, after 1707, British American Empire, the failure to find similar sources of wealth meant that the system of colonization through private agents persisted for well over a century after the first successful establishment of a colony in Virginia during the early decades of the seventeenth century. Before the 1730s all twelve of the English colonies established on the North American mainland and seven of the eight English colonies founded in the West Indies were the result of private initiatives by chartered companies or individuals or groups of landed proprietors. Only Jamaica, conquered from the Spaniards by an English force in 1655, was the result of a government effort.

If, in contrast to the Spanish colonies, the English colonies never yielded the English state enough revenue to enable it to impose metropolitan authority over them, these still small but expanding emblems of English power did well enough to prove their value as trading partners and to suggest that they might serve as the agents through which England could become a significant player in the emerging Atlantic world. Already by the middle of the seventeenth century in both North America and the West Indies, they had become the object of trade and territorial rivalries with the French and Dutch. As Adam Smith noted in 1776, the English government had "contributed scarce any thing . . . towards . . . the establishment" of these colonies. But, he added, as soon as "those establishments had been effectuated and they had become . . . considerable," metropolitan traders and officials began to demand regulation of their economies for the benefit of the metropolis. Hence, as Smith said, the principal view of the "first regulations" England made for the colonies in the 1650s and 1660s was "to secure to herself the monopoly of their commerce; to confine their market, and to enlarge her own at their expense."[11] Not extending beyond trade regulations, these navigation laws, similar in content to those made during the same period by the other European colonizing powers, suggested that the colonies, in the words of the colonial theorist and former governor of Massachusetts Thomas Pownall in the 1760s, were little more than "a kind of farms," "*mere plantations*, tracts of foreign country" that "the mother country had caused to be worked and cultured [solely] for its own use" and whose commodities the mother country had every right to appropriate to herself.[12]

Colonial opposition to these laws and the intensification of international rivalry in America soon led to the articulation of demands by London officials and merchants for the imposition of metropolitan *political* authority over the colonies. Perhaps inspired by Colbert's recent efforts to deprivatize the Canadian ventures and subject them to the direct authority of the French Crown, English officials during the 1670s and 1680s developed a tripartite policy to achieve this end. The first part of the policy was to recall the charters that formed the legal basis for most of the colonies, bringing them under the direct administration of the Crown. The second was to reorganize the colonies into fewer, larger, and presumably more easily managed and defended polities. The third was to reduce the extensive powers of the representative assemblies that in every colony, in imitation of the English House of Commons, exercised broad legislative authority and provided a sturdy institutional base for the expression of settler interests. The high-water mark of metropolitan efforts to implement these policies came in the 1680s with the Dominion of New England, which incorporated all of the New England colonies into a single polity to be governed with no representative institutions whatever. The theory behind these measures was that the colonies were not simply commercial enterprises in the service of the metropole but also adjuncts of royal power. Politically subordinate to the parent state, they might be governed from London *directly*, not through local colonial institutions *indirectly*. Crown officials encountered broad and deep resistance to these attempts to reduce the self-governing power of the colonies and to impose metropolitan authority upon them. Having long enjoyed a large amount of political autonomy with little interference from London, colonial leaders principally conceived of the colonies not as adjuncts of royal power, but as overseas extensions of the metropolis. Mostly English people or their creole descendants, they had constructed polities for themselves that would provide them with the fundamental guarantees of Englishmen: government by consent, rule by law, and the sanctity of private property, defined to include individual legal and civil rights as well as land and other forms of tangible wealth. As communities of English people, they furthermore expected to enjoy the traditional English legal safeguards of trial by jury and habeas corpus and "all the rights, privileges, and full and free exercise of their own will and liberty in making laws."[13]

Reinforced by the intensive constitutional discussion in the colonies about their relationship to England, the tenacity with which colonial leaders asserted and acted on these views largely frustrated metropolitan efforts at centralization. Over time, most colonists came to accept, at least outwardly, the principle of commercial monopoly explicit in the navigation acts, if such was to be the price of a metropolitan navy to protect their trade, and of access to a legal and constitutional tradition that would insure the security of their rights as English people. By 1730, London officials had also managed to bring fifteen of nineteen American colonies under direct royal control. But their attempts to reorganize the colonies and diminish the authority of the colonial assemblies were demonstrable failures. New Englanders seized upon the occasion of the Glorious Revolution to overthrow the Dominion of New England in 1689, and the metropolis never again sought to combine existing colonies or to govern a colony with a large settler population without benefit of representative institutions.

Although the British state spent considerable and slowly increasing sums to defend the colonies after 1680,[14] and although it assumed substantial portions of the direct costs of the establishment of Georgia in 1732 and the expansion of Nova Scotia in 1748, it was always reluctant to lay out funds sufficient to support the bureaucratic, military, and naval resources that might have enabled it to impose central authority without the consent of the dominant possessing classes in the colonies. To obtain that consent, metropolitan authorities had no choice but to negotiate. In these negotiations, the colonists frequently acted as if, in Koenigsberger's perceptive comment, "their association with England was essentially similar to that of states which had entered a union voluntarily or through heredity."[15] Repeatedly, the assemblies used their power of the purse to thwart metropolitan initiatives and to retain power in local hands. In this situation, royal officials, as Colin M. MacLachlan has said of the contemporary Spanish empire, largely "served as agents regulating and monitoring, rather than directing."[16]

If throughout the years after the earliest interventions of the English state into colonial affairs in the middle of the seventeenth century its relationship with the colonies was thus, as C. A. Bayly has observed, "largely . . . mediated through groups of complaisant mercantile elites and creoles,"[17] that relationship remained highly problematic and subject to persistent controversy. What colonial status meant, and what the nature of the empire was, remained questions to which metropolitans and colonials had very different answers, and metropolitan authorities continued to exhibit profound unease over their inability to impose metropolitan conceptions on the colonies.[18]

Notwithstanding these continuing problems with the administration of the empire, the English enjoyed phenomenal success as a nation during the late seventeenth and early eighteenth centuries. The Glorious Revolution in 1688–89 prevented the establishment of an absolute monarchical regime. The union with Scotland in 1707 created the new and greater entity of Great Britain. Naval successes during the wars of 1689 through 1713 established Britain as the dominant seapower in the Atlantic, and Britain's performance in those wars marked, as Lawrence Stone has noted, Britain's "dramatic return to the European stage as a major player in the game of power politics—after 250 years of virtual absence, ever since the battle of Agincourt."[19] Britain's status as a great power was vividly confirmed by its sweeping victories in the Seven Years' War. "The sudden emerging of Britain from the contemptible figure she made, to its present astonishing power," declared the polemicist Robert Wallace in 1764, "fills all Europe with amazement and jealousy."[20]

In trying to explain Britain's rapid rise to national greatness, many contemporary commentators pointed directly to the American colonies. If the metropolitan-colonial relationship continued to be a significant source of tension within the British Empire throughout the first six decades of the eighteenth century, the colonies themselves, most observers agreed, had done brilliantly. "Nothing in the history of mankind is like their progress," Edmund Burke announced in 1774. "I never cast an eye on their flourishing commerce, and their cultivated and commodious life, but they seem to me rather antient nations grown to perfection through a long series of fortunate events, and a train of successful industry, accumulating wealth in many centuries, than the Colonies of yesterday; than a set of miserable out-casts, a few years ago, not so much sent as thrown out, on the bleak and barren shore of a desolate wilderness three thousand miles from all civilized intercourse."[21]

To explain the phenomenal prosperity and development of the British colonies, observers pointed to two factors: their extensive commercial activity and their form of governance. In his impressive treatise on the colonies, Pownall was only one of many writers to hail the operation of "the spirit of commerce" in raising "*these plantations to become objects of trade*" at levels well "beyond what the mother country or the colonists themselves ever thought of, planned, or even hoped for." This development, as Pownall never tired of pointing out, was of enormous value to the parent state. By extending British commerce "through every part of the Atlantic Ocean," it at once "established the *British government on a grand commercial basis*" and contributed to the transformation of the British Empire into "A GRAND MARINE EMPIRE."[22] But the expansion of commerce and empire celebrated by writers such as Pownall also characterized France and the Netherlands during the same period, if to a smaller extent, and when analysts sought to explain the superior achievements of the British colonies and the British Empire, they pointed to the extraordinary liberty that British people enjoyed in the colonies. What "distinguished the English colonies" and what accounted for their impressive growth, said Montesquieu, was their "system of self-government."[23]

In the British tradition, self-government meant representative government. "From the earliest and first instance of the establishment of a BRITISH SENATE," wrote Pownall, "*the principle of establishing the Imperium of government, on the basis of a representative legislature*" had been the defining feature of British governance.[24] By extending "this beautiful part of our constitution" to the colonies, George Dempster told the House of Commons in October 1775, "our wise ancestors have bound together the different and distant parts of this mighty empire" and "diffused in a most unexampled manner the blessings of liberty and good government through our remotest provinces."[25] "In every thing, except their foreign trade," elaborated Adam Smith, "the liberty of the English colonists to manage their own affairs is complete and is in every respect equal to that of their fellow-citizens at home." Possessed of "the sole right of imposing taxes for the support of the colony government," colonial assemblies everywhere were able to provide the same security for liberty and property and the same protection against official misconduct as people enjoyed in the home islands.[26] "The annual meetings of their little assemblies," said Dempster, "have constantly restrained the despotism, and corrected the follies of their governors; they watch over the administration of justice, and from time to time enact such salutary regulations as tend to promote their happiness and well being."[27] "The government of the English colonies is perhaps the only one which, since the world began," said Adam Smith, "could give perfect security to the inhabitants of such "very distant . . . province[s]."[28] By thus permitting the colonies to adopt "the form of its own government," Montesquieu observed, Britain had effectively insured that the colonies would prosper, that "great peoples" would "emerge" from the "forests to which the nation sent them," and that the colonies would be able to think of themselves and be thought of by others as "intrinsically British."[29]

As they pondered the imperial system that had developed on the ground in colonial British America as a consequence of an ongoing process of bargaining between colonies and metropolis, a system defined, not by ex post facto theories, but by a century and a half of empirical relations, analysts decided that that system represented something without historical precedent. Unlike the Greek colonies, which, as early modern Europeans understood them, had been autonomous settlements in previously unoccupied lands by surplus population, they did not have de jure autonomy. Unlike the Roman colonies, which, as one eighteenth-century commentator remarked, had been "planted among vanquished nations to over-awe, and hold them in subjection," they were not primarily concerned with "keep[ing] conquered Countries in Subjection."[30] Rather, like most of the early modern European colonies in America, they were groups of people who, with the authorization of the monarch, settled in what were alleged to be vacant, lightly settled, or underutilized places for the specific purposes of cultivating the land and promoting trade "for the good of themselves and that [of the] state they belong[ed] to." Thus "intended to increase the Wealth and Power of their native Kingdom," these "Colonies of Commerce," people gradually came to realize, were an entirely "new species of colonizing, of modern date, and differing essentially from every other species of colonizing that is known."[31]

To try to understand British colonization by searching "the most respectable authorities, antient and modern," for parallels in "the experience of other states and empires," Burke declared in 1769, would only produce "the greatest errors imaginable." The British Empire, he insisted, was "wholly new in the world. It is singular: it is grown up to this magnitude and importance within the memory of man; nothing in history is parallel to it. All the reasonings about it, that are likely to be at all solid, must be drawn from its actual circumstance. In this new system," he contended, "a principle of commerce, or artificial commerce, must predominate," along with a recognition that, as "descendants of Englishmen" and themselves "men of free character and spirit," they had to be governed "with, at least, some condescention to this spirit and this character."[32]

As Burke's remarks suggest, implicit in British colonization were two new "principles of policy."[33] The first involved the primacy of commerce. The central objective of empire, as Daniel Baugh has noted, "was not territorial colonization or domination, but trade."[34] So long as the metropolis "pursued trade, and forgot revenue," Burke declared in 1774, the empire worked to Britain's enormous benefit. "You not only acquired Commerce," he told the House of Commons, "but you actually created the very objects of trade in America; and by that creation you raised the trade of this kingdom at least four-fold."[35] "The true connection between the Colonies and Great Britain," averred Charles Pratt, the 1st Baron Camden, in the House of Lords, "is commercial."[36] The second new principle was the distribution of authority between the metropolis and colonies through an implicit process of negotiation that left colonials with not just the "image" but the "substance" of the British constitution, with, in Burke's words, "every characteristick mark of a free people in all [t]he[i]r internal concerns."[37]

Indeed, the absence of metropolitan coercive force in the colonies during the empire's first century and a half powerfully and correctly suggested to many contemporaries that informal economic and cultural ties and shared traditions were more than sufficient to hold the British Empire together. Not fear or force, but consensus and accommodation, the experience of the early modern British Empire seemed to show, were the foundations for successful imperial governance. Fear, Richard Jackson advised the House of Commons in 1769, was a "poor engine of government." Especially at so great a distance, he was persuaded, laws could "not be carried into execution" and countries could "not . . . be governed" when there was "an universal discontent among the people."[38] "A system of force over the minds of free people," asserted General Henry Seymour Conway in the same forum a year later, could "never be a successful system."[39] "The immutable condition, the eternal Law of extensive and detached empire," Burke observed, was that "the circulation of power must be less vigorous at the extremities." "All Nations, who have extensive empire," he said, found that the authority of the center "derived from a prudent relaxation in" the peripheries and that to govern distant areas of empire at all it was necessary to govern them "with a loose rein."[40] In the early modern era, viable imperial governance had to be consensual governance.

However well the British Empire may have functioned for the enrichment and self-esteem of its members, metropolitan authorities and their associates in London and the colonies exhibited throughout the first half of the eighteenth century a persistent concern about what appeared to them to be severe and highly undesirable defects in its form and dynamics. Regarding the empire as severely underorganized,[41] they often deplored the continuing failure of the metropolis "to furnish [the] colonies with a clearly defined legal and civil status"[42]—without ever endeavoring to do much about it. However, by mid-century, the growing populations and wealth of the colonies and intensifying rivalries with France and Spain led to a significant deepening of such concerns. For the first time, metropolitan analysts engaged in intensive, elaborate, and systematic constitutional discussions about the nature and workings of the empire. Between 1748 and 1765, several men with experience in colonial governance, including James Abercromby, Henry McCulloh, Archibald Kennedy, William Bollan, William Douglass, Malachy Postlethwayt, Thomas Pownall, Francis Bernard, Henry Ellis, and John Mitchell produced a large literature on these questions.[43]

Starting from the assumptions that the very word *colony* implied subordination,[44] and that the "first principle in Colony Government" had "ever been . . . to make . . . Colonies . . . Subservient to the Interest of the Principal State,"[45] these writers mostly contended that the colonies had been initiated and established by the metropolitan state for the purpose of furthering state policy. For that reason, they argued, in Abercromby's words, that the colonies always had to be assessed not merely from "a Mercantile View" but "through the Eyes of State."[46] They needed, said another writer, to be considered in terms of "power and dominion, as well as trade."[47] From this perspective, in their view, there could be no doubt that the original purpose of colonization was to "add Strength to the State by extending its Dominions," and, to that end, emigrants to the colonies always "remain[ed] subject to, and under the power and Dominion, of the Kingdom" whence they came. So far, then, from being in any sense equal to the parent state, colonies were nothing more than "Provincial Governments . . . subordinate to the Chief State."[48]

To explain why British colonists did not behave like residents of "provinces of the British empire,"[49] these writers developed the myth—directly the reverse of the process by which imperial governance actually had developed within the empire—that the metropolitan government had originally exerted widespread authority over the colonies but had subsequently permitted it to slip into the hands of the colonial assemblies. They traced this development to various sources, including the prevalence of self-interested behavior among the colonists, the size and diversity of the empire, the growing wealth and populations of the colonies, and, most important, metropolitan neglect. They protested against the "loose" manner in which the metropolis had governed the colonies,[50] complained about the tendency of the colonists to act as if, in the words of Thomas Hobbes, their obligation to "their Metropolis or Mother" required "no more of them, than Fathers require of the Children, whom they emancipate and make free from their domestique government,"[51] and expressed alarm that the colonies often acted independently, not just of the metropolis, but of each other, in the process behaving "as if they thought themselves so many independent states, under their respective charters, rather than as provinces of the same empire."[52]

If successful empire was "the means through which national power and ascendancy could be proved and demonstrated,"[53] then these problems were indeed serious. Not just the security and survival of the empire but the international prestige of Britain itself, they suggested, demanded a deep reform of imperial governance. Frequently quoting a remark by the political economist Charles Davenant from early in the century that colonies were "a strength to their mother kingdom, while they are under good discipline, while they are strictly made to observe the fundamental laws of their original country, and while they are kept dependent on it,"[54] they pointed to the French as "paragon[s] of imperial management" who had proven "thoughtful and efficient in every respect in which the British proved wanting."[55] They called for the implementation of an imperial system that, like the contemporary Bourbon Reforms in the Spanish empire, would be "uniformly structured, depoliticized, and subject to rational direction," one that "demanded conformity and ruled out compromise," one in which political considerations would be "subordinated . . . to rational criteria" and "objectives and goals" be formulated "in advance of a crisis."[56] In the name of turning back the clock to a golden age of imperial governance in which the metropolis enjoyed its proper authority, they proposed to substitute a new *directive* mode of imperial governance for the traditional *consensual* one and thereby to reduce the colonies to a degree of economic and political subordination that few of them had ever experienced and those few only for a brief period in the 1680s, under the reign of James II.

The successful conclusion of the Seven Years' War provided the occasion for a "policy revolution" involving a shift from "a focus on commerce to a focus on control of territory and its inhabitants."[57] This "new Colony System," as Burke called it,[58] that British authorities endeavored to implement both tried to overturn the "ancient system of governing the colonies" and ignored the most important principles on which the empire had been constructed[59]: that "Liberty and Commerce" were "the true Basis of its Power."[60] This "new-fangled system"[61] involved direct metropolitan taxation of the colonies to help pay debts accumulated during the Seven Years' War and a variety of other measures that, as Burke subsequently complained, had the objective "of *rendering government* powerful and paramount over the several dependencies of the British Empire."[62] This "political offensive" immediately became what Koenigsberger has called "a flashpoint for rebellion, repression, and war."[63]

Of course, this quarrel was complicated by changes in the internal governance of Great Britain following the Glorious Revolution. Koenigsberger has recently analyzed the composite monarchies of early modern Europe in terms of a distinction he borrowed from the medieval English legal theorist Sir John Fortescue between *dominium regale*, a condition in which "the ruler could legislate and tax his subjects without their consent," and *dominium politicum et regale*, a situation in which "the ruler needed such consent and" in which that "consent usually had to be given by the representative assembly." Before 1688, the English had had a regime of dominium politicum et regale. But the Glorious Revolution and its attendent developments changed that regime "into something quite different, parliamentary government . . . in which there" was "no longer a balance between the monarchy and parliament as two basically independent authorities." As the repository of sovereign authority within Britain, the King-in-Parliament now became, Koenigsberger persuasively suggests, "an absolutist parliamentary regime," while the colonies and Ireland retained dominium politicum et regale regimes. Parliament's efforts to tax the colonies for revenue directly in the 1760s and 1770s and the colonists' refusal to accede to such taxation pointedly raised the fundamental theoretical problem of how to reconcile the sovereignty of the King-in-Parliament with the colonial demand for limitations on metropolitan political authority in accordance with their long "experience of *dominium politicum et regale* and . . . their mythology of liberty" arising out of their by then-ancient claims to identities as *British* peoples who enjoyed *British* forms of governance.[64]

In this situation, as Koenigsberger points out, the colonists were inevitably "driven back to the traditional solution of the composite monarchy made up of states with equal rights and held together only by a common allegiance to the crown."[65] Building upon the old idea that, as Henry Fox declared in the House of Commons in 1754, the "colonies are more immediately under the eye of the crown than any other part of the British dominions,"[66] colonial spokesmen argued that the colonies had "never [been] thought to be within the realm of England, any more than Scotland or Ireland," and were not therefore *"subject to England."* So far from being a unified entity, the British Empire, they declared in articulating a century and a half of experience, was a polity composed "of *different realms, subject to the same king*."[67]

The American withdrawal from the British Empire neither settled this controversy over the nature of the empire nor put an end to British efforts to enhance metropolitan authority over the colonies. Despite a temporary loosening of metropolitan controls in and the extension of a large measure of self-government to Ireland in the early 1780s, British colonial policy after the American War for Independence involved, in general, according to Bayly, "a systematic attempt to centralize power within colonial territories, to exalt the executive above local liberties and to remove non-European and non-British from positions of all but marginal political authority." As Bayly assesses them, these measures represented a bald "attempt to establish overseas despotisms which mirrored in many ways the politics of neo-absolutism and the Holy Alliance of contemporary Europe."[68] Such efforts derived from an old impulse. In one sense, they were merely continuations of the ongoing project referred to by Adam Smith in the passages quoted at the beginning of this chapter to turn the British Empire into an entity that would be tightly controlled from the center. In another sense, however, these post-1783 measures were also quite modern. They occurred in a new era when state power was expanding, and they represented an effort to create an imperial version of the centralized national state that would become the norm in the West following the French Revolution. Early modern empire, as defined by imperial organization and practice and as exemplified by the British Empire, had been something quite different.

Notes

1. Adam Smith, *An Inquiry into the Nature and Causes of the Wealth of Nations* (1776), ed. R. H. Campbell and A. S. Skinner, 2 vols. (Oxford: Oxford University Press, 1976), 2:946.
2. Ibid.
3. Charles Tilly, *Coercion, Capital, and European States, A.D. 990–1990* (Cambridge, Mass.: Blackwell, 1990), 43–44, 224.
4. Mark Greengrass, ed., *Conquest and Coalescence: The Shaping of the State in Early Modern Europe* (London: Edward Arnold, 1991), vii, 1–2, 3.
5. J. H. Elliott, "A Europe of Composite Monarchies," *Past and Present* 137 (1992), 52–53, 57, 69.
6. H. G. Koenigsberger, "Composite States, Representative Institutions and the American Revolution," *Historical Research* 62 (1989), 135–36.

7. Ibid., 136, 143, 149–50.
8. Jack P. Greene, "Negotiated Authorities: The Problem of Governance in the Extended Polities of the Early Modern Atlantic World," in Greene, *Negotiated Authorities: Essays in Colonial Political and Constitutional History* (Charlottesville, Va.: University of Virginia Press, 1994), 1–24.
9. Smith, *Wealth of Nations*, 2:586.
10. This and succeeding paragraphs are adapted from Greene, "Negotiated Authorities," 12–15.
11. Smith, *Wealth of Nations*, 2:590.
12. Thomas Pownall, *The Administration of the Colonies*, 4th ed. (London: J. Walker, 1768), 282–83.
13. Ibid., 69.
14. See Kurt William Nagel, "Empire and Interest: British Colonial Defense Policy, 1689–1748," Ph.D. diss., Johns Hopkins University, 1992.
15. Koenigsberger, "Composite States," 145.
16. Colin M. MacLachlan *Spain's Empire in the New World: The Role of Ideas in Institutional and Social Change* (Berkeley and Los Angeles: University of California Press, 1988), 125.
17. C. A. Bayly, *Imperial Meridian: The British Empire and the World 1780–1830* (London: Longmans, 1989), 5.
18. On this subject, see Jack P. Greene, *Peripheries and Center: Constitutional Development in the Extended Polities of the British Empire and the United States, 1607–1788* (Athens: University of Georgia Press, 1986).
19. Richard Koebner, *Empire* (Cambridge: Cambridge University Press, 1961), 70–71, 77; Lawrence Stone, ed., *An Imperial State at War: Britain from 1689 to 1815* (London: Routledge, 1994), 2.
20. Robert Wallace, *A View of the Internal Policy of Great Britain* (London: A. Millar, 1764), 159, as quoted by Peter N. Miller, *Defining the Common Good: Empire, Religion and Philosophy in Eighteenth-Century Britain* (Cambridge: Cambridge University Press, 1994), 179.
21. Edmund Burke, Speech on American Taxation, April 19, 1774, in Paul Lankford, ed., *The Writings and Speeches of Edmund Burke*, vol. 2, *Party, Parliament, and the American Crisis 1766–1774* (Oxford: Oxford University Press, 1981), 429.
22. Pownall, *Administration of the Colonies*, 282–83.
23. Quoted in Koebner, *Empire*, 92.
24. Pownall, *Administration of the Colonies*, 175; emphasis in the original.
25. George Dempster, Speech, October 27, 1775, in Richard Simmons and P. D. G. Thomas, eds., *Proceedings and Debates of the British Parliament Respecting North America, 1754–1783*, 6 vols. (Millwood, N.Y.: Kraus International Publications, 1982–87), 6:140.
26. Smith, *Wealth of Nations*, 2:584–85.
27. Dempster, Speech, October 27, 1775, 6:140.
28. Smith, *Wealth of Nations*, 2:586.
29. Quoted in Koebner, *Empire*, 92, 297.
30. Samuel Estwick, *A Letter to the Reverend Josiah Tucker, D. D.* (London: J. Almon, 1776), 92–93.
31. John Trenchard and Thomas Gordon, *Cato's Letters: Essays on Liberty, Civil and Religious, and Other Important Subjects*, 4 vols. (London: W. Wilkins, T. Woodward, J. Walthoe, and J. Peele, 1724), 3:283–84; William Douglass, *A Summary, Historical and Political, of the first Planting, progressive Improvements, and present State of the British Settlements in North-America*, 2 vols. (Boston: Rogers and Fowle, 1749–51), 1:205–7; Malachy Postlethwayt, *The Universal Dictionary of Trade and Commerce*, 2 vols. (London: John Knapton, 1757), 2:471; Estwick, *Letter to Josiah Tucker*, 92–93; Anthony Stokes, *A View of the Constitution of the British Colonies in North America and the West Indies* (London: B. White, 1783), 1–3.
32. Edmund Burke, *Observations on a Late State of the Nation* (London, 1769), in Langford, ed., *Writings and Speeches*, 2:194.

33. Miller, *Defining the Common Good*, 199.
34. Characterized by Lawrence Stone in his introduction to Stone, ed., *An Imperial State at War*, 25.
35. Burke, Speech on American Taxation, April 19, 1774, in Langford, ed., *Writings and Speeches*, 2:429.
36. Camden, Speech, March 11, 1766, in Simmons and Thomas, eds., *Proceedings and Debates of the British Parliament*, 2:342.
37. Burke, Speech on American Taxation, April 19, 1774, in Langford, ed., *Writings and Speeches*, 2:429.
38. Jackson, Speech, April 19, 1769, in Simmons and Thomas, eds., *Proceedings and Debates of the British Parliament* 3:153.
39. Conway, Speech, March 5, 1770, in ibid., 3:224.
40. Burke, Speech on Conciliation, March 22, 1775, in *Selected Writings and Speeches on America*, ed. Thomas H. D. Mahoney (Indianapolis: Bobbs Merrill, 1964), 136–37.
41. J. G. A. Pocock, *The Politics of Extent and the Problems of Freedom* (Colorado Springs: Colorado College, 1988), 10.
42. J. G. A. Pocock, "Empire, State and Confederation: The War of American Independence as a Crisis in Multiple Monarchy," in John Robertson, ed., *A Union for Empire: Political Thought and the British Union of 1707* (Cambridge: Cambridge University Press, 1995), 343.
43. The fullest treatment of this literature is Miller, *Defining the Common Good*, 195–213.
44. Charles Townshend, Speech, February 6, 1765, in Simmons and Thomas, eds., *Proceedings of the British Parliament*, 2:13.
45. Jack P. Greene, Charles F. Mullett, and Edward C. Papenfuse, Jr., eds., *Magna Charta for America: James Abercromby's "An Examination of the Acts of Parliament Relative to the Trade and the Government of our American Colonies" (1752) and "De Jure et Gubernatione Coloniarum, or An Inquiry into the Nature, and the Rights of Colonies, Ancient, and Modern" (1774)* (Phildelphia: American Philosophical Society, 1986), 45.
46. Ibid.
47. John Mitchell, *The Contest in America between Great Britain and France* (London: A. Millar, 1757), xvii, quoted in Miller, *Defining the Common Good*, 170.
48. Greene, Mullett, and Papenfuse, eds., *Magna Charta for America*, 26.
49. Smith, *Wealth of Nations*, 2:946.
50. Alexander Wedderborne, Speech, May 2, 1774, in Simmons and Thomas, eds., *Proceedings of the British Parliament*, 4:363.
51. Thomas Hobbes, *Leviathon, Or the Matter, Forme and Power of a Commonwealth, Ecclesiastical and Civil* (London, 1651), 131, as cited by J. M. Bumsted, "'Things in the Womb of Time': Ideas of American Independence, 1633 to 1763," *William and Mary Quarterly*, 3d ser., 31 (1974), 536.
52. *State of the British and French Colonies in North America* (London, 1755), 57, as cited in Miller, *Defining the Common Good*, 168.
53. Kathleen Wilson, "Empire of Virtue: The Imperial Project and Hanoverian Culture c.1720–1785," in Stone, ed., *An Imperial State at War*, 155.
54. Charles Davenant, "On the Plantation Trade," in *Political and Commercial Works*, 5 vols. (London: R. Horsfeld, 1771), 2:10, quoted in Jack P. Greene, "Metropolis and Colonies: Changing Patterns of Constitutional Conflict in the Early Modern British Empire, 1607–1763," in Greene, *Negotiated Authorities*, 57.
55. Miller, *Defining the Common Good*, 167; Koebner, *Empire*, 103.
56. MacLachlan, *Spain's Empire in the New World,* 89, 103, 127.
57. Stone, "introduction," in Stone, ed., *An Imperial State at War*, 26.
58. Burke, Speech on American Taxation, April 19, 1774, in Langford, ed., *Writings and Speeches*, 2:431.
59. Dempster, Speech, October 27, 1775, in Simmons and Thomas, eds., *Proceedings and Debates of the British Parliament*, 6:139.
60. Burke, Speech on the Repeal of the Stamp Act, February 21, 1766, in Langford, ed., *Writings and Speeches*, 2:56.
61. Dempster, Speech, October 27, 1775, in Simmons and Thomas, eds., *Proceedings and Debates of the British Parliament*, 6:139.

62. Burke, Speech on Irish Trade, February 15, 1779, in R. B. McDowell, ed., *The Writings and Speeches of Edmund Burke*, Vol. 9 (London, 1991), 9:527, emphasis in the original.
63. Koenigsberger, "Composite States," 147, 151.
64. Ibid., 136, 149, 150, 152.
65. Ibid., 152.
66. Henry Fox, Speech, December 16, 1754, in Simmons and Thomas, eds., *Proceedings and Debates of the British Parliament*, 1:36.
67. Joseph Priestley, "Address to Protestant Dissenters," 1774, in J. T. Rutt, ed., *The Theological and Miscellaneous Works of Joseph Priestly*, 25 vols. (London, 1823), 22:493, quoted in Miller, *Defining the Common Interest*, 239.
68. Bayly, *Imperial Meridian*, 8.

Perceptions from the Periphery

Colonial American Views of Britain's Asiatic Empire, 1756–1783

H. V. Bowen

Although undoubtedly of major importance in commercial, cultural, and strategic terms, Britain's eighteenth-century Atlantic colonies represented only one part of a far-flung and ever-expanding overseas empire. It cannot be denied that Britons long remained preoccupied with their "first" empire of settlement and plantations in North America and the Caribbean, but there were many signs after 1756 that they were becoming increasingly aware of the importance of their connections with other parts of the world. No straightforward "swing to the east" occurred in British interests before, or even after, the loss of the American colonies in 1783, but during the decades following the Seven Years' War and the conquest of Bengal in 1763–65 many Britons opened their eyes and minds to the various new opportunities offered to them by the development and extension of commercial activity in the Asia-Pacific region.[1] In the context of the core-periphery relations addressed in this volume, the gradual broadening of Britain's overseas horizons meant that "imperial" connections had to be established beyond those that had already been forged between England and its outlying provinces in Wales, Ireland, Scotland, North America, and the West Indies. Over time, many bridges had been built between the core and the peripheries of the Atlantic world, but now additional bridges were required to support and sustain ever-increasing levels of British activity in Africa, India, China, and the Pacific. These were established and then strengthened in order to facilitate flows of goods, people, ideas, and information of types that were often quite different from those that linked together the English-speaking parts of the Atlantic basin. As the balance of British imperial interests began the long-term process of shifting away from the Western Hemisphere to the East, a global empire emerged that was multinational and multifaith in character and contained a bewildering array of institutional and organizational forms. Its creation posed a whole series of challenges to those who had long defined British imperialism within the terms of reference applied narrowly to the Atlantic empire.

This essay will seek to examine some of the ways in which those in the colonial American world endeavored to come to terms with the globalization of British imperial interests. Set within a context provided by a redefinition of core-periphery relations in general, it explores the tenuous connections that were being established between some of the outlying parts of the empire. For, as several historians of Britain's eighteenth-century empire have recently acknowledged, it is important that appropriate weight and attention is given to the relationships that developed, directly and indirectly, between different peripheries. By focusing on "interprovincial dialogue" within the English-speaking Atlantic world,[2] a new dimension has been added to our understanding of how those at the outer and inner margins of empire saw themselves in relation to one another as well as to the metropolis. Thus, the position of "provincials" in Ireland, Scotland, North America, and the Caribbean is now being set within a theoretical framework that represents an adapted form of the core-periphery model that has served to bring a much greater sense of historical coherence to the early modern English Atlantic empire.[3]

To date, however, studies of interprovincial relationships within the eighteenth-century British Empire have been located narrowly within geographical terms of reference defined by what is now routinely described as an Atlantic or Anglo-American cultural system.[4] This was a "system" given some sense of form by the dogged adherence of many of those at the margins of empire to a set of common identity-forming benchmarks embracing language, liberty, fashion, manners, and so on. What has not yet been explored in any great depth, though, is the nature of any relationship that might have been emerging between provinces of the old "first" Atlantic empire and the new areas of sustained activity that were developing in the rapidly expanding empire of the East.[5] Of course, a range of fundamental differences existed between Britain's empire of settlement and its empire of conquest in the East, which almost defy the establishment of any meaningful connections between them. Nevertheless, it is important to examine how, if at all, provincial overseas members of the established empire, as well as those in Britain itself, responded to the challenges posed by the emergence of new forms of imperial activity, even though they were developing thousands of miles and several oceans apart.

This essay focuses upon how those at one periphery, in North America, perceived and responded to the distant and very different periphery that was emerging as a large territorial empire established by the British in Asia. As the American constitutional and political crisis of the 1760s and 1770s unfolded, the effects of the globalization of Britain's empire served ultimately to inflict considerable damage upon British relations with the part of the "old" periphery represented by the thirteen colonies. This occurred as the belief took hold in North America that, as a result of the actions of the East India Company, unwelcome "alien" influences from the East were being transferred, via the metropolis, to the Atlantic empire. Many American colonials further believed that these influences undermined, and ultimately threatened to destroy, long-standing imperial relationships, structures, and understandings.

Some of the ways in which people in Britain began to come to terms with their possession of an expanding global empire have been explored elsewhere.[6] From the "annus mirabilis," of 1759 onward, Britons (and to a lesser degree colonial Americans) were made aware through print, verse, song, and even landscape architecture that Britannia's influence was being felt, simultaneously, in all four quarters of the globe.

During the Seven Years' War, Americans rejoiced at news of local and faraway victories over France in much the same way as their counterparts in Britain,[7] and some were moved to express their views in poetic lines, especially after the death of General James Wolfe before Quebec in September 1759.[8] On several occasions, the theme of global triumph emerged from the verses published in colonial newspapers. For example, the author of "Panegyrical VERSES on the Death of General Wolfe," writing from Kent County, Maryland, concluded his work by suggesting that now "a new World, to GEORGE'S Empire won, Disowns a Bound, and tires th' unsetting sun."[9] The author of "Verses occasioned by the SUCCESS of the BRITISH ARMS in the YEAR 1759" produced a poetic review of military triumphs that covered two-thirds of the front page of the *Maryland Gazette* on January 3, 1760. The vast geographical scope of his subject was such that the author thought that

> From Pole to Pole my rambling Muse shou'd rove,
> and when o'er th' astonished World she drove,
> In ev'ry climate as she past along,
> Great GEORGE'S triumphs should adorn her Song.
> If chill'd with Cold, and in the North she mov'd
> O'er icy sea and frozen Lakes she rov'd,
> Attesting Nations shou'd with her rejoice,
> Join in the concert, and approve her voice.
> If in the *South* to warmer climes she goes,
> BOSCAWEN rides triumphant o'er his Foes.
> POCOCK in the *East* curbs their lawless Pride,
> and *Western* Nations court his conq'ring side.

Military success and commercial expansion had been secured at the expense of the Bourbon powers, and this prompted reflection upon the strengths and virtues of the British people, as well as the standing of the nation and empire in the wider world. A verse entitled "The Contrast" was published in the *Boston Gazette* on November 12, 1759, comparing Britain with France, and it included a roll call of the contemporary British heroes who had masterminded victories in the Eastern Hemisphere as well as the West. Admiral Edward Hawke, and by implication American colonists, were exhorted to

> Be ever dear to Britain's sons thy name
> O brave restorer of her naval fame!
> Such chiefs as Amherst, Forbes, Wolfe and thou
> Clive, Osborn, Keppel, Tyrrel, Lechart, How,
> Are formed to execute, by sea or land
> What Pitt and Legge may plan or George command,
> Each patriot heart shall bless your conquering sword,
> N-vr France dream of Louisbourg restor'd.

At one level, this type of verse was part of the collective expression of relief that was released when it was realized that French designs and ambitions in North America had been decisively thwarted by British and colonial forces. At a rather different level, however, such writings also represented a manifestation of the desire of many American colonists to assert their Britishness and loyalty to the Crown. As with others in the empire, notably in Scotland and Ireland, Americans willingly identified themselves with an increasing, sharply defined form of Britishness that, through its vigorous denunciations of Catholicism, intolerance, and despotism, helped to bring a sense of coherence, order, and common belonging to all parts of the Anglo-American world. This process, which accelerated after mid-century, led colonists into the belief that they were now partners in a successful expanding empire.[10] After 1760, future prospects seemed to suggest to the colonists that they themselves would extend the western wing of the British Empire across the North American continent,[11] while others would be engaged in their own forms of expansionist endeavor in Asia, Africa, and elsewhere. As one consequence of this, images associated with Britannia's triumphant global progress were given a variety of different artistic expressions, from decorative wooden carvings to elaborate iced sugar creations, by those who were swift to take commercial advantage of American association with the imperial and military achievements of Britain and its allies.[12]

Close observers of politics and empire did not simply bask in the reflected glory of military and naval success. They also began to consider the implications of the land and sea victories of the Seven Years' War, and as they did this they reformulated their notions of empire and imperialism. In particular, ideas about a global British Empire began to emerge and be refined in the metropolis. This does not mean that contemporaries suddenly ceased writing or speaking about Britain's North American empire or its empire of the East, for these constructions long survived in the minds and words of those who articulated thoughts about imperial affairs. Rather, it is to suggest that, in conceptual terms, ideas relating to the existence of a global empire began to be superimposed upon configurations of imperial thought that had long defined the British presence in different parts of the world. Of course, any vision of a global empire remained blurred and half-formed, and Edmund Burke later remarked that the general British failure to move beyond this elementary stage of the analytical process had played its part in causing the partial disintegration of the empire, and the loss of the American colonies, between 1775 and 1783.[13]

Nevertheless, individuals at both the core and periphery of the empire did begin to look beyond limited transatlantic horizons. In North America commentators disagreed about the constitutional form taken by Britain's empire, and there was a debate of gathering strength about the redefined terms of British imperial membership on offer to the colonists after 1763, but some were now prepared to acknowledge that the colonies needed to be properly located within a context defined by the existence of a greater worldwide imperial body.[14] As John Dickinson wrote of the American colonies when discussing parliamentary authority, "He, who considers these provinces as states distinct from the *British Empire*, has very slender notions of *justice* or of *their interests*. We are but parts of the *whole*."[15] Others established connections between different forms of imperial endeavor, and in Britain calls were made for the more effective economic and administrative integration of the overseas empire. From authors of surveys of the empire such as Adam Adamson, John Campbell, Arthur Young, through imperial theorists such as Thomas Pownall and William Knox, to prominent politicians such as Lord Clive and Sir George Colebrooke of the East India Company, it is possible to discern movement, albeit in the form of hesitant steps, toward the emergence of a view that stressed the need for Britain to be in possession of a well-ordered, rationally organized global empire rather than a loose collection of territories scattered seemingly at random across the world.[16]

Although some in the metropolis were struggling to come to terms with the expansion of empire on a number of different territorial and commercial fronts, most colonial Americans remained only dimly aware of their place in the very broadest, global, imperial scheme of things. In large part, of course, this was because of the realities of a situation in which formidable communication, geographical, institutional, and logistical barriers prevented easy access to other parts of the empire beyond the Atlantic. In a British maritime world still regulated by the navigation system and monopoly rights, there were no direct sea passages linking North America with India and the East Indies. And, unlike the Spanish, the British were not able to secure access to the Pacific from territorial staging posts in the Americas, which made it difficult for North Americans to follow any westward paths to the Orient.[17] As a result, very few colonial Americans ever acquired any direct firsthand knowledge of Britain's Asian empire through travel or temporary residence in the East. Indeed, the British communities in India were small in number, with the white populations of Madras and Calcutta being counted in hundreds rather than thousands, and there were only limited commercial openings even for those who were able to secure patronage and favor from the East India Company's court of directors.

Some Americans did, however, find their way into the Indian Ocean as illegal traders or privateers, and at the end of the seventeenth century, when buccaneers extended their activities way beyond the Caribbean, New York acted as a supply base for a sophisticated and well-funded pirate operation established on the island of Madagascar.[18] This type of presence in the region was by its very nature a precarious and fleeting one, and it only ever brought the individuals concerned into limited contact with local societies and cultures. A few Americans may have found their way to India as crew members of East Indiamen or Royal Naval vessels but this does not seem very likely, even in an age that saw the Anglo-American maritime fleet containing many individuals who have been described as being representative of the new "international working man."[19] Royal Navy crews usually contained a large number of "foreigners," including Americans,[20] but those who were recruited or pressed in the colonies almost always served their time in Atlantic waters. Indeed, to ensure that men were not removed too far from their home port, senior colonial officials such as Governor Thomas Pownall of Massachusetts sometimes sought assurances from the navy that seamen who enlisted for duty beyond their province would not eventually be transferred to Europe or the West Indies.[21]

Those who moved in colonial maritime circles might well have gathered scraps of knowledge about the East from their encounters with British seamen who had served there in the navy or onboard the East Indiamen, which plied the trade routes between London, the Indian Ocean, and China. One can only hazard a guess at how many British seamen ever found their way from India to North America, but there were several ways in which this might have happened. There were large numbers of seafaring men circulating in semiconstant motion from port to port around the Atlantic, and it has been noted that their oral culture was of an international type and form.[22] They were, literally as well as metaphorically, men of the world.[23] Included among them were naval officers who had served in the East or who in peacetime had found "respectable" employment on the ships of the East India Company.[24] Best known in the former context was perhaps Edward Boscawen (1711–61) who, after acting as commander-in-chief of Crown land and sea forces in India between 1747 and 1749, later served at the American station. During the Seven Years' War he took command of the squadron that covered the assault on Louisbourg in 1758. Also to be found in American waters were some of the ordinary seamen who were recruited or pressed for wartime naval service as they were returning home from Asia.[25] In the merchant fleet there were no doubt a few other adventurous men like Edward Barlow, who in his attempt to see the world chose to work passages that took him to all points of the compass.[26] In each case, as they touched land, even if only briefly, these individuals gathered experience of a variety of different cultural and social systems, and they acted as agents for the informal transfer of information from one hemisphere to another.

The transfer of cultural knowledge from East to West was not yet facilitated by movements of British soldiers from India to North America on any large scale. Regular troops did not serve in India in great numbers at this time, mainly because the East India Company possessed its own armed forces. Moreover, although individual soldiers sometimes found their way to the American colonies from Asia, the "rotational" arrangements that were in place within the British army did not take any units from Bengal or Madras to North America before 1783. Opportunities for career movement from the eastern wing of the empire to the West were thus limited, although one notable exception to this was provided by Sir Archibald Campbell (1739–91). Campbell had served in Highland regiments in North America between 1758 and 1764, but was then posted to India during the early 1770s. He returned to the American colonies during the War for Independence, his experiences between 1775 and 1778 ranging from prisoner of war to commander-in-chief in Georgia. Campbell went on to serve as governor of Jamaica between 1782 and 1785 before he made his way once more to India, where he endured an unhappy time as governor of Madras between 1786 and 1789. His career path provides a good, though wholly untypical, example of how imperial circumstances could dictate a pattern of administrative and military service that touched some of the farthest-flung corners of the overseas empire.[27] For the most part, though, there is little evidence of army personnel finding their way from East to West. Rather, any trend that might be discernible points to movement in the other direction, especially after 1783, when officers such as Gerard Lake and, most notably, Lord Cornwallis saw service in India having first been stationed in North America.

A small number of well-to-do North Americans had business and financial interests that were tied, even if only indirectly, to the fortunes of the British in India. This included a few who, through agents and attorneys in London, had purchased East India Company stock,[28] but this hardly represented a close interest in the East because such individuals were primarily concerned with financial returns and not any meaningful engagement with unfamiliar societies and cultures. Other Americans, or Britons temporarily residing in the colonies, were members of extended families who established branches throughout the British Empire during the course of the eighteenth century. For some, this opened the prospect of movement around, or contact between, Britain's imperial outposts, and there are examples of individuals in North America who were connected with kin whose commercial and business careers took them to the East. These types of networks were established on a global scale as entrepreneurs sought out and developed new business opportunities in different parts of the world.[29] The Franks family was long represented at the heart of the City of London, for example, but its members also fanned out across the world in search of opportunities and put down roots in Philadelphia, New York, Jamaica, Surat, and Bombay.[30] Family horizons broadened as the empire expanded, a trait most evident in the well-documented activities of descendants of James Russell (1708–88) who first focused their attention on their Scottish homeland before extending their interests to London, Maryland, and finally India.[31] This type of family was of course untypical, but correspondence and the relaying of news and business information between outlying branches helped to facilitate flows of information around the wider empire.

In spite of tenuous links such as these being established between East and West, few colonists had firsthand knowledge of the East and they seldom even encountered anyone who had traveled to Asia. The vast majority of Americans therefore found that their awareness of Britain's Oriental empire was shaped, first and foremost, by what they consumed and what they read. As far as goods were concerned, those in the colonies, like their metropolitan contemporaries, developed a voracious appetite for Indian and Chinese produce. Tea, textiles, spices, and pepper were reexported to them in ever-increasing quantities from Britain or they were smuggled across the Atlantic from Europe. Indeed, as far as legal commercial activity was concerned, 60 percent of the goods shipped to the continental colonies as reexports from Britain were East India goods.[32] Over time, tea came to represent the most important element of this trade as British and colonial merchants attempted to meet demand for the increasingly popular consumer item. Americans were initially rather slow to develop a taste for tea, and regular imports did not become established until the 1720s. By the 1760s, however, over 1,000,000 pounds of tea were being consumed in the colonies each year,[33] and this supports a calculation that suggests that by that time at least two-thirds of white adults were drinking the beverage every day.[34] Tea drinking became an established social ritual, and the gradual transfer of the habit to all classes was accompanied by the wider use of ceramic vessels or chinaware.[35] "Tea furniture" in the form of tables, chairs, and trays also became popular, and even China export porcelain was used to bring a sense of authenticity to children's tea services.[36] The importance of tea drinking was, in turn, reflected in the contents of inventories that in all social categories increasingly contained references to tea and different types of tea-related equipment.[37] This confirms the strength of the "transatlantic addiction" for tea which, it has recently been argued, helped to define some of the most basic social and cultural contours of the Anglo-American world.[38]

The extensive purchasing of goods imported from Britain helped to bring Americans into the same world of consumption as their metropolitan counterparts, and this played a leading part within the processes of "anglicization" that were at work in the colonies.[39] But, as T. H. Breen has recently remarked, by 1760 enthusiastic participation in the transatlantic marketplace also "had the capacity to influence how colonists imagined themselves within a larger empire."[40] Through their extensive purchases of a wide variety of imported goods, Americans were strengthening the commercial sinews that helped to integrate and sustain Britain's expanding empire. Indeed, as far as East India goods were concerned, this process, which was supported by a sophisticated supply and distribution system centered on the metropolis, allowed the produce of one imperial periphery to be marketed and sold in large quantities at another. Accordingly, an array of East India goods of different types was brought before the colonial consumer by British and American merchants. As far as fashionable textiles were concerned, markets in North America offered as wide a choice of products as did those in Britain. The New York company, Francis Lewis and Son, were able, for example, to advertise "a variety of India goods" on sale at their warehouse in 1773. These goods included "Taffeties, persians, damasks, lutestrings, pudosoys, sattens, amozeens, modes and peelongs, printed callicoes and cottons, muslins of various sorts, ambricks, lawns, dowlas, gaslix, tandems, plattilas royal, pistol lawns, white and black gauze, gauze handkerchiefs and aprons, and minionets."[41] Colonial consumption of Eastern produce was encouraged by newspaper advertisements and shop signs that suggested that the purchasers of Hyson tea, Bengal silk, or Nankeen cloth would be brought into contact with an exotic and far-distant world.[42] To that extent, the "larger empire" imagined by Americans, and invoked by Breen, embraced the interests that Britain was now controlling and exploiting in the East, even though the focus of contemporary attention and analysis undoubtedly remained firmly fixed on the Atlantic world during the 1750s and 1760s.[43]

Beyond consumption, colonists' awareness of and responses to the empire of the East was shaped by what they read in newspapers, periodicals, and pamphlets. As with Asian goods reexported from Britain, news and information about India almost always first passed through a metropolitan prism, arriving at the American periphery in the form of articles and essays reprinted from London publications. There was never a great number of these before the Seven Years' War, however, because news and views of India did not loom very large in the British press. The content of newspapers in Britain and America was always dominated by items relating to Europe and the British Isles and, as has recently been pointed out, this helped to ensure that the "mental map" of readers in Philadelphia was little different from that of readers in London, Norwich, or Bristol.[44] As far as the readers of the *Pennsylvania Gazette* were concerned, this meant that the world beyond the Atlantic barely impinged upon their consciousness at all, and it has been estimated that between 1740 and 1765 only 0.8 percent of news items and 0.8 percent of news space was devoted to Asia, Africa, and the Middle East. In spite of this, however, there are signs that items about India, which (as with so much else) took the form of letters, extracts, or "advices" from London, could command the attention of colonial American readers from time to time. This was especially the case during the Seven Years' War, when the success or failure of British arms in the wider world was deemed by publishers to be a matter of some interest to their local readers. Thus in 1759–60, for example, accounts of the siege of Madras and the actions of Vice Admiral George Pocock received extensive coverage in the colonial press. These accounts, based upon extracts from Pocock's letters, which had been published in a *London Gazette Extraordinary* on October 12, 1759, occupied all three columns on the front page of the *New Hampshire Gazette* of December 29, and all of the first page and some of the second of the *Boston Post Boy* of December 24.[45] Readers were treated to a blow-by-blow account of military and naval engagements, but the articles also contained plenty of incidental information about the climate, culture, and topography of South Asia.

After the war, news of British success in India continued to be relayed to North America, notably in 1765 when Lord Clive set the seal on a successful military campaign by securing the territorial revenues of Bengal, Bihar, and Orissa for the East India Company. The company was granted the *diwani* of these large provinces by the Mughal emperor Shah Alam II in the Treaty of Allahabad in August 1765, and news of this great turning point in the company's fortunes reached London on April 19, 1766. It was forwarded almost immediately to North America, with a letter dated April 22 arriving in Boston on June 19.[46] The news from India, presented in the form of "An extract of a letter from Bengal," was then reported in the *Boston Evening Post* on June 23, and the *New Hampshire Gazette* four days later.

Following Clive's great success in Bengal, the East India Company became a semipermanent fixture on the British domestic political agenda, and it was the subject of a considerable amount of coverage in the London press.[47] Concern about British conduct in India, rumors about extensive corruption, and, above all, condemnation of "nabobs" or returned company servants were all reported in great detail, alongside general items about the climate, geography, history, and topography of territories now controlled by the company.[48] Indeed, as the company began to lurch toward bankruptcy and crisis after 1765, "East India affairs" and proceedings at the company's legislative assembly, the general court, were often given prominence above parliamentary reports in the London press.

In time, this close interest in India was reflected in colonial newspapers, and considerable space was devoted to a wide variety of items related to the company and Britain's Indian empire. After 1765, for example, readers of the *Pennsylvania Gazette* were presented with "Extracts of letters from London," which contained information on East India stock prices,[49] accounts of proceedings at East India House,[50] and reports of parliamentary debates about the East India Company.[51] Those taking the *Virginia Gazette* were kept up to date on the East India trade, military success in India, and the general state of the East India Company,[52] while German-speaking readers of Henry Miller's *Staatsbote* were presented with a series of articles on the company and its traffic in tea during the summer of 1773.[53] As this last example suggests, it was, above all, against a background provided by the gradual breakdown of constitutional and political relations with Britain that attention was increasingly focused upon the East India Company's tea trade, and it was this issue that helped to cause a marked shift in American perceptions of the East. As this happened, colonists undertook a reassessment of their own position within the wider British Empire.

Until Charles Townshend's attempts in 1767 to raise revenue from tea imported into North America, few colonists were moved to express an opinion in print about the East India Company, India, or the empire of the East. Newspaper articles were undoubtedly read and digested, and those who were not indifferent about events in Asia would perhaps have welcomed British success in India, if only because company gains were often made at the expense of the French. Some North Americans no doubt sensed that the new territorial possessions in India added to the general wealth, power, and glory of the wider British Empire, but the form taken by British imperialism in the East remained largely ill-considered and ill-defined. For the vast majority, there were no direct repercussions to be felt from Britain's acquisition of its Indian empire.

All this changed during the early 1770s, however, and for the first time American colonists were obliged to consider the general implications of British imperialism in Asia, and the effects that these might have upon them and their own everyday lives. As this happened, opinions were formed and these were given expression in print alongside the routine reports about India and the East India Company that continued to emanate from sources in London.

During the tea crisis that unfolded between 1767 and 1773, colonial perceptions of the East India Company changed quite considerably. The company was not directly implicated in the political events surrounding the consumer action and colonial boycotts of tea organized between 1767 and 1770 in response to the imposition of the Townshend duties.[54] Although sales of tea to America were hard hit by nonimportation agreements, colonial anger was directed first and foremost toward British ministers, and the company emerged from the episode with its reputation largely unscathed. Colonial views changed markedly and abruptly, however, when it became known that the company had been empowered by the Tea Act of 1773 to trade with North America on its own account through consignees, or buyers of imported tea, who were to replace the merchants who had long managed the legal colonial tea trade. In October 1773 the Tea Act was printed on the front pages of colonial newspapers and this prompted an outpouring of letters on the subject of the tea trade and the threat that it posed to American liberties.[55]

In the months that followed, extensive coverage was devoted to the many town meetings held to coordinate action against the act. Tea, it was reported in the press in February 1774, "has of late been, and is now, the principal subject of conversation, and has occasioned such a vast number of town meetings upon this continent."[56] Different modes of resistance, both passive and active, were developed at these meetings and then implemented in the form of both individual and community action. As tea stocks were voluntarily and indiscriminately burned in large communal bonfires,[57] consignees and merchants were threatened and intimidated, and Americans were urged to boycott imported tea and consider growing their own.[58] Not all bowed to this pressure at once, however, and East India goods of a general type continued to be advertised widely throughout the colonies after the Boston Tea Party. One Boston merchant, Cyrus Baldwin, even took the considerable risk in late December 1773 of drawing public attention to tea "to be sold cheap for cash," although he was careful to add, "These [choice Bohea and Souchong] teas were imported before the East India Company tea arrived, or it was known that they would send any here on their own account."[59] Nevertheless, as a tidal wave of "patriotic" action gathered strength up to and beyond the famous events surrounding the Boston Tea Party, public attention was focused closely upon the East India Company. The company's methods and motives were subjected to a searching examination, and this gave rise to the expression of considerable fears about the quite alien forms of British imperialism it was held to represent.

Parliamentary action had been designed to enable the hard-pressed East India Company to dispose of its large accumulated stocks of tea in London, but in the ports of Boston, New York, and Philadelphia the measure was interpreted as a calculated attempt to force cheap but highly taxed tea onto colonial consumers.[60] It was claimed that this action would destroy the livelihood of those merchants and agents who were involved in the tea trade, but it was also believed that the monopoly would eventually be extended, with the company securing exclusive control over the importation of silk, spices, pepper, drugs, and chinaware into the colonies.[61] As the preamble to a notice of a town meeting held in Portsmouth, New Hampshire, asked when outlining the threat posed to the colonies by the company: "If they now succeed, where will they end? Will they not engross and monopolize every other article?"[62] The company's efforts to find a market for its teas in North America were thus firmly resisted by colonists whose resolve was stiffened by rumors that the company intended to establish its own warehouses in their midst.[63] The building of warehouses was seen to represent the first stage in a company attempt to engross and monopolize a large part of British-American trade, and the issue provoked dire warnings from those who perceived it as a very real threat to the economic well-being of the colonies. "A MECHANIC" predicted that the company would "soon send their own factors and creatures, establish houses among US, ship US all other East-India goods; and, in order to full freight their ships, take in other kind of goods at under Freight or (more probably ship) them on their own account to their own factors, and undersell our merchants, till they monopolize the whole trade."[64] The end result would be the destruction of colonial transoceanic trade and the shipbuilding industry. In the face of this threat, Americans developed a healthy appetite for news about the company and its activities. More basic information about the company's history and its structure was laid before readers, and the shortcomings of British rule in India were exposed to colonial newspaper readers through reports of proceedings that had taken place during the course of a lengthy parliamentary inquiry into East India affairs in 1772–73.[65] And, of course, the views of those in Britain who criticized company policy and the changes made to the tea trade were given due prominence in the colonial press.[66] Equipped with such information, Americans were able to broaden the base of the criticisms that they leveled against the company, and in doing this they now began to offer unqualified condemnation of the form taken by British imperial activity in Asia.

Under attack from authors such as "HAMPDEN" who produced the *Alarm* papers that were circulated through the streets of New York, the company was soon transformed into an instrument of tyranny and despotism being deployed by George III and his ministers in their attempts to coerce and oppress North America. One newspaper correspondent referred to Lord North's government and "their auxiliaries, the East-India slavemakers."[67] Elsewhere, the company was depicted as being a "servile tool" which, having been "enslaved" by North, was now being taken up as a weapon to attack America.[68] These sentiments, which had originally been expressed in London, clearly struck a chord, and were intended to strike a chord, in the colonies. The freeholders and inhabitants of Frederick County, Maryland, declared at a meeting held at Winchester that the company, "those servile tools of arbitrary power, have justly forfeited the esteem and regard of all honest men," and they resolved not to purchase any East India goods "except saltpetre, spices, and medicinal drugs."[69] Servile or not, the company's power and ambition was thought to be limitless, and this was held to pose a very real threat to the colonists because of the peculiar strength and potency of the "Asiatic" practices and principles that had been adopted by the British in the East. Indeed, the company became even more feared and despised because of the way that it was thought to have conducted itself in India. Reports from London fueled the belief that through the establishment of an empire of conquest the company had terrorized and forcibly subjugated the people of Bengal. This suggested to some that the company was well versed in the techniques of coercion and control that might now be applied in North America with the active support and encouragement of the British government. John Dickinson, writing as "RUSTICUS," declared in 1773 that the East India Company had "the assurance to step forward in aid of the minister [Lord North], to execute his plan of enslaving" the colonists. Referring to events in India, he continued, noting that "they have, by the most unparalleled barbarities, extortions, and monopolies, stripped the miserable inhabitants of their property, and reduced whole provinces to indigence and ruin . . . having drained the sources of their immense wealth which they have for several years past been accustomed to amass and squander away on their lusts and in corrupting their country, they now, it seems cast their eyes on America as a new theater whereon to exercise their talents of rapine, oppression, and cruelty. . . . It is something of a consolation to be overcome by a lion, but to be devoured by rats is intolerable."[70] Again, a handbill, which contained a forceful attack on the East India Company's tea scheme, was circulated through Pennsylvania by a group of tradesmen in the early winter of 1773. Later published in the *Pennsylvania Gazette*, it told readers about what would inevitably follow in the wake of any acceptance of company tea, warning, "The East India Company, if once they get footing in this (once happy) country, will leave no stone to become your masters. They are an opulent body, and money or credit is not wanting amongst them. They themselves are well versed in TYRANNY, PLUNDER, OPPRESSION, and BLOODSHED. Whole provinces, labouring under the distress of oppression, slavery, famine and the sword, are familiar to them. Thus they have enriched themselves,—thus they are become the most powerful trading company in the universe. Be, therefore, my dear fellow tradesmen, prudent,—be watchful,—be determined to let no motive induce you to favour the accursed scheme."[71]

In helping them to meet this powerful threat, it was believed that Americans were in possession of inherent characteristics, strengths, and virtues that were quite different from those that belonged to the peoples who seemingly had been so easily subjugated by the British in India. Because of this, it was hoped that the outcome of the hard-fought struggle between the forces of tyranny and freedom would not be the same in the western part of Britain's empire as it had been in the East. As John Dickinson put it, "The monopoly of tea is, I dare say, but a small part of the plan they have formed to strip us of all our property. But thank GOD, we are not Sea Poys, nor Marattas, but British subjects who are born to liberty, who know its worth and prize it high."[72]

It was also believed that because the company had been tainted with Eastern ways, it had played an important part in destroying the virtue and moral strength of those in the metropolis who had come into contact with powerful corrosive agents such as avarice, corruption, idleness, and luxury, which had found their way from India into British society and the body politic. The "decay of Britain" became an important theme among commentators on both sides of the Atlantic, and the supposed effects of the possession of an Asiatic empire were duly noted as an important cause of this worrying situation. Americans were already engaged in a vigorous debate about the extent to which their "virtue" was under threat from a form of consumerism that was heavily dependent upon imported luxury goods and commodities such as tea.[73] Some now also argued that Eastern vices would be reexported from Britain by the company and would find their way into American society, where they would have an equally damaging effect.[74] This was a primary concern among the residents of Ipswich, Massachusetts who, at a town meeting on December 23, 1773, expressed a strong collective desire to prevent the landing of company tea at any American port. Their first resolution, which also highlighted a strong undercurrent of tension that existed between port and inland towns, argued that tea was being imported "for the sole purpose of raising a revenue." It went on to suggest, however, that, if landed, the tea would "support, in idleness and extravagance, a set of miscreants, whose vile emissaries and understrappers swarm in seaport towns, and by their dissolute lives and evil practices, threaten this land with a curse more deplorable than Egyptian darkness."[75] Another Egyptian analogy had been used elsewhere in Massachusetts a month or so earlier, when the town meeting of Cambridge had resolved that the tea duty would be collected by a "set of worse than Egyptian Task-masters."[76]

Powerful Eastern influences emanating from one periphery of Britain's overseas empire were thus seen to have weakened the imperial core and it appeared that, in turn, they were now being brought to bear upon another periphery. This was a point made with some force by Governor William Livingston when he spoke before the Assembly and Council of New Jersey in 1776. He reviewed the events of recent years and concluded, "In a word, till the most scrupulous conscience could, on the maturest reflection, find itself justified before God and Man, in renouncing those tyrants, who, having ravaged the great part of Asia, and dissipated in venality and riot the treasures extorted from its innocent inhabitants by the hand of rapine and blood, finally meant to prolong their luxury and corruption by appropriating the hard earned competence of the American world."[77] Livingston's sentiments were wholeheartedly endorsed by one anonymous writer who declared that this passage "ought to be printed in letters of gold, that it might engage the attention of the most heedless American."[78]

In 1773 and the years that followed, Americans were warned, in a number of different ways and at a number of different levels, about the company's supposed evil designs. Those who read or heard such warnings could not avoid the conclusion that the company was seeking to introduce ideas and values into North America that were quite different from those that had hitherto defined and shaped the contours of Britain's Atlantic empire. If the company was successful in its attempt to force tea upon the colonists, slavery, moral decay, and general distress would soon follow. A rejection of company tea, now described as a "poisonous weed,"[79] thus represented a rejection not only of government policy but also of an alien form of imperial relationship of the type that had been forcibly imposed upon the people of Bengal.

Although Americans had many different reasons for rejecting British tea and East India goods, they were not seeking to seal themselves off from the wider world. On the contrary, they continued to acknowledge the material benefits that could be earned from contact with other continents. They had, however, arrived at a point at which they sought to reject some of the values, ideas, and imperial methods they believed were being imported along with British goods from the East. British trade was not simply anglicizing colonial society; it was also now thought to be Easternizing it as well, and this was widely thought to be unacceptable. Americans thus sought to establish new relationships of their own with the wider world, confident that, having been alerted to the dangers of Asian despotism and tyranny, they could avoid the pitfalls and problems encountered by the British in recent years. As they did this, they began to develop direct commercial contact with the peripheries of the empire they were leaving.[80] By building on these foundations, some Americans believed that their own empire of trade could then be established, as was made clear in one "oration on the advantages of independence." The author, Dr. Ramsay, suggested that in the new age "stately oaks" would soon "carry American thunder around the world." He continued, "Whole forests will be transformed into vessels of commerce, enriching this independent continent with the produce of every clime and every soil. The wealth of Europe, Asia, and Africa will flow upon America; our trade will no longer be confined by the selfish regulations of an avaricious step dame, but will follow wherever interest leads the way."[81] According to this projection, membership of one global empire would simply be replaced by membership of another, albeit one organized on very different commercial lines.[82]

For the British, the events of 1773 to 1783 served only to highlight how difficult it was to maintain a presence on more than one imperial front. Afflicted by a general crisis that touched the empire in India, Ireland, and the West Indies as well as North America, British enthusiasm about the possibilities offered by possession of a global empire gradually evaporated. The optimistic assessments about the benefits of empire that had so marked the "years of victory" at the beginning of the 1760s were replaced by gloomy predictions about Britain's future standing in the world. Deeply held fears about activity on a global scale had been realized, and by 1780 the empire seemed to many to be on the point of final collapse and disintegration. Viewed from the center it appeared that, in part, the problems generated by one periphery had been transplanted elsewhere, with devastating consequences. Partly in an attempt to prevent this from happening again, Britain embarked on a period of imperial reconstruction after 1783 that led to a fundamental redefinition of all its surviving relationships with different peripheries, near and far. The effects of this were seen in the methods that were now used to control and regulate the empire, in the recasting of overseas trade on new foundations, and in a growing awareness of the interdependence of different imperial outposts.[83] Indeed, the loss, in a formal sense, of one periphery was to have the most profound implications for British perceptions of its remaining possessions and interests in other parts of the world.

Notes

1. For a recent summary discussion that offers a balanced overview of these developments see P. J. Marshall, "Britain without America—A Second Empire?" in Marshall, ed., *The Oxford History of the British Empire*, vol. 2, *The Eighteenth Century* (Oxford: Oxford University Press, 1998), 576–95. The phrase "swing to the east" was first used by Vincent Harlow whose book provoked a considerable and lengthy debate about the direction, form, and purpose of British overseas activity during the second half of the eighteenth century. See V. T. Harlow, *The Founding of the Second British Empire, 1763–1793*, 2 vols. (Oxford: Oxford University Press, 1952, 1964).
2. This term is used in Patrick Griffin, "America's Changing Image in Ireland's Looking Glass: Provincial Construction of an Eighteenth Century British Atlantic World," *Journal of Imperial and Commonwealth History* 26:3 (1998), 29.
3. See, for example, ibid., and Ned Landsman, "The Provinces and the Empire: Scot-

land and the American Colonies" in Lawrence Stone, ed., *An Imperial State at War: Britain from 1689 to 1815* (London: Routledge, 1994), 258–87.

4. For Richard L. Bushman's use of the term *Anglo-American cultural system* see his "American High Styles and Vernacular Cultures," in Jack P. Greene and J. R. Pole, eds., *Colonial British America: Essays in the New History of the Early Modern Era* (Baltimore: Johns Hopkins University Press, 1984), 348. For a detailed elaboration of the concept see Bushman, *The Refinement of America: Persons, Houses, Cities* (New York: Knopf, 1992).
5. An important exception here is to be found in the significant number of works that explore different aspects of the relationship between Scotland and India. For a small sample of this work see G. J. Bryant, "Scots in India in the Eighteenth Century," *Scottish History Review* 64 (1985), 22–41, and J. Riddy, "Warren Hastings: Scotland's Benefactor?" in Geoffrey Carnall and Colin Nicholson, eds., *The Impeachment of Warren Hastings: Papers from a Bicentenary Commemoration* (Edinburgh: Edinburgh University Press, 1989), 30–57.
6. H. V. Bowen, "British Conceptions of Global Empire, 1756–1783," *Journal of Imperial and Commonwealth History* 26 (1998), 1–27.
7. For reports of some of the celebrations in towns across British North America see *Boston Evening Post*, October 15 and October 22, 1759; *Boston Post Boy*, October 22, 1759; *Maryland Gazette,* November 1 and 8, 1759; *New Hampshire Gazette*, October 19, 1759; and *Pennsylvania Gazette*, October 18 and 25, 1759. *The South Carolina Gazette* declared on November 17, 1759 that "the rejoicings through the British Empire in North America have been the greatest and most general ever known. . . ."
8. For examples of the type of verses inspired by the death of Wolfe see *New Hampshire Gazett*e, November 2 and December 29, 1759. An epic poem about Wolfe, "a second Scipio," was begun in the *South Carolina Gazette* on November 17, 1759. It was continued on November 24 and eventually concluded on December 22.
9. *Pennsylvania Gazette*, March 13, 1760.
10. For a recent expression of this argument, and full supporting references, see T. H. Breen, "Ideology and Nationalism on the Eve of the American Revolution: Revisions Once More in Need of Revising," *Journal of American History* 84 (1997), 22–28.
11. It was of course recognized that territorial expansion on such a scale would have the most profound implications for the future of the British Empire as a whole. For contemporary American discussion of this see Norbert Kilian, "New Wine in Old Skins? American Definitions of Empire and the Emergence of a New Concept," in David Armitage, ed., *Theories of Empire 1450–1800* (Aldershot: Ashgate, 1998), 315–17.
12. For a description of such a wooden mantelpiece decoration see the *Pennsylvania Gazette*, March 14, 1765, and for an advertisement drawing attention to the sugar work of a German confectioner see the *Pennsylvania Gazette*, June 20, 1765.
13. See Burke's comments of 1785 as quoted in Reginald Coupland, *The American Revolution and the British Empire* (London: Longrans, Green, and Co., 1930), 180.
14. For colonial American conceptions of empire and the debate about the North American position in the wider British Empire see Kilian, "New Wine in Old Skins?" 307–15.
15. *Letters from a farmer in Pennsylvania, to the inhabitants of the British colonies by John Dickinson with a historical introduction by R. T. H. Halsey* (New York: Krans Reprint, 1970), 13.
16. This emergence of this view is discussed in detail in Bowen, "British Conceptions of Global Empire."
17. For later British attempts to establish a permanent connection between South America, the Pacific, and India see Holden Furber, "An Abortive Attempt at Anglo-Spanish Co-operation in the Far East in 1793," *Hispanic American Historical Review* 15 (1935), 448–63.
18. Robert C. Ritchie, *Captain Kidd and the War against the Pirates* (Cambridge, Mass.: Harvard University Press, 1986), 26, 37–9, 83, 137.
19. Marcus Rediker, *Between the Devil and the Deep Blue Sea: Merchant Seamen, Pirates, and the Anglo-American Maritime World, 1700–1750* (Cambridge: Cambridge University Press, 1987), 79.

20. N. A. M. Rodger, *The Wooden World: An Anatomy of the Georgian Navy* (London: Collins, 1986), 158.
21. P. S. Haffenden, "Community and Conflict: New England and the Royal Navy 1689–1775" in *The American Revolution and the Sea. Proceedings of the 14th Conference of the International Commission for Maritime History* (Greenwich: National Maritime Museum, 1974), 91. Recruitment of colonial Americans into the Royal Navy, and the levels of resistance, are discussed in Jesse Lemisch, "Jack Tar in the Streets: Merchant Seamen in the Politics of Revolutionary America," *William and Mary Quarterly* 3d series, no. 30 (1968), 381–95.
22. Ian K. Steele, *The English Atlantic 1675–1740: An Exploration of Communication and Community* (New York: Oxford University Press, 1986), 262. Steele estimates that there were twenty-five to thirty thousand men working on Atlantic routes or in the fishing industry during the late 1730s.
23. Rediker, *Between the Devil and the Deep Blue Sea*. Rediker's book is a detailed study of the seaman as a "man of the world."
24. Rodger, *The Wooden World*, 269–70.
25. For this practice see ibid., 139–40.
26. For details of Barlow's extraordinary worldwide maritime career see Basil Lubbock, ed., *Barlow's Journal of His Life at Sea in King's Ships, East and West Indiamen and Other Merchantmen from 1659 to 1703*, 2 vols. (London: Hewst and Blackett, Ltd., 1934).
27. For the global career pattern of Lt. Col. Justly Watson (c. 1710–1757) see Jeremy Black, *European Warfare 1660–1815* (London: UCL Press, 1994), 144.
28. P. G. M. Dickson, *The Financial Revolution in England: A Study in the Development of Public Credit, 1688–1756* (London: Macmillan, 1967), 324. Some of these investors, along with colonial purchasers of other British stocks, are identified on 317, 330–31.
29. For a detailed study of this type of activity engaged in by a group of London merchants see David Hancock, *Citizens of the World: London Merchants and the Integration of the British Atlantic Community, 1735–1785* (Cambridge: Cambridge University Press, 1995).
30. Ritchie, *Captain Kidd*, 66–7.
31. Jacob M. Price, "One Family's Empire: The Russell-Lee-Clerk Connection in Maryland, Britain, and India, 1707–1857," *Maryland Historical Magazine* 72 (1977), 165–225.
32. John J. McCusker and Russell R. Menard, *The Economy of British America, 1607–1783* (Chapel Hill: University of North Carolina Press, 1985), 302, citing Lawrence A. Harper, *The English Navigation Laws*, 266 n. and 267 n.
33. Benjamin W. Labaree, *The Boston Tea Party* (New York: Oxford University Press, 1964), 7.
34. Carole Shammas, *The Pre-Industrial Consumer in England and America* (Oxford: Oxford University Press, 1990), 64.
35. Ibid., 187.
36. Rodris Roth, "Tea-Drinking in Eighteenth-Century America: Its Etiquette and Equipage," in R. B. St. George, ed., *Material Life in America 1600–1800* (Boston: Northeastern University Press, 1988), 439–62.
37. Bushman, *Refinement of America*, 184.
38. Philip Lawson, "Sources, Schools, and Separation: The Many Faces of Parliament's Role in Anglo-American History to 1783" in Lawson, ed., *Parliament and the Atlantic Empire* (Edinburgh: Edinburgh University Press for the Parliamentary History Yearbook, 1995), 20–21.
39. T. H. Breen, "An Empire of Goods: The Anglicization of Colonial America, 1690–1776," *Journal of British Studies* 25 (1986), 467–99.
40. Breen, "Ideology and Nationalism," 17.
41. *New York Gazette and Weekly Mercury*, November 1, 1773.
42. For a pictorial example of a shop sign which highlighted the availability of Eastern produce see Roth, "Tea-Drinking in Eighteenth-Century America," 457. Advertisements for East India goods are to be found scattered throughout colonial newspapers.
43. For colonial American attitudes toward the "mutually beneficial" empire of commerce see T. H. Breen, "Narrative of Commercial Life: Consumption, Ideology, and Com-

munity on the Eve of the American Revolution," *William and Mary Quarterly* 3d ser., no. 5 (1993), 481–83.

44. Charles E. Clark, *The Public Prints: The Newspaper in Anglo-American Culture, 1665–1740* (New York: Oxford University Press, 1994), 216.
45. See also the *Maryland Gazette*, January 3, 1760.
46. For details of the reduction in the age of London-datelined news arriving in the colonies between 1702 and 1744 see Steele, *English Atlantic*, 158–59. For the speed of news delivery from London by newspapers in the southern colonies see Robert M. Weir, "The Role of the Newspaper in the Southern Colonies on the Eve of the American Revolution: An Interpretation" in Bernard Bailyn and John B. Hench, eds., *The Press and the American Revolution* (Boston: Northeastern University Press, 1981), 127–31, 150.
47. H. V. Bowen, *Revenue and Reform: The Indian Problem in British Politics, 1757–1773* (Cambridge: Cambridge University Press, 1991).
48. For the upsurge in metropolitan interest in India see P. J. Marshall and Glyndwr Williams, *The Great Map of Mankind: British Perceptions of the World in the Age of Enlightenment* (London: J. M. Dent and Sons, Ltd., 1982), 74–8.
49. April 23, 1767; July 27, 1769; November 11, 1771.
50. December 11, 1766; January 6, 1773.
51. August 27, 1767; March 17, 1773.
52. March 16, 1769, April 5, 1770, and November 12, 1772.
53. Willi Paul Adams, "The Colonial German-Language Press and the American Revolution," in Bailyn and Hench, eds., *The Press and the American Revolution*, 196.
54. For discussion of the boycott of tea and general colonial resistance to the Townshend duties, see Labaree, *Boston Tea Party*, 15–57, and Breen, "Narrative of Commercial Life," 485–94.
55. See, for example, *Boston Evening Post*, October 25, 1773. For reporting of the Tea Act in North America see Labaree, *Boston Tea Party*, 87–89.
56. "From the *Massachusetts Spy*" in the *New Hampshire Gazette*, February 18, 1774.
57. For a report of the bonfire of all imported tea, Dutch as well as British, that took place at Lexington see *New York Gazette and Weekly Mercury*, December 27, 1773.
58. For practical advice on the growing of tea in North America see the article by "HOME MANUFACTURE" in *Boston Post Boy*, January 31–February 7, 1774.
59. *Boston Gazette*, December 27, 1773.
60. P. D. G. Thomas, *Tea Party to Independence: The Third Phase of the American Revolution, 1773–1776* (Oxford: Clarendon Press, 1991), 14–15. Labaree, *Boston Tea Party*, 89–103.
61. Different aspects of colonial fears about the establishment of a company monopoly are illustrated in Arthur Meier Schlesinger, "The Uprising against the East India Company," *Political Science Quarterly* 32 (1917), 71–75.
62. *Boston Post Boy* December 13–20, 1773.
63. This intended company action was reported in the colonial press before and after the Boston Tea Party. See, for example, *Pennsylvania Gazette*, May 3, 1773 and December 22, 1773. I have found no evidence in the company's records that suggests that any such measure was ever discussed.
64. Quoted in Schlesinger, "Uprising," 72.
65. See, for example, *Pennsylvania Gazette*, January 19, 1774. Even before the tea crisis broke in the autumn of 1773, colonial newspapers were taking an interest in the proceedings against Lord Clive who was facing corruption charges in Parliament (*Boston Evening Post*, July 19, 1773).
66. See, for example, the parliamentary speech of George Johnstone (MP for Cockermouth and former governor of West Florida) made on March 30, and reported in the *Pennsylvania Gazette* on May 18, 1774.
67. *Boston Post Boy*, December 6–12, 1773.
68. *Pennsylvania Gazette*, June 8, 1774.
69. Ibid., June 29, 1774.
70. John Dickinson, *A Letter from the Country* (Philadelphia: Belknap Press at Harvard University Press, 1773), quoted in Bernard Bailyn with the assistance of Jane N. Gar-

rett, ed., *Pamphlets of the American Revolution 1750–1776.* Vol. 1: *1750–1765* (Cambridge, Mass.: Belknap Press at Harvard University Press, 1965), 665. For a slightly different version of this passage see Schlesinger, "Uprising," 77.

71. *Pennsylvania Gazette*, December 8, 1773. See also *Boston Post Boy*, December 13–20, 1773.
72. This section of the letter from the American farmer "from the country to a gentleman in Philadelphia" was printed in, among other newspapers, the *Connecticut Courant* of February 1–8, 1774.
73. Breen, "Narrative of Commercial Life," 494–500.
74. For a discussion of this theme see Bernard Bailyn, *The Ideological Origins of the American Revolution* (Cambridge, Mass.: Belknap Press at Harvard University Press, 1967), 134–39.
75. *Boston Gazette*, January 3, 1774.
76. *Boston Post Boy*, November 22–29, 1773.
77. Ibid., October 9, 1776.
78. Ibid.
79. *Boston Evening Post*, November 29, 1773. Tea drinking was now widely attacked as a harmful habit. See, for example, Schlesinger, "Uprising," 78.
80. See, for example, Holden Furber, "The Beginnings of American Trade with India, 1784–1812," *New England Quarterly* 11 (1938), 235–65.
81. The oration of Dr. Ramsay, delivered at Charleston, South Carolina, and dedicated to the lieutenant governor, Christopher Gadsen, as reported in the *Pennsylvania Gazette*, January 20, 1779.
82. For discussion of the several different lines of thought evident in use of the term *empire* as it was applied to the new American situation by those in the former colonies after 1775 see Kilian, "New Wine in Old Skins?" 317–20.
83. For a recent study of some of these issues see C. A. Bayly, *Imperial Meridian: The British Empire and the World, 1780–1830* (London: Longman, 1989). See also Harlow, *Founding of the Second British Empire.*

"Empire for Liberty"

Center and Peripheries in Postcolonial America

Peter S. Onuf

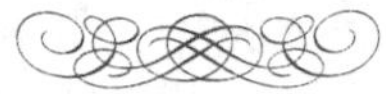

"Who can limit the extent to which the federative principle may operate effectively?" asked Thomas Jefferson in his second inaugural address in March 1805. The Louisiana Purchase had added a vast new domain to the United States, leading less optimistic observers to fear "that the enlargement of our territory would endanger its union."[1] But Jefferson looked forward to the proliferation of free republican states, bound together by ties of common principles and harmonious interests. The Enlightenment vision of a benign postimperial order, predicated on the reciprocity of benefits and the security of natural rights, would be fulfilled with the union's progressive expansion. Power would be diffused and decentered in the federal republic: The Americans would no longer be subject to the domineering rule of a distant metropolis, as they had been before declaring and securing their independence. Indeed, for Jefferson, the new nation was invulnerable—it had, as he had boldly pronounced in his first inaugural, "the strongest Government on earth"—precisely because it had *not* concentrated authority and resources in a single central place, so inviting the assaults of hostile, counterrevolutionary powers. The new nation's strength could not be measured in conventional military terms, but rather in the loyalty of the "honest patriot" who would rise up in defense of his own liberties and his country's independence whenever they were threatened.[2]

Jefferson's conception of a new republican, postimperial order in the American hemisphere met with considerable skepticism in his own day (the "candid apprehension" of antiexpansionist critics that he acknowledged in his second inaugural) and derision in our own. The thrust of the criticism then and now has been that Jefferson did not have a firm grasp of geopolitical reality, and that his penchant for ideological posturing and empty abstractions led him dangerously astray.

Federalists invoked the conventional wisdom of contemporaneous political science in warning against the centrifugal effects of an overextended polity. Federalists were not always opposed to expansion: national security might dictate an aggressive, expansionist policy, as when Federalists urged a preemptive strike against New

Orleans—before Jefferson's diplomacy (and good luck) gained the prize by peaceful means. But the premise of Federalist foreign policy was that there should be a correspondence between military force and strategic objectives, that the expansion of the union should never run ahead of the federal government's ability to enforce its authority against foreign and domestic threats. Yet if Federalists agreed that the annexation of New Orleans was imperative, they were equally certain that the acquisition of the Louisiana Territory was a potential disaster. The disproportion between its present extended domain and its pathetically inadequate military force already put the new nation at serious risk: Further expansion would weaken the bonds of union, exposing and exacerbating interregional conflicts of interest.[3]

Modern "realists" also denounce Jefferson for failing to acknowledge the imperatives of power politics. But they must account for a subsequent course of historical development—the rise of the United States within a few short decades to continental and then hemispheric hegemony—that would have left Jefferson's Federalist critics utterly baffled. Retrospective realists, chronicling the inevitable, inexorable rise of American empire thus emphasize the extraordinary dynamism of a continental economy that eventually would underwrite American power, the fortuitous circumstance of a collapsing European balance of power and the effective dismantling of European imperial regimes in the Americas. Had Jefferson and his followers been true to their idealistic professions, they might well have squandered these geopolitical advantages. But the history of Jeffersonian statecraft was one of ruthlessly exploiting regional power imbalances according to the pragmatic precepts of reason of state diplomacy—and of the hypocritical denial or, worse, the convenient self-delusion that republicans operated on a higher moral plane than their corrupt European counterparts.

The Federalist critique of Jeffersonian expansionism asserted that a polity of imperial dimensions could survive multiplying external challenges to its extended frontiers and corresponding centrifugal pressures from within only by modeling itself on the powerful nation-states with which it must necessarily contend. Visions of universal monarchy that had once inspired European imperialists could not be sustained in the modern era of great power politics; nor, as the American Revolution surely had demonstrated, was it possible to sustain a less autocratic, more liberal imperial regime dedicated to the pursuit of common interests and reciprocal benefits. Antiexpansionist Federalists concluded that the very idea of "empire" itself was an anachronism in the modern age, that the Jeffersonian-Republicanism quest for an "empire for liberty"—an empire that would dispense with concentrated power and metropolitan rule—would leave the new nation hopelessly ill-equipped to deal with pressing and pervasive threats to its vital interests and even to its survival.

The United States should become a stronger nation, consolidating authority in a central government that commanded the resources of the continent, before it recklessly risked the enmity of the great European powers. Federalists thus saw the new nation operating as a weak, secondary force in a postimperial balance of power. Modern critics, taking a much longer view, are more impressed with continuities between the old imperial regime and the new national dispensation. It would be only a matter of time before the United States would emerge as a new imperial power, despite its affectation of republican righteousness and despite the Jeffersonians' failure to follow the lead of Federalist nation builders. In this reductive perspective, *empire* and *nation* are not clearly distinguishable terms. *Empire* is read forward into our own time, and *nation* backward to its mythic origins in early modernity. Power is the great solvent, for we know nations and empires (powerful nations with hegemonic ambitions) for what they do to each other, not for the distinctive ways in which they are constituted and conceptualized.[4]

My premise in this essay is that the American Revolution precipitated epochal constitutional and conceptual changes reflected in controversy over the implications of territorial expansion for the future of the American union. Britain was the exemplar of an effective, modernizing nation-state that could best secure and project its vital interests. Federalist antiexpansionists embraced the logic of national sovereignty and the competitive struggle for relative advantage. It was most characteristically anti-imperial and therefore "modern" on the question of size, for it was convinced that an overextended union could never achieve a sufficient degree of national integration to function effectively in a dangerous world. Jeffersonian expansionsists, by contrast, rejected the consolidation of authority that they believed had destroyed the British Empire and Federalists persisted in advocating precisely that because they continued to think and act within an imperial framework. As reform-minded proponents of an idealized world order, made fully and finally compatible with natural rights, free exchange, the progressive diffusion of civilization, and the rights of self-government within and among confederated states, Jeffersonian-Republican imperialists looked backward.[5]

Under the republican aegis, the New World would be redeemed from the destructive struggles of European powers for dominion. The expanding American union would become an "empire for liberty." Jeffersonian avatars of the new dispensation thus invoked the most enlightened and advanced thinking of the modern age on behalf of an antique imperial vision. That Jeffersonian vision of republican empire ultimately failed, but not—as Federalist critics and neo-Federalist scholars contend—because it could not accommodate the realities of international power politics in the modern world. To the contrary, I hope to show, the most severe challenges to the American system came from within, not from without.

Ever anxious about the reimposition of an older, centralized style of imperial rule, vigilant republicans increasingly cast their domestic opponents as "foreigners" who were conspiring to seize the federal government and foster the development of a dangerously powerful national metropolis. In other words, memories of the old (British monarchical) empire tended to have a corrosive, ultimately subversive effect on the new (American republican) empire. Indeed, the existence of genuine threats from abroad, or from European imperial powers on the American frontiers, mitigated the tendency for American republicans to see the worst in their American foes. But without such threats, a kind of ideological regress set in, as Americans imagined themselves in the embattled situation of the Revolutionary fathers, vindicating their liberties against a despotic imperial regime. The American Revolution thus simultaneously served as the unifying, universalizing, nation-making myth for subsequent generations of Americans and as a paradigm for a potentially divisive, increasingly sectionalized, nation-breaking politics. The Civil War constituted the ultimate regression, as they resisted the relentless encroachments of northern despotism southern secessionists saw themselves as the true legatees of their Revolutionary fathers.[6]

The Revolutionaries' new republican empire finally failed because later generations of Americans could not, in moments of political and constitutional crisis, clearly distinguish it from the old monarchical empire that they had overthrown with independence. The imaginative conflation of old and new empires revealed the conservative, backward-looking ("classical") tendencies of American republican ideology, obsessively focused on the vindication of provincial liberties against the emerging power of the modern nation-state. This conflation also tended to obscure from view, both for contemporaries and for later commentators, the progressive, forward-looking dimensions of the "empire for liberty."

Jefferson and his fellow patriots imagined that there was a world of difference between monarchical and republican rule, between an extended polity held in place by consolidated, coercive power and a consensual union of free republican states in a regime of reciprocal benefits and perpetual peace. This notion of a republican imperium enlisted the modernizing discourses of Enlightenment political economy, social theory, and jurisprudence to envision a postmonarchical future in which power would be domesticated, diffused, and decentered. But when later generations—and Jefferson himself, in his later years—began to fear that this republican millennium would never be attained, the bright line between old and new became progressively dimmer. Insufficiently virtuous, Americans were really no different than Europeans; whatever its apparent form or constitution, monarchical or republican, power was essentially the same. These growing doubts, characteristically expressed in protestations of self-righteousness and the projection of anti-American tendencies onto partisan or sectional foes, led doctrinaire republicans to emphasize the fragility and tenuousness of their liberties, to reconceptualize the promise of a republican future as the endangered legacy of a glorious Revolutionary past.

As latter-day republicans refought the Revolution and paid homage to the Revolutionary fathers, they implicitly called into question the epochal, world-changing character of the movement that the fathers themselves had celebrated. It was not that Americans doubted the superiority of republican to monarchical governments in a general way, but rather that they were increasingly skeptical about the effectiveness, impartiality, durability, and republican character of their *federal* government. In other words, they doubted that their republican *empire* was such an epochal improvement on—or perhaps even a viable alternative to—the old monarchical imperial order. Antebellum Americans insisted that they had not lost their faith, but celebrations of the union and its manifest destiny betrayed the growing recognition of its problematic character in practice.

The apotheosis of perpetual union as an end in itself and as the object of patriotic devotion eloquently testified to the conceptual impoverishment of the Revolutionaries' republican empire. This was not the liberal, cosmopolitan idea of union as a republican alternative to the rule of domineering metropolis over subject provinces, but rather an exclusive, exceptionalist conception of American nationhood that put the Americans on the same plane as other nations, justifying the consolidation of power in the name of a single great, homogenous "people." The identification of union and nation was vigorously and bitterly contested by defenders of local, state, and sectional rights and interests. Opponents of federal power, fearful of its potential abuses, now invoked the discourses of modernity—free trade, the reciprocal distribution of benefits, government by consent—*against* the union.

The founders' conception of the federal republic as a progressive alternative to great power politics faded from memory. Jefferson and his fellow radical republicans had believed the Revolution would transform their world, rendering the conventional, coercive, and destructive exercise of power that sustained imperial rule over extended territories obsolete. The destruction of the union in the Civil War marked the ultimate failure of this vision of a republican empire. Before he died, Jefferson had a preview of this awful outcome: The Missouri "question, like a fire bell in the night, awakened and filled me with terror. I considered it at once as the knell of the Union."[7]

Jefferson's conception of republican empire grew out of his experiences as a leader of Virginia's revolution against British imperial rule.[8] In seeking to vindicate his colony's corporate rights and to impose radical limits on royal authority, Jefferson assumed a boldly republican stance. Yet Jefferson's animus against George III, culminating in the passionate denunciations of the Declaration of Independence, was inspired by a powerful identification with an idealized British Empire. The legacy of this imperial vision was apparent in Jefferson's conception of an American union in which his beloved Virginia would flourish.

Jefferson's challenges to royal authority before the Revolution provided the conceptual framework for his imperial vision. "Kings are the servants, not the proprietors of the people," he provocatively asserted in his *Summary View of the Rights of British America* (1774), thus deflating and reversing conventional formulations. Jefferson was determined to explode the "fictitious principle that all lands belong originally to the king," whose proprietorship thus defined his dominions and constituted his subjects as people.[9] Elaborating the theory of expatriation that Virginian Richard Bland had sketched out a decade earlier, Jefferson imagined a more direct relation between the king and his people, unmediated by property relations and the degrading implication that George III "owned" his Virginian subjects. "America was conquered, and her settlements made, and firmly established, at the expence of individuals, and not of the British public," Jefferson explained. "Their own blood was spilt in acquiring lands for their settlement, their own fortunes expended in making that settlement effectual; for themselves they fought, for themselves they conquered, and for themselves alone they have right to hold."[10] By identifying the king with *one* of the "peoples" over whom he ruled—"the British public"—Jefferson framed the issue in terms of the equal (property) rights of another, wholly distinct people, the Virginians, who had "submitt[ed]" themselves to the same common sovereign. In Jefferson's imaginative reformulation, the empire was constituted by the voluntary submission of its component communities to the authority of the king, "the central link connecting the several parts of the empire thus newly multiplied."[11]

The *Summary View* offered a rationale both for a radically diminished conception of royal authority and for denying Parliament—the legislature of the British people—any authority at all. For most commentators the conclusion was irresistible: Jefferson and his fellow radicals meant to make British America into an independent sovereignty and rival power. Yet there was a countertendency in Jefferson's Revolutionary writings, a quest for an enduring "union" that would sustain and expand the British Empire. George III might be a "servant" of his people(s), but he played an absolutely crucial role as "the only mediatory power between the several states of the British empire."[12] This union of peoples, the fundamental meaning of "empire" for

Jefferson, was a higher good, indeed the highest political good. "We are willing, on our part," he would have had the Continental Congress say, "to sacrifice every thing which reason can ask to the restoration of that tranquillity for which all must wish. On their part, *let them be ready to establish union* and a generous plan. Let them name their terms, but let them be just."[13]

Jefferson's hatred of monarchy, the animating premise of his political thought throughout his subsequent career, was a function of increasingly exaggerated expectations and their inevitable frustration. The sense of personal betrayal in the Declaration of Independence seems extravagantly excessive in Jefferson's recital of George III's "long train of abuses," inviting as it did the editorial excisions of his soberer colleagues and the psychological speculations of his biographers.[14] Yet Jefferson's indictment of the king in the Declaration was a measure of the importance he attached to imperial union, not of his guilty misgivings about assaulting patriarchal authority. This was much more than a case of disclaiming responsibility and projecting guilt in a psychodrama of national self-determination. George III's abuses carried enormous rhetorical weight for Jefferson because the constitutional controversies of the imperial crisis had eliminated every other "link" between British metropolis and the British-American provinces or "states." This was a union that Jefferson cherished, even as it was progressively ruptured, not only because he shared the Anglophiliac tendencies of provincial elites but because empire—his idealized version of the old regime—provided the conceptual framework for his enlightened, cosmopolitan republicanism.[15]

George III was important to Jefferson because his sovereign authority, constitutionally limited in order to secure the rule of law and legitimately exercised only in service to his subjects, was the last remaining link of imperial union. In one of the passages of the original draft of the Declaration that was excised by Congress, Jefferson recurred to the mythical history of Anglo-America he had outlined in the *Summary View*. The settlement of the colonies had been "effected at the expense of our own blood & treasure, unassisted by the wealth or the strength of Great Britain"; the empire was the product of *colonial* initiatives: "in constituting indeed our several forms of government, we had adopted one common king, thereby laying a foundation for *perpetual league & amity* with them." Significantly, this union, made possible by the "mediatory power" of the king, was between distinct peoples, or "states." It had been destroyed because George III had proven incapable of rising above a partial, self-interested identification with one of his peoples at the expense of the others. But the ultimate blame for this unhappy state of affairs lay not with George himself, but with the British people, those "unfeeling brethren" who in the final crisis encouraged *their* "chief magistrate" (he was no longer a "common king") to pillage and plunder the Americans, not to make peace with them and so perpetuate imperial union.[16]

Jefferson's antimonarchical turn was complete. Not only had the British monarchy proven incapable of preserving the complex and extended imperial polity, but it also worked to foment discord and enmity among peoples who were by virtue of ties of birth, culture, sentiment, and interest "natural" allies. Indeed, the unnatural behavior of "unfeeling" British brethren was eloquent testimony to the pernicious effects of a corrupt monarchical regime in making friends into enemies. True union would only be possible if monarchy and aristocracy were extirpated: To endure and prosper, an *empire* had to be *republican*.

The important work of Jefferson's Declaration was to persuade Anglo-Americans that loyalty to the king could no longer sustain union between Britain and the American colonies. But if these "political bands" were "dissolve[d]," Jefferson believed that declaring independence forged new bands. No longer united through the mediation of the British monarchy, the American states were now "Free and Independant," with "full Power to levy War, conclude Peace, contract Alliances, establish Commerce, and to do all other Acts and Things which Independant States may of right do." Yet as the American states dissolved their ties with Britain and recognized each other's free and equal status, they proceeded to form a new and more enduring union, stating "we mutually pledge to each other our Lives, our Fortunes, and our sacred Honor."[17] For Jefferson, this was no mere rhetorical flourish. As he wrote near the end of his life (in 1825), the Declaration was "the fundamental act of union of these States."[18]

Union, like the republican governments of its member states, was based on "the consent of the governed"; "the Laws of Nature and of Nature's God" entitled these *states* to a "separate & equal station," just as the creator endowed all *men* with "unalienable Rights."[19] In both cases the recognition of equal rights guaranteed closer ties, more perfect unions of men and of republican states, than had been possible under British monarchy. The monarchical connection had not only fostered unnatural divisions between metropolitan Britons and provincial Anglo-Americans, but it had set colony against colony in a mutually destructive competition for relative advantage.

The British Empire's radical flaw was the fundamental premise of inequality, manifest in the pretensions of the central government to exercise rule over distant provinces, in the unequal distribution of benefits in the imperial economy, and in the hierarchical order of monarchical society. The collapse of Britain's monarchical empire showed that such unequal pretensions could only be sustained by the exercise of coercive force that soon proved self-defeating, and disunion was the result. By contrast, Jefferson's republican empire would be built on the more durable foundation of equal rights.

Jefferson's conception of union was reflected in the way the Declaration recognizes the claims of a plurality of distinct states and at the same time speaks for them in a single voice. It would be a mistake to conclude either that Jefferson and his colleagues were themselves confused about the sources of their own authority—for whom were they speaking?—or that they meant to sow confusion at home and abroad as a cover for their bold assumption of authority. For Jefferson, recognition of the master principle of equality enabled Americans to discover and promote unity in diversity both within and among their state-republics. The genius of a republican empire, its great source of power, was that the singular and the plural would thus define and support one another, securing the rights of the parts—citizens and states—was the threshold for recognizing the transcendent claims of the whole. What could signify this recognition more powerfully than the willingness of congressmen to pledge their "Lives . . . Fortunes and . . . sacred Honor" to one another?

Jefferson's republican empire was predicated both on the rejection of monarchical rule and constitutional guarantees of the kind of provincial autonomy and self-determination that Anglo-Americans had long enjoyed. Certainly, as his biographers have emphasized, Jefferson was a loyal Virginian, dedicated throughout his long life to the interests of his "country" (and his class). But it was precisely because Jefferson was a "localist," so prosperously and self-confidently situated on the imperial periphery, that he could envision a republican alternative, that of an empire without a dominant metropolitan center that would expand across the continent, securing the rights of its member states and spreading its benefits equally.

Jefferson offered a blueprint for the new republican empire in his *Notes on the State of Virginia*. The "Old Dominion" may have once taken pride in its British connections, but the imperial crisis had revealed the ways in which proud Virginia was in fact subject to the commercial exploitation and despotic rule of a distant, "unfeeling" metropolis. Independent Virginia would not go its own way, however, despite its imperial dimensions ("This state is . . . one third larger than the islands of Great Britain and Ireland, which are reckoned at 88357 square miles") and the extraordinary prospects for future development so exhaustively cataloged throughout the *Notes*.[20] For Jefferson, Virginia's future and America's were inextricable, even indistinguishable.

The *Notes* constituted an imaginative effort to situate Virginia in a dynamic and expanding union. The first two "queries" tell contrasting stories of contracting territorial limits and expanding commerce and settlement. In the first query (on "Boundaries"), Jefferson recounted successive limitations on Virginia's vast domains, beginning with "the grant of Maryland to the Lord Baltimore" (in 1632) and culminating (for the time being at least) with "the cession made by Virginia to Congress of all the lands to which they had title on the North side of the Ohio" (in 1784). If Virginia diminishes in the first query, however, its prospective influence extends far beyond its contracted boundaries in the next query ("Rivers").[21] Indeed, Jefferson's horizon now extends to the limits of the union itself: "The country watered by the Missisipi and its eastern branches, constitutes five-eighths of the United States, two of which five-eighths are occupied by the Ohio and its waters: the residuary streams which run into the Gulph of Mexico, the Atlantic, and the St. Laurence water, the remaining three-eighths."[22]

Even while Virginia was bounded within increasingly narrow limits, Virginians found themselves favorably situated to participate in the boundless opportunities afforded by the great system of inland waterways. During the colonial period, boundary changes were imposed by the Crown as new colonies were created and international agreements negotiated. In theory, these changes violated Virginia's territorial integrity: Crown jurisdiction derived from—and therefore could not legitimately diminish—the corporate property rights of a community of expatriated Englishmen. But "our ancestors . . . were farmers, not lawyers," Jefferson wrote in the *Summary View*, and just as the colonists submitted to Crown management of public lands, they had tacitly accepted boundary limitations.[23]

At Jefferson's suggestion, the first state constitution (adopted in June 1776) insisted on Virginia's original territorial right even as it legitimized colonial boundary changes. It noted, "The territories contained within the Charters erecting the Colonies of Maryland, Pennsylvania, North and South Carolina, are hereby ceded, released, and forever confirmed to the People of those Colonies respectively, with all the rights of property, jurisdiction, and Government, and all other rights whatsoever which might at any time heretofore have been claimed by Virginia. . . ." This acknowledgment of the jurisdictional status quo would preempt boundary conflicts and facilitate union among the new American republics. Jefferson envisioned this process of progressive self-limitation continuing under the new republican dispensation. According to his draft of the constitution, the legislature would be empowered to lay off "one or more territories" west of the mountains as "new colonies . . . established on the same fundamental laws contained in this instrument, and shall be free and independant of this colony and of all the world." (As finally adopted by the convention, the Constitution authorized the legislature to form "one or two" new states in the west, but eliminated Jefferson's discussion of their future constitutional and political status.)[24]

Jefferson's conception of republican empire was encapsulated in his provision for "free and independant" new states in his draft constitution and in his subsequent Ordinance for Territorial Government, adopted by Congress in 1784, calling for the admission of new western states to the union "on an equal footing with the . . . original states."[25] His apparently paradoxical premise was that the recognition of the equal rights of political communities, and therefore of their complete independence of each other and of "all the world," was the necessary precondition for creating enduring, consensual bonds of union among them. State boundaries that were drawn to secure the rights and promote the real interests of republican citizens would preempt wars and facilitate peaceful exchanges. Empire thus was not simply the happy consequence of the natural affinity of republics; Jefferson also assumed that the boundaries that defined the effective limits of self-governing republics would be *permeable*, facilitating the proliferation of interdependent economic interests and social connections that would establish union on the most solid (and "natural") foundation.[26]

The *Notes on the State of Virginia* constituted both a promotional tract, celebrating the state's and the nation's prospects for economic development, and Jefferson's blueprint for completing the republican revolution in his beloved Commonwealth. In explicating this reform program, scholars have appropriately focused attention on Jefferson's dissatisfaction with the Virginia constitution of 1776 and on his frustrated efforts to effect a comprehensive revisal of the Commonwealth's laws (discussed at length in queries 13 and 14).[27] Jefferson thought that the ongoing process of making the state *smaller* was equally important to the progressive perfection of republican government in Virginia. (Jefferson's "ward republics" took this principle of territorial fission to its logical extreme, "distributing to every one exactly the functions he is competent to. . ., dividing and subdividing these republics from the great national one down through all its subordinations, until it ends in the administration of every man's farm by himself."[28]) But small republics presupposed a republican context, a consensual union of "Free and Independant" states. Making Virginia smaller only made sense to the patriotic Jefferson to the extent that it could freely exploit its advantageous situation in an ever larger, more perfect republican union. For Jefferson, contracting boundaries and boundless opportunity were inextricably, dialectically linked; this was his vision of republican empire.

Jefferson's vision was predicated on a faith in the beneficient, harmonizing, and civilizing effects of commerce that was widely shared by enlightened political economists of his day. The notion of reciprocal benefits in mutually beneficial exchange was particularly attractive to colonists who chafed under a mercantilist regime that they believed enriched the metropolitan core at the expense of the provincial periphery.[29] Indeed, the growing conviction among alienated American patriots that the British Empire was designed *not* to secure the rights of all Englishmen, but rather to make invidious distinctions and render unequal benefits among them, gave apparently trivial constitutional quarrels an ultimately revolutionary urgency. For Jefferson and many other revolutionaries, the specter of metropolitan domination and of the "enslavement" of subject provinces inexorably led to the rejection of monarchical authority and therefore of the British connection. But it did not lead, as Jefferson's *Notes* eloquently attest, to the rejection of empire.

Jefferson celebrated the prospective operation of a liberal regime of free trade within the framework of a more perfect republican empire. This would be an empire without a center, or *dominant metropolis*. Dynamic and expansive, it would spread, diffuse, and equalize benefits through the vast system of inland waterways, improved and extended by the art of man, to its farthest reaches: This would be an empire without peripheries. American "nature" made this great project possible. Indeed, Jefferson's imperial vision took on a reassuring concreteness and specificity in the inventories of resources and developmental opportunities in the *Notes* that stood in stark contrast to the unnaturalness and artificiality of the old imperial regime.

Jefferson's hostility to cities is well known, and frequently misunderstood. His main concern was not to forestall commercial development, but rather to preempt the (unnatural) concentrations of population, wealth, and power that would recapitulate the structural inequalities and inefficiences of the monarchical empire. The most eloquent statement of Jefferson's urban vision is not to be found in his famous strictures in query 19 ("Manufactures")—"the mobs of great cities add just so much to the support of pure government, as sores do to the strength of the human body"—but rather in query 3 ("Sea-Ports"). Jefferson left this query blank: "Having no ports but our rivers and creeks, this Query has been answered under the preceding one" on "Rivers."[30] Of course, Jefferson knew that this assertion was literally not true: America would not exist without links to the larger world through its ports—and even Virginia had them. But what Jefferson had imaginatively abolished were great port cities that dominated the hinterland; in their place, he projected a great system of inland commerce that rising cities, like the Chesapeake ports of Alexandria and Baltimore, would serve, but not dominate.

Jefferson turned westward when he imagined his republican empire, and away from the domination of a corrupt British metropolis and the colonial seaports through which it exercised its dominion. It was his profound aversion to the old imperial regime and the degrading dependency and subordination that it supposedly entailed that provided the animus for his assault on cities and celebration of agrarian virtue. When Jefferson railed against urban workers and mobs, he was conjuring up the pervasively corrupting effects of the monarchical empire on the American colonists generally: "Dependance begets subservience and venality, suffocates the germ of virtue, and prepares fit tools for the designs of ambition."[31] Like the opposition of slavery and freedom, the opposition of city vice and rural virtue was a compelling trope for provincial Americans: What fate could be more horrible than to be drawn into the metropolitan vortex?

Jefferson's conception of republican empire was premised on his profound hostility to metropolitan domination. His images of urban corruption expressed more generalized anxieties about provincial subordination and dependence. British influence penetrated far beyond the small port cities that serviced the transatlantic trade; at the same time, many city people demonstrated their independence and virtue in supporting the Revolution. During the 1790s, manufacturers and workers in northern cities would provide crucial support for the Jeffersonian opposition. Jefferson was not talking about real American cities in the *Notes*. Instead, he showed how the metropolis, operating through provincial proxies, could continue to exercise a pervasive, insidious influence on Americans even after independence.

Jefferson imaginatively sought to banish the metropolis from American soil when he famously concluded that we should "let our work-shops remain in Europe." A similar purifying impulse was apparent in his speculations on transatlantic commerce: "it might be better for us to abandon the ocean altogether, that being the element whereon we shall be principally exposed to jostle with other nations: to leave to others to bring what we shall want, and to carry what we can spare."[32] But, of course, Jefferson knew that such a complete separation from the trading world was impractical and undesirable. The fantasy was that Americans, having withdrawn from the carrying trade, would (thanks to competition among the remaining carriers) be able to meet its former imperial masters on a plane of commercial equality, trading agricultural surpluses ("what we can spare") for manufactured goods ("what we shall want"). Paradoxically, the next best thing to complete withdrawal from the carrying trade was complete engagement, free trade: "Our interest will be to throw open the doors of commerce, and to knock off all its shackles, giving perfect freedom to all persons for the vent of whatever they may chuse to bring into our ports, and asking the same in theirs."[33] Equality here was conceived in terms of commercial reciprocity—the presence of American merchants in European ports would balance that of Europeans in America—and of a free competition in which Americans actively participated. The common premise in both prescriptions (no trade or free trade) was Jefferson's determination to preserve the new republican empire from the pernicious effects of metropolitan domination. Indeed, Jefferson's vaunted agrarianism was an artifact of his devotion to a republican political economy, not its fundamental premise. It was only by means of commercial expansion through its great system of rivers that the American union could offer a viable alternative to the mercantilist regime of unequal benefits in a monarchical empire. Commercial expansion into the hinterland was the necessary precondition for the proliferation of Jefferson's freeholding farmers; similarly, Jefferson's apotheosis of the yeomanry ("I repeat it again, cultivators of the earth are the most virtuous and independant citizens") constituted his tribute, cast in the most self-consciously archaic, neoclassical, republican terms, to the dynamic, decentered, and progressive political economy of the postmercantilist age.[34]

Yet the distinction between symbolic representations and real people and places was never so clear in Jefferson's thought and practice as this analysis suggests. The binary oppositions—between aristocratic inequality and republican equality, city and country, slavery and freedom, vice and virtue—that enabled Jefferson to make sense out of the new nation's new relation to the old metropole suggested problematic and shifting identities, loyalties, and boundaries *among* Americans. In times of crisis, Jefferson and his coadjutors could imagine that the revival of metropolitan influence and monarchical sentiment had led to the gangrenous corruption of a geographically defined portion of the union. Even more devastating was the awful possibility that the American people as a whole were insufficiently virtuous—that is, resistant to metropolitan influence—to preserve their independence. This possibility cast a darkening shadow over the republican opposition to the High Federalist ascendancy of the late 1790s.

James Madison offered a particularly chilling image of the sociology and psychology of metropolitan corruption in an anonymous essay published in the Philadelphia *Aurora* in 1799. Beginning with an account of British traders in America, Madison proceeded to show how British trade could make Americans into foreigners. "Every shipment, every consignment, every commission," Madison wrote, "is a channel" through which British influence "flows." He continued, "Our sea-port towns are the reservoirs into which it is collected. From these, issue a thousand streams to the inland towns, and country stores. . . . Thus it is, that our country is penetrated to its remotest corners with a foreign poison vitiating the American sentiment, recolonizing the American character, and duping us into the politics of a foreign nation."[35]

This was the antithesis and negation of Jefferson's republican empire, for the very system of inland trade that promised to release the American economy from the commercial domination of the old metropole was now seen as the medium of British penetration and corruption. In this hyperbolic formulation, no American who participated in the market—participation that was here conceptualized in terms of the unequal relations of debtors and creditors—was safe from corrupting influences. Madison's pervasive anxieties pointed toward a truly atavistic, anticommercial, antimodern agrarianism, a despairing acknowledgment that a genuinely republican empire was a practical impossibility.

Madison's essay shows how the Jeffersonians' progressive, modernizing vision could regress under the stress of international, intersectional, and partisan conflict. That regress was toward the unwelcome knowledge that metropolitan power was ultimately irresistible and that, therefore, the Revolution itself was pointless. In other words, Jeffersonian-Republicans approached the "realistic" assessment of power politics, the hallmark of modern statecraft for modern diplomatic historians, by imagining a counterrevolutionary return to the old world of monarchical, mercantilist empires. The metropolitan center yet again threatened to rule subject provinces on the periphery. High Federalists, aided and abetted by their British sponsors, clearly intended to remodel the government of the union along these monarchical lines.

As Federalists demolished the constitutional forms of republican empire, embattled Jeffersonians despaired of the union, turning to their state governments to defend their liberties. Jefferson followed the logic of this descending spiral in his original draft of the Kentucky Resolutions (October 1798): Unless the lengthening train of Federalist abuses, culminating in the Alien and Sedition Acts, were "arrested at the threshold," they would "necessarily drive these States into revolution and blood, and will furnish new calumnies against republican government, and new pretexts for those who wish it to be believed that man cannot be governed but by a rod of iron."[36] The virtuous remnant would be forced to reenact the American Revolution. In doing so, however, they would have to make war on their once fellow Americans, recognizing the impossibility of sustaining a truly republican federal union. Of course, such an outcome would betray Jefferson's geopolitical vision in the *Notes*, a vision that linked Virginia's contracting boundaries and republican perfection with boundless opportunity in an ever expanding, ever more perfect "empire for liberty."

For Jeffersonians, the "Spirit of 1776" evoked both the Revolutionaries' vaulting ambition to inaugurate a new world order and the desperate measures they had been driven to by the collapse of the old imperial order. To enjoin the rising generation to reenact the Revolution may have revived dedication to the regime's first principles, but it also constituted the implicit recognition that the Revolution had failed to change the world. Indeed, the more faithful later generations were to Revolutionaries' original script, the more difficult it was for them to recapture the progressive, enlightened thrust of Revolutionary ideology. Resisting domination by a despotic central government became an end in itself, not what it had been for the young Jefferson, the means of redeeming and republicanizing empire.

Endemic divisions over early national foreign and commercial policy encouraged Americans to see each other as foreigners. Characteristically, Jeffersonians took this tendency to ideological extremes; eager anticipation of the free trade millennium, when competition among foreign consumers would bid up the prices of American staples, threw the pernicious operations of monopolizing capitalists into stark relief. Old Republican John Taylor of Caroline thus identified the manufacturing interests of the north who impoverished southerners by manipulating tariff policy as an emergent "foreign" power. "Let the capitalists or factories stand for Britain," Taylor wrote in *Tyranny Unmasked*, "and all the other occupations for the colonies, and very little difference between the two cases will appear."[37] If anything, Taylor suggested, American capitalists exercised a more tyrannical rule over agriculturalists than their foreign counterparts who, at least, had to compete with one another.

The language of liberal political economy fed into sectionalism, destabilizing and redefining ideas about who and what was foreign and inimical to the new nation's best interests. The discourse of federal constitutionalism reflected and legitimated these tendencies. Constitutional historian Andrew Lenner has shown that both Federalists and Jeffersonian-Republicans invoked law of nations doctrine throughout the formative party battles of the 1790s. In the subsequent era of republican ascendancy, the law of nations justified a radically circumscribed definition of federal authority and correspondingly robust conception of state sovereignty. In times of crisis, southerners would invoke Vattel and the other great treatise writers when their enemies sought to consolidate power and encroach on the reserved rights and vital interests of their states. The recourse to international law by patriotic southerners who sought to uphold the principles of self-determination and state equality was particularly conspicuous in the Missouri controversies.[38]

When Jeffersonians found themselves on the defensive in the competition for relative advantage in the federal political arena, they characteristically invoked the specter of metropolitan domination that had inspired the Revolutionary fathers. Thinking in terms of the old empire—and taught by Jefferson to be vigilant against the constant and pervasive dangers of an aristocratic, monarchical revival—these "Old Republicans" lost sight of the new, republican empire that inspired provincial Anglo-American Revolutionaries. As a result, the progressive strains of Enlightenment thought that had been integral to Jefferson's conception of the union were now increasingly turned against federal authority.

A growing sense of sectional distinctiveness and grievance was fostered by appeals to liberal political economy and to the jurisprudence of liberal internationalism. Both of these strains of thought linked latter-day sectionalists with the progressive, antimercantilist, antistatist impulses of the American Revolution, the great touchstone of Jeffersonian-Republican ideology. Yet these impulses were extricated from and ultimately directed against the Jeffersonian vision of republican empire. Obsessed with the dangers of an emergent American metropolis that would exercise despotic rule over subject provinces, these republicans were able to sustain an imaginative identification with Revolutionary founders who had fought the same good fight. But the appeal to the principles of 1776 also led an influential cadre of latter-day Jeffersonians to question the very possibility of continuing union with Americans from other regions whose fundamental interests and values seemed increasingly alien.

For the young Jefferson, the United States was something new under the sun, a new political order that Europe, should it ever achieve sufficient enlightenment, might one day emulate. In sharp contrast to Old World regimes, the independence and prosperity of the new republican empire did not depend on the massive concentration of coercive force, but rather on ties of affectionate union and harmonious interest. Jefferson's subsequent disenchantment was not simply a function of the inevitable disappointment of these vaulting expectations—though this is apparent enough in his later years. Instead, ironically, it was Jefferson's progressive, "modern" ideas, dissociated from the conceptual framework of republican empire, that led him and his followers to identify and demonize his enemies as America's enemies. This continuing, confusing process of defining the political nation obscured the pursuit of sectional advantage among partisan friends while projecting it on to enemies.

The tendency to conflate ideology and geography, to project the "idea of a geographical line" through the union, was best exemplified by Jefferson's ambivalent feelings toward New Englanders.[39] His alternating efforts to republicanize the Yankees and then to drive them out of the union altogether reveal a powerful dialectic in the new nation's revolutionary legacy; a cosmopolitan and inclusive conception of republican empire that was in tension with a paranoid particularism sanctioned by the fathers' opposition to despotic central authority. But it was the growing sense of a more fundamental national and racial boundary between whites and blacks that exposed and exacerbated this chronic tension, finally destroying the union.

Jefferson's ineffectual attempts to grapple with the problem of slavery, as a statesman and as a planter, called into question the viability of America's bold experiment in republican government. This was not because Jefferson failed to rise above his class interest, or found himself fatally tethered to an archaic institution. Rather, it was the way in which Jefferson embraced what seemed to him a progressive and enlightened solution to a profoundly unjust institution that led him to the threshhold of sectionalism—where he was soon overtaken by growing numbers of his followers.

In the American Revolutionary crisis, Jefferson suddenly came to see the situation of Virginia's slaves in *collective* terms. As he struggled toward a conception of (white) Virginian nationhood, he conceptualized enslaved Africans as a captive nation: Emancipation, expatriation, and colonization constituted the only conceivable basis of lasting peace and the equal enjoyment of natural rights for both peoples. Masters and slaves were two distinct nations, suspended in a permanent state of war.[40]

Jefferson's colonization scheme, first outlined in the *Notes on the State of Virginia*, may never have had any hope of success. It was yet another case where an enlightened, liberal prescription, designed in this case to do justice to enslaved blacks and to create the conditions under which white virtue could flourish, promoted unintended, ultimately tragic consequences. For the widely shared idea that southern slaves constituted a dangerous security threat made self-preservation, the first law of nature, a paramount and compelling concern for white southerners throughout the antebellum period. Indeed, this was the fundamental concern that colonization was supposed to address and that Jefferson tried to communicate to his northern correspondents. Facing potential insurrection from enslaved African Americans, dangerous foreigners in their own midst, southerners looked to their fellow Americans for succor. But if instead, northerners restricted the spread of slavery and the diffusion of slaves (the issue in Missouri), if they persisted in their efforts to impoverish the south (banks and the tariff), if they refused to cooperate in the great, redemptive project of colonization, it could only mean that they were really enemies of republican government and federal union. They must mean to use slaves as allies and proxies in a war of extermination: "Are our slaves to be presented with freedom and a dagger?" Jefferson asked John Adams in one of his more hysterical moments during the Missouri controversy.[41]

When Jefferson despaired of ever solving the slavery problem, all of his fears of sectional tyranny and oppression came to the fore. The lines of thought that had led Jefferson into the modern world—a liberal conception of political economy, his progressive jurisprudence, and his vision of consensual republican politics—led him to despair for the future of his beloved union, and to imagine his own death. Here, indeed, was the answer Jefferson had propounded in his second inaugural: "Who can limit the extent to which the federative principle may operate effectively?" It was the Americans themselves, not foreigners, who seemed determined to limit the operation of a principle that had once promised to transform the world. The failure of their union, Jefferson told former congressman John Holmes during the Missouri Crisis, would be an "act of suicide on themselves, and of treason against the hopes of the world."[42]

Notes

1. Thomas Jefferson [henceforth, TJ], Second Inaugural Address, March 4, 1805, in Merrill D. Peterson, ed., *Thomas Jefferson Writings* (New York: Library of America, 1984), 519.
2. TJ, First Inaugural Address, March 4, 1801, in Peterson, ed., *Jefferson Writings*, 493.
3. This case has been made most forcefully by Robert W. Tucker and David C. Hendrickson, *Empire of Liberty: The Statecraft of Thomas Jefferson* (New York: Oxford University Press, 1990), 125–56. For further discussion of the Louisiana Crisis, and citations, see Peter S. Onuf, "The Expanding Union," in *Devising Liberty: Preserving and Creating Freedom in the New American Republic*, ed. David Thomas Konig (Stanford, Calif.: Stanford University Press, 1995), 50–80, esp. 50–56.
4. Important contributions to this antiimperialist literature include Albert K. Weinberg, *Manifest Destiny: A Study in Nationalist Expansionism in American History* (Baltimore:

Johns Hopkins University Press, 1935) and Alexander DeConde, *This Affair of Louisiana* (New York: Scribner, 1976). For a typology of "empire" that focuses on transhistorical "generic features," see D. W. Meinig, *Continental America, 1800–1867*, vol. 2 of *The Shaping of America: A Geographical Perspective on 500 Years of History* (New Haven, Conn.: Yale University Press, 1993), 170–96, quotation at 179. Meinig writes, "To recast the history of Anglo-American expansionism into imperial terms is merely one basic shift in perspective that can help Euro-Americans gain a clearer view of our national past."

5. My debts to Anthony Pagden and J. G. A. Pocock will be apparent here. See Pagden, *Lords of All the World: Ideologies of Empire in Spain, Britain, and France c.1500–c.1800* (New Haven, Conn.: Yale University Press, 1995), esp. 156–200, and Pocock, "States, Republics, and Empires: The American Founding in Early Modern Perspective," in Terence Ball and J.G.A. Pocock, eds., *Conceptual Change and the Constitution* (Lawrence: University of Kansas Press, 1988), 55–77. On the conceptual history of federalism and union see Peter S. Onuf and Nicholas G. Onuf, *Federal Union, Modern World: The Law of Nations in an Age of Revolutions, 1776–1814* (Madison, Wisc.: Madison House, 1993). For an ambitious recent effort to reconceptualize the history of European states-systems, see Daniel Deudney, "The Philadelphian System: Sovereignty, Arms Control and Balance of Power in the American States-Union, ca. 1787–1861," *International Organization* 49 (1995), 191–228, and Deudney, "Binding Sovereigns: Authorities, Structures, and Geopolitics in Philadelphian Systems," in Thomas J. Biersteker and Cynthia Weber, eds., *State Sovereignty as Social Construct* (Cambridge: Cambridge University Press, 1996), 190–239.
6. For my preliminary thoughts on this theme see Peter S. Onuf, "Federalism, Republicanism, and the Origins of American Sectionalism," in Edward L. Ayers, Patricia Nelson Limerick, Stephen Nissenbaum, and Peter S. Onuf, *All Over the Map: Rethinking American Regions* (Baltimore: Johns Hopkins University Press, 1996), 11–37.
7. TJ to John Holmes, April 22, 1820, in Andrew A. Lipscomb and Albert Ellery Bergh, eds., *The Writings of Thomas Jefferson*, 20 vols. (Washington, D.C.: Thomas Jefferson Memorial Association, 1903–4), 15:249.
8. For a fuller treatment of this theme see Peter S. Onuf, *Jefferson's Empire: The Language of American Nationhood* (Charlottesville: University Press of Virginia, 2000).
9. TJ, *A Summary View of the Rights of British America* (1774), in Peterson, ed., *Jefferson Writings*, 119.
10. Ibid., 121.
11. Ibid., 107.
12. Ibid., 115.
13. TJ, *Summary View*, 121; emphasis added. For an excellent commentary on *The Summary View* see Stephen A. Conrad, "Putting Rights Talk in Its Place: *The Summary View* Revisited," in Peter S. Onuf, ed., *Jeffersonian Legacies* (Charlottesville: University Press of Virginia, 1993), 254–80.
14. See, for instance, Joseph J. Ellis, *American Sphinx: The Character of Thomas Jefferson* (New York: Alfred A. Knopf, 1997), 59: "His several arguments for American independence all were shaped around a central motif, in which the imperfect and inadequate present was contrasted with a perfect and pure future"; these were the "personal cravings" of a "young man" who failed to grow up. The most recent and best discussion of the editing of the Declaration is Pauline Maier, *American Scripture: Making the Declaration of Independence* (New York: Alfred A. Knopf, 1997), 97–153.
15. I am indebted to Gordon Wood's *Radicalism of the American Revolution* (New York: Alfred A. Knopf, 1992) for my understanding of republicanism.
16. TJ's "original Rough draught" of the Declaration of Independence," in Julian P. Boyd, et al., *The Papers of Thomas Jefferson*, 27 vols. to date (Princeton, N.J.: Princeton University Press, 1950–), 1:426–27.
17. The Declaration of Independence as Adopted by Congress, July 4, 1776, in ibid., 1:429, 432.
18. Minutes of the Board of Visitors, University of Virginia, March 4, 1825, in Peterson, ed., *Jefferson Writings*, 479.

19. The Declaration of Independence as adopted by Congress, July 4, 1776, in Boyd et al., eds., *Papers*, 1:429.
20. TJ, *Notes on the State of Virginia*, ed. William Peden (London, 1787; reprt., Chapel Hill: University of North Carolina Press, 1954), query 1 ("Boundaries"), 4.
21. Ibid., query 1, p. 4. My analysis here is indebted to John Seelye, *Beautiful Machine: Rivers and the Republican Plan, 1755–1825* (New York: Oxford University Press, 1991).
22. Ibid., query 2, p. 15.
23. *Summary View*, in Peterson, ed., *Jefferson Writings*, 119.
24. The Constitution as adopted by the Convention, [June 29, 1776], in Boyd et al., ed. *Jefferson Papers*, 1:383; Third Draft by Jefferson, [before June 13], ibid., 363. See the discussion in Peter S. Onuf, *The Origins of the Federal Republic: Jurisdictional Controversies in the United States, 1775–1787* (Philadelphia: University of Pennsylvania Press, 1983), 75–102.
25. For the text of the Ordinance, adopted by Congress on April 23, 1784, and commentary, see Peter S. Onuf, *Statehood and Union: A History of the Northwest Ordinance* (Bloomington: Indiana University Press, 1987), 46–49.
26. On "permeable" boundaries see Onuf and Onuf, *Federal Union, Modern World*, 135–39.
27. For a brief discussion and citations to the literature on the *Notes*, see Peter S. Onuf, "The Scholars' Jefferson," *William and Mary Quarterly* 3d ser., no. 50 (1993), 682.
28. TJ to Joseph C. Cabell, February 2, 1816, in Peterson, ed., *Jefferson Writings*, 1380.
29. Albert O. Hirschman, *The Passions and the Interests: Political Arguments for Capitalism before Its Triumph* (Princeton, N.J.: Princeton University Press, 1977); Pagden, *Lords of All the World*, 156–77.
30. *Notes*, ed. Peden, 165, 17.
31. Ibid., query 19 ("Manufactures"), 165.
32. Ibid.; query 22 ("Public Revenue and Expences"), 175.
33. Ibid., 174.
34. Ibid.
35. [James Madison], "Foreign Influence," *Aurora* (Philadelphia), January 23, 1799. For fuller discussion of this letter see Onuf, *Jefferson's Empire*, 90–93.
36. TJ, Draft of the Kentucky Resolutions, October 1798, in Peterson, ed., *Jefferson Writings*, 454. Not surprisingly, in view of later developments, TJ's reference to "nullification" (453) has elicited the most scholarly commentary, but it was the threat of war that most compellingly expressed his sense of desperation.
37. John Taylor, *Tyranny Unmasked*, ed. F. Thornton Miller (1821; reprt., Indianapolis: Liberty Press, 1992), 141.
38. Andrew C. Lenner, *The Federal Principle in American Politics* (Madison, Wisc.: Madison House, 2000) .
39. TJ to Hon. Mark Langdon Hill, April 5, 1820, in Lipscomb and Bergh, eds., *Writings of Jefferson*, 15:243. On TJ and New England, see Onuf, *Jefferson's Empire*, 121–29.
40. Onuf, *Jefferson's Empire*, 147–88.
41. Jefferson to Adams, Monticello, January 22, 1821, in Lester J. Cappon, ed., *The Adams-Jefferson Letters: The Complete Correspondence between Thomas Jefferson and Abigail and John Adams* (Chapel Hill: University of North Carolina Press, 1959), 569–70.
42. TJ to John Holmes, April 22, 1820 in Lipscomb and Bergh, eds., *Writings of Thomas Jefferson*, 15:250.

Index

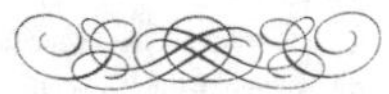